THE PUZZLE OF STRIKES

In this book Roberto Franzosi presents an analysis of the temporal dynamics of postwar Italian strikes in the industrial sector. The book is novel in a variety of ways. First, Franzosi adopts an unusual inductive approach to social-scientific explanations. He begins by highlighting a set of characteristics of the strike data that call for explanation: the pieces of the puzzle. Then, chapter by chapter, he uses a broad range of available strike theories – business cycle, economic hardship, resource mobilization, bargaining structure, political exchange, and Marxist – as clues to assemble the puzzle. As a result, the book has the narrative flavor of a mystery story, with its sequence of false steps, pat solutions, and unexpected twists and turns (typical is the complete reversal of the causal argument in the final chapters). Second, Franzosi combines the use of statistical, historical, ethnographic, newspaper, and survey material. A constant dialogue runs through the book between different methodological approaches (in particular, statistical versus historical) and theoretical approaches (in particular, Marxist versus non-Marxist). Third, strikes are viewed as the strategic interaction between organized interests ("It takes two to tango"). The focus is as much on employers' and state actions as on workers' actions. Finally, the book's aim is not merely descriptive, nor does it seek simply to test the explanatory power of existing strike theories. Rather, the goal is to disentangle the causal structure in the historical interactions among economic, institutional, and political processes. Two broad questions loom in the background: What moves history forward and what role does conflict play?

The result of Franzosi's eclectic methodological and theoretical approach is that, unexpectedly, each theory works, each theory contributes to fitting at least some of the pieces of the puzzle. Business cycle theories explain the periodic ups and downs of strike frequency: when unemployment soars, the frequency of strikes declines – although their duration increases. Resource-mobilization theories account for the close link between the availability of organizational resources and workers' capacity to mount collective action (particularly, successful actions). Institutionalization theories of collective bargaining are best equipped to deal with the periodic rhythm of industrial conflict imparted by the renewal of labor contracts. Political exchange theories explain the overall change in the shape of strikes (toward shorter, less frequent, but much larger strikes) during the late 1970s, as the Italian Communist Party was slowly being brought into a government coalition. Finally, strike waves emerge from the analyses as motors of sociopolitical change. Theories broadly conceived within a Marxist theoretical tradition provide the most plausible explanation for the occurrence of mobilization processes of such momentous proportions. Of course, if all theories are right, the puzzling theoretical questions are: Under what conditions will a given theory hold? How can we make predictions about future strike patterns?

CAMBRIDGE STUDIES IN COMPARATIVE POLITICS

General Editor

PETER LANGE Duke University

Associate Editors

ELLEN COMISSO University of California, San Diego
PETER HALL Harvard University
JOEL MIGDAL University of Washington
HELEN MILNER Columbia University
SIDNEY TARROW Cornell University
RONALD ROGOWSKI University of California, Los Angeles

OTHER BOOKS IN THE SERIES

Catherine Boone, *Merchant Capital and the Roots of Power in Senegal, 1930–1985*
Ellen Immergut, *Health Politics: Interests and Institutions in Western Europe*
Thomas Janoski and Alexander M. Hicks, eds., *The Comparative Political Economy of the Welfare State*
Herbert Kitschelt, *The Transformation of European Social Democracy*
Allan Kornberg and Harold D. Clarke, *Citizens and Community: Political Support in a Representative Democracy*
David D. Laitin, *Language Repertoires and State Construction in Africa*
Joel S. Migdal, Atul Kohli, and Vivienne Shue, eds., *State Power and Social Forces: Domination and Transformation in the Third World*
Paul Pierson, *Dismantling the Welfare State: Reagan, Thatcher, and the Politics of Welfare Retrenchment*
Theda Skocpol, *Social Revolutions in the Modern World*
Sven Steinmo, Kathleen Thelen, and Frank Longstreth, eds., *Structuring Politics: Historical Institutionalism in Comparative Analysis*
Sidney Tarrow, *Power in Movement: Social Protest, Reform, and Revolution*
Ashutosh Varshney, *Democracy, Development, and the Countryside: Urban–Rural Struggles in India*

THE PUZZLE OF STRIKES

CLASS AND STATE STRATEGIES IN POSTWAR ITALY

ROBERTO FRANZOSI
Rutgers University

Published by the Press Syndicate of the University of Cambridge
The Pitt Building, Trumpington Street, Cambridge CB2 1RP
40 West 20th Street, New York, NY 10011, USA
10 Stamford Road, Oakleigh, Melbourne 3166, Australia

© Cambridge University Press 1995

First published 1995

Printed in the United States of America

Library of Congress Cataloging-in-Publication Data

Franzosi, Roberto.
The puzzle of strikes : class and state strategies in postwar Italy / Roberto Franzosi.
p. cm. – (Cambridge studies in comparative politics)
Includes bibliographical references and index.
ISBN 0-521-45287-2
1. Strikes and lockouts – Italy. 2. Labor market – Italy. 3. Italy – Economic conditions – 1945–90.
4. Labor policy – Italy. 5. Collective bargaining – Italy. I. Title. II. Series.
HD5383.F73 1995
331.89'2945 – dc20

DNLM/DLC   93-51254
for Library of Congress   CIP

A catalog record for this book is available from the British Library.

ISBN 0-521-45287-2 hardback

Contents

List of tables, figures, and equations	page ix
Preface	xvii
Acknowledgments	xxiii

1 The puzzle box — 1
- 1.1 Why strikes? Why Italy? — 1
- 1.2 Meet the Italian strike — 2
- 1.3 Letting the data talk: the pieces of the puzzle — 4
- 1.4 How to fit the puzzle: the available theories — 7
- 1.5 Serious problems: dialogue among the deaf — 12
- 1.6 More serious problems: it takes two to tango — 15
- 1.7 Really serious problems: the automatic pilot (writing schemata and regression blenders) — 18
- 1.8 In search of a solution — 21
- 1.9 Organization of the book — 24
- 1.10 Pat solutions, red herrings, and paradoxes — 26

2 Labor-market conditions and bargaining power — 30
- 2.1 How the labor-market argument runs — 30
- 2.2 The economists' tradition of strike research: the Ashenfelter and Johnson model — 31
- 2.3 Test of the Ashenfelter and Johnson model: empirical results — 33
- 2.4 A word of caution — 35
- 2.5 Further problems: Is that all we can say? — 38
- 2.6 Examining the residuals — 41
- 2.7 Subsample analyses — 42
- 2.8 Checking the results against economic history — 47
- 2.9 Fitting the puzzle: the first step — 54

3 When do workers strike? How the economy matters — 56
- 3.1 Did I go wrong? — 56
- 3.2 Beyond strike-frequency models — 57
- 3.3 Beyond labor-market models — 57

3.3.1	Exploratory analyses	59
3.3.2	Multivariate analyses	67
3.4	Structural characteristics of the Italian economy	72
3.4.1	Long-term sectoral shifts in the occupational structure	75
3.4.2	The mode of production: technology and social organization	78
3.4.3	Labor-market structure	80
3.4.4	The industrial structure: the distribution of plant sizes	84
3.5	Even if bargaining parties had perfect knowledge: the Marxist view of conflict and the economy	89
3.6	Where we stand	92

4 Organizational resources and collective action — 96
4.1	Shifting gears	96
4.2	Hardship, discontent, and labor unrest	97
4.3	Resource-mobilization theories of collective action	99
4.4	*La longue durée*: moral economy and repertoires of collective action	101
4.5	Testing the organizational model	106
4.6	Back to exploratory analyses	109
4.7	More history: the organization of interests	114
4.7.1	Workers	114
4.7.2	Employers	119
4.8	Muddled causality: further probing into the role of organization	124
4.9	*Aiutati che il ciel t'aiuta*: the Marxist approach to organization	134
4.10	Fitting more pieces to the puzzle	139

5 The structure of collective bargaining — 143
5.1	Unanswered questions	143
5.2	Collective bargaining in postwar Italy: a brief historical overview	144
5.3	Does the structure of collective bargaining make a difference?	153
5.4	Back to the Ashenfelter and Johnson model	161
5.5	Unexplained residuals: Why models of the number of strikers perform so poorly	168
5.6	Plant-level bargaining	175
5.7	On the cost of strikes (the employers' view)	179
5.8	Unforeseen pieces fall into place	182
5.9	A false sense of security	185
5.10	The picture emerges	187

6 Class power, politics, and conflict — 190
6.1	Left to explain: the 1975–78 strike shapes	190
6.2	Political models of strikes: the long term	191
6.3	Political models of strikes: the short term	193

6.4	Italian postwar politics: blocked opportunities on the left	196
6.5	Political subcultures: Red regions, White regions	207
6.6	An overall model of power	212
6.6.1	On the cost of strikes (the workers' view), or, What happens to conflict when a group does not have power?	213
6.6.2	Corporatism *all'italiana*, or, What happens to conflict when a group does have power?	224
6.7	Short term and long term, economics and politics: the unions' dilemmas	231
6.8	Economic versus organizational/political models of strikes: Snyder's argument on Italy	237
6.9	The micro and the macro, the economic and the political: modes of regulation of labor	240
6.10	The power of statistics and the statistics of power	242
6.11	The finished picture?	253

7 Mobilization processes: the 1969 *autunno caldo* — 257

7.1	Clearly an outlier: 1969	257
7.2	Strike waves and cycles of struggle	258
7.3	The supermarket at Fiat Mirafiori: the workers	264
7.4	The tactics: "everyone did what they wanted"	267
7.5	The demands: *vogliamo tutto* ("we want everything")	272
7.6	The radical Left	283
7.7	Structure and culture	289
7.8	The limits of participation	293
7.9	Strike waves: political or economic explanations?	297

8 Countermobilization processes: reactions by the state and employers to strike waves — 301

8.1	Switching sides: the view from above	301
8.2	State responses	302
8.3	The long aftermath	306
8.4	The great fear: from paternalism to personnel management	308
8.5	Collective responses: reaffirming *la centralità dell'impresa*	314
8.6	Converging interests: *inquadramento unico* (*mobilità interna*)	317
8.7	Housecleaning (*mobilità esterna*)	323
8.8	Machines don't strike	328
8.8.1	Experimenting with new technologies	330
8.9	Small plants don't strike	332
8.10	Against the market and labor: the employers' dream of total flexibility	335
8.11	The puzzle is complete	338

9 The picture in the puzzle 343
9.1 Unexpected findings, one more time: class conflict as the *independent* variable 343
9.2 Summing up what we know (firm empirical grounds) 345
9.3 Summing up what we don't know (theoretical puzzles and tentative solutions) 349
9.4 Looking into the crystal ball: venturing predictions from the model 355
9.5 The test of history, one last time: the 1980s 359
9.6 Looking back, looking forth: the 1969 *autunno caldo* in historical perspective 368
9.7 Which road to the past? Methodological dilemmas 372

Epilogue 378

Appendix: the data 379

Notes 395
Bibliography 449
Index 485

Tables, figures, and equations

TABLES

2.1.	Test of the Ashenfelter and Johnson model	page 34
2.2.	Almon polynomial distributed lag coefficients for models in Table 2.1	36
2.3.	Seasonal model of strike frequency	39
2.4.	Subsample estimates for the Ashenfelter and Johnson model	44
2.5.	Almon polynomial distributed lag coefficients for models in Table 2.4	46
2.6.	Testing the effects of unemployment during the 1950s	47
2.7.	Unemployment rate in Lombardy and Italy (1959–65)	52
3.1.	Test of the Ashenfelter and Johnson model using numbers of strikers and hours lost as dependent variables	58
3.2.	Correlation coefficients between business-cycle measures and numbers of strikes, strikers, and hours lost	59
3.3.	Coherence values at seasonal frequencies between industrial production and numbers of strikes, strikers, and hours lost (manufacturing industry, 1950–01/1978–12)	66
3.4.	Testing the Ashenfelter and Johnson model with labor-market and product-market variables	68
3.5.	Almon polynomial distributed lag coefficients for models in Table 3.4	69
3.6.	Measuring the effects of product-market variables on numbers of strikes, strikers, and hours lost	71
3.7.	More on labor-market and product-market effects	73
3.8.	Nonperiodic cycles of numbers of strikes, strikers, and hours lost	74
3.9.	Chronology of Italian business cycles between 1945 and 1983	75
3.10.	Distribution of the labor force by sector and period (%)	76
3.11.	Hire rates for blue-collar workers in Milanese firms (1959–62)	81
3.12.	Historical transformation of the job hierarchy in Italian firms (1950–68)	83
3.13.	Distribution of Italian plants by size (number of plants per size class)	85
3.14.	Distribution of Italian plants by size (total number of employees per size class)	85

3.15.	Distribution of strike-free plants by plant size and strike issue (%)	87
3.16.	Confindustria survey data of absenteeism by year and plant size	88
4.1.	Testing the organizational model	107
4.2.	Signs and significance of the coefficients of the wage and union variables at various lags (0, 1, 2, 3) (estimates of equation 4.1)	108
4.3.	Correlation coefficients between numbers of strikes, strikers, and hours lost and union membership and unionization rate (1950–78)	112
4.4.	Correlation coefficients between numbers of strikes, strikers, and hours lost and union membership and unionization rate (1956–78)	113
4.5.	Correlation coefficients between detrended values of unemployment and numbers of strikes, strikers, and hours lost, by scope (manufacturing industry, 1955–II/1975–IV)	114
4.6.	Distribution of Confindustria member firms by firm size in 1969	121
4.7.	Distribution of commissioni interne elections by plant size (1969)	127
4.8.	Unionization by firm size in the Turin province in metalworking industry (1971)	128
4.9.	Organizational success and strike activity by firm size (1972)	129
4.10.	Distribution of Bolognese firms and employees by firm size and trade-union presence (1975)	130
4.11.	Plant-level characteristics of union structures and collective action mobilization by firm size (%)	132
5.1.	Number of plant-level agreements in industry (1953–61)	148
5.2.	Bargaining agents in plant-level agreements (%)	148
5.3.	Distribution of strike durations at Alfasud (%)	150
5.4.	Distribution of number of strikers by strike duration at Alfasud (%) (March 17, 1975, to July 31, 1975)	150
5.5.	Scala mobile coverage of wages in manufacturing industries	152
5.6.	Number of plant-level agreements in industry (1969–72)	157
5.7.	Number of firms involved in plant-level bargaining, and numbers of strikes and strikers	157
5.8.	Number of large-scale strikes and percentages of strikers involved	160
5.9.	Work stoppages for the renewal of the 1969 metalworkers' collective contract (dates and durations in hours)	161
5.10.	Correlation coefficients between numbers of strikes and strikers and the error components from model 4 of Table 2.1 and model 2 of Table 3.6	164

5.11.	Correlation coefficients between contract indicator and numbers of strikes, strikers, and hours lost at various levels	165
5.12.	Testing the role of the bargaining structure	166
5.13.	Almon polynomial distributed lag coefficients for models of Table 5.12	167
5.14.	Combining organizational and collective bargaining effects	168
5.15.	Checking the effect of unexplained observations (1974, 1975, 1977)	172
5.16.	Per capita spending for wages by firm size	178
5.17.	Hours worked and hours lost due to labor unrest and absenteeism	181
5.18.	Confindustria survey data on absenteeism by year and type	182
5.19.	Correlation coefficients between numbers of strikes, strikers, and hours lost and labor share of national income (economywide, detrended data, 1955–78)	185
6.1.	Testing a long-term political model of strikes	193
6.2.	Testing a short-term political model of strikes	195
6.3.	Workers' participation in strikes and unionization in the Red Valdelsa and White Bassano districts, by firm size (%)	210
6.4.	Repression of workers (1948–56)	214
6.5.	Number of injunctions and fines against employers	217
6.6.	Testing the effect of workers' layoffs	223
6.7.	Replication of Snyder's work	239
6.8.	Testing the effect of the compromesso storico	244
7.1.	Is 1969 an influential observation?	260
7.2.	Frequency distribution of firms holding elections for commissioni interne, by year and firm size	262
7.3.	Percentage of firms with no strikes, by firm size and year	262
7.4.	Unionization by firm size and year (%)	263
7.5.	CGIL-FIOM union growth in the Turin province, in metalworking, by firm size (% values, 1971/1964)	263
7.6.	Workers' participation in collective action	266
7.7.	Distribution of strike tactics adopted between 1969 and 1971, by firm size	270
7.8.	Strike demands in plant-level bargaining (1970–71)	273
7.9.	Wages by skill level in historical perspective	274
7.10.	Correlation coefficients between numbers of strikes, strikers, and hours lost and number of nonfatal work-related injuries (industry, 1950–I/1978–IV)	275
7.11.	Distribution of blue-collar workers by skill level and year in selected firms	279
7.12.	Distribution of work force in industry by skill level, sex, and year	280
7.13.	Percentages of workers at various skill levels in the textile and metalworking industries, by year	280

7.14.	Rates of participation in collective action of male and female blue-collar workers	296
7.15.	Rates of participation in collective action of blue-collar and white-collar workers	296
8.1.	Involvement of the Ministry of Labor in labor disputes	305
8.2.	Skill-grading system: the old and the new	318
8.3.	Distribution of blue-collar workers by skill level in metalworking industry	320
8.4.	People looking for job by reason (April 1975)	326
8.5.	Ratio between borrowed and internally generated capital, by firm size and year	330
8.6.	Percentage change in blue-collar employment by firm size and period	336
9.1.	Percentage of firms with egalitarian wage increases, by firm size	363
9.2.	Percentage of firm-level contracts characterized by wage incentives, by year and firm size	363
A.1.	Measuring the extent of bias in Italian strike data	382
N.2.1.	Strike frequency model with moving seasonality	397
N.3.1.	Cross-national productivity indices	403
N.3.2.	Distribution of Italian plants by size (6–99 employees)	405
N.4.1.	Correlation coefficients between unemployment rate and numbers of strikes, strikers, and hours lost, by cause (1959–II/1975–IV) (economywide data, first-differenced values)	408
N.5.1.	Absenteeism data for Fiat and Pirelli (1969–81)	419
N.6.1.	Economic and political strikes	432

FIGURES

1.1.	Distribution of strikes by numbers of strikers (median values 1976–80)	3
1.2.	Distribution of strikes by numbers of hours lost (median values 1976–80)	3
1.3.	Plot of yearly numbers of strikes in industry	4
1.4.	Plot of yearly numbers of strikers in industry	5
1.5.	Plot of yearly numbers of hours lost in industry	5
1.6.	Yearly shapes of strikes	8–9
2.1.	Plot of the residuals (model 2 in Table 2.1)	42
2.2.	Plots of observed and estimated values (model 2 in Table 2.1)	43
2.3.	Plots of measures of unemployment in industry	51
3.1.	Plots of the index of industrial production	60

3.2.	Plots of ISCO composite business-cycle indicator	61
3.3.	Plot of capacity utilization	61
3.4.	Plots of capacity utilization and number of strikes	63
3.5.	Plots of capacity utilization and number of strikers	65
3.6.	Bar charts of numbers of strikes in agriculture, industry, and services (1951–1980, five-year averages)	76
3.7.	Bar charts of numbers of strikers in agriculture, industry, and services (1951–1980, five-year averages)	77
3.8.	Bar charts of numbers of hours lost in agriculture, industry, and services (1951–1980, five-year averages)	77
3.9.	Plot of firm profits	91
4.1.	Plot of CGIL + CISL union membership (industry)	109
4.2.	Plots of CGIL and CISL union membership (industry)	111
4.3.	Plots of percentage of votes obtained by CGIL and CISL in yearly elections of commissioni interne	112
4.4.	Plots of smoothed data for number of strikers and CGIL + CISL union membership	125
4.5.	Plot of PCI membership	138
5.1.	Plot of monthly numbers of plant-level strikes and industrywide strikers	156
5.2.	Plot of the percentage of all strikers accounted for by contract-renewal strikes	158
5.3.	Plot of the percentage of all strikers accounted for by solidarity strikes	159
5.4.	Plot of the percentage of all strikers accounted for by industry-wide strikes	159
5.5.	Plots of the number of large-scale strikes and of the percentage of strikers involved	160
5.6.	Plot of the residuals (model 2 in Table 2.1) with quarters of contract renewal and high strike frequency in metalworking industry clearly marked	163
5.7.	Plot of the yearly percentage of industrial workers subject to contract renewal	170
5.8.	Plot of the number of strikes involving the largest time lost ("most costly strikes")	171
5.9.	Plot of the percentage of total number of hours lost accounted for by strikes with the largest number of hours lost	171
5.10.	Plot of the percentage of workers on strike for "other" reasons	175
5.11.	Plot of quarterly number of hours worked in the manufacturing industry	180
5.12.	Plot of rate of change of contractual minimum wages (metalworking industry)	184

6.1.	Plot of number of layoffs of members of commissioni interne	221
6.2.	Plot of the percentage of layoff procedures fought by the unions	227
6.3.	Plots of Tarantelli's measures of workers' market power	228
6.4.	Plot of the durations of governments between 1947 and 1980	245
6.5.	Plot of the durations of government crises between 1947 and 1980	246
6.6.	Bar chart of number of government crises per year between 1950 and 1980	246
6.7.	Plot of monthly number of strikers (economic strikes)	248–9
6.8.	Plot of monthly number of strikers (political strikes)	251
7.1.	Plots of the number of work-related injuries and of the number of hours worked in industry	276
8.1.	Plot of transfer rate (1965–I/1977–IV)	321
8.2.	Plot of transfer rate (1958–01/1964–12)	322
8.3.	Plots of the numbers of individual layoffs for giustificato motivo and giusta causa	324
8.4.	Plots of the numbers of workers laid off and firms requesting layoffs	324
8.5.	Plot of layoff rate (1965–I/1978–IV)	325
8.6.	Plot of number of hours covered by cassa integrazione guadagni	328
8.7.	Plots of investment in industrial equipment and rate of change of capital-to-labor ratio (K/L)	329
9.1.	Causal structure of an economic model of strikes	349
9.2.	Causal structure of a power model of strikes	350
9.3.	Causal structure of a power model of strikes	352
9.4.	Plots of unemployment rate and numbers of hours of cassa integrazione guadagni	364
9.5.	Plot of the number of strikes in industry	365
9.6.	Plot of the number of strikers in industry	366
9.7.	Plot of the number of hours lost in industry	366
9.8.	Plot of union membership in industry (CGIL + CISL)	367
9.9.	Plot of GNP growth	368

EQUATIONS

(2.1)	The original Ashenfelter and Johnson strike frequency model	32
(2.2)	A respecification of the Ashenfelter and Johnson strike frequency model for the Italian case	32
(3.1)	Extending the Ashenfelter and Johnson model to the numbers of strikers and hours lost	57
(3.2)	Extending the Ashenfelter and Johnson strike frequency model beyond labor-market variables: the effect of product-market variables	67

(3.3)	Extending the Ashenfelter and Johnson strike frequency model: combining labor-market and product-market variables	67
(3.4)	Problems of simultaneous-equation bias: strike frequency and product-market variables (a detrended, first-differenced model)	70
(4.1)	An organizational model of the numbers of strikes, strikers, and hours lost	106
(5.1)	A respecification of equation (2.2) to account for the effect of the bargaining structure	164
(5.2)	A respecification of equation (3.2) to account for the effect of the bargaining structure	165
(5.3)	A respecification of equation (3.3) to account for the effect of the bargaining structure	165
(5.4)	A respecification of equation (4.1) to account for the effect of the bargaining structure	165
(5.5)	A respecification of equation (5.4) to account for the effect of unexplained observations (1974, 1975, 1977)	170
(6.1)	A long-term, political model of the numbers of strikes, strikers, and hours lost	192
(6.2)	A short-term, political model of the numbers of strikes, strikers, and hours lost	194
(6.3)	Testing the effect of workers' layoffs on the numbers of strikes, strikers, and hours lost	221
(7.1)	A respecification of equation (4.1) for the number of hours lost to account for the effect of the 1969 autunno caldo	258
(7.2)	A respecification of equation (5.4) for the number of hours lost to account for the effect of the 1969 autunno caldo	258
(7.3)	A respecification of equation (6.1) for the number of hours lost to account for the effect of the 1969 autunno caldo	258
(7.4)	A respecification of equation (6.2) for the number of hours lost to account for the effect of the 1969 autunno caldo	258
(7.5)	A respecification of equation (6.3) for the number of hours lost to account for the effect of the 1969 autunno caldo	259

To Maddalena and Marianna, my daughters,
in fulfillment of a long-standing promise.

To those who dream
and upon whom circumstances
force the courage to struggle
to make their dreams come true.

So do flux and reflux – the rhythm of change –
alternate and persist in everything under the sky.
Thomas Hardy (1978, p. 399)

Nescire autem quid ante quam natus sic acciderit, id est semper esse puerum. Quid enim est aetas hominis, nisi ea memoria rerum veterum cum superiorum aetate contexitur?
(To be ignorant of what occurred before you were born is to remain always a child. For what is the worth of human life, unless it is woven into the life of our ancestors by the records of history?)
Cicero (1962, pp. 394–5 – xxxiv, 120)

Preface

> We know more and more about less and less
> until at the end we know everything
> about nothing.

This book took four years to write and ten to rewrite (in an ideal sense, anyway, because the actual rewriting took place between April 1992 and September 1993, with further spells of writing between April and December 1994). It started as a dissertation project in the Department of Sociology (back then, Social Relations) at The Johns Hopkins University in 1978. I carried out the empirical work and the final writing of the dissertation at the Centro Studi Confindustria in Rome, during the two years I spent there as a researcher, from September 1979 to August 1981. I began the rewriting during the 1981–82 academic year at the Center for Research on Social Organizations at the University of Michigan and continued it at the University of Wisconsin.

Several people back then thought the dissertation to be of sufficient quality to be publishable as a book (it was accepted as such in 1986 by another press). Over the years they encouraged me, pushed me, threatened me to "get it out." Why, then, has it taken me ten years to do so? The answer to this question is bound up with both professional and personal strands of my life. In 1982, I believed that the dissertation was a good piece of statistical analysis. After all, I had taken great care in digging out long forgotten and buried data, in teasing out the statistical details of the arguments, in always being true to the data and what they had to tell me.

But there was the problem: *statistics*. I did not want to publish just a piece of statistical virtuosity. By the end of my empirical work on the dissertation, I had realized that there was a lot more behind the statistical paraphernalia of the dissertation. The finding that economic, institutional, and organizational variables all contributed to determine the temporal movements of Italian strikes was an important story. After all, the prevailing theories concerning strikes in Italy painted a somewhat different picture. Even at the level of popular culture, the notion that there were empirically discernible and predictable patterns in the temporal movements of Italian strikes seemed to contradict basic gut feelings about the irrationality of Italian labor relations, particularly during the 1970s. Nonetheless, the story left me somewhat uneasy. I felt that it told only half of the truth. Both the data and the detailed statistical work were bringing out a much more complex picture. The final picture seemed to be one in which the determinants of strikes (the "independent variables") changed over time with the levels and forms of conflict. But at the time, I was not ready to accept such a reversal of the causal argument. Neither was I ready to accept the idea that a worker's diary, an employer's interview, or three data points could constitute empirical evidence. The quantitative strike literature could no longer help me in making sense of this new picture. Unfortunately, I knew no other literature. I had exhausted the limits of my historical/theoretical knowledge. In pursuing a mathematical/statistical background, I had had no time to expand my historical/theoretical knowledge beyond the limits of a literature review. Yet my own data, my own findings, the very products of my intensive quantitative background, were now crying out to me: "There is history behind your *time* series." Or, as Michelle Perrot (1968, p. 120) would have it, "there are people behind numbers." Where had sociology gone among all of this? Where had history? Where had theory?

But if conflict itself changed the parameters that shaped its course, these parameters were not under workers' control. Only conflict itself was. What else was behind my strike data, my spectral coherences and regression coefficients? What other actors in the picture had been obscured by the emphasis on quantitative strike research? My empirical findings on the relationships between strikes and the bargaining structure, strikes and the business cycle, offered some suggestions: The state had institutionalized in the law the broad framework in which collective bargaining took place; both employers and the state made the economic decisions (investment, monetary, labor policies) that determined the outline of the business cycle. But employers and the state rarely enter into the picture in quantitative strike research. The connections were right there in the data, but I did not know how to draw them. I had dug myself deeper and deeper into the hole of specialization of knowledge and statistical expertise. I did not know how to read history except through the coefficients of time-series analysis. There was no other meaning, for me, behind the immediate meaning of the coefficients. It was a time of terrible personal frustration with the scientific enterprise, with the emptiness and narrowness it can foster, with the "one-dimensional man" that is all too common among social scientists.

A meeting I had in 1980 with a union cadre at CGIL best illustrates where I stood then and how far I still had to journey. The cadre, intrigued by the fact that I had studied for years in the *United States*, that I was working for *i padroni* of Confindustria (both class enemies), and that I was using computers to study strikes, worriedly asked me: "So, what have you found?" "Well," I proudly replied, "my main findings are that unemployment rate has a negative effect on the frequency of strikes and that strike size and unionization seem to go together, although I have to do further work to disintagle the causal direction of the relationship." After some translating of statistical jargon into plain Italian, the union cadre paused for a second and, then, with a broad smile (the class enemies apparently did not have one up on him) he said to me: "Is that it? You mean to tell me that someone is paying you good money and that you are using computers to discover *that*? Well, next time," he concluded, "come talk to me first and I will tell you the same things and you can take a two-year vacation at the expense of *i padroni*." He did not seem to be too impressed with the fact that I had used the most approppriate data and the most up-to-date statistical techniques to tease out those results. Neither was he impressed with the fact that my findings contradicted Snyder's work on Italy – the best econometric analysis of Italian strikes. He had never heard of Snyder, and, perhaps, "he too should have come talk to me." At the time I found consolation in the fact that at least I had not distorted reality. But, in fact, is that enough to justify years of training, a good income, and the use of cutting-edge technology?

Slowly at first, at the University of Michigan, and at an increasing pace at the University of Wisconsin, I began a long journey in history and theory. History (and theory) was creeping in through the courses I was teaching, through the Ph.D. preliminary examinations I was correcting, the seminars in which I was participating, the informal conversations with colleagues and students, the corridor gossip, the network of friendships. In the Class Analysis Program, the struggle between history and theory ("us") and "number crunching" ("them") was being waged daily. But the historical and theoretical knowledge necessary to reframe my manuscript was not forthcoming, not, at least, as fast as I thought it should be. And while I was waiting for that to happen, the manuscript, too, was waiting in a drawer. Not that I forgot about it. On the contrary. Throughout all those years the manuscript was haunting me, as I kept thinking about the arguments, as I kept trying to find answers to my questions: How can I overcome the limitations of a statistical approach to the study of strikes? How can I provide a broader picture of the actors and actions involved?

By 1985, I was probably ready to get the manuscript out, casting it in the kind of historical/theoretical framework that I had been developing – at least so it seems, judging from an unpublished paper from that year. Unfortunately, by that time, a new project had rolled in. Frustrated by the poverty of information content in the official strike statistics that I had used in my dissertation, in 1982 I had started exploring new ways of studying industrial conflict. Influenced by the work of Charles Tilly and his use of newspapers as sources of historical data, I started developing a methodology of data collection from text sources that would allow me to collect highly qualitative data to be analyzed statistically. The goal was that of achieving quantity without sacrificing quality. In January 1986 I set up a project of data collection in Genoa, Italy. From 1986 to 1991, when I finally completed data collection on the 1919–22, 1968–72, and 1986–87 periods in Italy, the new project entirely absorbed my energies. It periodically kept me away from Madison for long stretches of time. The development of an entirely new linguistic- and computer-based approach to content analysis proved to be more problematic than originally anticipated. I spent incredibly long and unrewarding hours doing computer programming. No less problematic was the long-distance supervision of the project, despite modern computer-communications technology. Only stubborn determination to finish what I had set out to accomplish saw me through it. In the meantime, the practical problems of completing the data collection and some extensive writing about the new methodology did not allow me the peace of mind necessary to work on the manuscript. In 1991, data collection on those projects finally came to an end. In April 1992, having been denied tenure at the University of Wisconsin and having no job, I finally had the time and no choice but to write this book. My earlier solution to the problem of obtaining richer data had led to the development of a methodology that would combine quality and quantity within a single approach. In this book, I offer yet a different solution based on the simultaneous use of a variety of both quantitative and qualitative methodologies. The eclectic approach to data and method that I embrace in this book is the cumulative result of my personal agony over the question how to avoid throwing the baby out with the bath water. Having lost faith in the legerdemain of high-powered statistics, I agonized for years over the fate of the manuscript, striving to find a format that not only would be statistically elegant but also would be true to the historical record. *The Puzzle of Strikes* is thus, first and foremost, an attempt to solve the personal puzzle of how to approach the problem of scientific explanations in the social sciences.

If the decade-long agony over the fate of this manuscript had been trying, it was the fifteen months of final writing that brought out a stormy process of personal understanding and substantive breakthroughs that made the writing of this book an incredibly emotional experience. As I was glued to the computer for months on end, relentlessly, the ghosts of history that I was bringing back to life kept me good company, making me laugh and cry with them. And with those ghosts of history came the ghosts of my own past, caught as I had been in the dilemma of "a contradictory class location." Born to a well-to-do father and a mother from a poor family and raised in the extended paternal family that never fully accepted my mother, the experience of class had been part of my most formative years. The ambiguity of early childhood permanently marked my personality and my life with the stamp of contradictory polarity: living in Italy or in the United States, a bourgeois or a Marxist, a theorist or a methodologist, and so forth. The "hidden injuries of class"[1] have imbued my work over the years with moral overtones and have provided much of the emotional charge. I am well aware of the dangers involved in holding a moral position of truth in the social sciences. But there is even more danger in upholding the truth that comes from the uncritical acceptance of scientific paradigms.

For years I was blown about by the contradictions of my childhood experience, without much idea of what was happening. Only recently have I understood the roots of my personality, through trying years of introspection over the motivations and the actions of the players involved in the social relations of my family. And lately I have come to think that it is time to "forgive and forget." Interestingly enough, just as in my life I was trying to understand and overcome personal contradictions, in this book I try to overcome contradictions between modes of social-science productions (historical, ethnographic, statistical, etc.) and theoretical approaches (economic bargaining, resource mobilization, Marxist and non-Marxist, etc.). During the months of final writing, I was playing out my personal dilemmas and contradictions in the dilemmas and contradictions of historical actors. The strategic interactions among the people who populated my childhood blurred into the interactions among Rico, Barbisin, Giuseppe Dozzo, Paolo Migliaccio, Aris Accornero, Roberto Sibona, Cesare Cosi, Nico Ciarciaglino, Giovanni Agnelli, Leopoldo Pirelli, Guido Carli, Fiorentino Sullo, Carlo Donat Cattin, Enrico Berlinguer, Romolo Gobbi, Guido Viale, and the countless others who crowded the stage of history during the period studied in this book. And so, during the final writing, I gave everyone a voice: workers, the unions, employers, state officials, radicals. I listened to what each had to say. I analyzed what each did and could have done. I empathized and understood. But my heart, I have to admit, was and is with those who tried and, perhaps, lost. Given my personal biography, that is indeed how it should be, perhaps the only way it could have been.

Writing as an Italian far from home and writing in a second language gave me some of the distance necessary to at least try to keep the passion and emotional involvement in check. Writing with no job, with virtually no professional ties to the discipline, and facing the serious possibility of having to get out of academia, further gave me the freedom to maintain my independence from professional camps for the sake of a career . . . that I did not have. So, with a tragic sense of battles lost and won, of the strong passions that animated all sides, of high hopes and despair, it is time to put it all to rest. The view of history that emerges is one of people making their own history – but not just as they please. If there is any sense to C. Wright Mills's "intersection between biography and history," that has indeed been the personal experience behind this book.

Acknowledgments

Given the long history of this book, I have accumulated many debts along the way, involving many different people and institutions in the United States and in Italy.

I started the work at Johns Hopkins under the direction of Richard Rubinson. While at Hopkins, my friends Francesco Caramazza and Alberto Devoto helped me to make my first steps in econometrics and spectral analysis. I carried out some of the early work of data collection and data analysis in Italy at the Centro Studi Confindustria (Confederazione Generale dell'Industria Italiana) between September 1979 and August 1981. Throughout that entire period, Paolo Savona, Confindustria director general, and Enzo Grilli, the director of the Centro Studi, granted me the material support and the research freedom necessary to pursue my interests and follow my research agenda. I can truly say that without Enzo Grilli's constant help and friendship this work would never have been possible. There is no other single person to whom this book owes more.

Many other people at Confindustria were generous with their time. Librarians, computer operators, secretaries, and colleagues (my office mate Mauro La Noce, in particular) were always more than supportive and patient with me – this despite the fact that I always pressed them to work at my maniacal pace, even in the more relaxed atmosphere of Roman work habits. Franco Adolini, Gianna Bargagli, Massimo Chirichini, Angelo Farcis, Giovanna Guidi, Franco Martone, Maurizio Tarquini, Anna Maria Carandente, and, in particular, Giuseppina Jagher provided invaluable help with data collection. The endless conversations I had with Giulio de Caprariis greatly helped me to clarify my ideas. For over a decade, until the day before sending off the manuscript for copyediting, Giulio was always there ready to grapple one more time with *The Puzzle*, providing bibliographical references and data and sharing with me his views on the current state of labor relations. Isidoro Mariani's and Massimo Pagani's knowledge of the details and hidden idiosyncrasies of many Italian data series was invaluable. More than ten years have now lapsed, and so has much of my arrogant belief in high-powered statistics. Gwillym Jenkins, already dying from leukemia, once announced in a class I took with him, "You must fall in love with your data. You must take your data to bed not for a one-night stand but for a long-term relationship, so as to get to know their most intimate aspects." These simple lessons not only have stuck in my mind, but also have become part of my standard approach to data analysis.

The long years of rewriting started in the Fall of 1981 at the Center for Research on Social Organizations (CRSO) at the University of Michigan, where I spent an academic year as a postdoctoral fellow thanks to a grant from Consiglio Nazionale delle Ricerche, Confindustria's Giovani Imprenditori, and Associazione Imprenditori Marche. At CRSO, Charles Tilly taught me an unforgettable lesson in history and theory. There, I opened a window on the wide world behind regression coefficients. It took me several years of work, as an assistant professor at the University of Wisconsin, to explore that world.

At the University of Wisconsin, many people contributed to my intellectual development. My colleagues and friends Ron Aminzade, Richard Lachman, and Erik Wright helped me through the years along my new path. They were always there to give me books and articles, to suggest historical and theoretical readings, to include me among the circle of those who appreciate history and theory – "our camp." They never talked about the fact that I was teaching a seminar in advanced statistics – the "other camp." In particular, Erik Wright helped me to clarify my arguments. Alberto Palloni shared with me from the beginning my anguish over the tension between theoretical and empirical work.

Throughout the long period of both writing and rewriting, I have always been able to count on another friend: Alberto Devoto. During the last year of terrible isolation, his daily electronic messages to the cry of *Forza Paris* made life more bearable. Svetlana Kropp read and reread drafts of chapters, ran statistical analyses, and prepared tables. She was not always understanding of my obsession with *The Puzzle* (yet always supportive), but it is hard for me to imagine having written this book without her. For several years she was forced to share the anxieties and fears that have accompanied the book. Joseph Kepecs played a significant role in exploring the personal, deep seated roots of those fears.

Many other people provided either data or a sympathetic ear to my arguments: Lorenzo Bordogna, Giorgio Calcagnini, Eugene Cleur, Gino Giugni, Alberto Heimler, Rogers Hollingsworth, Nino Magna, Ross Matsueda, Doug Maynard, Carol Mershon, Giorgio Sola, Vittorio Valli, and Wolfgang Streeck. A special mention should go to Aris Accornero, Gian Primo Cella, and Sidney Tarrow for their faith in my work even when I jealously kept it away from public scrutiny.

At Istituto Centrale di Statistica, Lorenzo Settanni was always available to explain the idiosyncracies of official strike data. Luigi Alinari made the contract-renewal data from his senior thesis available to me. Fabrizio Barca shared with me his data on firm profits, as did Francesco Batteggazzorre with his cabinet-crisis data. Annalisa Spotti collected from *Il Corriere della Sera* the data on the relationship between strike activity and cabinet crises.

Toni Schulze, Virginia Rogers, Patricia McDaniel, and Mirjana Sotirović helped with some of the typing. At the end, preparing a "camera-ready" copy of the manuscript was truly a nightmare. My friend Charles Palit provided invaluable support in that process. I spent countless hours at his house. Svetlana Kropp, Piero Squillante, and Eric Newman, production editor at Cambridge, pitched in at the end. As frustrating as it was at times to stretch the limit of what WordPerfect can do as a typesetting tool, the technical support staff at WordPerfect was always courteous and occasionally even helpful.

I owe much of what I have learned about writing in the English language to the patience of Ann Althouse. Editors at Cambridge University Press carefully went over the manuscript, thoroughly eliminating the many inaccuracies that come from writing in a second language. Gloria Cook helped me in reviewing some of those changes. Vivek Chibber, Denis O'Hearn, Katharine Jones, Fulvio Venturino, and Erik Wright read and provided comments on individual chapters. Gerald Friedman, Richard Lachman, Kenneth Land, John Markoff, Patricia McDaniel, Nader Sohrabi, and Mirjana Sotirović generously offered comments on the entire manuscript at different stages of production. I am particularly indebted to Gian Primo Cella, Samuel Cohn, Giulio de Caprariis, and Michael Shalev for their close reading of the final manuscript. Samuel Cohn's inspirational review of the manuscript gave me much of the determination to continue. As I was debating whether I had crossed the fine line between determination and delusion, his review gave me the courage to write the kind of book that I had always dreamt of and that I eventually wrote. The title is a combination of suggestions from the Cambridge Syndicate and Gerald Marwell.

Last but not least, I would like to acknowledge the great intellectual debt that I have incurred over the years with two scholars and friends: Charles Tilly and Erik Wright. In different ways, they have provided role models for me to follow, through their relentless pursuit of broad issues, through the depth and breadth of the historical and theoretical questions they asked. I will never forget Charles Tilly asking a bewildered speaker, in all friendliness: "Can you explain to me in three minutes or less why I should be here listening to you?" I have asked that same question always of myself and, occasionally, of others. Why is the problem at hand worth pursuing? What is its relevance? If it is not worth an hour of a listener's time, then, why should it be worth years of ours?

To all these institutions, to all these and many more people who, without necessarily agreeing with the opinions expressed in this book or the conclusions reached, have contributed their time, ideas, and expertise, I wish to express my gratitude. It is no fault of theirs that I have done no better.

1

The puzzle box

Strikes ... always instil fear into the capitalists, because they begin to undermine their supremacy.... Every strike brings thoughts of socialism very forcibly to the worker's mind, thoughts of the struggle of the entire working class for emancipation from the oppression of capital.
V.I. Lenin (quoted in Clarke and Clements, 1977, pp. 58–9)

We have no intention whatever of doubting or despising the "revelation of history," for history is all and everything to us.
Friedrich Engels (Lapides, 1987, p. xviii)

Without use of history and without an historical sense of psychological matters, the social scientist cannot adequately state the kind of problems that ought now to be the orienting points of his studies.
Mills (1959, p. 143)

Exploratory data analysis can never be the whole story, but nothing else can serve as the foundation stone – as the first step.
Tukey (1977, p. 3)

1.1. WHY STRIKES? WHY ITALY?

It has been twenty years since Shorter and Tilly's *Strikes in France: 1830–1968* and Pizzorno's *Lotte operaie e sindacato in Italia: 1968–1972* were published – two books unsurpassed in the strike literature, even as the levels of industrial conflict reached during the turbulent 1960s remain unsurpassed, and not only in France and Italy. The 1960s saw a great resurgence of conflict across a range of industrial nations, and with that renewed conflict came a revival of scholarly interest, as researchers began trying to make sense of what had happened. Just as eventful as the 1960s had been on the stage of historical reality, the 1970s saw the development of new theoretical approaches to the study of strikes. Resource-mobilization and political-exchange theories of strikes date back to those years. A burgeoning historical, sociological, and political literature showed beyond doubt that the factors involved in strikes are too complex to be accounted for by the purely economic models in vogue until then. Within the sociological tradition, old caryatids came tumbling down, like the prevailing Durkheimian theories of collective action.

And then came the 1980s, a long decade of silence. With working-class quiescence came a decline in scholarly interest in strikes. Silence fell, but not because we had found all the answers. That is hardly ever the case. No, we simply lost interest. After all, history itself had relegated strikes to the background. Access to research grants and the trend in academic publishing had begun to follow different routes. Yet a stormy decade of scholarly production had left behind many unanswered questions, many unexplained discrepancies, many findings that did not fit together.

Italy, for one, did not fit the known patterns. Neither economic models nor organizational or political models seemed to properly explain the Italian case, and the case was mostly ignored. Yet, in retrospect at least, Italy offers fascinating opportunities for testing the available theories of strikes. What is fascinating is that, unexpectedly, all my efforts toward historical reconstruction and empirical testing appear to have led to the unsettling conclusion that all theories work, all theories contribute to an understanding of at least part of the Italian experience. Even more fascinating is the fact that Italy provides an unusual opportunity to work with two scholarly traditions, the Marxist and non-Marxist, that have mostly kept each other at arm's length. Historical reality pushes me in that direction.

Within the economic and political choices that have torn Italian society and its organizations, within the cultural and political traditions of the Italian working class, one can trace the painful dilemmas of that class: between short- and long-term actions, between economic and political actions. The patterns discernible in Italian strikes clearly reflect those dilemmas and the ensuing choices. Tracing the determinants of the temporal patterns of strikes will put us in close touch with the theoretical tradition that brought out the dilemmas and informed the choices: the Marxist tradition. But, by and large, Marxist scholarship has neglected empirical studies of strikes. The Italian historical experience provides a unique opportunity to examine Marxist and non-Marxist social theories in close encounters.

1.2. MEET THE ITALIAN STRIKE

Ross and Hartman (1960), in a comparative analysis of strike trends, classified fifteen countries in North America, Europe, Asia, and Africa, as well as Australia, into five different categories on the basis of their levels of industrial conflict. In their scheme, Italy belongs to the Mediterranean-Asian pattern, together with France, Japan, and India (Ross and Hartman, 1960, pp. 75–7, 120–6). The characteristics of conflict in this pattern are short durations and large worker participation. In Ross and Hartman's words, "the Italian rates of participation have been fantastically high."[1] Not greatly different from the French strike (Shorter and Tilly, 1974), "the typical Italian strike is clearly a demonstration rather than a trial of economic strength, regardless of its causes" (Ross and Hartman, 1960, p. 124).

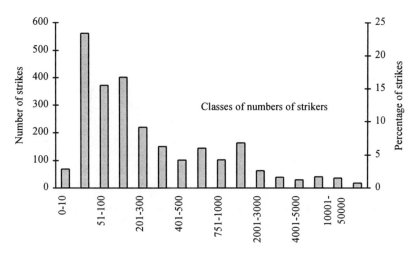

Figure 1.1. *Distribution of strikes by numbers of strikers (median values 1976–80)*

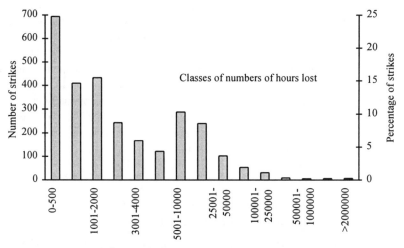

Figure 1.2. *Distribution of strikes by numbers of hours lost (median values 1976–80)*

This picture of the Italian strike based on aggregate data, however, is somewhat misleading. An examination of strike data by size, first published by the Istituto Centrale di Statistica (ISTAT) in 1976, reveals a different picture (Figures 1.1 and 1.2). Although there were a few "fantastically" large strikes (the "demonstrative" strike), that in fact was not "the typical Italian strike." As Figure 1.1 shows, the

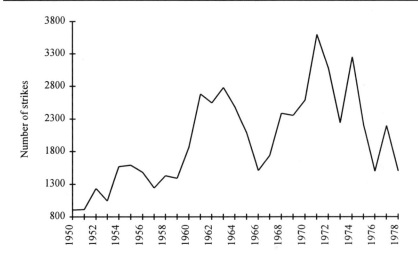

Figure 1.3. *Plot of yearly numbers of strikes in industry*

most typical Italian strike (in terms of relative frequencies) was rather small in size, involving between 11 and 50 workers. During the period 1976–80, the cumulative frequencies of strikes by numbers of workers involved show that 63% of all strikes involved less than 300 workers, 79% less than 750 workers, 90% less than 2,000 workers, and 98% less than 10,000 workers (Figure 1.1), hardly a picture of "fantastically high" strike sizes. Italian strikes also tended to be short, from just a few minutes to a few hours in duration (Figure 1.2). Again, during the period 1976–80, each striker lost an average of 5 to 10 hours a year due to strikes. Thus, the typical Italian strike is small and brief, with a few exceptionally large but just as short "demonstrative" strikes (for a definition of strikes, as collected by ISTAT, Istituto Centrale di Statistica, and an assessment of the reliability of the data, see the appendix on data). What combination of cultural, institutional, and structural factors accounts for this picture of Italian strikes?

1.3. LETTING THE DATA TALK: THE PIECES OF THE PUZZLE

The bar charts of Figures 1.1 and 1.2 hardly exhaust the characteristics of Italian strikes that call for an explanation. An attentive examination of the available strike data would reveal many such characteristics, so many pieces of a jigsaw puzzle awaiting to be put together. To get a firsthand idea of what these characteristics are, let us start by looking at some time plots of the three main indicators of strike activity: number of strikes, number of strikers, and number of hours lost.[2]

All three plots (Figures 1.3, 1.4, and 1.5) reveal the uneven nature of Italian industrial conflict. All three strike indicators fluctuate up and down, with sudden advances and deep retreats. The plot of the number of strikes shows an inverted-U

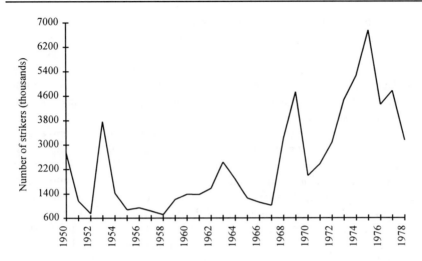

Figure 1.4. *Plot of yearly numbers of strikers in industry*

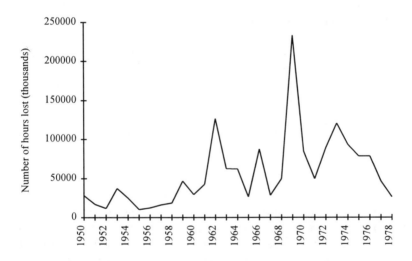

Figure 1.5. *Plot of yearly numbers of hours lost in industry*

shape, peaking in the early 1970s. It also shows distinct peaks at approximately three-year intervals during the 1970s. The plot showing the number of strikers is characterized by a trend toward increasing worker participation, after a sharp decline in the early 1950s. The plot of the number of hours lost also reveals an upward trend, with a decline in the second half of the 1970s. The number of strikes and number of hours lost indicate two distinct waves of conflict in the early and late 1960s.

Even more revealing than these simple time plots are the graphic representations of the "shapes" of strikes.[3] The *shape* of a strike is a parallelepiped whose sides are the frequency, duration, and size of strikes, and whose volume is the product of the three sides.[4] Figure 1.6 shows the yearly shapes of strikes in the Italian manufacturing industries from 1954 to 1978.[5] The 1950s strikes are characterized by rather homogeneous shapes and by low volumes. Only 1954 shows a larger strike size and a higher frequency.

For the 1960s, the shapes have higher volumes. Strikes, on the average, were longer and more frequent than a decade earlier. Strike sizes, although showing an upward trend, were at rather low levels until the end of the 1960s.[6] The strikes of 1962 and 1966 had durations longer than average. Long durations seem to characterize those strikes that are power struggles between workers and employers. Hardly ever have strikes in Italy assumed these characteristics, which are more typical in the British and American institutional contexts.[7] The shape for 1969 provides a dramatic picture of the unprecedented (and unsurpassed) volume of conflict during that year. Only 1959 has a shape similar to that of 1969, although on a smaller scale.

The 1970s trends accentuate the tendency of the previous decade toward higher volumes. The average size, in particular after 1975, becomes the characteristic indicator of the decade. The years 1959, 1962, 1966, 1969, and 1973 show marked differences in shapes with respect to surrounding years.[8] The three- to four-year intervals between these years seem to confirm a cyclical, periodic component of strike activity in Italy. Finally, the annual shapes changed drastically from 1975 onward. Strikes during the latter part of the 1970s were shorter and less frequent but larger than ever before, and with a tendency for the overall volumes to go down.

Exploratory analyses of the three strike indicators, based on various time-series techniques [spectral analysis, decomposition methods, autoregressive integrated moving-average (ARIMA) models] confirm our initial impression of the cyclical behavior of strikes; for detail of these analyses, see Franzosi (1980). Spectral analyses, in particular, show the existence of both short-term, seasonal periodic cycles and medium-term, three-year cycles. Furthermore, they reveal a one-year delay, or shift, between (1) the series of number of strikes and (2) the series of number of strikers and number of hours lost. The series of number of strikers and number of hours lost peak every three years. These peaks are followed, one year later, by similar peaks in the number of strikes. Decomposition analyses based on moving averages also show the existence of nonperiodic cycles of a few years' duration.

The exploratory analyses also illustrate the multifaceted nature of strikes. The correlation coefficients and the spectral coherences among the numbers of strikes, strikers, and hours lost are high, but not so high as to imply complete linear dependence. Furthermore, correlation, spectral, and principal component analyses all point in the same direction: The number of strikers and the number of hours lost are more closely related than either is to the number of strikes. The indicators used to quantify strike activity are independent of each other, even though they have a common denominator (especially numbers of strikers and hours lost). Given these differences, we would expect these three indicators to be related to different underlying causal structures (particularly, those related to the number of strikes would be expected to differ from those related to the numbers of strikers and hours lost).

In summary, the exploratory analyses of strike indicators provide the following pieces of the puzzle that I am attempting to put together:

1. The numbers of strikes, strikers, and hours lost constitute similar, but slightly different, measures of strike activity (in particular, the numbers of strikers and hours lost are empirically closer to each other than either is to the number of strikes).
2. The numbers of strikes, strikers, and hours lost show nonperiodic cyclical components of a few years' duration.
3. The numbers of strikes, strikers, and hours lost show periodic cyclical behavior, with both a seasonal periodicity and a three-year periodicity.
4. The numbers of strikes, strikers, and hours lost do not peak at the same time in the three-year cycle; they typically show a one-year shift, with number of strikes peaking first, followed a year later by peak numbers of strikers and hours lost.
5. There are upward trends in numbers of strikes, strikers, and hours lost. The 1950s were characterized by low levels of strike activity. Then, strike activity was high in the late 1960s and early 1970s. The numbers of strikes and hours lost began declining after 1975.
6. The strike indicators (particularly the numbers of strikes and hours lost) show two peaks of conflict: 1959–63 and 1968–72.
7. The strike shapes for 1962 and 1966 show longer-than-average durations.
8. The strike shapes for 1959 and 1969 show higher overall volumes, more closely resembling a cube than a rectangular parallelepiped.
9. All strike indicators point to 1969 as a true outlier.
10. The relationships among numbers of strikes, strikers, and hours lost are not stable over time. In particular, the 1970s introduced a new pattern of relationships.
11. The strike shapes for the years 1975–78 are different from the typical postwar shapes; strikes in that period were brief and infrequent, but the few strikes that occurred involved greater numbers of workers than the average.
12. In the context of relatively homogeneous strike shapes for the period 1975–78, the strike shape for 1978 indicates that strikes were even more infrequent and larger in size than in the other years of that period.

1.4. HOW TO FIT THE PUZZLE: THE AVAILABLE THEORIES

This book takes an inductive approach to explanations in the social sciences. Its point of departure is a set of characteristics of Italian strikes: the pieces of a jigsaw puzzle. It then applies the available theories to try to assemble the puzzle. To some extent, the data themselves have much to say as to where each piece of the puzzle fits. But, by and large, it is the available theories of strikes that have guided my search for explanations, that have provided clues, and have indicated which direction to take. And the strike literature is particularly rich, mostly with empirical analyses, but also offering some work that is more theoretical.[9] At least five

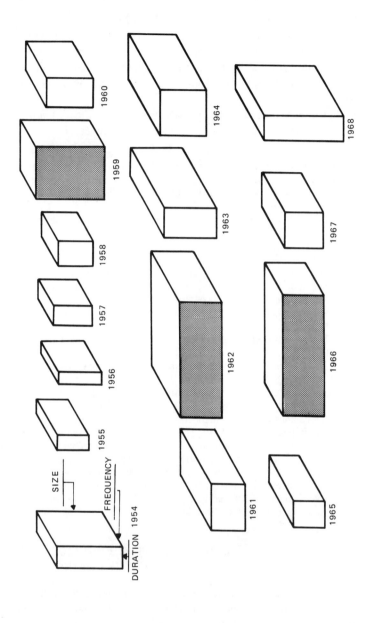

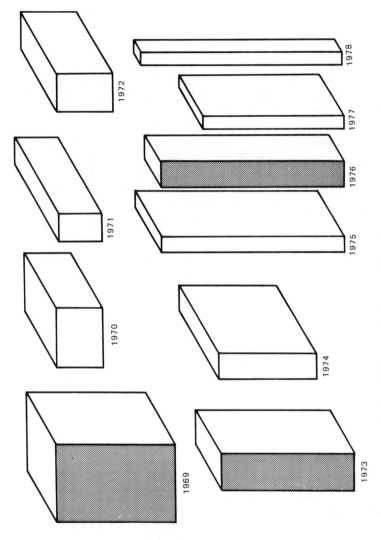

Figure 1.6. *Yearly shapes of strikes*

different approaches to the study of strikes have emerged: studies of business cycles, studies of economic hardship and relative deprivation, theories of resource mobilization, the institutional approach, and political-exchange theory.

Business-cycle explanations of strikes have the longest tradition in the literature. They focus on the relationships among business cycles, the bargaining position of labor, and strikes. According to business-cycle models (e.g., the Ashenfelter and Johnson model), the state of the labor market modifies the bargaining position of workers vis-à-vis employers and influences their propensity to strike.[10] During boom periods, the labor market is tight (i.e., workers are in demand) and workers are more willing to take the risk of mobilization, because they can find other jobs more easily. Employers, on the other hand, have difficulty in finding replacement workers. They are also less willing to have their production interrupted at a time when orders and profits are high. Under conditions approaching full employment, workers are thus in a relatively more favorable position than employers and are more willing to go on strike. During busts, with unemployment high and rising, the situation is reversed: Workers are less willing to mobilize, because they know that employers can easily replace troublesome workers. Also, employers can fill orders out of their stockpiled inventories. Thus, employers are in a better position, and the incidence of strikes goes down.

Economic hardship theories hypothesize that workers' grievances are the basis for their collective actions. When the level of grievances becomes intolerable, workers will act. They will act when they "can't take it anymore." That is more likely to happen during times of economic recession and crisis, when their working conditions deteriorate and grievances mount. Whereas business-cycle theories of strikes assume a rational cost–benefit analysis of the short-term economic returns to collective action, relative deprivation and economic hardship theories of collective action (strikes included) seek to exclude these "economic" calculations. The prediction of business-cycle theories of strikes is that people will act collectively during times of prosperity. The prediction of economic-hardship models is that people will act collectively during hard times. Both business-cycle and economic-hardship models deal with the relationship between economics and collective action, but, whereas the former models stem from the economic tradition, the latter arise from the sociological tradition.[11]

Resource mobilization theories seek to explain collective action in terms of a group's capacity to mobilize resources and organize.[12] Contrary to relative-deprivation and economic-hardship theories, they view collective action as the product of social organization, rather than disorganization. For relative-deprivation and economic-hardship theories, collective action is seen as almost a "natural" consequence of a group's grievances. For resource-mobilization theory, grievances are seen as more or less constant – groups always have gripes. Without organization, however, there can be no collective action, certainly no sustained and successful collective action. Working within this theoretical tradition, Shorter and Tilly (1974) attempted to explain the long-term patterns of strikes in terms of increased organizational capacities of the working class: Although economic and structural factors are certainly important, it has been workers' greater organizational capacities that have deeply transformed the nature of strikes, increasing participation and frequency while at the same time reducing duration.

Those who advocate institutional theories would argue that the institutionalization of collective bargaining has imprinted a periodic pattern on strike activity, the period being determined by the durations of collective contracts. This is particularly true when contract expirations cluster together in the same quarter or in the same year. Sellier (1960) and Clegg (1976) further argued that the level at which contract negotiations are held is associated with specific dimensions of strike activity. In particular, centralized economywide or industrywide bargaining should lead to a pattern of a few large strikes, potentially involving all the workers in a specific economic sector. It could be millions of workers for the larger sectors. Local bargaining at the level of the single firm should lead to fragmentation of conflict, with each firm negotiating with labor to settle its individual local disputes. There is potential for the frequency of strikes to be high, but the average strike should be small (up to the size of the average firm).

Political-exchange theories have focused on long-term developments in strike patterns, developments related to changes in the political position of labor in the national power structure. Contrary to the claims of those whose thesis is that strike activity is "withering away" (Ross and Hartman, 1960, pp. 4–5), comparative political research has shown that in capitalist countries, the incidence of strikes has declined only when labor-oriented social-democratic parties have acquired stable and lasting control of their governments, such as in Scandinavian social democracies and in Austria (Hibbs, 1978; Korpi and Shalev, 1980, p. 320). In those cases, direct access to political power has provided labor with alternative, less costly means to achieve a more favorable distribution of resources: the government machinery itself, rather than the strike (Korpi and Shalev, 1980, p. 325). When the working class has control of the government, the locus of conflict over the distribution of resources, the national income in particular, shifts from the labor market and the private sector, where strike activity is the typical means of pressure, to the public sector, where political exchange prevails. Thus, redistributive, welfare policies instituted by labor governments reduce conflict.

By and large, Marxist scholarship has ignored the quantitative study of strikes, despite the central role that the "class struggle" plays in the Marxist theoretical framework.[13] And the strike literature has greeted the Marxist framework with silence. In a literature where the game is played on the basis of estimation methods, signs and significance of coefficients, what Marxism might have had to say about strikes has been of absolutely no interest. Yet no other social theory has evoked so much hard thought, and for so long, about conflict. Indeed, Marxist theory offers its own solutions to many of the issues dealt with in this section.

Contrary to the premises underlying the economic-bargaining approach, for classical Marxists the rise of class conflict is linked to long-term immiseration, rather than to prosperity. Only recently, scholars working within a broad Marxist theoretical framework (e.g., the U.S. theory of the "social structure of accumulation" and the French "regulation" theory) have postulated the existence of long-term cycles (crises) in capitalist economic systems and have studied the relationship of these cycles to heightened levels of class confrontation. The long-term crisis cycles differ from both the short-term business cycles of neoclassical economics and the long-term economic immiseration of capitalism postulated by classical Marxism. Furthermore, a Marxist approach to economic relations in capitalist societies would fundamentally undermine another premise of economic-bargaining models: that perfect knowledge by the bargaining parties of each other's concession curves would eliminate all reasons for striking. Strikes are the results of capitalist social relations of production, rather than the results of faulty negotiations. For Marxists, perfect knowledge may eliminate the short-term reasons for striking, but not the long-term ones.

Marxists do not have much to say specifically about the relationship between the bargaining structure and the pattern of strikes. Yet the choice of the most appropriate bargaining level has been at the heart of their political strategy. Thus, for instance, in the 1950s, the CGIL, the union close to the Italian Communist Party, rejected plant-level bargaining as divisive of the working class and put all its eggs in one basket, centralized bargaining, a choice for which later the CGIL (and the Italian working class) was to pay very dearly.

Marxist theory shares with resource-mobilization theories an emphasis on organization. Yet Marxist theory goes beyond. Marxists have agonized over the nature of the organization (economic, such as unions, or political, such as the vanguard party) and its goals (class compromise within bourgeois democracies, or revolutionary politics). They have theorized extensively about the costs of each choice. Political exchange is at the heart of Marxist thinking, at the heart of the dilemma between short-term and long-term goals, between economic action and political action, between class compromise and revolutionary politics. With the strongest Communist Party in the West, the Italian working class has painfully agonized over these issues throughout the postwar period. It would be hard to understand Italian class conflict without understanding the theoretical framework that has informed these choices.

1.5. SERIOUS PROBLEMS: DIALOGUE AMONG THE DEAF

The quantitative literature on strikes has been quite successful in explaining various aspects of strikes. The economic approach has explained the cyclical behavior of strike activity (number of strikes, in particular) and its connection with the business cycle. The sociological and political approaches have pinned down the long-term movement of strike activity (number of strikers, in particular). The former approach has viewed the long-term movement of strikes as the result of workers' organizational capacities, whereas the latter has seen it to be the result of changes in the political position of labor in national power structures. Despite this success, many problems still remain. One of the most serious problems in the literature is the lack of integration between competing approaches. Never mind that Marxist and non-Marxist theories have ignored each other. Even within the non-Marxist tradition, the various theoretical approaches to the study of strikes have addressed different sets of questions, have explained different aspects of strike activity.

In studying strikes, the economic approach has mainly been concerned with the questions of why and when strikes occur. The answer has been that they occur because economic systems go through cycles of expansion and recession that affect the amount of wealth produced in the system at any given time. Furthermore, strikes occur when expansion puts workers in a better bargaining position. Typically, under capitalism, the distribution of increased (or decreased) wealth is carried out through the "invisible hand" of market mechanisms. Bargaining between workers and employers is the way to ensure an advantageous distribution of scarce and fluctuating resources in a market economy. The strike is a means to acquire knowledge about the other party's concession curve in a bargaining situation characterized by limited information.

However, the distribution of resources through market mechanisms is not the only way to redistribute resources. Political mechanisms can also be used. What happens to industrial conflict when resources are distributed in the polity rather than in the market? Furthermore, is the presence of fluctuating economic conditions sufficient cause for strikes to occur? Are there any mediating factors that affect the occurrence of strikes? In other words, is the probability of strikes conditional upon economic factors alone, with all other factors assumed to hold constant? From the postulate that strikes are the result of changing economic conditions, does it follow that most strikes should occur during prosperity, when labor-market tightness puts workers in a better bargaining position? What does it take for labor to recognize its better bargaining position and take advantage of it? The questions of why and when do strikes occur have always been at the heart of economists' concerns. Sociologists have addressed different questions: How can strikes occur? Is it enough to be in a better bargaining position for there to be a strike? Their answer is that it is organization that makes strikes possible; without organization there can be no collective action. Political scientists' basic concern flows from yet another question: What happens to strike activity when workers' organizational capacities succeed in imposing new distributive mechanisms, based in the political rather than in the economic market?

These different theoretical concerns have led the different disciplines to focus on particular components of strike activity and time horizons. Thus, economists have concentrated mainly on strike frequency (i.e., on the occurrence or nonoccurrence of strikes), sociologists on the mobilization aspect of strikes (i.e., on the number of workers involved, or strike size), and political scientists on the overall levels of strike activity (as measured by strike volume). Furthermore, economists' models are mainly short-term models; their basic time frame is the length of the business cycle. Resource-mobilization and political-exchange theories, on the other hand, focus on the medium term and long term. They are interested in the outcome of labor strategies aimed at maximizing long-term organizational and/or political goals rather than short-term economic goals, a strategy that would promote strike activity even in the face of repeated economic defeat, a strategy in which the conflict is about, rather than within, the rules of the game. Within the confines of bargaining models, based solely on a cost–benefit analysis of economic gains and losses, much of French or Italian strike activity, for instance, makes little sense. As Shorter and Tilly (1974, p. 68) write,

> The outcomes of French strikes have been so dismal over the years, and their growing lack of success so palpable, that one wonders why the workers bothered. Indeed, anyone who insisted that the true purpose of strikes was to achieve the stated grievances would be absolutely at a loss....

Few serious attempts have been made to understand the discrepancies and to explain the divergences among the different approaches.

Snyder (1975, 1977) put forward a theoretical explanation that attempts to account for such discrepancies. Snyder's basic argument is that organizational/political models of strikes prevail in institutional settings (countries and time periods) where labor institutionalization is low (prewar United States and prewar and postwar France and Italy), whereas economic models prevail in institutional settings of the opposite type (postwar United States). If Snyder's argument were correct, then we would expect that (1) economic bargaining models, such as the Ashenfelter and Johnson model, would perform poorly in the Italian context and (2) organizational/political models would best explain the Italian postwar experience.

Contrary to Snyder's dichotomous strike model, Korpi[14] argued for an integrated strike model. In Korpi's "power difference" model, economic factors play significant roles in strike activity to the extent that these factors, particularly the level of unemployment, affect the current balance of power between workers and employers by improving the tactical position of labor (Korpi, 1974, p. 1577). This model is similar to bargaining models. In Korpi's model, however, bargaining power is affected not only by short-term economic changes but also by long-term changes in the locus of conflict, caused by shifts in the political position of labor. Economic variables are central to bargaining models. Differences in power, as perhaps affected by economic conditions, form the core of Korpi's model.

Marxist scholars similarly argue that classes strategically take advantage of changes in economic, organizational, institutional, political, and other conditions in order to either increase their class capacities – the organizational resources that enable a class to act collectively in pursuit of its interests, much as in resource-mobilization theories – or diminish the capacities of other classes. However, Marxists argue, it is not simply that class capacities are unequal in capitalist societies; capitalists also are better able to shape the very factors that affect these capacities. Through their control over production and investment decisions, capitalists can directly affect the performance of the economy (Offe and Ronge, 1975; Block, 1977). The level of economic performance is not only a key determinant of conflict, as bargaining models argue; in bourgeois democracies it also ensures that the state is a "capitalist state" (i.e., a state that broadly works in the interests of the capitalist class). Furthermore, in organizing and fostering their interests, workers pay a much greater price than do capitalists (Offe and Wiesenthal, 1980). This gap in organizational costs tends to widen during times of recession. For Marxists, as well, then, economic factors play significant roles in strike activity, to the extent that they alter class capacities.

The fitting of the puzzle of strikes thus requires not only the fitting of different pieces of empirical evidence, but, first and foremost, the fitting of theoretical strands that have been deaf to each other's words.

1.6. MORE SERIOUS PROBLEMS: IT TAKES TWO TO TANGO

The strike literature is overwhelmingly quantitative. The ready availability of government-collected data in most industrialized countries since at least the end of the nineteenth century has made it all too easy for quantitative researchers to treat strikes as little more than an excuse for statistical exercises. Unfortunately, all too often, statistical work tends "to deny (and even to block the cognitive access to) the reality of class" (Offe and Wiesenthal, 1980, p. 71). This is particularly true for quantitative strike research. The aseptic language of statistical discourse has mystified the object of study: class conflict. Few studies in a very abundant literature have made a connection between "strikes" and "class struggle," between employees and the working class, between employers and the capitalist class. Fewer yet have attempted an explanation of strikes in class terms. Nowhere in the literature does one see the streets and the squares filled with workers. Neither does one feel the excitement or the fear aroused by the sight of the crowds, the lines of police, the signs and placards, leaflets, clenched fists, red banners, the hammer and sickle – the markers of class identity and the symbols of revolutionary discourse.[15] These images have dissolved into countless correlation coefficients, regression coefficients, t statistics, power spectra, spectral coherences, graphs, plots. The class nature of strikes has been effectively "exnominated" from discourse, hidden behind the language of statistical objectivity and truth.

Part of the problem stems from the fact that strike statistics themselves reflect class relations. Strikes were originally viewed as crimes under "combination acts." Their recording was police business; data were kept secret in the hands of ministries of the interior (Perrot, 1974). Only after the conception of strikes shifted from one of crime to one of "social illness" did strikes become the concern of specialized labor ministries – in Italy, however, strike data are still collected through local police departments. Despite the shift from "repression" to "cure," however, the kind of information collected still reflected state concern with rising labor militancy, as information was collected on the presence of working-class organizations during strikes, the occurrence of violence, and the outcomes of strikes.[16] If governments were eager to collect information on strikes, they were not nearly as eager to make such information available. During the nineteenth century in Italy, publication of strike data was never timely; often two years or more passed before strike statistics were made available; in any case, data were published at a highly aggregated level. As such, strike statistics were of little use to working-class organizations (Lay, Marucco, and Pesante, 1973, pp. 108–9).

The question is, How can one study the class nature of "industrial" conflict, when not only the category of class has been eliminated from the discourse of strike data, but also all the significant actors involved? In fact, if data are available on what workers do, data on what employers and the state do are much less readily available. Neither ISTAT (the Italian central statistical institute) nor the Ministry of Labor, for instance, has ever collected data on the forms and levels of labor repression used by employers, nor have they collected data on the timing of employers' introduction of new technologies and new forms of organization of production that offer opportunities for breaking up worker solidarity.

Strikes emerged in the nineteenth century in most Western countries as the predominant expression of grievances of a class generated by industrial capitalism (Thompson, 1978, pp. 146–50). They emerged out of the ongoing interactions among the main groups involved – workers, employers, and the state – and it was those interactions that ultimately defined the rules and the acceptable forms of protest (Tilly, 1978, p. 161). It is not possible to understand what workers do without at the same time understanding what employers and the state do. With the exception of a handful of studies, strike research has been particularly silent on the roles of employers and the state.[17] Yet if it takes two to tango, it takes at least two to fight. The interactions among strike activity and economic, organizational, institutional, and political factors that I tease out in this book were interactions among actors organized in the pursuit of their interests.

But strikes are not simply multiple-actor phenomena (most of which never make it into the picture); they also are multiple-action phenomena. In part, this statement is tautological. If there is a multiplicity of actors, each actor will engage in different actions. On the one hand, workers themselves engage in an array of collective actions: The strike is only part of a wider repertoire that workers use (e.g., strikes, mass meetings, rallies inside and outside the plant). On the other hand, the state intervenes in various institutional settings (police, courts, parliament, arbitration boards) and at a variety of levels (local, regional, central). Employers hire and fire workers, make investment decisions, reorganize production, and open, move, or close plants. More specifically, in this book I will show that employers' reactions to the 1969 *autunno caldo* ("hot autumn") and later strikes fundamentally changed the forms of organization of production, which in turn changed the class structure. By the end of the 1970s, the unskilled worker who had fought the struggles of the late 1960s and early 1970s was no longer "central" to the new forms of organization of production. Through decentralization, robotization, and other restructuring plans, in the span of a decade the Italian employers had virtually eliminated from the class structure the type of worker who had been one of the key actors in the previous cycle of struggle (Accornero, 1981). Unfortunately, the whole political and economic organization of the class, its economic and political strategy throughout the 1970s, had been based on that type of worker (the "mass worker") (Accornero, 1981; Rieser, 1981). The elimination of that type of worker from the class structure represented a long-term defeat for the Italian working class as a whole.

In short, in the preceding section I argued that disciplinary parochialism is responsible for the lack of integration among the various theoretical approaches, with their localized focus on specific strike components, time horizons, and social processes. In this section I have argued that the ready availability of government-collected data since the 1800s in most Western countries and the preponderantly quantitative nature of the strike literature have been responsible for another shortcoming: the strategic interactions among the players involved have been lost in the literature. Even those models presumably based on the interactions among several players (e.g., the Ashenfelter and Johnson model) have, in the final analysis, closely focused on workers and their actions. All that an economic model of strikes is saying is that workers' rational calculations and decisions to strike are functions of wages, prices, and unemployment rate. It does not say anything about how other actors may affect these economic variables. The social relations behind the economic relations have been lost; the interests of the different actors and their strategic interactions are gone. In these models, workers merely react to impersonal forces that no one controls, no one directs, no one benefits from. *A strike is the result of the strategic interactions among several social actors with specific interests and specific capacities.*

But that is not all. The quantitative strike literature has largely ignored what is probably the single most important characteristic of strikes: the fact that in most industrialized countries over past the 150 years, labor militancy seems to have erupted in massive movements of defiance against employers and the state in a handful of historical conjunctures, or strike waves, as in the British 1926 "general strike," the 1968 French May, the Italian 1919–20 "red years," and the 1969 *autunno caldo* ("hot autumn").[18]

The salience of strike waves is their radical challenge to constituted authority, both inside and outside the workplace. Not only do strike indicators reach record highs at these times, but tactics and demands become more radical. The strike movement reaches out to draw in parties that are typically uninvolved. Entrepreneurs and political authorities respond, usually with massive concessions at first, to be followed later by repression. Even when these mass mobilization movements are partly in the hands of formal organizations (i.e., unions, but also working-class parties) they have many of the characteristics of the mass movements of disruption that Piven and Cloward (1979) so vividly described. Unfortunately, in econometric modeling, a strike wave becomes just another data point in a time series. If we were more careful with our econometric work, perhaps we would be more aware that these data points result in unexplained outliers. We then could use "dummy variables" to account for outliers from a statistical viewpoint. But, in most cases we simply ignore outliers. In any case, whether we choose to dummy-out the outliers or to ignore them, we leave unresolved the problem of explaining these momentous mobilization processes. That the working class in any capitalist country is typically quiescent is certainly something that needs to be explained. As Batstone, Boraston, and Frenkel (1978, p. 26) write: "If we want to understand strikes we have also to understand non-strikes." But in light of this quiescence, that the working class should, at times, massively rise and become defiant of economic and political relations is perhaps even more astonishing.

1.7. REALLY SERIOUS PROBLEMS: THE AUTOMATIC PILOT (WRITING SCHEMATA AND REGRESSION BLENDERS)

The strike literature is both old and abundant. For more than a century researchers have been picking at the issue. Government data gave researchers, particularly those looking for quantitative results, material that was easy to work with. Yet despite this wealth of production, the literature seems to have repeatedly and parochially focused on the same (often marginal) issues and, worse, ignored the most fundamental aspects of strikes: the strategic interactions among the actors involved and the phenomenon of strike waves. By and large, the strike literature is neither intellectually exciting nor innovative. Worse yet, one does not get from it a sense of cumulation of knowledge. Why?

Semantic linguists have shown that literary genres (e.g., narrative, scientific journal articles, news) are characterized by *deep structures* or schemata that are invariant for the genre (like an *ideal type*, to put it in more familiar terminology).[19] Thus, for instance, a scientific journal article may have the following schema: *introduction, literature review, hypotheses, data and methods, empirical results, conclusions*. The headings for the schema may vary in actual articles (the *literature review* and *hypotheses* may become *theory*; the *empirical results* may be labeled *findings*). The material in an article may not be efficiently organized under the headings of the schema (thus, one may find some literature review in the *hypotheses* section or even in the *empirical results* section, or some *data and methods* in the *empirical results*). But, by and large, each article organizes the material (or, in any case, this material can be reorganized) according to a schema that is fixed within the genre.

Schemata help to routinize both writing and reading, production and consumption of linguistic material. Schemata help the reader to organize knowledge, to understand. Text understanding, in fact, seems to proceed via the construction of an organizational framework, a set of drawers where we place the material as we encounter it (Kintsch and van Dijk, 1978; van Dijk, 1980). Schemata help readers to place the material in the appropriate drawers, to know what to expect.

As writers, all we have to do in the process of production is to follow steps. There is little creative process involved, at least as far as the organization of the material. The creative steps are not in the construction of a schema per se, but in the content of the *hypotheses* and the *empirical results* sections. And that, perhaps, is how it should be. That is where, supposedly, we make our scientific contribution, with a new way of conceptualizing a problem or of testing old propositions, or both. Unfortunately, in quantitative research, even these creative steps have become routinized. Our *hypotheses* are narrowly conceived, so that they are indeed amenable to multivariate, empirical testing. Our empirical testing is an excuse to apply the latest and "sexiest" technique available (until someone figures out that the technique has problems that undermine the results). More specifically, empirical testing has increasingly come to rely on the *regression blender* for answers. We toss everything in (the more the better, because thereby we think that we are *controlling* for as many factors as possible), we let the blender mix up the data, and then we write up the results.

We cannot simply blame statistics per se for this. Undoubtedly, as Freedman (1991, p. 300) writes: "regression models make it all too easy to substitute technique for work." Exclusive reliance on statistical data and an overwhelming emphasis on methodological sophistication do make it more difficult to look beyond what is quantifiable and analyzable within high-powered methodologies. Yet the use of statistics (particularly exploratory techniques) has proved quite fruitful in this book. The problem is not one of journal production versus book production, either. Certainly space limitations in journal publishing force researchers to gloss over (if not hide under the carpet) ambiguities, inconsistencies, and discrepancies (only those between the author's work and other people's work are highlighted). Complexities are simplified in the name of a clean "punch line." But sometimes book publishing can enlarge the scope of these problems, simply providing more of the same.

The problem, in fact, is deeper than either the choice of publishing medium or the choice of methodological approach and empirical evidence. The problem is that under the combined pressures of forces that all urge us in the same direction (career, space constraints, data availability, limitations of statistical techniques, etc.), we have come to theorize in very narrow ways, we tend to call off our investigative work at the first hint of an answer to a question. Whether qualitative or quantitative in orientation, there is a tendency for researchers to rely exclusively on one or another form of empirical evidence and methodology. Within the quantitative approach, what this means is that anything that is not quantifiable is not included in one's model. What is not included in the model is not part of the causal structure, not part of the explanation. The problem is brushed aside, soon to be forgotten. What it also means is that data and methodological limitations foster mental habits whereby the complexities of historical reality are intentionally overlooked, problems are brushed aside, and coefficients are evaluated for their own inherent interest. Statistical results rarely translate back into an interpretation of historical reality. In the regression-blender approach, regression results *become* the explanation. Whatever comes out of the regression blender we faithfully write up in the *empirical results* sections of the research papers that fill our journals.

Typically, in our statistical work, we become absorbed in the technical aspects of model building and estimating. Historical change comes to be seen as a problem of instability in the structural parameters, causality a problem of model building (e.g., single- vs. multiple-equation models, variables with lagged or contemporaneous effects). Causality yields to additive, seriatim explanations for sociohistorical processes whereby complexity is built by adding, piecemeal fashion, new variables to a model. Innovation is measured in terms of new variables added to a model, in terms of selecting a different sample or estimation technique.

As regression results are merely interpreted, not explained, hardly any cumulation of knowledge is achieved. (For instance, consider this example: When expanding the sample size to include the 1960–63 observations, the coefficient of the unemployment rate changes from negative to positive, and the wage variable loses its significance. This is contrary to Ashenfelter and Johnson's findings.) Differences in empirical findings are simply reported, rather than explained. In that way, the social sciences have come to be made up of sets of disconnected, contradictory, and unexplained information.

There is real pressure toward narrowly conceived theorizing, particularly, theorizing that leads to propositions that can be easily tested empirically. Otherwise, in the face of grand-scale theorizing, one's empirical work would look too simplistic, the balance between theoretical and empirical claims too tilted toward the latter. Not surprisingly, theoretical and empirical work typically mirror each other perfectly. In order not to clutter the argument and not to leave too many holes in the fabric, data and methodological constraints tend to force one into theoretical narrowness. Consider Chomsky's (1968, p. xi) scathing words:

Modern linguistics shares the delusion – the accurate term, I believe – that the modern "behavioral sciences" have in some essential respects achieved a transition from "speculation" to "science" and that earlier work can be safely consigned to the antiquarians. Obviously any rational person will favor rigorous analysis and careful experiment; but to a considerable degree, I feel, the "behavioral sciences" are merely mimicking the surface features of the natural sciences; much of their scientific character has been achieved by a restriction of subject matter and a concentration on rather peripheral issues. Such narrowing of focus can be justified if it leads to achievements of real intellectual significance, but in this case, I think it would be very difficult to show that the narrowing of scope has led to deep and significant results.

And so we busy ourselves to produce, with the forgiving hand of the writing schemata and the regression blender. As readers, to keep up with such abundant production, we learn the technique of skim reading, and we learn to pick up the *important points* (i.e., whether a coefficient is positive or negative, significant or insignificant). And thus it goes, from mindless producers to mindless consumers, both running on automatic pilot: normal science made subnormal, where production for the sake of production (volume production, by large numbers) seems to have become the name of the game.

Cui prodest? When we put the problem of scientific production in these terms (*Who benefits?*), then we must see ourselves as involved not just in a process of scientific production, but in a process of ideological production (i.e., of producing and reproducing meaning in the service of dominant social relations). By relying on data that allow us to address only a narrow set of questions, over and over again, by keeping the spotlight fixed on the same actors, on the same actions, on the same issues, we (consciously or unconsciously) become involved in the process of mystification of the reality of unequal social relations. The fact that some things are left in the darkness does not mean that they are not there, of course, but the mechanism of the spotlight can soon make us forget that there is a wider world out there. Qualitative work certainly is not synonymous with critical work, but the danger of quantitative work is that for lack of available data it repeatedly focuses on the same set of narrowly conceived questions. When that is coupled with the fact that data (particularly government data or data produced by large-scale organizations) typically are not collected for the purpose of illuminating unequal social relations, quantitative social (scientific) production can become dangerously involved in ideological production.

1.8. IN SEARCH OF A SOLUTION

Unfortunately, reciting a litany of more or less well known problems that beset our research practice will not make those problems go away. Particularly in quantitative research, it is scholars not involved in the day-to-day muddling through of practical, empirical research who point out the problems; sometimes it is scholars who have made their fortunes with quantitative research and, on their way to building new fortunes, have become more royalist than the king himself. But where does this leave us? If one's research agenda is theory-driven, rather than method-driven, if one is genuinely interested in understanding substantive, historical problems, what can one do? What have I done in this book to deal with these problems? How have I approached the methodological and theoretical problems involved in overcoming at least some of the deficiencies of the automatic-pilot approach?

I dealt with the statistical problem of historical change and periodization in several ways. First, in the case of longer-term econometric models, I always formally tested the temporal stability of structural parameters. Second, I relied on my knowledge of the historical record to target particular periods for more careful analysis. That knowledge, however, all too often failed me. Early on, during the phase of data analysis, I used a third approach. I devised a methodology that would allow me to compute subsample analyses automatically.[20] I then carefully inspected the estimated coefficients, often plotting them against time, and looked for changes in sign and magnitude. That approach had the advantage of being independent of my knowledge of the historical record. The data themselves forced me to look for explanations. Particularly at the beginning of the analyses, that approach increased my understanding of the historical unfolding of labor conflicts in postwar Italy.

But, in fact, the emphasis on historical change in this book goes well beyond the limits of even careful statistical analysis of subsamples. The view of history embraced here, being the result of the strategic interactions of organized groups (i.e., classes and the state) in the pursuit of their individual and collective interests, forces me to put at the heart of this monograph the changing nature of these groups' strategies as they each act and react to the choices of the others. An important feature of these strategies is that they change; they are continually in a state of flux. Econometric solutions to the problem of historical change, as important as these solutions are within the context of quantitative analysis, only begin to capture this continual process of change and strategic interaction. Historical change and causality are not just statistical problems; most important, they are problems of agency.[21] Thus, while dealing with problems of historical change at a statistical level, I consistently used history to guide my understanding of the actions and motivations of the social actors (workers, employers, their organizations, the state or states) and how the actions of these actors may change the course of history at any given time. Although it may be difficult to see from the vantage point of regression coefficients, history is about people. It is about actors struggling in the pursuit of their interests. History is, first and foremost, a question of agency.

The uncertainty of the outcomes of these struggles in which antagonistic groups engage, even under conditions of structural imbalance in these groups' resources and forces, is what gives history much of its heroic flavor, tinting these struggles with the colors of passion. I tried to capture some of that passion, the human side of the struggles behind the regression coefficients, by using the rich ethnographic material of field research,[22] workers' diaries and interviews. Throughout this book I bring in "guest speakers" (mostly workers, but also many employers and managers) to interpret for us the econometric results, to give meaning to a negative or positive coefficient. Their testimony, taken from surveys, diaries, and interviews, brings in much of the pathos, the heroism, the fears, and the contradictions of those struggles, but also some of the more comic situations, "Because, you see, the class struggle is also comedy."(quoted in Accornero and Rieser, 1981, p.16). Indeed, the class struggle as comedy is what Paolo Migliaccio, known as "the rat" (*u rattu*), a former mine worker from Carloforte, must have had in mind when he told me the story of a strike in which he had been a protagonist:

See, one day one of the tunnels in the mine collapsed, and a miner was injured. I, myself, was a welder. You wouldn't get me there in those pits to die years later of asbestosis or silicosis with rotted lungs. I saw many of these kids coming in, young, strong as bulls, and bullies too: "I'll destroy this mountain!" "Yeah, yeah, you just wait," I used to think, "and the mountain will destroy you." And sure enough. It was just a question of time, and they'd drop like flies, skinny as ghosts and gray in the face. But I was a welder and kept as far away from the pits as I could. But, that day, it was a friend of mine that had been injured down there, and no one knew whether it was safe to continue work. And the supervisor insisted that everything was OK, "nothing to worry about." But he wasn't the one going down there, and the workers went on strike. The supervisor was furious, and he was cursing and threatening, all red in the face. But the guy that was injured was a friend of mine. I wasn't about to just stand there. And there was the donkey that the supervisor rode around. So, when no one was watching, I welded the iron shoe of the donkey's right fore and left hind hoofs to the cart tracks. And the donkey just stood there. The supervisor pushed him, he shoved him, he kicked him, but the damned donkey just wouldn't move. And the carts couldn't go anywhere. Everyone was standing around there. They couldn't figure out what was wrong with the donkey. The engineer came to see what the fuss was all about. So I told him about my friend, the strike, the supervisor, and how I had welded the donkey's hoofs. Everyone was laughing like crazy. Even the engineer couldn't help laughing. And so, he sent everyone home with pay.

I used history to make sense of statistical results. I used survey and ethnographic material not simply to spice up the historical narrative and to contextualize statistical results.[23] Most importantly, I used survey and ethnography to fill in the vacuum left by the paucity of time-series data. Rather than ignore a problem simply because no time-series data were available, I amply utilized, as empirical evidence, both qualitative data and quantitative data that, for lack of sufficient numbers of observations, could not be used in econometric modeling.

Of course, the use of ethnographic material may seem selective. Why did I use that particular quotation from that particular worker? How would my story have changed, had I let someone else speak? These are legitimate and worrisome questions (incidentally ... does anyone worry about the selection process involved in quantitative research, the way we pick a few regression models out of the hundreds we run, with the coefficients of some regressions going one way, and those of others going another way?) My answer to these questions is that, of course, the particular choices were selective. But they were selective only in the sense that I picked the ones that were most expressive and engaging. They were *not* selective in the sense that I chose them simply for rhetorical reasons, because they would fit well with my argument (although I would invite fellow social scientists to a serious and healthy reflection on the rhetorical foundations of our work). Rather, they were representative of converging set of meanings. The stories point in the same direction. They "saturate" the field of meaning (Bertaux, 1981). I was no less critical in my acceptance of qualitative evidence than I was with the quantitative evidence.

For all my claims regarding ethnography and history, the book may appear to the more qualitatively inclined readers as a statistical tour de force. A great deal of the empirical basis of the book is provided by a wealth of tables, graphs, plots, charts, and equations. Yet I should warn quantitatively inclined readers at the outset that in this book they will not find multiple-equation strike models that can properly account for the complexity of the historical processes from a statistical viewpoint. The problems of data and methods were overwhelming.

How confident am I of the statistical results? To put it in more concrete terms: How much money would I be willing to bet on these results? As social scientists, we do not normally bet money on our models – and perhaps a good thing it is, because if we did, not just our models but we too would be bankrupt. Indeed, I do not have great faith in the results of any single regression equation. Each is encumbered with too many problems for me to really believe what the statistics books say. I never took regression results at face value, as *the* explanation. Rather,

I did the opposite. My most enlightening breakthroughs came not from what statistics *could explain*, but from what it *could not explain*. They came from pursuing unusual patterns in the residuals, systematic inconsistencies in the signs of coefficients, and unexpectedly low R^2 values. I doggedly followed what regression could not explain, and the unexplained often provided insights. Searching for explanations, I formulated hypotheses. Sometimes the pursuit of those hypotheses led to more regression work; most often, it simply led to a search for historical or ethnographic evidence. In line with the narrative spirit of the book, regression provided fruitful leads for me to follow. In the end, the empirical evidence had to be true to the historical record; the historical record had to find support in the empirical evidence.

But this is leading me astray from the original question: Am I ready to bet money on my results? The answer is a qualified yes. I am ready to bet money on the overall picture that emerges from the use of combined statistical, historical, survey, and ethnographic evidence. For the quantofrenics, certainly, the empirical evidence is thin, when it is not based on multivariate techniques. For the historians, all that statistical baggage may be little more than silver lining. My statistical modeling is simple, my narrative limited. So perhaps the book provides only a partial combination of history and sociology (particularly, quantitative sociology).[24] Yet I believe that the overall picture that emerges is quite sound. I carefully checked it and rechecked it, playing statistics against statistics, statistics against history, and history against ethnography and survey research. But, this book is not simply about the meeting of history and statistics, or ethnography and statistics. It is about the historical embedment of empirical results and the empirical testing of theoretical explanations of historical processes. In fact, history and statistics had to meet in a coherent theoretical framework. I tested the explanatory power of different theoretical approaches, pointing out similarities and differences among them, contradictions and limitations within them. I am ready to bet money on this process of theory building and theory testing via the combination of historical, statistical, survey, and ethnographic material, via the interplay between different theoretical approaches. Thus, not only do I believe in the overall results. I also believe in the process, a process based on simultaneous use of different forms of empirical evidence, on a constant dialogue between *teoria* and *empiria*.

1.9. ORGANIZATION OF THE BOOK

Like any respectable puzzle box, this book comes complete with hardware and software, with all the pieces of the puzzle (the characteristics of the strike data) and a set of instructions (strike theories). Each chapter addresses one of the main theories of strikes and tests its potential for understanding these characteristics, for fitting the puzzle together.

Chapter 2 offers an analysis of the relationship between strikes and the state of the labor market. I test the Ashenfelter and Johnson model, the best-known among the economic models of strikes. The business cycle seems to contribute an explanation of the temporal movement of, at least, the frequency of strikes. This runs counter to Snyder's theoretical expectations and empirical evidence on Italy. Why are my findings different from Snyder's?

In Chapter 3, in order to answer that question, I expand the analyses to different strike indicators (number of workers involved and number of hours lost) and different business-cycle indicators (capacity utilization, industrial production, etc.). The results leave no doubt about the fact that economic factors played a fundamental role in shaping the temporal patterns of Italian strikes. Chapter 3 analyzes not only the short-term relationships between the economy and strike activity, but also the relationships involving secular, structural characteristics of the economy (e.g., distribution of the labor force, distribution of firm sizes, technical and social modes of production).

However, the results of Chapter 3 also point to the limits of a purely economic interpretation of Italian strikes. After two chapters of economic analysis, too many pieces of the puzzle still lay about without explanation. Chapter 4 explores the relationship between strike activity and union organization. The organization of Italian labor in "class unions" goes a long way toward explaining the particular characteristics of Italian strikes: brief and large. The econometric results confirm a widespread finding that economic factors weigh more heavily in determining the number of strikes, whereas unionization weighs more heavily on the number of workers involved and the number of hours lost. The analyses also show that smaller firms have historically been outside of union control. Not surprisingly, these firms have shown much lower strike rates.

Chapter 5 fits the last few pieces to the puzzle. The two-tier bargaining structure (plant-level bargaining and national, industrywide bargaining) explains the temporal pattern of Italian strikes: the three-year cycle and the one-year lag between number of strikes and number of strikers. The analyses also show that collective bargaining has mostly been confined to large and medium-size plants. Plant-level bargaining, in particular, is related to higher-than-average wages. The puzzle is now almost complete, except for two pieces: the anomaly of 1969, the year with the highest number of hours lost due to strikes in the whole period, and the characteristics of conflict during the 1975–78 period, when conflicts became very brief and infrequent, but also much larger than ever before.

Chapter 6 provides an explanation for the 1975–78 strike shapes. The changes in the characteristics of strikes during those years reflect the gradually increasing power of the Italian Communist Party in the aftermath of the 1969 "hot autumn" and up until its 1978 participation in a government coalition. The changes in the shapes of strikes between 1975 and 1978 reflect a change in labor strategy away from the economic market and into the political market.

Finally, Chapter 7 takes a closer look at the many little events that make up the biggest *event* in Italian labor history: the 1969 *autunno caldo*, the "hot autumn" of *anno Domini* 1969. I show that working-class, large-scale mobilization processes (also known as strike waves or cycles of struggle) are characterized not only by higher levels of conflict but also by new and more radical tactics and demands. The wave front hit large factories particularly hard. Strike waves typically also force concessions from both economic and political authorities, and thus they have many of the characteristics of Piven and Cloward's mass disruption movements (Piven and Cloward, 1979). The strikes during the "hot autumn" and subsequent years indeed had these characteristics.

Large-scale mobilization processes are followed typically by equally momentous countermobilization processes. Chapter 8 analyzes the reactions of both state and employers to the 1969 *autunno caldo*, the subtle balance between soft and hard violence, between the carrot and the stick. The 1968–72 strike wave changed the forms of institutionalization of labor and the balance of class forces in the political arena. Indirectly, via employers' reactions, the strike wave significantly transformed Italy's very economic structure. As Italy's large-scale employers tried to stem the tide of workers' mobilization, the large factories shrank in average size and number and small factories mushroomed. Contrary to Shorter and Tilly (1974), who view strike waves as the outcomes of national, political processes, I argue that strike waves are related to the long-term cycles of capitalist economies. Strike waves tend to occur around the peak of the upward phase of long-term cycles.

In Chapter 9, I step back and take a final look at the complete picture. One more time, I make sure that all the pieces fit tightly together in the proper places, I check both the local and global coherence of the picture, I go over the main themes embedded in its narrative and the theories that have been most helpful in creating that narrative. If Chapter 9 is a conclusion, it is not simply a summary of previous chapters, a picture of *déjà vu*. To evaluate the basic soundness of the picture that has finally emerged from fitting the puzzle, I bring in more evidence, I look at the picture from the angle of broader theoretical frameworks, I put it all to the test of history, one final time. If the puzzle of strikes started in Chapter 1 by setting for itself the task of fitting together different pieces of empirical evidence, the puzzle ends with the task of fitting theoretical pieces.

1.10. PAT SOLUTIONS, RED HERRINGS, AND PARADOXES

Unlike most puzzle boxes, this particular box comes without a picture of the complete puzzle. Furthermore, many pieces are missing. If this makes the work ahead of me more challenging, it also makes it that much more uncertain. I do not have the luxury of knowing beforehand what the puzzle should look like. In fact, I do not even know if there is a coherent picture among these scattered pieces. I am forced to proceed somewhat blindly, with different strands of theories, my own intuition, and my sociological "craft" providing the only guidance to my work. As a consequence, I fit and refit pieces throughout the book in search of a coherent picture. Pieces that seem to fit perfectly in one chapter show a tight squeeze in another, in light of new evidence, of new theories. I continually have to dig up new pieces to fill a hole, to cover a vacuum. The complete picture does not emerge until the very end. As a result, this book tells a story, a story of many leads that lead nowhere, of theories that go only part of the way toward explaining the data. The story builds its own suspense, with continual setbacks and new resolutions. What seems to be a plausible explanation in one chapter, I reject in the next. Why a certain theory cannot fully account for the empirical evidence becomes apparent only in light of another theory. Within this narrative framework, the story that unfolds does not proceed as smoothly as the description of the organization of the book in the preceding section might make it appear.

In chapter after chapter, as I find new answers, I also raise new questions. Thus, in Chapter 4, the econometric results point to differentiated effects (negative and positive) of the wage variable on the numbers of strikes and strikers. Why is that so? In Chapter 5, we see that the characteristics of strikes during contract-renewal years are quite different from those in surrounding years. Why, then, are the characteristics of strikes in 1976, a contract-renewal year, not any different from those of 1975 or 1977? In Chapter 7, I focus on an unprecedented historical event, the 1969 *autunno caldo*, and its highly disruptive (revolutionary?) characteristics. In Chapter 8, I explore the causes and consequences of that event and I locate its structural roots (see Braudel, 1980, pp. 27–38, 74–6; Le Roy Ladurie, 1979, pp. 111–31). But that exploration into the relationship between event and structure unexpectedly leads me to completely reverse the causal argument of the book. Conflict becomes the independent variable, the main mechanism of change in the economic, organizational, institutional, and political spheres.

More generally, in chapter after chapter, parts of the empirical evidence seem to be incompatible with the proposed theoretical framework. I call these inconsistencies *paradoxes*, because the theory fails to explain what it should be best equipped to explain. Thus, in Chapter 2, the empirical evidence seems to point to a certain peculiar behavior of Italian workers: swept up by optimism during boom times, they struck more often than would be predicted by economic-bargaining models; overcome by discouragement during busts, they struck less frequently than would be predicted. Does this behavior have something to do with the character of the Italian people, as the eighteenth-century literature would have it *(paradox of the génie d'un peuple)*? Still in Chapter 2, we discover that strike activity during the 1970s remained at high levels, and sometimes increased, in spite of rising unemployment. According to economic-bargaining theories, strike activity and unemployment should be inversely related *(paradox of the 1970s)*.

In Chapter 3, economic analysis cannot explain why the shapes of strikes in 1962 (a year of economic boom) and 1966 (a recessionary year) are so remarkably similar. Economic-bargaining theories would lead us to expect strikes to be shorter during the downswing phase of the business cycle and longer during the upswing *(paradox of the 1962 and 1966 strike shapes)*. Furthermore, the analysis of the structural characteristics of the Italian economy bring out two other paradoxes. Italian strikes have tended to be either smaller in size than the work force of the average large plant (the ones that have struck) or larger than the work force of even the largest plants *(paradox of strike size)*. Contrary to all the available evidence that would link greater levels of class consciousness and conflict to larger plants, the Italian evidence suggests that the very largest plants have fewer strikes and are less unionized than large and medium-size plants *(paradox of large firms)*.

The analyses of Chapter 4 on plant-level organizational structures leave no doubt about the fact that small firms are largely outside of union control. If so, how can we explain the fact that regions with high percentages of small-scale industrial production (e.g., Emilia-Romagna, Tuscany) are the most highly unionized in Italy *(paradox of small-scale-production regions)*?

Chapter 5 adds another twist to the *paradox of small-scale-production regions*: Analyses of diffusion of plant-level bargaining and working conditions in large firms versus small firms leave no doubt about the fact that plant-level bargaining typically is absent from small firms. Furthermore, in small firms, working conditions and salaries typically are lower than those in larger firms. If so, however, how can we explain the fact that regions with an industrial infrastructure of small-scale plants (e.g., Emilia-Romagna, Tuscany, but also Veneto) show the highest per capita incomes and the highest quality-of-life indices in Italy?

Each chapter in the book focuses narrowly, and almost exclusively, on one aspect of strikes (economic, organizational, institutional, political). In each chapter I even keep separate the historical treatment of these various aspects. I deal with economic history in Chapter 2, with the history of labor and employer organizations in Chapter 4, with the history of the institutionalization of conflict in Chapter 5, and with political history in Chapter 6. Each chapter begins the story all over again (1950–78), looking at historical reality from a different angle. Just as in choosing an inductive organization for the book, I take this approach quite intentionally, and for two reasons. First, this approach squares well with the rhetorical device of the puzzle, for I cannot give away in Chapter 2 what I do not discuss until Chapter 6. Most important, I use this approach as a heuristic device. By keeping various aspects of social reality separate, in each chapter I answer only some of the questions, I fit only a few of the pieces. The limitations of this approach leave me with unanswered questions, unfitted pieces – all the more so because the interplay between theory and data, in each chapter, brings up new and unforeseen questions, new pieces of the puzzle that cannot be accounted for by the body of theoretical knowledge amassed to that point. This approach forces me to revise and update interpretations continually, to keep rearranging the pieces until they bring out a coherent picture. Unfortunately, in our quantitative work we often tend not only to look at social reality from a limited angle but also to stop fitting our pieces after the first apparently successful trial.

Thus, many running threads weave in and out of this book. I engage the reader on different levels:

1. an explanation of the temporal patterns of Italian postwar strikes at different levels of temporalities and in light of four different classes of factors and theories: economic, organizational, institutional, and political;
2. a dialogue with the social-scientific enterprise, regarding how we go about building and testing theories and what constitutes acceptable empirical evidence (which involves a

dialogue between different methodological approaches, i.e., qualitative and quantitative, and, within the quantitative approach, between multivariate statistical modeling and simple exploratory analysis);
3. a dialogue between competing theoretical frameworks (i.e., the Marxist and non-Marxist traditions, but also involving lower-level theories, such as economic-bargaining, resource-mobilization, and political-exchange theories);
4. an interpretation of Italian postwar history in light of the strategic interactions of classes and the state as they pursue their interests within the constraints and possibilities of given structural and historical conditions;
5. a narrative framework (the puzzle metaphor) that envelops all the other viewpoints.

Some of the characteristics of the book (e.g., its inductive approach, its reliance on different types of empirical evidence, the use of exploratory and confirmatory statistical techniques, the one-sided view of historical reality adopted in each chapter, the interplay of different theoretical approaches) come from this complex weaving of the cloth, and the different threads running through it.

That is the story that this book tells, complete with plots and subplots. The book, however, does not just tell a story. Despite its narrative framework, the book abides by the rules of scientific method. It satisfies the burden of proof. As such, its narrative is embedded in a wealth of historical/empirical evidence. If it is successful, other researchers engaged in similar projects will be able to replicate my findings. Whether or not I have succeeded in combining all these different levels, only the reader can tell. As narrative work, the success of the book ultimately will depend on how well it tells the story. As scientific work, its success will depend on its ability to account for historical reality, to integrate statistical, historical, and theoretical work, to manipulate data and methods. But . . . on with the story!

2

Labor-market conditions and bargaining power

How do the fluctuations in economic activity affect the number of strikes? Obviously, through their effect on unemployment. When this goes down, when the working day gets longer in the factories, due to new orders, when workers are employed six or seven days a week, instead of four or five, they realize (without having to consult the statistics) that business is going well and they try to take advantage of the situation. Hence, strikes. When, on the contrary, unemployment soars, when workers see some of their fellow workers being dismissed, and the number of working hours and days curtailed, they hesitate to strike, at least over wage issues, for fear of being replaced by the army of the unemployed. The curve of strikes dwindles. Therefore, there is a relationship of cause and effect between the fluctuations of unemployment and those of strikes.

Rist (1907, p. 402)

2.1. HOW THE LABOR-MARKET ARGUMENT RUNS

Labor-market theories of strikes claim that union behavior and the propensity to strike are heavily dependent on the state of the labor market. As early as the beginning of the twentieth century, in two seminal articles, Rist (1907, 1912) argued that there exists a strong relationship between the business cycle and strike activity, but that this relationship is mainly indirect, mediated by the state of the labor market. According to Rist (1912, pp. 748–9), "the rise or fall of strikes is related to the fluctuations of unemployment, because it is through the rise or fall of unemployment that industrial hardship or prosperity is felt by the workers." Rist (1907, p. 406) found such a close relationship between the number of strikes and unemployment, across several countries, as to suggest that in the absence of a good measure of unemployment, one could use the measure of strikes as a proxy.

Unfortunately, Rist's work did not set a new paradigm in strike research. Partly because of the lack of reliable unemployment data prior to World War II, Rist's work remained an isolated milestone in a mainstream of empirical strike research focused on prices and production, rather than unemployment, as determinants of strikes.

It fell to an American economist, Albert Rees, to popularize, some fifty years later, the relationship between labor-market conditions and strike activity. According to Rees (1952), in times of rising employment, workers can more easily find jobs elsewhere, in case retaliatory actions are taken by their employers, and/or they can find part-time jobs during a strike. On the other hand, during a strike, employers can less easily replace strikers with outsiders, and in any case are less willing to interrupt production, being afraid of losing their share of an expanding market. Also, demonstration effects of rising wages everywhere are likely to induce employers to give in to strikers. Under conditions of full employment, workers are thus in a more favorable position than employers and are more willing to go on strike. In times of falling employment, the situation is reversed. Workers are afraid to take a militant stance, because troublesome workers can easily be replaced. Employers can fill orders out of existing inventories. Several other factors – the general tendency for wages to be "sticky downward," fixed-term union contracts, and falling consumer prices – help to explain the unions' more cautious approach in the bargaining process and their reluctance to strike. Employers may actually welcome a strike, in order to avoid variable costs. As Engels (Lapides, 1987, pp. 127–8) wrote, "Strikes . . . often enough have been brought about purposely during the last few years of bad business by the capitalists to have a pretext for closing down their factories and mills."

2.2. THE ECONOMISTS' TRADITION OF STRIKE RESEARCH: THE ASHENFELTER AND JOHNSON MODEL

Although Rees's explanation, based on the relative bargaining powers of the negotiating parties, has some intuitive appeal, it has a fundamental flaw. If the relative bargaining power of workers and that of employers change with the business cycle, going in opposite directions, why should these changes be reflected in strike activity? If one party has more power, and the other less, only the level of wages should be affected (Cousineau and Lacroix, 1976, 1986). There is no a priori reason to believe that a change in bargaining power should affect strike activity (Gramm, 1986). Indeed, as Hicks (1932) pointed out, if the actors involved in the negotiations were rational and well informed, there would be no reason to strike. Each party would know exactly the other party's concession curve, and they could agree immediately on the wage level, fixed by the point of intersection of the two concession curves (essentially the wage level they would agree on after a strike) thus saving both sides the costs of a strike. Because strikes do occur, it must be that all or some of the actors involved either are irrational or hold imperfect information. The assumption of irrationality, however, flies in the face of strike research, which has shown that there are predictable patterns in the fluctuations of strike activity over time (Mauro, 1982, p. 536). Why should irrationality follow predictable patterns? We are rather accustomed to think of irrationality as a random factor. The levels and types of information available to the bargaining parties, on the other hand, are more likely to vary systematically and in different directions for the bargaining parties under different conditions. Hicks (1932, pp. 146–7) wrote that "The majority of . . . strikes are doubtless the result of faulty negotiation . . . adequate knowledge will always make a settlement possible."

Ashenfelter and Johnson (1969) extended Hicks's two-party model, based on management and trade unions, to a three-party model, based on management, trade unions, and workers. Ashenfelter and Johnson's work depends heavily on Rees's argument, but it also draws on the theoretical contributions of wage-determination models (e.g., Zeuthen, 1930; Hicks, 1932) as well as the mathematical elegance of bargaining models (e.g., Nash, 1950; Harsanyi, 1956; Bishop, 1964). Contrary to Rees and Hicks, who never tested their models empirically, Ashenfelter and Johnson provided extensive econometric evidence. They proposed the following single-equation model of strike frequency:

$$S_t = \beta_0 + \beta_1 D_{1t} + \beta_2 D_{2t} + \beta_3 D_{3t} + \beta_4 \sum_{i=0}^{n} \mu_i \Delta R_{t-i} + \beta_5 UN_t + \beta_6 \pi_{t-1} + \beta_7 T + \epsilon_t \quad (2.1)$$

where S_t is the quarterly number of strikes; D_{1t}, D_{2t}, and D_{3t} are a set of quarterly seasonal dummies introduced to approximate the seasonal pattern of contract renewals; $\sum \mu_i \Delta R_{t-i}$ is a moving average of changes in real wages in the previous n quarters; UN_t is the current level of unemployment; π_{t-1} is the previous level of profits; T is a time-trend variable introduced to approximate long-term structural changes; and ϵ_ts an error term. The expected signs of the coefficients are as follows: $\beta_4 < 0$, $\beta_5 < 0$, $\beta_7 > 0$ and β_6 has an undetermined sign.

Ashenfelter and Johnson estimated equation (2.1) using quarterly U.S. manufacturing data for the 1952–67 period. The results strongly support the model. Among four different variations of the basic equation, the lowest estimated R^2 was .938. All coefficients of the explanatory variables (except for previous level of profits) were highly significant and had their expected signs. The combination of a tight mathematical formulation and sophisticated econometric work has made the Ashenfelter and Johnson model a standard in the economic strike literature. For that reason, I will test the Ashenfelter and Johnson model for the Italian case.

The model I propose to verify is a modified form of the Ashenfelter and Johnson equation (2.1), without the previous level of profits and the time trend, as shown in equation (2.2):

$$S_t = \beta_0 + \beta_1 D_{1t} + \beta_2 D_{2t} + \beta_3 D_{3t} + \beta_4 \sum_{i=0}^{n} \mu_i \Delta R_{t-i} + \beta_5 UN_t + \epsilon_t \quad (2.2)$$

Contrary to the original specification, I did not include a time-trend variable in the specification of the Ashenfelter and Johnson model for the Italian case [equation (2.2)], because the residuals obtained from the estimates of the model did not present any significant linear trend that would justify its inclusion (Draper and Smith, 1966, pp. 86–103). Furthermore, I did not include the previous level of profits because reliable quarterly data on profits are not available for Italy. Ashenfelter and Johnson themselves dropped the profit variable from the specification of their model because the variable yielded inconclusive results. Pencavel (1970) did the same in his estimate of the Ashenfelter and Johnson model for the United Kingdom. Nonetheless, what are the likely effects of leaving out the profit variable from the specification of the model? From a substantive viewpoint, just as the unemployment rate measures workers' willingness to mount collective actions, the profit variable measures employers' willingness to grant concessions. The inclusion of both variables in the model measures the give-and-take involved in labor relations, the strategic interaction between workers and employers. From a methodological viewpoint, if we assume that the original Ashenfelter and Johnson model is correctly specified, then equation (2.2) for the Italian case is misspecified, with all the statistical consequences of model misspecification, namely, unbiased but inefficient estimates and invalid inference procedures.

Both substantive and methodological problems thus seem to weaken our confidence in the specification of the Ashenfelter and Johnson model for the Italian case. On the one hand, the main advantage of the model is lost: the ability to describe the frequency of strikes resulting from the strategic interaction between workers and employers. On the other hand, the statistical results may be problematic and that would seem to be quite worrisome. Yet, I will not pretend to be worried. We might as well squarely and honestly face the fact that all our statistical models are hopelessly misspecified. Assuming, as we typically do, that the effects of omitted variables cancel each other out is naive and optimistic, and perhaps even self-deceiving. Why should a model based on unemployment, wages, and profits, rather than on unemployment and wages, provide the correct specification for the number of strikes? What basis do we have to assume that all other effects (e.g., legal framework, political repression, availability of organizational resources) either are negligible or cancel each other out? I would like to be able to make the comforting assumption that the omission of the profit variable is inconsequential. Unfortunately, I will spend the rest of this book arguing that that is not so. The strategic interaction between employers and workers is at the heart of the conceptual framework adopted here. Even the inclusion of a profit variable would merely mimic the nature of this interaction. Rather than ignore the problems raised by the scarcity of the quantitative data that are available, I will try to substantiate the nature of this strategic interaction through the combined use of different forms of empirical evidence. I will return many times to the issue of employers' willingness and ability to grant concessions.

2.3. TEST OF THE ASHENFELTER AND JOHNSON MODEL: EMPIRICAL RESULTS

To test equation (2.2), I used standard Ordinary Least Squares (OLS) on quarterly, manufacturing-industry data from 1959–I to 1978–IV.[1] Following Ashenfelter and Johnson, I applied the Almon polynomial distributed-lag procedure to estimate the relationship between strikes and wages.[2] Because of the controversies surrounding the Almon procedure, I carried out several preliminary analyses to determine the correct specification of the degree p of the polynomial and of the length n of the lag structure.[3] Such painstaking care should provide some confidence in the basic soundness of the statistical work and lend credence to the results obtained and the conclusions reached. The statistical results strongly suggest a second-degree polynomial and a twelve-quarter length for the lag structure.

Models 1 and 2 of Table 2.1 show the results of the estimates of equation (2.2) obtained with and without the application of end-point constraints to the Almon lag structure. Unemployment rate has the expected negative effect on the number of

Table 2.1. *Test of the Ashenfelter and Johnson model*

Dependent variable: Number of strikes
Aggregation level: Manufacturing industry; quarterly series
Sample period: 1959-II/1978-IV
Estimation method: Almon polynomial distributed lags for all models (models 1 and 3 estimated with end-point constraints; models 2 and 4 estimated without end-point constraints); OLS for models 1 and 2; GLS (Cochrane-Orcutt) for models 3 and 4

	Model 1	Model 2	Model 3	Model 4
Constant	818.94*	790.31*	460.94*	460.89*
	(80.24)	(83.24)	(108.36)	(109.55)
1st-quarter dummy	96.64*	83.47*	58.39*	52.66*
	(39.93)	(41.03)	(20.38)	(22.01)
2nd-quarter dummy	23.27	15.75	44.75*	40.04**
	(39.13)	(39.59)	(21.58)	(22.49)
3rd-quarter dummy	-94.45*	-103.45*	-85.13*	-90.14*
	(38.79)	(39.37)	(18.02)	(19.25)
Unemployment rate	-83.45*	-76.99*	-33.14*	-32.18*
	(13.45)	(14.41)	(14.34)	(14.69)
Change in real wages (%)	179.53*	177.06*	247.69*	247.22*
	(21.83)	(22.75)	(59.05)	(59.30)
Adjusted R^2	.55	.55	.79	.79
Durbin-Watson	.63	.64	1.86	1.84
Wallis	1.85	2.28	1.91	2.23

Note: Standard error in parentheses. **Significant at the .05 level; *significant at the .01 level.

strikes. The percentage variations of the index of real wages contrary to the results obtained by Ashenfelter and Johnson, have a positive effect on strikes. Bordogna and Provasi (1979, pp. 259–66) obtained a similar result for postwar Italy, which they interpreted as a demonstration effect typical of periods of high levels of worker mobilization (*la lotta che paga*: the more you strike, the more you get; the more you get, the more you strike). The set of seasonal dummies reveals a significant seasonal pattern in the number of strikes, as we would have expected on the basis of the exploratory analyses summarized in Chapter 1 (for the analyses see Franzosi, 1980). It is the summer months of the third quarter that register a slowdown in strike activity.

The values of R^2 indicate that the Ashenfelter and Johnson model explains almost 60% of the total variance for the Italian case. The low values of the Durbin-Watson statistic (0.6) show that the residuals suffer from serial correlation (or autocorrelation), with the following effects: inefficient estimates, suboptimal forecasts based on the regression equation, and lack of validity of the usual statistical tests of significance. Together with the low values of the R^2, this result provides a good indication of omission of relevant variables from the model.

Cochrane and Orcutt (1949) suggested a procedure to eliminate autocorrelation from the error vector.[4] Models 3 and 4 show the results obtained from estimating equation (2.2), with and without end-point constraints, using this procedure. The Durbin-Watson statistic now reaches acceptable levels (1.8); I eliminated the problem of first-order serial correlation of the residuals. The application of the procedure, besides stabilizing the estimates, has also improved the exploratory power of the model: R^2 goes from .55 to .79 for models 1 and 3 and from .55 to .79 for models 2 and 4. However, using quarterly data, the error component may also be affected by fourth-order serial correlation, due to unexplained seasonality: There is correlation between the residuals of corresponding quarters of successive years, rather than between the residuals of successive quarters (Thomas and Wallis, 1971, p. 64). It is for this reason that I included a set of seasonal dummies in the specification of equation (2.2.). But the residual component may contain an unexplained portion of seasonal variation, despite the inclusion of seasonal dummies in the model – all the more so because the dependent variable is affected by moving seasonality (Franzosi, 1980). The Durbin-Watson test is not an appropriate test for higher-order autocorrelations. The Wallis test (Wallis, 1972), however, indicates that none of the four models show evidence of fourth-order serial correlation of the residuals (Table 2.1).[5]

Table 2.2 presents the estimated coefficients for the distributed-lag structures of models 1–4 of Table 2.1. The lag structures have a U, rather than an inverted-U, shape of the weights, where successive quarters have increasing weights up to a certain point, and decline thereafter. The coefficients for each lag are always significant and stable. Only the far-end effects (contemporaneous and most remote in time), in these and other models, yield insignificant results without the application of the Cochrane-Orcutt procedure. The lag structure has a three-year length, which could explain the pattern of a three-year cycle in strike indicators picked up by the exploratory data analyses. Direct comparison of the first and second columns of Table 2.2 shows that applying end-point constraints with the Almon method produces much more uniform shapes. In fact, the coefficients of the distributed lags of models 1 and 3 are perfectly symmetrical around central values (which does not happen when no end-point constraints are imposed). This result, according to Schmidt and Waud (1973), is an artifact of the end-point imposition, rather than an observable empirical relationship. Furthermore, a direct comparison of the coefficients of models 1 and 2 and of those of models 3 and 4 shows that constraining the end points to zero produces a systematic effect of overestimation of the coefficients, thus widening the region of acceptance.

2.4. A WORD OF CAUTION

Despite the generally good results obtained in my estimate of the Ashenfelter and Johnson model for the Italian case, a word of caution is in order. In fact, the model has been heavily criticized on both methodological and theoretical grounds.[6]

Methodologically, the Ashenfelter and Johnson model has a major limitation: the use of aggregate, sector-level data to test what is essentially a microlevel, firm-level model.[7] Econometric work by Mauro (1982), Cousineau and Lacroix

Table 2.2. *Almon polynomial distributed lag coefficients for models in Table 2.1*

	Percent change in real wages$_{t-i}$ for model			
Lag i	1	2	3	4
0	5.92*	10.48**	8.17*	13.98*
	(0.72)	(5.82)	(1.95)	(5.22)
1	10.85*	14.82*	14.98*	18.50*
	(1.32)	(4.05)	(3.57)	(4.85)
2	14.80*	18.10*	20.42*	22.02*
	(1.80)	(3.07)	(4.87)	(5.39)
3	17.76*	20.30*	24.51*	24.55*
	(2.16)	(2.86)	(5.84)	(6.18)
4	19.73*	21.43*	27.23*	26.09*
	(2.40)	(3.04)	(6.49)	(6.83)
5	20.72*	21.50*	28.59*	26.63*
	(2.52)	(3.22)	(6.81)	(7.18)
6	20.72*	20.49*	29.59*	26.18*
	(2.52)	(3.22)	(6.81)	(7.18)
7	19.73*	18.42*	27.23*	24.73*
	(2.40)	(3.05)	(6.49)	(6.83)
8	17.76*	15.27*	24.51*	22.29*
	(2.16)	(2.92)	(5.84)	(6.21)
9	14.80*	11.06*	20.42*	18.85*
	(1.80)	(3.23)	(4.87)	(5.49)
10	10.85*	5.77	14.98*	14.42*
	(1.32)	(4.31)	(3.57)	(5.09)
11	5.92*	-0.58	8.17*	8.99
	(0.72)	(6.15)	(1.95)	(5.65)

Note: Standard error in parentheses. **Significant at the .05 level; *significant at the .01 level.

(1986), and Gramm (1986) has been based on more appropriate microlevel data. The use of these new data has allowed economic strike research to go beyond strike models based solely on unemployment and prices – which predominantly affect workers' concession schedule. New variables include the duration and timing of collective agreements, the sizes and demographic characteristics of the industry and of the bargaining unit, the firms' or industry's profits, the concentration ratio, the level of stockpiling, and the existence of escalator clauses. The empirical results, however, confirm not only the dialectic nature of industrial conflict and the importance of previously neglected microlevel variables but also the close connection between the business cycle and the strike cycle.

Theoretically, a major problem with the Ashenfelter and Johnson model is that two of the parties (union and management negotiators) are perfectly informed, whereas the rank and file are completely uninformed. It is not unrealistic to assume that management and union leadership will be better informed than the rank and file. After all, involvement in the bargaining process is mainly a prerogative of management and union leadership. As Reder and Neumann (1980, p. 870) have argued, the development of bargaining "protocols" (the "rules and conventions governing the procedure for negotiating collective agreements") and continuous involvement in the bargaining process contribute to the decrease in uncertainty between bargaining pairs. It is unrealistic, however, to assume that management and union leadership will have perfect knowledge, but that workers will have no knowledge at all.

As a result of these assumptions, the Ashenfelter and Johnson model wrongly depicts bargaining as a situation in which workers make demands, and management either accepts them or rejects them. In that model, there is no give-and-take between management and workers during negotiations; the workers will change their concession curve, as a function of changes in the levels of unemployment and/or prices (Kaufman, 1981, p. 335). In fact, Ashenfelter and Johnson hold that a strike will occur when workers' unreasonable level of wage demands comes to clash with the employer's acceptable level. Union leaders are aware of the gap between the wage increase demanded by workers and that which management would accept. But they must declare the strike for "political reasons," because they fear the consequences for their leadership positions of signing an agreement that would not be accepted by the rank and file, given their current level of wage demands. The strike, however, lowers "the rank and file's expectations due to the shock effect of the firm's resistance and the resultant loss of normal income" (Ashenfelter and Johnson, 1969, p. 37). It is only when workers' demands have fallen to a level at which their leadership "can safely sign with management" (Ashenfelter and Johnson, 1969, p. 37) that the strike ends. Thus, "the basic function of the strike is to square up the union membership's wage expectations with what the firm may be willing to pay" in a bargaining situation in which management and union leaders have perfect knowledge of each other's concession curves, but workers do not (Ashenfelter and Johnson, 1969, p. 39).

Because of the unrealistic assumptions of the Ashenfelter and Johnson model, several recent studies have gone back to Hicks's original model, based on the assumptions of rationality and imperfect knowledge for all of the bargaining parties. But whereas Hicks never attempted to specify the variables that affect the levels of information held by the negotiating parties, the main goal of current work is to specify theoretical models of misinformation. Thus, Reder and Neumann (1980), Kaufman (1981), Mauro (1982), Cousineau and Lacroix (1986), and Gramm (1986) strongly argue that strikes occur as a result of the imperfect information held by all parties involved (not just workers) as they use such information strategically during the course of the interaction typical of the bargaining process.

Mauro (1982) argues that misinformation results not only from (1) lack of previous negotiations – as Reder and Neumann would have it – but also from (2) each party's use of different variables in drawing up its concession schedule[8] and (3) past failures to adopt mechanisms, such as pattern bargaining or automatic cost-of-living adjustment clauses, that would limit the scope of future bargaining and effectively reduce the extent of uncertainty. For Kaufman (1981), as well, strikes occur as a result of imperfect information. Economic variables play important roles in making information more or less readily available. Inflation, in particular, is an important predictor of strike frequency, as it increases the uncertainty about future wage levels.

Work by Gramm and Cousineau and Lacroix is similarly based on the assumption of imperfect information. For Cousineau and Lacroix (1986), the sets of information available to the negotiating parties are not the same in terms of quality and quantity, nor are the costs of a strike the same for the two parties; furthermore, such cost differentials are not fixed over time or across industries. Gramm's work is mainly directed at specifying "the forces influencing both the unions' willingness to strike and employers' willingness to take a strike" (e.g., gender composition of the labor force, or union density in the industry) (Gramm, 1986, p. 361). The work by Perrone (1983, 1984) and by Wallace, Griffin, and Rubin (1989) on positional power seems to confirm the economists' argument about strikes being the results of imperfect information. In those firms and sectors where the positional power of workers (i.e., their capacity to inflict damages not only to the immediate employer but also to the broader economy) is high, strike activity is lower. Knowledge by employers that workers hold a position of strength is usually a sufficient condition for prompt settlement of a dispute. The mere threat of a strike by highly positioned workers is as good as a strike. As Marx (quoted by Lapides, 1987, p. 47) wrote, "Under certain circumstances, there is for the workman no other means of ascertaining whether he is or not paid the actual market value of his labour, but to strike or to threaten to do so."

The contribution of recent economic strike research is twofold. Methodologically, Mauro, Cousineau and Lacroix, Gramm, and others have tested their bargaining models at the more appropriate level of the individual bargaining unit, using microlevel data. Theoretically, these authors have squarely placed the strategic interaction between all parties involved at the heart of strike activity. Furthermore, in their attempt to find an answer to Hicks's basic dilemma ("Why do strikes occur at all?" Why don't both parties adjust their expectations and tactics over the course of the cycle?), economists have successfully specified the environmental variables that affect the negotiating parties' knowledge of each other's concession schedules. To explain the discrepancy of information available to the bargaining parties, economists have moved beyond strictly economic factors, such as unemployment, wages, and prices. In particular, frontier work in the economic approach has shown that much of the variation in strike activity over time is related to the structure of collective bargaining, particularly the timing of contract expirations.[9]

2.5. FURTHER PROBLEMS: IS THAT ALL WE CAN SAY?

Methodological and theoretical shortcomings with the Ashenfelter and Johnson model should certainly caution us in drawing substantive conclusions from their model of labor-market effects on strikes. But, that is hardly all of the problem.

Table 2.3. *Seasonal model of strike frequency*

Dependent variable:	Number of strikes
Aggregation level:	Manufacturing industry; quarterly series
Sample period:	1959-I/1978-IV
Estimation method:	OLS

Number of strikes = 517.83* (constant) 32.71** (1st-quarter dummy)
(70.61) (19.81)

59.74* (2nd-quarter dummy) -73.02* (3rd-quarter dummy)
(22.53) (19.46)

Adjusted R^2 .74
Durbin-Watson 1.60

Note: Standard error in parentheses. **Significant at the .05 level; *significant at the .01 level.

Mayhew (1979, p. 10), for instance, argued that strike-frequency models "might be saying little more than that strikes have increased over time, and that they have a seasonal pattern."

The results of Table 2.3 confirm that a strike model based solely on a set of seasonal dummies explains over 70% of the total variance, even for the Italian case. Mayhew seems to have a point, and one should guard against overly optimistic assessments of the explanatory power of strike models, if, indeed, most of their power could come from seasonality and/or trend alone. Mayhew's warning is all the more troubling because the explanation of seasonal or trend components of strikes in econometric models usually is confined to a set of dummy variables (seasonality) and to an increasing function of time (trend). Both solutions leave unresolved the problem of pinning down the correlates of strike activity at the very high (seasonal) and very low (trend) frequency bands.

First, seasonality and trend are only two of the components of time series. There is much to be learned on the cyclical aspects of strikes. Partial F tests confirm that cyclical variables, unemployment in particular, contribute significantly to explaining total variance in my strike model.

Second, there is a great deal that one can read into even a simple monthly distribution of strikes. Strikes come "with the cherry blossoms," said Perrot (1974, p. 103). "Winter is the time of silence" (Perrot, 1974, p. 112). That was certainly true for the last century. Very few strikes occurred during the winter months[10], and when they did, the likelihood of success was much lower (Perrot, 1974, p. 112). The difficulties of daily life, for a working class barely living at a subsistence level, were greater during the winter – the greater necessities for such items as clothing, heating, and better nutrition, the greater likelihood of illness (Perrot, 1974, p. 112). As the land lies idle, workers cannot rely on the garden patches through which many of them acquire a modicum of "country independence" during the summer months (Perrot, 1974, p. 111). As Aminzade (1980, p. 76) wrote, "Severe economic hardship, which the winter-time typically brought to a much larger segment of the working-class population, reduced the collective resources at the disposal of workers, and therefore their capacity to carry on strikes." According to Perrot, the seasonal cycle is not the only cycle that reflects the availability of resources to launch and, most importantly, to sustain a strike. Both the weekly and the daily cycles show a flurry of strikes during the first week of the month and on Mondays, reflecting the "rhythm of paychecks" (Perrot, 1974, p. 108).

In modern times, the rhythm of hunger and paychecks may be less relevant in determining the seasonal fluctuations of strikes. Other causes are more telling, such as the calendar, a country's institutional context, and seasonal weather changes (Granger, 1976).[11] Christmas generally has a negative effect on the propensity to strike in most countries.[12] In Italy, surprisingly, the month of December (particularly after the 1969 *autunno caldo*) features the highest peaks for all strike indicators (Franzosi, 1980). This happens at a time when the need for cash at hand should be highest. There are several reasons for this anomaly. In Italy, for accounting reasons, wage cuts due to strikes show up in the next month's paycheck. Thus, wages lost for strikes in December are deducted from the January paycheck. The high conflict levels even during the month of November tend to discredit the system of postponed payment as an explanation. Rather, the thirteenth monthly paycheck that Italian workers receive for Christmas (*tredicesima*) could offer a more plausible explanation. However, institutional reasons are more likely to explain high end-of-year strike activity. Unions usually present their claims to single employers or to employer associations at the beginning of spring and autumn. Consequently, strike activity tends to peak in July and December, to underscore the unions' desire to reach an agreement before the summer and Christmas vacations. Production, in some sectors, is concentrated in particular months of the year. Workers will tend to mobilize when production is at peak.[13] But this close seasonal relationship between production series and strike activity is high not only in those productive sectors that are most sensitive to seasonal variations, such as agriculture, construction, and tourism industries; we will see at greater length in Chapter 3, there is always a strong relationship between seasonality in production and seasonality in strike activity (de Wasseige, 1952; Sapsford, 1975).

But is that all we can say? Does a regression-based strike model have anything else to say beyond the basic fact that work stoppages are seasonal and that they go up and down with unemployment? Can we read any more than this from the statistical evidence? In estimating the Ashenfelter and Johnson model with the Cochrane-Orcutt procedure, I eliminated the *statistical* problems of both first- and fourth-order serial correlation, as confirmed by the values of the Durbin-Watson and Wallis tests, but the *substantive* problems remain. In fact, the real meaning of serial correlation of any order is that of model misspecification: Some relevant variables, having been omitted from the model, show up in the error component, making it autocorrelated (Johnston, 1972, p. 243).[14] One should be very cautious about drawing conclusions based on regression equations with low Durbin-Watson values, because autocorrelated error components could hide even "nonsense regressions" (Granger and Newbold, 1974; Plosser and Schwert, 1978). Although excluding this possibility,[15] the low Durbin-Watson values bear witness to the explanatory limits of the Ashenfelter and Johnson model for the Italian situation.

An examination of the regression coefficients estimated with and without the Cochrane-Orcutt procedure can provide valuable indications of the nature of these omitted variables. Comparisons of models 1 and 3 and of models 2 and 4 in Table 2.1 show that the coefficients of the percentage variations of real wages go from 179.53 to 247.69 in the equations estimated using the Almon method with end-point constraints, and from 177.06 to 247.22 when constraining the end points to zero. Even more dramatic is the descrease in the unemployment-rate coefficient, which goes from -83.45 to -33.14 and from -76.99 to -32.18. If this is any indication, we should be looking for variables that will raise the effect of real wages, while simultaneously lowering that of unemployment. Equivalently, we should be searching for the causes that modified the traditional trade-off between money wages and unemployment rate, as expressed by the Phillips curve.[16] Without getting involved in the debate that has surrounded the Phillips curve,[17] the changes in the magnitudes of the coefficients (1) confirm the hypotheses of temporal instability of structural parameters and (2) offer some indications of the explanatory limits of an econometric model that tries to explain short- and medium-term movements of strikes in Italy with market mechanisms alone. Thus, although I do not find any evidence to reject an economic-bargaining model of strikes, the evidence is not strong enough to accept it wholeheartedly.

2.6. EXAMINING THE RESIDUALS

A close examination of the residuals and of the observed and estimated values for the models in Table 2.1 confirms the need to consider variables other than economic variables in a strike model for Italy. Figure 2.1 shows a plot of the residuals obtained from estimating model 2. The Ashenfelter and Johnson model seems to leave an unexplained cyclical pattern in the residuals (the peaks in 1969, 1972, 1974, 1978). Is this a pattern left over from the wage–strike relationship (with its three-year cycle), or is there more to it? Furthermore, the plots in Figure 2.2 of the observed and estimated values show that, for the Italian case, the Ashenfelter and Johnson model underestimates the number of strikes for the three periods 1961-I/1962-III, 1968-I/1969-IV, and 1971-I/1972-IV and overestimates the same for the periods 1965-III/1967-III (although a slight overestimate is apparent since 1964-II) and 1974-III/1976-III. On the basis of this observation, it would seem that economic variables alone cannot explain the periods of high worker mobilization, such as 1961–62, 1968–69, and 1971–72.[18] On the other hand, periods of short-run economic hardship, such as the recessions of October 1963–January 1965 and June 1974–September 1975, seem to have affected the propensity to strike among the Italian working class well beyond the level that unfavorable labor-market conditions would warrant. Thus, from the analyses there emerges a picture of the Italian working class more than willing to resort to strikes

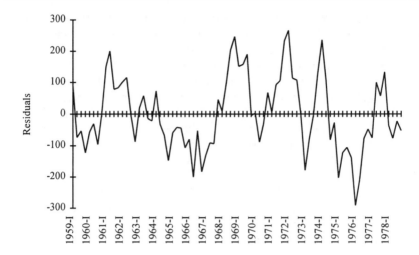

Figure 2.1. *Plot of the residuals (model 2 in Table 2.1)*

in the up-phase of the business cycle and very reluctant to strike during short-term severe hardship. There also emerges the picture of an industrial-relations system based on conflict rather than on bargaining and mediation. Industrial conflict in Italy is an integral part of the bargaining process. Conflict does not occur simply because there has been a breakdown in negotiations; often it both precedes and follows negotiations, regardless of outcome (Mershon, 1986, p. 3). Strikes, in this context, are simply a bargaining-pressure tactic.

The application of the Cochrane-Orcutt procedure downplays this form of labor strategy based on conflict.[19] Undoubtedly, explicit inclusion of noneconomic variables would result in better performance of the model. But then the model would no longer be a "bargaining model," based on the assumption that market forces alone regulate the incidence of strikes. In any case, which variables could account for the fact that periods of economic boom and bust heighten or dampen industrial conflict well above or below what a purely economic model would predict? Do we have to invoke eighteenth-century theories of the *génie d'un peuple* linked to the character of Italian workers? Do, indeed, Italian workers get so easily demoralized during busts and so easily carried away by enthusiasm during booms (the *paradox of the génie d'un peuple*)?

2.7. SUBSAMPLE ANALYSES

The econometric estimates of the Ashenfelter and Johnson model of equation (2.2), like any econometric estimate, are based on the assumption of temporal stability of the structural parameters. Translated into substantive terms, that assumption means that the relationships among unemployment, wages, and strikes were constant over the entire twenty years of the sample period used to test the model

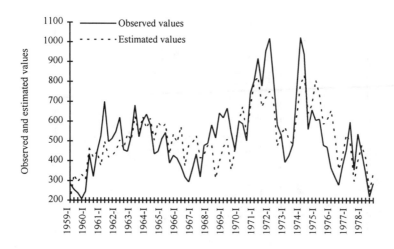

Figure 2.2. *Plots of observed and estimated values (model 2 in Table 2.1)*

(1959–78). Yet, history is about change as much as it is about continuity. What reasons do we have to believe that the set of relationships postulated by the model should hold constant over time? After all, one of the pieces of the puzzle unveiled in Chapter 1 pointed to changing patterns of relationships among strike indicators, particularly during the 1970s. Indeed, a statistical test of the assumption of temporal stability of the structural parameters shows that the assumption is untenable.[20] The results of the test imply that some relevant variables, capable of modifying those relationships, have been omitted from the model. Thus, the results of the test seem to support the conclusions reached previously that economic determinants alone (or at least, wages and unemployment), however significant, are not sufficient to explain the pattern of Italian strikes.

Further evidence on the instability of the structural parameters comes from the estimates obtained from various subsample analyses. Table 2.4 presents some of the results obtained by estimating equation (2.2) over different sample periods.[21] The estimates bring out two short periods of optimal behavior, according to the criteria of the adjusted R^2 and the significance of the coefficients: the early 1960s and the mid-1970s. The coefficients are all significant. The values of R^2 are very high, being all above .9. The results of the Durbin-Watson test exclude first-order serial correlation of the residuals, implying that the Ashenfelter and Johnson model can reach high explanatory levels for the Italian situation also, even if for only short periods. The sign of the wage variable changes from one decade to the next, as we can see from models 1–4, and models 5–7. Throughout the 1950s, unions' ability to pressure employers into wage concessions was low. It does not come as a surprise, therefore, that during that period past positive changes in the level of real wages had a negative effect on strike frequency, as in the American model: Conflict subsides after workers obtain higher wages.

Table 2.4. Subsample estimates for the Ashenfelter and Johnson model

Dependent variable: Number of strikes
Aggregation level: Manufacturing industry; quarterly series
Sample period: 1959–63 for model 1, 1959–64 for model 2, 1960–62 for model 3, 1962–64 for model 4, 1969–78 for models 5 and 6, 1973–76 for model 7
Estimation method: Almon polynomial distributed lags for all models (all models estimated with no end-point constraints); OLS for models 1–5 and 7; GLS (Cochrane-Orcutt) for model 6

Variables	Model 1	Model 2	Model 3	Model 4	Model 5	Model 6	Model 7
Constant	1147.26*	1094.64*	788.53*	928.83*	968.20*	183.81	1089.49*
	(63.05)	(66.01)	(94.16)	(30.09)	(295.67)	(313.04)	(316.77)
1st-quarter dummy	238.34*	248.90*	164.08*	280.18*	32.85	13.09	-20.37
	(37.26)	(37.33)	(46.01)	(15.47)	(63.89)	(33.62)	(51.20)
2nd-quarter dummy	85.53*	84.94*	193.47*	169.18	-40.06	-13.83	-99.74**
	(28.52)	(30.04)	(22.94)	(8.37)	(66.10)	(42.18)	(52.96)
3rd-quarter dummy	-119.41*	-103.77*	-78.07*	-70.51*	130.54**	-148.20	-221.54*
	(29.35)	(30.35)	(26.05)	(8.69)	(64.29)	(47.71)	(32.38)
Unemployment rate	-121.65*	-119.94*	-64.37*	-112.97*	-100.23*	-29.86	-137.83*
	(10.13)	(10.92)	(18.20)	(7.60)	(39.66)	(37.53)	(39.40)
Change in real wages (%)	-368.32*	-239.02*	-182.10*	-57.92*	179.67*	393.81*	227.01*
	(84.45)	(59.41)	(62.09)	(18.28)	(39.66)	(82.54)	(44.24)
Adjusted R^2	.91	.87	.96	.99	.57	.83	.92
Durbin-Watson	1.73	1.77	1.85	2.36	0.64	1.78	2.54
Wallis	2.02	1.83	2.33	1.12	2.21	2.55	2.47

Note: Standard error in parentheses. **Significant at the .05 level; *significant at the .01 level.

The 1970s reversed the situation. The mobilization process that began in 1969, with the *autunno caldo* ("hot autumn"), set off a spiral of "demonstration" effects: Favorable results obtained through strike activity (e.g., wage increases, fringe benefits) increase the likelihood of further use of the strike by a highly mobilized base. Higher participation in the next strike round, in turn, increases the chance of yet more favorable results, and so on. Such a relationship, if sustained over a long period, can explode in a spiral effect, leading to hyper-inflation. For this reason, it cannot have been constant throughout the twenty-year period considered in this analysis. Table 2.5 reports the distributed lag structures of the coefficients of the wage variable for models 1–7. The lag structures clearly highlight the demonstration effects typical of high periods of mobilization. While all the coefficients for the 1970 estimates are positive (models 5, 6, and 7), the coefficients for the 1960 estimates have positive signs for the closest lags, and negative for those further away in time (see models 1– 4 in Table 2.5). However, a positive lag structure is a short-term effect. Reflecting the downturn of the 1964–65 recession, the econometric results (for brevity, not reported here) worsen from 1966 onward, with lower R^2, unclear lag structures (unstable and very sensitive to the specification of their length), and positive but nonsignificant coefficients for the unemployment rate. Throughout the whole period from 1966 to 1971 the simple correlation coefficient between the number of strikes and the unemployment rate is quite close to zero; only during the 1970s are the coefficients high and negative again (for the 1970–78 period the simple correlation coefficient $r = -.66$ and for some subsamples r even presents values larger than -.8, the highest in the twenty years considered).

In view of these correlations, we would expect a negative, significant effect of the unemployment rate on the number of strikes during the 1970s. Models 5 and 6 in Table 2.4 present the results of estimates of equation (2.2) for the 1969-I/1978-IV period. Model 5 seems to confirm my expectations: The coefficient for the unemployment-rate variable is significant and has a negative sign, whereas the significant coefficient for the percentage variation of real wages has a positive sign, reflecting the high worker mobilization that characterized the early 1970s. The low Durbin-Watson values, however, show that the residuals are affected by first-order autocorrelation. With the application of the Cochrane-Orcutt procedure (model 6), the unemployment-rate coefficient loses its significance, although keeping its negative sign. This is a result that occurs throughout the whole period, even for the estimates that have not been reported here. Only the estimates for the period of the severe 1974–75 recession retain significant coefficients for the unemployment-rate variable.

The finding that the labor market played a less significant role in strike activity during the 1970s than during the 1960s runs counter to Snyder's (1975) prediction of an increasing role over time for economic effects on strike activity in capitalist societies. But was the weaker relationship between strike frequency and unemployment during the 1970s a short-term phenomenon, or was it indicative of a longer, postwar decline in the effectiveness of labor-market mechanisms as

Table 2.5. *Almon polynomial distributed lag coefficients for models in Table 2.4*

Lag i	Percent change in real wages$_{t-i}$ for model						
	1	2	3	4	5	6	7
0	3.56	16.49	65.83*	8.59	8.59	23.46*	29.14*
	(13.69)	(11.73)	(20.27)	(5.34)	(8.03)	(6.34)	(4.73)
1	-21.79**	-5.68	26.18**	17.79*	14.05*	31.31*	33.34*
	(11.47)	(7.97)	(13.56)	(3.62)	(6.73)	(6.49)	(5.06)
2	41.26*	-22.96*	-6.30	20.13*	18.22*	37.32*	35.33*
	(11.24)	(7.64)	(11.29)	(3.12)	(6.29)	(7.56)	(6.22)
3	-54.85*	-35.35*	-31.61*	15.61*	21.10*	41.48*	35.12*
	(11.7)	(8.83)	(11.42)	(3.43)	(6.32)	(8.71)	(7.10)
4	-62.54*	-42.86*	-49.75*	4.22	22.69*	43.80*	32.69*
	(11.88)	(9.71)	(11.21)	(4.01)	(6.43)	(9.56)	(7.4)
5	-64.36*	-45.47*	-60.73*	-14.03*	22.99*	44.27*	28.05*
	(11.41)	(9.75)	(9.56)	(4.81)	(6.36)	(9.97)	(7.13)
6	-60.28*	-43.19*	-64.54*	-39.14*	22.00*	42.90*	21.20*
	(10.38)	(9.15)	(7.07)	(6.07)	(6.01)	(9.9)	(6.53)
7	-50.32*	-36.03*	-61.18*	-71.11*	19.72*	39.68*	12.14**
	(9.53)	(8.95)	(8.28)	(8.06)	(5.41)	(9.35)	(6.31)
8	-34.48*	-23.97*			16.15*	34.61*	
	(10.43)	(10.91)			(4.76)	(8.43)	
9					11.30*	27.70*	
					(4.61)	(7.35)	
10					5.15	18.94*	
					(5.65)	(6.65)	
11					-2.29	8.34*	
					(7.98)	(7.21)	

Note: Standard error in parentheses. **Significant at the .05 level; *significant at the .01 level.

regulators of labor militancy? To properly answer this question, we have to take a longer historical perspective. For instance, what was the relationship between strikes and unemployment during the 1950s?

Unfortunately, ISTAT survey data on unemployment on a quarterly basis have been available only since 1959. We cannot use ISTAT data to test the relationship between strike frequency and unemployment in the 1950s. However, employment office data[22] on unemployment have been available since 1950. We can use these data to test the relationship between unemployment and strikes in the first half of the period being studied in this book (1950–65).

As we can see from Table 2.6, the coefficient for unemployment rate is more than sixfold its standard error. The results show a more significant negative relationship between unemployment and number of strikes during the 1950s and early 1960s than in later periods (models 5–7 in Table 2.4).[23] Some caution is in order in the interpretation of the results, given the difference in the data sources for unemployment. Notwithstanding, there appears to be a tendency for strikes to become less sensitive to the labor market over the course of the 1950–78 period.

Table 2.6. *Testing the effects of unemployment during the 1950s*

Dependent variable:	Number of strikes	
Aggregation level:	Manufacturing industry; quarterly series	
Sample period:	1950-II/1965-IV	
Estimation method:	OLS	

Number of strikes =	908.22* (constant) (89.78)	144.79* (1st-quarter dummy) (23.63)
	70.87* (2nd-quarter dummy) (22.18)	-51.91* (3rd-quarter dummy) (0.91)
Unemployment rate	-.272E-3* (.396E-4)	
Adjusted R^2	.79	
Durbin-Watson	2.11	

Note: Standard error in parentheses. **Significant at the .05 level; *significant at the .01 level.

The finding that the labor market played a less significant role in strike activity during the 1970s is not only bewildering in light of Snyder's work, but it is also somewhat paradoxical. After all, strike activity during the first half of the decade remained at very high levels despite the high and rising levels of unemployment. Why did labor-market mechanisms cease to regulate conflict during the 1970s *(paradox of the 1970s)*? How can we explain these results?

2.8. CHECKING THE RESULTS AGAINST ECONOMIC HISTORY

Careful statistical work is the best antidote against sloppy results. We can use the most appropriate techniques, and we can guard against a variety of specification errors. However, regardless of what statistical tests say about confidence levels (90%, 95%, etc.), ultimately it is against the test of history that time-series results have to stand up. How do my results fare in this test? To find the answer to this question, let me quickly trace the main threads of Italian postwar economic history.[24]

Throughout the postwar period the Italian economy experienced high rates of growth. In comparative perspective, Japan was at the head of the pack among industrialized countries, but Italy was one of Europe's fastest-growing economies. The growth rate peaked during the years 1959–63, the years of Italy's "economic miracle" (*miracolo economico*). All major economic indicators rose during that five-year period. Investment soared to over 25% of gross national product (GNP), not only the highest figure in Italian economic history but also one of the highest among Western countries (Salvati, 1984, p. 60). Industrial development was concentrated in the northern regions of the "industrial triangle" (*triangolo industriale*, Genoa-Milan-Turin). Growth rates, however, declined thereafter, particularly during the 1970s. During the 1964–66 period, growth plummeted. Italy was all alone among Western economies in that mid-1960s recession. Most other economies continued to grow throughout the 1960s.[25] In the 1970s, on the other hand, Italy was in good company; its decline paralleled a general slowdown in the world's economies.

During the 1950s and 1960s, the recipe for rapid growth was production for export and a cheap and abundant supply of labor. In the period between 1958 and 1968, the rate of growth for Italian manufacturing export was by far the world's largest. Only after 1968 was Italy surpassed by Japan (Fondazione Giovanni Agnelli, 1973, pp. 64–5). But unemployment levels were staggering, with over 2 million people out of work. Even higher were the levels of underemployment, particularly in agriculture and services (Meldolesi, 1972). Wages not only were low, but also differed from city to city, from industry to industry, and for males and females (despite the fact that the constitution called for equal pay across genders) – a veritable "wage jungle" (*giungla retributiva*) (Gorrieri, 1973). The labor market in Italy, in principle, has traditionally been under extensive and rigid control by the state (Reyneri, 1989b, p. 131). In reality, in light of the low administrative capacities of the Italian state, it has been the balance of class forces that has regulated the labor market. Historically, and at least until the late 1960s, that balance had been particularly unfavorable to the working class (Meldolesi, 1972; Paci, 1973).

The 1947, 1950, and 1965 agreements between employers and the unions on layoffs and dismissals increasingly tended to reduce "in theory" the limits of management prerogatives (Gruppi di studio, 1968, p. 14). Although those agreements provided for "arbitration colleges" for the resolution of controversial cases, the college rulings were not binding for employers (Gruppi di studio, 1968, p. 21). As a consequence, employers increasingly settled dismissal disputes financially, typically by providing one or two months' severance pay (Gruppi di studio, 1968, p. 25).

Entrance into the labor market was similarly regulated by the Ministry of Labor through its territorial offices, largely outside of union control (Reyneri, 1989b, pp. 134, 136). Individuals looking for jobs were required to register at the employment office, putting their names on "placement lists" (*liste di collocamento*). Area firms were required to make new hires from the placement lists. Firms, however, preferred to use private channels, such as important or petty officials of political parties in the government (particularly the Christian Democrats), the Catholic Church, or the non-Communist unions (the "free" unions, as these were called at the time) (Reyneri, 1989a, pp. 377–9).[26] In a labor market such as that of the 1950s, highly discriminatory against Communist and unionized workers, those channels provided better guarantees of "political" control over the work force. Political screening of new hires through parish churches was quite common.[27] As Rico, a young Socialist worker looking for a job in 1950, tells the story,

I started knocking at every door for a job, particularly in large companies. . . . A recommendation by the DC [Christian Democrats], or by the Church, or by the PLI [Partito

Liberale Italiano], or by the "free unions" [CISL, Confederazione Italiana Sindacati dei Lavoratori, and UIL, Unione Italiana del Lavoro] would have been useful. Then, companies would hire you. . . . Everyone knew that there were two big bosses that provided jobs in my company as well as in other companies. One was Don Mariano, and the other one was Capponi [who] had become the secretary of the new "free union." He hired, he promoted, he fired people at his will; he was really a boss. (Brentano, 1975, pp. 101–7)

Of course, the Don Marianos and the Capponis of this world did not simply provide jobs with no conditions. For Don Mariano, the Catholic priest, the condition was that Rico should "kneel a few times at his masses" (Brentano, 1975, p. 106). For Capponi, it was anti-Communist zeal. During a meeting with Capponi, Rico knew all too well what was expected of a worker who had found a job through the Don Mariano/Capponi job services:

I remembered at that time the incredible stories of workers who had to hand out leaflets of the "free union" at the factory gates and in the main square. They had to hand them out to their ex-comrades, Socialists and Communists, members of the CGIL [Communist] union. I myself had once spat on the feet of one of these "traitors". . . . I instinctively stared down at my shoes, in fear of already finding spit there. (Brentano, 1975, p. 111)

In the 1950s and 1960s, the labor market was characterized by continual drainage of labor from agriculture. Until the mid-1950s, the majority of new immigrants to northern industrial cities, particularly to the cities of the industrial triangle, came from the countryside of the northern regions (Piedmont, Valle d'Aosta, Lombardy, Veneto). During that period, southern immigrants contributed only 20% to northern urbanization (Ascoli, 1979, p. 110). Southern immigration picked up in the second half of the 1950s, after the failure of the government land reform. As one of them put it: "Here [Calabria, a poor southern region], it is the peasants of the Reform, hand laborers and youth that emigrate. They come from country villages" (Mauro, 1973, p. 101).

During the boom years of the "economic miracle," some 1.3 million people migrated from the South to the North (Ascoli, 1979, p. 117), "a massive exodus of biblical proportion" (Ascoli, 1979, p. 52).[28] From 1957 to the end of the decade, sixty to seventy thousand new immigrants each year settled in Lombardy, the most industrialized Italian region, around Milan, and a hundred thousand per year came during the 1961–63 period (Paci, 1973, p. 159). At first, the exodus was "regulated," mostly informally, by word of mouth, through the "migration chain." But, later, toward the end of the 1960s, large northern companies started hiring locally and directly, mostly young workers for unskilled jobs on the assembly lines.

Immigrants, particularly southern immigrants, tended to be young, unmarried males with low educational credentials (Ascoli, 1979, p. 123). Many did not even have an elementary-school diploma (Paci, 1973, p. 59). Some 20–40% were functionally illiterate (Ascoli, 1979, p. 123). The dream for all of them was industrial employment in large concerns. Fiat, the Turin automaker, the largest Italian industrial conglomerate, was everyone's great hope. As Pasquale De Stefani, an immigrant working at Fiat, put it, "Even in my village, people thought that to be hired by Agnelli [the family that controls Fiat] was a godsend. My mother in law said that Fiat was like Divine Providence, and Agnelli a benefactor" (Polo, 1989, p. 125).

Reality forced a harsh awakening from such dreams. Most immigrants did not immediately land a job in a large firm. Most started out in the construction industry and in the small craft shops and later moved to the larger manufacturing plants. Immigrants often occupied the most dangerous, the most toxic, and the hardest jobs in the factories (Ascoli, 1979, pp. 125–7). A study conducted in Genoa in 1962 found that "There is a tendency for southerners to be located in those parts of the plant where work is harder and more dangerous" (Cavalli, 1964, p. 105). Similarly, in Turin, southern immigrants "are employed in the heaviest, most uncomfortable, and often dangerous jobs" (Zaccone Derossi, 1962, p. 237). Immigrants were more likely to occupy the lowest echelons of the job hierarchy. Southern immigrants, in particular, were at the very bottom of the ladder. According to a survey conducted in Turin in 1962, "64% of the immigrants interviewed were hand laborers and unskilled workers, 30% were peddlers and artisans, while only 1.5% were skilled workers and technicians" (Canteri, 1964, p. 128). In Genoa, as one looks at the occupational hierarchy from hand laborer to skilled or specialized worker to gang boss, "The proportion of southerners decreases, while correspondingly that of others increases" (Cavalli, 1964, p. 104). A study in the construction industry in Milan reported substantially similar results (Paci, 1973, pp. 42–5). Job stability at the bottom of the occupational hierarchy was much more tenuous than at higher levels. A 1959 survey of employment turnover conducted by Assolombarda (Associazione Industriale Lombarda, 1961, p. 12), the employers' association of the province of Milan, showed that the rate of turnover of unskilled workers was almost ten times as high as that of skilled workers. If we set the level of turnover of unskilled workers at 100, that of semiskilled workers would be 41, and that of skilled workers 11.[29] Immigrants had a higher-than-average turnover.[30]

If for southern immigrants things were not good inside the factories, they were not much better outside. Southern immigrants often were forced to live in the attics, basements, and shanties, in the old, run-down neighborhoods or peripheral areas of northern cities (Alasia and Montaldi, 1960; Cavalli, 1964; Canteri, 1964; Alberoni and Baglioni, 1965; Fofi, 1975). The "better" neighborhoods, particularly in Turin, often posted signs "We do not rent to southerners." Thus, for most immigrants, marginalization on the job was coupled with social and cultural marginalization.

Throughout the 1950s, the levels of unemployment were staggering. Official statistics do not really reveal the extent of the weakness of the labor market (see Figure 2.3 for plots of the measures of unemployment). Much of the unemployment was hidden by phenomena such as "discouraged unemployment." Women and youth, as well as massive underemployment in agriculture, services, and petty craft production, provided the great "reserve army" of labor during the period, functioning like a great accordion, expanding during booms in the areas of low-cost, marginal employment in small-scale production and contracting during

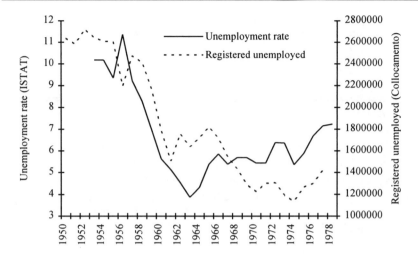

Figure 2.3. *Plots of measures of unemployment in industry*

busts (Paci, 1973, pp. 104–5). The people living on the fringes of the market, the discouraged unemployed, knew better than to waste time looking for nonexistent jobs. An exemplar is the "full employment" experiment attempted in 1955 by the minister of labor, Vigorelli. Following the announcement of a plan to provide enough jobs to cover the "official" number of unemployed looking for jobs in fourteen poor communes, that number rose sharply, particularly bringing in women (Meldolesi, 1972, p. 34).

But by the late 1950s, the labor market was approaching full employment.[31] The unemployment rate in Lombardy, the most industrialized Italian region, declined steadily from 3.9% in 1959 to 1.7% in 1963, as shown in Table 2.7. With the economy in full swing, the bargaining position of labor improved, and the level of industrial conflict rose. In terms of strike frequency and hours lost, the 1959–63 strike wave reached unprecedented levels (the number of hours lost in 1962 was second only to 1969 in the postwar period). During those first successful strikes, Michele Dimanico, a Fiat-Spa worker, recalled that

For the first time, I saw many comrades who had not given up, but rather endured, who had been losers, inevitably, given their work, family, and economic situations, and who had regained the strength to say no to the *padrone*. I saw many workers cry like I don't believe I have ever seen, and cry such joyful tears that it is really a feeling I will never forget. (quoted in Lanzardo, 1979, p. 108)[32]

That strike wave resulted in the highest wage increases of the postwar period to that date. In the presence of full employment and wage increases, one of the terms of the equation of postwar Italian growth disappeared: a seemingly unlimited supply of cheap labor. With inflation on the rise, in the fall of 1963 the Bank of Italy imposed severe monetary restrictions that suddenly brought the economy to a

Table 2.7. *Unemployment rate in Lombardy and Italy (1959–65)*

Area	1959	1960	1961	1962	1963	1964	1965
Lombardy	3.9	2.5	1.9	1.7	1.7	2.3	3.7
Italy	5.2	4.0	3.4	3.0	2.5	2.7	3.6

Source: Valli (1976, p. 76).

grinding halt. Investment fell sharply. The number of bankruptcies soared. Even some larger manufacturing groups that had overinvested during the years of euphoria went belly-up, leaving many brand-new plants that never even started producing (Fondazione Giovanni Agnelli, 1973, p. 133) – the class struggle often requires drastic measures that can deeply affect at least some segments of the capitalist class itself.

The decline in investment and production led to increasing unemployment rates (Figure 2.3). With unemployment on the rise, employers regained control over the work force. Furthermore, they intensified the pace of "industrial restructuring," totally reorganizing productive processes. Through shift work, speedups, overtime, and shop-floor mobility, employers greatly increased the pace of production. In the face of plummeting levels of investment, the high productivity increases of those years seemed to come at workers' expense (Salvati, 1984, p. 96). As a Sit-Siemens female union representative put it in an interview,

At the assembly line, when I was first hired, I think we did 160 or 180 pieces a day, with 18 women. Today they produce 320 pieces, with 25 women. So the number of women has not kept up with the speed. That is the way speedups were done. They would "cut the line." For example, if there were 18 women, they would cut back to 14, but they wouldn't cut the number of pieces that much. Or else they would cut the line and then bring it back up to 25 women and increase the speed. (Regalia, 1975b, p. 43)

With one's job in jeopardy, again, industrial conflict declined. During the mid-1960s, "The shop-floor climate is that of the 1950s" (Salvati, 1984, p. 96). A good indicator of labor's increasing difficulties is the longer strike durations of 1966 (see the shapes of strikes in Chapter 1, Figure 1.6, pp. 8–9).

By 1968, economic recovery was again under way, triggering a second wave of migration from the South to the North between 1968 and 1970 (Ascoli, 1979, p. 117). As Paci wrote (1973, p. 168): "For the first time [in Italian history], the balance of forces between labor supply and demand . . . is not inevitably tilted in favor of demand, because of the availability of endemic pockets of 'reserve' labor." As the labor market expanded toward increasing employment, strike activity picked up in 1968, reaching the highest levels in Italian labor history in the fall of 1969 (*autunno caldo*). Workers began to break off in a series of spontaneous and uncontrolled strikes, often against unions' directives. It was the high point of a strike wave that was to characterize the years 1968–72 as the years of "permanent conflict" (*conflittualità permanente*).[33] Strikers' demands were deeply rooted in the everyday working conditions inside and outside the factories. Aside from wage issues (centered on egalitarian principles of equal pay for equal work, and wage increases equal for all workers regardless of their positions in the firm's hierarchical structure), their demands centered around the issues of speedups, factory environments, the abolition of job classification, Tayloristic organization of production, union representation on the shop floor, and social services.

The *autunno caldo* resulted in the highest wage increases of the postwar period. Prices started climbing. To bring inflation under control, in 1970 the government implemented restrictive policies in both the monetary and the fiscal areas. Those policies, however, did not produce in 1970 the same effects on the labor market as they had in 1964. The 1973 contract renewals brought more wage increases and, with them, more inflation. In order to stimulate sluggish investment and export, in February 1973 the Bank of Italy attempted to stabilize matters via a fluctuation-devaluation of the lira (Valli, 1976, p. 88). The oil shock of 1974 caused a deep international recession and further added to Italy's economic problems. To stem a worsening economic and monetary situation, in March 1974 Italy applied for a standby loan from the International Monetary Fund (IMF). Inflation kept rising, until at the end of the decade it was running at double digit figures, the highest rate among industrialized economies. Government spending and the public deficit also began to increase, slowly at first, until by 1990 the public debt had soared to a staggering 100.5% of GNP, up from 66.4% in 1982.[34]

The Italian economy crawled along at an average annual growth rate of 2% in the second half of the 1970s. Other Western economies, however, were faring no better (Salvati, 1984, pp. 132–3). The recession hit larger firms particularly hard. Employment decreased sharply in large firms (-13.5% among the class of firms with more than 500 employees) (Salvati, 1984, p. 134). Unemployment started to increase, particularly after 1975 (Figure 2.3). Yet despite the poor performances of large Italian firms in the 1970s, the decade was not one of economic decline. In the shadow of stagnant monopoly giants, a host of small firms provided the economic system incredible vitality. Employment increased (+11.5%), both in the small firms (10–100 employees) and in very small ones (< 10 employees) (Salvati, 1984, p. 134). New regions, mostly in central Italy and in the Northeast, which had been unaffected by the economic miracle of the late 1950s, experienced their own miracle that brought growth and diffusion of smaller firms – the "Third Italy," *Terza Italia*, as Bagnasco (1977) defined these new areas of economic growth. By the end of the decade, Italy had joined the ranks of the seven largest industrialized economies.

In conclusion, the statistical findings seem to hold up well against the test of history. The historical narrative has basically confirmed the negative relationship between strike frequency and the business cycle, the state of the labor market in particular. Indeed, when strike activity was low, unemployment was high, such as throughout most of the 1950s and in the period 1963–67; vice versa, when strike activity was high, unemployment was low, such as during the years of Italy's economic miracle (1959–63) and the years between 1968 and the early 1970s. The interplay between history and statistics has proved informative. It encourages me to keep up this approach in the following chapters. Yet even the historical account fails to shed further light on an important question: Why was strike activity high in the 1970s in the face of growing unemployment? Economic history does point to the growing difficulties of the Italian economy, particularly among larger firms. Yet those difficulties did not translate into a decline in industrial conflict. The labor market in the 1970s seems to have ceased to operate as a mechanism for the regulation of conflict. Could the growth of the *Terza Italia* explain the unabated high levels of labor militancy? Possibly. But wouldn't that be somewhat paradoxical? Doesn't the accepted wisdom point to a positive relationship between labor militancy and plant size? Given the decline of larger firms and the growth of smaller firms during the 1970s, as highlighted by economic historians, shouldn't we expect to have seen a decline in strike activity? I am afraid that neither statistics nor economic history has provided an explanation for the *paradox of the 1970s* – the paradox of increasing unemployment, simultaneously high and expanding levels of strike activity – at least not at this point.

2.9. FITTING THE PUZZLE: THE FIRST STEP

The findings presented in this chapter seem to confirm, for the Italian case, the dependence of strike frequency on labor market conditions, or, more generally, on the business cycle. In particular, strikes were related to the upward phases of the cycle. This implies rational behavior by trade unions, aimed at maximizing the bargaining power stemming from their favorable position in the labor market. Indeed, the labor market has historically been one of the most important mechanisms for the regulation of industrial conflict in capitalist societies. For the United States in the early 1900s, Montgomery wrote that "Large-scale strikes erupted whenever the level of unemployment fell off sufficiently to give the strikers a ghost of a chance of success."[35] For the Rouen textile workers in 1848, Demier (1982, pp. 21–2) similarly noted that the "Great passivity of the workers [was] a result of the constant pressure of an overabundance of laborers, of the order of 15,000–20,000 even in times of prosperity." Things were not much different for textile workers in St.-Etienne. The available historical evidence leaves no doubt that economic crises severely curtail workers' capacities to launch collective protests (Aminzade, 1984, p. 449). Even under precapitalist social relations shortages of hands came to favor direct producers. Rodney Hilton (1977, p. 154) thus commented on the results of the population decline following the Black Death of the fourteenth century: "The immediate impact of the Black Death had been that both agricultural and other workers demanded, according to the strength of their local bargaining power, up to twice or even three times their previous wages."

Thus, the econometric and historical evidence presented in this chapter helps to put together the first few pieces of the puzzle. The business cycle, with its swings of a few years' length, can help explain the nonperiodic cyclical pattern of strikes. Furthermore, the three-year length of the lag structure of the coefficients of the wage variable may provide an explanation for the three-year cycle of strike indicators (at least the number of strikes).

Although the econometric evidence in this chapter seems to support an economic-bargaining model of strikes for the Italian case, the explanatory power of such a model has its limits. Both the problem of first-order serial correlation of the residuals and the problem of the percentage of unexplained variance (20%) reveal, even for strike frequency, the explanatory limits of a strike model based on economic determinants alone. Furthermore, the subsample results point to a decreasing role of labor-market effects on strikes. This is a particularly disturbing point. How can we explain the fact that throughout the 1970s, both strike activity and unemployment were high? Why did the labor market cease to be a mechanism for the regulation of industrial conflict? How can we explain the *paradox of the 1970s*?

These limits call for a more careful examination of the relationship between strike activity and the business cycle. In this chapter I have focused on strike frequency. If the other strike indicators represent independent and partly unrelated measures of conflict, as the exploratory data analyses reported in Chapter 1 suggest, then an understanding of strikes cannot rest solely on the study of just one of its components. Furthermore, economic-bargaining models rely heavily on labor-market mechanisms. However, we need to consider different measures of the business cycle in order to firm up our understanding of the relationship between the economy and strike activity. I will take up both tasks in the next chapter, where I will extend the analyses in two different directions: (1) other strike indicators as dependent variables and (2) other business-cycle indicators as independent variables.

3

When do workers strike? How the economy matters

> It can be shown for all countries for which statistics exist that strikes are somewhat sensitive to the trade cycle – indeed it would be surprising if this were not so.
>
> Knowles (1952, p. 144)

3.1. DID I GO WRONG?

Studies of the economic determinants of strikes (i.e., their relationships to the level of general economic activity) have not been based exclusively on unemployment. Actually, given the novelty of labor-force surveys in most industrialized countries,[1] it was only in the postwar period that unemployment became the most commonly used cyclical indicator in empirical investigations of strikes. Various other economic series have been used as proxies for the business cycle: price and wage indices, the value of imported raw materials, industrial production, composite cyclical indicators, and GNP.[2]

The empirical evidence put forward in this literature strongly supports the hypothesis of a positive relationship between strike activity and the business cycle, however measured, with one major qualification: The number of strikes is the factor that is most sensitive to business-cycle fluctuations.[3] The findings reported in Chapter 2 confirm that strike frequency in Italy was related to the movements of real wages and unemployment. These findings run counter to those reported by David Snyder (1975) in one of the few econometric analyses of Italian strike data. According to Snyder, there is no evidence in favor of an economic model of strikes for the Italian case.

In order to address this discrepancy between Snyder's findings and my findings, in this chapter I will take up at greater length the question of economic determinants of strikes. I will consider both other strike measures (number of strikers and number of hours lost) and other business-cycle measures (industrial production, capacity utilization, a composite business cycle indicator, and GNP). The statistical results presented in this chapter, however, confirm the findings in Chapter 2: Strike activity (particularly strike frequency) tracks the temporal movements of the business cycle. In this chapter, I will also address more general questions about the relationship between strike activity and state of the economy. Who pays the bill for the loss of production due to strikes ("the cost of strikes")? What are the effects on strikes of the structural features of the Italian economy (namely, the sectoral distribution of the labor force, the technical modes of production, the labor-market structure, and the size distribution of productive units)?

3.2. BEYOND STRIKE-FREQUENCY MODELS

As early as 1913, in direct contrast with Rist's findings on the relationship between strike frequency and unemployment, French economist Lucien March (1913, p. 114) argued that "The movement of strikes, as measured by the number of strikers, bears no close relationship to the movement of economic activity.... [Only] the number of strikes depends, in a fairly large part, upon the level of unemployment." Could March be right? Could, indeed, a model specification such as that of Ashenfelter and Johnson work only for the number of strikes as the dependent variable? To answer this question, in this section, I will test the Ashenfelter and Johnson model using the numbers of strikers and hours lost as dependent variables. The specification of the model is virtually the same as in equation (2.2) in Chapter 2 (p. 32) with the sole difference of the dependent variable, Y_t, which now measures either the number of strikers or the number of hours lost.

$$Y_t = \beta_0 + \beta_1 D_{1t} + \beta_2 D_{2t} + \beta_3 D_{3t} + \beta_4 \sum_{i=0}^{n} \mu_i \Delta R_{t-i} + \beta_5 UN_t + \epsilon_t \qquad (3.1)$$

The estimates of equation (3.1) are presented in Table 3.1. The econometric results seem to support March's claim. Although the coefficients of unemployment rate are always negative in both the models of the number of strikers and hours lost, they are also never statistically significant at the conventional levels of acceptance. The effect of the wage variable has also changed, as shown by the lag coefficients. There seems to be a negative relationship between wages and number of strikers and hours lost for the most recent quarters, and a positive relationship for the more distant ones. Finally, the explanatory capacity of the model is very low, as highlighted by the values of the adjusted R^2. The high R^2 values obtained estimating a model of number of strikes are mostly due to the seasonal pattern of the series (see Table 2.3 in Chapter 2, p. 39). Seasonality plays a much lesser role in the series of number of workers and hours lost (see Franzosi, 1980), as confirmed by the t values of the seasonal dummies in Table 3.1. Nonetheless, the insignificance of the coefficients of the unemployment rate and the wage variable (for model 2) and the low R^2 values point to the greater difficulties of an economic model of the Ashenfelter and Johnson type in explaining the series of numbers of strikers and hours lost.

3.3. BEYOND LABOR-MARKET MODELS

In this section I extend the analyses of Chapter 2 beyond the labor market and into the product market. I use the numbers of strikes, strikers, and hours lost as dependent variables. As independent variables I use an index of industrial production in the manufacturing industry and the GNP.[4] I also use a composite business-cycle indicator of the type developed by Burns and Mitchell (1947) at the

Table 3.1. *Test of the Ashenfelter and Johnson model using numbers of strikers and hours lost as dependent variables*

Dependent variable: Number of strikers for model 1; number of hours lost for model 2
Aggregation level: Manufacturing industry; quarterly series
Sample period: 1959-II/1978-IV
Estimation method: Almon polynomial distributed lags and GLS (Cochrane-Orcutt)

Variables	Model 1	Model 2	Lag i	Model 1	Model 2
Constant	1,097,289	35,584.85**	0	-88,230.48**	-2,143.54**
	(689,748)	(16,044.49)		(43,820.14)	(990.89)
1st-quarter dummy	269,708.2	935.98	1	-48,639.03	-1,519.08**
	(226,558.5)	(4,827.35)		(31,698.67)	(733.72)
2nd-quarter dummy	-123,352.5	-4,898.05	2	-14,182.26	-973.48
	(234,737)	(5,004.0)		(26,000.82)	(627.33)
3rd-quarter dummy	-505,815.8*	-8,890.7**	3	15,139.83	-506.73
	(208,141)	(4,375.91)		(25,750.40)	(637.45)
Change in real wages (%)	420,000.**	-1,856.2	4	39,327.25	-118.83
	(220,000.)	(5,478.6)		(27,640.93)	(686.72)
Unemployment rate	-86,684.	-2,616.5	5	58,379.98**	190.21
	(1,21,160.3)	(2,787.5)		(29,083.99)	(721.19)
			6	72,298.02*	420.40
Adjusted R^2	0.18	0.06		(29,062.08)	(720.24)
Durbin-Watson	2.00	1.96	7	81,081.39*	571.73
Wallis	1.98	2.01		(27,659.98)	(685.79)
			8	84,730.08*	644.21
				(26,097.75)	(643.13)
			9	83,244.08*	637.84
				(27,118.06)	(650.75)
			10	76,623.40**	552.61
				(33,758.31)	(781.45)
			11	64,868.05	388.53
				(46,630.25)	(1059.23)

Note: Standard error in parentheses. **Significant at the .05 level; *significant at the .01 level.

U.S. National Bureau of Economic Research (NBER). The Italian indicator is an index computed by ISCO (Istituto Italiano per lo Studio della Congiuntura), the Italian equivalent of the American NBER, based on a weighted average of twenty-seven macroeconomic series. The expected behavior of the index is the same as that of industrial production and GNP. Being based on several series, however, the composite index should not be as sensitive to the irregularities of any given product market, as with production series. A composite business-cycle indicator is therefore better suited to reflect the overall state of the economy. Finally, I use what is now commonly regarded as one of the most appropriate cyclical indicators: a measure of capacity utilization, based on the peak-to-peak interpolation of industrial-production series (Klein and Summers, 1966; Klein and Preston, 1967). In Italy, the index is computed by the research unit of the Bank of Italy.

I use product-market variables, such as the index of industrial production and GNP, under the assumption that when the market expands and industrial output

Table 3.2. *Correlation coefficients between business-cycle measures and numbers of strikes, strikers, and hours lost*

Variables	Strikes	Strikers	Hours lost
Industrial production[a]	.63	.45	.31
Detrended industrial production[a,b]	.51	.14	-.03
Capacity utilization[c]	.09	-.38	-.57
Composite business-cycle indicator[d]	.23	-.32	-.39

[a]Manufacturing industry, 1950-I/1978-IV.
[b]Fourth-differenced values for industrial production and number of strikes, strikers, and hours lost.
[c]Manufacturing industry 1953-II/1978-IV.
[d]Manufacturing industry 1967-II/1978-IV.

increases, there will be more reasons for striking: The higher work intensity and the higher prices that come with periods of increased production are likely to spur labor unrest (Knowles, 1952, p. 146) – all the more so because during the upswing phases of the business cycles, greater opportunities for employment put workers in a more favorable bargaining position (Gomberg, 1944, p. 93). As Hobsbawm (1964) and Rist (1907) remarked, workers do not have to look at production figures to know that things are going better for the employer and that times are favorable to demand higher wages. One breathes a special atmosphere in a plant where a slump is giving way to a full productive swing: Trucks are coming and going, the pace of production picks up, and working hours get extended into overtime. Workers have only to look at their employer's face to know whether or not their demands are likely to be met.

3.3.1. Exploratory analyses

Table 3.2 shows the correlation coefficients between the quarterly values of the numbers of strikes, strikers, and hours lost and the index of industrial production. The coefficients reveal positive relationships between industrial production and all three measures of strikes. However, the relationship for the number of strikes is stronger ($r = .63$) than those for the numbers of strikers ($r = .45$) and hours lost ($r = .31$). These findings would thus seem to confirm the stronger dependence of the number of strikes on the business cycle commonly observed in the literature.

The correlation coefficients between the three strike indicators and the composite business-cycle index and the index of capacity utilization, however, show a quite different picture (Table 3.2). The correlation coefficients in both series are weak, although positive, with respect to the number of strikes, whereas they are strong and negative with respect to both the number of strikers and the number of hours lost. These results are troubling. First, it appears that when using more appropriate business-cycle measures (particularly capacity utilization), the positive relationship between the number of strikes and the state of the economy vanishes. Furthermore, how can we interpret the negative relationships between capacity utilization and the numbers of strikers and hours lost ($r = -.57$)? Do such

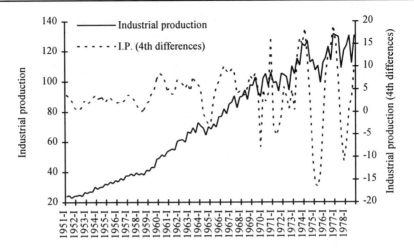

Figure 3.1. *Plots of the index of industrial production*

findings mean that as utilization of industrial installations approaches the maximum and the economy produces ever more frantically, fewer hours will be lost to strike activity (although rare strikes may still occur, for $r = .09$ with the number of strikes)? On the one hand, that interpretation would run counter to the economic-bargaining model for which I found some support in Chapter 2. On the other hand, if industrial capacity is being fully utilized, then industrial production should also be booming. In that case, why should the results for capacity utilization and industrial production differ? How can we explain these mixed signals? To answer these questions, let me take a closer look at the data.

Figures 3.1, 3.2, and 3.3 show time plots for the index of industrial production, the ISCO composite business-cycle indicator, and capacity utilization. Both the index of industrial production and the composite business-cycle indicator show high linear trends. Capacity utilization is a strictly cyclical series, varying cyclically from 0 to 100, at which point productive capacity is fully utilized. Could the positive relationships between the number of strikes and industrial production and the composite business-cycle indicator be due to trend effects? The problem with measuring the linear relationship between trended variables is that trended series are increasing functions of time. Two trended series may spuriously appear to be correlated simply because they have in common the time-trend component, leading to "nonsense regression" (e.g., a high correlation between income and sunspots).[5] Is it possible that the correlation coefficients between industrial production and strike measures simply reflect the correlation between their common time-trend components? To answer this question, let me eliminate the trend components from all the series (numbers of strikes, strikers, and hours lost, industrial production, composite business-cycle indicator) using the method of differencing[6] and then recompute the correlations (Table 3.2). The plots of Figures 3.1 and 3.2 of the

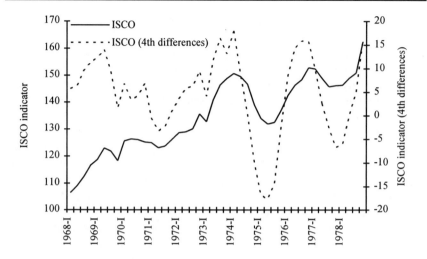

Figure 3.2. *Plots of ISCO composite business-cycle indicator*

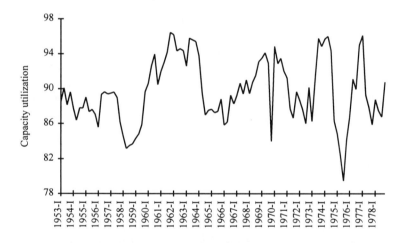

Figure 3.3. *Plot of capacity utilization*

differenced values of industrial production and ISCO indicator show that, indeed, differencing has eliminated the trend component from both series. The three series of capacity utilization and detrended industrial production and ISCO indicator now reveal a basic similar pattern with an increase in output capacity in the early and late 1960s (confirming the basic economic history traced in the preceding chapter).

The correlation cofficients among strike indicators and detrended production series change quite drastically: Only the number of strikes shows a high linear relationship with industrial production, although it is somewhat lower than before, as is typically the case with detrended variables (.51 instead of .63). The coefficient of the number of hours lost is very close to zero and is negative. These results are now more like those obtained using capacity utilization. However, even a detrended measure of industrial production seems to confirm my previous findings that (1) strike frequency is more sensitive to the level of economic activity than are the other two strike components and (2) strikes are more likely to flare up in times of economic expansion than in times of depression.

The negative coefficients between the numbers of strikers and hours lost and the product-market variables could mean either two things, depending on how we want to read the direction of causation between variables. First, they could mean that the larger the number of people on strike and the larger the number of hours lost due to strikes, the larger will be the loss in production. After all, hours lost in strikes are lost to production. Alternatively, they could mean that periods of sluggish production are characterized by longer strikes. The little evidence available on the relationship between strike durations and the business cycle consistently supports this interpretation.[7] My own data on the longer duration of the strike shape (Figure 1.6) for 1966, the last year of the deep 1964–66 recession, is consistent with this view.

I certainly cannot infer causation from correlation (*Ve vobis!*). What I can do, however, is to probe further into the empirical evidence to search for clues that may help me to explain the negative coefficients and infer the causal direction. I will take two different approaches. The first is based on point-by-point comparisons of the time plots of numbers of strikes and strikers, and capacity utilization.[8] The other route is statistically more sophisticated. I used spectral analysis to determine if the relationships between industrial production and the numbers of strikes, strikers, and hours lost differed at different frequency bands. In spectral analysis, one can compute correlation coefficients (*coherences,* as they are called in spectral terminology) at different frequencies.[9] In plain language, the questions that spectral analysis allows me to address are as follows: At which frequencies are the series most linearly related? At the seasonal frequencies, or at some longer cycle? What would be the length of these cycles? Would the relationships be positive or negative? At which cycles would they be positive or negative? Perhaps answers to these questions would also provide some clues about the negative coefficients found in Table 3.2 and their causal reading. Let me start with some simple time plots.

The plot in Figure 3.4 relates the number of strikes to the pattern of capacity utilization.[10] As a general impression, one can say that the number of strikes closely follows the business cycle, as measured by capacity utilization, although the movements of the two curves may not necessarily be perfectly synchronous. In fact, capacity utilization seems to rise and fall much more sharply than does the number of strikes. This is probably due to the fact that the effects of capacity utilization on strike frequency are likely to be indirect, mediated by the trend of

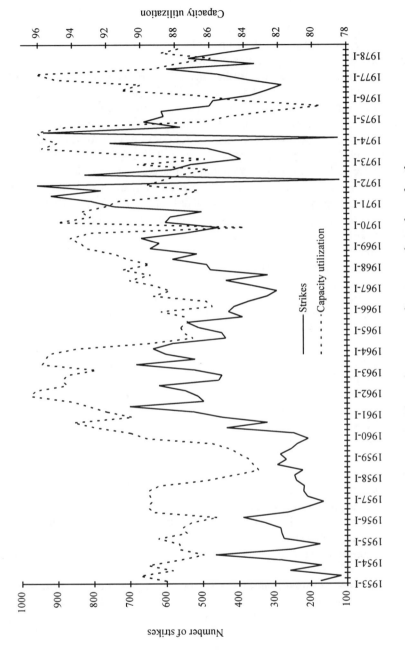

Figure 3.4. Plots of capacity utilization and number of strikes

employment, which is a less sensitive business cycle indicator than is capacity utilization. For one thing, it may not be rational economically for firms to adjust their production levels by firing workers when product demand slackens and re-hiring them when production picks up again. Also, in the presence of strong unions, that may not even be possible politically.

More specifically, the number of strikes increased in the early 1960s in the wake of economic expansion, closely followed capacity utilization until the 1964-II drop, and reached a minimum in 1966-IV, when capacity utilization had already been going up for a couple of quarters. From then on, the number of strikes picked up, once again following the cycle very closely, with a first peak for each series in 1969-II, followed by a trough in 1969-IV, and a similar peak in 1970-I. From 1970 onward, the relationship between the number of strikes and capacity utilization, previously positive, became negative. When strike frequency was up, capacity utilization was down, and vice versa. Capacity utilization, in fact, went down from 1970-III for four quarters, while strikes were on the upswing. From 1972-I until 1973-I, strike frequency sharply declined, and capacity utilization showed oscillating behavior. The first quarter of 1973 represented a lower turning point for both curves, which went up together until the upper turning point of 1974-I. On the way down, the two curves took slightly different routes: Capacity utilization sharply dropped to its historical minimum in the third quarter of 1975 in a sudden severe (though short) recession. The number of strikes, on the other hand, did not fall so abruptly, but showed a minor peak in 1974-IV and continued to drop until 1976-III, at which point capacity utilization had already been rising for a year. The relationship from then on became positive once more, with almost coincident upper and lower turning points in both series.

What can we infer from this detailed description? It would seem that the number of strikes and capacity utilization were, overall, positively related, except for a few subperiods when the relationship was negative (notably 1970-I/1971-III and until, perhaps, 1973-I and 1975-III/1976-III). It should also be noted that throughout the whole period, short, intense outbursts of industrial unrest seem to be negatively related to capacity utilization, as in 1954-II, 1956-I, or the early 1970s, the years of "permanent conflict" (Giugni et al., 1976). But the highest levels of conflict registered in the postwar period did not prevent capacity utilization from reaching one of its historical highs in 1974-I and 1974-II. In short, the long- and medium-term relationship between strike frequency and capacity utilization was positive, although in the short term outbursts of strikes obviously lowered production.[11]

The relationship between capacity utilization and the number of strikers is not as clear-cut, as one can see from Figure 3.5, because long-, medium-, and short-term effects cannot as easily be disentangled. Quite clearly, peaks in the number of strikers are inversely related to capacity utilization, as in 1953-III, 1954-II, 1956-I, 1963-I, 1966-I, 1969-IV, 1973-I, 1974-IV/1976-I, 1976-II/1976-IV, and 1977-IV. But, again, the peaks in worker participation in 1955-I, 1959-II, 1960-III, 1961-IV, 1962-III, 1964-II, 1970-IV, and 1974-II do not correspond to troughs in capacity utilization.

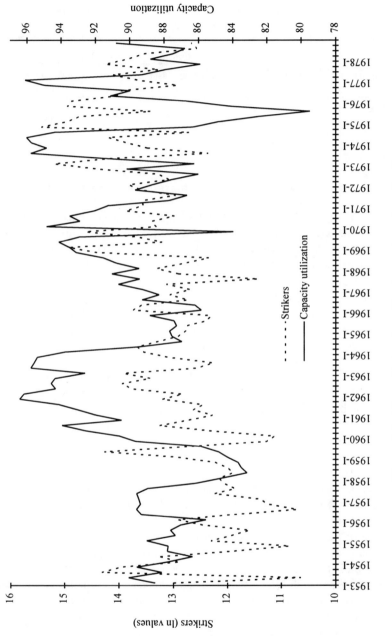

Figure 3.5. *Plots of capacity utilization and number of strikers*

Table 3.3. *Coherence values at seasonal frequencies between industrial production and numbers of strikes, strikers, and hours lost (manufacturing industry, 1950–1/1978–12)*

		Coherence square (cycle/month)		
Frequency	Period (months)	Number of strikes	Number of strikers	Number of hours lost
0.0833	12	0.54	0.50	0.16
0.1667	6	0.76	0.47	0.19
0.2500	4	0.80	0.42	0.28
0.3333	3	0.94	0.12	0.14
0.4167	2.4	0.74	0.58	0.57
0.5000	2	0.93	0.42	0.27

The results of a bivariate spectral analysis confirm the existence of a strong relationship between production and strike activity.[12] Not surprisingly, the relationship with the number of strikes is particularly strong. At the seasonal frequencies, the values of the spectral coherences are very high, as one can see from Table 3.3. As expected by now, the seasonal coherence values with the numbers of strikers and hours lost are not nearly as high, this being particularly true for the number of hours lost. Spectral coherences between numbers of strikes, strikers, and hours lost and industrial production show distinct peaks not only at the seasonal frequencies but also at lower frequencies. The number of strikes, for instance, shows a peak at the .0312 frequency, which corresponds to a period of 32 months.[13] The number of strikers shows relatively high coherence values at the .0312 and .0417 frequency bands (coherence values of .33 and .38), for periods of 32 and 24 months, and the number of hours lost peaks at the .0521 frequency (.69 coherence value), for a period of 19 months. These peaks are so strong that high coherence values are generated at subharmonic frequencies as well. Furthermore, at these lower frequencies, the values of the co-spectrum are negative. How can we interpret these negative relationships between strike indicators and industrial production at two- to three-year intervals? Why should there be such a relationship? After all, Granger and Newbold (1977, p. 33) argue that macroeconomic series present no periodic components, other than the seasonal component. If a cycle in a production series is observed at higher frequencies, it must be caused by institutional, noneconomic processes. As we saw in Chapter 1, one of the pieces of the puzzle is a cyclical component in strike activity with an average three-year length. Perhaps the cyclical component in an Italian production series is caused by strike activity, with periodic bouts of conflict leading to temporary decreases in production (negative co-spectrum). Perhaps institutional factors can explain the cyclical movements of Italian strikes (e.g., collective bargaining).

In conclusion, the correlation coefficients, graphic displays, and spectral coherences show that of all strike indicators, frequency most closely follows production, being particularly sensitive to short-term variations in the level of economic activity. The numbers of strikers and hours lost are much less dependent on short-term economic conditions. If anything, peaks in labor unrest, in terms of the number of workers involved and hours lost, have a negative effect on production (as Figures 3.1, 3.2, and 3.3 and the spectral results confirm). These peaks seem to crop up at three-year intervals.

3.3.2. Multivariate analyses

Will the conclusions of the preceding section based on univariate and bivariate analyses stand up in a multivariate context?[14] The multivariate regression models that I propose to test are essentially variations of the basic Ashenfelter and Johnson model presented in equation (2.2) (Chapter 2, p. 32). I propose to estimate the following two models:

$$S_t = \beta_0 + \beta_1 D_{1t} + \beta_2 D_{2t} + \beta_3 D_{3t} + \beta_4 BC_t + \beta_5 \sum_{i=0}^{n} \mu_i \Delta R_{t-i} + \epsilon_t \qquad (3.2)$$

$$S_t = \beta_0 + \beta_1 D_{1t} + \beta_2 D_{2t} + \beta_3 D_{3t} + \beta_4 UN_t + \beta_5 BC_t + \beta_6 \sum_{i=0}^{n} \mu_i \Delta R_{t-i} + \epsilon_t \qquad (3.3)$$

where S measures the number of strikes, D_1, D_2, and D_3 are a set of seasonal dummies, UN measures the unemployment rate, BC is a business-cycle measure (industrial production, or capacity utilization) and $\Sigma\mu_i \Delta R_{t-i}$ measures real wages (distributed-lag specification), and where $\beta_4 > 0$ in equation (3.2) and $\beta_5 > 0$ in equation (3.3) for the reasons just discussed regarding the expected relationship between strike frequency and economic conditions, $\beta_4 < 0$ in equation (3.3) for the reasons discussed in Chapter 2 (expected negative relationship between unemployment rate and strike frequency) and $\beta_5 > 0$ in equation (3.2) and $\beta_6 > 0$ in equation (3.3) also as explained in Chapter 2 (workers will be less inclined to strike if their recent wages have been rising). To estimate the two equations I used generalized least squares (Cochrane-Orcutt procedure) in order to avoid problems of first order serial correlation. I also applied the Almon technique[15] because the wage variable is in the form of distributed lags.

The results of the econometric estimates for equations (3.2) and (3.3) are shown in Table 3.4 and Table 3.5. Overall, the results leave no doubt about the significance of the effect of the business cycle, however measured, on strike activity. The coefficients of all economic variables are in the expected directions: negative for unemployment rate and positive for both industrial production and capacity utilization. The coefficients of capacity utilization fall below the usual acceptance levels, but they are positive, and their effects, in terms of size, are as strong as or stronger than those of industrial production. Contrary to the expectations of the original Ashenfelter and Johnson model, but in line with the results of Chapter 2, the coefficients of the wage variable are positive and significant. Constraining to zero the end points of the lag structure of the wage variable has a systematic effect on the sizes of the coefficients of the economic

Table 3.4. *Testing the Ashenfelter and Johnson model with labor-market and product-market variables*

Dependent variable: Number of strikes
Aggregation level: Manufacturing industry; quarterly series
Sample period: 1959-II/1978-IV
Estimation method: Almon polynomial distributed lags for all models (models 1, 3, and 5–8 estimated with end-point constraints; models 2 and 4 estimated without constraints); GLS (Cochrane-Orcutt) for all models

Variables	Model 1	Model 2	Model 3	Model 4	Model 5	Model 6	Model 7	Model 8
Constant	-363.81	-320.94	-38.91	-13.40	-342.49	-257.27	-100.76	37.96
	(344.27)	(337.57)	(287.08)	(287.03)	(330.71)	(347.39)	(353.54)	(366.16)
1st-quarter dummy	43.08*	36.75**	59.60*	54.85*	34.66**	29.85	51.78	48.20**
	(17.30)	(18.46)	(19.44)	(21.08)	(18.39)	(19.76)	(20.76)	(22.52)
2nd-quarter dummy	57.58*	51.29*	45.55*	41.59**	61.92*	56.53*	48.00*	48.20**
	(23.11)	(20.74)	(20.38)	(21.33)	(20.83)	(22.62)	(22.30)	(23.59)
3rd-quarter dummy	-43.73**	-51.60**	-58.06*	-63.28*	82.34*	-87.97*	-87.50*	-91.20*
	(19.42)	(24.50)	(23.26)	(24.38)	(18.02)	(19.90)	(18.46)	(20.10)
Change in real wages (%)	324.98**	320.27*	317.09*	312.96*	256.15*	256.33*	234.59*	238.71*
	(75.95)	(76.23)	(73.47)	(73.81)	(64.71)	(65.51)	(56.93)	(58.67)
Unemployment rate			-26.71**	-26.36**			-28.39**	-27.75**
			(13.75)	(14.12)			(15.25)	(15.60)
Industrial production	4.55*	4.35**	3.48**	3.34**				
	(2.07)	(2.08)	(2.01)	(2.02)				
Capacity utilization					6.79**	5.89**	6.16**	5.40
					(3.47)	(3.63)	(3.51)	(3.66)
Adjusted R^2	.79	.78	.79	.79	.77	.77	.78	.77
Durbin-Watson	1.92	1.89	1.94	1.93	1.74	1.72	1.81	1.79
Wallis	2.07	2.04	2.15	2.12	2.15	2.13	2.20	2.18

Note: Standard error in parentheses. **Significant at the .05 level; *significant at the .01 level.

Table 3.5. *Almon polynomial distributed lag coefficients for models in Table 3.4*

	Percent change in real wages$_{t-i}$ for model							
Lag	1	2	3	4	5	6	7	8
0	10.71*	16.18*	10.45*	15.40*	8.44*	13.33*	7.73*	12.14*
	(2.50)	(5.24)	(2.42)	(5.19)	(2.13)	(5.46)	(1.88)	(5.38)
1	19.64*	23.06*	19.16*	21.96*	15.48*	18.64*	14.18*	16.97*
	(4.59)	(5.52)	(4.44)	(5.4)	(3.91)	(5.19)	3.44	(4.89)
2	26.78*	28.45*	26.13*	27.14*	21.11*	22.79*	19.33*	20.76*
	(6.26)	(6.65)	(6.06)	(6.45)	(5.33)	(5.86)	(4.69)	(5.33)
3	32.14*	32.35*	31.36*	30.93*	25.33*	25.79*	23.20*	23.54*
	(7.51)	(7.81)	(7.27)	(7.56)	(6.6)	(6.74)	(5.63)	(6.07)
4	35.71*	34.75*	34.84*	33.33*	28.15*	27.63*	25.78*	25.29*
	(8.35)	(8.67)	(8.07)	(8.39)	(7.11)	(7.46)	(6.26)	(6.7)
5	37.50*	35.67*	36.59*	34.35*	29.56*	28.32*	27.07*	26.01*
	(8.76)	(9.12)	(8.48)	(8.83)	(7.47)	(7.85)	(6.57)	(7.05)
6	37.50*	35.10*	36.59*	33.98*	29.56*	27.86*	27.07*	25.72*
	(8.76)	(9.12)	(8.48)	(8.83)	(7.47)	(7.86)	(6.57)	(7.07)
7	35.71*	33.03*	34.84*	32.22*	28.15*	26.24*	25.78*	24.39*
	(8.35)	(8.67)	(8.07)	(8.41)	(7.11)	(7.5)	(6.26)	(6.76)
8	32.14*	29.48*	31.36*	29.09*	25.33*	23.47*	23.20*	22.05*
	(7.51)	(7.83)	(7.27)	(7.6)	(6.4)	(6.83)	(5.63)	(6.19)
9	26.78*	24.43*	26.13*	24.56*	21.11*	19.55*	19.33*	18.68*
	(6.26)	(6.71)	(6.06)	(6.55)	(5.33)	(6.02)	(4.69)	(5.56)
10	19.64*	17.90*	19.16*	18.65*	15.48*	14.47*	14.18*	14.29*
	(4.59)	(5.7)	(4.44)	(5.64)	(3.91)	(5.48)	(3.44)	(5.25)
11	10.71*	9.87**	10.45*	11.35**	8.44*	8.24*	7.73*	8.87*
	(2.50)	(5.57)	(2.42)	(5.62)	(2.13)	(5.87)	(1.88)	(5.87)

Note: Standard error in parentheses. **Significant at the .05 level; *significant at the .01 level.

variables, with an upward bias that widens the acceptance region. Indeed, whereas the coefficient of capacity utilization is never significant when estimating the model with no end-point constraints (results not reported), the significance of industrial production goes from a 99% level of confidence (when constraining the end points to zero) to a 95% level.

These estimates, however, are likely to suffer from simultaneous-equation bias, that is, from problems arising from the reciprocal relationship (simultaneously both cause and effect) between strike activity and production. As the analyses of the foregoing section have revealed, production variables are likely to be endogenous, that is, determined by simultaneous interactions between dependent and independent variables, between strike and production variables (Johnston, 1972, pp. 341–3). Ordinary least squares (OLS) procedures assume that causation goes in one direction only, from independent variable to dependent variable. Using OLS to estimate a model with current endogenous variables will cause the endogenous "independent" variables to be correlated with the disturbance term of the equation and will cause the parameter estimates to be biased and inconsistent (Johnston,

1972, p. 376). The problem can be overcome by applying either single-equation simultaneous methods [two-stage least squares (2SLS) and limited information single equation (LISE)] or complete-system simultaneous methods [three-stage least squares (3SLS) and full information maximum likelihood (FIML)] (Johnston, 1972, p. 380). I chose 2SLS for its simplicity and estimated the following detrended model:[16]

$$\Delta S_t = \beta_0 + \beta_1 D_{1t} + \beta_2 D_{2t} + \beta_3 D_{3t} + \beta_4 \Delta IP_t + \epsilon_t \qquad (3.4)$$

where ΔS measures the fourth-differenced values of number of strikes, D_1, D_2, and D_3 are a set of seasonal dummies, and ΔIP measures the fourth-differenced value of unemployment rate, and where $\beta_4 > 0$. Models 1 and 2 of Table 3.6 show the results obtained estimating equation (3.4) with both OLS and 2SLS. A direct comparison between the two sets of coefficients clearly highlights the distorting effect of simultaneous-equation bias. The 2SLS estimates show that once the negative effects on production caused by peaks in strike frequency are accounted for, the relationship between production and strike frequency is even more strongly positive and significant than OLS estimates would lead one to believe.

If these multivariate estimates have further clarified the relationship between strike frequency and the state of the economy, they have left unresolved the problem of pinning down the effects of economic determinants on other strike components, such as worker involvement and hours lost. We have already seen that the relationship can be strongly negative, because peaks in the numbers of strikers and hours lost significantly lower production at three-year intervals.

In order to focus on these middle-term negative effects of a few years' duration without any blurring due to trend, I reestimated equation (3.2) using fourth-differenced values of industrial production (Granger and Newbold, 1974; Plosser and Schwert, 1978). The econometric estimates of models 3–6 in Table 3.6 confirm that indeed these periodic bouts of strike activity negatively affect production. The production variables are in fact highly significant and have negative signs. The values of the Durbin-Watson statistic exclude serial correlation problems. The R^2 values are low, as one would expect with the use of detrended data,[17] but they are also generally lower that those obtained when using the number of strikes as the dependent variable (see, e.g., model 1). This implies that there is more to the numbers of strikers and hours lost than economic variables alone can explain.

In order to explain the negative signs of the statistical relationships between strike indicators and the index of industrial production, the composite business-cycle index, and the index of capacity utilization, I have proposed thus far a short-run causal reading from strike activity to production variables, rather than vice versa. Spectral results confirmed the validity of that interpretation. The econometric findings in this section provide further support; after all, the unemployment-rate coefficient, which is not as sensitive to short-term fluctuations in the level of industrial conflict, maintains unaltered its expected negative sign. There is yet another way to confirm my causal reading of the relationship. An

Table 3.6. *Measuring the effects of product-market variables on numbers of strikes, strikers, and hours lost*

Dependent variable: Number of strikes for models 1 and 2; number of strikers for models 3 and 4; number of hours lost for models 5 and 6
Aggregation level: Manufacturing industry; quarterly series
Sample period: 1959-II/1978-IV
Estimation method: OLS for models 1 and 6; 2SLS for model 2; GLS (Cochrane-Orcutt) for models 3–5. Instrumental variables in model 2: constant, 1st-, 2nd-, and 3rd-quarter dummies, first differenced values of capacity utilization, unemployment rate, number of hours worked in manufacturing industry

Variables	Model 1	Model 2	Model 3	Model 4	Model 5	Model 6
Constant	21.24	1.80	1,271,560*	727,450*	282,44.1*	13,456.8*
	(26.63)	(31.83)	(295,182)	(187,886)	(6,015.1)	(3,482.5)
1st-quarter dummy	20.51	41.13	-1,016,520*	-437,323	284,50.0*	-11,653.2*
	(37.61)	(39.94)	(419,773)	(317,754)	(7,924.2)	(5,037.1)
2nd-quarter dummy	-5.68	6.62	-1,795,590*	-1,436,260*	-3,2891.0*	-23,750.8*
	(32.94)	(33.89)	(345,783)	(283,219)	(7,643.8)	(5,984.0)
3rd-quarter dummy	-111.26*	-76.19	-2,035,700*	-1,050,160*	-44,579.0*	-17,454.7*
	(47.77)	(52.08)	(511,160)	(311,383)	(10,067.3)	(4,858.5)
Unemployment rate			-326,799*	-275,579	-5,883.3*	-5,559.8*
			(136,952)	(123,870)	(3,022.5)	(2,469.2)
Industrial production	6.38*	8.73*	-652,501*		-1,823.8*	
	(.47)	(2.82)	(21,427)		(463.2)	
Capacity utilization				-135,542*		-4,398.0*
				(29,372)		(569.9)
Adjusted R^2	.44	.44	.32	.41	.28	.45
Durbin-Watson	1.63	1.64	2.06	2.00	2.10	2.07
Wallis	2.37	2.27	1.75	1.94	1.63	1.95

Note: Standard error in parentheses. **Significant at the .05 level; *significant at the .01 level.

eight-hour strike in a plant will halt production for eight hours. This negative effect, however, is unlikely to affect monthly production figures for the company (because lost time can be compensated by overtime) and is even less likely to affect the macroeconomic production series for the sector in which the plant operates. The more disaggregated (in regard to both time and sector) is the series that we use, the more likely it is that production losses due to strikes will show up; the more aggregated the series, the less likely it will be to detect any effect of strikes on production. Indeed, when we consider more highly aggregated data at the economywide level, such as quarterly values of GNP, the coefficients of production variables, as one can see from Table 3.7, are positive and significant for all strike components.

3.4. STRUCTURAL CHARACTERISTICS OF THE ITALIAN ECONOMY

In Chapter 2 and in the preceding sections I have traced the relationships between short- and middle-term business fluctuations and strike activity. The evidence seems to point to a strong relationship between labor conflict and the labor market. More specifically, whereas the number of strikes decreases with rising levels of unemployment, the number of hours lost seems to increase as both labor and capital retrench on the defensive during recessions. The longer duration of strikes during the 1966 recession (see the strike shapes in Chapter 1, Figure 1.6) is a case in point (although . . . why is the strike duration during the boom year of 1962 just as exceptionally long?).

The relationship with the product market is more difficult to disentangle, blurred as it is by problems of trend and reciprocal causation at different frequency bands (with temporary bouts of strike activity leading to a decrease in production, particularly noticeable at regular, two- to three-year intervals, and long-term periods of booming production leading to increases in labor unrest). Nonetheless, there appears to be little doubt that strikes and the production cycle go hand in hand.

Yet even a cursory comparison between the beginning and ending dates of strike cycles (Table 3.8)[18] and the Italian postwar business cycles, as identified by ISCO (1985), the Italian institute for the study of business cycles (Table 3.9), shows that the two sets of cycles do not match for any of the three strike series.[19] Thus, if there is a relationship between the business cycle and strike activity, it must be somewhat looser than would be implied by a strict periodization of the business cycle. Undoubtedly, the relationship between the cycle (as measured by ISCO) and strike activity is mediated by the labor market, which is less sensitive than the product market to the fluctuations in business activity. To the extent that industrial conflict is regulated by labor-market mechanisms, the relationship between the business cycle and industrial conflict will have some temporal lags, due to indirect effects, and perhaps will even be mediated by noneconomic mechanisms (e.g., union strength, institutional mechanisms of collective bargaining). All of this may explain

Table 3.7. *More on labor-market and product-market effects*

Dependent variable:	Number of strikes for models 1 and 2; number of strikers for models 3 and 4; number of hours lost for models 5 and 6
Aggregation level:	Economy; quarterly series
Sample period:	1954-II/1975-IV for models 1, 3, and 5; 1959-II/1975-IV for models 2, 4, and 6
Estimation method:	GLS (Cochrane-Orcutt) for all models

Variables	Model 1	Model 2	Model 3	Model 4	Model 5	Model 6
Constant	17.13	-32.94	-1,200,290.0	-9,5644.5	-4,349.23	21,722.4
	(259.17)	(493.44)	(812,621.0)	(1,773,720.0)	(11,753.1)	(26,218.8)
1st-quarter dummy	138.10*	240.01*	437,430.0	878,193.0*	-100.71	835.29
	(40.08)	(67.76)	(299,498.0)	(476,214.0)	(5,353.13)	(8,203.09)
2nd-quarter dummy	125.77*	119.52*	-3,727.0	-259,455.0	-587.36	-6,159.63
	(34.53)	(40.06)	(319,795.0)	(411,681.0)	(5,699.83)	(7,480.26)
3rd-quarter dummy	-83.68	-131.88*	-790,774.0*	-1,125,010.0*	10,029.6**	-15,040.0*
	(28.33)	(31.08)	(281,258.0)	(354,146.0)	(5,115.13)	(6,623.22)
Unemployment rate		-64.04*		-374,688.0		-3,289.82
		(24.19)		(265,788.0)		(4,320.47)
GNP, in 1970 lire	.073*	.100*	252.11*	326.96*	2.91*	2.45*
	(.020)	(.035)	(63.77)	(114.63)	(.91)	(1.54)
Adjusted R^2	.84	.83	.45	.40	.28	.17
Durbin-Watson	1.70	1.64	1.80	1.38	1.93	1.92
Wallis	1.63	2.09	1.55	1.74	2.00	2.10

Note: Standard error in parentheses. **Significant at the .05 level; *significant at the .01 level.

Table 3.8. *Nonperiodic cycles of numbers of strikes, strikers, and hours lost*

	Number of strikes		Number of strikers		Number of hours lost	
	Date	Duration^a	Date	Duration	Date	Duration
1	Jan. '50–Sep. '51	20	Apr. '53–Nov. '54	19	Feb. '53–Oct. '54	20
2	Sep. '51–May '53	20	Nov. '54–Dec. '56	25	Oct. '54–Dec. '56	26
3	May '53–Dec. '54	19	Dec. '56–Jun. '58	18	Dec. '56–Jun. '58	18
4	Dec. '54–Dec. '56	24	Jun. '58–Jan. '60	19	Jun. '58–Jan. '60	19
5^b	Dec. '56–Nov. '59	35	Jan. '60–Jul. '61	18	Jan. '60–Jul. '61	18
6^c	Nov. '59–Dec. '66	85	Jul. '61–Jul. '63	24	Jul. '61–Jul. '63	24
7	Dec. '66–Dec. '69	36	Jul. '63–Nov. '65	28	Jul. '63–Nov. '65	28
8	Dec. '69–Mar. '73	39	Nov. '65–Feb. '67	15	Nov. '65–Feb. '67	15
9	Mar. '73–Jun. '76	39	Feb. '67–Nov. '71	57	Feb. '67–Nov. '71	57
10	Jun. '76–Dec. '78	30	Nov. '71–Dec. '73	25	Nov. '71–Dec. '73	25
11	Dec. '73–May '75	17	Dec. '73–May '75	17		
12	May '75–Dec. '76	19	May '75–Dec. '76	19		
13	Dec. '76–Dec. '78	24	Dec. '76–Dec. '78	24		
Mean		29		20.9^d		21.1^e

^{a}In months.
^{b}5a Dec. '56–May '58 17
   5b May '58–Nov. '59 18
^{c}6a Nov. '59–Dec. '62 37
   6b Dec. '62–Oct. '64 22
   6c Oct. '64–Dec. '66 26
^{d}Including cycles nos. 5 and 6.
^{e}Excluding cycles nos. 1 and 10.

some of the ambiguities in the findings, some of my uneasiness about their interpretation.

Yet if we back away from all the problems of simultaneous-equation bias, model misspecification, structural instability of the parameters, and specification of the business cycle (labor- or product-market variables), the historical record is, surprisingly, rather clear. Strike activity was low in the 1950s, when unemployment and underemployment were at staggering levels. It picked up in 1959–62, when unemployment went down and production soared. It declined in 1964–66, when the recession hit labor hard before it had had a chance to consolidate the gains of the 1959–63 strike wave (*ricatto congiunturale*). Conflict exploded in 1969–72, when, again, the labor market tightened up. Finally, it started to decline toward the end of the 1970s, as unemployment kept growing. Now, if we are willing to lean out of the temporal window of this book and peek into the 1980s, then we see that during the 1980s, industrial conflict almost "withered away" to the levels of the early 1950s, as the *cassa integrazione guadagni* (temporary unemployment benefits), layoffs, early retirements, and plant closings kept reducing the size of the industrial labor force, particularly in the larger firms. According to this reading of the economic data, the postwar period was characterized by two main cycles, rather

Table 3.9. *Chronology of Italian business cycles between 1945 and 1983*

Cycle	Beginning		Peak		End trough		Number of months		
I	May	1945	Sep.	1947	Mar.	1948	28	6	34
II	Mar.	1948	Apr.	1951	May	1952	37	13	50
III	May	1952	Sep.	1957	Aug.	1958	64	11	75
IV	Aug.	1958	Oct.	1963	Jan.	1965	62	15	77
V	Jan.	1965	Oct.	1970	Oct.	1971	69	12	81
VI	Oct.	1971	Jan.	1974	Sep.	1975	32	15	47
VII	Sep.	1975	Feb.	1977	Dec.	1977	17	10	27
VIII	Dec.	1977	Mar.	1980	Jun.	1983	27	39	66

Source: ISCO (1985).

than the eight cycles identified by ISCO (Table 3.9): one long upward swing from 1950 to the early 1970s (except for the short and severe 1964–67 recession), and the slow decline thereafter.

If that is the case, then perhaps the relationship between industrial conflict and the labor market must be viewed in a somewhat longer perspective than the four- to seven-year business cycle. Viewed in this longer perspective, the focus, historically and empirically, shifts from an emphasis on the yearly fluctuations of unemployment rate, industrial production, or GNP to the structural characteristics of the economy and how they slowly changed over time. I will turn next to those issues, focusing, in particular, on the following long-term aspects: Changes in the occupational structure, in the productive structure (technical organization of production, and size distribution of productive units), and in the labor-market structure.

3.4.1. Long-term sectoral shifts in the occupational structure

In the process of economic growth during the postwar decades, the structure of the Italian economy shifted from agriculture to industry and to services, following a well-known trajectory (Clark, 1940).

As Table 3.10 shows, agricultural employment steadily declined throughout the entire period (in particular, self-employment, which masked the high levels in underemployment of the Italian economy and provided much of the "reserve army" during the 1950s). Industrial employment went from 23.1% in 1951 to a peak of 36.0% in 1970 and slowly declined thereafter. Service-sector employment, on the other hand, grew steadily (tripling in the state sector).

Shifts of workers from one productive sector to another entail parallel shifts in the forms of worker organizations and collective consciousness. As the class structure changes, so does class consciousness and conflict.[20] As Hobsbawm put it, it takes time for newcomers to learn the ropes of solidarity.

The three-dimensional plots of Figures 3.6, 3.7, and 3.8 report five-year averages for the numbers of strikes, strikers, and hours lost in agriculture, industry,

Table 3.10. *Distribution of the labor force by sector and period (%)*

Period	Agriculture			Industry			Services		
	Employed	Self-employed	Tot.	Employed	Self-employed	Tot.	Employed	Self-employed	Tot.
1951–60	9.2	28.4	37.6	26.2	6.8	33.0	19.6	9.8	29.4
1961–70	7.6	16.9	24.5	33.6	6.5	40.1	23.8	15.6	39.4
1971–80	5.8	9.7	15.5	32.7	5.1	37.8	32.4	14.3	46.7
1951	11.5	32.4	43.9	23.1	6.4	29.5	17.9	8.7	26.6
1981	5.0	7.8	12.8	31.2	5.1	36.3	35.7	15.2	50.9

Source: ISTAT (1986).

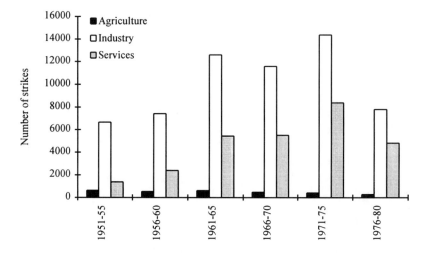

Figure 3.6. *Bar charts of numbers of strikes in agriculture, industry, and services (1951–1980, five-year averages)*

and services over the period 1951–80. The plots clearly show how conflict closely followed the long-term shifts in the labor force (Troiani, 1978, p. 89). Still a powerful threat in the 1950s and 1960s, agricultural conflict (with its widespread movements of land occupation, particularly in the South), declined in later years. On the other hand, all three indicators of strikes in the service sector steadily increased during the postwar period.[21]

Within these broad sectors, no less significant was the distribution of the work force in subsectors, characterized by different levels of economic vitality. According to Graziani (1976, pp. 201–2), the Italian economy during the 1950s and 1960s was characterized by a dualistic structure: traditional sectors that were sluggish (the food-processing, shoe, textile, wood working, and construction

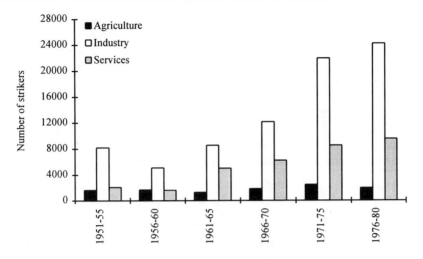

Figure 3.7. *Bar charts of numbers of strikers in agriculture, industry, and services (1951–1980, five-year averages)*

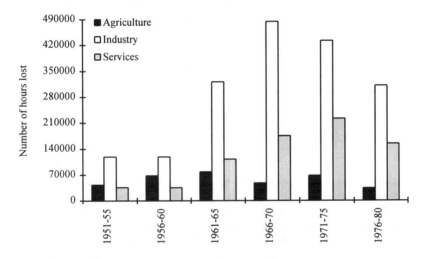

Figure 3.8. *Bar charts of numbers of hours lost in agriculture, industry, and services (1951–1980, five-year averages)*

industries) and modern sectors that were dynamic (the metalworking, chemical, and rubber industries).[22] Between 1951 and 1972, the textile, food-processing, and metalworking sectors declined in their share of total gross manufacturing production, whereas the mechanical, automobile, and chemical sectors kept growing. The mechanical sector showed the fastest growth, from 20% to 27%, followed by the chemical sector (Fondazione Giovanni Agnelli, 1973, pp. 24–5).

Comparative research on the interindustry propensity to strike has shown that there were significant sectoral differences in strike activity.[23] Indeed, the available evidence suggests that interindustry strike propensities in Italy closely followed Graziani's dual sectors: Strike activity was higher in the metalworking industry (accounting for some 50% of all hours lost to strikes in the period 1967–76) and chemical industry (with some 10% of all hours lost), and lower in the others (Troiani, 1978, p. 95).

In conclusion, whereas the business cycle helps to explain the short-term and middle-term fluctuations in strike activity, secular shifts in the occupational structure help to explain the long-term patterns of strikes.

3.4.2. The mode of production: technology and social organization

In 1938, at the time of the last industrial census under the Fascist regime, the degree of mechanization in Italian industry was low, the average plant size was small, and the average industrial equipment inventory was old and technically obsolete (CISIM, 1952, pp. 74–6; Romeo, 1961, p. 179).[24] Modern forms of organization of production (e.g., Taylorism) were regarded as only distant curiosities even in the larger firms (CISIM, 1952, pp. 101–3; Caracciolo, 1969, p. 167; Sapelli, 1976, p. 161). The survival of such a stagnant industrial economy had been made possible by the autarchic policies of the Fascist regime which had sealed off Italy from international competition (Romeo, 1961, p. 190; Grassini, 1969, p. 270; Castronovo, 1980, p. 299). "Italian industry practically lived closed within itself from the 1929 crisis to the outbreak of the war" (Grassini, 1969, p. 270). Although the war effort forced considerable expansion and improvement in Italian industrial capacity (Daneo, 1975, pp. 4–5), the overall result of the Fascist industrial policies was that "Italian industry in 1940 was on average some twenty years behind the United States, in terms of level of technology" (Caracciolo, 1969, p. 160). Such problems were further compounded by the destruction of much productive capacity (calculated at around 20%) during the war (Daneo, 1975, p. 5).

Postwar reconstruction, which was aided by the Marshall Plan, featured large-scale purchases of American industrial equipment. The decision of the republican government to liberalize trade made rapid modernization of Italy's industrial structure imperative for the survival of the bourgeoisie in an internationally competitive environment. The Stanford Research Institute, commissioned by the Italian government to evaluate metalworking firms at the end of the 1940s, concluded that "Facilities, though generally adequate, are far from modern. Equipment layout is poor. Space utilization is not efficient" (CISIM, 1952, p. 67; see also Grassini, 1969, p. 264). In the late 1940s, industrial production was still based on general-purpose machinery (e.g., lathes, boring mills) operated by skilled craftsmen. Equipment was far less specialized than in the United States (CISIM, 1952, p. 75). Modern conveyor systems (of the assembly line type) were virtually unknown, "probably the greatest deficiencies in the Italian mechanical industries" (CISIM, 1952, p. 79). During the 1950s, production (at least in larger plants) increasingly came to be based on single-purpose machines organized in assembly lines (Grassini, 1969, pp. 254–5).[25] By 1960, mechanization and rationalization of Italian plants along both Fordistic and Tayloristic lines had become quite advanced (Sapelli, 1976, p. 163).[26] Indeed, the 1950s were the decade of Italy's "technological leap" (Valcamonici, 1977, p. 223), as confirmed by the high levels of investment in industrial equipment during those years (see Figure 8.7 in Chapter 8, p. 329). Productivity gains were high. By 1955, Italy had already achieved one of the highest productivity levels among Western industrialized economies, and by 1960, it was second only to Norway.[27]

The pace of technological innovation, with the widespread diffusion of machines for use in assembly lines, picked up in the early 1960s, and extensive rationalization of the organization of production took place during the recession in the middle of the 1960s. "After the 1961 struggles, white-coated technicians entered the factories, the stop-watch men, the capitalist rationality" (Ferraris, 1965, p. 33). In the 1960s, in many sectors (e.g., textiles, metalworking), productivity gains were achieved more through extensive reorganization of production than through capital investment (Valcamonici, 1977, p. 217). As the Italian economist Roberto Valcamonici (1977, p. 201) put it, "The history of the decade 1961–1971 is a history of deep restructuring of productive processes." As firms faced higher labor costs and as the recession downsized employment, productivity gains were achieved mostly through more efficient production (Valcamonici, 1977, p. 200).

Although Italy arrived late to the use of modern technical (Fordism) and social (Taylorism) forms of organization of production, by the late 1960s that process had come to full maturity.[28] The stopwatch, piecework, minute divisions of labor, repetitious tasks, "scientific" determination of the time allowed for each operation, and increasing encroachment on workers' "dead time" (*saturazione dei tempi*) had become all too familiar in the Italian factory world.[29] A study conducted in the early 1970s by Federlombarda, the territorial association of Lombardy employers, provided an empirical assessment of the levels and types of technology available in firms with less than 500 employees. Although the data are fairly crude, they do show that the prevalent mode of production in larger firms was based on automated or semiautomated equipment, requiring workers simply to tend machines (over 80% of the firms in the sample with more than 100 employees). The percentage of firms in the sample that based their production on nonautomated technology declined linearly with plant size: 45.8% of firms with 1–19 employees, 34.4% of those with 20–49, 35.1% of those with 50–99, and 22.2% of those with 100–249 (Bergamaschi, 1977a, p. 196). Firms employing more than 250 workers all used automated technology.[30]

There are two questions that arise here: How does the technical organization of production affect industrial conflict? Do workers' modes of consciousness and forms of conflict vary when they are faced with different styles of workplace organization? From the literature, it would appear that, indeed, there is a strong relationship among technology, consciousness, and conflict. In conducting a comparative analysis of production technologies,[31] Blauner (1964) concluded that alienation was high among workers who tended machines and worked on an assembly line, whereas it was low among workers in craft and automated production (process, continuous-flow).[32] And alienation goes hand in hand with conflict. Similarly, Woodward (1965, pp. 50–67) found that both intermanagerial relationships and employer–employee relationships were better at the extremes of the scale of technical complexity. It was among those involved in mass-production technology, according to Woodward, that relationships were worse.[33]

Against Blauner's and Woodward's views of process industries (e.g., oil refining and plastics) as the site of more harmonious labor relations, Mallet (1965, 1975) argued that automation does not foster industrial peace, but rather industrial conflict.[34] According to Mallet, workers in automated industries have better educational credentials and enjoy higher wages and greater job security than do workers in traditional industries. As a result, these workers experience a potentially explosive contradiction between their integration into a challenging technical environment and their subjection to the firm's authority structure. Having satisfied their basic economic needs, these workers begin to demand control of production. They truly constitute the new revolutionary element of the working class – indeed, a new working class.[35]

If the future of production lies in automated technology, the arguments of Blauner, Woodward, and Mallet would lead to divergent predictions about the future of labor relations in industry. Despite their divergent views on the future of industrial relations, Blauner, Woodward, and Mallet basically agree that the social organization of production around the assembly line is the most dehumanizing form of production and is a continuing source of conflict. This consideration brings up a question: Given that assembly line technology in Italy had increasingly spread throughout the 1960s, was the explosion of conflict in 1968 and 1969 simply a coincidence, or did it reflect the long-term maturity of a technical mode of production based on Fordism? More generally, the arguments on the historical transformations of technical modes of production have shown that the changes are never purely technical, but involve different forms of social organization of production and different distributions of skills within the working class. Changes in the technical mode of production, in other words, are linked to changes in the class structure. As Fordism was becoming the predominant form of organization of production throughout the 1950s and 1960s, was, in fact, the structure of the Italian industrial working class changing correspondingly? Was there a general decrease in the level of workers' skills? Let me tackle these questions next.

3.4.3. Labor-market structure

In 1950, Italian firms classified workers into four basic skill categories: skilled workers at the top, semiskilled and unskilled workers, and common hand laborers at the bottom of the hierarchy.[36] Women were traditionally grouped in a category of their own – needless to say, at the bottom of the hierarchy. In the period between 1950 and 1970 in Italy, the tendency was for increasing percentages of workers to

Table 3.11. *Hire rates for blue-collar workers in Milanese firms (1959–62)*

	Small firms (<250 workers)				Large firms (>250 workers)			
	OS[a]	OQ	MS	MC	OS	OQ	MS	MC
1959	7.2	11.7	26.1	43.3	2.2	5.4	23.9	53.0
1960	7.8	14.8	34.8	65.6	4.8	9.4	38.4	76.9
1961	10.9	17.0	42.0	77.3	4.9	10.7	48.6	94.8
1962	11.3	19.1	43.3	80.4	4.9	10.7	47.6	113.5

[a]OS, *operai specializzati* (skilled); OQ, *operai qualificati* (semiskilled); MS, *manovali specializzati* (unskilled); MC, *manovali comuni* (unskilled).
Source: Associazione Industriale Lombarda (1960, 1961, 1962, 1963, 1964).

be classified in the lowest skill categories (Paci, 1973, pp. 160–1). On the basis of the 1951 and 1961 census data, Bianchi and D'Ambrosio (1970, p. 60) estimated that the percentage of skilled workers in the steel industry went from 12.9% in 1951 to 11.2% a decade later; the percentage of semiskilled workers declined from 29.3% to 27.3%. Similar declines occurred in all other economic sectors (see also Cella, 1976b, p. 170). In 1967, a survey conducted in the Turin province found that 50.2% of blue-collar manufacturing jobs were concentrated in the very lowest hierarchical echelons (hand laborers and unskilled workers) (Cella, 1976b, pp. 176–7); in the automobile industry, the figure was 66.3%. In textiles, only 6.8% of the blue-collar work force was classified as skilled. In the province of Milan, with a more diversified industrial base, 38.5% of the manufacturing work force was classified in the lowest categories (44% in automobiles, and 52.9% in electrical machinery, both based on assembly line technology). At the national level, 40% of the work force was concentrated in the lowest two categories.

The large industrial plants employed much higher percentages of unskilled workers. According to a survey conducted in 1968 in Lombardy (Paci, 1973, p. 161), workers classified as unskilled in their current jobs and experiencing downward reclassification were 19% in factories employing less than 50 workers, 22% in factories employing between 50 and 1,000 workers, and 38% in larger factories (Reyneri and Tempia, 1974, pp. 67–8).[37] The yearly surveys of labor turnover conducted by Assolombarda in the boom years of the "economic miracle," between 1958 and 1962, in the most industrialized province in the country provide some valuable information on the workers being hired by Milanese firms in those days (Table 3.11). The rates of hiring for workers in the lowest skill grade were much higher, and became increasingly so over the years, than those for workers in any other grade. Considering that the majority of workers were classified at the lowest skill levels, these figures indicate that firms were hiring huge numbers of mostly unskilled workers. Large firms employing more than 250 workers were even more likely to hire workers at the lowest level.

The skill requirements for the various job levels were the ostensible criteria for these classifications. Yet Blackburn and Mann (1979), on the basis of a comparative analysis of skill requirements for almost 300 job categories in an

English industrial city, concluded that the absolute level of skill needed for all but a handful of the very highest jobs is minimal. In Blackburn and Mann's words (1979, p. 280), most blue-collar jobs differ only in one respect: "They involve different levels of debasement. 87% of the workers [in the sample] exercise less skill at work than they would if they drove to work." In basic confirmation that skill requirements provide only a partial basis for an objective classification of jobs, a yearly survey conducted by the Istituto per la Ricostruzione Industriale (IRI) and Ente Nazionale Idrocarburi (ENI), Italy's two giant state-owned conglomerates, showed that jobs basically involving the same level of skill were classified differently in different firms (Cella, 1976b, p. 177). In the factory world, nearly all manual workers constitute relatively homogeneous labor power at the semiskilled level of machine-tending operations. Aside from differences related to sex, race, and health, all workers have indistinguishable market capacities.

In the absence of any intrinsic satisfaction deriving from the use of one's skills, the major systematic source of variations in work rewards has been from the *internal labor market* operating within large firms.[38] The internal labor market provides workers with job security and with opportunities for advancement up a career ladder.[39] To the individual worker, the phantom of a career is made more plausible by the fact that, particularly in larger firms, workers tend to pile up at the bottom of the hierarchy. The Assolombarda survey (Associazione Industriali Lombarda, 1961, p. 13) of worker turnover showed that the probability of promotion was high for workers in the lowest echelons, but rapidly declined toward the top. Job classifications and the distribution of the work force in a hierarchical ladder of positions, with increased rewards along the ladder, develop "in the labor force a kind of 'hierarchy fetishism' – a continual craving for more and better job titles and status, the satisfaction of which leads eventually to intensified hunger for still more and better job titles and job status" (Gordon, 1978, p. 77).[40]

The extensive classification of jobs thus provides the phantom of a career, internal to the company and seemingly based on skills. Yet the transition from one job level to the next only minimally involves the acquisition of new skills by the workers. Rather, it is an administrative decision that reflects the employer's willingness to reward *docile bodies*. Survey research, in both Italy and elsewhere, has found that the real criterion for promotion is not the mustering of skills (in any case minimal) but worker cooperation (Reyneri and Tempia, 1974; Blackburn and Mann, 1979). As Blackburn and Mann[41] put it, "Responsibility, stability, trustworthiness – such are the qualities by which (reasonably enough) [employers] wish to select and promote."

Thus, perhaps the persistence of extensive classifications of jobs purportedly based on skill, but where the skill content has been so profoundly diluted, also serves the interests of capital in a *divide et impera* strategy (Braverman, 1974; Marglin, 1974; Cella, 1976b, p. 182; Rubery, 1978). For the workers' logic based on skill and craft tradition (Stone, 1974) the modern firm has substituted a logic based on authority and hierarchy; furthermore, it has transferred control over job hierarchies from the workers into its own hands (Paci, 1973, p. 151).

Table 3.12. *Historical transformation of the job hierarchy in Italian firms (1950–68)*

Hierarchical levels[a]	1950	1963[b]	1966[b]	1968[c]
1st super *operaio specializzato provetto*			x	x
1st *operaio specializzato* (OS)	x[d]	x	x	x
2nd *operaio qualificato* (OQ)	x	x	x	x
3rd super				x
operaio comune di prima (OC2)		x	x	x
3rd *manovale specializzato* (MS)	x			
operaio comune di seconda (OC1)		x	x	x
4th women	x	x	x	x
5th *manovale comune* (MC)	x	x	x	x
6th women	x			
7th women	x			

[a] Skilled worker (1st super, OS), semiskilled worker (OQ), unskilled worker (MS, OC1, OC2, MC).
[b] Introduced with the national metalworkers' contract.
[c] Introduced with the national chemical workers' contract.
[d] x marks the availability of the skill level at the time.
Source: Cella (1976b, pp. 170, 172, 173), Regini and Reyneri (1971, pp. 94–5).

Despite capitalists' interests in the creation and perpetuation of job hierarchies in the factories, to underestimate the role that workers and their unions play in structuring labor markets would be a mistake. In all countries and in all times, workers have organized to control the supply of labor in order to defend themselves against competition.[42] Unions may similarly have a stake in creating and maintaining a system of job hierarchies (Rubery, 1978).[43] After all, often the creation of new job categories may be the only way to obtain wage increases for large numbers of workers (e.g., Reyneri and Tempia, 1974).

The data in Table 3.12 clearly bear this out.[44] The table summarizes the historical changes in the hierarchical classification of blue-collar jobs in Italian firms (Regini and Reyneri, 1971; Cella, 1976b). To the basic four-level structure of the *sistema delle qualifiche* of the 1950s, the 1963 contract renewal with the metalworker unions added a new level by splitting the *manovali specializzati* into two categories: *operai comuni di prima* and *operai comuni di seconda*. In 1966, the metalworkers obtained yet another new level at the top (1st super). Chemical workers introduced another level with their 1968 contract (3rd super). Typically, after the introduction of a new level in one sector, other sectors followed suit.

In conclusion, the analyses of this section confirm the long-run changes in the distribution of skills and the basic transformation of the structure of the working class due to the diffusion of Fordism as a prevailing mode of production. Not only was the class structure in postwar Italy changing because of long-term shifts in the labor force from agriculture to industry and to services, but also the structure of the industrial working class itself was changing under the effects of the diffusion of a technical mode of production (the assembly line) based on unskilled labor, rather than skilled labor.[45] If the structure of the working class changed along the lines outlined in this section, we should be able to observe a parallel historical change in the types of actors (i.e., from skilled workers to unskilled workers) involved in industrial struggles. Is there empirically observable evidence regarding the class actors and class struggles for the Italian case? As Fordism in Italy had come to maturity by the late 1960s, was the resurgence of conflict during the 1969 *autunno caldo* in the hands of the unskilled workers? Had the struggles of the 1950s mainly involved skilled workers? We must wait until Chapter 7 for an in-depth, ethnographic analysis of the types of class actors involved.

3.4.4. The industrial structure: the distribution of plant sizes

Not only will the structure of the labor market change with the changes in technical modes of production, but also the concentration of firms in a sector and the average firm size will change with the prevailing form of production technology (for Italy, see Valcamonici, 1977, p. 221). The general historical trend has been toward greater concentration and larger sizes for both firms and productive units. Marx argued that increasing concentration of capital in fewer and fewer hands and socialization of labor in ever larger factories were the two fundamental contradictions that would eventually bring capitalism down ("So few of them, so many of us"). By 1920, giant oligopolies and large mills had begun to emerge in most industrialized countries. Italy followed a similar path. Census data confirm the trend toward larger plant sizes during the period between 1911 and 1938, with a 17% increase during the decade 1927–38 in the number of plants with more than 500 employees (Caracciolo, 1969, pp. 169–70).

Despite that growth, however, fascism, with its petit bourgeois ideology and its highly protective policies, did not put Italian industry on equal footing with other industrialized economies. According to the 1951 industrial census, the average number of employees per productive unit in the Italian manufacturing industry was still quite low (5.5 employees per unit; 7.4 in 1961 and 8.4 in 1971). By international standards, the weight of small firms in the Italian economy was very high.[46] In 1961, 28% of the workers in Italian manufacturing worked in firms with less than ten employees, compared with 2.1% in the United Kingdom, 3.3% in the United States, 7.4% in Belgium, 7.9% in the Netherlands, and 13.2% in West Germany. Conversely, only 13.7% of the work force worked in factories with more that 1,000 workers, compared with 30.5% in the United States, 28.2% in West Germany, 28.1% in the Netherlands, and 24.8% in Belgium.

Just as atypical was the degree of concentration of Italian industry, with its relatively small number of larger industrial groups. According to a 1973 report by the Fondazione Giovanni Agnelli, in 1971 there were some forty private groups and three state-owned corporations that operated in a multinational or at least European environment. If we add to that figure all the corporations that operated on a national scale, we arrive at some "two hundred families" (Fondazione Giovanni Agnelli, 1973, p. 60). As compared with that figure, there were more than 400 large-scale foreign corporations operating in Italy.[47]

Table 3.13. *Distribution of Italian plants by size (number of plants per size class)*

Employees	1951	1961	1971	1981
<2	445,107	352,648	297,705	333,256
3–5	75,396	91,923	83,530	109,591
6–10	21,007	35,325	40,060	62,943
11–50	18,298	32,125	42,182	63,465
51–100	3,106	5,106	6,483	7,049
101–500	2,741	3,858	4,862	5,174
501–1,000	353	381	427	422
>1,000	199	186	235	233

Source: ISTAT (1986, pp. 210, 221, 226).

Table 3.14. *Distribution of Italian plants by size (total number of employees per size class)*

Employees	1951	1961	1971	1981
<2	555,937	457,048	383,695	432,133
3–5	271,614	337,349	309,325	410,996
6–10	155,404	262,794	303,749	480,939
11–50	397,495	694,831	906,967	1,261,841
51–100	219,764	357,102	454,549	491,909
101–500	570,577	779,480	959,926	994,924
501–1,000	247,359	263,874	296,747	285,742
>1,000	424,101	428,880	596,122	564,156

Source: ISTAT (1986, pp. 210, 221, 226).

Tables 3.13 and 3.14 show data on the distributions of firms and of employment by firm size in the manufacturing industry in 1951, 1961, 1971, and 1981 (the years of the industrial censuses). On the one hand, the census data reveal the persistent weight of small-scale production in the Italian manufacturing industry. In 1971, productive units with less than ten workers represented almost 89% of the total number of units. Only 16% of employees in manufacturing worked in large-scale settings (>1,000 employees); 44% of the manufacturing labor force was employed in units with less than 50 people (Valcamonici, 1977, p. 179–80).

On the other hand, the data reveal a sharp break in the historical transformation of the productive structure. In the period between 1950 and 1970, the Italian productive system grew across the entire spectrum of plant size classes, according to a process of *diffused* development, particularly in the area of middle-sized plants (Caracciolo, 1969, p. 174). The average plant size grew from 57.2 workers in 1961 to 76.8 in 1971.[48] After 1970, however, there appears to have been a marked slowdown for large firms, in terms of both number of units and total employment, and a great expansion of small firms in the class of 3–5 workers, and even more in the class of 10–19 workers (61.75% increase during the decade) (Barca and

Magnani, 1989, pp. 196–7).[49] The decline in average firm size in the 1970s was clearly highlighted by the decline in the entropic mean, from 76.8 in 1971 to 56.7 in 1981 (Barca and Magnani, 1989, p. 196).

Again, the question of interest is how the particular distribution of Italian plant sizes may have affected industrial conflict. Given the highly skewed distribution toward smaller productive units, it is perhaps no surprise that most Italian strikes have been smaller in scale when viewed in comparative perspective. After all, the average strike can be only as large as the average plant. Furthermore, perhaps the handful of larger plants could explain the handful of exceptionally large strikes in Italy. These seem to be plausible explanations. But, more generally, is there any effect of plant size on conflict? Marx certainly thought that larger work settings offered increased possibilities for solidarity. In large plants, there are better opportunities for rapid circulation of ideas and wide-scale communication – the preconditions for solidarity. Social relations between workers and employers are also unencumbered by elements from outside of the "cash nexus" (Westergaard, 1970). As Newby (1979) has shown, class relations based on traditional ideologies of paternalism and authority, rather than class, prevail in small and isolated settings, where oppositional and radical class imageries are not readily available.

The work of Blauner and Woodward reviewed earlier on the relationship between the technology of production and labor relations, would lead us to make differential predictions about workers' behaviors in larger and smaller plants. Large plants typically are characterized by either mass production technologies (in many mechanical companies, e.g., automobiles, large home appliances) or process technologies (e.g., chemical, steel). Because, according to Blauner and Woodward, process technology reduces the likelihood of conflict, larger firms can be sites of either more or less labor unrest, depending on the kind of technology used (assembly line or process). And if we believe Mallet's argument on the greater likelihood of radicalism among the more highly educated technicians of process-based firms (the new working class), we end up predicting higher rates of conflict for all large-scale plants, regardless of production technology.[50]

No official microlevel data on strikes are available in Italy, and so we cannot empirically test the relationship between plant size and the characteristics of conflict. However, there have been several surveys that do provide some evidence on the relationship between plant size and strike activity. For the 1960s, indirect support for a linear relationship between conflict and plant size comes from Farneti's survey of Piedmont entrepreneurs. According to that survey, organizational issues were employers' main concerns regardless of firm size, rather than issues of productivity or labor relations (i.e., conflict). But, whereas the importance of productivity issues steadily declined with firm size, labor-relations issues steadily increased (Farneti, 1970, p. 123). A Federlombarda survey of 354 Lombardy firms confirmed that in 1969 the probability of a firm being strike-free was inversely proportional to size: 78.3% of firms with less than 20 workers were strike-free, compared with 54% in the 20–49 class, 41.2% in the 50–99 class,

Table 3.15. *Distribution of strike-free plants by plant size and strike issue (%)*

Issue	Number of employees						Total
	51–100	101–250	251–500	501–1,000	1,001–5,000	>5,000	
Industry contract	15.4	7.8	6.2	8.1	2.0	4.3	7.4
Firm contract	36.6	30.5	19.6	13.7	7.6	1.9	20.8
Social reforms	24.3	19.2	10.3	10.6	5.0	4.9	13.7
Solidarity	41.2	33.8	27.2	20.1	14.4	17.8	27.2
Political events	53.0	48.4	39.0	35.5	42.1	25.5	42.6

Source: Buratto et al. (1974, pp. 329–32).

10.5% in the 100–249 class, 23.1% in the 250–499 class, and 0% in the 500–999 class (Bergamaschi, 1977b, pp. 260–4).

According to a 1971 Isvet survey of workers' attitudes, plant size was one of the most telling predictors of workers' militancy.[51] Workers' levels of participation in collective action, union and party membership all increased with plant size.[52] More generally, a class view of industrial relations based on an opposition of interests and confrontation goes along with larger work settings; employers' ideologies of being on the same team were more often found among the workers in smaller plants (De Masi, 1972, p. 125): 11.7% of the workers in smaller firms (50–100 workers) reported that there had been no strikes in their plants for the preceding two years; that figure decreased steadily to 0.4% for plants with more than 5,000 workers (Buratto et al., 1974, p. 323).[53] Furthermore, regardless of the issue involved, workers in small plants were much more likely to report that there had been no instances of strikes in their plants (Table 3.15).[54] The only exceptions to the linearity of the relationship seem to have involved firms with more than 5,000 employees, where strike activity over some issues appeared to decline. This result could simply reflect the particular situation in the handful of larger firms in the Isvet survey. Nonetheless, the inversion of a linear relationship between plant size and militancy showed up in the Isvet survey not just in the levels of strike activity, but in many other indicators as well (e.g., politicization, unionization).

Confindustria survey data on absenteeism recorded yearly during the 1970s basically support these findings (Table 3.16). A row-wise reading of the table shows that in each year in the period from 1972 (when the survey was started) to 1985, absenteeism[55] increased linearly with firm size. A column-wise reading of the table shows that within each class of plant sizes, the number of hours lost due to absenteeism peaked around 1973–74, remained above the 10% mark in all size classes (except for the smaller plants), and steadily declined after 1980. Again, the firms in the largest size class (>1,000) appear to have been less conflict-prone than were smaller firms in many years. It is curious that workers in the largest firms, the ones where achievement of solidarity and communication should be easiest, were not consistently the most militant *(paradox of large firms)*.

Still in the 1980s, two surveys conducted in 1983 and 1984 by Federmeccanica, the association of private metalworking employers, confirmed that plant size was

Table 3.16. *Confindustria survey data of absenteeism by year and plant size*

Year	Plant size (number of employees)				
	1–50	51–250	251–500	501–1,000	>1,000
1972	8.3[a]	11.1	12.8	13.8	14.3
1973	9.6	12.5	13.8	17.3	15.3
1974	9.3	14.1	16.3	17.4	15.7
1975	10.7	12.4	14.3	14.8	14.9
1976	9.3	12.1	13.5	15.2	15.1
1977	9.3	11.5	12.2	12.1	14.5
1978	7.3	11.7	12.0	13.2	13.5
1979	8.5	13.9	15.7	15.7	16.8
1980	8.2	11.3	13.0	12.6	14.8
1981	9.9	11.4	11.6	11.7	9.8
1982	9.5	9.4	9.6	11.6	8.6
1983	6.9	10.1	11.0	10.5	9.3
1984	6.0	8.5	8.9	8.5	7.9
1985	7.0	7.2	8.2	8.0	8.0

[a]Ratio of the numbers of hours lost due to strikes and to medical reasons to the total number of hours worked (blue-collar and clerical workers).
Source: Barca and Magnani (1989, p. 131), from Confindustria, *Rassegna di statistiche del lavoro*.

directly related to conflict: the larger the plants, the greater the likelihood of worker mobilization (Mortillaro, 1986, p. 204). Furthermore, strikes in larger plants tended to be more disruptive, as they typically were accompanied by various other forms of collective action (e.g., internal and external pickets, rallies, blockade of goods); the probability that none of these actions would occur was much higher in smaller plants (47% vs. 3%) (Mortillaro, 1984, p. 147; 1986, p. 204).

In conclusion, the survey data presented here provide strong support in favor of a positive relationship between strike rates and plant size.[56] Perhaps with the exception of the very large plants, the larger industrial units appear to be the typical, if not the exclusive, setting for industrial conflict in Italy.[57] These empirical findings shed new light on the locus of conflict. Unfortunately, the findings also cast some doubt on the explanation that would link the smaller sizes of Italian strikes to the prevalence of smaller productive units. After all, if industrial conflict is found mostly in the larger units typical of other industrialized countries, why should Italian strikes be smaller on average?

Unfortunately, these results also force me to dismiss the only explanation I could find in Chapter 2 for the paradox of simultaneous increases in the levels of unemployment and strikes during the 1970s *(paradox of the 1970s)*. Given the stagnation and slow decline of large firms and the vigorous performance of the smaller firms of the *Terza Italia*, I had wondered if the high levels of strike activity in the 1970s could be related to the economic vitality of smaller firms during the decade. The data presented in this section have confirmed the decline of the larger firms and the blossoming of the smaller ones, but they have also incontrovertibly shown that the smaller firms were not the sites of workers' conflict. The solution to the *paradox of the 1970s* must lie elsewhere.

Furthermore, even the tentative explanation put forward earlier regarding the peculiar distribution of the sizes of Italian strikes (a handful of exceptionally large strikes, and a host of small strikes) now crumbles. The hypothesis that I had entertained was this: Could a handful of exceptionally large plants account for the handful of exceptionally large strikes? In the face of the available empirical evidence, the answer has to be no. In fact, how large would these plants have to be? The handful of larger strikes involved tens or even hundreds of thousands of workers (see Figure 1.1 in Chapter 1, p. 3), a much larger size than the work force of even the largest plants. No less intriguing is the problem of the small sizes of the majority of Italian strikes. If, by and large, industrial conflict were a prerogative of large plants, what could account for the fact that most strikes were much smaller than the work force of large plants? A focus on plant size alone cannot fully explain the elusive problem of Italian strike size *(paradox of strike size)*.

Acquisition of new knowledge thus seems to come at the expense of what once seemed plausible. Furthermore, it leaves me with no explanation for the *paradox of the 1970s*. Worse yet, it introduces two other paradoxes: the *paradox of large firms* and the *paradox of strike size*. First, the largest firms which, by all accounts should be easier to mobilize, seem to have been less conflict-prone than medium-size firms. Second, Italian strikes either were smaller in size than the average work force of striking plants, or were much larger than the work force of even the largest plants. What, then, explains Italian strike sizes?

Notwithstanding these setbacks, the analysis of the structural characteristics of the Italian economy has shed a great deal of light on the relationship between strike activity and long-term economic factors. Furthermore, it has clearly linked industrial conflict to the structuring of class. Within the working class, it has focused the spotlight on specific actors (e.g., skilled or unskilled workers, but also, technicians). It has alerted me what to look for when in Chapter 7 I will analyze the available empirical record regarding the types of actors involved in the postwar struggles. Similarly, the findings in these sections may point to possible explanations for the explosion of conflict during the 1969 *autunno caldo*, in linking strike waves to sociotechnical modes of production: specifically, the Fordism that had come to maturity in the late 1960s.

3.5. EVEN IF BARGAINING PARTIES HAD PERFECT KNOWLEDGE: THE MARXIST VIEW OF CONFLICT AND THE ECONOMY

The economic-bargaining literature on strikes that I reviewed in Chapter 2 rests on the belief that perfect knowledge would eliminate strikes. The argument is that if bargaining parties had perfect knowledge, there would be no reason to strike. Employers would know exactly what workers would be willing to accept to settle an issue; workers would know precisely how much employers could give. Strikes are seen as the result of faulty negotiations and imperfect information. Inflation and unemployment make matters worse by reducing the level of information available to the bargaining parties and increasing the uncertainty about future expectations (Kaufman, 1981; Gramm, 1986). Institutionalized mechanisms of collective bargaining, on the other hand, work in the opposite direction, helping each party to achieve a moderate amount of knowledge about the other's concession curve (Mauro, 1982; Reder and Neumann, 1980).

But, in fact, would perfect knowledge of the parties' concession curves necessarily result in a "withering away of strikes"? The answer depends on some basic tacit premises of the "perfect knowledge" argument: that workers and employers agree on the overall framework of a capitalist society, that they share a fundamental agreement regarding the form of the distribution of resources (profit and wages), and that workers question only the terms of that distribution.

Marxists would disagree with that view. In fact, the classical Marxist position is that workers' and employers' interests are fundamentally opposed and that the role of class conflict (and, thus, of strikes) is to eliminate the "wage form" altogether. Class conflict, in other words, is not *within* the rules of the game, but *about* those rules (Hyman, 1975, 1989).

Marxists not only do not share the basic assumptions of economic-bargaining theories of strikes; they also do not share the conception of the business cycle. In economic-bargaining theories of strikes, both workers and employers come to grips with the "invisible hand" of the market (the business cycle), taking advantage of their favorable positions at different times. The vagaries of the business cycle are factors with which both workers and employers must deal. A change in the level of strike activity is the result of changes in the business cycle. Conflict is strictly a dependent variable. Contrary to that view, for Marxists, the invisible hand is mostly invisible to the workers. Employers can typically guide that hand where they want it to be. Kalecki (1943), for instance, argued that as the economy reaches full employment, labor is in a better bargaining position vis-à-vis employers (a position Marxists share with business-cycle theorists of strikes). Labor will use this change in the balance of class power to push for a larger share of resources (typically via strikes). The result will be a squeeze on the profits of capitalist enterprises. Kalecki seems to have a point.

Indeed, as the time plot of Figure 3.9 shows, firm profits in Italy were lowest when labor conflict was highest, and vice versa (Barca and Magnani, 1989, p. 29). The levels of profit for Italian firms were high during the 1950s, when industrial conflict was at its lowest. During the years of Italy's "economic miracle" toward the end of the 1950s, profits reached record highs. Profits began to decline as labor conflict increased prior to the 1962 and 1963 contract renewals. Profits went up again during the middle of the decade, when the recession clipped the wings of labor. The 1968–72 strike wave put an end to profit altogether. Profits did not begin to rise steadily again until well into the second half of the 1970s, when a general deterioration in economic conditions (the labor market in particular) put labor on the defensive.

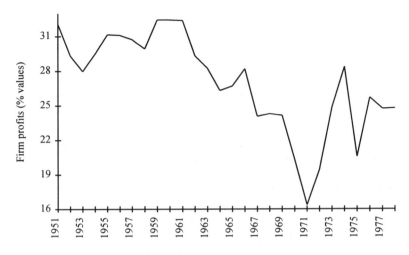

Figure 3.9. *Plot of firm profits*

As conflict and wages rise and profits decline, business confidence declines. Capitalists have less incentive to invest, or if they do, they direct their investments toward labor-saving technologies. In either case, the result is a decline in the level of employment and, with it, a decline in the levels of conflict.[58] Arguing against the hopes of Keynesian full-employment policies, Kalecki wrote that "unemployment is an integral part of the 'normal' capitalist system.... Indeed, under a regime of permanent full employment, the 'sack' would cease to play its role as a disciplinary measure" (Kalecki, 1943, p. 326). With the balance of class forces reestablished, the (politically induced)[59] business cycle can start anew.

For Marxists, however, the cycle does not start anew each time in quite the same way in a sort of social "perpetual motion." Marxists see these short-term cycles as being embedded within a long-term tendency of capitalism toward ever-decreasing rates of profit.[60] The result of this secular decline implicit in the Marxist view of the capitalist logic of accumulation will be bankruptcy of the economic system, followed by immiseration. In fact, it is at that point that a social revolution by the proletariat will bring the system down.[61] In the postwar period, Marxist scholars have stressed the cyclical nature rather than the trend aspects of capitalist crises. Long cycles bring about periodic crises in capitalist economic relations without necessarily changing capitalist political relations (Aglietta, 1979, pp. 351–2).[62]

Kondratieff, Sweezy, and Mandel all introduced cyclical long-term fluctuations in their Marxist economics. For Kondratieff (1935), capitalist economies are characterized by long-term waves of development. It is changes within economic institutions, particularly the cyclical replacement of long-lived capital goods, that cause these long-term cyclical fluctuations in capitalist economies (Kotz, 1987, p. 25).[63] Long waves are both predictable and regular, of some fifty years in length (Kotz, 1987, p. 19).[64]

In more recent years, the American "social structure of accumulation" theory and the French "regulation" theory have similarly argued for the existence of long cycles, while rejecting the strict periodicity of these cycles.[65] For both theories, capital accumulation is not simply an economic process. It does not rest solely on the smooth working of economic institutions proper, but also on political and ideological institutions. Thus, an economic crisis is both a crisis of accumulation in economic institutions and an ideological crisis in sociopolitical institutions. The resolution of the crisis thus requires a double-edged solution, on both the economic and political fronts. Particularly for the social structure of accumulation theory, a new set of sociopolitical institutions[66] is a necessary condition for restoration of the possibility of sustained and rapid accumulation of capital after a period of economic crisis (Gordon, 1980, p. 21). To the extent that there is no guarantee that a new set of sociopolitical institutions will emerge at a time of crisis,[67] crises open up political opportunities for labor.

The social structure of accumulation theories put greater emphasis on the role of the class struggle in producing a crisis (Bowles et al., 1983, chap. 6). A long period of accumulation requires "social stability" (i.e., relative quiescence of both interclass conflict and intraclass conflict). The role of sociopolitical institutions in the social structure of accumulation view is precisely that of regulating conflict. For the "regulation" theories, changes in the structure of demand and markets distinguish the transitions between upward and downward portions of the cycle. Class conflict is not the cause but rather the outcome of such transition.

In conclusion, a Marxist theory of economic cycles considers conflict to be both cause and effect of the business cycle, or, in statistical terms, to be both an independent variable and a dependent variable. Furthermore, a Marxist theory of economic cycles keeps an eye on cycles of different lengths (the business cycle of a few years' duration, the economic crises that occur approximately fifty years apart, and, at least among classical thinkers, the secular decline of capitalism). Finally, a Marxist theory of economic cycles opens the window of capital–labor relations beyond the economic and into the political. For Marxists, an understanding of economic relations involves an understanding of the social actors (i.e., classes and their institutions, such as the state) involved in those relations, as well as their historical interests and the specific ways in which they have pursued those interests. Given that not only Marxist theory but also the statistical and historical evidence of this and the preceding chapters point in that same direction, perhaps the time has come to look through that window.

3.6. WHERE WE STAND

In this chapter I have considered both the medium-term (five to ten years) and long-term (several decades) relationships between strikes and the economy. On the one hand, I have probed further into the relationship between strike activity and the short-term business cycle. I have extended the analyses of Chapter 2 (based on the number of strikes and unemployment) to the number of workers involved and the number of hours lost, as well as to a variety of business-cycle measures (e.g., index of capacity utilization, index of industrial production). On the other hand, I have considered the effects on strikes of the structural characteristics of the economy and their long-term changes, particularly shifts in the occupational structure, the technological basis of production, the distribution of plant sizes, and the labor-market structure. The findings have been enlightening.

For the short run, despite problems of trend and reciprocal causation, the statistical evidence confirms the findings of Chapter 2: Beyond doubt, strike activity, frequency in particular, follows the temporal movement of the year-to-year fluctuations of the business cycle. Short-term economic hardship has a strong negative effect on strike activity, especially strike frequency. The analyses have also revealed a systematic negative relationship between strike activity (especially the numbers of strikers and hours lost) and production at two- to three-year intervals. Beyond the finding that the causation in this relationship goes from strike activity to production (i.e., cyclical bouts of strike activity result in systematic losses of production), the causes of these cycles remain unexplained. However, two- to three- year cycles keep popping up in the analyses. In Chapter 1 we saw how all strike indicators are characterized by periodic two- to three-year cycles. In Chapter 2 we saw how these same cycles characterize the relationship between the number of strikes and wages. In this chapter we have learned that production as well is affected by the two-to-three years periodicity of strike patterns. Yet I have no explanation for these cycles.

For the long run, these analyses have shown the effects of structural characteristics of the economy on strikes. The strike trends closely follow the long-term shifts in the occupational structure. Furthermore, the empirical evidence leaves no doubt that large plants are the primary sites of conflict (with the exception of the very large firms that seem to experience lower levels of conflict, *paradox of large firms*). The analyses have also highlighted the rapid expansion of mass-production technology (notably, the assembly line) in Italian manufacturing industries during the 1950s and 1960s. At the same time, the factory world was undergoing a process of sweeping rationalization. By the late 1960s, that combination of Fordism and Taylorism had laid the cornerstone for a new technical and social organization of production. With the expansion of Fordism and Taylorism, increasingly larger proportions of the blue-collar work force came to be concentrated in the lower levels of the job hierarchy, particularly in the larger plants. In the spring of 1969, Fiat alone announced plans to hire some fifteen thousand new workers in Turin. Although many of those workers had specialized high-school diplomas (*i ragionieri in fabbrica*, accountants on the shop floor), they basically entered the factory world at the lowest levels of the job hierarchy, as unskilled workers.

In short, during the course of the 1960s, the process of transformation of the class structure, linked to shifts in the occupational structure and to changes in the technical modes of production (e.g., the wide diffusion of assembly line technology) reached new heights. To the shift in skill levels inside the factory there corresponded a parallel shift in culture both inside and outside the factories. The new unskilled workers were mostly southern immigrants to the industrial North. They came to replace northern skilled workers. What effects did those changes in the class structure (both in skill levels and in cultural background of the "typical" worker) have on the capacity of the working class to organize and mobilize? Can those structural transformations in the economy help us to interpret the 1969 *autunno caldo*? Was the relationship between the heightened levels of class conflict and the structural break in the economy, as demonstrated by the empirical evidence for the late 1960s and early 1970s, purely a coincidence or a relationship of cause and effect? If the latter obtained, which was the cause, and which the effect?

The structural characteristics of the economy, however, affect not only the structure of the working class, but also that of the capitalist class. In this respect, census data on the distribution of plants by size show the historical persistence (in fact, growth) of small-scale industrial production well into the 1990s. If we are willing to make the assumption that 1 capitalist = 1 or 2 productive units, then, the census data provide a snapshot of the Italian capitalist class: a large number of small entrepreneurs and a handful of large-scale capitalists. That assumption seems to be justified by the available data on the Italian class structure.[68]

The findings in this chapter have added new pieces to the puzzle (e.g., strike activity explains the empirically observable dips in production variables) and confirmed that the pieces put together in Chapter 2 are firmly in place. But of course the puzzle is far from complete. For one thing, the fact that only a few of the pieces have fallen into place confirms that we have only scraped the surface of the topic of Italian strike patterns. Second, the empirical evidence on the size distributions of Italian plants and strikes has left unresolved the puzzle of the sizes of Italian strikes: a large number of small strikes and a handful of exceptionally large strikes *(paradox of strike size)*. The seemingly obvious explanation of small strikes by the prevalence of smaller firms in the Italian setting is contradicted by the fact that strikes in Italy seem to have occurred predominantly in larger firms. On the other hand, the few large strikes were much larger than the work force of even the largest firm. The only plausible explanation that I could put forward at the end of Chapter 2, based on the growth of small-scale production, particularly in the *Terza Italia*, does not seem to hold in light of the analyses of this chapter on the relationship between strike activity and plant size.

Unfortunately, economic models of strikes have also left unexplained the simultaneous growth of unemployment and increased strike activity *(paradox of the 1970s)*. Worse yet, the economic analyses of this chapter appear to introduce yet another paradox: The *paradox of the 1962 and 1966 strike shapes*. Those shapes (Figure 1.6 in Chapter 1) are very similar to each other and very different from the shapes of all other years. That longer strike durations are related to poor economic conditions is a well-known – albeit little studied – fact in the literature. It should not come as a surprise that the strike shapes of 1966, the year of Italy's worst postwar recession, should show longer strike durations. What does come as a surprise, however, is the fact that the duration of strikes in 1962, the peak year in

Italy's "economic miracle," should show durations that are just as long. Similar outcomes for different underlying causes can only leave us quite baffled.

My analyses of the structural characteristics of the Italian economy have been aimed at disentangling short-term and long-term relationships between strikes and the economy. Business-cycle theories argue that capitalist economies are characterized by medium-term fluctuations of a few years' duration. Are the structural changes in capitalist economies also cyclical? Although neoclassical economics has little to say about this, Marxist economics does provide a conceptual tool for the analysis of long-term effects: the "long waves." Furthermore, Marxist economics not only shifts the emphasis from the short term to the long term in its analysis of capitalist economies but also shifts the emphasis from purely economic variables to political variables.

Clearly, there is more to strikes than economics. Much more work lies ahead. Again, I have raised more questions and broader questions than I have answered. The seminal debate between Rist (1907, 1912) and March (1911, 1913) at the beginning of the twentieth century was the forerunner of a scholarly controversy between those who claimed that strike activity was related to the business cycle and those who opposed such a view. Recent econometric investigations have confirmed, across several countries, that strictly economic models can offer satisfying estimates only for strike frequency (Andreani, 1968, pp. 119, 136, 195, 267–8; Skeels, 1971; Walsh, 1975, p. 53; Bordogna and Provasi, 1979).

What are the variables that can explain strike indicators other than frequency? Furthermore, economic activity can be statistically significant in explaining strikes, without, however, being the main or exclusive influence (Vanderkamp, 1970). Finally, Snyder (1975, 1977) has questioned even the dependence of the number of strikes on the business cycle, particularly in institutional contexts different from the postwar Anglo-American context, for which economic models offer the most satisfying explanations (Vanderkamp, 1970). Indeed, Paldman and Pedersen (1982), on the basis of a comparative econometric analysis of the number of strikes in fifteen countries, have concluded that the Ashenfelter and Johnson model performs well only for the United States; in other countries, the effects of unemployment and wage and price variables are much less clear-cut. In the next three chapters I will explore the contributions from the noneconomic strike literature (in particular, resource mobilization and political-exchange theories) and will try to find answers to the many unanswered questions.

4

Organizational resources and collective action

A challenger, to be effective, needs organization . . . to pry loose time, money and commitment . . . to focus prism-like these resources upon the arena of central state politics.
Shorter and Tilly (1974, p. 147)

Trades unions in England, as well as in every other manufacturing country, are a necessity for the working classes in their struggle against capital . . . If a whole trade of workmen form a powerful organization . . . then, and then only, have they a chance.
Karl Marx (Lapides, 1987, p. 105)

Trade unions . . . are the types of proletarian organization specific to the historical period dominated by capital. In a certain sense it can be argued that they are an integral part of capitalist society, and that they have a function which is inherent in the regime of private property.
Antonio Gramsci (1954, p. 36)

4.1. SHIFTING GEARS

The findings in Chapters 2 and 3 have shown that economic models go a long way toward explaining Italian strikes. Yet the findings have also revealed the limits of this type of model for the Italian case. In particular, economic models do not explain why the statistical relationships to economic factors should be stronger for strike frequency than for other strike components, nor can they identify the noneconomic determinants that lie behind strike size, duration, and volume. The economic literature has very little to say on these points (Skeels, 1971). The economic strike literature has even less to say about why, under unfavorable labor-market conditions, the Italian working class has been less militant than would seem warranted by economic factors alone *(paradox of the génie d'un peuple).* Most important, economic-bargaining models do not seem to be able to explain the *paradox of the 1970s,* when rising levels of unemployment went hand in hand with rising labor militancy. Furthermore, economic factors cannot explain three other paradoxes encountered in Chapter 3: the *paradox of strike size,* the *paradox of large firms,* and the *paradox of the 1962 and 1966 strike shapes.*

The time has come to shift gears and move away from a focus on economic factors and to consider organizational, institutional, and political factors. I start in this chapter by looking at the relationship between organization and strikes. The expectation is that organizational variables should be highly related to strikes in the Italian case. First, Shorter and Tilly's work on France highlighted the role of labor organizations in shaping the prevailing patterns of French strikes (Shorter and Tilly, 1974), and the Italian and French working classes show many similarities, namely, the presence of strong Communist Parties and Communist-led unions and the persistence of radical ideologies in the labor movement. Second, with specific reference to Italy, Snyder (1975) argued that Italian strikes should conform to an organizational/political model, rather than to an economic model. Although in Chapters 2 and 3, I found no evidence against an economic model of strikes, the analyses also revealed the limits of a purely economic interpretation of Italian strikes. In examining the role of organization, I will use resource-mobilization theories of collective action. I will also explore the contributions of the Marxist approach to organization.

Much of the empirical work described in this chapter will focus on the relationship between strikes and organizational strength, as measured, in particular, by union membership levels. I will also consider other measures of organizational strength (e.g., the results of the elections for the *commissioni interne*). Finally, I will rely on a great deal of survey-research material to pin down the relationship between the availability of organizational resources and strike activity at the plant level.

4.2. HARDSHIP, DISCONTENT, AND LABOR UNREST

The business-cycle theories that I considered in Chapters 2 and 3 relate industrial conflict to the improved short-term economic conditions during the upswing phases of the business cycle. We have seen that there is a great deal of empirical evidence, not only for Italy but also for other countries, in support of this view. But not all would agree with this view. For one thing, we have seen how classical Marxism linked the possibilities of revolutionary outcomes to long-term immiseration and the economic collapse of capitalism. Even among non-Marxist scholarship, there are authors who see collective action as being linked to both short-term and long-term economic hardship and relative deprivation. For instance, Gurr (1969, p. 603) wrote that "both short-term [deprivation] and persistent deprivation are significant causes of the various forms of civil strife." Under the headings "economic hardship" and "relative deprivation" we can group a set of theories that relate conflict and protest to the worsening of economic conditions. According to these theories, the deterioration of a group's material life leads to discontent and hence to protest and collective action.

In spite of the emphasis on the relationship between the state of the economy and collective action, we are dealing with psychological theories rather than with economic or sociological theories of collective action (Davies, 1969, pp. 692, 728).

Durkheim, "useless Durkheim" (Tilly, 1981), with his concepts of anomie and social disorganization provides the basic theoretical underpinning for the relative-deprivation and economic-hardship approaches to collective action. Collective action, particularly violent collective action, is based on frustration/aggression mechanisms. Frustration stems from the fact that one or more fundamental needs of an individual go unsatisfied.[1] Frustration and discontent are directly proportional to the expectation–achievement gap: the higher one's expectations relative to past achievements, the higher one's discontent. The more intense and widespread the individual discontent in a society, the more likely is civil strife (Gurr, 1969, pp. 596–7). Davies (1969, p. 690) is more explicit on the precise timing of protest, which is "more likely to take place when a prolonged period of rising expectations and rising gratifications is followed by a short period of sharp reversal, during which the gap between expectations and gratifications quickly widens and becomes intolerable [the J curve]."

Although economic-hardship and relative-deprivation arguments have been used primarily to explain violence and/or revolutions in cross-national studies, similar arguments have been invoked for strike activity. Jackson, Turner, and Wilkinson (1972, pp. 37, 39, 89, 95) and Soskice (1978, pp. 379, 390–1, 399, 404), for instance, argued that the increasing "sense of relative deprivation of major social groups" deriving from the inflationary process of the mid-1950s was largely responsible for the wave of industrial conflict that swept Western economies in the late 1960s. De Masi and Fevola (1974a) provided an interpretation for the heightened levels of conflict during and after the 1969 *autunno caldo* in Italy, similarly based on frustration/aggression mechanisms, tempered by a consideration of structural (particularly class) mechanisms.[2] It was Kornhauser (1954a) who provided the best example of a psychological explanation for industrial conflict.

Kornhauser's 1954 essay is a good compendium of a Durkheimian approach to collective action. For Kornhauser, "Labor unrest is part of the general disorganization and unsettlement of our time" (1954a, p. 77), the "individual insecurity and the confusion of values" (1954a, p. 78), the worker's "feelings of lostness in a world beyond his comprehension and control" (1954a, p. 78), "a sense of not belonging" (1954a, p. 78), with "varying degrees of satisfaction and frustration" (1954a, p. 78), "different aspirations, frustrations, and demands" (1954a, p. 79), "a perpetual state of unsatisfied aspirations" (1954a, p. 80), and "the rapid expansion of working people's expectations" (1954a, p. 82). A careful analysis of the most bitter strikes would no doubt reveal for each of them "a long history of misunderstandings ... a cluster of fighting traditions" (1954a, p. 82).

Does the empirical evidence for the Italian case provide any support for a relative-deprivation or economic-hardship explanation of strikes? For the purpose of empirical testing, there are two different formulations of the economic-hardship argument.

The first formulation (by Gurr) links collective actions to short-term or persistent economic hardship. In the case of strikes, we should observe higher levels of strike activity during the downswing phases of the business cycle. The second formulation (by Davies) claims that not all economic recessions lead to collective action and protest. It is more likely that protest will take place only during those recessions that follow relatively long periods of prosperity.

The overwhelming empirical evidence accumulated in the preceding two chapters leads me to reject the first formulation: Strike activity does go up and down with the business cycle, but it goes up during booms, and down during busts. Perhaps it is only because the bitter, long-drawn-out strikes that occur during recessions tend to receive greater publicity that there is such a widespread popular belief that strike activity tends to increase in times of hardship.[3] And, indeed, strikes tend to be longer during recessions and more bitter, with greater likelihood of violence, as both workers and employers retrench. Once again, the strike shape of 1966, a year of severe economic crisis, with its longer durations bears this out (see Figure 1.6, pp. 8–9). But strike frequency does go down during recessions.[4]

The Italian data likewise do not support the second formulation. If anything, strike activity tended to increase sharply after recessions, as economic conditions improved: the two major Italian strike outbreaks of the postwar period (1959–63, 1968–72) occurred after some years of economic hardship, but not until improved labor-market conditions gave labor a fighting chance (see also Cronin, 1979, p. 64).

4.3. RESOURCE-MOBILIZATION THEORIES OF COLLECTIVE ACTION

The economic literature has viewed strikes as resulting from uncertainty in the bargaining process ("Strikes are the result of faulty negotiations"). The North American sociological literature, on the other hand, has viewed collective action (and strikes) as resulting from social dislocation, strain, and disorganization deriving from processes of social differentiation, along Durkheimian lines. Against this last approach, resource-mobilization theorists during the 1970s mounted a devastating critique, viewing strikes as the result of organizational resources.[5]

According to resource-mobilization theories of collective action, psychological theories are based on scarcely tenable hierarchies of human needs of supposed universal validity. Furthermore, they cannot easily be tested empirically, because the expectation–achievement gap is hard to measure. Even assuming that the gap could be measured satisfactorily, when is it exactly that discontent becomes unbearable, thus leading to protest? Finally, frustration and deprivation may well be necessary conditions, but they are not sufficient conditions for strike activity. To be sure, with no frustration and discontent, there would be no reason for collective action. As Hobsbawm (1964, p. 136) noted, bad conditions provide explosive material ready to be set off by a spark. For Ross and Hartman (1960, p. 43):

Generally the strike reflects worker dissatisfaction, to be sure; but . . . industrial discontent is only a raw material. Strikes may or may not be fashioned out of it. The economic and institutional context of employment relations will determine the gradient or channel in which discontent is directed.

Undoubtedly, grievances constitute a precondition for any collective action. But one cannot understand collective actions without taking into account such mediating factors as the internal organization within groups, the opportunities to act effectively, the available forms of action, and the wider context of social relations.[6]

Without organization there can be no collective action, at least no successful collective action. An organization, however minimal, is a necessary condition in order to control, coordinate, and manage the resources involved in mobilization processes and collective actions. The importance of an organization was recognized even by the authorities who first collected data on strikes in Italy. The questionnaire of 1898, sent out to the prefects charged with the collection of strike data, included a question on the presence and degree of worker organization (Lay et al., 1973, p. 103). The quantitative strike literature has similarly acknowledged the importance of the relationship between organization and strikes (Griffin, 1939, pp. 101, 111; Knowles, 1952, pp. 140, 150; Goetz-Girey, 1965, p. 146). However, most scholars who have studied strikes have preferred a strictly economic interpretation of strike activity. Even when they have explicitly tried to test the role of unionization in strike activity, they have ultimately centered their models on strictly economic variables, such as unemployment and wages (e.g., Ashenfelter and Johnson, 1969; Pencavel, 1970). But most important, their work has lacked any theoretical conceptualization and understanding of the role of worker organizations beyond the mere acknowledgment of an empirical relationship between unionization and strikes.[7] It is the theories of resource mobilization that have provided much of the theoretical basis for understanding the role of organization.

According to resource-mobilization theories, collective action requires the pooling of group resources toward common ends (Tilly, 1974, pp. 212, 217; Shorter and Tilly, 1974, p. 5). Resources include both material resources (jobs, income, savings, property) and nonmaterial resources (authority, commitment, loyalty, trust, friendship, skills, etc.) (Oberschall, 1973, p. 28). Some resources are for individual, private use, whereas others are collectively owned or controlled by a group (Oberschall, 1973, p. 28; Gamson, 1975, p. 137). Both individuals and groups continually create, destroy, borrow, and exchange resources – a process called "resource management" (Oberschall, 1973, p. 27). From the point of view of resource management, collective actions involve the transfer of control over resources from individuals to a group (i.e., collectivization of effective control, if not ownership) (Etzioni 1968, p. 392). The acquisition of collective control over resources is called mobilization, however the transfer occurs (Tilly, 1974, p. 214; Etzioni, 1968, p. 380).

The numbers and types of organizations that control resource management will affect both the level and form of mobilization (Etzioni, 1968, p. 408). According to Tilly (1975, 1978), the main organizational types run along a communal–associational dimension. The idea is not new in sociology. Communal structures are small and localized, with a relatively simple division of labor. They can be quite effective in mobilizing normative resources, such as loyalties and commitments to groups and ideas. Associational structures are large and complex (Tonnies, 1963). They are most effective for mobilizing utilitarian resources, defined on the basis of material and economic goods (Tilly, 1975, p. 505; Etzioni, 1968, p. 380). A hierarchical organization of authority structures and a more elaborate division of labor can allow associational groups to maximize their bargaining power with actions that are well organized, disciplined, and carefully planned (Tilly, 1975, pp. 505–6). The modern labor union is one example of this type of associational structure.

The forms of collective action in which groups engage will be affected not only by the organizational basis of the group (communal vs. associational) but also by the position of the group in the power structure of the population to which the group belongs. Along this line, collective actions can be defensive (or reactive, i.e., they resist encroachment on the resources currently under group control), offensive (or proactive, i.e., they lay claim to resources under the control of contending groups), or competitive (i.e., they compete for resources that either group can control). Within this double categorization, the strike is an associational and offensive (proactive) form of collective action (Tilly, 1975, p. 508). The strike is one of the various means by which the working class can lay claim to resources controlled by the bourgeoisie, be those resources political or economic.

Taking a longer historical perspective, over the past few hundred years in Europe, the uses of different forms of collective action have waxed and waned in sequence (Tilly, 1978, p.148; 1986). From the seventeenth century to the nineteenth century, the use of reactive forms spread (e.g., food riots, tax rebellions). During the nineteenth and twentieth centuries, reactive actions declined, and collective proaction became more typical (e.g., strikes, demonstrations, rallies).[8] As the spread of the capitalist mode of production was changing traditional ways of life from *Gemeinschaft* to *Gesellschaft*, also changing were people's forms of collective action and ideologies regarding group relations. These forms of collective action did not change in isolation, one collective action here, another one there, in a random way. Entire sets of collective actions changed in predictable ways, making available to people new repertoires of actions. Particularly during the course of the 1700s in England, two forms of social relations in the workplace, two ideologies, and two sets of collective actions clashed throughout the century: the new, fast-rising market economy (*Gesellschaft*) and the traditional, dying moral economy (*Gemeinschaft*) (Thompson, 1978, p. 155). Let us take a closer look at this historical change from manor to market, from reactive to proactive forms of collective actions.

4.4. *LA LONGUE DURÉE*: MORAL ECONOMY AND REPERTOIRES OF COLLECTIVE ACTIONS

Work-related struggles have a long history. We can trace them back to the ancient world (De Ste. Croix, 1981) and to the Middle Ages and Renaissance (Crouzel, 1887). But in fact, workers' struggles as we know them today have resulted directly from the capitalist world and wage relations (Tilly, 1975, 1978, pp. 143–59; 1986).

During the course of the past century, the strike emerged on the European scene as part of a new repertoire of collective actions.[9] That repertoire included many varieties of strikes (the sit-down, general, checkerboard, walkout, wildcat, and more) and different forms of demonstrations (the march, the mass meeting, the temporary occupation of premises). It also included petitioning, the organization of pressure groups, electoral rallies, and so forth. That new repertoire came to replace centuries-old forms of collective actions, such as machine breaking, food riots, tax rebellions, charivari, and "rough music" (Thompson, 1978, p. 145).

The logic of people's behavior in the two repertoires of collective actions is different. The "modern" repertoire is proactive, the other reactive; the modern one industrial, the other preindustrial; the modern one forward-looking, the other backward-looking; the modern one offensive, the other defensive (Thompson, 1978, p. 136).[10] People involved in the traditional repertoire sought to return to a golden age imagined somewhere back in time (Thompson, 1978). People struggled against the encroachment of new historical forces in their lives, such as the modern state and its ever-increasing tax burden, capitalist agriculture in the countryside, and industrial forms of production (Mousnier, 1970; Tilly, 1986). In applying the new repertoire, people accepted the new forms of social relations; instead of struggling against them, they struggled around them.

Reactive actions were rooted in the cultural context of feudal ideologies of class relations based on reciprocity and exchange (Bendix, 1974, pp. 60–73). However unequal the terms of exchange, people traded obedience and deference for protection. John Stuart Mill best summarized that kind of ideology:

The lot of the poor in all things which affect them collectively, should be regarded for them, not by them. They should not be required or encouraged to think for themselves . . . . It is the duty of the higher classes to think for them, and to take the responsibility of their lot . . . . This function the higher classes should prepare themselves to perform conscientiously, and their whole demeanor should impress the poor with a reliance on it, in order that, while yielding passive and active obedience to the rules prescribed for them they may resign themselves in all other respects to a trustful insouciance, and repose under the shadow of their protectors. The relation between rich and poor should be only partially authoritative; it should be amiable, moral, and sentimental; affectionate tutelage on the one side, respectful and grateful deference on the other. The rich should be in loco parentis to the poor, guiding and restraining them like children. Of spontaneous actions on their part there should be no need. (quoted by Bendix, 1974, p. 47)

In that traditional view, it was the duty of the higher classes to take care of the lower classes in times of need and distress. If the lower classes were nothing but children, the higher classes had to assume responsibility for guiding them.[11] The ideology of capitalist class relations (laissez-faire) denies that responsibility: the upper classes cannot and should not take care of the lower classes; the lower classes must take prime responsibility for themselves (Bendix, 1974, pp. 86–99).

The reactive actions of the traditional repertoire were the common people's weapons against this new laissez-faire ideology and against the social practices that the new ideology justified and rationalized (e.g., enclosure of common lands, sale of grain at a higher price outside one's district). A sense of being deprived of justice is at the root of all forms of reactive actions (Moore, 1978). As E.P. Thompson (1978, pp. 78–9) wrote:

[Reactive actions are] grounded upon a consistent traditional view of social norms and obligations, of the proper economic functions of several parties within the community, which, taken together, can be said to constitute the moral economy of the poor. An outrage to these moral assumptions, quite as much as actual deprivation, was the usual occasion for direct action.

People in the "moral economy" were "rebellious, but rebellious in defense of custom" (Thompson, 1978, p. 154). Their aim was to redress a wrong that they perceived in the light of class ideologies based on reciprocity and exchange, to bring things back to the way they had always been. In one of the oldest forms of collective action, the "bread riot," ordinary people would seize a mill or baker, roll back the price of flour according to traditional standards, and then sell it to the crowd at that price. The remarkable thing about reactive actions was their discipline and the familiarity of their routines (Thompson, 1971, p. 108). The traditional forms of collective action did not require much organizing – in the sense in which we conceive of organization today (Calhoun, 1982, pp. 211–13). Such an action was the result of the sudden gathering of a crowd, of perceived infringements against customary rights, of moral outrage, of a consensus of support in the community, and of familiar patterns of collective actions (Thompson, 1971, pp. 112, 119). A sense of community and the solidarity of traditional bonds provided the basis for collective action in the moral economy (Calhoun, 1982, pp. 211–13; Aminzade, 1981, 1984).

The concepts of *moral economy* and *repertoires of collective actions* allow us a long historical perspective on the role of strikes in the European scene of the past several hundred years. Furthermore, they help put strikes in proper perspective vis-à-vis a variety of other forms of collective action. But within the modern repertoire of collective actions, strikes have undergone extensive historical transformations since their appearance during the industrial revolution. In particular, the shape of strikes, the combination of strike frequency, size, and duration that we encountered in Chapter 1, has changed drastically over the last one hundred years (Shorter and Tilly, 1974, pp. 51–8; Tilly, 1978, p. 96). During the 1800s strikes were characterized by low frequency, small size, and long duration. A century later strikes had become mass phenomena, very frequent and short. Not all national experiences followed that pattern. In comparative perspective, the shape of North American strikes still looks today very much like it did a century ago. But in France and Italy strike shapes have changed as suggested (Shorter and Tilly, 1974, pp. 306–31; Bordogna and Provasi, 1979).

Several structural factors have contributed to this change, particularly industrialization and urbanization (Shorter and Tilly, 1974, pp. 194–235, 267–83).[12] Structural transformations such as industrialization and urbanization undoubtedly are important in modifying the long-term shapes of strikes. After all, historically industrialization resulted in the mass proletarianization of the work force, bringing increases in the number and average size of industrial establishments. Urbanization created the conditions for rapid exchange of ideas by concentrating large numbers of workers in small areas. Industrial establishments in urban areas became the new sites for class confrontation. More industrial establishments and larger concentrations of workers provided the ingredients for increased numbers of strikes and larger strikes.

But according to Shorter and Tilly (1974), it was mainly organization that contributed to that transformation. The strike is intimately bound up with the historical development of labor organizations (Perrot, 1974, pp. 424–49; Shorter and Tilly, 1974, pp. 147–93; Aminzade, 1981, pp. 69–95).[13] On the one hand, modern workers' organizations, with their centralized bureaucratic structures, have been increasingly capable of commanding great numbers of workers. That has resulted in an increase in the average size of strikes. On the other hand, the institutionalization of strikes, their integration into the legislative apparatus of modern industrial democracies, and the development of procedures for consultation and negotiation have tended, at the same time, to reduce direct prolonged confrontations, leading to a decrease in the average duration of labor disputes.

A great deal of historical research seems to bear out quite clearly the impact of organization on industrial conflict. In historical perspective, strikes and unionization, taken as measures of organization, go together: In the long run, the higher the percentage of unionization, the higher the strike propensity (Andreani, 1968; Shorter and Tilly, 1974). In particular, unionization shows a high correlation with the number of strikers, for a well-organized union can call upon many workers simultaneously from several regions, industrial sectors, and factories.[14] Complex strikes, in particular, require the experienced hands of an organization. With regard to late nineteenth-century strikes in Italy, Merli (1972, p. 550) wrote that "The city-wide, regional, and national general strike can only be attempted by a solid and experienced organization." Complex strike tactics, such as revolving strikes (by firm, location, sector), are also the least costly and the most successful for the workers (Perrot, 1974, p. 487). Needless to say, they are also the most dreaded by the employers (Perrot, 1974, p. 489). Unionization and organizational growth in a sector are inversely related to the number of spontaneous strikes (Procacci, 1970, p. 68). Recent historical work by Louise Tilly on the Milanese working class at the turn of the century highlights the strong connection between workers' ability to engage in collective action and availability of organizational resources (Tilly, 1992, pp. 123–79).[15] In fact, in opposition to theories of industrialism and convergence, strikes and unions appear to be the only universal characteristics of industrial societies.[16]

Trade unions have contributed to increase the percentage of strikes that have ended with favorable outcomes for the workers (Merli, 1972, p. 513).[17] Better organization had the effect of shifting the timing of strikes from periods of economic hardship (the moral economy) to periods of prosperity. That shift in the timing of strikes resulted in shorter strikes. Longer strikes tend to occur during times of economic hardship, when employers are psychologically less disposed and financially less able to meet workers' demands, and thus long-drawn-out strikes have a low probability of success (Snyder and Kelly, 1976; Colasanti, 1982). Ross and Hartman (1960, p. 56) showed that in the United States, the percentage of strikes ending in success for the workers was inversely proportional to strike length. Furthermore, industrial disputes of long duration are more likely to produce episodes of violence (Snyder and Kelly, 1976).[18] Violent strikes have a lower probability than nonviolent ones of ending favorably for the workers (Snyder and Kelly, 1976; De Santis, 1979).[19]

Ultimately, strike success entailed a longer-term cost: Unions increasingly came to conceive of the strike as a means to achieve concrete, bread-and-butter goals, rather than as a revolutionary tactic (Lester, 1958). Strike success may thus simply reflect a change in the overall meaning of the strike within the general framework of increased institutionalization of labor in Western capitalist societies. Strike success was the result of organizational success in the framework of class compromise. Perhaps labor's short-term (economic) success should be viewed in the context of long-term (political) failure of the working class in its quest for power. As Dahrendorf (1959, p. 259) wrote, "Every act of organization is as such a process of institutionalization." Thus, organizational success for the lower classes is itself a sign of renunciation of radical demands for political control. "Organizations endure by abandoning their oppositional politics" (Piven and Cloward, 1979, p. xxi).

Whereas organization plays a positive role in the declaration of a strike (particularly an offensive strike), an organization is indispensable to keep a strike going, however it began (Shorter and Tilly, 1974, p. 192). Long strikes, more than sudden outbreaks of workers' protest, require a complex organization (De Santis, 1979, pp. 31–2). That has become even more important over the years: In Italy, at the beginning of the century, most strikes lasting ten days or more were managed by an organization, and the rare cases of strikes of some months' duration were always under the control of an organization (Procacci, 1970, p. 71; Lay et al., 1973, p. 103; De Santis, 1979, p. 46). Over time, the strike increasingly became a trade-union matter (Perrot, 1974, p. 426). In the 1899 *Statistica degli scioperi avvenuti nell'industria e nella agricoltura durante l'anno 1897*, one reads that "Strikes can go on for a longer period of time, wherever leagues of resistance are formed" (quoted in De Santis, 1979, p. 9), and that was precisely because of the collection and management of strike funds (Spriano, 1958). An organization is also necessary to manage the benefits obtained through a successful strike (Aguet, 1954, p. 371). Without an organization to monitor implementation of the newly won contract, an employer could easily renege and not carry out the new provisions, rendering them purely nominal (Stearns, 1968; Merli, 1972, p. 513). The presence of an organization makes it easier to remobilize workers, in case employers are reluctant to deliver on their promises (Aguet, 1954, p. 371). As Piven and Cloward (1979, pp. 34–5) wrote:

When protest subsides, concessions may be withdrawn. Thus when the unemployed become docile, the relief rolls are cut even though many are still unemployed; when the ghetto becomes quiescent, evictions are resumed. The reason is simple enough. Since the poor no longer pose the threat of disruption, they no longer exert leverage on political leaders; there is no need for conciliation.

4.5. TESTING THE ORGANIZATIONAL MODEL

In quantitative strike research, multivariate testing of resource-mobilization theories of collective action typically has been based on single-equation econometric models that combine business-cycle measures (i.e., unemployment rate and real wages) with measures of organizational strength. Union membership and unionization rate have been the most popular (if not the exclusive) organizational measures.[20] The model that I propose to verify closely follows this traditional specification:

$$Y_t = \beta_0 + \beta_1 UN_t + \beta_2 UNION_t + \beta_3 \Delta W_{t-1} + \epsilon_t \tag{4.1}$$

where Y, the dependent variable, measures the number of strikes, strikers, or hours lost; among the independent variables, UN measures the unemployment rate, $UNION$ measures the level of union membership as given by the combined membership of the two main unions (CGIL and CISL) (no data are available for a third, smaller union, UIL; see the Appendix for data), and ΔW_{t-1} measures the percentage change in real blue-collar wages in the previous year. On the basis of the literature, one would expect unionization to be positively related to the number of strikers. The relationship with the number of strikes should be positive, but weaker than that with the number of strikers. Unemployment and wages should behave in the manner discussed in Chapter 2: Unemployment should have negative effects on all strike indicators except perhaps the number of hours lost (strikes tend to be longer during recessions); high wages in the past should have a negative effect on strikes (there will be less reason to strike if workers have already obtained much of what they want).

I tried several specifications for the functional forms of the $UNION$ and W variables. In Chapter 2 we saw that the number of strikes is a function of the percentage variation in real wages during the preceding twelve quarters (three years). When using yearly data, a three-year lag structure may be too short for proper estimation. For that reason, I used alternative specifications: a three-year distributed-lag structure, a one-year lagged relationship, and a contemporaneous relationship. For the organizational variable, I adopted a similar specification of contemporaneous and lagged effects.[21]

Table 4.1 summarizes the "best" econometric results, in terms of overall fit (adjusted R^2) and significance of the coefficients. The results provide overall support for the organizational model of equation (4.1). The coefficients for the union-membership variable (CISL + CGIL) are positive and significant in the models for the numbers of strikers and hours lost. The best estimates, in terms of R^2 and signs and significance of the coefficients, are those obtained with the number of strikers as the dependent variable, as we can see from the estimates for

Table 4.1. *Testing the organizational model*

Dependent variable: Number of strikes for models 1 and 2; number of strikers for model 3; number of hours lost for model 4
Aggregation level: Industry; yearly series
Sample period: 1955/1978
Estimation method: GLS (Cochrane Orcutt) for all models

Variables	Model 1	Model 2[a]	Model 3	Model 4
Constant	3,003.92*	3,002.24*	632.12	124,650.7*
	(666.05)	(679.45)	(989.64)	(43,917.54)
Unemployment rate	-221.31*	-236.13*	-367.96*	-15,129.69*
	(86.21)	(84.96)	(131.40)	(5,871.72)
Change real wages$_{t-1}$ (%)	45.80**	-68.66*	-135.80**	-3,935.35
	(25.90)	(21.54)	(59.09)	(2,959.94)
Union membership	.17E-3	.50**	.26E-2*	.29E-1**
	(.25E-3)	(.26)	(.38E-3)	(.17E-1)
Adjusted R^2	0.31	0.43	0.69	0.18
Durbin-Watson	1.91	1.89	1.86	1.96

Note: Standard error in parentheses. **Significant at the .05 level; *significant at the .01 level.
[a] In model 2, the wage variable is lagged at time t-3; in all other models the wage variable is lagged at time t-1.

model 2 in Table 4.1. The estimates for models 1 and 2 confirm that strike frequency is less dependent on unionization. Also, the adjusted multiple correlation coefficients, R^2, are lower than those obtained with the number of strikers (model 3). The number of hours lost (model 4) shows the worst overall fit to equation (4.1). The value for the adjusted R^2 is particularly low. Even in this model, however, all variables are significant and have the expected signs. For all three models, the values of the Durbin-Watson statistic exclude first-order autocorrelation of the residuals. These results confirm, for the Italian case, the hypothesis that relates worker organization, as measured by the level of union membership, to strike activity and, in particular, to the number of strikers. Organization acts on the shapes of strikes by increasing the size of strikes, rather than their frequency, that is, by calling on strikes a higher percentage of workers. Furthermore, the estimates confirm that worsening labor markets, as measured by unemployment rate, have the expected negative effect on strike activity. Somewhat puzzling are the relationships between real wages and the strike indicators: High wages in the preceding year are positively related to the current number of strikes (model 1), but negatively related to the numbers of strikers and hours lost, as one can see from the signs of the coefficients of ΔW_{t-1} in model 3. Furthermore, even in the model for the number of strikes, the coefficient of the wage variable is negative when lagged three years. Is this a statistical artifact, or does it reflect real substantive differences in the relationships among variables?

Typically, fluctuating signs of coefficients are symptoms of multicollinearity (Belsley, Kuh, and Welsch, 1980, pp. 85–116). Various measures of multi-

Table 4.2. *Signs and significance of the coefficients of the wage and union variables at various lags (0, 1, 2, 3) (estimates of equation 4.1)*

Variable	Lag	t		t-1		t-2		t-3	
Strikes	t	-[a]	+	-	+	-	-	-	-
	t-1	+**	+	+**	+	+**	-	+**	-
	t-2	+	+	+	+	+	-	+	-
	t-3	-*	+**	-*	+	-*	+	-*	-
Strikers	t	-	+*	+	+*	+	+*	+	+*
	t-1	-**	+*	-**	+*	-+*		-	+
	t-2	+	+*	+	+*	+	+*	+	+**
	t-3	-	+*	-	+*	-**	+*	-**	+
Hours lost	t	+	+	+	+	+	+	+	+
	t-1	-	+	-	+	-	+	-	+
	t-2	+	+	+	+	+	+	+	-
	t-3	-	+	+	+	+	+	+	-

Note: Standard error in parentheses. **Significant at the .05 level; *significant at the .01 level.
[a] Wage coefficient in the first column of each pair; union coefficient in the second column.

collinearity, however, have revealed no sign of it in my data. When dealing with time-series data, fluctuating signs can also be an indication of cyclical behavior of the series: Different lags will then pick up different stages in the relationship between two equally cyclical variables. Indeed, we saw in Chapter 1 that strike indicators were characterized by cyclical behavior, with a period of three years. Furthermore, in Chapter 2, we saw that the relationship between wages and the number of strikes featured a three-year distributed lag structure. Finally, in Chapter 3 we saw that both strike and production variables showed high correlations (coherences, in spectral language) at that frequency band. In order to probe further into the nature of a three-year cycle in strike indicators and its relationships to other variables, I estimated equation (4.1) using various lags (0, 1, 2, 3 years) for both the wage and unionization variables.

Table 4.2 shows the signs and significance of the coefficients of these variables obtained estimating equation (4.1) with various combinations of lagged relationships. In each pair of columns, the first entry refers to the wage variable, and the second refers to the union membership variable. The results seem to support the existence of a doubly cyclical relationship between strike indicators and wages (a column-wise reading of the signs of the wage coefficient, the first column in each pair of columns): Signs fluctuate systematically for the numbers of strikes, strikers, and hours lost. The signs of the coefficients of the union variable are more stable (particularly in the estimates of the number of strikers). When they do change, however, they usually do so at three-year intervals.[22]

In conclusion, the econometric findings confirm the expectations of both the economic-bargaining and resource-mobilization models of strikes. The temporal pattern of these Italian strikes seems to have been determined by both the conditions of the labor market and the availability of organizational resources. In

Organizational resources and collective action

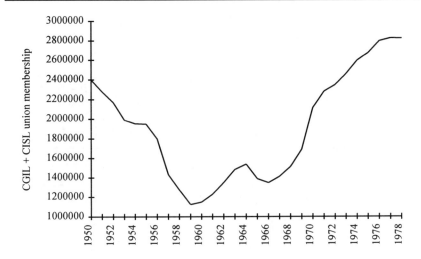

Figure 4.1. *Plot of CGIL + CISL union membership (industry)*

particular, the fluctuations in the number of strikes seem to have been more sensitive to the fluctuations in economic conditions, whereas the number of strikers was more closely related to the workers' organizational capacities.

4.6. BACK TO EXPLORATORY ANALYSES

The more qualitatively and historically minded readers (I hope they are still with me) may wonder if all of this econometric work really means anything. The richness of the historical analysis has been squeezed into a regression coefficient and a single measure of organizational resources: union membership. The signs and significance of the coefficients seem to shift, magically appearing and disappearing like rabbits from a conjurer's hat. These readers may even hold the opinion that quantitative researchers can always find a specification for a model that will bring out statistical results that will fit the theory (or a theory that will fit the data, for that matter). Qualitative, historical research is certainly not immune from these problems, but the point is well taken. To satisfy these readers' skepticism, let me further probe into the role of organization using simple statistical tools (time plots, correlations) and different measures of organizational strength.

Let us begin these exploratory analyses with a time plot of total union membership in industry (Figure 4.1). The plot shows a drastic decline in membership between 1950 and 1959, a reversal of that trend thereafter until 1964, and a further sharp increase after 1969. The relationship between the temporal patterns of union membership and strikes is quite clear (see Figures 1.3, 1.4, and 1.5, pp. 4–5). The 1950s were generally a period of working-class demobilization, with both strike activity and union membership steadily declining. The 1959–63 strike wave was accompanied by a parallel increase in union membership. The 1964 recession hit labor hard as shown by the declines in both strike activity and union membership. During the 1968–72 strike wave, organizational growth skyrocketed.

Two years, in particular, stand out in the plot of union membership: 1956 and 1969: 1956 was the year of the most dramatic postwar decline in union membership (20%); 1969, on the contrary, with an 11.7% increase over the preceding year, was second only to the 1970 record (+25.2%). In the 1970s, Italian unions achieved one of the highest rates of membership growth in Western labor history. On the basis of the hypotheses of the resource mobilization literature, we would expect a direct relationship between organizational capacities (as measured by union membership) and strike activity (particularly between years with high numbers of strikes and increasing unionization). Looking back at the strike plots of Chapter 1, 1956 does not seem to present any feature that would single it out from the strike patterns typical of the 1950s; 1969, on the other hand, was one of the most strike-prone years of the entire postwar period. In 1969, the number of strikers jumped from 3,206,000 in the preceding year to 4,734,000, for a 47.7% increase (the fifth highest value, after 1953, 1968, 1959, and 1963), and the number of hours lost reached a record value for the period under consideration going from 49,831,000 to 232,881,000, with more than 35 hours lost per worker, and 49 hours per striker, for a 367.4% increase over the preceding year.

One thing is clear: The strike variable cannot explain both cases. If a mobilization hypothesis, related to strike activity, can explain 1969, for 1956 we cannot as readily invoke a demobilization hypothesis linked to a decline in worker participation. True enough, the 1950s were characterized by a gradual demobilization process, as measured by both strike activity and union membership. It was that demobilization process, which was occurring in most Western nations in the immediate postwar years, that prompted many to predict the "end of ideology." However, in 1956, unionization rates experienced a sharp decline that cannot be explained by a parallel decline in strike levels.

Given that I have aggregated union membership data across different unions, could these problems be the result of cross-sectional aggregation? Let us go back to the basic time plots and look at union membership data for CGIL and CISL separately. Indeed, the time plots of Figure 4.2 reveal interesting differences in the temporal behavior of union membership for the two organizations. CGIL and CISL present very similar patterns starting around 1960, with sharp increases in membership up to 1964, a reversal of that tendency during the mid-1960s recession (the "recession blackmail," *ricatto congiunturale*, from the unions' perspective), and then rapid and prolonged growth after 1967 (most visibly after the 1969 *autunno caldo*), as both the labor market and strike activity picked up again. Membership growth was particularly spectacular for CISL. Whereas at the end of that prolonged growth period in 1978 CGIL had barely reached its 1950 membership levels, CISL had grown almost fivefold compared with any time in the past. If CGIL and CISL grew according to similar patterns during the 1960s and 1970s, the two organizations had declined in different ways during the 1950s. CGIL membership took a sharp dive throughout the entire decade (with the exception of

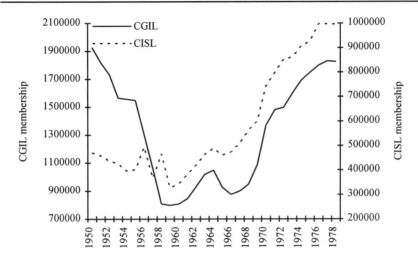

Figure 4.2. *Plots of CGIL and CISL union membership (industry)*

a couple of years around 1953–54 averaging a 19.5% annual decline between 1955 and 1958). CISL also declined during the 1950s to a postwar low in 1959, but CISL's decline was slower than that of CGIL until 1954. After 1954, CISL membership bounced up and down along a declining slope, in a pattern very different from that for CGIL. In fact, after 1954, while CGIL membership plummeted, CISL membership actually rose. In 1956, CISL membership went from 401,606 to 494,277 for a 23.1% increase (the highest after 1958 and 1970).[23]

The plots of Figure 4.3 show the percentages of votes received by CGIL and CISL in the yearly elections held in every plant for the *commissione interne*, the workers' representative bodies in the plants in the period 1945–69.[24] The elections of *commissioni interne* were the only means for worker participation within the plant until the late 1960s, when the *commissioni interne* were replaced by new representative bodies. They provided the battleground for determining the national fortunes of CGIL, CISL, and the Unione Italiana del Lavoro (UIL), the three largest unions.[25] The plots confirm the basic differences in behavior in the temporal movements of the CGIL and CISL unions. Throughout the early 1950s, CGIL kept losing ground to CISL in plant-based elections. The statistical evidence based on electoral results parallels that based on unionization figures. It suggests clear differences in the ways CGIL and CISL were affected by the demobilization process of the 1950s. Why? Furthermore, why did CGIL and CISL show the same relationship to strike activity after 1956–57?

Cross-sectoral aggregation does make a difference. It hides the fact that the temporal patterns of unionization in the 1950s were different for the two main organizations of labor. From all of this, we may be able to draw an important lesson: that we cannot simply treat data as potato sacks, that we have to look inside from time to time. What we have not yet learned, however, is what accounts for the

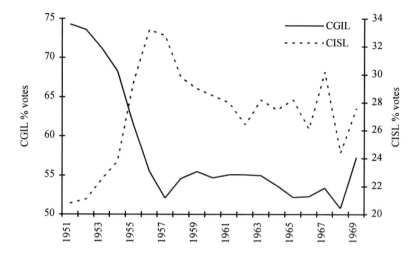

Figure 4.3. *Plots of percentage of votes obtained by CGIL and CISL in yearly elections of* commissioni interne

Table 4.3. *Correlation coefficients between numbers of strikes, strikers, and hours lost and union membership and unionization rate (1950–78)*

	Strikes	Strikers	Hours lost
CGIL + CISL union membership	.052	.659	.070
CGIL + CISL unionization rate	-.280	.393	-.155
CGIL union membership	-.154	.498	-.086
CGIL unionization rate	-.428	.201	-.272
CISL union membership	.396	.760	.322
CISL unionization rate	.245	.728	.231

similarities and differences in the temporal patterns of union membership for CGIL and CISL. We only know that these differences cannot be explained by strike patterns.

Let me now turn to some simple measures involving linear relationships. Table 4.3 reports the Pearson simple correlation coefficients between numbers of strikes, strikers, and hours lost and union membership and unionization rate. The findings confirm that the number of strikers shows the highest linear relationship with organization, as measured by both the absolute level of union membership and the unionization rate. The correlation coefficients for the number of strikes and the number of hours lost are very low.[26]

The correlation coefficients between strike indicators and union indicators for the two largest unions (CGIL and CISL) reveal interesting differences: CISL seems to have been more effective than CGIL in mobilizing workers ($r = .76$ for CISL membership, and $r = .728$ for CISL unionization rate, as compared with $r = .498$

Table 4.4. *Correlation coefficients between numbers of strikes, strikers, and hours lost and union membership and unionization rate (1956–78)*

	Strikes	Strikers	Hours lost
CGIL membership	.228	.783	.147
CISL membership	.251	.788	.191
Total membership	.238	.790	.165
CGIL unionization rate	.159	.751	.102
CISL unionization rate	.207	.765	.168
Total unionization rate	.180	.766	.129

for CGIL membership and $r = .201$ for CGIL unionization rate). Furthermore, correlation coefficients between the numbers of strikes and hours lost are positive for CISL, whereas those involving CGIL are negative. These differences in sign and magnitude between the two unions show that the low and negative coefficients for total unionization (CGIL + CISL) are due to CGIL. Somewhat paradoxically, CGIL, compared to CISL, would therefore seem to have kept conflict down, rather than having stirred it up (Colasanti, 1982).

The time plot, however, had revealed marked fluctuations in union membership figures for the early 1950s. In particular, the years 1956–57 seem to have been key years, marking a historical turning point. The correlation coefficients for the 1956–78 period, shown in Table 4.4, confirm this: Not only have the negative signs for CGIL disappeared, but also the magnitudes of the coefficients are now similar to those for CISL. Thus, starting in 1956, both organizations show positive relationships to all strike components, size in particular.

The correlation coefficients in Table 4.5 between detrended values for unemployment and the numbers of strikes, strikers, and hours lost, by the scope of strikes, provide further evidence on the relationships among organizational strength, labor-market tightness, and strike behavior. The only positive coefficients are those between industry and multiple-industry strikes and the unemployment rate. It would appear that workers rely on centralized, politicized, large-scale actions, as measured by industry and multiple-industry strikes, when their economic-bargaining power is low, as measured by the unemployment rate. On the contrary, when their economic power is high, workers seem to favor local, plant-level actions. This finding thus provides empirical support for Pizzorno's argument on economic versus political strength. In fact, according to Pizzorno (1973, p. 129),

Labor unions lean on political parties when they are strong, i.e., able to mobilize support to impose their programs, and when, furthermore, the labor-market power of the working class is weak. But when the parties do not operate as channels of participation and when, furthermore, the labor unions become the main instruments of mass participation, then the situation is reversed; the unions do not need the parties anymore, and they become autonomous.

In conclusion, the exploratory analyses in this section have confirmed that organization plays a fundamental role in workers' mobilization processes. This is

Table 4.5. *Correlation coefficients between detrended values of unemployment and numbers of strikes, strikers, and hours lost, by scope (manufacturing industry, 1955–II/1975–IV)*

	Plant			Industry			Multiple industries		
	S^a	W	H	S	W	H	S	W	H
Unemployment rate	-.10	-.27	-.22	-.10	-.07	.13	-.05	-.07	.14

^{a}S, number of strikes; W, number of strikers; H, number of hours lost.

particularly true for the number of strikers, whereas the relationships are weaker for the other strike components (numbers of strikes and hours lost). Thus, the findings confirm that strike activity is a multidimensional phenomenon, whose various components are characterized by different underlying causal structures. As we have seen in the preceding chapters, the number of strikes is most strongly dependent on the fluctuations of the business cycle, but strike participation is more closely related to organizational strength. In particular, the two main surges in the growth of union membership seem to have coincided with periods of intense strike activity (1959–63, 1968–72).

The exploratory analyses should have dispelled the qualitatively inclined readers' worst fears about the trickery of multivariate statistics. Not only have the exploratory analyses confirmed the multivariate econometric results, but they have shed further light on the relationship between organization and strike activity. First, the analyses have revealed a strategic use of the strike weapon by the unions: a tendency to rely on large-scale *political* actions when their bargaining position in the labor market was weak, and reliance on microconflict at the plant level when the business cycle afforded them a better bargaining position. Second, the analyses have highlighted differences in the relationships of strike variables with CGIL and CISL union membership. Did those differences reflect underlying organizational characteristics of the two unions? Why did they disappear after 1956?

4.7. MORE HISTORY: THE ORGANIZATION OF INTERESTS

In order to find an answer to these questions, in this section I will take a closer look at the organization of Italian labor. In line with the view of strikes as strategic interaction (as it takes two to tango, it takes at least two to fight), I will look at both the organization of workers and that of employers.

4.7.1. Workers

With the collapse of the Fascist regime, which had prohibited strikes and lockouts, Italian workers organized, with the 1944 Pact of Rome, the Italian General Confederation of Labor (CGIL).[27] The CGIL united the Communist, Catholic, and Secular forces that had participated in the underground Resistance and, later, in the liberation movement against the Nazis. The Communists, led by Di Vittorio, had the majority and controlled the union. But in the climate of cold war confrontation in the postwar years, trade-union unity was soon to crumble.[28] Disagreements arose over the political use of mass actions by the unions (Turone, 1984, pp. 109, 117). Against Article 9 of the CGIL statute that allowed political strikes, Grandi, the leader of the Catholic wing, thundered that "the republic is defended in Parliament" (Turone, 1984, p. 117). The defeat of the Popular Front in the 1948 elections, and the attempted assassination of Palmiro Togliatti, the Communist Party leader, on July 14, 1948, hastened the pace of disintegration (Turone, 1984, p. 145). A general strike broke out. Italy appeared to be on the verge of a revolutionary outbreak (Turone, 1984, p. 145; Marino, 1991, pp. 13–28). Condemning the strike, the Catholic faction of CGIL withdrew from the unitary union, the first step toward setting up an independent organization.

In 1950, CGIL, already without the Catholic faction since 1948, split along political lines into three deeply antagonistic organizations: CGIL, the Italian General Confederation of Labor, the largest union, affiliated with the Communist and Socialist parties, which kept the original name; the Italian Confederation of Workers Union (CISL), affiliated with the Christian Democrat and Social Democrat parties; and the smaller Italian Workers Union (UIL), with Republican and Social Democrat ties. La Palombara stated that "American financial assistance was vital for the survival of the free federations [CISL and UIL]" (as they were then called) (La Palombara, 1957, p. 57). American money was instrumental in setting up in Florence the CISL school for the training of CISL union cadres. Anti-Communist pressure on Italian labor came mostly through the American Federation of Labor (AFL.) As Filippelli noted, "Denying Communist control over European labor was an essential goal of American policy for the reconstruction and stabilization of Europe, but had to be accomplished without the appearance of American government involvement."[29]

The three unions had similar organizational structures. They all organized workers along both "vertical" (by economic sector) and "horizontal" (by territory) lines.[30] The vertical organization included, at the top, the confederations *(confederazioni,* e.g., CGIL, CISL, and UIL) and, below, several federations *(federazioni)* or national category unions *(sindacati nazionali di categoria)* organized along industry lines (e.g., metalworking, chemical, textile). There was a separate federation for each major economic sector and for each of the three confederations [e.g., FIOM (the CGIL metalworking federation), FIM (the CISL metalworking federation)]. The horizontal organization included both the local branches of the federations at the regional and local levels, and the local and regional "labor chambers" *(camere del lavoro).*[31]

At the plant level, until the late 1960s, the grievance committees *(commissioni interne)* were the main organizational structures inside the factories. A 1947 agreement between Confindustria, the main employer organization, and the CGIL, CISL, and UIL stripped the *commissioni interne* of their capacity to conduct bargaining negotiations with employers and to sign collective agreements. The *commissioni interne* function became largely symbolic. It was only in 1960 that the unions attempted to set up union organizational structures inside the Italian plants, with the *sezione sindacale aziendale* (plant-level trade-union section), or Ssa. The Ssa were instituted in 1960 to be truly representative union bodies at the plant level. Employers, however, never widely recognized those new representative bodies. Workers themselves never transferred their allegiances from the *commissioni interne* to the Ssa, and the Ssa never took root. In fact, they never even performed those plant-level bargaining functions for which they supposedly had been set up (Treu, 1971, p. 148; Romagnoli, 1976, pp. 140–1).[32]

Throughout the 1950s and much of the 1960s unions could count on only limited organizational resources. The resources commanded were mostly ideological. The ties between the unions and political parties were strong for all three unions. Given their low levels of economic power in an unfavorable labor market, unions relied for support on political parties with the proper ideological affinities ("twin parties:"mostly Communist but also Socialist parties for CGIL, mostly Christian Democrat but also Social Democrat parties for CISL, and Republican and Social Democrat parties for UIL) (Pizzorno, 1973, pp. 117–20). Political parties, on the other hand, relied on labor unions to mobilize workers around political issues. Union activity was subordinated to party agendas. Union leaders were active in politics: They were party members, and they held elected political positions in both the Parliament and local governments (Weitz, 1975, p. 228). For CGIL, the relationship between the union and the Communist Party in the 1950s was best summarized by the concept of "transmission belt" (*cinghia di trasmissione*): the trade union as a bridge between the party and the working-class base.[33] Given the different political affiliations of the three unions, relations among the unions were strained, in a mirror image of the political rift among the sets of "twin parties."

CGIL, CISL, and UIL differed in the their basic views of the nature of unions. For the Communist-led CGIL, unions should be *class unions* (i.e., vehicles for revolutionary politics). A class union should reject any compromise with the capitalist system during the day-to-day negotiations of economic matters. Union involvement in such matters could only lead to economism and to the pursuit of particularistic interests by the better-placed workers. CISL and UIL, on the other hand, accepted the basic political framework of a capitalist society. They saw the role of a union as being that of aggressive pursuit of a fair share of the economic resources that capitalist development made available. Both CISL and UIL rejected a political role for the unions and confined their actions to the economic sphere, the bread-and-butter issues.

The practice whereby an employer would have separate agreements (*accordi separati*) with different unions, particularly with CISL and UIL, was quite widespread. Many companies would not even bother to negotiate with CGIL representatives. A CISL member of the *commissione interna* (CI) at the Innocenti automobile plant remembers that

Management was willing to deal with CISL and UIL only. This was not officially declared, but while two CISL and UIL members went to a bargaining meeting with management, I, being the youngest, waited outside with the CGIL member. Afterward, ... once the deal was agreed upon, we all went back in with the CGIL CI member for the farce of a bargaining meeting *ex novo*. (quoted in Reyneri, 1974a, p. 131)

Many companies even gave CISL and UIL a free hand in hiring and firing in exchange for their cooperation (e.g., Regalia, 1975b, p. 38). Finally, many companies offered special bonuses to those workers who would drop their CGIL membership (e.g., Reyneri, 1974a, p. 121). CISL and its Christian Democratic leadership used their *parentela* relationship with the majority Christian Democrat Party in government to obtain resources and protection (La Palombara, 1964, pp. 306–48). For example, in 1951, the government appointed Giulio Pastore, secretary general of CISL, to the International Labour Organization (ILO) in Geneva, despite the fact that CGIL was larger than CISL (Turone, 1984, p. 182).

With the 1962–63 strikes in the metalworking industry, the traditional political hostility among the unions began to decline. But it was the 1969 *autunno caldo* that accelerated the drive toward unity among the unions. A new generation of highly militant workers, with little understanding of the ideological squabbles that had kept the unions apart, was pushing in that direction. According to the 1971 Isvet survey of workers' attitudes, 52.4% of the workers interviewed believed that union unity was "very useful" for the workers (30.2% believed it was "rather useful") (De Masi and Fevola, 1974a, p. 795). The figures were even higher among highly militant workers, among workers concentrated in larger plants, and among those belonging to (or at least sympathetic to) CGIL or the Italian Communist Party. The percentage of workers who believed that union unity was "very beneficial" for workers jumped from 27.6% among low-militancy workers to 75.3% for highly militant workers. Under pressure from the rank and file, in 1972, CGIL, CISL, and UIL established joint decision-making bodies with the creation of the United Federation (Federazione Unitaria). Although the Federazione Unitaria did not result in a full merger, it provided a common forum for working together.[34]

The revolutionary ferment of the 1969 *autunno caldo* quickly prompted Parliament to pass favorable labor legislation, on May 20, 1970: the law no. 300, or the "Workers' Charter" (*Statuto dei Lavoratori*). The Workers' Charter granted legal recognition to the unions' representative bodies inside the plants – at least in plants with more than 15 workers – in the form of *rappresentanze sindacali aziendali* (plant-level union representative bodies), or Rsa. The charter further guaranteed union rights in the workplace, such as time off and leaves of absence for the plant-level union representatives for their union activities. It legalized mass meetings inside the factories, to allow workers to discuss labor issues, and it allowed each worker a number of paid hours each year to attend such meetings.[35] Discrimination against workers engaged in union activity became illegal. That new legal framework substantially protected worker-activists who previously had been harassed, fired, and blacklisted for their political and union activities. As a worker at the Falck ironworks put it,

At one time, to be an activist meant to lose your job. That was a strong negative incentive; one works so that one can eat, and then you end up losing your job. ... Now, instead, you have recognitions of all kinds, from the church to the company. Then there is the fact that if the company touches an activist, in general, at least there is protest. One feels better protected. (quoted in Carabelli, 1974, p. 148)

What form were the Rsa to take? Should the *commissioni interne* simply change their name? If not, what should the relationship be between the new Rsa and the old *commissioni interne*? Or should the *commissioni interne* simply disappear? While those questions were being hotly debated by the leadership, the workers provided their own answer. In the heat of the 1969 *autunno caldo* strikes, workers set up new forms of representation, such as the *comitati unitari di base* (base unitary committees, or CUB), the *consigli di fabbrica* (factory councils, or Cdf), and the *delegati* (workers' delegates) (Regalia, 1978; Romagnoli and Della Rocca, 1989, pp. 117–20).[36] By and large, the Cdf and *delegati* movements grew out of the workers' grass-roots activities.[37] Particularly at the beginning, those new forms of representation were set up by the workers themselves, rather than by the unions. In fact, in many instances (especially the CUB; see Avanguardia Operaia, 1971) the new structures were set up in open opposition to the official unions.[38]

All workers were eligible to vote for the *delegati*. Contrary to the practices of the *commissioni interne*, where each union provided the names of candidates, workers entered their choices for delegates on blank ballots. The electoral basis for the *delegati* was the homogeneous work group at the shop level.[39] As a consequence, the number of workplaces with *delegati* was quite high and representation was widely diffused. There had been three *commissioni interne* members in plants with 41–175 workers, and the numbers ranged up to a maximum of 15 members in plants with more than 10,000 workers (Romagnoli and Della Rocca, 1989, p. 115). On the basis of data on *delegati* and Cdf collected from a sample of firms in the province of Milan, Romagnoli concluded (1976, p. 120; see also, 1971, p. 56) that "there [was] a shift from an average of 1 representative [for] every 478 workers in 1969 [including both *commissioni interne* and Ssa] to an average of 1 representative [for] every 86 workers in 1970 and 1 [for] every 54 in 1973."

Another survey conducted in 1972 by Romagnoli among a sample of 85 firms in the Milan province found an average of 37 workers per delegate (Romagnoli, 1973, p. 33). A survey conducted by the Milan Camera del Lavoro in 1974 among a sample of 124 Milanese firms found an average of 33 workers per delegate (Celadin, 1974, p. 175).[40] Undoubtedly, both workers' representation and decision-making processes became more democratic during the crucial years of the 1968–72 strike wave.

The ensemble of *delegati* formed the Consiglio di fabbrica (factory council), the Cdf. The Cdf, in turn, elected a restricted number of *delegati* to be part of its *esecutivo* (executive).[41] Memberships in both the Cdf and executive bodies were typically limited-term and rotating. In most companies, workers could revoke the mandate to their delegates before the end of the term.[42] The Cdf included aspects of both the *commissioni interne* and Ssa, since they were both workers' representative bodies, regardless of union affiliation, and union representative structures at the plant level.[43] Unlike the *commissioni interne*, the Cdf, in particular its executive body, enjoyed considerable bargaining power (as sanctioned in the law, the 1970 Workers' Charter).

The majority of Cdf members belonged to a union; only 8.9% did not, according to Celadin's data (1974, p. 49) and 5% according to Romagnoli (1976, p. 147). Many of them belonged to a political party – 34% according to Romagnoli (1973, p. 53). Although the Communist, Christian Democrat, and Socialist parties were the most common choices, some 12–15% of the delegates had had some contact or frequent contacts with radical extraparliamentary groups (Romagnoli, 1973, p. 56). It was mostly the young, unskilled immigrants from the South (some of them student-workers) who were involved in extraparliamentary groups. Considering that those groups (e.g., Lotta Continua, Potere Operaio) arose out of the student movement, the presence of such groups in the factories shows the close contact between the student movement and the labor movement during the late 1960s. Many of the delegates in Romagnoli's 1971 sample were unskilled workers. That was quite a change from the *commissioni interne*, whose members typically were skilled workers.[44] The changes in the occupational structure were highlighted in Chapter 3, and undoubtedly the changes in the sociotechnical forms of organization of production affected not only the occupational structure but also the organizational forms of the class.

Between 1970 and 1972 the *commissioni interne* were completely swept away. The transition from *commissioni interne* and Ssa to the delegates and Cdf was not always one of complete rejection of the past. In more than 47% of the firms in a 1970 sample, current or former *commissioni interne* members were elected as delegates (Romagnoli, 1976, p. 147). As the old *commissioni interne* died, the *delegati* movement quickly spread from the larger to the smaller factories, from industry to services (Regalia, 1978). According to FIOM-CGIL data,[45] in 1970, in the industrial North, 1,176 new Cdf were set up, compared with 5,945 Rsa, the representational bodies envisioned by the Workers' Charter.[46] The Rsa were slowly disappearing, engulfed by the Cdf movement.[47] The number of new Cdf kept growing year after year, from 8,101 in 1972 (with some 82,923 delegates) to 9,813 in 1973, 16,000 in 1974, and 32,000 in 1978 (with some 210,000 delegates).[48]

Under the pressure imposed by a highly mobilized base of rank-and-file workers, in the span of a few years, not only workers' representation at the plant level had become more democratic,[49] but also union organizations themselves had become more democratic. Responding to workers' demands, unions debated the problem of rotating the trade-union offices and set aside the principle of the "transmission belt" (although more frequently in theory than in practice) to adopt incompatibility rules that prohibited union officials from also holding party positions or elected offices. Union officials had to choose one or the other.

4.7.2. Employers

Italian employers are organized into several associations that differ for the various economic sectors (agriculture, craft production, industry, commerce).[50] Within each sector there operate different associations, depending on the type of ownership (private or state), the affiliations with political parties (Christian Democrat or Socialist and/or Communist parties), and firm sizes (small firms, large firms) (Becchi Collidà, 1989, pp. 135–6; Lanzalaco, 1990, pp. 59–60). Thus, in agriculture, large farmers are organized in Confagricoltura, while small farmers are organized in Confcoltivatori, with close ties to the Communist Party, and in Coldiretti, with Christian Democrat ties. Similarly, small commercial firms are organized around Confcommercio (close to the Christian Democrat Party) and Confesercenti (close to the Socialist and Communist parties). In industry, the main association is the Confederazione Generale dell'Industria Italiana (Confindustria), which organizes private entrepreneurs, whereas Intersind and Asap organize public, state-owned companies. In industry there is also a smaller association, Confederazione della Piccola e Media Industria (Confapi), which organizes small private firms. By and large, Confindustria has been the most powerful employer organization, since 1910 the symbol of Italian capitalism, with an influential role in labor and political relations.[51]

Confindustria is a confederation of both territory-based sectoral associations and sector-based national associations. It provides both collective-bargaining services for member firms and technical assistance on labor and commercial matters. Smaller firms, without specialized technical staffs of their own, are the main beneficiaries of Confindustria's technical services (Martinelli et al., 1981, p. 266). In comparative perspective, Confindustria presents a twofold peculiarity among employer associations: sectoral specialization (it represents only industrial firms) and territorial differentiation (not only is the number of territorial organizations, 106, larger than that of sectoral organizations, 98, but also the decision-making weight of territorial associations is much greater) (Martinelli and Treu, 1984, p. 272; Lanzalaco, 1990, pp. 63–6).[52] According to its 1946 charter, each Confindustria member firm must also take (voluntary) memberships in both a territorial association (typically at the provincial level) and a sectoral association. The territorial associations in the provinces of Milan and Turin [Associazione Industriale Lombarda (Assolombarda) and Unione Industriale di Torino] are the most powerful territorial associations, given the Confindustria electoral system. In fact, the electoral weight of a territorial association in the election of all Confindustria governing bodies is directly proportional to the number of employees represented by that association. Given that most large firms are concentrated in the Milan and Turin provinces, the associations of Milan and Turin control more than half the votes in the general assembly of Confindustria (Martinelli and Treu, 1984, pp. 72–3).

In the late 1940s, Confindustria represented 68,354 industrial firms, with a total of 1,922,256 employees; 95.3% of the firms had less than 100 employees, 3.0% had 100–250 employees, and only 1.7% had more than 250 employees.[53] Throughout the 1950s, the percentage of Confindustria member firms with less than 10 employees consistently remained above 60% of the total (Mattina, 1991, p. 106). In 1969, most member firms were small in size, as can be seen from Table 4.6.[54] The great number of small firms in the organization is not surprising, given

Table 4.6. *Distribution of Confindustria member firms by firm size in 1969*

	Number of employees							
	<10	11–50	51–100	101–250	251–500	501–1,000	>1,000	Total
A[a]	54,698	20,192	4,441	2,530	847	338	199	83,245
B	65.71	24.26	5.33	3.04	1.02	0.41	0.24	100
C	232,026	481,445	305,925	382,979	286,592	230,471	548,361	2,467,799
D	9.4	19.51	12.4	15.52	11.61	9.34	22.2	100

[a]A, number of firms; B, percentage of firms; C, number of employees; D, percentage of employees.
Source: Confindustria, *Annuario*, 1970, pp. 744–9.

the Italian industrial base discussed in Chapter 3 (Mattina, 1991, pp. 106–7). Despite the much greater number of smaller firms, larger firms took control of Confindustria at the outset and maintained that control over the years (Mattina, 1991, pp. 98–102, 105–11). The financial contributions by member firms to Confindustria are based on the number of employees. The 199 firms with more than 1,000 employees each, which in 1969 constituted only 0.24% of Confindustria membership, accounted for 22.2% of all workers in Confindustria member firms (see Table 4.6). The inherent contradiction in having member firms of such disparate sizes has led to polarization between small and large firms, one of the main sources of conflict within Confindustria.[55] That contradiction has occasionally led to explosive disagreements, particularly during periods of heightened class confrontation with labor.[56] In such cases, the willingness of larger firms to buy industrial peace by paying higher wages has clashed with smaller firms' need to keep the cost of labor low.

In the late 1940s and early 1950s, Confindustria's main goal was to recast a bourgeois order under the protective umbrella of American financial and military aid. Under Angelo Costa's presidency, Confindustria, on the defensive, doggedly retrenched, struggling to put control over layoffs back into the hands of management, to keep wages down, and to resist any form of workers' control and/or participation within the firms.[57] Costa strove to centralize power in Confindustria, rather than in the territorial or sectoral organizations, and to present a united front against labor. As part of that plan, Costa pushed for highly centralized bargaining (Martinelli et al., 1981, p. 242; Mattina, 1991, p. 100).

Throughout the 1950s, Confindustria policies and politics were shaped by a frail compromise between the interests of small firms and the interests of the minority oligopoly giants (Martinelli et al., 1981, p. 243). That compromise broke down in the late 1950s. The round of negotiations for the collective contract renewals of 1959 and 1962, held under conditions of a tight labor market that put labor in a better bargaining position, helped to crystallize the differences between the interests of small firms and large firms, between private firms and state-owned firms. The newly created public employer association, Intersind, played a key role in those negotiations, on both occasions signing agreements favorable to the workers. Although in both cases Confindustria held out longer before signing similar agreements, in the end it followed suit. The chasm between the interests of small firms and big business within Confindustria widened further in the early 1960s because of the plans of the Center-Left government for nationalization of the electric industry and for centralized economic planning. Confindustria opposed both measures (La Palombara, 1966, pp. 72, 123; Pirzio Ammassari, 1976, pp. 94–105; Mutti and Segatti, 1977, p. 118).

Small entrepreneurs joined with the financial and electric oligopolies that controlled the Confindustria leadership in an effort to derail the plans of the Center-Left government. The electric-industry bourgeoisie was able to maintain tight control over smaller industrialists via its discretionary use of electric tariffs (Martinelli, 1978, pp. 48–9; Martinelli et al., 1981, p. 243). What Pietro Ferrerio, chief executive officer of Edison, the main electric company, had told the Commissione Economica per l'Assemblea Costituente in 1946 still held in 1963: "To me, the most unbridled disorganization is preferable even to the best of planning" (quoted in De Carlini, 1972, pp. 69–70; see also Pirzio Ammassari, 1976, p. 31).

Large firms, on the other hand, were interested in inexpensive energy (and a state-owned electric company promised just that). These firms also needed more market predictability (and the kind of planning that the Center-Left wanted to introduce was, again, just that).

In the 1960s, the frail compromise between small and large firms, private and public bourgeoisie, broke down. While the large public and private oligopolies operating in the modern sectors supported the Center-Left modernizing strategy, Confindustria, still in the hands of the traditional capitalists and an economically aggressive and innovative but politically backward class of small entrepreneurs, retrenched, supporting both right-wing parties and right-wing currents within the Christian Democrat Party.[58] Vittorio Valletta, Fiat general manager, shocked the Confindustria leadership when on June 26, 1962, in an interview with the Roman daily *Il Messaggero*, he declared that

> The Center-Left government is a product of the times. We cannot and we should not turn back. I am in favor of the Center-Left. . . . Not only the trade unions commit severe mistakes, but Confindustria, as well. It is my impression that soon enough groups inside the employer organization will put pressure on the Confindustria leadership responsible for the current strategy so as to abandon its principled and rigid positions. (quoted in De Carlini, 1972, pp. 65–6)

Times change and strategies change: the man who had purged Fiat of all Communist workers in the early 1950s was extending the olive branch. But the old guard in Confindustria would not die easily. During the years of the Center-Left governments, Confindustria survived – having lost its privileged (*clientela*) access to the state, having lost the battles against labor in the contract renewals of 1959 and 1962, and finally having lost the battle with the Christian Democrats over both the nationalization of electric companies and centralized economic planning – but the old leadership was without political spark. Confindustria became mostly an organization that provided technical services for smaller firms (Martinelli et al., 1981, p. 266).

It was the resurgence of conflict in 1968 and during the 1969 *autunno caldo* that brought the old leadership down. In March 1969, Confindustria set up a commission, headed by Leopoldo Pirelli, the Milan-based tire manufacturer, "with the mandate to investigate and prepare changes and adjustments to the confederal charter" (Pirzio Ammassari, 1976, p. 130). That probably was long overdue, because the 1946 charter had simply reinstituted the pre-Fascist 1919 and 1921 charters. That strategic choice to revise the 1946 charter was to lead to major organizational problems (Lanzalaco, 1990, p. 158). On February 20, 1970, Confindustria made public the final report (the so-called *Rapporto Pirelli*) (Pirzio Ammassari, 1976, pp. 130–3; Lanzalaco, 1990, pp. 167–71). The *Rapporto Pirelli* called for radical changes in three areas: (1) greater integration among territorial and sectoral associations and Confindustria, and rationalization of membership in territorial and sectoral associations; (2) revision of Confindustria's organizational structure, with the creation of specialized *lines* (the lines for *rapporti interni, rapporti esterni, rapporti sindacali*, and *rapporti economici*);[59] (3) greater direct participation by Italian entrepreneurs in the cultural, political, and social life of Italian society (Lanzalaco, 1990, pp. 167–71).

The most serious organizational changes envisioned by the Pirelli report, such as the rationalization of dual membership in territorial and sectoral associations, were never implemented (Lanzalaco, 1990, p. 172).[60] In that sense, the *Rapporto Pirelli* and the *Riforma Pirelli* that followed were failures. The *Rapporto Pirelli* had its impact elsewhere, as a new political and ideological banner of the Italian bourgeoisie (Pirzio Ammassari, 1976, p. 130; Lanzalaco, 1990, p. 172). The report emphasized an ideological break with the past. It represented the "neocapitalist" vision of the leaders of the large oligopolies operating in the modern sectors of the economy (Fiat, Pirelli, Olivetti, etc.). Those leaders (e.g., Giovanni Agnelli, majority stockholder of Fiat) viewed Confindustria as an institution to organize the ideological and political interests of the bourgeoisie (Pirzio Ammassari, 1976, p. 142).[61] Consistent with Pirelli's and Agnelli's view of a Confindustria unencumbered by the conflicts surrounding labor contract renewals, on December 11, 1971, a new sectoral association was created, Federmeccanica, the federation of metals and mechanical industries. Federmeccanica was specifically set up to handle labor relations and deal with the aggressive and powerful metalworking unions (CGIL-FIOM, CISL-FIM, UIL-UIM) and the Federazione Unitaria.

A survey conducted by Federmeccanica among its member firms in 1973 showed that of some 8,000 member firms, with a total of 900,000 employees, 91% had less than 200 employees each, for a total of some 300,000 employees.[62] Its 85 largest firms employed 43% of all its workers (382,000 employees). The remaining 7.5% were medium-size firms, and they accounted for the other 25% of total employment by all Federmeccanica firms. Not surprisingly, the makeup of firms in Federmeccanica reproduced Confindustria's rift between small firms and big business. Indeed, mediating and reconciling the different interests of its small and large firms were the main problems facing Federmeccanica leadership (Pirzio Ammassari, 1976, p. 143). In 1973, after the signing of the metalworkers' collective contract, Walter Mandelli, president of Federmeccanica, declared in an interview that the contract could have been signed a few months earlier except that then "We were not able to have it accepted by our members, in particular, small and medium firms" (quoted in Pirzio Ammassari, 1976, p. 145). Again, in 1975, the small and medium-size industrialists of Lecce rebelled against Confindustria's strategy of political trade-offs with unions and the state (Pirzio Ammassari, 1976, p. 185).

Consistent with Pirelli's and Agnelli's suggestions for direct participation by industrialists in "the management of their common affairs," the cream of the Italian bourgeoisie took up key positions in the organizational structure of Confindustria. Agnelli himself took the presidency in 1973. Guido Carli, former governor of the Bank of Italy, followed in 1976. During those years, Confindustria opted for a high profile, with its leadership firmly in the hands of the large oligopolies. The small entrepreneurs (the vast majority of Confindustria membership) followed the new line, but they did so reluctantly. Nicola Resta, president of Confindustria's commission on small business, best expressed such feelings in an interview in March 1973 on the eve of Confindustria's annual general assembly:

What does small business need? A strong and united organization . . . that provides certain services and bargaining representation with both the political and labor worlds. . . . Because big industrialists can well defend themselves by themselves, but small entrepreneurs . . . do not need a [political] organization. We need services and bargaining power. (quoted in Pirzio Ammassari, 1976, p. 161)

A host of employers' surveys showed that smaller entrepreneurs, even when they belonged to Confindustria, did not feel that their interests were fairly represented by Confindustria, which they perceived to be in the hands of big capital controlled by rich families (Farneti, 1970, pp. 194–5). For those reasons, small employers typically viewed their local associations more positively than they did Confindustria, which they perceived to be involved in backroom dealings with the government and the unions at the expense of small entrepreneurs (Guala, 1975, p. 124; Bagnasco and Trigilia, 1984, p. 224). Those same surveys revealed the kinds of services that small employers needed from their organizations (Martinelli, 1977, p. 336; Urbani, 1977a, p. 392; Guala, 1975, p. 125). On the one hand, they wanted a tougher stance toward the political class and the trade unions, as well as cultural initiatives to polish the "image" of the employers. On the other hand, they wanted technical assistance with union bargaining, export, credit, and fiscal matters.

4.8. MUDDLED CAUSALITY: FURTHER PROBING INTO THE ROLE OF ORGANIZATION

Rosa Luxemburg (1971, p. 66) wrote in her 1906 essay *The Mass Strike* that "The organization does not supply the troops for the struggle, but the struggle, in an ever

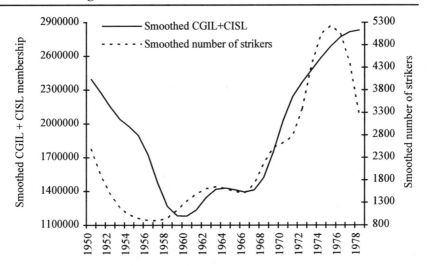

Figure 4.4. *Plots of smoothed data for number of strikers and CGIL + CISL union membership*

growing degree, supplies recruits for the organization." Rosa Luxemburg did not spend her time collecting data and running regressions; she spoke from her experience as an organizer and a militant. Is there any empirical support for her statement? Do workers tend to join an organization after they have participated in a strike? Is unionization the organizational reward for successful strikes?

The exploratory plots of union membership data (Figure 4.1) have already revealed how deeply the 1959–63 and 1968–72 strike waves affected union membership.[63] The similarity between the growth pattern for the number of strikers and that for union membership (CGIL in particular) is certainly remarkable. Unionization figures show wave-like temporal patterns similar to the trends for strikes (size in particular). Yet the picture is somewhat blurred by differences in short- and long-term behaviors for the union membership and strike series. Institutional arrangements (e.g., automatic withholding of union dues by employers) make it more difficult for workers to cancel their union membership than to abstain from collective action.[64]

Given these differences in the short- and long-term fluctuations in unionization and strike series, let me smooth out the rough edges from the two series of number of strikers and union membership (CGIL + CISL). By eliminating some of the year-to-year fluctuations, we should be able to bring into sharper focus the common underlying, long-term temporal patterns. The plots in Figure 4.4, based on resistant smoothers,[65] show how closely the unionization series follows in time the series for the number of strikers.[66] The patterns for strike activity and unionization go hand in hand, with unionization progressing by big jumps, in the wake of major cycles of industrial conflict.

Indeed, so closely do the strike and unionization curves go together (and not only for the Italian case) that the same variables used in strike models are used in union-growth models: In the former, a strike indicator is the dependent variable, and unionization is one of the independent variables; in the latter, the reverse is true.[67] On the basis of an analysis of unionization and strike data in Italy during the 1950–86 period, La Valle (1989, p. 40) concluded that the temporal pattern of unionization closely followed that of strikes: The upward turning points, the peaks, and the lower turning points followed the patterns of strikes by some years.[68] Research based on microlevel union data makes this connection even clearer. According to an analysis of trade union data for the province of Milan, unionization peaked after each wave of conflict, perhaps a year later (CISL Milano, 1975a).[69] A similar analysis of unionization data for the province of Turin and selected firms confirmed a tendency for union growth to soar after bouts of strike activity (Cavallo Perin, 1980).

But in fact, not only membership but also the unions' personnel changed after the two major postwar outbursts of industrial conflict (Della Rocca, 1978). The first major change occurred in the early 1960s, after the 1962 strikes preceding the renewal of the metalworkers' collective agreement (Della Rocca, 1978, p. 67). In the 1962 metalworkers' contract with state-owned firms, unions won the concession of dues checkoff by employers. Private firms and other sectors followed suit in the 1966 collective contracts. That victory stabilized union membership and revenues, and set off both quantitative and qualitative changes in the organization of unions. The bureaucratic apparatus increased in size, and a new group of officials with backgrounds quite different from those of their older colleagues entered the union bureaucracies. Prior to the early 1960s, union officials had come, at first, from the political and labor-union apparatus of the pre-Fascist era, and later they came from the scores of workers (mostly skilled workers) who, in the repressive climate of the 1950s, had lost their jobs because of their political beliefs and activities. After the 1959–63 strike wave, and particularly after the 1969 *autunno caldo*, a new generation of cadres took up full-time positions in the unions. The newcomers generally were semiskilled assembly line workers without professional qualifications and without previous political apprenticeship in the party (at least for CGIL). In a brief span of time, approximately one-third of the whole leadership apparatus was replaced, via co-optation of those workers who had actively participated in the struggles, usually in informal leadership roles.

Finally, the basic organizational structure within unions changed after each strike wave (Della Rocca, 1974, 1981). After the 1959–63 strike wave, the balance of power within the unions shifted from the confederal level, which had dominated the labor-relations scene during the 1950s, to the federal level (e.g., metalworkers, textile workers). That shift toward decentralization of structures was carried even further after the 1969 *autunno caldo*. New organizational structures sprouted and quickly spread [the base unitary committees, *comitati unitari di base* (CUB); the plant-level union representative bodies, *rappresentanze sindacali aziendali* (Rsa); and factory councils, *consigli di fabbrica* (Cdf), alongside the traditional "internal commissions," *commissioni interne*]. Within a few years, the factory council became the typical organizational structure at the plant level, supplanting all other organizational forms.

Table 4.7. *Distribution of* commissioni interne *elections by plant size (1969)*

	Number of employees						
	<10	11–50	51–100	101–250	251–500	501–1,000	>1,000
Plants with elections	9	179	202	218	98	44	24
Member firms	54,698	20,192	4,441	2,530	847	338	199
Percentage of firms	.02	.89	4.5	8.6	11.6	13.0	12.1

Source: Confederazione Generale dell'Industria Italiana (1973).

If union membership growth and, more generally, union organizational change follow rather than precede conflict, where does this leave resource-mobilization models of collective action? Is organizational growth a consequence of mobilization and collective action? What is the role of organization? To answer these questions, I have to abandon the use of econometric modeling and the focus on aggregate year-to-year unionization data. Instead, I will examine the available data on the presence of unions at the plant level, these data coming from several workers', employers', and firms' surveys conducted at different times over the postwar period. Although these data cannot be used in the context of time-series econometric modeling (for lack of year-to-year continuity in the data), they do provide a wealth of information, and all of this information seems to point in the same direction: Historically, the union presence has been very weak in smaller firms, and strong in larger firms, although not as strong as in medium-size firms.[70] Furthermore, it has been stronger in the "industrial triangle" of the Northwest and in central Italy, and it has been stronger in the metalworking and chemical sectors (Romagnoli and Rossi, 1980, pp. 45–73).

The 1956 Commissione Parlamentare d'Inchiesta sulle Condizioni dei Lavoratori in Italia conducted the first systematic surveys of working-class organizational resources inside the factories. The data collected by the Commissione Parlamentare showed that the presence of commissioni interne in Italian firms was quite uneven, by region, sector, and firm size. Firms located in the industrial North were more likely to have *commissioni interne* than were firms located in central Italy and, particularly, firms in the South (Commissione Parlamentare, 1958b, pp. 31–5, 42). Textile firms were less likely to have *commissioni interne* than were metalworking or chemical firms (1958b, p. 34). Of the 195 manufacturing firms inspected by the Commissione Parlamentare, 145 of them (74%) had *commissioni interne* and 50 (26%) did not. The presence of *commissioni interne* (CI) was linearly related to plant size: 48% of firms with 51–100 workers had them, as did 79% of those with 101–500 employees and 100% of firms with more than 500 employees (1958b, p. 40). "CI were nonexistent in smaller firms," one reads in the final report.[71]

Data collected by Confindustria provide even clearer evidence of the diffusion of *commissioni interne* by plant size (Table 4.7). During the 1950s and 1960s, Confindustria systematically collected from its member firms data on the yearly elections of workers to the *commissioni interne*. Even more informative than union-

Table 4.8. *Unionization by firm size in the Turin province in metalworking industry (1971)*

	Number of employees					
	10–50	50–100	100–250	250–500	500–1,000	>1,000
Employees	7.3[a]	22.8	29.3	32.9	25.8	12.0
Firms	9.5	50.0	71.3	84.7	100.0	100.0

[a]Percentage values.
Source: Cavallo Perin (1980).

membership figures (often artificially inflated by the unions, and known only to the unions), those yearly plant-level elections provided both unions and employers a barometer with which to gauge the working-class mood and power relationships within the firm. Table 4.7 shows only the data for 1969, in order to allow comparisons with the available Confindustria membership data for the same year (Table 4.6).[72] Although voting data are by plant and Confindustria membership data are by firm (one firm could own more than one plant), the data leave little doubt that *commissioni interne* were much more likely to be found in the larger industrial units.[73]

The *commissioni interne* were swept away by the workers' movement of the late 1960s and early 1970s, with the Rsa and Cdf coming to replace them. The distribution, by firm size, of these new forms of workers' representation follows a pattern similar to that of the *commissioni interne*. A one-time survey conducted by Confindustria in 1970 showed that the percentage of firms with a Cdf was directly proportional to firm size. Whereas 26.5% of firms with fewer than 200 employees had a Cdf, the figure rose to 62.8% for the large firms (with more than 1,000 employees).[74]

The presence of a form of workers' representation in the factory, whether *commissioni interne*, Rsa, or Cdf, was certainly a good indicator of the available organizational resources. Unlike the Rsa, however, neither the *commissioni interne* nor the Cdf were formally part of the union organizational structure.[75] Thus, data on *commissioni interne* and Cdf distributions may not really reflect the degree of union penetration into the industrial texture. To the extent that unions may provide connecting links between workers in different factories, data on the distributions of otherwise disconnected *commissioni interne* and Cdf may have overestimated the unions' organizational resources. To address this issue, let us look more specifically at the few available data on unionization by firm size.

According to a study by Cavallo Perin (1980) on unionization in the metalworking industry in the province of Turin in the years between 1964 and 1971, firms with less than fifty employees seem to have been impenetrable to the unions: unions had a foothold in only 9.5% of those firms and unionized only 7.3% of the work force (see Table 4.8).[76] The likelihood of a firm being unionized rapidly increased with firm size. Whereas the relationship between firm size and the

Table 4.9. *Organizational success and strike activity by firm size (1972)*

	Number of employees					
	1–19	20–49	50–99	100–249	250–499	500–999
A[a]	22.4[b]	62	83.8	94.3	100.0	100.0
B	22.9	58.7	57.6	64.2	68.2	83.3
C	25	66	94.4	92.9	100.0	100.0
D	70	57.1	31.8	20.7	8.3	0.0

[a] A, firms with a union organizational structure; B, work force unionized; C, firms unionized; D, firms with no strikes.
[b] Percentage values.
Source: Bergamaschi (1977b, pp. 256, 258, 262).

number of firms unionized was perfectly linear, that between firm size and the percentage of the work force unionized was curvilinear: In both small and large firms, the proportion of the work force unionized was much lower than that in midsize firms (100–500 workers). Surprisingly, only 12.0% of the work force in firms with more than 1,000 employees was unionized.[77]

A 1975 Federlombarda survey allows us to look closer into the world of the smaller firms (1–50 workers), which seem to have been particularly impenetrable to unions (Table 4.9). The survey confirmed that the presence of any form of union organizational structure at the plant level[78] was directly related to plant size. Unions always had an organizational structure in larger firms (employing more than 250 workers). Still in 1975, however, at the height of union growth, unions had an organizational foothold in only 22.4% of firms with 1–19 employees (Table 4.9). The proportion of firms with a union organizational structure increased in each successive class of firm sizes, but the largest jump occurred in going from the 1–19 class (22.4% with a union organizational presence) to the 20–49 class (62%).

The findings of significant organizational weakness in firms with less than 20 employees and of an increase in plant-level organizational resources above the 20-employee level were confirmed by survey data collected in 1975 for the Emilia Romagna region by the united metalworkers' union of Bologna, FLM (Capecchi, 1978). According to the Bologna FLM survey, there was a strong linear relationship between a firm's size and the likelihood of a union presence in the firm. Among firms with 1–19 workers, trade unions were present in only 6.2% (Table 4.10). Among firms in all other size classes, the union presence was quite strong, including firms in the 20–49 class (88.8% of the firms unionized). Bagnasco and Trigilia's research on labor relations in the area of Bassano, characterized by small-scale production, provided further information on the availability of organizational resources among small firms. In fact, unionization levels were quite low among smaller firms (16.9% among firms with fewer than 10 employees), but increased rapidly for larger firms (43% among firms with 10–50 employees; 60% among firms with more than 50 employees) (Bagnasco and Trigilia, 1984, p. 216).[79]

Table 4.10. *Distribution of Bolognese firms and employees by firm size and trade-union presence (1975)*

Employees	Total		Union presence		Percentages	
	Firms	Workers	Firms	Workers	Firms	Workers
1–19	8,869	30,209	550	3,000	6.2	9.9
20–49	260	9,078	231	6,521	88.9	71.8
50–99	112	8,177	107	7,748	95.5	94.8
100–249	85	12,543	77	11,478	90.6	91.5
250–499	19	6,577	17	5,958	89.5	90.6
500–999	10	7,398	10	7,398	100.0	100.0
>1,000	4	6,331	4	6,331	100.0	100.0
Total	9,359	80,313	996	48,434	10.6	60.3

Source: Capecchi (1978, p. 84).

Information on whether or not unions were present in small firms, however, does not tell the whole story. First, even when unions were present in smaller firms, the organizational structure tended to be very simple. Regalia's research on delegates showed that smaller firms had a lower degree of differentiation of functions (e.g., the presence of various commissions, *esecutivo*). Regalia found no differentiation in 82% of small firms versus only 3% for the large ones (Regalia, 1984a, p. 169).[80] Second, even when unions were present in smaller firms, they operated under difficult conditions. No one knew that better than the delegates themselves. According to the survey conducted by Regalia, delegates in smaller firms were more likely to view the organizational strength of the Cdf in their firms more negatively than were delegates in larger firms (Regalia, 1984a, p. 95).

A good indicator of the difficulties that delegates encountered in small firms was the lower rate of turnover among delegates, as well as the lower frequency of elections. According to a 1975 survey of 452 metalworking firms in the province of Bologna, the average number of renewals of the Cdf was linearly related to class size: minimum among firms with 1–49 workers (0.9), and maximum among firms with 500–999 workers (3.0).[81]

The lower figures for delegate turnover and elections in smaller firms do not mean a lack of democratic representation or of commitment to industrial democracy among workers in smaller firms. Rather, elections were not held because there was no one there to take the job of elected representative. For one thing, no real advantages accrued to workers in smaller firms if they did become delegates. The available evidence shows that it was larger firms that were more likely to grant permits for trade-union activities and to keep workers on the payroll while they were engaged in full-time trade-union activities.[82] Second, the cost of militancy typically was higher in smaller firms. The prevalence of face-to-face relationships tended to discourage direct confrontation, but when confrontations occurred, they were likely to be more personal and passionate. As a Federmeccanica survey in 1984 showed, in 72% of the smaller firms (fewer than 100 employees), employers themselves carried out the labor-relations functions (Mortillaro, 1986, p. 194). In all larger firms, those functions were delegated, typically to managers. Small employers often took confrontations with labor as personal affronts. No wonder that small employers so strongly resisted the unionization drive of the early 1970s. One such employer wistfully recounted that "We kept unions out for two years, but then we had to give in because we were reported for anti-union practices" (quoted in Martinelli, 1978, p. 60). To gain that end, employers would use almost any means: providing individual incentives to keep workers divided, transferring and laying off radical workers, granting small concessions before a union could organize workers to demand them, making the lives of labor activists miserable to the point of forcing them to resign, as employers' own data show (Associazione Industriale Lombarda, 1983, pp. 47, 53–4).

Not only may data on the presence of union organizational structures inside the factories have overestimated the extent of workers' real power, particularly for smaller firms, but also unionization data were not without problems. Aggregate data do not provide a clear picture of the organizational resources available within a firm. To shed some light on this problem, let us go back to Cavallo Perin's data in Table 4.8 (p. 129): 7.3% of the work force in smaller firms (10–50 workers) was unionized and 9.5% of the firms had at least some union members. That gives a total of 2,345 unionized workers in 144 firms, for an average of 16 unionized workers per firm. As for the other size classes, we have an average of 31 workers unionized in each firm in the 50–100 class, 62 workers in the 100–250 class, 127 in the 250–500, 191 in the 500–1,000 class, and 545 workers in each of the 43 firms with more than 1,000 workers each. If for each class we take the midpoint value (e.g., 75 for the class 50–100), we can then compute the average unionization rate for each size class: 53% (16 workers divided by an average firm size of 30, the midpoint of the 10–50 class), 41.3%, 35.4%, 33.9%, 25.5%. For the largest 43 firms employing more than 1,000 workers, we do not have an upper bound, and so we cannot compute a midsize value. But we do know from Cavallo Perin that the average firm size was 4,543 workers. Furthermore, we know that the overall unionization for FIAT (which alone accounted for 77.2% of total employment in the largest category) was 8.4% and that for Olivetti (which accounted for another 20% of employment) was 23.3%. We also know that the average unionization rate in the largest (>1,000) class, without Fiat and Olivetti, was 24.7%. Unfortunately, Cavallo Perin did not provide the number of Fiat and Olivetti productive units employing more than 1,000 workers, and so we cannot know exactly the average unionization rate in the larger firms. However, we can safely assume that it was a number somewhere between 8.4% and 24.7%.

What this long story tells us is that there appears to have been a negative linear relationship between firm size and the percentage of the total work force unionized: Smaller firms were much less likely to be unionized than larger ones (which always were unionized), but when they were unionized, that unionization tended to

Table 4.11. *Plant-level characteristics of union structures and collective action mobilization by firm size (%)*

	Number of employees				
	1–50	50–250	250–500	500–1,000	>1,000
Weak	79.1	55.9	16.7	0.0	33.3
Strong	20.9	44.1	83.3	100.0	66.7
Militant	31.1	40.5	50.0	50.0	28.6
Nonmilitant	68.9	59.5	50.0	50.0	71.4
Mobilizing	9.2	22.4	36.4	28.6	50.0
Nonmobilizing	90.8	77.6	63.6	71.4	50.0

Source: Biagi (1976, pp. 397, 399).

encompass a much higher proportion of the work force (more than 50%, compared with 20% or lower).[83] The scanty empirical evidence available supports this finding. Beccalli (1971), in a seminal study of the relationship between organization and strike activity in Italy, found that in small firms, unionization occurs in "islands": In many small firms, the unions are virtually nonexistent (which never occurs in the large firms), but where they exist, they tend to unionize a much higher proportion of the work force. The 1983 Assolombarda survey confirmed that smaller firms tended to have much higher percentages of workers unionized than larger firms (even higher than 90%, and, never below 50%).[84] Because workers would be more vulnerable to employers' retaliatory actions, unionization in smaller firms tended to be an all-or-none proposition.

In conclusion, both data on the type of union organizational presence (e.g., *commissioni interne*, Cdf, Rsa) and data on the extent of unionization (either as number of firms unionized or as percentage of work force unionized) often do not readily reveal the reality of workers' plant-level organizational strength and tend to distort the extent of union penetration, particularly for smaller firms.

Given that uneven distribution of organizational resources, it is perhaps no surprise that, as we saw in Chapter 3, smaller firms seldom suffered strikes (or, for that matter, that certain economic sectors and areas seldom had strikes). The Federlombarda data in Table 4.9 clearly show the close connection between the availability of organizational resources and strike activity. But there is empirical evidence that links, even more directly, the availability of organizational resources at the plant level and workers' ability to mount collective actions. Field research directed by Treu (1975, 1976a) on the proceedings of labor courts based on the 1970 Workers' Charter showed that unions were very weak in smaller settings (among firms with 1–50 workers, 79.1% had "weak" unions, and 20.9% had "strong" unions) (Table 4.11).[85] Union strength translates directly into workers' ability to mount collective actions for various reasons, even for reasons related to a firm's involvement in labor-court proceedings. In most firms employing fewer than 50 workers, labor-court proceedings occurred without provoking any form of collective mobilization by the workers (90.8% of small firms did not mobilize). Treu's data also confirm the puzzling behavior in the very largest firms *(paradox of large firms)* where unions were not as strong and workers were not as militant as in midsize firms.

Furthermore, the uneven distribution of organizational resources among the very small and very large firms can perhaps help explain the *paradox of strike size*: a handful of large strikes, larger than even the work forces of the largest plants, and a host of small strikes, smaller than the average work-force size in the plants that most typically strike (for this paradox, see Section 3.4.4. in Chapter 3, p. 84). The evidence discussed here would seem to account for this second aspect of the paradox: When unions called a strike in the larger firms, they could count on active support from only a minority of the work force. When coupled with the historical internal divisions of Italian unions along political lines, the picture that emerges is that workers in the vast majority of small firms did not strike, and in the larger firms, only a fraction of the work force did, bringing the average strike size below the average work-force size in large firms. Thus, the lower unionization rates in the largest firms can explain the lower levels of conflict in those firms, as borne out by several surveys. The explanation, however, begs the question of why unions were not able to organize more workers in the largest firms, which would seem to be the easiest to organize.

The wealth of empirical evidence available on the diffusion of workers' representative structures and on unionization rates (in terms of both the number of firms unionized and the percentage of the total work force unionized) leaves no doubt about their uneven distribution by economic sector, territory, and firm size. The Italian working class had stronger organizational resources in the "industrial triangle" of the Northwest and in central Italy, in the metalworking and chemical sectors, and in larger firms. Elsewhere, the Italian working class had fewer organizational resources. With particular emphasis on firm size, the different schemes used to classify firms' work forces into size groups (1–10, 1–20, 1–50, 10–50, 40–100, etc.) make comparability across studies difficult. Furthermore, the unions' rates of success in gaining a foothold in firms of various sizes have fluctuated at different times. Nevertheless, the available evidence shows that, by and large, unions were kept out of the smaller firms. In particular, unions never made significant inroads in firms employing fewer than 20–40 workers.

The available evidence also shows that the presence of an organizational structure at the plant level is positively related to the workers' ability to mount collective actions: Organizational resources are indispensable to collective action, just as resource-mobilization theories of collective action would argue. However, given that smaller firms were evenly dispersed among larger firms in the same territory, then the structural weakness of the trade unions in the smaller firms could be counteracted by relative strength in nearby large firms (Bagnasco and Trigilia, 1984, pp. 63–4). But such dispersion only partially obtains. Clustering of smaller firms seems to be a distinct characteristic of the industrial infrastructure of certain socioeconomic areas. Economic growth in such regions as Veneto, Emilia

Romagna, Tuscany, and, more generally, of the areas of Bagnasco's *Terza Italia*, is based on a diffused process of small-scale industrial production. Under these conditions, it would seem that the structural organizational weakness of smaller firms should translate into generalized weakness in a whole area. Yet that is not the case. In fact, some of these regions of small-scale production (e.g., Emilia Romagna, Tuscany) are also the most highly unionized in Italy. How can we explain yet another paradox *(paradox of small-scale production regions)*?

4.9. *AIUTATI CHE IL CIEL T'AIUTA*:[86] THE MARXIST APPROACH TO ORGANIZATION

The empirical and historical analyses in this chapter have shown that during the 1950s the Italian labor movement was deeply divided into opposing camps. CGIL, on the one hand, and CISL and UIL, on the other, organized workers according to different ideological principles: class unionism and trade unionism. Class unionism had a long tradition in the Italian labor movement. After the collapse of the Fascist regime, CGIL's class unionism came to represent the main organizational force, with almost twice as many members as CISL. Needless to say, class unionism had its roots in the Marxist tradition. How did that tradition approach the problem of organization?

It has often been argued that Marx failed to understand the importance of working-class organization; that he believed that one day the contradictions within capitalism (i.e., the concentration of capital, the socialization of labor) would, by themselves, bring on the revolution. Although it is true that Marx never theorized extensively about the process involved in creating a revolutionary class, certainly he did not believe that it would arise by itself, or he would not have spent his life in revolutionary practice as a union and party organizer, pamphleteer, journalist, and political commentator. The volume edited by Lapides (1987) that collects the writings of Marx and Engels on trade unions clearly illustrates that commitment.

Whereas there is little doubt that Marx was correct that "All serious success of the proletariat depends upon an organisation" (Lapides, 1987, p. 67), a question remains: What kind of organization did Marx envision? In his early writing, Marx insisted that the working class had to be organized first, into national unions and then into international unions (Lapides, 1987, pp. 61, 67). In his later writings, however, Marx had become increasingly pessimistic about the revolutionary possibilities of trade-union activity alone; he began to stress the need for a political organization of the class. The imperative for general political action stemmed from the fact that "in its merely economic action capital is the stronger side" (Marx, in Lapides, 1987, p. 94). Thus, for Marx, organization implied organization in both the economic and political realms:

In a political struggle of class against class, organisation is the most important weapon.... At the side of, or above, the unions of special trades there must spring up a general union, a political organisation of the working class as a whole. (Lapides, 1987, pp. 128–9)

Despite Marx's growing awareness of the limits of trade union actions, he vehemently rejected the notion that one should avoid economic struggles so as not to muddle the purity of the ultimate revolutionary cause.[87] Throughout his life, Marx was well aware that "the history of these Unions is a long series of defeats, interrupted by a few isolated victories" (Marx, in Lapides, 1987, p. 5). Twenty-six years later, he still wrote that

> The trade unions of this country [England] have now for nearly sixty years fought against [the law of wages] – with what result? Have they succeeded . . . ? [No. But] far be it from us to say that trades unions are of no use because they have not done that. On the contrary. . . . (Lapides, 1987, pp. 104–5)

Marx believed that economic struggles would prepare the terrain for political struggles. The political movement of the class would arise out of the separate economic movements (Marx, in Lapides, 1987, p. 113). Organization would be a prerequisite for those movements, but the movements, in turn, would help to develop the organization (Marx, in Lapides, 1987, p. 114).

Marx's insistence on working-class organization found an amplified echo in the writings of his twentieth-century followers such as Lenin, Luxemburg, Kautsky, Lukacs, and Gramsci.[88] But those authors shared the increasing pessimism of Marx and Engels about reliance solely on economic class organizations. In the pamphlet *What Is to Be Done?* Lenin insisted that on their own, workers could never achieve revolutionary consciousness (Lenin, 1989, p. 98):

> The history of all countries shows that the working class exclusively by its own effort is able to develop only trade-union consciousness, i.e., the conviction that it is necessary to combine in unions, fight the employers, and strive to compel the government to pass necessary labour legislation, etc.[89]

Revolutionary consciousness would have to be "brought from without" via a revolutionary party. "The normal activities of trade unions as such pose no threat to the stability of the capitalist order" (quoted in Hyman, 1971, p. 12). For Gramsci (1954, p. 40) "Socialist parties are increasingly taking on a revolutionary and internationalist profile; trade unions, on the other hand, tend to incarnate the theory (!) and the tactic of reformist opportunism . . ." Even Rosa Luxemburg was quite skeptical about the revolutionary role of the unions:

> The trade union leaders, constantly absorbed in economic guerrilla war whose plausible task it is to make the workers place the highest value on the smallest economic achievement, every increase in wages and shortening of the working day, gradually lose the power of seeing the larger connections and of taking a survey of the whole position. (Luxemburg, 1971, p. 87).

For Trotsky (quoted in Clarke and Clements 1977, p. 77), "The trade union bureaucracy had definitely become a part of the capitalist apparatus, economic and governmental."[90] Gramsci (1954, p. 41, 45) similarly wrote:

Trade union activity is absolutely incapable of overcoming, it its own sphere and with its own means, capitalist society; it is absolutely incapable of emancipating the proletarian ... trade unionism is nothing but a form of capitalist society, not a potential means of transcending capitalist society.

Thus, unions, as working-class organizations, suffer from the ambiguity of being simultaneously institutions that can gain power *for* the working class and institutions that can exercise power *over* the working class (Offe and Wiesenthal, 1980, p. 99; see also Mann, 1973). As a consequence, Lenin, Lukacs, and Gramsci more fully theorized the relationship between economic (trade-union) organization and political (party) organization of the working class that Marx had only briefly discussed. Lenin, in particular, added to that tradition a theory of the "vanguard party" as the only way to achieve revolutionary goals. Nonetheless, one thing is clear: From Marx onward, the entire classical Marxist tradition has insisted on the central role of organization in working class mobilization. The difference lies not in opinions on whether or not an organization is necessary, but rather on what the role of the latter is to be (e.g., economic or political).[91]

The Marxist theory of organization is not a stand-alone. It is intimately linked to the Marxist economic theory. In fact, not only Marx but also Lenin, Trotsky, Luxemburg, and Kautsky were acutely aware that immiseration and economic hardship were powerful incentives for working-class mobilization. Yet, in their opinion, immiseration by itself is not sufficient to produce effective (read "revolutionary") mobilization. For the latter to occur, there must be a sufficient pool of suitable resources at the disposal of the working class, a view that Marxists share with resource-mobilization theory. The most important resource in this respect is organization. Thus, economic hardship is a necessary but not sufficient condition for working-class mobilization. An additional factor is required, namely, organizational capacity. What is more, because capitalism is prone to booms and busts, Marxists can plan strategies of collective action. While waiting for the next economic crisis, they can prepare to take full advantage of the favorable historical conditions by building an organization. As Rosa Luxemburg (1971, pp. 68–9) wrote:

The Social Democrats are the most enlightened, most class-conscious vanguard of the proletariat. They cannot and dare not wait, in a fatalist fashion, with folded arms for the advent of the "revolutionary situation," to wait for that which in every spontaneous peoples' movement, falls from the clouds. On the contrary, they must now, as always, hasten the development of things and endeavor to accelerate events.

Thus, Marxist theory shares with resource-mobilization theories an emphasis on organization, and with economic-hardship theories an emphasis on immiseration and economic hardship as causes of mobilization. But here lies the difference between the Durkheimian and Marxist approaches to economic hardship. In the Durkheimian view, economic hardship and immiseration function as a psychological mechanism that triggers social unrest. In the Marxist view, the claims about the effects of immiseration are embedded in a theory of economic crisis that attempts to explain the cyclical tendency within capitalism toward boom and bust. In doing so, Marxists not only claim to predict an important effect of immiseration – working-class mobilization – but also suggest that capitalism has structural tendencies toward periodic economic crises. Having carried out adequate organization, one can then take advantage of these favorable historical conjunctures for revolutionary purposes.

For Marxists, working-class organization means both economic organization and political organization of the class. True to that dogma, while CGIL organized Italian workers in the economic arena, its "twin" political party, the Italian Communist Party (PCI), organized workers in the political arena. Given the strong empirical relationship between strikes and the "economic wing" of the working class, did that relationship similarly characterize the "political wing?" What was the relationship between strikes and the PCI, the hegemonic party on the left in Italy, the second largest party (whose share of the electoral vote had ranged from 20% to more than 30%), and the largest Communist Party in the West? At the polls, in the period 1950–78, the PCI improved its share of the vote with every new election (Farneti, 1983, p. 183). That positive trend in the political fortunes of the Italian working class may provide some insight into the long-term positive trends for strike indicators highlighted in Chapter 1. But the lack of temporal variability in the electoral trends renders this political indicator of PCI strength ill-suited to be related to the cyclical components of strike data. There is another indicator of PCI strength that is much more appropriate for this: the number of party members (Barbagli and Corbetta, 1978; Farneti, 1983, p. 183).

Figure 4.5 underscores the close relationship between the economic and political wings of the working class. The temporal contour for PCI membership follows very closely that for CGIL membership (Figure 4.2, p. 111) and *commissioni interne* electoral results (Figure 4.3, p. 112). These results basically confirm the close relationship among strike activity, unionization, and political support for left-wing parties, in terms of membership. It is indeed this close relationship that qualifies strike activity as a form of working-class political action (Shorter and Tilly, 1974, p. 343).[92]

Other characteristics highlight the close relationship between the economic and the political in the world of the Italian working class. The institutional and legal separation between economic struggles and political struggles that seems to be a general characteristic of bourgeois democracies was never achieved in Italy, at least not to the extent we see in other national experiences.[93]

First, political strikes have never been explicitly prohibited by Italian law.[94] As a consequence, strikes often have occurred over purely political issues: the Vietnam war, police repression, government economic policies, and many others. Typically, political strikes have been large-scale, national displays of working-class strength. But political strikes also have occurred "spontaneously" at the shop level. In either

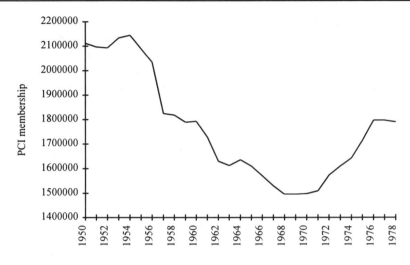

Figure 4.5. *Plot of PCI membership*

case, they often have been symbolic displays, varying in duration from only a few minutes to a few hours.

Second, the "primacy of politics" in Italy has been clearly highlighted by surveys of union personnel. A survey conducted in December 1972–January 1973 among Lombardy metalworking-union cadres found that only 29.7% of the respondents were not members of some party (Cella, 1973, pp. 24–8). Party membership often preceded union membership, particularly for the Communist metalworking union, FIOM (75.7%). A similar survey conducted by CGIL among the delegates to territorial union congresses in Lombardy showed that a high percentage of the delegates (73%) belonged to a political party. Furthermore, party membership had preceded or coincided with union membership for well over two-thirds of those delegates (Baccalini et al., 1981).[95] Extensive research on the CGIL union by Biagioni, Palmieri, and Pipan (1980) showed that in 1977, of the 29,810 members of the *comitati direttivi*,[96] only 18% did not declare any party affiliation.[97] The figure was even lower (6%) for the 14,570 members of the *consigli generali*.[98] Of the full-time personnel in both the vertical and horizontal structures, 69.7% belonged to the Italian Communist Party and 25.7% to the Italian Socialist Party, with a negligible 1% unaffiliated (Biagioni et al., 1980, p. 250). The effects of the close connection between the economic and political wings of the labor movement were not limited to union officers; both the 1971 and 1980 Isvet surveys of workers' attitudes showed that party membership and union membership went hand in hand for many workers (De Masi and Fevola, 1974a; De Masi et al., 1985).

Third, until 1969, union leaders were allowed to hold positions in political parties and also run for election to parliamentary positions, and many did (Bechelloni, 1968; Morisi and Vacante, 1981; CESOS-CISL and IRES-CGIL, 1982, 1984, 1986).[99] The parliamentary experience of trade-union leaders in the

1950s and 1960s must be evaluated in the context of a widespread conception of labor unions as "transmission belts" between a political-party vanguard and its base in the rank-and-file workers.[100] Political parties relied on labor unions to effect rapid mobilization around the political themes that were centrally debated. Trade unions, in exchange, found in ideologically allied parties ("twin parties," in the Italian expression) the support that compensated for their structural weakness inside the factories (Pizzorno, 1973). That support was not only legislative but also organizational and financial (Feltrin, 1991, p. 341).

Finally, regarding the few prominent union leaders who became members of Parliament at one point or another during their careers, that achievement was the result of a political career within the party, rather than a career within the union. Leadership positions in the union were not sufficient qualifications to access Parliament. In fact, a good deal of the leadership for both CGIL and CISL was supplied directly by the parties (the Italian Communist Party and the Christian Democrat Party, respectively) (Ferrante, 1982, p. 673; Feltrin, 1991, p. 339). That practice of personnel exchange (mostly from the party to the union) declined at the national level during the 1960s as a result of the institutionalization of a career ladder internal to union organizations (Feltrin, 1991, p. 340). Yet the practice was still quite widespread at the local level (Ferrante, 1982, p. 674). Furthermore, even in 1977, around 5% of CGIL personnel came from the ranks of the party (15% for adjunct secretaries general) (Biagioni et al., 1980, p. 330).

In conclusion, the economic and political organizational wings of the working class seem to go hand in hand over time. Furthermore, both organizational assets seem to fluctuate in close coordination with the long-term fluctuations in strike indicators. In particular, in the 1970s all three indicators – union (CGIL), party (PCI), and strikes – were on the increase. Did the working class translate the mobilization movement after the 1969 *autunno caldo* into organizational strength? Was the increased organizational strength of labor responsible for the increased rigidity of the labor market? We saw in Chapter 2 that the traditional negative relationship between unemployment and strike frequency hypothesized by the Ashenfelter and Johnson model broke down in the 1970s. Strikes kept increasing in the face of rising unemployment *(paradox of the 1970s)*. Was that the result of the unions' increased organizational strength? How did the unions expend that strength, by bargaining with employers in the economic market or by bargaining with the state in the political market? The answers to some questions in this chapter have raised many further questions. The flood of light shed on some aspects of Italian strikes (economic and organizational) seems to have faintly illuminated other aspects as well (e.g., institutional, political). I will address those aspects next.

4.10. FITTING MORE PIECES TO THE PUZZLE

The Durkheimian theories of collective action that prevailed in the North American social sciences during the 1950s and 1960s viewed collective action as the result of social disintegration, economic hardship, and relative deprivation. Arguing against that paradigm, resource-mobilization theories of the late 1960s and 1970s claimed that mobilization and collective action were the result of organization. In strike research, mobilization and organization have been measured by a strike indicator (typically, the number of strikers) and unionization. Unfortunately, on the basis of the statistical work presented in this chapter, it appears that major increases in unionization follow, rather than precede, outbursts of industrial conflict.

The causal sequence from strike activity to unionization, from mobilization to organization, may seem to put resource-mobilization theories in jeopardy. After all, these theories claim that organization is the basis for mobilization, rather than the other way around. Against that shortsighted view of temporal causality, we have seen that although increases in unionization do follow escalations in strike activity, higher levels of unionization make mobilization easier the next time around. Furthermore, through the use of a great deal of microlevel data, we have seen that small plants are, by and large, outside of union control. Even in the 1970s and early 1980s, at the height of unions' organizational successes, workers in smaller firms (1–50 employees) had weak organizational resources inside the factories. Workers in firms with 1–20 employees were particularly underorganized. That lack of organizational resources went hand in hand with the serious difficulties encountered in trying to mount collective actions in small firms, particularly offensive collective actions.

There are good reasons that smaller firms should be more difficult to unionize than larger firms. On the one hand, organizing smaller firms is much more time-consuming than organizing larger ones. "Ten firms with twenty employees each pose problems ten times bigger than a single firm with 200 employees" (Centro Studi Federlibro, 1974, p. 84). Even after small firms are organized, it is more difficult and more costly to maintain regular contact with them (Amoretti, 1981).[101] Even in the 1970s, at the peak of union expansion in Italy, outside union representatives rarely participated in the life of the small firm.[102] As a consequence, workers in smaller firms often felt abandoned. As a union representative put it, "The problems arise when trade-union representatives cannot, humanly, intervene in all firms; and often workers get mad at us . . . when we tell them that we cannot be present in the firm during bargaining" (Moni, 1980). Such feelings of abandonment can lead to wholesale rejection of unions. As a 1981–82 Assolombarda survey showed, once out of a small firm, it is almost impossible for a union to get back in (Associazione Industriale Lombarda, 1983).

That unions should encounter more difficulties in organizing smaller firms is hardly a surprise. Somewhat surprising, on the other hand, is the finding that unions were stronger in midsize firms, rather than in larger firms. It would seem to make sense that the same factors that make it difficult to unionize smaller firms should make it easy to unionize larger ones. Furthermore, on the basis of the arguments reviewed in Chapter 3 on the relationship between workers' militancy and plant size, we would have expected a positive, linear relationship between plant size and unionization. Yet both the Isvet data on workers' participation in strikes (see Table 3.15, p. 87) and Confindustria's data on absenteeism (see Table 3.16, p. 88) showed an unexplained tendency toward lower strike propensities in the largest firms. The unionization data discussed in this chapter have added further evidence on this *paradox of large firms*, without, however, providing an explanation.

The analysis of organizational resources has helped to elucidate a solution for the *paradox of strike size*. The large majority of Italian strikes have been small, but not because Italian plants are small. After all, small plants tended not to suffer strikes. Strikes were small even in the larger plants, and that was because the organization of labor traditionally had been weak at the point of production and had been divided among politically competing unions. Thus, when CGIL would call a strike, CISL and UIL would abstain (or actively campaign against the strike). When CISL would call a strike, CGIL would ask its members to boycott the strike in the hope of embarrassing its rival. But if strikes generally were small, a handful of them were exceptionally large. Again, the organization of Italian labor provides an explanation: Weakness in terms of organizational resources in the plants and the "class" character of Italian unions had forced the unions into close relationships with their supporting political parties. The close connection between economic and political action translated into a handful of mass displays of working-class solidarity (i.e., large strike sizes). Furthermore, the unions' lack of financial resources explains yet another characteristic of Italian strikes: their brevity.

The use of the strike as a political weapon would certainly seem to go a long way in providing an explanation for the large sizes of some Italian strikes. And there is certainly plenty of evidence on the continuous political involvement of the unions throughout the postwar period. Except for one problem: political strikes were never included in the counts of official strike statistics (and only after 1975 were they recorded separately; see Appendix on data). Thus, if some strikes were large it was not because those were political, "demonstrative" strikes. I am afraid we still do not have a full solution for the *paradox of strike size*.

The empirical results also help to pin down other unexplained differences in the behavior among the number of strikes, strikers, and hours lost within econometric models. In Chapters 2 and 3, we saw that strike activity was strongly related to the business cycle, even in the Italian context. In this chapter, we have seen that there was a strong relationship between strike activity and organization, as measured by various indicators (in particular, unionization). However, the relationships between economic factors and strike activity were not equally strong for all strike indicators; strike frequency seems to have been more sensitive to the upswings and downswings of the business cycle. Similarly, organization was more strongly related to strike size.

The historical and empirical evidence presented in this chapter leaves no doubt about who wins in the contest between Durkheimian theories of collective action and resource-mobilization theories. However, resource-mobilization theories are not alone in underscoring the effects of organization on mobilization and collective action. Marxist thinkers had already emphasized the importance of organization. Thus, Marxist economic theory shares with bargaining theories of strikes an emphasis on the positive short-term relationship between cyclical economic prosperity and strike activity, and it shares with Durkheimian theories of collective action an emphasis on a positive long-term relationship between economic hardship and class conflict, particularly revolutionary conflict. Contrary to Durkheimian theories of economic hardship, however, Marxists suggest that economic hardship is a result of the structural tendencies of capitalism toward periodic crises. For Marx, Lenin, Trotsky, Luxemburg and Kautsky, economic crises and immiseration should provide opportunities for mobilization and revolutionary actions when capitalism can no longer afford to buy consensus and as moral outrage inflames the spirits of the lower classes. Contrary to traditional Marxist thinking, my analyses of the organization of Italian capitalism have pointed out that the capitalist class is fragmented among different interests, particularly small versus large capitalists, financial versus manufacturing capitalists, and private versus public capitalists.

In conclusion, the work reported in this chapter has added a few more missing pieces to the puzzle; it has explained some of the differences in behavior among the numbers of strikes, strikers, and hours lost. Notwithstanding, I have only a partial solution for the *paradox of strike size* and no solution for the *paradox of the 1970s* or the *paradox of the 1962 and 1966 strike shapes*. Neither have I answered a question raised in Chapter 2: Why is it that Italian labor is more vulnerable to unfavorable labor-market conditions than purely economic strike models would predict, or, conversely, why is it that when times are good, Italian labor is much more militant than economic considerations alone would warrant (the *paradox of the génie d'un peuple*)? The sharp decreases in the levels of conflict revealed by the time plots of strike indicators (see Figures 1.3, 1.4, and 1.5, pp. 4–5) and by the strike shapes (Figure 1.6, p. 8) between 1954 and 1958 seem to characterize the levels of unionization as well, particularly for the more militant, Communist CGIL. Was the decrease in the level of conflict "caused" by the weakening of organizational strength? Or was it the other way around, with organizational decline causing the reduction in conflict? But either way, we are still left with no answer to our question. Alternatively, were there other factors that caused the decline of both conflict and organization? For all the answers that this chapter has provided, there are still many questions that remain unanswered.

5

The structure of collective bargaining

Collective bargaining is the great social invention that has institutionalized industrial conflict. In much the same way as the electoral process and majority rule have institutionalized political conflict in a democracy, collective bargaining has created a stable means for resolving industrial conflict.

Dubin (1954, p. 47)

Collective bargaining provides one of the more important bulwarks for the preservation of the private-enterprise system. . . . Collective bargaining is an institution which bolsters the existing economic order. . . . A union movement which emphasizes collective bargaining is inevitably a conservative movement, for collective bargaining is inseparable from private enterprise.

Harbison (1954, pp. 274, 277, 278)

5.1. UNANSWERED QUESTIONS

In Chapters 2 and 3 we saw that economic models of strikes can explain the nonperiodic, medium-term fluctuations in strike activity. In Italy, however, strike activity also shows distinct periodic, two- to three-year cycles. Furthermore, the cycles in numbers of strikes and strikers peak at different times: the cycle in the number of strikers peaks approximately one year earlier than the cycle in the number of strikes.

The evidence confirming the existence of a three-year periodic cycle has been accumulating over the preceding three chapters. The exploratory data analyses summarized in Chapter 1 revealed the basic pattern (Franzosi, 1980). The empirical testing of the Ashenfelter and Johnson model in Chapter 2 showed the existence of a three-year lag structure in real wages, thus pointing to a relationship between a three-year strike cycle and a three-year wage cycle. Traces of this pattern remained unexplained in the residuals obtained from the econometric estimates of the Ashenfelter and Johnson model. The spectral results reported in Chapter 3 brought out the existence of a negative relationship between strikes and production at a three-year interval.

What explains the three-year periodic cycle in strikes? Why does a three-year cycle also characterize both the wage and production series? After all, according to Granger and Newbold (1977, p. 33), there is no empirical evidence that modern macroeconomic series contain cyclical components of a periodic nature, other than the seasonal ones. If they do, it must be for extraeconomic, institutional reasons.

In this chapter, I will try to answer those questions. Following Granger and Newbold's suggestion about the institutional nature of periodic cycles in macroeconomic series, I will focus on the Italian system of industrial relations and, more specifically, on the structure of collective bargaining. Could the periodic renewal of collective agreements explain the three-year cycle in strike indicators? But then why should the curve for the number of strikes peak one year later than the curve for the number of strikers?

5.2. COLLECTIVE BARGAINING IN POSTWAR ITALY: A BRIEF HISTORICAL OVERVIEW

In the 1950s, the Italian system of collective bargaining was highly centralized. The three main confederations of labor (CGIL, CISL, UIL) typically sat together at the negotiating table facing a highly centralized employer association (Confindustria).[1] Negotiations were conducted at the national level, across different occupational categories and industrial sectors.[2] Negotiations at lower levels (particularly the plant level) were excluded or reduced to a minimum. At the national, industrywide level, unions and employers signed agreements for all the workers in a specific sector (e.g., metal, textile, chemical workers). Typically, those agreements had a two- to three-year duration.[3] In the political and economic climate of the 1950s, highly unfavorable to workers, agreements would not be renewed at the time of expiration, but only after delays, sometimes of several years. Between 1949 and 1954, the employers and their associations (e.g., Confindustria) became increasingly hostile to plant-level bargaining. Oddly enough, on this issue, the employers found themselves on the same side of the Communist CGIL union, albeit for opposite reasons.

The employers rejected plant-level bargaining for fear that it would lead to high levels of conflict and that it would cut too deeply into profits (Mattina, 1991, pp. 100–1). In particular, the large number of small-scale employers belonging to Confindustria pushed for centralized bargaining. Small firms had never had the experience or the expertise to deal with the legal implications of plant-level bargaining. The available survey research shows that as late as the 1970s, most bargaining activity in smaller firms was informal and verbal, the result of the employers' direct involvement in the bargaining process. Bargaining took place directly on the shop floor or in the employer's office. When plant-level bargaining became more formalized, small employers tended to shift the site to the headquarters of the employers' association, for technical and legal support. Furthermore, small employers rejected plant-level bargaining for fear that it would lead to higher wages. Indeed, the available evidence suggests that owners of smaller firms (1–9 employees) kept very close to the minimum wage increases set in the national contracts, whereas wages varied considerably in larger firms (Brusco, 1975, p. 15).

CGIL rejected plant-level bargaining, for fear that it would lead to an exclusive focus on bread-and-butter concerns, to a decrease in class spirit, and to divisions within the working class along corporatist, particularistic lines (Gallessi, 1981, p. 21). In his intervention at CGIL's second national congress in 1949, Luciano Lama, the future secretary general of CGIL, asserted that "We are against the institution of plant-level trade unions . . . because this solution can mean and does mean in many cases the degeneration of the unitary trade union in a plant-level, corporatist organization" (quoted in Accornero, 1974, p. 91). Again in 1954, "CGIL . . . stresses its aversion to any type of plant-level unions that [would] divide workers and lead to a degeneration of the labor movement" (Foa, 1975, p. 103). Unfortunately, that strategy left employers with a great deal of room for implementing paternalistic policies. Centralized, industrywide bargaining or, worse yet, economywide bargaining, by its very nature, cannot provide more than a minimum low common denominator (for wage increases) for all firms in one sector (or in the economy as a whole). It must strive to keep in business even the marginal firms, in marginal sectors.[4] Paradoxically, by rejecting plant-level union representation and bargaining, which, CGIL believed, would lead to internal divisions among workers according to the market mechanisms of firm and sector profitability, CGIL gave employers a free hand to promote just such divisions (Accornero, 1974, p. 92). And employers did precisely that, but on the basis of their own standards. Those standards were hardly sympathetic to the Left. In many plants, wage increases, productivity bonuses, and promotions were doled out in a manner highly discriminatory against CGIL or Communist workers.

The end result of employers' use of the carrot and the stick was a highly demoralized, highly fragmented working class in which workers individually reaped the benefits or paid the price for their political beliefs, a pattern that continued for most of the 1950s and for a good part of the 1960s. According to a Sit-Siemens worker, "It was the company that handed out the bonus; it wasn't bargained. They gave it out at Christmas – to some workers 2,000 lire, to some 5,000, to some 20,000. It was the bonus of discord" (quoted in Regalia, 1975b, p. 38). Often, when workers successfully struck for concessions, the most paternalistic companies would unilaterally grant benefits without signing any agreement, thus preserving the principle of managerial prerogatives (Abbatecola, 1974, p. 126). Companies often made concessions "anticipating" the provisions to be signed in the national, industrywide contracts. Thus, at Frau, a furniture manufacturing company, (1) in 1963, the company introduced the 44-hour workweek, as later won by workers in their national contract; (2) in 1967, the company anticipated the reduction of the workweek to 40 hours; (3) in 1970, it anticipated a production bonus (Masiero, 1974, p. 316). As Mr. Borghi, the owner of Ignis, a manufacturer of large household appliances, put it to the workers' representatives: "What is it that you want? A five-per-cent increase? Fine, here it is. And if the unions obtain more with the national agreement, I'll give you the difference. And if they obtain less, you keep the five per cent and we go on" (quoted in Santi, 1974, p. 131).

Contrary to CGIL, CISL accepted the basic premise of bread-and-butter unions ("What is good for General Motors is good for the country"). CISL saw its union role as one of guaranteeing profits while demanding wages. Unions should go after profit wherever profit could be found (a strategy that Mann, 1973, called "aggressive economism"). In CISL analysis, the best way to achieve that goal was through "union organizations located both inside and outside the plants" (Foa, 1975, p. 102) and through both centralized, national bargaining and decentralized, plant-level bargaining:

National, intercategory and category bargaining remains a valid instrument to pursue the equilibrium between wages and productivity increases at the intercategory and category levels; [but] it [also] requires the introduction and development of a system of plant-level agreements, integrative of the national agreements. (Foa, 1975, pp. 100–1)

In 1955, CGIL, for the first time, lost in the elections for the *commissioni interne* at Fiat, the largest Italian factory, an old symbol of a highly militant working class. The news came as a shock. A poster showing the red flag being lowered at Fiat appeared all over Italy (Pugno and Garavini, 1974, p. 15). CGIL defeats in other factories soon followed, across the country (see the plot of the electoral results for the CGIL *commissioni interne*, Figure 4.3, p. 112). We saw how those losses dramatically affected CGIL membership (see Figure 4.2, p. 111). In the wake of that defeat, CGIL began a slow process of self-criticism (Sclavi, 1971). The debate centered on an old question: Which is the most appropriate bargaining level for a class union? Is it the national, interconfederal level, involving several economic sectors (e.g., industry as a whole) or the category level (e.g., metal-working, textiles, chemicals)? Or is it the branch level (e.g., shipyards, the steel sector within metalworking, the cotton or wool sector within textiles) or even the plant level (Foa, 1975, p. 80)? Furthermore, what should the bargaining issues be at each level? The heated debate continued through the fifth CGIL national congress in 1960. But in the end, the new strategy of decentralized bargaining won out, with all its risks of particularistic demands (Cella, 1976a).

The unfavorable labor-market conditions, the lack of plant-level organizational structures, the limited resources, a trade-union role subordinated to general political goals, and a highly centralized level of bargaining can help us to understand some of the peculiar characteristics of strikes during that period: their large size, low frequency, and short duration (Horowitz, 1963, p. 292; Giugni et al., 1976, p. 26). Large, general strikes were quite common throughout the period. Strike activity was marked by strident political overtones. Centralized bargaining further contributed to that typical pattern of large-scale strikes. But strikes were infrequent. The state of the economy did not allow workers much bargaining clout, in line with the arguments of Chapter 2. Strikes were also very short: Given their limited resources and inability to amass strike funds, unions could not afford long, protracted contests of strength. Strikes typically were symbolic displays of working-class strength ("demonstrative" strikes) (Shorter and Tilly, 1974, pp. 343–4).

A major development in the Italian labor-relations system occurred in the aftermath of the 1962–63 strikes in the metalworking industry: *contrattazione articolata*, "articulated bargaining." Articulated bargaining introduced a two-tier bargaining structure, with bargaining allowed both at the national, industrywide level and at the local, plant level. Plant-level bargaining was to be restricted to issues specifically set out in the clauses of the national, categorywide contract (the so-called *clausole di rinvio*, "deferment clauses"). Furthermore, the national contract included no-strike clauses and arbitration provisions *(pause di tregua)*. Intersind and Asap, the two newly created organizations to handle labor affairs for companies belonging to the state-owned corporations, IRI and ENI (Intersind for IRI and Asap for ENI), played a fundamental role in shaping the new system of industrial relations, by introducing *contrattazione articolata* in their July 5, 1962, and December 20, 1962, contracts with the metalworkers. Confindustria, the private employers' association, bitterly opposed plant-level bargaining. In March 1961, the minister of labor, Fiorentino Sullo, introducing a practice that was to become typical by the end of the decade, summoned the unions (CGIL, CISL, and UIL) and the employers' associations (Confindustria and Intersind) to a meeting (Pirzio Ammassari, 1976, p. 106). After several postponements and extensive polemics, the unsuccessful meeting took place on November 14. In an article titled "Confindustria and trade unions" that appeared two weeks later in the journal *Politica*, Minister Sullo publicly chastised Confindustria. Concerning Confindustria's rejection of an agreement that would have included provisions for plant-level bargaining, the minister wrote that

It has to do more with the role of the unions . . . than with economic reasons. There is a suspicion by workers that, through more or less unilateral concessions, Confindustria wants to mortify organized labor. Industrial peace will not be effective without trade union collaboration. (quoted in Pirzio Ammassari, 1976, p. 107)

A letter of reply from the Confindustria vice-president, Angelo Costa, was published in financial newspapers:

We find it odd that a minister who took upon himself the task of mediation would deem it appropriate to publicly express his thoughts and his endorsement of the point of view of one of the parties. (quoted in Pirzio Ammassari, 1976, pp. 107–8)

To that, Minister Sullo replied in *Politica* that plant-level contracts between *commissioni interne* and management were quite common, despite Confindustria's official stance on the issue, despite the existence of specific clauses in all national, industrywide contracts against plant-level bargaining, and despite an interconfederal agreement between Confindustria and the unions that barred *commissioni interne* from collective bargaining.[5]

The minister had a point. Of the 145 firms inspected in 1956 by the Commissione Parlamentare d'Inchiesta sulle Condizioni dei Lavoratori in Italia (1958b, p. 119) that had *commissioni interne*, 28% signed plant-level agreements.

Table 5.1. *Number of plant-level agreements in industry (1953–61)*

Economic sector	May 1953–May 1957	1960	1961
Metalworking	287	225	800
Textiles	78	115	338[a]
Clothing	26	12	–
Chemicals	105	101	50
Construction	51	36	500
Wood processing	18	7	–
Food processing	61	32	55
Glass and ceramics	30	14	187
Mining	17	5	60
Polygraphic	17	15	43
Total	670	562	2,033

[a]Includes clothing.
Source: Guidi et al. (1974, pp. 384, 385, 391).

Table 5.2. *Bargaining agents in plant-level agreements (%)*

Period	Trade unions	Trade unions and CI	CI
1953–57	49.0[a]	–	51.0
1960	49.0	14.3	36.7
1961	47.9	17.0	35.1

[a]Trade unions and trade unions + CI.
Source: Ammassari and Scaiola (1962, p. 159).

The data in Table 5.1 confirm that informal plant-level contracts were becoming more widespread throughout the 1950s.[6] In the years between 1953 and 1957, nearly 700 formal agreements, involving over 500 companies, were signed. In 1960 alone, almost as many agreements were signed as during the 1953–57 period (562), for a total of 558 companies. The trend continued in 1961. In many of those agreements, the *commissioni interne* (CI) were directly involved in the bargaining process and in the signing of the agreement (Table 5.2).

It was 1968, however, that was to become "the year of plant-level bargaining," with a generalized spreading of bargaining at that level while waiting for the categorywide contract renewals of 1969. The system of *clausole di rinvio* and *pause di tregua* was completely swept away by the high tide of the 1969 *autunno caldo* (Bordogna, 1985, p. 180). The 1970 Workers' Charter formally institutionalized both plant-level bargaining and union organizational structures [factory councils, *consigli di fabbrica* (Cdf), and delegates, *delegati*]. During the early 1970s, plant-level bargaining became the most militant level of bargaining. The new workers' representative bodies, such as *delegati*, Cdf, and *esecutivo,* were actively involved in plant-level bargaining, often outside of the unions' control.

It was the diffusion of the new, highly autonomous and militant organizational structures at the plant level that kept conflict at unprecedented highs throughout the first half of the 1970s. Particularly in the period 1970–72, shop-level conflict became almost endemic in a number of large factories, as Pizzorno's research on the 1968–72 strike wave well documents (Pizzorno, 1974–75). According to Sit-Siemens management, in the first four months of 1970 "there were 746 work stoppages in various shops, with 83,900 lost hours on record" (quoted in Regalia, 1975b, p. 76).

To understand how microconflict operates, let us look at the data assembled by Salerni (1980) in his case study of conflict at the Alfa-Romeo plant in Pomigliano d'Arco, near Naples. As the data in Table 5.3 show, in each year, the most common strike duration was between half an hour and an hour (with approximately 35% of all strikes concentrated in this category), with strikes of fifteen to thirty minutes being almost as frequent (around 27%). Over the three-year period, 70% of all strikes at Alfasud lasted less than an hour, and only 16% lasted more than two hours.

Table 5.4 provides some limited data on the sizes of Alfasud strikes. Most strikes (40.3%) involved 11–25 workers. Strikes lasting less than fifteen minutes and involving fewer than 25 workers composed the most frequent category of strike (14.7%). These data depict a situation of permanent conflict on the shop floor. Although the situation at the Alfasud plant was notoriously bad, things may not have been much better elsewhere. In France, the resurgence of conflict in May 1968 was sudden and brief; in Italy, it began slowly in 1968, skyrocketed during the 1969 *autunnno caldo*, and dragged on for several years thereafter.[7] For Accornero (1992, p. 49), it was precisely the long duration of the period of conflict that explained the much deeper effects of labor mobilization on Italian society than on French society.

In the heat of the strike wave (1969–70), the mass movement, rather than the union organization, had been at the forefront of the struggles. After their initial stumbles, however, the unions appropriated some of the workers' more radical demands and tactics. The unions tried their best to "ride the tiger" of the movement (*cavalcare la tigre*), as the Italians put it. The unions' strategy was to try to restrain the most radical expressions, to expand the struggle to involve workers in quiescent firms, sectors, and regions, and to extend to all workers the benefits won by workers in vanguard firms and sectors. That their strategy paid off is clearly illustrated by the growth of all labor organizations during that period, as we saw in Chapter 4 (see the plots of union memberships of Figure 4.2, p. 111). But the vanguard of the movement often was outside of union control.

By 1973–74, however, the unions had restored much of their control over a highly militant and often vehemently antiunion working class. It was a slow process of co-optation of leaders, isolation of noncooperative leaders, and increased centralization of bargaining. At the plant level, homogeneous work groups, the voting base for *delegati*, often would be enlarged to reduce the voting strength of radical groups of workers (e.g., Carabelli, 1974, p. 161). In many plants, the unions

Table 5.3. *Distribution of strike durations at Alfasud (%)*

Duration[a]	1973	1974	1975
≤ 15	3.5	7.0	11.4
16–30	27.0	26.1	29.3
31–60	35.9	32.1	35.8
61–120	16.0	15.2	11.4
> 120	17.6	19.4	12.1
Total	100.0	100.0	100.0
Number of strikes	(563)	(1,452)	(1,520)

[a] In minutes.
Source: Salerni (1980, p. 214).

Table 5.4. *Distribution of number of strikers by strike duration at Alfasud (%) (March 17, 1975, to July 31, 1975)*

Number of strikes	Duration[a]				
	≤15	16–30	31–60	61–120	>120
≤10	**0.4**[b]	5.8	6.6	1.6	1.2
11–25	14.7	10.9	9.3	2.7	2.7
26–50	4.7	10.8	5.8	4.1	1.9
51–100	0.6	4.9	3.1	0.8	2.1
101–200	0.6	0.8	2.3	0.2	0.8
>200	–	0.2	0.2	–	0.2
Total	21.0	33.4	27.3	9.4	8.9
Number of strikes	-102	-162	-132	-46	-43

[a] In minutes.
[b] Microconflict area in bold.
Source: Salerni (1980, p. 214).

themselves initiated the *delegati* and the Cdf – and many of these never became too involved or too radical.[8] The mass meetings inside the plants increasingly came under union control. The meetings became more and more formalized, favoring the union representatives, who were better trained and more experienced at controlling an agenda, and as unions came to control the agenda for meetings, the array of issues increasingly narrowed (Regalia, 1975a, p. 107). The mass meeting ceased to be a decision-making forum in the hands of the workers (Regalia, 1975a, p. 107). Rather, it became the setting for unions to inform workers about contract negotiations held elsewhere, or, at best, for workers to rubber stamp decisions made elsewhere (i.e., the territorial organizations of the unions for plant-level bargaining, the federal unions for category bargaining, and, after 1975, the confederal unions). In particular, the reappropriation of plant-level bargaining by the territorial organizations gave unions their most effective tool for the management of conflict (after all, plant-level bargaining was responsible for the majority of strikes).

Throughout the early 1970s, in a climate of "permanent conflict" at the plant level, confederal-level unions lost their dominant position of power to both category and territorial organizations. Confederal agreements became very rare (Bordogna, 1985); more typical were the national, industrywide agreements. The unions bargaining at that level often attempted to extend to the workers of a whole sector the provisions won in the most innovative plant-level agreements (Cella and Treu, 1983, p. 104). In an effort to offset the detrimental effects of plant-level bargaining (the tendency toward economism and labor fragmentation in a multitude of local disputes that ultimately favored the better-placed workers) and to halt the erosion of their power, confederal-level organizations became involved in a broad program of socioeconomic reforms, punctuated by repeated meetings with the government and brief (e.g., two hours) general strikes (Accornero and Cardulli, 1974). CGIL, CISL, and UIL did not simply pressure the government to implement modernization programs in housing, health care, education, social security, and economic development of the South;[9] they confronted the government with specific platforms of their own, and they used the general strike as a pressure tactic against a politically vulnerable bargaining partner.

By the middle of the decade, the confederations had slowly taken back their power from the federations vis-à-vis not only the state (through the drive for sociopolitical reforms) but also the employers (Cella and Treu, 1983, pp. 107–11). On January 25, 1975, Confindustria, under the presidency of Giovanni Agnelli, the majority owner of Fiat, Italy's largest private conglomerate, signed an interconfederal agreement with the three major unions (CGIL, CISL, UIL) for automatic adjustments of wages to offset increases in the cost of living (*scala mobile*).[10] The agreement covered almost 100% of wages at the lower end of the wage spectrum (i.e., the unskilled workers), but it did not fully protect skilled workers, technicians, and white-collar employees from wage erosion due to inflation. On May 20, 1975, Parliament extended the *scala mobile* provisions to public employees as well (law no. 164).

As the data in Table 5.5 show, however, even in the best of times, on average, across skill levels, the agreement provided only 80% coverage. Yet for large-scale employers it was a costly agreement (Somaini, 1989). After all, as we have seen, in large-scale factories based on Fordism as a mode of production, the majority of workers were unskilled. Why would large-scale employers want such an agreement? What Giovanni Agnelli told Eugenio Scalfari in an interview for the weekly *L'Espresso* in 1972 about the metalworkers' high wage demands still held in 1975 (quoted in Provasi, 1976, p. 291):

Scalfari: Would employers be able to economically bear it [cost increases due to the metalworkers' contract]?
Agnelli: No.

Table 5.5. Scala mobile *coverage of wages in manufacturing industries*

	1970	1971	1972	1973	1974	1975	1976	1977	1978
Percentage of cost of living	62	53	59	59	39	61	59	80	81
	1979	1980	1981	1982	1983	1984	1985	1986	
Percentage of cost of living	70	61	80	77	72	54	60	55	

Source: Bank of Italy data; Somaini (1989, p. 324).

Scalfari: Then, why do you accept it?
Agnelli: To buy a period of social peace, in the hope that in the meantime we can recuperate firm-level . . . efficiency.[11]

In the first half of the 1970s, continual processes of contract negotiations (with their inevitable outcome of industrial unrest) were being carried out by management in the large firms: for category, conglomerate, division, plant, and even shop-level contracts.[12] Between 1969 and 1980, Pirelli signed 102 agreements at all levels, and 753 piece-rate agreements with shop-floor representatives, quite "an intense bargaining activity" (Negrelli, 1982, p. 492). The jurisdiction at each level was not well defined, and as a consequence, issues were continually being renegotiated at various levels.[13] Although the number of hours lost in strike activity typically were higher during years of national-contract renewals, most strikes occurred over plant-level bargaining.[14] The continual interruptions due to small, short strikes could be more disruptive to production than an eight-hour strike of the whole work force – all the more so because national contracts were always under the direction of the unions (with their traditional aversion to the more damaging strike tactics), whereas microconflict often is in the hands of a highly militant vanguard.[15] For employers, plant-level bargaining was the most onerous bargaining level. By granting their unskilled workers automatic wage increases, large-scale employers were trying to eliminate one of the main sources of conflict in their plants (Pirzio Ammassari, 1976, p. 183).

Time told that the employers' strategy paid off. For one thing, the changes in the shapes of strikes between 1975 and 1978 reveal the sharp decline in the number of strikes. Furthermore, after the signing of the new *scala mobile* agreement in 1975, bargaining came to center less on wage issues and increasingly on forms of worker–employer collaboration at the plant level (e.g., the right of trade unions to be informed about a firm's broad investment policies, and workers' participation in firm-level decision-making bodies) (Cella and Treu, 1983, p. 109). A content analysis of the leaflets distributed at the Fiat auto plant in Cassino further confirms the change in mood (Bagnara and Diani, 1980). The research findings show that the percentage of plant-level issues among all issues being negotiated dropped from 51.2% in 1974–75 to 40.4% in 1976–77, whereas that for broader territorial or national issues increased from 13.9% to 23.1%. Case-study data on firms that had experienced high levels of conflict during the 1968–72 period confirm those trends.

At Pirelli, in the period 1976–80, the amount of bargaining required to settle wage issues and piece rates dwindled, whereas bargaining over the organization of production and skill levels increased. The piece rate, once responsible for some 30% of the total wage packet of a worker, came to account for less than 10% of a worker's gross pay, with automatic mechanisms making up over 60% (Negrelli, 1982, p. 495). Bargaining, once fragmented and conducted on a multitude of levels, became increasingly centralized, moving away from the Cdf (Negrelli, 1982, p. 494). Similarly, at Fiat, the average hourly wage went from 721.7 lire in 1969 to 4,267.2 in 1980. That increase derived from a variety of sources: (1) 15.9% from national metalworkers' contracts, (2) 7.9% from plant-level contracts, (3) 2% from national, interconfederal agreements, (4) 6.4% from unilateral managerial concessions, (5) 7.4% from miscellaneous bonuses, and 6) 60.4% from the interconfederal agreement on *scala mobile* (Becchi Collidà and Negrelli, 1986, p. 170). An analysis of all agreements signed in five large firms in the period between 1969 and 1981 similarly shows a sharp break in 1975: The total number of agreements in those firms dropped, and the number of wage agreements declined by half after that year (Della Rocca and Negrelli, 1983, p. 563).

In light of those findings (the decline in both strike frequency and in plant-level bargaining), it is clear why employers, particularly large-scale employers, were willing to sign a costly agreement.[16] But why should the unions sign such an agreement? The agreement favored unskilled workers rather than skilled workers, blue-collar workers rather than white-collar workers, thus continuing the trend toward more egalitarian wages promoted by the unions after the *autunno caldo*. The danger of splitting the working class (skilled vs. unskilled, white-collar vs. blue-collar workers), of creating particularly well protected segments of the work force, was real. Furthermore, it had been plant-level bargaining that had resurrected workers' militancy and reversed the almost two-decade-long decline in union organizational strength. Given the general failure of the reform experience at the confederal level, plant-level bargaining had been the unions' most successful level of bargaining during the 1970s. Most of the gains obtained, both for workers and for the unions as organizations, had come at that level. Why, then, would the unions willingly give up a weapon of such success (*la lotta che paga*, "the struggle that pays off," as Italian union leaders put it)? Why did the unions sign that agreement? What were they hoping to get in return? What was their strategy?

5.3. DOES THE STRUCTURE OF COLLECTIVE BARGAINING MAKE A DIFFERENCE?

These are important questions if we are to understand the course of Italian labor history in the 1970s and beyond. But for now, other questions urge us on. In particular: Does the pattern of strike activity reflect the historical changes in collective bargaining outlined in the preceding section? If so, how? Unfortunately, available scholarly research is of little help in answering these questions: there has been very little work on the relationship between collective bargaining and strikes.

At a general level, U.S. industrial-relations scholars in the 1950s argued that as the strike becomes more institutionalized, it loses much of its violence and excitement.[17] Under collective bargaining, strikes become cold-blooded bargaining maneuvers in the hands of professional negotiators (Kornhauser, Dubin, and Ross, 1954, p. 12). Collective bargaining provides an avenue for peaceful resolution of conflicts of interest through compromise and cooperation (Harbison, 1954, p. 271). "Collective bargaining is the great social invention that has institutionalized industrial conflict. . . . collective bargaining has created a stable means for resolving industrial conflict" (Dubin 1954, p. 44). As labor–management relations "mature" (Kornhauser et al., 1954, p. 508), strikes not only become less violent but also become less frequent. On the basis of a comparative analysis of Britain and Scandinavia, Ingham (1974, p. 35) showed that the institutionalization of conflict and the adoption of collective bargaining reduced both the level of conflict and its dependence on economic conditions. Reder and Neumann (1980) and Mauro (1982) further argued that the establishment of negotiating rules, the adoption of bargaining mechanisms, and the use of pattern bargaining effectively reduce the extent of uncertainty by limiting the scope of future bargaining and, implicitly, the level of conflict that comes with uncertainty.

Those arguments make only generic claims that the institutionalization of collective bargaining reduces the level of industrial conflict; they say nothing about the specific nature of this relationship. Given the differences in national industrial-relations systems (Clegg, 1976; Cella and Treu, 1982; Bean, 1985; Visser, 1989), how do specific systems affect strike patterns? Which strike indicators are affected? How? Sellier (1960) and Clegg (1976) argued that the bargaining structure and the level at which negotiations are held (the central nationwide or industrywide level, the local plant level) are associated with specific dimensions of strike activity.[18] Let me briefly review those arguments.

Centralized, economywide bargaining can be expected to be characterized by low levels of industrial conflict. Bargaining issues are general and abstract at such a high level of negotiations, remote from the workers' daily experience in the factories and offices. The motivation to act collectively is low.[19]

Centralized, industrywide bargaining tends to be accompanied by large numbers of workers on strike at times of contract renewals. Often the workers in a whole sector of the economy will go on strike to prompt renewal of their collective contract; that could be millions of workers in the largest sectors, such as metalworking. Industrywide strikes tend to have the characteristics of general strikes: infrequent, but very large in size.

Plant-level bargaining is very decentralized; it tends to lead to high strike frequencies, but small sizes, as the work forces in thousands of firms, independently of one another, renew their contracts locally. The probability of a strike is high, but the number of strikers in each individual strike tends to be low, given that the size of the work force in each plant sets much lower limits to the population at risk. On the other hand, the total number of workers willing to engage in strikes should be high. According to Sellier (1960) and Baglioni (1963, 1966, pp. 265–302), workers' involvement in labor activities is directly proportional to the bargaining level: The more the strike issues affect the worker's personal interests (such as in plant-level bargaining), the more likely it is that the worker will participate in the strike.

Does the pattern of Italian strikes conform to the expectations of bargaining-structure models? Is there any empirically observable relationship between strike activity and bargaining structure in Italy? In postwar Italy, as the bargaining structure changed over time, were those changes reflected in the patterns of strikes?

At a general level, the evidence seems to be consistent with those arguments. Indeed, as Clegg would have it, between 1955 and 1975, not only did the strike frequency increase, as the industrial-relations system was becoming more decentralized, but also the percentage of plant-level strikes jumped from 70% to 90% of all quarterly strikes. Furthermore, the growing decentralization of bargaining during the 1960s and 1970s went hand in hand with positive trends in strike size and volume, just as Sellier and Baglioni argue. But the changes in the level of bargaining affected not only strike activity but also the content of workers' demands. In general, at lower negotiating levels, the focus is on job-control issues or, more generally, on management prerogatives versus workers' rights (Pizzorno, 1977, p. 158). The development of plant-level bargaining was also characterized by a diversification of bargaining issues, away from purely economic and wage issues. According to trade-union data (Guidi et al., 1973, p. 15), the percentage of wage demands in plant-level bargaining between 1969 and 1972 went from 54% to 25%, while the percentage of environmental and health demands increased from a mere 2.9% in 1969 to 16.1% in 1972. In general, the issues that directly and most immediately concerned workers' lives within the plants became, over time, the central focus for collective bargaining: working hours, job ratings, and so forth (Bellardi et al., 1978).

But there is also more direct evidence in favor of Sellier, Baglioni, and Clegg's arguments. As we saw, spectral analyses of the series of numbers of strikes, strikers, and hours lost show high-power spectra at three-year frequency bands (i.e., bouts of strike activity at three-year intervals) and a phase shift of approximately one year between the series for number of strikes and the series for numbers of strikers and hours lost (i.e., a one-year lag between peaks in the number of strikes and peaks in the numbers of strikers and hours lost) (Franzosi, 1980). That those patterns are related to the Italian bargaining structure can be clearly seen from the plots in Figure 5.1. The plots are based on metalworking-industry data, in order to avoid blurring effects due to sectoral aggregation. The dotted line shows the number of workers involved in industrywide strikes, and the solid line shows the number of plant-level strikes. The black vertical bars mark the quarters for renewals of metalworkers' collective contracts. One thing is clear: The months prior to contract renewals were characterized by peaks in the number of strikers, while at the same time the number of strikes reached a trough. The number of plant-level strikes peaks approximately a year after the signing of the industrywide collective agreement.

The available data on the number of plant-level agreements provide further evidence of the close relationship between strike frequency and plant-level

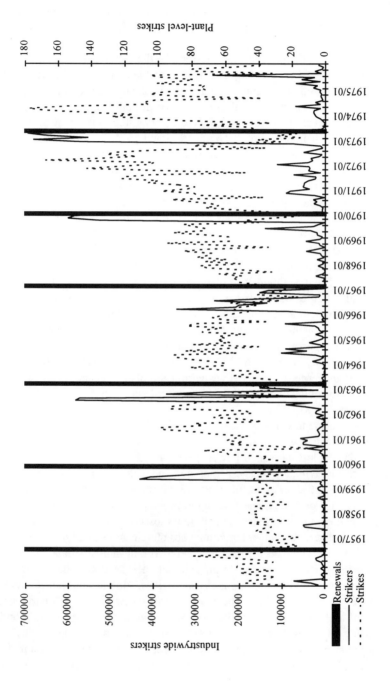

Figure 5.1. Plot of monthly numbers of plant-level strikes and industrywide strikers

Table 5.6. *Number of plant-level agreements in industry (1969–72)*

	1969	1970	1971	1972
Number of agreements	3,330	3,975	4,568	2,899

Source: Guidi et al. (1973, p. 6).

Table 5.7. *Number of firms involved in plant-level bargaining, and numbers of strikes and strikers*

	1979–I	II	III	IV	1980–I	II	III	IV	1981–I
Number of firms	464	321	295	421	1,168	1,170	765	769	614
Number of agreements	363	286	255	176	486	573	401	182	486
Percentage of firms	1.5	1.0	0.9	2.8	3.7	9.7	4.4	4.2	3.9
Percentage of agreements	1.1	0.9	0.8	1.2	1.6	4.8	2.3	1.0	3.1
Number of strikes	328	267	198	165	222	324	295	264	365
Number of strikers	1,260	2,939	328	976	438	942	1,907	1,359	577

Source: Confederazione generale italiana dell'industria, *Indagine congiunturale sul mercato del lavoro e la contrattazione aziendale*; ISTAT, *Bollettino mensile di statistica*.

bargaining. For instance, the trade-union data reported in Table 5.6 show that the number of plant agreements in various industrial sectors (including construction) went up in 1970 and 1971 after the signing of categorywide collective agreements in late 1969, but went down again in 1972 as those contracts were approaching their expiration dates (late 1972). Table 5.7 presents data on the numbers of firms and workers involved each quarter in plant-level bargaining. The information was collected by the Confederazione Generale dell'Industria Italiana among a sample of member firms.[20] One can see that the number of firms involved in plant-level bargaining was inversely proportional to category-level bargaining. In particular, plant-level bargaining in manufacturing industries peaked in 1980, several quarters after the signing of major categorywide collective agreements. The table not only shows that plant and category bargaining were inversely related, described by two out-of-phase sine waves, but also confirms that plant-level bargaining and strike frequency went together.

The empirical evidence of Figure 5.1 and Tables 5.6 and 5.7 clearly highlights the relationship between the patterns of conflict and the bargaining structure. However, there is more information that we can squeeze out of the strike data. Strike data by cause (e.g., contract renewal) have been available since 1961. We can use this information to compute the percentage of all strikers who were on strike for reasons of contract renewal (Figure 5.2). The plot clearly shows how the three-year periodicity of labor contracts (1962–63, 1966, 1969–70, 1973, 1976, 1979, 1983) produces a pattern of surges in workers' mobilization. During those bouts of mobilization for the renewal of industrywide collective contracts, 30–60% of all strikers were involved in contract-renewal strikes. Although that figure might

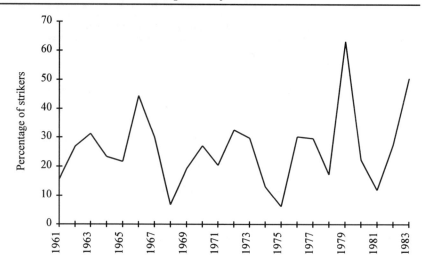

Figure 5.2. *Plot of the percentage of all strikers accounted for by contract-renewal strikes*

seem low, note that the plot of Figure 5.3 for the percentage of all strikers accounted for by solidarity strikes (available only since 1967) shows that during contract renewals, some 50% of all strikers were on strike for reasons of solidarity. Despite the current of denial of class categories that operates at the level of public discourse via the denial of working-class solidarity and unity (particularly in the news media)[21] the plot in Figure 5.3 clearly highlights the classwide strategies of Italian unions.

That the peaks in mobilization revealed by Figure 5.2 were related to large-scale strikes is highlighted by the plot in Figure 5.4, which shows the percentage of all strikers accounted for by industrywide strikes. That there were only a few of these strikes is apparent from the fact that the troughs in the number of strikes correspond to the peaks in the number of strikers in Figure 5.1. The use of data on the distribution of strikes by their sizes would bear out this point even more clearly. Unfortunately, ISTAT, the central statistical office, has made these data available only since 1976, too late to explain the pattern of Italian strikes during the 1954–78 or 1959–78 period. Nonetheless, there is a great deal that we can learn by looking at those data for the years 1976–87. Of the sixteen classes of strike sizes provided by ISTAT, let us focus on the top class of largest strikes, involving at least 50,000 workers (see also Figure 1.1 in Chapter 1, p. 3).

Table 5.8 shows the number of strikes involving more than 50,000 workers and the percentage of the total number of strikers accounted for by those largest strikes. Figure 5.5 provides a graphic display of the same information. The plot confirms the three-year cycle in the eruption of large-scale strikes, clearly linked to the timing of the renewal of national collective contracts. But the data also show that it was indeed just a handful of strikes (among several hundred or even thousand

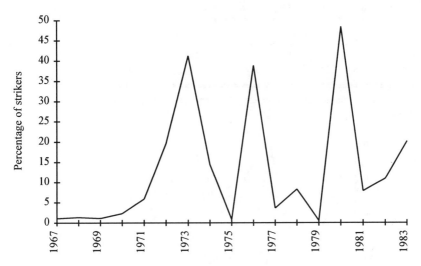

Figure 5.3. *Plot of the percentage of all strikers accounted for by solidarity strikes*

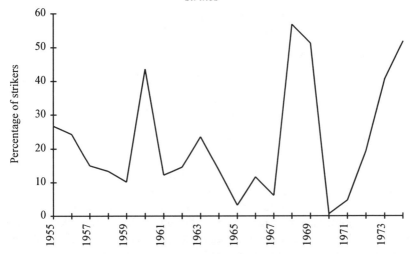

Figure 5.4. *Plot of the percentage of all strikers accounted for by industry-wide strikes*

each year) that accounted for a large percentage of the number of strikers.[22] The data of Table 5.9 confirm that and further highlight the characteristics and the temporal pattern of strike activity related to the renewal of collective contracts. The data refer to the strikes declared by the metalworkers' unions for the renewal of their 1969 national contract. Between the beginning of September and the end of December, the unions called a total of 190 strike hours, spread out among tens of

Table 5.8. *Number of large-scale strikes and percentages of strikers involved*

	1976	1977	1978	1979	1980	1981	1982	1983	1984	1985	1986	1987
A[a]	73	53	51	81	71	34	78	70	54	26	57	36
B	18	14	14	26	19	10	16	20	7	3	11	6

[a] A, percentage of total number of strikers; B, number of strikes involving more than 50,000 workers.

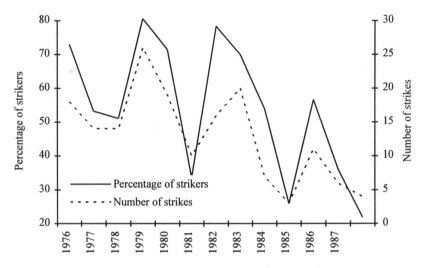

Figure 5.5. *Plots of the number of large-scale strikes and of the percentage of strikers involved*

individual work stoppages, only three of which had a one-day duration (8 hours). The rest of the work stoppages lasted fewer than 8 hours each.

In conclusion, the strike activity surrounding the renewal of industrywide collective contracts was characterized by a handful of very large and brief strikes involving all workers in the industry subject to contract renewal. After the signing of an industrywide collective agreement that set minimum wage increases and other terms of concern to a whole industry, hundreds of firms throughout the country would renew their plant agreements locally. At that contractual level, the bargaining process was characterized by a multitude of brief, small, local strikes. Frequency was the most revealing strike component.[23] Thus, the analyses support, at least for the Italian case, Clegg's hypothesis about the relationships between strike measures and bargaining level.[24] The analyses also cast further light on some little-known aspects of the relationships between institutional arrangements (such as a country's bargaining structure) and strike activity.

Table 5.9. *Work stoppages for the renewal of the 1969 metalworkers' collective contract (dates and durations in hours)*

Sep. 11	8	Oct. 6–12	8	Nov. 10–15	12
Sep. 15 or 16	3	Oct. 7	4	Nov. 17–22	12
Sep. 19	3	Oct. 13–19	12	Nov. 24–29	12
Sep. 15–20	6	Oct. 17	8	Dec. 1–7	12
Sep. 25	8	Oct. 20–26	12	Dec. 9–13	12
Sep. 22–27	4	Oct. 27–31	12	Dec. 15–22	12
Sep. 29–Oct. 5	12	Nov. 3–8	12	Dec. 22–24	6

It is the bargaining structure that can explain the shapes of Italian strikes highlighted in Chapter 1. Plant-level strikes made up more than 95% of all strikes. Unlike that pattern, industry-level strikes (e.g., metalworking, chemicals) and interindustry strikes were responsible for 70–90% of all strikers and time lost. Thus, a handful of very large strikes accounted for the majority of strikers and time lost due to strikes.[25] It was that handful of large, industrywide or even interindustry strikes that accounted for at least part of the *paradox of strike size*. Some strikes were larger than the work forces of even the largest plants, because some strikes went well beyond the boundaries of the single factory. We still do not know, however, why the rest of the strikes (the plant-level strikes) were, on average, smaller than the work forces of the large factories (the ones that suffered strikes).

5.4. BACK TO THE ASHENFELTER AND JOHNSON MODEL

Given the close relationship between the number of plant-level agreements and strike frequency, one must wonder why I did not explicitly include the number of plant-level contracts in my strike-frequency models. The answer is simple: Contract information is available only for limited sample periods and few industrial sectors.[26] Problems of data availability similarly prevented Ashenfelter and Johnson from including the number of contract expirations in a quarter, N_t, in their equation. Instead, they approximated N_t, observing that strike frequency is directly proportional to the number of contract expirations in a quarter. Thus, $N_t = \sum_{j=1}^{4} X_j N_{jt}$, where X_j is the (constant) number of contract expirations in the jth quarter of each year, and N_{jt} is a quarterly dummy to adjust for seasonal variations, set equal to 1 in the jth quarter of the year, and 0 otherwise. This probably can solve the problem of the short-term, seasonal fluctuations in the number of contract expirations. But the Ashenfelter and Johnson assumption of a constant number of contract expirations in the jth quarter of each year, is untenable for the Italian case. The figures given earlier on the number of plant agreements and the results of exploratory analysis of strike data summarized in Chapter 1 pointing to the presence of a regular periodic strike cycle of two to three years' duration clearly indicate periodic behavior (not constant behavior) of collective bargaining in Italy. My examination of the residuals from the estimates of the Ashenfelter and Johnson model in Chapter 2 seemed to reveal an unexplained periodic component. In light of the findings in this chapter concerning collective bargaining in Italy, let me probe further into the pattern of the residuals.

Let me go back to the plot of the residuals obtained from estimating the Ashenfelter and Johnson model in Chapter 2 (Figure 2.1, p. 42).[27] Let me reproduce here that plot for convenience (Figure 5.6); but in order to highlight the pattern in the residuals, let me mark the quarters of contract renewals for the metalworkers with black bars below the horizontal axis. Above the x-axis, let me mark with gray bars the quarters of highest plant-level numbers of strikes in the metalworking industry. Again, I single out the metalworking sector for clarity's sake. In any case, plant-level strike activity in metalworking firms represents, on average, 40–60% of all plant-level strikes in manufacturing. With the help of these reference bars, we can see that the residuals from the estimates of the Ashenfelter and Johnson model are characterized by a distinct pattern, with low values around contract renewals and high values in between, when plant-level bargaining (characterized by high strike frequency) was at a peak.

A plot of the residuals obtained by estimating with two-stage least squares equation (3.4) in Chapter 3 (model 2 in Table 3.6, p. 71) would show a similar pattern. Again, the renewal of metalworking collective agreements dampened strike frequency, whereas plant-level bargaining raised it. Thus, regardless of the model specification adopted, strike-frequency models based solely on economic variables overlook an important aspect of strike activity related to the peculiar institutional arrangements of the Italian industrial-relations system.

The correlations between those two sets of residuals and the numbers of strikes and strikers further support these conclusions. As Table 5.10 shows, the error components are correlated positively with the number of strikes and negatively with the number of strikers. Furthermore, if one considers the number of plant-level strikes and the number of workers involved in categorywide strikes, the sizes of the coefficients tend to get even larger, further underscoring the differences between the numbers of strikes and strikers. What that means is that when the number of plant-level strikes is high, so is the error component, and when the number of strikers involved in categorywide strikes is high, the error component is low. But the error component, as we have seen, is low around the time for renewal of categorywide collective agreements, for metalworkers in particular. So the error components of the strike-frequency models are characterized by fluctuations clearly related to the Italian bargaining structure.

From a statistical viewpoint, the fact that the regression residuals show both predictable and unexplained patterns implies that the regression model is misspecified: One or more relevant variables that could account for the residual pattern have been excluded from the model. The end result is that coefficient estimates are biased, and the estimates of their variances are likely to be inflated (Johnston, 1972,

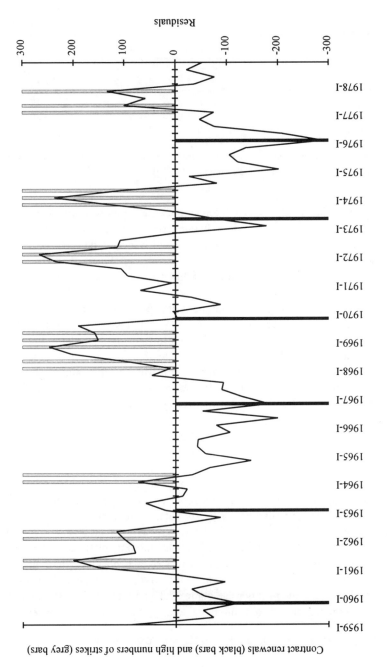

Figure 5.6. Plot of the residuals (model 2 in Table 2.1) with quarters of contract renewal and high strike frequency in metalworking industry clearly marked

Table 5.10. *Correlation coefficients between numbers of strikes and strikers and the error components from model 4 of Table 2.1 and model 2 of Table 3.6*

	Error vector (model 4, Table 2.1)		Error vector (model 2, Table 3.6)	
	1959-II 1978-IV	1959-II 1975-IV	1959-II 1977-IV	1959-II 1978-IV
Strikes	.31	.29	.28	.28
Strikers	-.26	.28	-.21	-.20
Strikes (plant level)[a]		.29		.28
Strikers (industry level)[a]		.38		-.32

[a] Plant- and industry-level strike data available only until 1975.

pp. 168–9). But inflated variances are likely to increase the probability of rejecting the role that a variable plays in a model.[28] In our case, the exclusion from the model of a bargaining variable may have decreased the significance of the unemployment-rate variable.

We need to respecify the original Ashenfelter and Johnson model [equation (2.2), p. 32], and include a variable that can account for the cyclical behavior of industrial conflict stemming from the periodic expirations and renewals of collective agreements. The number of plant-level contracts expiring each quarter would be the ideal measure for that variable. Unfortunately, just like in the U.S. case, information on plant-level agreements is available only for selected periods and industries. To overcome that problem, I constructed a bargaining variable given by the percentage of workers subject to industrywide contract renewal in each quarter (*CONTRACT*).[29] In light of the arguments in this chapter on the relationship between strike frequency and plant-level bargaining, and strike size and industry-level bargaining, it is expected that the effect of this contract-renewal variable will be negative on strike frequency and positive on the number of workers involved.

The correlation coefficients between the contract-renewal variable and plant-level and industry-level strike indicators reported in Table 5.11 confirm that expectation. Whether using quarterly or yearly data, the renewals of industrywide collective agreements tend to dampen strike activity at the plant level and raise it at the industry level. At the industry level, whereas the relationship between collective contract renewals and the number of strikes is negative, that with the numbers of strikers and hours lost is higly positive, as expected. Will these bivariate results hold in the multivariate context? To answer that question, let me respecify the Ashenfelter and Johnson model adding the *CONTRACT* variable:

$$S_t = \beta_0 + \beta_1 D_{1t} + \beta_2 D_{2t} + \beta_3 D_{3t} + \beta_4 \sum_{i=0}^{n} \mu_i \Delta W_{t-i} + \beta_5 UN_t + \beta_6 CONTRACT_t + \epsilon_t \quad (5.1)$$

A contract variable should also be added to equation (3.2) and equation (3.3) of Chapter 3 (p. 67):

Table 5.11. *Correlation coefficients between contract indicator and numbers of strikes, strikers, and hours lost at various levels*

	Plant level			Industry level		
	Number of strikes	Number of strikers	Number of hours lost	Number of strikes	Number of strikers	Number of hours lost
Contract renewal[a]	-.58	-.45	-.48	-.28	.49	.36
Contract renewal[b]	-.32	-.36	-.39	-.26	.41	.70

[a] Quarterly data (1959/I–75/IV)
[b] Yearly data (1955–74).

$$W_t = \beta_0 + \beta_1 D_{1t} + \beta_2 D_{2t} + \beta_3 D_{3t} + \beta_4 \sum_{i=0}^{n} \mu_i \Delta W_{t-i} + \beta_5 BC_t + \beta_6 CONTRACT_t + \epsilon_t \quad (5.2)$$

$$H_t = \beta_0 + \beta_1 D_{1t} + \beta_2 D_{2t} + \beta_3 D_{3t} + \beta_4 \sum_{i=0}^{n} \mu_i \Delta W_{t-i} + \beta_5 UN_t + \beta_6 BC_t + \beta_7 CONTRACT_t + \epsilon_t \quad (5.3)$$

where S, W, and H measure the number of strikes, strikers, and hours lost, and D_1, D_2, and D_3 are a set of seasonal dummies, UN measures the unemployment rate, BC is a business cycle measure (industrial production or capacity utilization), and $\sum \mu_i \Delta W_{t-i}$ measures real wages (distributed-lag specification); also, $\beta_4 > 0$ in all three equations, $\beta_5 < 0$ in equation (5.1) and equation (5.3) for the reasons explained in Chapter 2, and $\beta_5 > 0$ in equation (5.2) and $\beta_6 > 0$ in equation (5.3) for the reasons explained in Chapter 3 concerning the expected relationships between strikes and product-market variables.

Finally, a contract variable should be added to the organizational model, equation (4.1) of Chapter 4 (p. 106):

$$Y_t = \beta_0 + \beta_1 UN_t + \beta_2 UNION_t + \beta_3 \Delta W_{t-1} + \beta_4 CONTRACT_t + \epsilon_t \quad (5.4)$$

In equation (5.4) Y, the dependent variable, measures the number of strikes, strikers, or hours lost, and among the independent variables, UN measures the unemployment rate, and $UNION$ measures union membership (CGIL + CISL).

Tables 5.12 and 5.13 show estimates for equations (5.1), (5.2), and (5.3). The findings confirm the existence of a significant relationship between strike activity and bargaining structure. The coefficients for the contract-renewal variable are significant and with the expected negative sign in all models involving the number of strikes as the dependent variable (models 1–6), significant and positive, as expected, with number of hours lost (model 8), but they are not significant (although with the expected positive sign) with number of strikers as the dependent variable (model 7). The inclusion of the contract variable in the Ashenfelter and Johnson model has also improved the explanatory power of the model, with higher values of the adjusted R^2, particularly for the estimates obtained without the application of the Cochrane-Orcutt procedure. For instance, the value of the adjusted R^2 goes from .55 (model 2 in Table 2.1, Chapter 2, p. 34) to .66

Table 5.12. *Testing the role of the bargaining structure*

Dependent variable: Number of strikes for models 1–6; number of strikers for model 7 and number of hours lost for model 8
Aggregation level: Manufacturing industries; quarterly series
Sample period: 1959-II/1978-IV
Estimation method: Almon polynomial distributed lags (all models estimated with no end-point constraints) for all models; OLS for model 1; GLS (Cochrane-Orcutt) for models 2–8

	Model 1	Model 2	Model 3	Model 4	Model 5	Model 6	Model 7	Model 8
Constant	842.82*	546.27*	170.17	550.79*	-97.15	118.90	927,151.5	26,443.39**
	(73.17)	(99.46)	(297.33)	(150.06)	(338.54)	(348.85)	(695,362.2)	(15,083.90)
1st quarter dummy	77.84**	47.94**	31.10**	48.02	24.81	48.76**	281,208.2	1,061.27
	(35.70)	(21.51)	(18.0)	(21.92)	(18.80)	(21.61)	(228,054.0)	(4,836.94)
2nd quarter dummy	15.92	34.80	47.33**	34.68**	50.98*	37.88**	-115,612.9	-4,883.64
	(34.43)	(21.97)	(20.18)	(22.20)	(21.48)	(22.27)	(235,671.5)	(5,003.10)
3rd quarter dummy	-125.98*	-105.07*	-68.25*	105.36*	-95.48*	101.37**	-462,947.2**	-73,717.06**
	(34.54)	(19.47)	(24.37)	(22.91)	(19.70)	(19.88)	(213,938.0)	(4,526.70)
Change in real wages (%)	162.17*	202.76	267.91*	201.93*	207.94*	202.7*	.46E+6*	977.75
	(20.01)	(51.52)	(75.36)	(55.02)	(57.7)	(48.12)	(.21E+6)	(4,676.9)
Unemployment rate	-71.58*	-33.24*		-33.45*		-33.16*	-84,461.38	-2,427.72
	(12.58)	(14.20)		(14.41)		(14.25)	(119,754.3)	(2,593.16)
Industrial production			3.83**	-.02				
			(1.99)	(1.46)				
Capacity utilization					4.92	.70		
					(3.55)	(3.54)		
Contract renewal	-2.84*	-1.58*	1.37*	-1.59*	-1.59*	-1.57*	5,137.85	237.76**
	(.58)	(.56)	(.55)	(.56)	(.57)	(.56)	(4,990.63)	(107.55)
Adjusted R^2	.66	.81	.80	.80	.80	.81	.18	.08
Durbin-Watson	.81	1.96	1.99	1.96	1.89	1.95	2.03	2.03
Wallis	1.86	2.13	2.01	2.13	2.02	2.07	2.03	1.97

Note: Standard error in parentheses. **Significant at the .05 level; *significant at the .01 level.

Table 5.13. *Almon polynomial distributed lag coefficients for models of Table 5.12*

Lag i	Percent change in real wages$_{t-i}$ for model							
	1	2	3	4	5	6	7	8
0	12.75*	12.25*	14.25*	12.24*	11.52**	10.62**	85,510.96**	-1,533.90**
	(5.08)	(5.01)	(5.12)	(5.13)	(5.24)	(5.10)	(43,462.57)	(936.94)
1	14.20*	15.45*	19.57*	15.41*	15.37*	14.27*	-43,925.66	-956.17
	(3.53)	(4.48)	(5.47)	(4.69)	(4.81)	(4.37)	(31,438.53)	(681.14)
2	15.26*	17.95*	23.73*	17.89*	18.39*	17.17*	-8,056.20	-463.65
	(2.73)	(4.82)	(6.60)	(5.11)	(5.30)	(4.55)	(25,986.57)	(567.56)
3	15.93*	19.73*	26.74*	19.66*	20.56*	19.32*	22,097.42	-56.34
	(2.64)	(5.46)	(7.75)	(5.79)	(6.07)	(5.11)	(25,960.24)	(569.41)
4	16.20*	20.81*	28.60*	20.73*	21.90*	20.71*	46,535.20	265.77
	(2.85)	(6.00)	(8.60)	(6.37)	(6.71)	(5.63)	(27,918.50)	(612.45)
5	16.08*	21.18*	29.29*	21.09*	22.40*	21.35*	65,257.14**	502.67
	(3.01)	(6.30)	(9.04)	(6.67)	(7.05)	(5.93)	(29,291.31)	(642.28)
6	15.56*	20.85*	28.84*	20.76*	22.05*	21.23*	78,263.25*	654.37
	(2.97)	(6.29)	(9.02)	(6.65)	(7.05)	(5.94)	(29,097.97)	(638.19)
7	14.65*	19.81*	27.23*	19.72*	20.87*	20.36*	85,553.52*	720.85
	(2.76)	(5.97)	(8.56)	(6.31)	(6.7)	(5.66)	(27,453.74)	(602.63)
8	13.34*	18.06*	24.46*	17.98*	18.85*	18.74*	87,127.95*	702.13
	(2.57)	(5.43)	(7.71)	(5.73)	(6.07)	(5.18)	(25,654.41)	(562.90)
9	11.63*	15.41*	20.54*	15.54*	15.99*	16.36*	82,986.54*	598.20
	(2.81)	(4.85)	(6.58)	(5.09)	(5.35)	(4.70)	(26,648.17)	(581.45)
10	9.54*	12.45*	15.46*	12.39*	12.29*	13.22*	73,129.30**	409.07
	(3.83)	(4.66)	(5.54)	(4.81)	(4.93)	(4.62)	(33,626.41)	(727.69)
11	7.04*	8.59**	9.22**	8.54	7.75	9.34**	57,556.21	134.73
	(5.57)	(5.41)	(5.38)	(5.48)	(5.47)	(5.44)	(47,032.62)	(1,013.34)

Note: Standard error in parentheses. **Significant at the .05 level; *significant at the .01 level.

(model 1 in Table 5.12), with a 20% increase in the amount of total variance explained.

Furthermore, in Chapter 2, I showed that when correcting the estimates for first-order serial correlation, R^2 increased from .55 (model 2 in Table 2.1) to .79 (model 4 in Table 2.1), with a 45% increase due to the effect of omitted variables. The results for model 1 in Table 5.12 show that nearly half of that effect (44.16%, to be precise) is due to the bargaining structure. Finally, the coefficients of the wage and unemployment variables are lower. The inclusion of a measure of institutionalization of collective bargaining seems to reduce the effect of unemployment on strike activity, supporting the argument that collective bargaining partly insulates labor negotiations from the vagaries of the labor market. The ratio of the unemployment-rate coefficient to its standard error (t-statistic), however, does not change.

Table 5.14 shows the econometric estimates for equation (5.4). A comparison with the findings in Chapter 4 (see Table 4.1, p. 107) shows that inclusion of the contract-renewal variable in an organizational model does not fundamentally alter

Table 5.14. *Combining organizational and collective bargaining effects*

Dependent variable: Number of strikes for models 1 and 2; number of strikers for model 3; number of hours lost for model 4
Aggregation level: Industry; yearly series
Sample period: 1955/1978
Estimation method: GLS (Cochrane-Orcutt) for all models

	Model 1	Model 2[a]	Model 3	Model 4
Constant	3,135.77*	3,956.01*	381.12	78,015.64**
	(747.69)	(726.35)	(1,048.37)	(44,904.49)
Unemployment rate	-193.63*	-217.45*	-368.49*	-13,784.04*
	(93.32)	(89.37)	(131.93)	(5,715.10)
Change in real wages$_{t-1}$ (%)	42.15**	-55.93*	-131.61*	-2,992.93
	(21.62)	(24.22)	(60.29)	(2,281.36)
Union membership	.115E-5	.43E-3	.266E-2*	.297E-1**
	(.290E-3)	(.28E-3)	(.383E-3)	(.165E-1)
Contract renewal	-6.33*	-3.18	5.81	990.13*
	(2.64)	(2.94)	(7.65)	(284.85)
Adjusted R^2	.39	.54	.68	.41
Durbin-Watson	1.71	1.91	1.90	1.94

[a]In model 2, wage variable lagged at time t-3.
Note: Standard error in parentheses. **Significant at the .05 level; *significant at the .01 level.

either organizational or labor-market effects. Furthermore, it improves the overall fit of the model, as shown by the increases in the adjusted R^2 values. The change in sign from positive to negative, for the wage variable in the estimates of the number of strikes (models 1 and 2 of Table 5.14) confirms the argument for a relationship between strike activity and wages, as mediated by the bargaining structure. The contract-renewal variable has the expected negative effect on the number of strikes and positive effects on the numbers of strikers and hours lost. In short, the econometric evidence in Tables 5.12 and 5.14 confirms that the structure of collective bargaining deeply affects the prevailing patterns of strikes in the Italian context.

5.5. UNEXPLAINED RESIDUALS: WHY MODELS OF THE NUMBER OF STRIKERS PERFORM SO POORLY

The historical and statistical evidence in this chapter has shown not only that a great deal of strike activity centers around issues of contract renewal but also that the very temporal pattern of strikes is shaped by the prevailing structure of collective bargaining. More broadly, the empirical evidence in this chapter and in Chapters 2 and 3 seems to point to a strike model for Italy in which the structure of collective bargaining and the business cycle provide the timing for the periodic and nonperiodic medium-run fluctuations in strike activity. Econometric work for other countries has shown that much of the variation in strike activity over time is similarly related to the structure of collective bargaining and, in particular, to the timing of contract expirations.[30]

Although those findings are quite encouraging, I find it somewhat puzzling that the contract variable that I constructed in order to account for the effects of collective bargaining on strike patterns should perform better in equations involving the number of strikes as the dependent variable (models 1–6 in Table 5.12), rather than the number of strikers (models 7 in Table 5.12).[31] After all, that variable measures the percentage of workers subject to contract renewal. It should shape, very closely, the temporal pattern of the series for the number of strikers. Surprisingly, however, it does not. I took the yearly data on the percentage of workers subject to contract renewal from Alinari (1979). Could there be errors in the Alinari data?[32]

Furthermore, whereas the series for the number of strikes provides a better fit when using quarterly data, the series for the number of strikers provides the best fit when using yearly data. On the one hand, this may simply confirm that a great deal of the variability in the series for the number of strikes is accounted for by seasonality alone (see Section 2.5 in Chapter 2, p. 38). On the other hand, the lack of statistical significance for the seasonal dummies in Table 3.1 of Chapter 3 (p. 58), and the contract-renewal variable in model 7 of Table 5.12 may simply reflect the greater fuzziness and lower predictability of the series for the number of strikers. The fact that a handful of large-scale strikes can account for an average of 70% of all strikers in a year confirms that the series for the number of strikers is more subject to outlying observations than is the series for the number of strikes. It would take thousands of separate, plant-level strikes to create an outlier in the series for the number of strikes, but perhaps only one general strike to create an outlier in the series for the number of strikers, clearly a more likely occurrence in the Italian industrial-relations context. Could the presence of some outlying observations explain the poor performance of the contract variable in model 3 of Table 5.14 involving the number of strikers as the dependent variable?

To answer the two questions raised by the mixed performance of the contract variable in my econometric estimates, let me probe further into the empirical evidence. The plot in Figure 5.7 excludes the problems raised by the use of Alinari's data. The plot follows closely the temporal contour of my own quarterly data, and the peaks in the series correspond to the timing of major contract renewals and expirations. As for outliers, box plots of the numbers of strikes and strikers would confirm that the series for the number of strikes is better behaved than the series for the number of strikers, which shows an outlier for the 1975 observation. Indeed, the plot for the number of strikers (Figure 1.4, in Chapter 1, p. 5) shows that in 1975, the series for the number of strikers achieved a historical peak, with the values for 1974 and 1977 trailing at a close distance. A direct comparison of the plots for the percentage of workers subject to contract renewal and for the number of strikers (Figure 5.7 and Figure 1.4) reveals that 1974, 1975, and 1977 were not years for contract renewals. Certainly, the fact that the three largest observations for the number of strikers are unaccounted for by the contract-

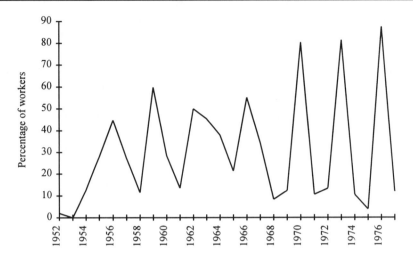

Figure 5.7. *Plot of the yearly percentage of industrial workers subject to contract renewal*

renewal variable could explain the poor performance of this variable in a strike-size model.

Evidence based on the number of hours lost brings into even sharper focus the unusual character of the 1974, 1975, and 1977 observations. The plot in Figure 5.8 showing the number of strikes with the highest number of hours lost and the plot in Figure 5.9 showing the percentage of total yearly hours lost to strikes accounted for by strikes involving at least 2 million hours lost[33] confirm both the three-year cycle of contract-renewal strikes and the uncharacteristic values for 1974, 1975, and 1977 unexplained by the renewal of collective agreements.

How can we deal with the fact that the values for 1974, 1975, and 1977 find no explanation in an econometric model of the yearly number of strikers, based on economic, organizational, and institutional effects? There are various statistical solutions that we could adopt. We could respecify a strike-size model, including among the regressors a set of three dummy variables (one for each year). Alternatively, we could modify the dependent variable itself, eliminating from the series for the number of strikers the values from the handful of largest strikes for 1974, 1975, and 1977. Unfortunately, this second alternative runs into problems of data availability for the 1977 observation and I have to rely exclusively on dummy variables.[34] In summary, the model that I propose to estimate is a modified specification of equation (5.4) with the inclusion of three dummy variables for the years 1974, 1975, and 1977.

$$W_t = \beta_0 + \beta_1 UN_t + \beta_2 UNION_t + \beta_3 \Delta W_{t-1} + \beta_4 CONTRACT_t + \beta_5 D\text{-}74 + \beta_6 D\text{-}75 + \beta_7 D\text{-}77 + \epsilon_t \quad (5.5)$$

Table 5.15 reports the econometric results obtained from estimating equation (5.5). The results show that a model properly specified to account for unexplained large

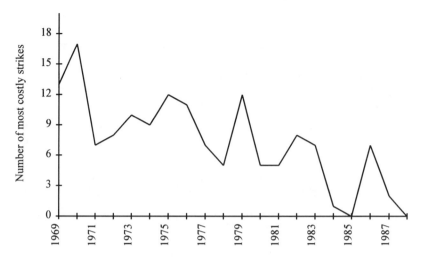

Figure 5.8. *Plot of the number of strikes involving the largest time lost ("most costly strikes")*

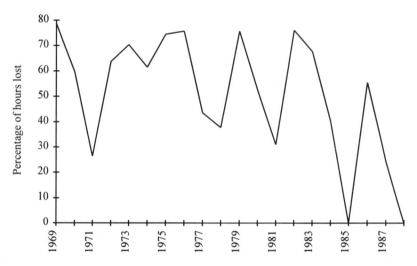

Figure 5.9. *Plot of the percentage of total number of hours lost accounted for by strikes with the largest number of hours lost*

residuals greatly improves the performance of the contract-renewal variable, just as expected. The results also show that the values for 1974 and 1975, in particular, are not only outliers, in the sense that they create large residuals, but also influential observations, to the extent that they change both individual coefficient estimates, their significance, and the overall fit of the model, as measured by the

172   The puzzle of strikes

Table 5.15. *Checking the effect of unexplained observations (1974, 1975, 1977)*

Dependent variable:	Number of strikers for all models			
Aggregation level:	Industry; yearly series			
Sample period:	1955/1978			
Estimation method:	GLS (Cochrane-Orcutt) for all models			

	Model 1	Model 2	Model 3	Model 4[a]
Constant	381.12	191.59	220.51	233.61
	(1,048.37)	(933.16)	(822.29)	(829.86)
Unemployment rate	-368.49*	-233.73**	-294.17*	-273.72*
	(131.93)	(122.41)	(106.09)	(103.65)
Change in real wages$_{t-1}$ (%)	-131.61*	-37.15	-95.90**	-104.00*
	(60.29)	(62.99)	(59.22)	(50.50)
Union membership	.266E-2*	.17E-2*	.22E-2*	.21E-2*
	(.383E-3)	(.44E-3)	(.35E-3)	(.30E-3)
Contract renewal	5.81	16.36*	13.02**	14.73*
	(7.65)	(6.76)	(6.88)	(6.47)
1974 dummy		2025.87*	1920.52*	
		(868.99)	(860.96)	
1975 dummy		3275.09*	2417.64*	
		(1058.70)	(975.28)	
1977 dummy		1310.58		
		(913.42)		
Adjusted R^2	.68	.75	.81	.69
Durbin-Watson	1.90	1.90	2.11	.2.08

[a]In model 4, the values of the number of strikers for 1974 and 1975 were modified.
Note: Standard error in parentheses. **Significant at the .05 level; *significant at the .01 level.

adjusted R^2 [compare the estimates of model 2 with those of model 1, reproduced in Table 5.15 for convenience and obtained from estimating equation (5.4) – model 3 in Table 5.14]. Given the lack of statistical significance of the 1977 dummy in model 2, model 3 estimates a variant of equation (5.5) without the 1977 dummy. Both the overall fit of the model (R^2 goes from .75 to .81) and the significance of individual variables have improved. The last model (model 4) reports the results obtained by estimating equation (5.4), having modified the values of the 1974 and 1975 observations, by substracting a handful of large-scale strikes.[35] Although the overall fit is not much better than that of the original model (.69 vs. .68) the significance of the coefficients of all independent variables has greatly improved and the effects are in the expected direction.

As good as those findings may be from a statistical viewpoint, they leave unresolved the problem of pinning down the causes for the three largest observations in the series for the number of strikers in the entire postwar period. If the purpose of sociological inquiry is to gain knowledge about social processes, rather than to play the statistical game of fits and significances, then the pursuit of an explanation for these points will certainly require further "footwork and shoe leather."[36] Each data point will require careful inspection and explanation. An account of both overall patterns in the data and individual observations that make sense in light of history should be the standard by which we evaluate our work.

One place to start our inquiry is among the monthly strike statistics. Close scrutiny of these statistics reveals high numbers of strikers from September through December of 1974, with totals above 2 million workers, and from January through April and again in December of 1975. In 1975, the monthly number of workers on strike for purely economic reasons twice (once in January and once in April) exceeded the unprecedented mark of more than 3 million workers. The average levels for 1977 were lower, but strike sizes remained high throughout the year, with numbers over the 1 million mark in June, July, November, and December, and high values also in February through April. That those strikes were of the general type (whether or not the unions labeled them as such), industrywide or even interindustry strikes, is clearly highlighted by the fact that a total of only four strikes in 1974, fourteen in 1975, and fourteen in 1977 accounted for the high numbers of strikers in those years.

Perusal of any Italian newspaper of the time will confirm the nature of those strikes: the large-scale strikes to press for a new *scala mobile* agreement in the fall of 1974 (general strike on December 4) and in the spring of 1975 (general strikes on January 23 and April 22). The *scala mobile* agreement was signed on January 25, 1975, with private employers, and a law passed on May 20, 1975, extended the benefits to public employees as well. Throughout that period, the unions mounted several large-scale strikes for various "general" causes: in defense of employment, to prompt private and public investments in the South, to reform the state-controlled retirement system. To give the reader a flavor of the times, let me focus on 1977 and on the months for which official strike statistics show the highest levels of workers on strike in that year (February, March, April, June, July, November, and December). The pages of *Il Corriere della Sera* (Cds) read like a war bulletin from the front. The year begins and ends with two massive general strikes (in March and December); in between, the unions call a series of national, large-scale strikes against both the government and employers.[37]

Friday, March 18, 1977 (Cds, p. 1). General strike (involving over 10 million workers) called by CGIL, CISL, UIL. Duration: From 4 to 12 hours depending upon the region. Reasons: against the government's wage and industrial policies.

Wednesday, April 27, 1977 (Cds, p. 2). National strike of large firms. Duration: 4 hours. Reasons: Increase in employment levels, productive investment in the South, youth employment, containment of inflation, plant-level bargaining.

Friday, June 3, 1977 (Cds, p. 7). National strike of workers in large conglomerates. Duration: 4 hours. Reasons: Industrial growth and employment.

Wednesday, June 22, 1977 (Cds, p. 2). National strike in industry. Duration: 4 hours. Reasons: Productive investment in the South and employment.

Thursday, November 3, 1977 (Cds, p. 6). National strike of textile workers (CGIL, CISL, and UIL). Duration: the entire day. Reasons: Employment and growth in the textile sector.

Thursday, November 3, 1977 (Cds, p. 2). National strike of state workers. Duration: 24 hours. Reasons: Prompt renewal of state workers' collective contracts.

Monday, November 7, 1977 (Cds, p. 18). National strike of state-owned food-processing firms. Duration: 8 hours. Reasons: Employment and restructuring of the food-processing sector.

Thursday, November 10, 1977 (Cds, p. 18). National strike of construction workers. Reasons: Press goverment intervention in public works and public housing.

Tuesday, November 15, 1977 (Cds, p. 1). National strike of the entire industrial sector. Duration: 4 hours. Reasons: Government policies to promote new jobs and productive investment.

Thursday. November 24, 1977 (Cds, p. 6). National strike of agricultural workers. Duration: 24 hours.

The tempo of mobilization picked up in a crescendo during the month of December: national strike of mass-media workers (December 1), national strike of metalworkers and national strike of all stock-exchange workers (December 2), national teachers' strike (December 6), general strike in Sardinia (December 7), national strike of all public transportation (December 9). The year 1978 saw more of the same, with the unions mounting an all-out political offensive against employers and the state, punctuated by brief and large displays of working-class mobilization capacity. When compared with the years of *conflittualità permanente* in 1968–72 with its diffused microlevel conflict, frequently involving a handful of workers for a handful of minutes, the years of *compromesso storico* in 1975–78 brought out quite a different pattern of conflict behavior.

Reading through the newspapers in search of an explanation for the 1974, 1975, and 1977 outliers will not only confirm the change in unions' strategies in the mid-1970s (from local bargaining to more centralized bargaining, from plant-level, small-scale actions to national and centralized mobilization), as highlighted at the beginning of this chapter; it will also give real meaning to the record levels of mobilization that tend to get mystified by econometric coefficients, with their pictures of huge masses of workers filling the streets and the squares of Italian cities (particularly Rome), of clenched fists and red banners – an impressive display of working-class solidarity. The clearly political markers in those pictures (the large masses, the hammer and sickle, the marches through downtown Rome, the political capital, rather than through Milan or Turin, the economic capitals), as well as the fact that those strikes often involved the state directly as an actor in the drama, illustrate the limitations of a view of industrial relations as being centered around only workers, unions, and employers. In the mid-1970s, Italian unions were pressuring both employers and the state via a barrage of large-scale, classwide strikes. We may, indeed, have to "bring the state back in" in order to understand the 1974, 1975, and 1977 outliers. That there was something more to the strikes in those three crucial years can clearly be seen in Figure 5.10, which plots the percentage of workers on strike for "other" reasons – other than for contract

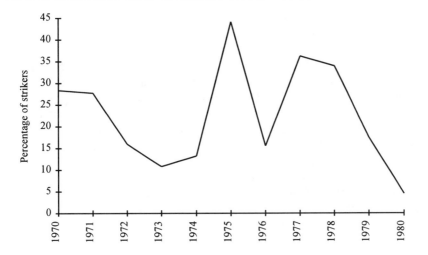

Figure 5.10. *Plot of the percentage of workers on strike for "other" reasons*

renewal, wage and economic issues, banning layoffs, and solidarity, according to the ISTAT categories of strike causes. If not contract renewal, wage and economic issues, a ban against layoffs, and solidarity, what else, then? For what "other" reasons were Italian workers striking in those years? In Chapter 6, I will look elsewhere, outside the strict realm of workers–employers economic relations and in the wider sphere of their political relations as mediated in the state, to find an answer to these questions. But despite such a limit to an explanation of industrial conflict based on the bargaining structure, this line of inquiry is far from having exhausted all of its explanatory power. To prove that, let me pursue an argument that I started developing in the preceding chapter while examining the distribution of workers' plant-level organizational resources by plant size. Let me probe further into the relationship between plant size and workers' ability to demand concessions and even more so to obtain concessions from their employers.

5.6. PLANT-LEVEL BARGAINING

Whereas national, categorywide contracts set minimum standards for all workers in all firms in an economic sector, many of the actual variations in working conditions and wages were determined within each firm via plant-level bargaining. Throughout the 1950s and 1960s, plant-level bargaining was rare. Although it picked up during the 1959–62 period, as we saw earlier in this chapter (see Table 5.1), it remained confined mostly to larger firms throughout the 1960s. However, in the 1970s, bargaining at that level became increasingly widespread. There are plenty of survey data that provide valuable information on the diffusion of plant-level bargaining during that decade and its relationship to firm size.

One of the first surveys was conducted in 1972 by the Bergamo FLM (the united federation of metalworkers). According to that survey, the use of plant-level bargaining was directly related to plant size: Only 4.4% of firms with fewer than 10 workers carried out plant-level bargaining, compared with 33.8% of firms employing 10–49 workers, 73.2% of firms with 50–99 workers, and 100% of firms in all other classes (100–249, 250–499, >500) (FLM di Bergamo, 1975, p. 208).

A later study on the diffusion of plant-level bargaining in the Veneto region during the 1979–81 period, involving firms with more than 20 employees, found 1,223 firms (for a total 1,296 agreements) involved in plant-level bargaining and an additional 450 firms involved in territorywide bargaining (Giubilato, 1982; Castegnaro, 1983). All in all, some 42% of firms with more than 20 employees were involved in collective bargaining, either at the plant level or at the territory level.[38] This aggregate figure, however, hides remarkable differences in bargaining practices across firms of different sizes. In fact, plant-level bargaining was linearly related to plant size: Whereas only 19% of firms in the 20–49 size class were involved, the figure jumped to 79% for the class of firms employing more than 500 workers. Thus, large numbers of workers were excluded from plant-level bargaining, because 60% of all workers were employed in the 20–49 size class.[39]

Data available from the Osservatorio Cesos on the state of labor relations in Italy for the years 1983–84[40] and 1984–85[41] confirm that plant-level bargaining was linearly related to firm size: 23.7% of smaller firms (20–99 workers) were involved in plant-level bargaining, as were 44.3% of medium-size firms (100–499), and 51.8% of larger firms (Camonico, 1986). Similarly, Regalia's research on *consigli di fabbrica* showed that large firms were more likely than smaller firms to engage in plant-level bargaining.[42] In fact, many large plants (61% of them) carried out both plant-level bargaining and shop-level bargaining.

An analysis of FLM data on plant-level bargaining in metalworking firms in Lombardy during the period October 1979 to July 1980 indirectly confirms the positive relationship between plant-level bargaining and firm size (Moro, 1980). The average size for the firms where plant-level bargaining was practiced was rather high (118 workers). Furthermore, the Lombardy FLM data show that only 42.9% of unionized firms were involved in plant-level bargaining. As we saw in Chapter 4, the percentage of unionized firms was particularly low in the class of smaller firms. Finally, Bagnasco and Trigilia's studies (1984, 1985; Trigilia, 1986) of two industrial districts featuring small-scale production showed that 73.6% of craft firms employing less than 10 workers had no plant-level bargaining, compared with 8.9% of large industrial firms.[43]

The fact that plant-level bargaining is used is certainly a good indicator of workers' organizational capacities in a plant. However, plant-level bargaining does not tell the whole story about labor relations in smaller firms. In fact, not only were small firms less likely to carry out plant-level bargaining than larger firms, but when they did engage in plant-level bargaining, the agreements that they signed were also less distinctive. The data from the Osservatorio Cesos show that the content of the labor agreements in smaller firms was "poorer"[44] and more standardized[45] (Camonico, 1986). They were predominantly concerned with wage issues (Associazione Industriale Lombarda, 1983, p. 153). Giubilato's analysis of plant-level contracts signed in the Veneto region similarly showed that "richness" in contract issues was linearly related to firm size.[46] Furthermore, regardless of firm size, workers were more likely to use plant-level bargaining in situations in which firms were in crisis and/or were restructuring than in times of prosperity. According to Camonico's analysis of the Osservatorio Cesos data, even smaller firms could experience fervid bargaining periods when facing crises (73% of the firms), not much different from those in larger firms (93%). In prosperous times, however, the difference in behavior between smaller and larger firms widened (27% vs. 66%).[47] That pattern tended to make things worse for workers in small firms, because they were more likely to bargain at the plant level when management had little to offer.

More generally, the overall styles of labor relations were different in larger and smaller firms. Regalia's 1981 survey of 63 *consigli di fabbrica* showed that smaller firms (100–200 employees) were characterized by a much greater degree of informality in the electoral process, in the style and frequency of delegates' meetings and channels of communication with workers and with the outside unions (Regalia, 1984a).[48] Regalia's findings were confirmed by the data collected by the Osservatorio Cesos: Labor relations were less formal in small firms (20–99 employees), with fewer regular meetings among the delegates.[49] In smaller firms, plant-level contracts often were informal and verbal (Associazione Industriale Lombarda, 1983, p. 153). Typically, negotiations were held within the firm. Only when outside union representatives were involved did employers shift the negotiations to the employers' association headquarters.[50]

Not only were labor relations more informal and plant-level bargaining less frequent in smaller firms, but also the workers in smaller firms were less militant during the bargaining process. A study of small firms sponsored by Giovani Imprenditori, the association of "young entrepreneurs" within Confindustria, showed that strike activity was very low in firms with fewer than 50 employees. Workers participated in strikes pending the renewal of national, categorywide contracts, but plant-level strikes were rare (Pastorino and Ragazzoni, 1980, p. 92). Those findings were confirmed by the Assolombarda survey: Workers in smaller firms typically struck prior to the renewal of national, collective contracts, but rarely struck for plant-level contracts. They never participated in political strikes (Associazione Industriale Lombarda, 1983, p. 139). During plant-level contract renewals, the only form of conflict concerned a ban on overtime.[51] Strikes had an impact only when they were called at the end of a shift or on Friday afternoon; then workers simply went home (Associazione Industriale Lombarda, 1983, p. 135). The research conducted by Giubilato among small firms in Veneto confirmed that strike activity during plant-level bargaining was linearly related to plant size: 36% of agreements in firms with 20–49 employees had been preceded by strikes, compared with 85% for firms with more than 500 workers.

The lower figures regarding militancy, plant-level bargaining, and the content of collective contracts in small plants, revealing though they may be, only scratch the surface of the state of labor relations in smaller firms. After all, it is one thing to ask, but quite another to reach a collective agreement, and still another to ensure

Table 5.16. *Per capita spending for wages by firm size*

	20–49	50–99	100–199	200–499	500–999	1,000–4,999	>5,000
1961	–	844	892	1,025	1,148	1,227	1,497
1971	1,916	2,298	2,520	2,805	3,129	3,477	3,585

Source: Fondazione Giovanni Agnelli (1973, p. 32).

its provisions are carried out. Giubilato's research among small firms in Veneto showed that evasion of contract provisions by management was more typical in smaller firms: 26% in smaller firms (for an average evasion rate of 11%), 17–18% in larger firms.[52] Smaller firms often evaded even health and environmental issues, the issues most commonly dealt in small-firm contracts: In one study, 14 of 21 clauses that required environmental inspections were never enforced; 9 of 13 firms that allowed environmental inspections did nothing about correcting any deficiencies; in 4 of 10 firms that required medical checkups of workers, the checkups were never done, and in 4 others they were done only superficially (Castegnaro, 1983). The Bergamo FLM research similarly showed that all firms with more than 100 employees complied with the provisions of the national, categorywide contract and practiced plant-level bargaining, whereas only 60% of firms employing fewer than 10 workers did so (Brusco, 1975, pp. 12–13).

The available data on wages by firm size show that regardless of whether or not workers demanded higher wages, they were not paid as much in smaller firms. On the basis of an extensive analysis of Ministry of Labor survey data, disaggregated by firm size, labor economist Dell'Aringa concluded that "without doubt, larger firms pay higher wages" (Dell'Aringa, 1976, p. 62). The survey of Bergamo metalworking firms showed that wages increased linearly with increasing firm size (Brusco, 1975, pp. 210–13). Wages in larger firms were 30–50% higher than those in smaller firms (Brusco, 1975, p. 14). In fact, according to Dell'Aringa, in 1969, workers in larger factories were making monthly salaries 79% higher than those in smaller factories (Dell'Aringa, 1976, p. 89). Wage differentials were wider in smaller firms, with widespread disregard for official union policies of wage egalitarianism, at least during the 1970s.[53] A study by d'Ambrosio showed that hourly earnings in small firms were some 60% lower than those in larger firms, with even wider gaps in some sectors (81% in clothing, 82% in printing, 97% in rubber) (d'Ambrosio, 1972, p. 27). The data compiled by a research team from the Fondazione Giovanni Agnelli showed that in both 1961 and 1971, per capita spending for wages was directly proportional to firm size (Table 5.16). Still in the first half of the 1980s, wages were higher in larger firms.[54]

Not surprisingly, working conditions in smaller firms were worse. In addition to the lower wages, higher wage differentials, evasion of contract provisions and social security payments, and the classification of workers predominantly in the lower skill grades, the work environment tended to be more hazardous to one's health, the pace of production was harsher, and working hours were longer. Already in the early 1950s, a report by the Christian Association of Italian Workers

(ACLI, 1953) and the material assembled by the Commissione Parlamentare d'Inchiesta sulle Condizioni dei Lavoratori in Italia (1958a, 1958b, 1958c) documented all too well such practices among the smaller firms.[55] Still in the 1970s, smaller firms were more likely than larger ones to expect employees to work overtime at no pay. In the 1971 Isvet survey of workers' attitudes, 8.1% of the workers in firms employing 50–100 workers reported that they worked overtime at no pay; the figure was 2.5% in firms employing 500–1,000 workers (Buratto et al., 1974, p. 192). Well into the 1980s, the rhythms of production were more intense and the work-environment conditions worse in smaller firms. Survey research, including research sponsored by employers' associations, painted a fairly negative picture of life in the smaller firms (e.g., Brusco, 1975; Pastorino and Ragazzoni, 1980; Associazione Industriale Lombarda, 1983). A good indicator of the more adverse conditions of life inside the small industrial firms was the fact that the most common issues dealt with in plant-level bargaining (aside from wages) were precisely those that revealed the poor state of affairs: health, environment, and time (Cagnato, 1981; Giubilato, 1982; Associazione Industriale Lombarda, 1983; Camonico, 1986).

In conclusion, the empirical evidence leaves no doubt about the positive linear relationship involving plant size, plant-level bargaining, and working and wage conditions: workers in large firms were better off economically than workers in small firms. That finding would seem to provide empirical support for Doeringer and Piore's theory (1971) of the existence of a dual labor market: a primary market characterized by job stability and higher wages, and a secondary market where low wages, poor social benefits, and poor working conditions are more typical.

If "small is beautiful," I certainly find no evidence of it in small Italian firms, and apparently neither did Italian workers. Only 13% of blue-collar workers in the 1971 Isvet survey would rather have worked in a smaller firm (Buratto et al., 1974, p. 171); the first choice (55% of the workers) was overwhelmingly for the larger firm. That finding, however, introduces yet another paradox: During the 1970s, areas where small-scale production was predominant (e.g., Emilia Romagna, Veneto) showed faster rates of growth, higher per capita incomes, and lower unemployment rates than did the rest of the country (Brusco, 1982). Research by Palanca (1979) confirmed that by the mid-1970s, some of the areas of small-scale production had indeed prospered sufficiently to attain the highest levels of income in Italy. Furthermore, industrial growth did not come at the cost of social dysfunction. The quality of life index was also highest for some of those areas (Palanca, 1983). How can we reconcile those findings that seem to support the slogan "small is beautiful" with the considerable body of evidence stacked against that argument in this section *(paradox of small-scale production regions)*?

5.7. ON THE COST OF STRIKES (THE EMPLOYERS' VIEW)

Workers and unions have historically been quite creative in devising forms of collective action that would hit employers the hardest at the lowest cost to the workers. Thus, a series of short, often unannounced, strikes, such as several half-

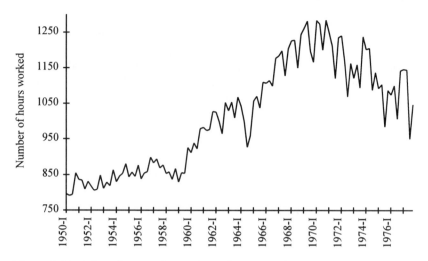

Figure 5.11. *Plot of quarterly number of hours worked in the manufacturing industry*

hour stoppages at different times during a day, could inflict great damage at low cost (Mershon, 1986, pp. 2, 335). The ability to implement effective strike tactics involves a good understanding of the production process in the factory. As an Italian shop-floor steward put it, "each department has been studied so that we may have maximum effect on production; and within each department [the strike assignment] varies by task. This way, production falls by 90 percent with two hours of strikes in the day" (quoted in Mershon, 1986, p. 335). It was those effects on output that often prompted firms and the conservative press to rail against what they alleged to be the high costs of strikes, in terms of both lost output and loss of competitiveness against foreign firms. Many scholars have attempted to measure the economic impacts of strikes with elaborate schemes, taking into account the numbers of consumers, producers, and suppliers directly and indirectly involved, as well as the length of the strike.[56]

Indeed, the exploratory analyses in Section 3.3.1 (p. 59) revealed decreases in industrial output at three-year intervals. The analyses also showed a remarkable correspondence between the timing of those periodic slumps in production and the timing of high levels of strike activity. We now know why: The renewals of industrywide collective contracts set the temporal pattern for the strike figures, which in turn set the pattern for production figures. Figure 5.11, showing the total number of hours worked in manufacturing,[57] makes that very clear: The troughs of 1969-IV, 1973-I, and 1979-II correspond to the timing of the handful of large-scale strikes that preceded the renewal of industrial contracts; the troughs of 1974-IV, 1975-I, and 1977-IV correspond to the handful of general strikes discussed earlier; the peaks in total hours worked were achieved in the years between contract-renewal years. Those were also the years of plant-level bargaining. In light of this evidence, the frequent refusals of Italian employers to engage in plant-level

Table 5.17. *Hours worked and hours lost due to labor unrest and absenteeism*

Cause	1968	1969	1970	1971	1972	1973	1974	1975
Hours lost to[a]	9.6	14.3	12.6	13.5	15.3	17.2	17.8	18.0
Labor unrest	1.3	4.7	2.5	1.9	2.4	3.3	3.1	2.2
Absenteeism	8.3	9.6	10.1	11.6	12.9	13.9	14.7	15.8

[a]Percentage of total hours worked.
Source: Mediobanca, reported in Troiani (1978, p. 163).

bargaining appear to be quite odd (hypocritical?): Accustomed as employers are in general to calculating losses and profits, time worked and time lost, why would they favor the bargaining level that had the most serious negative effects on production? Obviously, the employers' lamentations about the "cost of strikes" hid more than they revealed.

Notwithstanding the evidence presented here, by and large the "costs" of strikes have been greatly exaggerated (Kornhauser et al., 1954, p. 8; Harbison, 1954, p. 275). First, strikes can lead to technological progress and improvements in the organization of production that in the long run may offset their costs (Turner, 1969). Becchi Collidà and Negrelli (1986, p. 165), in their analysis of Fiat, concluded that "With hindsight, one could say that the explosion of industrial conflict in 1968–72 has stimulated, above all, technological innovation." Second, a high level of strike activity was the exception rather than the rule. For the Italian case, Ross and Hartman (1960, p. 124) remarked that "The fact remains that the average striker has remained away from work only two or three days." Third, lost output due to labor disputes can be recouped through overtime and increased work intensity before and after the strike (Turner et al., 1967, p. 54; Knowles, 1952). Indeed, we saw that not all peaks in the curve describing time lost due to strikes negatively affected even sensitive quarterly series of capacity-utilization data. Fourth, lost time due to strikes during recessions would not have been used productively anyway, because workers probably would have been put on shorter work schedules or even laid off. Finally, compared with strikes, often more time is lost because of work accidents deriving from unsafe working conditions, particularly in smaller firms (d'Ambrosio and Biz, 1974), unemployment,[58] and the common cold. Turner (1969, p. 35) wrote that "An effective anti-influenza serum would probably be of more measurable benefit to the economy than an effective anti-strike law – and perhaps be less difficult and less costly to produce."

Mediobanca survey data from a sample of Italian firms (Table 5.17) confirmed that the loss of time due to absenteeism was, on average, four times as high as that due to strikes.[59] Such highly aggregated data, however, may be somewhat misleading. The more disaggregated data of Confindustria on absenteeism (Table 5.18), collected among a sample of member firms, do not seem to confirm Turner's point. If we take the figures on nonprofessional illnesses (nonchronic diseases contracted on the job) lasting less than three days as indicators of absenteeism due to the common cold and influenza, then the time lost due to strikes each year during

Table 5.18. *Confindustria survey data on absenteeism by year and type*[a]

	1972	1973	1974	1975	1976	1977	1978
Work-related injuries[b]	.98	.85	.82	.69	.61	.69	.69
Nonprofessional illnesses	6.48	6.97	7.45	7.47	7.12	6.86	7.09
Nonprofessional illnesses (<3 days)	.68	.64	.96	.88	.97	.87	1.04
Marriage permits	.14	.14	.15	.13	.12	.09	.09
Maternity leave	1.38	1.50	1.66	1.77	1.33	1.08	1.14
Permits	1.13	1.23	1.32	1.33	1.46	1.37	1.45
Unjustified absences	.13	.13	.17	.22	.11	.08	.12
Disciplinary suspensions	.00	.01	.03	.01	.00	.00	.00
Strike activity	1.37	2.26	2.12	1.37	2.12	1.37	.76
Total	11.65	13.09	13.72	12.98	12.87	11.54	11.34

[a]The data refer to the rates of incidence (*tassi di gravità*). They include male and female blue-collar and white-collar workers.
[b]Includes professional illnesses.
Source: Confindustria, *Rassegna di statistiche del lavoro*. Rome.

the 1970s (with the sole exception of 1978) was consistently higher than the time lost to such illnesses.[60] However, even Confindustria data basically support the Mediobanca findings that time lost due to strikes is only a minor fraction of the total work time lost for all reasons. Furthermore, the 1970s, with their higher-than-average strike levels, may not be the proper reference period. Unfortunately, the Confindustria survey on absenteeism was begun only in 1972.[61] An earlier survey, between 1953 and 1957 and between 1963 and 1967, conducted by Assolombarda, the association of private employers in the province of Milan, did not provide data on absenteeism due to short-term illnesses. Nonetheless, time lost due to strikes was lower than time lost due to any other reason. Summarizing the 1953–57 period, Assolombarda reported the following:

> Among male workers, illnesses are the main reason for absenteeism, with 63–65% of hours lost. Absences due to work accidents and professional illnesses (12–16% combined) and strike activity follow, in decreasing order of importance.... During the five-year period, time lost due to strikes represents 5–10% of total time lost among male workers and 2–4% among female workers. (Associazione Industriale Lombarda, 1958, p. 31)

Confindustria data for the 1980s confirm the Assolombarda findings for the 1950s and 1960s. As strike activity continued to decrease during the 1980s, the ratio between time lost due to strikes and that due to short-term illnesses went from 1.08 in 1981 to 3.02 in 1982, and 2.52 in 1983, decreasing thereafter to .98, .73, .73, .5, .59, and .62 in 1989.

5.8. UNFORESEEN PIECES FALL INTO PLACE

Over the past several chapters we have been accumulating evidence concerning the relationship between strikes and wages. In Chapter 2, we saw that the number of strikes was positively related to the percentage variations in real minimum contractual wages. We also saw that the plot of the coefficients of the three-year lag structures in the estimates of the Ashenfelter and Johnson model describes concave-down parabolas. Finally, in Chapter 4 we saw that the one-year lagged effects of real wages were positive for the number of strikes and negative for the number of workers involved. Thus far, I have made no attempt to pin down the relationship among wages, prices, and strikes. The findings in this chapter, however, should now allow me to pull those scattered pieces of empirical evidence together and try to make sense of them.

First, that the lag structures extended over twelve quarters should come as no surprise. After all, most collective agreements had three-year durations.

Second, Bordogna and Provasi (1979, pp. 259–66) interpreted the positive signs of the wage lag structures as typical of high-mobilization periods (*la lotta che paga*; "the more you get, the more you want"). That explanation is indeed plausible, and therefore I provisionally accepted it in Chapter 2. But in light of the analyses in this chapter, I now have to reject that interpretation. Instead, I propose the following: The positive sign of the wage structure was due to the peculiar institutional arrangements that came to characterize the Italian industrial-relations system during the late 1960s and 1970s, regardless of the levels of worker mobilization. Let us see why and how.

The renewals of workers' collective agreements (characterized, as we have seen, by soaring numbers of strikers) led, approximately every three years, to sharp increases in minimum contractual money (and real) wages, as can be seen from Figure 5.12.[62] Between those peaks in both curves of number of strikers and wages, the curve of strike frequency describes a concave-down parabola (see Figure 5.1, p. 156). Such institutional arrangements resulted in the following pattern: a peak in real wages, a concave-down parabola in strike frequency, a peak in real wages, a concave-down parabola, and so on every three years. The shape and sign of the lag structure for the wage variable only reflected that type of institutional arrangement.

Those same arguments can now help us to understand the data reported in Table 3.1 (p. 58) regarding the negative signs of the distributed-lag coefficients for the first year and the data in Table 4.1 (p. 107) concerning the relationships between the lagged values for contractual minimum wages and the number of strikes (positive coefficients) and number of strikers (negative coefficients).[63] The signing at time t-1 of a categorywide collective contract will lead to higher contractual wages (the wage indicator used here). With the contract signed, at time t the strike component associated with categorywide bargaining (the number of strikers) will decline (leading to a negative relationship between wages at time t-1 and the number of strikers at time t, as shown in Table 4.1, p. 107). The end of category-wide bargaining at time t-1 will be followed at time t by plant-level bargaining, characterized by a high number of strikes. Thus, higher wages at time t-1 will be related to higher strike frequencies at time t, leading to a positive lagged relationship between wages and the number of strikes, precisely as shown in Table 4.1. The

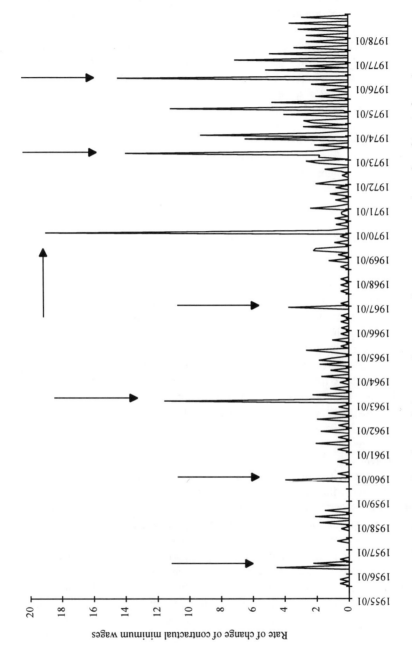

Figure 5.12. Plot of rate of change of contractual minimum wages (metalworking industry)

Table 5.19. *Correlation coefficients between numbers of strikes, strikers, and hours lost and labor share of national income (economywide, detrended data, 1955–78)*

	Strikes	Strikers	Hours lost
Labor share of national income	-.072	.34	-.13

statistical game that we often play of lagging different variables at different times (needless to say always justified on substantive and theoretical grounds) shows all its frailty. By lagging variables, we can always obtain a positive or a negative coefficient, depending on the result we want to show. Yet the analyses in this chapter leave no doubt that the interpretations of those coefficients are different and that, furthermore, they simply reflect different underlying causal structures.

Third, it was an important part of Italian unions' tactics that renewals of industrywide collective agreements be clustered together, so that in a contract-renewal year they could confront the employers' association at the national level with a wide mobilization front. That characteristic of the Italian system of industrial relations during the 1960s, and particularly during the 1970s, had periodic, short-term effects on both income distribution and industrial production. First, the wage increases resulting from the more or less contemporaneous renewals of several major collective agreements were likely to modify the distribution of national income in the workers' favor. However, the correlation coefficients in Table 5.19 show that strike size, rather than frequency, was positively related to the labor share of national income. That is hardly surprisingly. After all, it was the size component of strike activity that characterized the renewal of collective agreements, where minimum wage increases were fixed. Second, in Chapter 3, we saw that industrial production showed a characteristic three-year periodic cycle. The large strikes that preceded the renewal of major collective contracts under conditions of a union ban against working overtime (such as during the 1970s) did cause short-term decreases in industrial production.

In conclusion, the structure of collective bargaining not only helps us to understand much of the temporal pattern of Italian strikes highlighted by the exploratory analyses of strike data (Franzosi, 1980) but also helps explain the empirically observable relationships encountered in preceding chapters, such as those between strikes and wages, strikes and income shares, and strikes and industrial production.

5.9. A FALSE SENSE OF SECURITY

The analyses in this chapter have highlighted a little-known problem with quantitative research. The accepted wisdom is that the great advantage of quantitative research versus qualitative research lies in the numbers. What degree of credibility can be attributed to the findings of historical or ethnographic work?

How can one generalize from the handful of cases (often just one) on which most such studies are based? The best example of ethnographic research on Italian strikes (Pizzorno, 1974–75) was based on eleven factories: Autobianchi, Candy, Dalmine, Ercole Marelli, Falck, GTE, Ignis-IRE, Innocenti, Magneti Marelli, Redaelli and Sit-Siemens. How can we expect that what works for Dalmine or Falck will also work for Fiat, Italcantieri, Marzotto, or Pirelli? The greater, in-depth knowledge that one can acquire through qualitative research will be of little help if it cannot be generalized.

Quantitative research, on the other hand, albeit at the cost of some loss of information, encompasses much larger sample sizes. Furthermore, both the rules for sample selection and those for mapping the particular into the universal are known and "objective" (i.e., the rules of statistics). Indeed, compared with the handful of strikes that one can study via qualitative methods, any of the regression equations in this book can "crunch" some 46,290 strikes – that many occurred in industry during the period from 1950 to 1978, according to ISTAT. Unfortunately, however, such a large sample size provides only a false sense of security. In reality, the regression equations do not deal with 46,290 individual strikes. The unit of analysis for my time series regressions is not the individual strike, but the single year or quarter. In all, this leaves me with 29 observations when using yearly data, and 116, at best, when using quarterly data – a far cry from 46,290 observations.

The nature of the substantive relationship between variables can further reduce this number. For instance, in this chapter, we have seen that the relationship between wages and strikes was mediated by the structure of collective bargaining. Because wage negotiations were held every three years at the central, national level, the effective number of data points on which the relationship between wages and strikes can be tested is 29/3, or 9 data points (perhaps only 6, if one considers that this structure of bargaining was shaped during the 1960s and 1970s). Consider another example: In Chapter 4, we saw that strikes and unionization flared up together during strike waves. That being the case, the number of effective data points on which an empirical test of the relationship between unionization and strikes could be based would be only 2: the 1959–63 and 1968–72 strike waves.

When working with such small samples, one or two outlying observations may weigh disproportionately on the magnitudes and signs of the estimated coefficients, further reducing the effective sample size. Estimates may change drastically under the influence of one or two outliers in the sample (Franzosi, 1994). Temporal aggregation may frther add to the problem of "influence." For instance, in the relationship between strikes and wages, strikes related to the renewals of industrywide contracts went up in 1962, 1969, and 1972, whereas wages due to the collective contracts went up, in each case, in the following year. In 1957, 1959, and 1966, on the other hand, both contract-related strikes and wages went up in the same year. When looking at time-series correlations, that first set of years would lead to a negative correlation, and the second set to a positive correlation.

Thus, from our original 46,290 observations, we have gone down to 29 or 116, and to 9 or even 2, fewer than the number of cases studied by Pizzorno's team, fewer than all the workers cited in this book as expert witnesses: Aris Accornero, Giampiero Carpo, Pasquale de Stefani, Giovanni Dozzo, Luciano Parlanti, Roberto Sibona, and the many more who remain anonymous. The fact that we estimate our econometric models perhaps using even large samples only obscures the simple reality that oftentimes the effective number of observations is no larger than the number of cases typically studied via qualitative methods. The trouble is that, as quantitative researchers, we are mostly unaware (or we choose to be) of those potentially damaging effects. As a result, the likelihood of bold confidence in one's frail empirical work is much greater in quantitative research than in qualitative research, where apologetic caution is always part of the way the story is told.

But the analyses in this chapter have dealt a fatal blow to another "certainty" most of us hold very dear: unshakable faith in the causal structures reflected in our statistical models. The clues were all there in the preceding chapters: the negative distributed-lag coefficients for the most recent quarters in the estimates of the Ashenfelter and Johnson model with the numbers of strikers and hours lost as dependent variables (Table 3.1, p. 58), and the reciprocal relationships between production and strike variables (Section 3.3.1, p. 59), and that between unionization and strikes in Chapter 4. We simply cannot ignore the problem any longer.

In Chapter 2, I painstakingly measured the "distributed-lag relationship" between wages and strikes. I carried out several exploratory analyses to estimate precisely the degree p of the Almon polynomial and the length n of the lag structure. At the end, I was quite confident that Italian workers had based their strike decisions on *rational* calculations based on the movement of wages over the preceding three years. Now we discover that what all those painstaking analyses amounted to was measurement of a spurious relationship between strikes and wages – spurious because of the Italian bargaining structure, with its three-year cycle of contract renewals. Much ado, it now seems, about nothing, if it weren't for one simple fact: In pursuing those nagging and unexpected reguliarities in our statistical findings we have learned a great deal about our substantive problem.

5.10. THE PICTURE EMERGES

The arguments and findings in this chapter confirm that there is indeed more to strike activity than economic determinants can explain – in fact, more than either (or both) economic-bargaining or resource-mobilization models can explain. The characteristic wavelike pattern of strikes, where the series for the numbers of strikes and strikers describe two out-of-phase sine waves of three-year periodicity, is not due to economic factors, but to institutional factors, in particular, to the bargaining structure. The bargaining structure affects strikes in two ways.

First, the renewal of major industrial collective contracts approximately every three years induces periodic, wavelike patterns in strike components that follow three-year cycles. Second, the two-tier system of bargaining (national, industrywide agreements, and local, plant-level agreements) explains the out-of-phase pattern between the numbers of strikes and strikers. I showed that the renewals of national, industrywide collective agreements were accompanied by few, short, very large strikes (all the workers in a particular economic sector, e.g., metalworkers, striking a handful of times in brief, "demonstrative" strikes). In contrast, the renewals of plant-level agreements were characterized by large numbers of small, brief strikes. The time lag whereby plant-level bargaining took place after the industrywide contract had been settled explains the observed lag between the series of data for the numbers of strikes and strikers. Thus, my analysis of the structure of collective bargaining has nailed down the *paradox of strike size*. In Chapter 3, we found that plant-level strikes were smaller than the average work force in the largest factories (the factories that were more likely to suffer strikes), because unions were able to organize only a fraction of the work force in large factories (I do remind the reader that I have yet to determine why Italian unions were less successful in organizing the largest plants, the *paradox of large firms*). Furthermore, the three major unions, competing for workers' allegiances in the same plants, continued their antagonistic relationships throughout most of the period studied in this book, further reducing the likelihood of any united participation by the whole work force. In Chapter 4, I entertained the possibility that Italian strike sizes were much larger than even the largest plants because of the unions' use of the strike as a political, "demonstrative" weapon. Unfortunately that explanation runs against a basic problem: Political strikes were not included in the official strike counts. What would then explain the presence of some very large strikes? In this chapter we have finally found an answer to that question: A handful of strikes were much larger than the work force in even the largest plants, not because of the unions' widespread use of demonstrative strikes over political issues (which they did), but because the Italian system of bargaining had been centralized either at the economy- or industry-wide level.

More generally, institutional arrangements not only shaped the patterns of strikes but also affected the relationships among variables. The renewals of collective contracts resulted in comparatively high wage increases. The curve for money wages shows marked peaks every three years, in correspondence with the renewals of major industrywide collective contracts. Given that industrywide contracts were preceded by large-scale strikes, it is easily seen why money wage rates were positively related to strike size rather than frequency. The bargaining structure can thus explain the varying patterns of positive and negative coefficients between the wage variable and the different strike indicators that we encountered in Chapters 3 and 4.

In conclusion, institutional arrangements do make a difference. A great deal of the temporal pattern of strikes was related to the bargaining structure, to the particular historical forms of institutionalization of conflict. The findings in this chapter have added several pieces to the larger puzzle. The overall picture is now beginning to emerge.

First, institutional arrangements provide explanations for the empirically observable two- to three-year cycles in strike indicators and for their interrelationships.

Second, they shed light on some of the empirical findings in the preceding chapters, particularly the relationships among strikes, wages, and production.

Third, the shapes of strikes in 1959, 1962, 1966, 1969, and 1973 show marked differences with respect to those for surrounding years. A collective-bargaining argument helps to explain this finding, because major contract renewals occurred in those years.[64]

Fourth, the historical analyses of this and the previous chapter have solved the *paradox of the 1962 and 1966 strike shapes*. Among contract-renewal years, the years 1962 and 1966 brought out strikes whose durations were longer than average. Rarely did strikes in Italy assume those characteristics, which are more typical in the British or American institutional contexts (Shorter and Tilly, 1974, pp. 306–34; Hibbs, 1976). The 1966 recession may help to explain the longer strike duration in 1966. As we have repeatedly seen, strikes during recessions tend to be longer. In 1962, however, Italy was at the pinnacle of its "economic miracle." We cannot invoke economic-hardship arguments to explain both years. There is another interpretation for the 1962 strike shape: the vigorous resistance with which Confindustria and private employers greeted the workers' demands. The protracted 1962 struggles surrounding the renewal of industrywide collective contracts (particularly metalworkers) marked a change in the balance of class power.[65] As the years of chronically high unemployment and underemployment came to an end during the boom years of the "economic miracle," labor timidly began to test its strength. But a resolutely conservative Confindustria would not yield ground easily.

Fifth, the changes in the institutional context of labor relations introduced by the Workers' Charter in 1970 help to explain another piece of the puzzle: a new pattern, during the 1970s, of relationships among strike indicators. Could that change also help explain the *paradox of the 1970s* (high strike levels and high unemployment levels)? Could the change in institutional context help explain the poor performance for the 1970s of an economic-bargaining model of strikes solely based on unemployment (specifically, the Ashenfelter and Johnson model)?

Finally, the findings in this chapter help to explain (at least in part) the transformation in strike shapes during the period 1975–78. The dramatic declines in the frequency and duration of strikes during those years clearly were related to the 1975 agreement on extended coverage of wage escalators to offset inflation. Less clear, however, is why the sizes of strikes dramatically increased during the same period. Wage indexing alone cannot explain that. Furthermore, the shapes of strikes during industrywide contract renewal years characteristically were different from those of surrounding years. Why, then, is the strike shape for 1976 (a renewal year) so uncharacteristically similar to those for 1975 and 1977? Could the 1975 *scala mobile* agreement also explain this anomaly, or is there more to it? Finally, if the number of strikers surged at times of contract renewals, why did 1974, 1975, and 1977, which were not contract-renewal years, show the highest levels in the number of strikers in the entire postwar period? Ever more questions for a handful of answers – the frustrating experience of scientific inquiry, in case we had any illusion that our knowledge had brought us too close to the Gods.

6

Class power, politics, and conflict

> The business cycle is the cause of the main fluctuations, indeed of the very nature of strikes themselves; by itself, however, it cannot explain the depth of certain retreats, the amplitude of certain offensives. Political circumstances weigh very heavily and provide the key to the understanding of the major silences and thrusts.
> Perrot (1974, p. 722)

> Politics constitutes an important kind of precondition for the eruption of large-scale worker movements, though not being in itself a sufficient one.
> Shorter and Tilly (1974, p. 104)

> The apolitical nature [of trade unions] is a lie, because it cannot exist. Trade unions must have a political outlook . . . to protect the interests of all workers of any political party or even without a party. To accomplish their goals, trade unions often need the support of political parties. Trade unions have often turned to popular and democratic parties and to their parliamentary groups, in order to lobby for the approval or rejection of a given law, in the workers' best interests.
> Di Vittorio (quoted in CESOS-CISL and IRES-CGIL, 1984, p. 303)

6.1. LEFT TO EXPLAIN: THE 1975–78 STRIKE SHAPES

Little by little, chapter by chapter, I have used the available theories about strikes to investigate the meaning of the data presented in Chapter 1 (the pieces of the puzzle). I have fitted almost the entire puzzle. I am left with only one of the original pieces (the 1975–78 strike shapes) and one theory: political exchange. But in fact, do we not already have an explanation for the 1975–78 strike shapes? Did we not see, in Chapter 5, that the 1975 wage escalator agreement between labor and capital could account for the lower frequency, shorter durations, and larger sizes of strikes in that and subsequent years? Considering that most strikes occur over wage issues, an automatic link between prices and wages would certainly reduce the frequency of strikes. Furthermore, considering that most strikes occurred at the plant level, if we eliminate the main reason for conflict at that level, we should be left with only industrywide and economywide strikes – precisely those strikes that were brief in duration and large in size, as highlighted by the 1975–78 strike shapes.

That explanation would certainly account for all pieces of the puzzle, although it would leave one strike theory unaccounted for. It would also leave unresolved several of the paradoxes that we have encountered in earlier chapters: the *paradox of the génie d'un peuple*, the *paradox of the 1970s*, the *paradox of large firms*, and the *paradox of small-scale production regions*. Furthermore, that explanation begs some very important questions. Why would the Italian capitalists want to be locked into an agreement that would leave them with no bargaining power vis-à-vis the working class and in a vulnerable position vis-à-vis foreign capitalists, for whom the cost of labor might be more flexible? Why would the Italian working class want to give up the only weapon at their disposal – conflict – which seemed to have paid off in the early 1970s? Finally, given that conflict over the 1975–78 period took on the typical demonstrative character of political strikes, was that an indication of a drastic shift in labor's strategy from the economic arena to the political arena? If so, what characteristics did the bargaining process take? What was being bargained? Did the state become a new bargaining partner during that period? These are some of the questions I will take up in this chapter.

6.2. POLITICAL MODELS OF STRIKES: THE LONG TERM

Business-cycle theories of strikes contend that strikes are the products of favorable economic conditions, the state of the labor market in particular. Not all share that view. For one thing, scholars working in either the Durkheimian or Marxist tradition are more likely to view collective action as the result of economic hardship. More generally, during the 1950s, many scholars put forward a variety of arguments (the "embourgeoisement" of the working class, the "end of ideology," the "withering away of strikes") that all predicted a long-term decline in industrial conflict following the advent of prosperity in the Western world.[1]

Those various labels, "embourgeoisement," "end of ideology," and "withering away of strikes," have not fared well as explanations for either the short-term or long-term characteristics of industrial conflict. For the short run, the empirical evidence overwhelmingly suggests a positive relationship between prosperity (i.e., the upswing phase of the business cycle) and conflict. The empirical findings presented in this book confirm a positive short-term relationship between industrial conflict and the business cycle, even for the Italian case.[2] "The resurgence of conflict" in industrialized countries during the 1960s proved those theories wrong in regard to the long run as well (Crouch and Pizzorno, 1978). The plots of the numbers of strikes, strikers, and hours lost (Figures 1.3, 1.4, and 1.5) provide little evidence in favor of any "withering away of strikes" in the Italian economy.

While history itself was empirically refuting the theories of a "withering away of strikes," social scientists were busily at work providing both a critique of those theories and alternative explanations for the long-term trends of strikes. For Shorter and Tilly (1974, pp. 306–31), long-term changes in the levels and forms of industrial conflict can be understood only in terms of the long-term shifts in labor's political position in national power structures. Admission of the working class to the polity in Western bourgeois nations has led to deep structural changes in the shapes of strikes: Strikes have become much shorter, but also more frequent and larger.[3]

Where the strike rate soared, revolutionary unionism acquired new organizational resources in a drive for political representation. Where the strike rate fell, workers had been accepted into the polity, and now needed no longer to use strikes as a means of pressing political demands. Where the strike rate fluctuated, as in North America, labor had discarded the industrial work stoppage as a means of political action, turning instead to political parties. (Shorter and Tilly, 1974, p. 317)

Hibbs (1976, 1978) and Korpi and Shalev (1980) put forward similar theories of political exchange (rather than an "end of ideology" or a "withering away of strikes") to explain the long-term decline of strikes in many Western countries.[4] In capitalist countries, strike volumes (Hibbs, 1978) and strike sizes (Korpi and Shalev, 1980) have gone down only when labor-oriented social-democratic parties have acquired stable and lasting control over governments, such as in the Scandinavian social democracies and in Austria (Korpi and Shalev, 1980, p. 320). Direct access to political power offers labor alternative and less costly means to achieve a more favorable distribution of resources: the government machinery itself, rather than the strike (Korpi and Shalev, 1980, p. 325). When the working class has control of the government, the locus of conflict over the distribution of resources, national income in particular, shifts from the labor market and the private sector, where strike activity is the typical means of pressure, to the public sector, where political exchange prevails. According to Marx, whereas "In its merely economic action capital is the stronger" (Lapides, 1987, p. 94), in the public sector "The political resources of the organized working class are more telling" (Hibbs, 1978, p. 167). In particular, Hibbs and Korpi and Shalev argued that it was the redistributive, welfare policies instituted by labor governments that reduced conflict; their empirical work, based on cross-national, time-series data confirmed that hypothesis.

To carry out an empirical test of the explanatory power of a long-term political model of strikes, let me specify an econometric model that includes a measure of government welfare spending along with the economic, organizational, and collective-bargaining variables that were found in earlier chapters to be important determinants of the patterns of Italian strikes:

$$Y_t = \beta_0 + \beta_1 UN_t + \beta_2 UNION_t + \beta_3 CONTRACT_t + \beta_4 WELFARE_t + \epsilon_t \qquad (6.1)$$

where Y measures the number of strikes, strikers, or hours lost, UN measures the unemployment rate, $UNION$ measures the union membership for CGIL and CISL, $CONTRACT$ measures the percentage of workers subject to national, categorywide contract renewal, and $WELFARE$ measures the government spending for welfare as a proportion of gross national product. I did not include a wage variable in this specification of the model because, as we saw in Chapter 5, the sign and signifi-

Table 6.1. *Testing a long-term political model of strikes*

Aggregation level:	Industry; yearly series		
Sample period:	1955/1978		
Estimation method:	GLS (Cochrane-Orcutt) for all models		
	Number of strikes	Number of strikers	Number of hours lost
Constant	4,894.91*	-1,483.10	6,871,9.35
	(729.84)	(1,899.12)	(6,777,5.28)
Unemployment rate	-340.32*	-209.86	-1,256,6.59*
	(65.40)	(171.10)	(6,048.29)
Union membership	.107E-2*	.134E-2	.210E-1
	(.336E-3)	(.873E-2)	(.312E-1)
Contract renewal	-5.99**	6.27	1,031.46*
	(3.09)	(7.65)	(296.72)
Welfare spending	-159.20*	177.20	-125.60
	(59.34)	(153.26)	(5,534.88)
Adjusted R^2	.56	.53	.39
Durbin-Watson	1.87	1.78	1.94

Note: Standard error in parentheses. **Significant at the .05 level; *significant at the .01 level.

cance of the wage variable in an econometric model of number of strikes, strikers, or hours lost changed, depending upon the particular choice of dependent variable, simply reflecting the structure of collective bargaining, rather than any presumed relationship between workers' purchasing power and their propensity to strike.

As argued in earlier chapters, the expected sign for *UN* is negative, that for *UNION* is positive, and that for *CONTRACT* is positive for the numbers of strikers and hours lost and negative for the number of strikes. The *WELFARE* variable should have negative effects on all strike measures, to the extent that higher levels of government welfare spending give workers access to resources for which they do not have to struggle. The political struggle replaces the economic struggle.

The econometric findings reported in Table 6.1 for the long-term political model confirm that higher levels of welfare spending are indeed associated with changes in the overall shapes of strikes, as predicted. In particular, the redistribution of public resources in favor of the working class reduces both the frequency and the durations of strikes. Strike sizes, however, seem to increase. As we saw, the growth in welfare spending typically is linked to pro-labor governments, which may engage the unions in an exchange involving an increase in welfare resources for a reduction in the level of conflict (perhaps limited to quick and demonstrative actions of political significance). Can this type of political exchange explain the coefficients of the *WELFARE* variable?

6.3. POLITICAL MODELS OF STRIKES: THE SHORT TERM

Whereas stable and durable control of the executive branch by labor parties along neocorporatist lines may tend to decrease strike activity, short-lived labor governments may actually lead to increases in strike activity, because workers, perceiving such a government to be sympathetic to their interests, will seek to gain concessions before the government is toppled. A great deal of econometric research has attempted to test the effects of short-term political processes on strike activity.[5] Several measures have been used: in the United States, the percentage of Democrats or of votes favorable to labor cast in the House of Representatives, or, for other countries (e.g., France or Italy), the number of yearly cabinet changes. Most typical, however, is the use of dummy variables to capture the effects of extraordinary "political" events (e.g., wars, the passage of significant labor legislation, such as the 1947 Taft-Hartley Act, and the 1959 Landrum-Griffin Act in the United States) or the effects of the prevailing political climate (e.g., the party in power in Congress, the party of the president, an election year dummy).[6] Short-term government crises may have similar intensification effects on industrial conflict. For Snyder (1975, p. 263) a "political crisis . . . increases the vulnerability of government to the collective demands of labor unions," as expressed through strikes. The reasons were best explained by Shorter and Tilly, who saw political crises as providing "an opening for a redefinition of the relative positions of the actors in the national political structure, including the representatives of organized labor" (Shorter and Tilly, 1974, p. 80).

In order to test the political-crisis theory, I propose a modified specification of equation (6.1), where I replace the *WELFARE* variable with different measures of political instability and crisis: the number of cabinet crises per year, the number of days involved in government crises, and an election-year dummy variable. Without necessarily considering an election dummy variable a measure of political crisis, election years may nonetheless provide opportunities for mobilization and collective action.

$$Y_t = \beta_0 + \beta_1 UN_t + \beta_2 UNION_t + \beta_3 CONTRACT_t + \beta_4 CRISIS_t + \epsilon_t \qquad (6.2)$$

The expected sign of the *CRISIS* variable is positive, if indeed those government crises provide political opportunities for labor, and labor uses collective mobilization to try to take advantage of those opportunities.

The econometric findings in Table 6.2 show that a short-term political model for Italy does not yield the predicted behavior: The coefficients for the *CRISIS* variable often have negative signs, although they are never statistically significant.

Thus, the econometric evidence regarding the effects of political processes on Italian strikes is mixed. The results using the long-term, redistributive model are statistically stronger and more in line with underlying theories. But for the short-term model, the findings are weaker and are not what theory would have predicted. Perhaps the fact that the political variables are mostly in the form of dummy variables, of one sort or another, can provide an explanation for the poor econometric performance of short-term political models. Such variables can provide only crude approximations of the complexities of underlying political processes. Unfortunately, I cannot even play the authority game by invoking other studies. There has been almost no empirical work on the relationship between strike

Table 6.2. *Testing a short-term political model of strikes*

Dependent variable: Number of strikes for models 1, 4, and 7; number of strikers for models 2, 5, and 8; number of hours lost for models 3, 6, and 9
Aggregation level: Industry; yearly series
Sample period: 1955/1978
Estimation method: GLS (Cochrane-Orcutt) for all models

	Model 1	Model 2	Model 3	Model 4	Model 5	Model 6	Model 7	Model 8	Model 9
Constant	3,367.60*	416.80	67,569.21	3,276.06*	251.76	69,858.35**	3,282.75*	130.82	72,570.52**
	(718.16)	(1,297.16)	(43,132.98)	(700.31)	(1,211.72)	(41,550.65)	(685.17)	(1,189.78)	(42,013.88)
Unemployment rate	-229.58*	-335.79*	-12,501.52*	-224.40*	-348.96*	-12,596.57*	-223.01*	-320.56*	-12,739.16*
	(81.40)	(149.74)	(4,925.70)	(80.44)	(144.75)	(4,974.14)	(78.62)	(139.11)	(4,907.10)
Union membership	.263E-3	.222E-2*	.216E-1	.276E-3	.238E-2*	.213E-1	.254E-3	.225E-2*	.217E-1
	(.269E-3)	(.447E-3)	(.144E-1)	(.272E-3)	(.456E-3)	(.156E-1)	(.259E-3)	(.417E-3)	(.147E-1)
Contract renewal	-6.32*	7.09	1,025.47*	-6.32*	8.12	1,028.71*	-6.45*	7.20	1,029.19*
	(2.89)	(7.86)	(301.32)	(2.94)	(7.72)	(302.02)	(2.97)	(8.12)	(292.52)
Number of crises	-61.67	-137.14	1,727.68						
	(91.35)	(254.85)	(9,915.89)						
Crisis duration				-.82	-5.97	11.88			
				(1.89)	(5.15)	(205.10)			
Election-year dummy							-24.48	-61.66	-9,888.41
							(186.46)	(502.82)	(18,084.32)
Adjusted R^2	.31	.49	.39	.30	.52	.40	.30	.54	.40
Durbin-Watson	1.82	1.78	1.95	1.83	1.76	1.94	1.83	1.84	1.93

Note: Standard error in parentheses. **Significant at the .05 level; *significant at the .01 level.

activity and political power for the Italian case, and the only two studies available reached different conclusions. On the one hand, Snyder (1975) found that the higher the number of cabinet changes per year, the lower the numbers of both strikes and strikers. The election-year dummy seemed to lead to predictions of increased strike size and decreased frequency. On the other hand, Santagata (1981) studied the relationship involving the timing of elections, the performance of the economy, and the behavior of unions and workers, along the lines of the political/business-cycle hypothesis (Nordhaus, 1975). Santagata's analyses revealed a tendency toward greater conflict after the electoral year (16.5 hours per worker lost to strike activity) as compared with either the electoral year (9.5 hours) or the preelectoral year (8.7 hours) (Santagata, 1981, p. 293).[7] The econometric findings in Table 6.2 seem to support Snyder's findings on the effects of a cabinet-crisis variable and Santagata's findings on the effects of political elections.[8]

The inadequacy of the small body of statistical work leaves us with a great many questions. Did working-class parties in Italy ever acquire stable and durable control over the executive? Was there ever a labor-friendly government in power on which the Italian working class could count to institute extensive welfare policies? Did political crises in Italy provide political opportunities for labor, such that labor was able to mobilize and act collectively so as to seize those opportunities? Let us turn to history for possible answers to these questions.

6.4. ITALIAN POSTWAR POLITICS: BLOCKED OPPORTUNITIES ON THE LEFT

On June 2, 1946, Italy held both a referendum and general elections.[9] The referendum was to decide the fate of the monarchy, its image tarnished by its involvement with the Fascist regime. Italians opted for a republic, with 54% of the referendum votes. The general elections were to decide the seats each party would have in the Constituent Assembly, the body entrusted with the task of drafting a new constitution. In the interim, Italy was governed by a broad coalition of "national unity" that included Catholic, Socialist, Communist, and secular/liberal forces. Over a dozen parties participated in the elections, ranging from the far right (e.g., MSI, the Movimento Sociale Italiano, a party of Fascist ideology), through the center, with its host of parties (e.g., PRI, the Republican Party, and DC, the Christian Democrat Party), to the far left (e.g., PCI, Partito Comunista Italiano, a party following the Marxist tradition). Three parties emerged from the elections for the Constituent Assembly with considerable electoral clout: the Christian Democrats, with 35.2% of the votes; the Socialists (then PSIUP), with 20.7%; and the PCI, with 18.9% (Corbetta, Parisi, and Schadee, 1988). In fact, despite the great number of parties, the Italian political spectrum was dominated in the mid-1940s (as it still was three decades later) by three main forces: the Catholic, Socialist/Communist, and conservative forces (Farneti, 1983, pp. 43, 50–60).

The Catholic forces were rooted in a religious tradition that was particularly strong in the countryside, as well as in the Northeast and in the South. They organized their interests around the Democrazia Cristiana (DC), with support from both the United States and the Vatican. In terms of electoral results at the polls, the DC was the strongest party throughout the postwar period. Whether alone or as a majority partner in a coalition with other parties, the DC participated in every government during the postwar period. Until 1983, it had also provided all the prime ministers. In the 1950s, the DC built its strength by taking control of all the key positions in the government and in a number of semigovernmental organizations (e.g., railroad services). In particular, it was the DC's control and expansion of conglomerates that were wholly or partly state-owned, such as IRI and ENI, that increasingly provided the party with economic and financial independence and strength (Becchi Collidà, 1976). In the 1950s and 1960s, that systematic "occupation of the state" made the DC a powerful political machine.

The Socialist tradition had long been particularly strong among peasants and industrial workers. It organized its interests around two parties: the Partito Socialista Italiano (PSI) or Socialist Party, and the Partito Comunista Italiano (PCI) or Communist Party. The Socialist Party had long been torn between reformism and revolution, between opposition to and alliance with the DC. It split and reunited several times during the postwar period, but beginning in the late 1950s it resolved its dilemma and resolutely took the path of reformism and of participation in government coalitions with the DC. In the 1960s, with the creation of Center-Left coalitions, the PSI began to be admitted to the spoils system that the DC had so successfully set up for itself. The small Republican Party (PRI) organized secular forces around moderate-left-wing positions. It represented the enlightened bourgeoisie, comprising the owners and managers of the large firms operating in the technologically advanced sectors, people interested in a more rational approach to state intervention in the economy.

The conservative forces were organized around a handful of minor parties. The defeat of the Fascist regime and the involvement of even some liberal forces with that regime had discredited the political appeal of the Right in the eyes of the Italian electorate. On the extreme right wing was found the Movimento Sociale Italiano (MSI), which had reconstituted the defeated Fascist forces. Similarly, the Partito Liberale Italiano (PLI) or Liberal Party was rooted in a tradition that antedated the Fascist regime. Throughout the postwar period, the Right had been unable to offer a serious political alternative. The only times that the MSI and the PLI gained votes were when the Christian Democrats initiated "openings" to the Left (Farneti, 1983, p. 55).[10]

The Constitution drafted by the Constituent Assembly became effective on January 1, 1948. The Constitution was a compromise reached among competing and often violently opposed social forces. Surprisingly enough, neither Nenni, the Socialist leader, nor Togliatti, the Communist leader, pressed too hard for imposition of their radical views (in particular, their views on state planning). Togliatti was content with a moderate outcome – a "progressive democracy," he called it. Thus, the Constitution enshrined private property as a chief pillar of the new republic, but as a concession to the Left, it granted labor the right to organize and strike, and it stated a vague right to work. The Left's insistence on economic planning was recognized, but was diluted to a generic statement about the need for state intervention to regulate the market "toward social ends" (La Palombara, 1966, pp. 19–20). The republican Constitution sanctioned a division of powers, but fearful of Fascist nostalgia and backlashes, it assigned the central position to Parliament. It relegated the president to a weak, ceremonial role (similar to that of the monarch in England), and it subjected the executive branch (composed of a prime minister and a Council of Ministers) to the constant threat of a no-confidence vote in Parliament. Parliament was to be elected by the people under universal suffrage and according to the rule of proportional representation. The proportional rule ensured that there would be a high degree of democratic representation, but it also ensured that a large number of parties would continue to clutter the political landscape. It made the formation of government coalitions difficult and their survival precarious.[11] The Constitution also had provisions for certain constitutional guarantees and direct democracy (such as referenda and regional governments), but fearful of the Left, the DC dragged its feet in implementing them (Kogan, 1981, p. 3). The Constitutional Court (Corte Costituzionale), the body that would oversee the constitutionality of laws and government decrees, was not established until 1956. The Superior Council of the Magistracy (Consiglio Superiore della Magistratura), a self-governing body in the judiciary that would oversee appointments, transfers, promotions, and disciplinary actions against judges, came even later, in 1958. Until then, the Ministry of Justice had exercised those powers. Because the Ministry of Justice was a political body within the government, for a decade Italy lived with a dangerous mix of executive and judicial powers. Certain measures of direct democracy were implemented only in the 1970s, when the balance of political forces made them inevitable. The law that would make it possible to hold a referendum was passed only in 1974, soon followed by the first referendum, on divorce. Regular regional governments were not set up until 1970.

In the new climate of cold-war confrontation, the interference of the United States in Italian political affairs was quite strong. Both government bodies (e.g., the U.S. State Department) and nongovernment institutions (the unions, particularly the American Federation of Labor, AFL) became actively involved in Italian politics, with a clear anti-Communist stance.[12] In the late 1940s and early 1950s, American purchase orders to Italian firms, working under the provisions of the Marshall Plan, became the typical tool for exerting anti-Communist pressure.[13] Consider the minutes of a February 4, 1954, meeting in Rome between the U.S. ambassador, Clare Booth Luce, and Fiat executives:

Ambassador Luce told us [Fiat] that after the [June 7, 1953] elections the United States were worried about the Italian situation. . . . In light of the sacrifices made by the United States (more than 1 billion dollars), communism in Italy seems to be progressing rather than regressing. . . . As a consequence, more aid would seem useless, even that currently in offshore.[14] . . . The U.S. Senate in its March meeting will examine this situation, taking into account: the general state of the country; the specific condition of industrial firms, particularly in large cities; it will certainly not be encouraged to extend aid, but, in fact, to limit even that in offshore orders. (Migone, 1974, p. 258; see also Reyneri, 1974a, p. 173)[15]

As Maier (1991a, p. 188) concluded, "The Marshall Plan thus irrevocably split the European labor movement between 1947–49." In January 1947, Alcide De Gasperi, the Christian Democrat leader who headed the broad-coalition government of "national unity" that included both Socialists and Communists, paid a state visit to Washington. The question of Communist participation in the government was the critical issue. On his return, De Gasperi resigned his position as prime minister and formed a new coalition government without the Socialists and the Communists. For the PCI, it would be another thirty years before it entered another government coalition, and that, too, would be short-lived.

In the 1948 elections, the PSI (PSIUP at the time) and PCI ran jointly under the banner of the Democratic Popular Front. The United States heavily subsidized the electoral campaign for the Christian Democrats. Italian politicians, in their campaign against the Popular Front, emphasized the economic ties between Italy and the United States. In a campaign speech delivered on February 17, 1948, Alcide De Gasperi affirmed that

Personally, I would not like to see the day when those who have compromised themselves with an anti-American struggle went to power . . . because I would fear that the Italian people, while waiting ashore for the [American] ships full of grain and coal, would see them turning their bows toward other shores. (quoted in Daneo, 1975, p. 246)

The Popular Front lost the 1948 elections. In a telegram of congratulations from AFL leaders to the union leaders Pastore, Canini, and Parri for their 1948 electoral victory over the Popular Front, one reads that the "AFL trusts that free Italian unions will move soon to eliminate Communist control of the unions" (quoted in Turone, 1984, p. 151). After the 1948 elections, the PSI and PCI never again ran as a single ticket. In the 1953 general elections, the PCI emerged as the hegemonic party on the left, as the working-class party par excellence, with 22.6% of the votes (compared with 12.7% for the PSI). It maintained that lead throughout the postwar period.

The political formula for the 1950s was a coalition government based on political parties located near the center of the political spectrum (a formula also called centrism, *centrismo*). The first legislature (1948–53) saw the golden years of a symbiotic relationship[16] between Confindustria and the Christian Democrats, the main government party (Martinelli et al., 1981, p. 244; Mattina, 1991, pp. 203–36). Confindustria's capacity to influence the government on issues of industrial policy would never again reach such heights. The influence of Confindustria on the new democratic state was not based on direct participation by Italian employers in the parliamentary game.[17] Their number in Parliament, even counting "friends" and "affiliates," was always quite small (Mattina, 1991, pp. 251–62). However, that handful included people who were strategically placed in all the key parliamentary commissions, the real decision-making bodies of the

Italian Parliament (Mattina, 1991, pp. 262–73). Furthermore, Confindustria's influence was based on a *clientela* relationship with the Italian state, particularly strong with the Ministry of Industry and the Ministry of Foreign Trade (La Palombara, 1964, pp. 264–71; Pirzio Ammassari, 1976, pp. 61–2; Mattina, 1991, pp. 203–36). Confindustria provided much of the technical support (staff, data, policy memoranda) that those government ministries needed to handle issues of economic policy. The technical inadequacies in the Italian civil-service administration made it virtually imperative that the ministries rely on Confindustria's support (Mattina, 1991, p. 225). Confindustria also provided funds for the Christian Democrat Party and for individual leaders. In exchange, the DC implemented industrial and labor policies favorable to the capitalists (Martinelli et al., 1981, p. 244; Mattina, 1991, pp. 238–51). Furthermore, the DC intervened to mediate the conflicts of interest between small business and big business, attempting to select government economic policies that would be most fair to both interests.[18]

During the 1950s, the relationship between Confindustria and the DC rested on a frail compromise: The Italian capitalist class nominally accepted the DC's ideological hegemony in exchange for tight controls on labor and for government subsidies to business (Martinelli, 1978, p. 48). The compromise involved two quite different social groups: a political social group of lower-middle-class extraction, mostly from the South, and an entrepreneurial class of Northern origin. Dialogue between the two groups was not always easy – all the more so because the DC ideology was based on a Christian creed of interclass compromise (*interclassismo*) and fair treatment for the lower classes, a doctrine ill-suited to a business class immersed in the process of primary accumulation. Not surprisingly, that compromise broke down in the late 1950s, during the first round of contract renewals under conditions of a labor market favorable to the workers. But the end of the compromise had been in the making for quite some time. As Confindustria resolutely maintained its defensive and sternly antilabor stance, the left wing of the Christian Democrat Party, under the leadership of Amintore Fanfani, became increasingly dissatisfied with its relationship with the dominant bourgeoisie (Mutti and Segatti, 1977, pp. 109–11; Mattina, 1991, pp. 125–68).[19] The DC Left had a different view of the near future for Italian society, a future based on large, efficient corporations, a future in which labor would occupy a central role, albeit in a subordinate position to capital. The route that the left wing of the DC took to realize its goal was toward control and expansion of state-owned corporations: first IRI, and later, ENI.[20]

IRI (Istituto per la Ricostruzione Industriale) was a legacy of the Fascist regime.[21] IRI was involved in steel production, heavy-machinery industries (the defense industry, automobiles), the electric industry, ocean transport, petroleum, and banking (Banca Commerciale Italiana, Credito Italiano, Banco di Roma, among Italy's largest banks). In 1953, the DC consolidated all petroleum-related companies into a new state-owned conglomerate, ENI (Ente Nazionale Idrocarburi). In December 1956, Parliament passed a law proposed by the DC for the formation of a new ministry, the Ministero delle Partecipazioni Statali (Pirzio Ammassari, 1976, pp. 75–81). The ministry was to deal specifically with state-owned companies. In November 1957, Giorgio Bo, head of the new ministry, announced the withdrawal of ENI and IRI companies from membership in Confindustria, as called for by the law. On trade-union matters, ENI and IRI interests were thereafter to be represented by their own trade associations, Intersind, formed in 1958, and Asap, formed in 1960. Confindustria vigorously opposed the secession of public companies and the creation of Intersind (Pirzio Ammassari, 1976, pp. 75–81; Mutti and Segatti, 1977, p. 113; Mattina, 1991).

Throughout the 1950s and 1960s, both IRI and ENI grew to become true corporate giants in the landscape of Italian capital.[22] In 1962, state-owned companies accounted for 26.5% of Italy's total capital investment (up from 13% in 1955) (Mutti and Segatti, 1977, p. 123). During the decade 1963–72, the weight of public-sector companies among the top 150 manufacturing companies increased from 19% to 24% in terms of assets, from 28% to 35% in terms of investment, and from 20% to 24% in terms of employment.[23]

It was the firm control exercised by the left wing of the DC over those powerful economic machines that gave the DC financial independence from the bourgeoisie, and that control made the DC both a major political force and an economic power (Mutti and Segatti, 1977, p. 125). To further rid itself of its *clientela* relationship with Confindustria, based on Confindustria's provision of technical staff and support to many government ministries, the DC began an intensive technical training program for its own managers and for the managers of state corporations, mostly at the Università Cattolica of Milan (Mutti and Segatti, 1977, p. 129; Mattina, 1991, pp. 289–92). The managers of the state oligopolies shared with the left wing of the DC a modernizing, "neo-capitalist" vision of society, but so did some of the leaders of the private oligopolies. After all, ENI promised to provide cheap energy to the large oligopolies, and IRI provided steel at state-subsidized prices.

While the left wing of the DC was slowly consolidating its hegemony in the party, the Socialist Party was slowly moving toward the center of the political spectrum. Following the de-Stalinization process in the Soviet Union promulgated by the Twentieth Congress of the Communist Party of the Soviet Union (CPSU) in 1956 and the Polish and Hungarian uprisings in that same year, relationships between the Socialists and the Communists in Italy had become strained. The Socialists began voicing their willingness to participate in a coalition government with the DC.

Following the 1958 elections, with labor conflict soaring again after nearly ten years of quiescence, the political situation became very confused and unstable. In 1960, Fernando Tambroni, a member of the Christian Democrat Party and former minister of the interior, formed a new government with the active support of the MSI, the Italian Fascist Party. The MSI decided to hold its party congress in Genoa, which had been at the center of the Resistance against the Nazis, and remained a Communist stronghold. The Genoese perceived the MSI decision and the government approval for MSI to hold its congress in Genoa as outrageous acts of provocation. The population took to the streets in Genoa and elsewhere (Turone, 1984, pp. 262–6), and the Tambroni government was forced to resign.

The pendulum of history was swinging to the left. The new pope, John XXIII, and the new U.S. president, John Kennedy, began to relax their opposition to the inclusion of Socialists in any coalition government. In 1961, many central and northern Italian cities formed Center-Left (*centro-sinistra*) local governments based on alliances between Christian Democrats and Socialists (typically, Christian Democrats, Social Democrats, Republicans, and Socialists) (Kogan, 1981, p. 12). But the road toward a coalition involving DC and PSI at the national level remained long, for the PSI still insisted on the need for broad social reforms and economic planning. The days of the Popular Front, with its radical overtones, were not so far in the past as to have been erased from people's memories. Throughout the 1950s, centrist governments had carefully shied away from "economic planning," which smelled too much of Soviet-style industrialization. The DC had intervened in directing the economy mainly through the state-owned corporations (particularly, IRI and ENI) and the Cassa per il Mezzogiorno (an agency for the development of the South), in addition to instituting moderate land reform, spending for infrastructure, and granting loans to industry for reconstruction and conversion (La Palombara, 1966, p. 21).[24]

But after the stormy process of industrialization in the late 1950s and Italy's "economic miracle," even the DC came to accept the need for some economic planning. In 1962, Pasquale Saraceno, a leading economic adviser to the DC, put forward an economic plan based on (1) creation of a planning office, (2) nationalization of the electric industry, (3) fiscal reform, and (4) modernization of agriculture (La Palombara, 1966, pp. 65–6). The PSI introduced a similar plan of its own, but the PSI plan further called for radical reforms in education and science, for greater commitment to the development of the South, and for increased participation in democratic processes through the creation of regional governments, as outlined in the Constitution (La Palombara, 1966, p. 68).

In 1962, Amintore Fanfani, leader of the left-wing groups of the DC, formed a new government. In a parliamentary vote of confidence, the Socialists abstained, rather than vote against the government, as they had traditionally done.[25] The new government moved quickly to take the first steps toward economic planning. It introduced a Ministry of the Budget and Economic Programming, headed by the Republican Party leader Ugo La Malfa, a strong advocate for modernization and economic rationalization (La Palombara, 1966, p. 87). It also introduced the National Committee for Economic Programming (CNPE) (La Palombara, 1966, p. 95). In the summer of that year, the government introduced a bill to nationalize electric companies. The bill passed in the fall. Conservative forces were in shock. They flogged the government daily in the conservative press, alleging that the Fanfani government was extending a red carpet to the Communists, that nationalization of the electric industry was but the beginning of the collectivization of the whole of Italy (La Palombara, 1966, p. 72). Not surprisingly, Confindustria campaigned desperately against planning and nationalization (La Palombara, 1966, p. 123), for the Confindustria leadership was composed of people close to the electric industry (Becchi Collidà, 1989, p. 141).

By and large, Confindustria was successful in blocking the reformist drive of *centro-sinistra* governments, but that success came with a high price tag. A number of fiscal abuses, such as the employers' practice of granting higher wages to compensate for the lack of social reforms, the inefficiency in state-owned companies caused by party involvement in managerial decisions, and the tight control that banks exercised over small firms because of DC control over the banks, had resulted partly from Confindustria's lack of vision and political wisdom during the crucial early years of the *centro sinistra* (Martinelli, 1978, p. 51).[26] Interestingly enough, surveys of employers' attitudes showed that the cost of labor, the cost of borrowing money, and the high operating costs of state-run firms ranked highest on the list of employers' complaints (Martinelli, 1977, pp. 327, 350, 1978, p. 51; Urbani, 1977a, p. 385; see also Ottone, 1965). Few, if any, would admit to any responsibility.[27]

In the April 1963 general elections, both the Left and the Right gained, at the expense of the DC. The small Liberal Party (PLI) and the PCI each gained an additional 1 million votes. For the PCI, that was its strongest surge forward since 1946. The PLI based its campaign on criticizing the DC for having gone too far to the left. The PCI ran an electoral campaign based on accusing the PSI of splitting the working class.[28] Under pressure from both the Left and the Right, the Fanfani government fell (La Palombara, 1966, p. 76). In December of that year, Aldo Moro formed the first Center-Left government based on a four-party coalition that included the PSI. The government platform called for economic planning (but no further nationalization) and for the use of IRI and ENI as instruments of planning. The provisions for economic planning were to be mandatory, inscribed in law, rather than simple guidelines. The Moro government came to power espousing the two issues of monetary stability and economic planning, with five-year plans (La Palombara, 1966, p. 84). The high interest rates imposed by the Bank of Italy in 1963 were drastic measures. They took care of the inflationary process that had been set in motion by the recent rounds of labor agreements, and they "took care" of labor along with inflation. Those drastic economic measures plunged the economy into a deep recession, such that it would be another five years before industrial militancy would rise again. As for the second issue, it was not until early 1967 that Parliament finally passed the law that introduced the first five-year plan for the period 1965–69.[29]

Had the Center-Left project of economic planning and social reforms been successful, the outcome probably would have been a variant of the Scandinavian welfare-state model. But the project was not successful. Of the billions of dollars paid out by the government in compensation for the expropriation of electric companies, very few went back into productive investment. Social reforms were never implemented. Salvati (1976, p. 244) claimed that the only "success" of the Center-Left project was that it co-opted and corrupted a labor movement that in the immediately preceding years had shown renewed vitality. Indeed, the Center-Left governments "massively" co-opted the trade unions in their economic planning from its very beginning (Roccella, 1979, p. 34). The so-called triangular conferences (*conferenze triangolari*), involving the government, the trade unions, and the employers' associations, the main industrial-relations innovation of the time, became routine practices under Center-Left governments (Roccella, 1979, p. 34). The results were meager (Roccella, 1979, p. 35), but at least the new practices marked the end of another set of government practices typical of just a decade earlier: outright repression of union activities.

In the period 1968–75, unions began to make political demands. They launched massive, nationwide general strikes to press their demands. The pictures of the "human flood" of workers (often up to 1 million at a time), with their red banners and signs, in the major cities, particularly Rome, remain imposing symbols of the times. The unions became political actors in their own right. Using the same pressure tactics and contractual-bargaining strategy that they were using at the plant level, the unions engaged the government directly to advance their political demands for reforms. For some years, the unions, rather than political parties, channeled people's political demands (*supplenza dei partiti*).[30] While the categorywide and territorial unions aggressively pursued plant-level issues of work organization and wages (with strong egalitarian tendencies in both domains), the confederal unions became involved in struggles for social reforms (*stagione delle riforme*).[31] In 1970, the CGIL secretary general, Agostino Novella, defended the unions' political actions: "In order that they may become firm and long-lasting, trade-union conquests must necessarily transform themselves into goals of reform and power. . . . To those who rebuke us that to want reforms and power is to be political, we reply that to want only wage demands is to be corporatist" (quoted in Accornero, 1981, p. 14).

Soaring on the wings of the mass movement, the working class turned its fortunes around (Sebastiani, 1982; Pasquino, 1985). In 1969, the membership of the Italian Communist Party (PCI) began to rise, after a long period of decline (see the plot of Figure 4.5, p. 138). Radical ferment was running high. Throughout the 1960s, and increasingly so after the 1967–69 student movement, a host of radical political groups had been challenging the PCI from the left (the extraparliamentary Left, *sinistra extra-parlamentare*, i.e., radical Marxist groups, particularly Maoists and Trotskyites not in Parliament). In 1969, the PCI expelled a group of minority dissidents from the party. Those dissidents later founded their own party, the Manifesto. The radical Communist Party of Italy (Marxist-Leninist) was also founded at that time. The two parties ran as a single ticket in the 1972 national elections, receiving 1.3% of the votes.

The extreme Right reacted quickly to the new climate. The years 1969–1974 saw an increase in right-wing political violence, "black terrorism," *terrorismo nero* (Della Porta and Rossi, 1985). As workers were engaged in negotiating the contract renewals of the *autunno caldo*, the Right was engaged in promoting a "strategy of tension" (*strategia della tensione*). The year 1969 was punctuated by a series of bomb explosions set off by right-wing groups. On December 12, 1969, a bomb went off at the Banca dell'Agricoltura in Piazza Fontana in Milan during regular business hours; sixteen people were killed, and ninety injured. In many regions there was widespread violence resulting from arguments over which cities should be the seats of the newly instituted regional governments (e.g., L'Aquila, Reggio Calabria). In the South, the MSI, the party of the neo-Fascists, was maneuvering to reap the political benefits of violence. In the 1970 administrative elections, the MSI received 5.2% of the votes, a 21% increase over its previous high. Historically, the MSI, and to some extent the PLI (the Liberal Party), gained votes when the DC was moving left and lost them when the DC clashed with the PCI head-on (Farneti, 1983, p. 55). With government crises arising one after another, and widespread right-wing political violence, the PCI played a very cautious hand, not wishing to further endanger the political system (Kogan, 1981, pp. 76–7). No one had forgotten that the Fascists had come to power in 1922, only a few years after the period of Italy's highest labor mobilization prior to the *autunno caldo*, the so-called Red years (*biennio rosso*).

In that tense and confused climate of political instability, in September 1972 came the news that a military coup d'etat, with backing from the U.S. Central Intelligence Agency (CIA), had overthrown President Salvador Allende's Communist government in Chile. The dramatic overthrow of that popularly elected regime in one of the few Latin American countries with strong democratic traditions deeply impressed Enrico Berlinguer, the PCI secretary general. It reinforced in Berlinguer's mind Togliatti's earlier assessment of the limits of the possibility of revolutionary change in a country belonging to the Western bloc. Fearing for the survival of democracy in Italy, in the fall of 1973 Berlinguer had published a series of three articles in *Rinascita*, the party intellectual weekly (Berlinguer, 1973a–c), outlining a new political strategy for his party: *compromesso storico* ("historic compromise"). The premise of Berlinguer's *compromesso storico* was that "even if the political parties and the social forces on the left could attain 51% of the votes and of parliamentary representation, this fact alone could not guarantee the survival and the operation of a government that reflected this 51%" (quoted in Pasquino, 1985, p. 132). For Berlinguer, the PCI would have to accept "the fundamental fact that Italy belongs to a political bloc dominated by the United States, with all the inevitable pressures that come with it" (quoted in Pasquino, 1985, p. 132). The debate that followed the publication of those three articles cast a harsh light on some of the basic ambiguities that have long bedeviled the PCI, particularly the party's policy positions regarding (1) Italy's alignment in the international arena (the Soviet bloc vs. the Western bloc), (2) the economic organization of society (market economy vs. planned economy), and (3) the decision-making process and internal representation within the party (democratic centralism vs. decentralization) (Farneti, 1983, p. 33).

Thus, to some extent, the new strategy rejected Togliatti's "Italian way to socialism," a strategy that had never been quite clear but that certainly rejected both the northern European social-democratic path and the Soviet path of revolutionary confrontation with the bourgeoisie. Togliatti's strategy rested on the premise of acceptance of the multiparty principle and periodic elections, in the style of bourgeois democracies. But it also called for (1) a "government of the Left," that is, a government coalition of only forces on the left (e.g., Socialists), (2) a commitment to an international alliance with the Soviet Union, and (3) a gradual, long-term transition away from a market economy to a planned economy. Instead, Berlinguer called for PCI participation in a broad coalition government that would draw together several democratic forces, particularly the Catholic forces represented by the DC (not unlike the coalition of the 1944–47 period), and for Italy's continued commitment to the Western bloc and to the North Atlantic Treaty Organization (NATO) alliance in particular.

Over the course of the next three years (1974–76), the PCI scored three electoral victories in a row: in the 1974 divorce referendum, in the 1975 administrative elections, and in the 1976 national elections. In the 1976 elections, the PCI jumped to 34.4% of the votes, its highest share in the postwar period. In part, the 1975 and 1976 electoral victories had resulted from the lowering of the voting age to eighteen years in 1975, just before the administrative elections, but the victories also reflected a genuine popular demand for change (Pasquino, 1985, p. 139). Those three victories created "a diffused climate of great expectations" (Sebastiani, 1982, p. 212), at least on the left. Conservative forces saw it differently. As an entrepreneur put it on the eve of the 1976 election, "We should have stayed and fought, but our money is already in Switzerland" (quoted in Przeworski and Wallerstein, 1982, p. 143). Although that answer may have been typical of small entrepreneurs, large-scale capitalists were bracing for change. In an interview for the weekly *Panorama* on December 4, 1975, Giovanni Agnelli, the majority stockholder of Fiat, declared that

It is likely that there will be institutional changes. We must find new answers to old questions: To whom do firms belong? Stockholders? Managers? What should the workers' role be? More or less, political power is subject to constant social control. But who controls the top of the firms? (quoted in Pirzio Ammassari, 1976, p. 186)

In 1976, the PCI supported the single-party, minority government formed by the Christian Democrats. Although not formally in the government, the PCI, for the first time since the 1947 Popular Front government, was not in the opposition. The PCI was even given some honorary positions, such as some chairs of parliamentary committees and the presidency of the chamber (Sebastiani, 1982). Those were the first parliamentary offices for the PCI since 1947. Finding that they had a reliable ally edging ever closer to a role in government, the unions felt safe in abandoning the contractual-bargaining approach to the state that had been typical of the first half of the 1970s; they developed relationships with both the economic and political powers along neocorporatist lines.

As an alliance between the DC and PCI was slowly being hammered out in the two camps, by Moro in the DC and by Berlinguer in the PCI, Red terrorism skyrocketed. After a slow start in the first part of the decade, the number of leftist terrorist groups shot up from 8 in 1975 to 24 in 1976, 77 in 1977, 179 in 1978, and 217 in 1979 (Della Porta and Rossi, 1985, p. 420). The number of terrorist actions followed a similar trend. The extraparliamentary Left and the groups involved in leftist terrorism were not pleased with the PCI politics of national solidarity (Pasquino, 1985, p. 141). They viewed the PCI strategy as a complete sellout. They feared that direct involvement of the PCI in a coalition government would inevitably lead to embourgeoisement of the working class and, in the long run, to the demise of revolutionary politics in Italy.

On March 16, 1978, the PCI joined the DC, Socialists, Social Democrats, and Republicans in a broad coalition of national solidarity. The PCI retained its committee chairs and the presidency of the chamber.[32] On that same day, the Red Brigades, the most active leftist terrorist group in those years, kidnapped Aldo Moro, the architect of the DC-PCI alliance. After fifty-four days, on May 9, 1978, Moro's body, riddled with bullets, was found in the back of a car in downtown Rome. In tragic symbolism, the car was parked halfway between the DC and PCI headquarters (Mammarella, 1990, pp. 444–8). With the *compromesso storico* under strain, in December 1978 the PCI withdrew from the coalition government. The politics of *compromesso storico* had drawn to a tragic end.

6.5. POLITICAL SUBCULTURES: RED REGIONS, WHITE REGIONS

The preceding section has shown that the Italian political scene was dominated by the Christian Democrats (drawing votes from groups in the center and the right) and by the Communists (increasingly winning votes from groups on the left). Given their different positions in the political spectrum, it is no surprise that the social bases for the electorate in the two parties were different.[33] Thus, blue-collar workers were more likely to vote for the PCI, clerical workers for the DC, students for the PCI, housewives and the elderly for the DC. Furthermore, the likelihood of a PCI vote increased linearly with the size of the voter's commune of residence and with levels of education. It was also a young people's vote: the ratio of PCI/DC votes was favorable to the PCI in groups below age forty, but it was favorable to the DC for the older generations.

Certainly differences in the social basis for the electorate in the two parties were important, but they were not as important as it might seem: By and large, the two parties drew their votes from similar electorates in terms of social origins (Sani, 1978). Much more important was the fact that the strengths of the two parties were rooted in two distinct political subcultures: Catholic and Socialist.[34]

What was quite distinctive about those subcultures was that they were geographically based. In the postwar period, the areas of the Northeast (Veneto and some provinces of Lombardy, such as Bergamo and Brescia) overwhelmingly voted for the Christian Democrats (between 55% and 45% of the votes), though that trend decreased over time. The areas of central Italy (Emilia-Romagna, Umbria, and Tuscany) consistently and increasingly gave most of their votes to the

PCI (between 35% and 45%). Those two areas of distinct political traditions have been called the White area and Red area (Galli, 1968, p. 75).[35] In those areas, the two political traditions go back as far as the nineteenth century.[36] Not even the dismantling of all Socialist cultural and organizational structures carried out by the Fascists had succeeded in eradicating the Socialist tradition in the Red area of central Italy. Those traditions survived in underground, clandestine organizations and in the "historic memory" of the people (Baccetti, 1987).

Family traditions appear to have provided the breeding grounds for those two political cultures, passed on from one generation to the next. But family traditions do not grow in a vacuum; they are supported by a network of institutions and cultural forms. In the White area, a host of Church-sponsored institutions provided the basis for political socialization. The Christian Democratic Party had simply reaped the benefits of that socialization process in a symbiotic relationship with the church. In the Red area, the Communist Party itself had set up an impressive organizational structure made up of cultural, political, and economic institutions.[37] In both areas, a person's life was patterned around events (e.g., the yearly Festa dell'Amicizia held by the DC or the Festa dell'Unità of the PCI, the Sunday card game at the Casa del Popolo), institutions, and a network of friendships closely knit around and by the parties.[38]

Political preferences for the DC and the PCI in the two areas translated into union preferences as well (Sani, 1978, p. 118). Unionization in the White area was predominantly in the CISL; in the Red area it was predominantly in the CGIL.[39] But unionization was lower in White areas than in Red areas. The Red regions of Emilia Romagna, Tuscany, and Umbria had the highest unionization rates of any Italian regions, higher than the more heavily industrialized Piedmont and Lombardy.[40] The characteristics of strikes were also different in Red and White regions. The frequencies of strikes were similar in the two areas, but strike sizes were larger and strike durations shorter in the Red regions (Trigilia, 1986, p. 193). Longer strike durations, as we have seen, typically are found in situations of greater employer resistance (e.g., during periods of economic downturn). The much larger sizes, on the other hand, indicate a greater availability of organizational resources (the unions can call out a larger proportion of the work force, thus producing large-scale "demonstrative" strikes).

Bagnasco and Trigilia's comparative studies (1984, 1985) of two industrial districts featuring small-scale production (one Red, Valdelsa, in Tuscany; one White, Bassano del Grappa, in Veneto) brought those differences in levels of organization and militancy into sharp focus. Unionization rates were lower in firms of all sizes in the White Bassano district than in the Red Valdelsa district. But the scarcity of organizational resources was clearly related to workers' ability to mount collective actions. The local political culture provided a sympathetic forum for labor in the Red areas, where certain employers' practices were not tolerated. An empirical investigation, directed by Treu, covering 4,317 cases of appeals to the labor courts on the basis of the Workers' Charter in 57 provinces between 1970 and 1973 showed that the probability of a decision favorable to workers was higher in

Red provinces than in White provinces (Melucci and Rositi, 1975, pp. 145, 174, 178). The same research showed that even for larger firms, unions' appeals to the Workers' Charter either to demand the organizational and political rights envisioned by the charter or to protest employers' abuses on these issues tended to predominate in the White areas, indicating stronger ideological opposition from employers (Melucci and Rositi, 1975, p. 169). The only comparative data available on employers' attitudes in White and Red regions (data for the 1980s) confirm the tougher stance taken by employers in White areas toward labor and unions (Trigilia, 1986, p. 235).[41]

The overwhelming presence of a Communist culture in the Red areas tended to limit employers' antiunion practices by providing workers in small factories with organizational resources from outside the firms, even for firms that were not organized, thereby affording unions better opportunities to make inroads in smaller firms.

In conclusion, party control over the local political machinery and institutions, as well as a sympathetic political subculture, provided labor in Red regions with organizational resources that could be spent to labor's advantage in the market arena (Trigilia, 1986, p. 191).[42] Such political facilitation translated into union (CGIL) success in penetrating even the world of smaller firms, a world that elsewhere would have been out of their organizational range.[43] The effects of political facilitation, however, should not be exaggerated. Not even in the Red Emilia Romagna region were unions (the CGIL in particular) able to make significant inroads into firms in the size class of 1–20 employees, a class that in the course of the 1970s spread like wildfire. A Bologna FLM survey of metalworking firms showed that 90% of all firms (93.8% in the size class 1–20 employees) and some 40% of all metalworkers were completely outside of union control (Capecchi, 1978). Considering that unions were strongest in the metalworking sector and that in some sectors (e.g., textiles and clothing) most of the firms were concentrated in the size class of 1–19 employees, where unions were weaker, one can estimate that some 50–60% of all Emilia-Romagna industrial workers were without union protection (Capecchi, 1978, p. 24).

If that was the case, how can we explain the much higher unionization rates in Red regions? The Bologna FLM data in Table 4.10 (p. 130) and the data of Bagnasco and Trigilia in Table 6.3 can help us find an answer to this question, as they clearly highlight the limits and strengths of the organizational resources in Red regions: Unionization was higher in those regions because unions had been able (1) to enter firms that would have been well beyond their reach elsewhere (even the 1–10 class) and (2) to enroll a much higher proportion of the work force within each firm.

In conclusion, a Socialist political subculture has explained at least one aspect of the *paradox of small-scale production regions* encountered in Chapter 4: In general, small firms had low levels of unionization, and yet some regions, such as Tuscany and Emilia Romagna, based largely on small-scale industrial production, had the highest levels of unionization in Italy. But an analysis of political

Table 6.3. *Workers' participation in strikes and unionization in the Red Valdelsa and White Bassano districts, by firm size (%)*

	Number of workers		
	<10	11–50	>50
Valdelsa (Red)			
Strikes			
Plant level	76	85	92
Political	67	79	87
Unionization	41	89	99
Bassano (White)			
Strikes			
Plant level	19	49	79
Political	8	34	65
Unionization	17	43	64

Source: Trigilia (1986, p. 230).

subcultures can also help to explain the other aspect of the *paradox of small-scale production regions* encountered in Chapter 5: Wages in small firms were low, and yet regions based on small-scale production (e.g., Veneto, Emilia Romagna) had some of the highest per capita incomes and quality-of-life indices in Italy.

Local governments in Italy had almost no funds to promote economic development directly, but both Red and White local governments actively pursued a development strategy based on small-scale production. They passed zoning laws favorable to small businesses (and discouraged large industrial units), they actively supported small-business applications for low-interest loans from the local banks, they lobbied the branches of the central government on behalf of their districts, they provided publicly funded training programs for the work force, and they promoted consortia among small firms to achieve joint commercialization of their products (Trigilia, 1986, pp. 183–4). Particularly in the Red regions, direct party involvement with local economic development was much higher than elsewhere in Italy (Trigilia, 1986, p. 186).

In both Red and White regions, the local governments actively participated in providing infrastructural resources: investments in good communications and transportation networks, child-care institutions, low-income housing.[44] In the Red textile district of Prato in Tuscany, labor collective contracts contained, after 1974, a provision that firms would contribute funds equal to 1% of each worker's salary to an organization managed by both unions and employers. That organization would then use the funds for social projects such as public transportation, workplace medical care, child care, cafeterias, and training programs for workers (Moni, 1980).[45]

That growth strategy to promote small-scale, localized industrial production contributed to preserve, more or less intact, the traditional structure of the extended peasant family. Furthermore, it encouraged people to continue residence in their small communities, for workers had to travel only short distances to get to work. The temporal continuity in local residence meant that the agricultural heritage of those workers (in both land and know-how) was never lost. In the White district of Bassano del Grappa studied by Bagnasco and Trigilia, 74% of the workers interviewed owned a field or an orchard through which they supplemented the family income (Bagnasco and Trigilia, 1984, p. 169).[46]

The trend toward larger families with several income-producing members also allowed individual members much greater freedom in the labor market. Under the income umbrella of the extended family, each family member could afford periods of unemployment while seeking a better job. Larger family units with several income-earning members, all living in a house long owned by the family, and with their basic subsistence needs met by farming their land, also meant far greater possibilities for capital accumulation – capital waiting for an opportunity to be invested productively in small-scale industrial enterprises. The same tightly knit family structures and friendship networks provided the basic socialization necessary to learn the managerial skills required to make the transition from worker to employer. Technical and product innovations traveled along the same informal family and community networks. Indeed, the proportion of the work force classified in the ranks of the self-employed (small entrepreneurs) was higher than elsewhere.

In areas with large concentrations of big business (e.g., Piedmont, Lombardy) small firms often lived in a symbiotic relationship with large firms.[47] Consider Agnelli's description:

Among Fiat suppliers there are several thousand [small] firms. These firms are run by first- and second-generation entrepreneurs; many of them were supervisors or sons of workers;[48] they head small firms of fifteen to twenty workers, often located around Turin, that typically sell over 50% of their product to Fiat and 50% elsewhere. (Levi, 1983, p. 14)

But particularly in the White and Red regions in which small-scale production dominated, many of those small firms flourished in an interdependent network of firms localized in a particular area, the so-called industrial districts, where many small firms operated in symbiotic relationships among themselves, rather than in subordination to larger firms (Bagnasco and Trigilia, 1984, p. 133; Trigilia, 1986, p. 173).

The higher-than-average income distributions in those regions (Palanca, 1979) derived not so much from the higher wages of factory workers as from more general socioeconomic characteristics of those regions, characteristics that were carefully nurtured by both the Red and White political subcultures throughout the postwar period: (1) a higher-than-average rate of participation in the labor force, (2) greater possibilities for supplementing industrial wages via agricultural production, (3) greater reliance on family assets (e.g., housing), (4) lower per capita fixed living expenses within the extended family (e.g., housing, transportation), and (5) excellent systems of publicly subsidized housing, transportation, and child care. The higher quality-of-life indices in those areas (Palanca, 1983) similarly reflected

(1) higher welfare spending by local governments (particularly Red governments), (2) a more important role for family and local community in a person's life, and (3) the presence of only small urban concentrations.

In conclusion, differences in local political subcultures (Red and White) can fully explain *the puzzle of small firms* encountered in Chapters 4 and 5. The Red subculture gave labor access to organizational resources located outside the firm, rooted in a diffuse culture of pro-labor sentiment and in PCI control of the local political machinery and of powerful economic institutions (e.g., cooperatives). Both Red and White cultures pursued a growth strategy of small-scale industrialization that helped to create diffused entrepreneurial wealth and open up opportunities for income far greater than elsewhere, while at the same time avoiding many of the evils of large-scale industrialization (e.g., congested urban areas, immigration, the dismantling of traditional cultural forms and of the extended family).

6.6. AN OVERALL MODEL OF POWER

For resource-mobilization theories, the likelihood of collective action is inversely proportional to its cost (Tilly, 1978, pp. 98–9). The higher the costs to the group and its members, the lower the probability that the group will mobilize for collective purposes. People do not need to be accountants to calculate such costs. Neither do they have to be historians to keep a record of past collective actions and the responses they evoked in the elites. Collective memories (*la memoria storica*) linger on:

> The poor do not have to be historians of the occasions when protestors have been jailed or shot down to understand this point. The lesson of their vulnerability is engraved in everyday life; it is evident in every police beating, in every eviction, in every job lost, in every relief termination. (Piven and Cloward, 1979, p. 26)

We have, indeed, encountered many examples of the various costs of collective actions. Workers in smaller firms, for instance, faced much stiffer prices. So did workers under conditions of an unfavorable labor market. Different theories of strikes have suggested different mechanisms for the rise and fall in the costs of collective action.

For economic-bargaining models, the upswing phases of the business cycle put workers in a more favorable bargaining position vis-à-vis employers. The costs of going on strike and of "taking" a strike vary inversely for workers and employers as the business cycle runs its course. For resource-mobilization theories, it is the presence of an efficient union organization that decreases the costs of strikes (e.g., by shifting the timing of strikes to a period of more favorable conditions, or by providing strike funds) and increases the likelihood of success. The presence of a union organization effectively lowers the cost/benefit ratio. For political-exchange theories, the shift in the site for regulation of conflict from the labor market to the political market provides labor a less costly means to achieve economic ends:

Through the welfare state, the working class obtains a more favorable distribution of national income.

Implicitly, all three theories point to changes in a group's power as the basis for changes in its cost of collective action, if we take "power" to mean simply control over resources (whether economic, organizational, or political) (Korpi, 1974): The greater a group's power, the lower the cost of collective action; the lower its power, the higher the cost. Given that the probability of collective action is closely related to a group's power, let me address two questions – What happens to conflict when a group does not have power? What happens to conflict when a group does have power? – using the available survey, ethnographic, and historical evidence.

6.6.1. ON THE COST OF STRIKES (THE WORKERS' VIEW), OR, WHAT HAPPENS TO CONFLICT WHEN A GROUP DOES NOT HAVE POWER?

Mobilization poses a threat to dominant groups (Tilly, 1978, pp. 52–142). Depending on the severity of the threat and the willingness of a dominant group to share its power and make room for the challenging group, the dominant group may resort to repressive measures in order to preserve its position of power and privilege. Repression has the effect of lowering the level of mobilization by raising the cost of collective action to those who participate in it. Repression also reduces the probability of future collective action.

In Italy, repression was part and parcel of many workers' lives, both inside and outside the factories. The defeat of the first cycle of labor struggles in the immediate postwar period and the expulsion of the Communist Party from the coalition government of national unity in 1948 were followed by a decade of harsh repression at the hands of the state and the employers. The aims of those combined actions by government and employers were to limit union prerogatives, to control workers' behavior, and to defeat workers' vanguards, particularly Communists, within the plants (Treu, 1976a, pp. 560–1; Della Rocca, 1976, pp. 623–7):

> In January 1950, the labor dispute at Fonderie Riunite in Modena ended with 6 people dead and hundreds of workers wounded and on trial. From January 1, 1949, to August 31, 1952, police repression against agricultural laborers in the province of Ferrara resulted in the deaths of 4 laborers, the serious wounding of 17 others, thousands of workers beaten up, 679 arrested, 4,628 put on trial and many of them condemned, for a total of 683 years and 8 months in prison. Several workers, before being acquitted at the trials, spent a total of 48 years and 8 months in prison. (Caleffi and Mietto, 1980, pp. 6–7)

The brutality described in that account was not limited to the "red" cities of Modena or Ferrara. Scenes of that kind were becoming more and more typical throughout the country as the "recasting of bourgeois Italy" took place. As Table 6.4 shows, in the early 1950s thousands of workers, Communists in particular, were imprisoned, many were wounded, and quite a few were killed. Because of the

Table 6.4. *Repression of workers (1948–56)*

Outcome	Jan. 1948–Jul. 1950	Jul. 1950–Sep. 1954	Sep. 1954–1956	Total
Killed	62	13	5	80
Communists	48	6	3	57
Wounded	3,123	1,981	642	5,746
Communists	2,364	1,673	535	4,572
Convicted	19,313	41,930	7,765	69,008
Communists	15,420	36,075	6,791	58,286
Years of prison	8,441	11,985	2,112	22,538[a]
Communists	7,598	10,135	1,949	19,682

[a] 24 life sentences (19 of which to Communists) should be added to the total number of years in prison.

Source: *VIII Congresso Nazionale del Partito Comunista Italiano. Forza e attività del partito. Dati statistici. Documenti per i delegati.* Rome, 1956.

widespread use of highly repressive methods to control the labor movement during that period, Italian economist Michele Salvati (1976, p. 220) labeled that whole period of Italian history "repressive development." Undoubtedly, the structure of the labor market in the 1950s, with its high unemployment levels, and the "reserve army" of the agricultural exodus, gave employers the upper hand, but it was the legal framework set up and guaranteed by the state that allowed employers to use a heavy hand.

A 1939 law on domestic migrations from one region to another, left over from the Fascist regime and repealed only in 1961, required immigrant workers to have a job in order to establish residence, but one could not get a job without an established residence (Ascoli, 1979, p. 110). Most immigrants thus worked "illegally, exposed to the worst employer harassments and to the worst working conditions" (Ascoli, 1979, p. 111).

Prime Minister De Gasperi attempted to bring industrial conflict under control with the proposal of the Rubinacci law of December 4, 1951. The proposed statute met fierce opposition from the Left and did not pass. Later governments made no further legislative attempts to curb the use of strikes. The courts moved into that statutory vacuum. Employers' cries found a sympathetic ear in the courts of the time, whether to restrict the use of the most damaging forms of strikes or to ban the loudspeakers used to incite workers to strike. Furthermore, several forms of pressure exerted by the executive on the judicial branch, typical of the Fascist era, persisted well into the postwar democratic years and increasingly went in the direction of guaranteeing social order (Treu, 1976a, p. 568).

Prefects became the typical agents for government intervention in labor disputes. They were entrusted with both arbitration and repressive roles (denial of permission for public meetings and demonstrations, harassment of trade-union leaders, etc.). The intervention of the Ministry of Labor (Ministero del Lavoro) in arbitrations of labor disputes became increasingly unfavorable to workers.

Similarly, the regulations governing individual and collective dismissals played into the employers' hands, for arbitration committees (*collegi arbitrari*) had no real power to enforce rulings against employers. What governments, judges, prefects, and arbitrators did not do, the police did. The use of police in labor disputes was quite common. Beginning with the fall of the Popular Front government in 1948, massed police charges to disperse workers on strike, often resulting in the use of firearms, became increasingly frequent, first in the agricultural South, and later in the industrial North.[49] Vladimiro, a Michelin blue-collar worker in Turin, recalled the late 1950s: "When we were face-to-face with the police, they provoked us, spitting on our faces; they whispered 'bastards,' 'your mother is a whore,' so that they could start beating us up" (quoted in Lanzardo, 1979, p. 94).

More generally, the state, in its attempts to control class conflict, artificially divided wage earners, fixing in the law differential statuses, benefits, and forms of workers' organizations for wage workers and salaried employees (Pizzorno, 1974a; Kocka, 1980, pp. 26, 1983). In Italy, throughout the 1950s and 1960s, wage differentials between blue-collar and white-collar workers were "exceptionally high" compared with those in other industrialized countries (Valli, 1976, p. 21). Valli suggested that that "highly anomalous fact" must have been related to the politics of the Italian state, aimed at buying consensus among the strata of the petite bourgeoisie (Valli, 1976, pp. 50–2). Indeed, according to Pizzorno (1974a), the postwar Italian state pursued a strategy of consent based on the middle classes (old and new) as buffer strata between the bourgeoisie and a highly militant working class. The strategy was based on the theory of unequal incentives (*disuguaglianze incentivanti*) comprising both economic benefits (modern consumption) and political benefits (state-protected firms and clientelistic distribution of state resources). Berger (1974) and Weiss (1984) similarly argued that the persistence and growth of craft and small-scale industrial units in postwar Italy could be attributed to the deliberate policies of Christian Democrat governments to preserve a pluralistic class structure (see also Mattina, 1991).

Whereas the state provided the legal and political framework for a repressive-industrial relations system, much of the actual repression was carried out directly by employers, within the factories. Trade-union structures at the plant level came under attack from employers. First, the August 7, 1947, agreement between Confindustria and CGIL, CISL, and UIL stripped *commissioni interne* of all the bargaining functions they had previously enjoyed. Second, all political forms of workers' organizations set up in the plants during the Resistance against the Nazis, in particular the *consigli di gestione*, were dismantled (Treu, 1976a, p. 559).[50] Little by little, the *commissioni interne* lost a series of prerogatives: the freedom for their members to move around the plants to pursue trade-union activities, the right to hold meetings, to post memoranda, to have an office in a plant, and so forth (Della Rocca, 1976, pp. 620ff.). Political screening of new workers was widespread, with parish priests and the "free unions" (CISL and UIL) often being the basic sources for recruitment of new workers.[51] As a worker at the Dalmine steelworks recalled, "We had the documentation of letters of reference that said that the person to be

hired was a 'good' person, did not read the political press of a certain kind, etc."
(quoted in Abbatecola, 1974, p. 38). At the height of repression at the Fiat factory
in Turin, a Communist worker, Giuseppe Dozzo, wrote the following in his diary:

Monday (March 11, 1957)
We [Communist activists] try our best to talk to the workers. They listen, but they are very afraid.

Tuesday (November 26, 1957)
A female worker asks me how I ended up at shop 24. She thinks I am a new hire. I tell her I am a Communist. She screams out in terror. She tells me never to say something like this again, or I'll get fired.

Monday (December 30, 1957)
Shop 10; I get some workers to sign up for FIOM [the Communist federation of metalworkers belonging to CGIL]. I talk to many, but there is great fear. (in Pugno and Garavini, 1974, pp. 189, 218, 222; Accornero et al., 1960)

With labor's organizational structures excluded from the factories, employers began to implement a wide range of antilabor tactics: blacklisting, punishments for low productivity, cuts in pay, frisking, discrimination against union activists and politicized workers, awards of anti-CGIL and antistrike bonuses, separate agreements with the CISL and UIL "free unions" at the expense of the Communist-led CGIL, a ban against political and trade-union activities within the plants, the use of company unions, management interference in *commissioni enterne* elections, and so forth (Treu, 1976a; Della Rocca, 1976).[52] In many of the larger factories, the employers set up shops (sometimes physically separated and geographically distant from the main plant) where all the radicals who had not already been fired would be assigned to work (*reparti confino*).[53] Pressure tactics during strikes included house calls by company messengers to convince reluctant workers to report for work "even if only for a few minutes," "the police will protect you" (Lanzardo, 1979, p. 89). Vladimiro, Michelin worker in Turin, recalled that Mr. Dubrée, Michelin general manager, was determined to break a 1962 strike:

The strike was a political confrontation, and to win it he spent millions. Just think of how he "used" clerical workers and how much this cost him. Since he couldn't bring them into the offices [because of the pickets], he put them all up in several hotels around town, because he wanted to show that they didn't strike. (quoted in Lanzardo, 1979, p. 92)

A worker in a food-processing plant in the Milan area in 1952 complained that

In our firm, workers live in a state of fear. . . . A manager, standing next to the exit door the evening before a strike, thus summons the workers: "Tomorrow, there is a strike; those of you who participate will have to deal with me." (ACLI, 1953, p. 26)

The rates of exploitation of labor were high. According to the data collected by the Stanford Research Institute for the Italian government's commission of investigation into the state of the metalworking industry, almost 70% of all workers in the industry worked more than 40 hours per week, sometimes 60 hours, despite

Table 6.5. *Number of injunctions and fines against employers*

	One-day weekly rest		Workplace safety		Workplace hygienic conditions	
	Injunctions	Fines	Injunctions	Fines	Injunctions	Fines
1951	1,887	554	6,104	431	5,127	365
1955	2,972	3,791	14,721	3,338	8,893	2,038

Source: Commissione Parlamentare d'Inchiesta sulle Condizioni dei Lavoratori in Italia (1958a, pp. 130, 136, 139).

the high levels of unemployment at the time (CISIM, 1952, p. 255). The numbers of injunctions and fines against employers for forcing their workers to work seven days a week grew severalfold in the early 1950s (Table 6.5). Employers' disregard for labor laws on safety issues, social security, health, working hours, and so forth was quite widespread, and again, the numbers of injunctions and fines levied by the inspectors of the Ministry of Labor grew steadily in the early 1950s (Table 6.5). As high as those numbers were, it is likely that they were grossly underestimated. In fact, the frequency of inspections was quite low, with only one firm out of six being inspected, and with inspections concentrated mostly in the larger plants (Commissione Parlamentare d'Inchiesta sulle Condizioni dei Lavoratori in Italia, 1958a, pp. 106, 114). Notwithstanding the employers' low probability of being inspected and found in violation of the labor laws, a good indicator of the generally very poor working conditions and widespread breaches of labor and welfare laws was the fact that on many of the items of inspection, some 50% or even 60% of the firms inspected were found to be at fault (Commissione Parlamentare d'Inchiesta sulle Condizioni dei Lavoratori in Italia, 1958a, pp. 147, 149). Furthermore, both subtle pressures and heavy-handed measures to control workers were not uncommon during the labor inspectors' visits. A female textile worker complained that "Labor inspectors on visits to the plant are always accompanied by the entrepreneur himself in their rounds through the plant. This is an obstacle for a poor woman who would have something to say" (ACLI, 1953, p. 47). Workers' complaints to the Ministry of Labor grew in number from 25,845 in 1950 to 27,477 in 1951, and 39,489 in 1954 (Commissione Parlamentare d'Inchiesta sulle Condizioni dei Lavoratori in Italia, 1958a, p. 109).

The main instrument of repression remained the employers' unrestricted freedom to fine, transfer, or even fire workers (Onofri, 1955, pp. 40–64). In a labor market such as that in Italy during the 1950s, characterized by chronic underemployment and by an almost unlimited supply of labor, to be laid off was to be sentenced to a life of poverty. Older, married workers with family responsibilities were particularly vulnerable (Perrot, 1974, p. 505; Regini, 1974, p. 46). Often, men perceived the weight of their responsibilities in "the anxious, worried faces of the wives" (Perrot, 1974, p. 505). At work, women often were quite militant; at home, as housewives, the responsibilities of putting food on the table and facing the daily struggle to make ends meet turned them more conservative.[54] Employers knew that all too well. In the 1950s and 1960s, Italian companies would send suggestive letters to workers' homes in an attempt to involve their families in applying pressure to militant workers. One such letter from Fiat read as follows:

To the mothers and wives of Fiat workers:
In the course of last year, thanks to the victory of the democratic unions CISL and UIL and to the defeat of FIOM [the Communist metalworking federation belonging to CGIL], Fiat workers have not lost a single penny due to strikes and agitation, in previous years regularly organized by the FIOM *commissioni interne*. . . . Fiat workers have obtained much more without struggles, without strikes and strife, *without imposing useless sacrifices on the family, and finally without running any risk.* (Pugno and Garavini, 1974, p. 86; emphasis added)

Consider another example:

Open letter to the families of Fiat Avigliana workers:
The head of your household has received an important letter addressed to him personally. If he did not receive it . . . it probably means that, because of his labor and political attitudes, he is not considered a loyal Fiat employee.

Talk about it at home and consider whether this characterization is right. In any case, the outcome of the next elections for the *commissioni interne*, with its indication of the number of FIOM votes, will tell how many workers *have not thought about their families before casting their votes.*

Wives, mothers, sons and daughters, in your interest and in that of the people you love, make sure that your husband, your son, or your father is not one of them. (quoted in Pugno and Garavini, 1974, p. 88; emphasis added)

It was that argument of financial responsibility to the family that seemed to crush even the most militant workers. As Giuseppe Gullino, a Fiat militant in the 1950s, recalled,

I had heard that Bellini [a co-worker] had been a scab two or three times already. We had worked together in the past . . . he was a comrade. . . . I sent for him and said: "So, Bellini, how are you? You are doing everything possible to win the scorn of your comrades." That really set him off! "When I have nothing left to *feed my wife and son* at home, your comrades don't feed them. . . . I give it to you straight: I want those 'collaboration' bonuses."[55] (quoted in Accornero and Rieser, 1981, p. 93; emphasis added)

One day in the mid-1950s, Barbisin, a factory guard at Fiat particularly hated by the workers for his anti-Communist zeal, had been spying on a Communist worker. The workers caught Barbisin and reacted angrily, pushing him against the wall. As Giovanni Dozzo, the worker being spied upon, noted in his diary,

Barbisin understands that this time things are taking a bad turn for him. He waves his hands and tries to defend himself. "*I have a family*, and I was ordered to come here to spy on you." (Pugno and Garavini, 1974, p. 209; emphasis added)

Game and hunters, surveyed and surveyors – all caught up in that tragic game of life in which someone else called the shots. And some succumbed:

R., a gang supervisor, ... that day of the strike for the dismissal of Padroni [a co-worker], he too walked out. He did not like being a scab, but he was terribly afraid of participating in the strike; and fear once, fear twice, fear three times, that time was the last straw, and he quit his job, even though he was younger than I. (quoted in Accornero and Rieser, 1981, p. 136)

Among the firms that had *commissioni interne* (CI) and had been inspected by the 1956 Commissione Parlamentare d'Inchiesta sulle Condizioni dei Lavoratori in Italia (1958b, p. 162), 23% had fired some CI members, half of them for trade-union activities. Larger firms were more likely to mount attacks on workers' representative bodies: Only two firms in the size class employing 51–100 workers had fired CI members, compared with eleven in the 101–500 class and twenty in the class with more than 500 workers (Commissione Parlamentare, 1958b, p. 162). Larger firms also were more likely to fire CI members for no other reason than their trade-union involvement: twelve firms in the 51–100 class, three in the 101–500 class, and eleven in the class with more than 500 workers (Commissione Parlamentare, 1958b, p. 163). What the data show is that larger firms took the lead in dismantling workers' organizational structures at the plant level in the late 1940s and early 1950s.

In 1971, a Ministry of Justice investigation at Fiat revealed a huge filing system to keep track of its systematic "political" screening of workers: 354,077 files collected between 1949 and 1971, 203,422 collected during the period of greatest employer repression during the 1950s and early 1960s (an average of 12,000 files per year), and 150,655 collected between 1967 and 1971 (an average of 37,500 per year) during the years of the strike wave (Guidetti Serra, 1984). The screening system had been based on information provided by zealous and corrupt police officers, national-security agents, state-department employees, and parish priests. "With shock and sincere regret" Giovanni and Umberto Agnelli declared that they knew nothing about such "negative activity."

Fiat was not alone. An in-depth study of a sample of 190 firms in the project directed by Treu on labor's appeals to the Workers' Charter showed that the likelihood of repressive management was inversely related to firm size: 91.1% of firms employing fewer than 50 workers were repressive, 81.1% of firms with 50–250 workers, 68.8% of firms with 250–500 workers, and 20.0% of firms with 500–1,000 workers (Biagi, 1976, p. 395).[56] Interestingly enough, however, the probability of finding a repressive management increased to 42.9% among large firms employing more than 1,000 workers.

It should come as no surprise, then, that in the late 1960s the largest firms had lower levels of unionization than did middle-size firms (Cavallo Perin, 1980), nor should it be surprising that the findings accumulated in this book reveal a decline in workers' ability to mount collective action in the largest factories. During the long years of labor repression in the 1950s and 1960s, labor survived best in the midsize firms. Biagi's data confirm that the lower levels of both unionization and conflict in the very large firms were directly linked to employer repression. Repression has thus finally explained the *paradox of large firms*. The high levels of labor repression also explain Romagnoli's variant of this paradox:

[In 1969] we are confronted with an apparent paradox, i.e., large factories characterized by highly mechanized technologies are at the same time sites of low unionization and high capacity for conflict. (Romagnoli, 1976, p. 134)

Beginning in the early 1950s and extending throughout the 1960s, Italian employers ruthlessly repressed shop-floor workers' organizational structures. Large factories working under contracts deriving from the Marshall Plan led the antilabor and anti-Communist campaign. In many of those factories, unionization fell to very low levels. It was those same large factories, characterized by assembly line technology, that during the 1960s greatly increased the pace of production. When improved labor-market conditions toward the end of the 1960s gave the workers in those factories a fighting chance to make inroads against the employer, they seized it with a vengeance.

Militants, of course, and shop-floor activists were the people who absorbed the brunt of employers' repressive tactics. The diaries of Giovanni Dozzo and Aris Accornero[57] clearly illustrate the daily trickle of fines, suspensions, and layoffs designed to erode the resolve of the workers' vanguard.[58] The document *La classe lavoratrice si difende* (The working class defends itself) (ACLI, 1953), compiled by the Christian Association of Italian Workers, provides several examples from Milanese firms: "As for fines, it's a disaster: You are forced to pay for every trifle" (p. 38). "With fines and threats of layoffs, the workers' lives are made unbearable" (p. 44). "Fines are plentiful, and for minor reasons" (p. 46). "Heavy fines are levied for minor infractions" (p. 49). "The employer sends in his seven-year-old son to take down the names of the women who talk, and then fines them" (p. 50).

A survey conducted in 1971 by Romagnoli among the *delegati* of eighty-five Milanese factories showed that 20.4% of the delegates had experienced one form or another of disciplinary punishment for trade-union activities; 7% of them had been fired (Romagnoli, 1973, pp. 48–9). Figure 6.1 confirms that the members of the *commissioni interne* (the plant-level workers' representative bodies) were always the prime targets, particularly prior to 1955 and again from 1960 onward during the first strike wave.

Typically, the specifications of econometric models of strikes do not include a measure for layoffs; yet layoffs, even more than unemployment, have quite negative effects on workers' morale and on their willingness and ability to engage in collective action. When workers see people around them being fired, they begin to wonder if they will be next. Indeed, Skeels (1971) argued that layoffs should be included in a strike model, along with the unemployment rate. The two variables "conceptually might have different effects on the bargaining parties" (Skeels, 1971, p. 519).[59] There is no doubt that layoffs mainly reflect labor-market conditions and

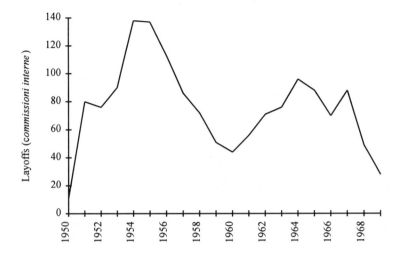

Figure 6.1. *Plot of number of layoffs of members of* commissioni interne

employers' needs to shed excess labor in the face of shrinking production and/or increasing competition. Nevertheless, layoffs tended to be used against the most politicized and most militant workers,[60] as means to curb labor militancy. As Mr. Bezzi, an entrepreneur in the early 1950s, candidly admitted to union representatives,

I called for twenty layoffs, not for reasons of redundancy, but because in the plant I have seven or eight troublesome workers I want to get rid of. You want to include these workers in the list of the Commissione Interna, and I fire them before you can do that. This much I have decided, and nothing can change my mind. If you stand in the way, I will shut down the plant and retire to the Riviera, because, in any case, I am tired of being an industrialist. (quoted in Onofri, 1955, p. 205)

Considering the importance of layoffs, let me carry out some multivariate analyses, using various measures of layoffs. The model that I propose to test basically follows the specification of the organizational model of equation (4.1), with the addition of a contract-renewal variable and different measures of layoffs:

$$Y_t = \beta_0 + \beta_1 UN_t + \beta_2 UNION_t + \beta_3 CONTRACT_t + \beta_4 LAYOFFS_t + \epsilon_t \qquad (6.3)$$

where Y measures the numbers of strikes, strikers, or hours lost, UN measures the unemployment rate, $UNION$ measures the union membership for CGIL and CISL, $CONTRACT$ measures the percentage of workers subject to national, categorywide contract renewal, and $LAYOFFS$ provides three different measures of layoffs: Number of firms requesting layoffs, number of workers laid off, and number of members of *Commissioni Interne* laid off. The $LAYOFFS$ variable has an expected negative sign. All other variables have the expected signs already discussed at the beginning of this chapter and in other chapters, namely, *UN* negative, *UNION* positive, *CONTRACT* positive for number of strikers and number of hours lost, and negative for number of strikes.

The specification of equation (6.3), including measures of both layoffs and unemployment, allows me to test the effects of separate aspects of the labor market. Table 6.6 shows the econometric results obtained from estimating equation (6.3). The results indeed show that the number of layoffs, however measured, always has negative effects; and so does the unemployment rate. Model 6 in Table 6.6 shows that the coefficient of the number of layoffs of *commissioni interne* members, representing the worker vanguard within the plant, are highly significant. In short, layoffs do raise the cost of mobilization and reduce the likelihood of workers' collective action, above and beyond what labor-market conditions alone would warrant.

We can hardly shed a tear over a negative and significant coefficient. Economists are in the habit of interpreting econometric coefficients in terms of the unitary changes that they produce in the dependent variables: so many layoffs, so many fewer strikes, or strikers. Even so, it is difficult to muster sympathy for the plight of workers simply on the basis of an econometric coefficient. This does not translate aseptic statistical measures back into the human meaning that they hide. Let us listen to how the workers themselves would interpret the "significance" of our statistical findings. The testimony comes from the impressive *cahiers de doléances* assembled in 1952 in the Milan area by the Christian Association of Italian Workers (ACLI):[61]

With the threat of layoffs, the employer tries to shut up trade-union activists.... Individual layoffs have been carried out with the sole purpose of intimidating labor. (ACLI, 1953, p. 43)

In the plant there exists a perfect spying organization: You cannot make a gesture or say a word that the employer won't know. All must bend under the threat of layoffs. (ACLI, 1953, p. 24)

Yet as statistically significant as the number of layoffs are, the official number of layoffs may have been considerably underestimated. Many workers' resignations were layoffs in disguise:

With cunning, workers to be fired are asked to resign. In two years, more than thirty have resigned because of their political and trade-union activities. (ACLI, 1953, p. 46)

We point out the special treatment reserved for several members of the Commissione Interna: one, hired as a mechanic, was moved... to be a porter... another one was assigned to prepare corn mush for the pigs. These workers endured for a while, and when they got tired they resigned. (ACLI, 1953, p. 27)

The undisputed right to hire and fire workers at will gave employers the upper hand in their relationship. The way employers put it,

Table 6.6. Testing the effect of workers' layoffs

Aggregation level: Industry; yearly series
Sample period: 1955/1975 for models 1 through 6; 1955/1969 for models 7, 8, and 9
Estimation method: GLS (Cochrane-Orcutt) for all models

	Number of strikes			Number of strikers			Number of hours lost		
	Model 1	Model 2	Model 3	Model 4	Model 5	Model 6	Model 7	Model 8	Model 9
Constant	2,818.06*	2,743.72*	1,769.25*	-732.84	710.27	-1,004.52*	52,987.37	52,096.84	-34,991.81
	(641.01)	(633.22)	(655.19)	(1,863.78)	(1,807.25)	(4531.36)	(47,855.34)	(45,085.37)	(38,118.43)
Unemployment rate	-220.43*	-217.67*	-190.62*	-200.89	-197.18	-180.25*	-11,780.36*	-11,254.94*	-7,991.39*
	(58.53)	(60.00)	(57.98)	(184.74)	(182.77)	(38.96)	(4,199.21)	(4,084.89)	(3,052.70)
Union membership	.593E-3*	.61E-3*	.15E-2*	.25E-2*	.25E-2*	.47E-2*	.34E-1*	.34E-1*	.13*
	(.226E-3)	(.23E-3)	(.53E-3)	(.68)	(.67E-3)	(.40E-3)	(.17E-1)	(.16E-1)	(.36E-1)
Contract renewal	-5.40	-5.31	-6.80*	10.75	10.66	-.61E-1	1,307.76*	1,304.00*	1,322.01*
	(3.40)	(3.97)	(3.17)	(8.55)	(8.49)	(3.14)	(348.09)	(343.39)	(390.87)
Firms requesting layoffs	-.10E-1			-.42			-21.87		
	(.20)			(.55)			(15.40)		
Workers laid off		-.28E-2			-.21E-1			-1.09**	
		(.92)			(.24E-1)			(.67)	
Commissioni interne laid off			-7.15			-38.92*			-1,284.14*
			(4.16)			(3.32)			(305.59)
Adjusted R^2	.57	.55	.52	.47	.48	.95	.57	.59	.83
Durbin-Watson	1.60	1.60	1.96	1.648	1.47	1.76	2.06	2.06	2.25

Note: Standard error in parentheses. **Significant at the .05 level; *significant at the .01 level.

if you want, this is like it is, otherwise there are plenty of people out there who would love to have your job. (ACLI, 1953, p. 28)

If you don't like it, the door is open. (ACLI, 1953, p. 36)

The role of repression in an overall model of power and collective action has been extensively theorized (e.g., Tilly, 1978, pp. 98–142). Repression plays a fundamental role in an overall causal model of strikes (Aguet, 1954; Ludtke, 1979). Yet in quantitative strike research, because of the difficulties of obtaining reliable data on repression, we typically leave a measure of repression out of our econometric models – "Out of sight, out of mind," what is not there is soon forgotten. The reality of statistical modeling comes to be seen as historical reality. Leaving repression out of the picture altogether can be quite misleading. Indeed, the low levels of industrial conflict throughout the 1950s probably would defy comprehension, in view of the later outbursts of labor unrest, without some understanding of the repressive climate of the time both inside and outside the plant. The high level of unemployment cannot, by itself, explain the depth of labor's defeat during that decade. Workers themselves seemed to know all too well that their situation reflected the balance of class forces:

Before 1948, before the political elections, employers did not use these despotic methods – reason: fear of communism. Now, democracy is weak ... workers live in the constant fear of being fired. (ACLI, 1953, p. 37)

The "withering away of strikes" and "the end of ideology" in the 1950s must be understood in the context of the highly repressive, antilabor climate of the cold-war years. The oral-history accounts of the period (e.g., Brentano, 1975), workers' diaries (e.g., Accornero, 1959, 1973; Accornero et al., 1960), interviews with workers (e.g., Carocci, 1960; Accornero and Rieser, 1981), labor documents (e.g., CGIL, 1953; ACLI, 1953), and the voluminous material gathered by the commission of inquiry[62] set up by Parliament in 1954 to investigate employees' working conditions all bear witness to the harshness of the repression. It is indeed the high levels of repression during the 1950s that can explain why economic-bargaining models of strikes tend to overestimate strike frequency during recessionary periods *(paradox of the génie d'un peuple*; see Section 2.6, p. 41).

6.6.2. CORPORATISM *ALL'ITALIANA*, OR, WHAT HAPPENS TO CONFLICT WHEN A GROUP DOES HAVE POWER?

The argument of political-exchange theories of strike activity is based on the assumption that with a friendly government in power, the working class can use its privileged access to the government to obtain a more favorable distribution of resources. Over the thirty-year period from 1950 to 1978, was there ever a time when the Italian working class could count on finding a friendly presence in the halls of government? Emilio Reyneri, an attentive scholar of the Italian labor movement, answered in the negative:

> Even at times of greater strength in the "political market," Italian unions never had a really "friendly government" in power; at best, they dealt with weak governments that sought to satisfy union demands without sacrificing the traditional interests of employers' and their bureaucratic or political clienteles.[63]

Luciano Lama, secretary general of CGIL, put it this way in a 1976 interview with Massimo Riva:

> We have always had to deal with a political leadership of the country that, in substance, refused any change in economic and social strategies; it refused change in practice, even when it did not at all reject dialogue and openness with the labor movement. (Riva, 1976, p. 91)

Certainly, the Center governments of the 1950s were not friendly. After all, the 1950s were the years of the greatest political repression of labor in postwar Italy. In the late 1950s and the 1960s, a new balance of class forces emerged in the economic and social arenas. But not even the Center-Left governments that represented that new class alignment at the political level were very friendly to labor. True, outright political repression declined, but successive Center-Left governments failed to implement the thorough structural reforms espoused in their original platform. The Socialist Party (PSI) failed in its attempts to force the Christian Democrats (DC), the leading party in the Center-Left coalition, to implement policies of modernization and rationalization of the state bureaucracy. After an enormous volume of rhetoric, countered by predictions of dire consequences from the conservative side, the Center-Left failed to implement economic planning. Rather, the DC succeeded in co-opting even the PSI to the spoils system that had served its political interests so successfully. Center-Left governments raised the systematic division of government posts along clientelistic lines to an art: so many votes, so many posts. Party politics came to pervade every sphere of Italian life, with representation along party lines in all areas: the boards of directors of the large, state-owned corporations, the government railroad company, the TV channels (one per party), and even the governing bodies of the magistracy (Dente and Regonini, 1989).

But in the end, it was the PCI, not the PSI, that in the immediate postwar period seized the hegemonic position on the left, maintaining it and even improving it over the decades. But the PCI never acquired "stable and durable" control of the executive branch, the necessary condition for a long-term "withering away of strikes," according to Shorter and Tilly, Hibbs, and Korpi and Shalev. Nevertheless, during the 1970s, the political position of the PCI gradually improved, with party membership and electoral returns continuing to rise.

Both the unions and the PCI used that increasing power to "occupy the state" (Cosi and Pugliese, 1977; Treu, Roccella, and Ferrari, 1979; IRSI, 1981). By the late 1970s, Italian unions had some 26,058 representatives in a variety of large and small, important and trivial public institutions (Roccella, 1979, p. 32) – "a huge apparatus," accounting for more than half of trade-union personnel, an apparatus larger than even the largest categorywide unions (Treu, 1979, pp. 5–6).[64] Research on the boards of directors of the sixty-three largest public institutions found that 22.7% of such board members (283 out of 1,252) were union representatives (Cosi and Pugliese, 1977). "Over 26,000 union representatives are certainly too many; as well as the number of committees and boards of which they are members" (Treu, 1979, p. 12; see also Accornero, 1992, pp. 201–4). Thus, it would appear that in the early 1970s, Italian unions adopted a strategy similar to that of the DC in the 1950s (the occupation of the state).

Unlike the DC, however, the unions were never able to gain access to the real centers of power, the boardrooms, in their efforts to infiltrate the state. In only 20% of cases were union personnel involved in the governing boards of institutions (Ferrari, 1979, p. 65). In fact, the union presence on the boards of state ministries did not even succeed in eliminating personnel practices based on paternalism and *clientela* (Roccella, 1979, p. 25). The unions' nominal participation thus provided an alibi for those in charge to continue their authoritarian and hierarchical decision-making practices, with the unions' role confined to rubber-stamping decisions made elsewhere (Ferrari, 1979, p. 54).

The unions also used their power to control labor market mechanisms. After all, workers knew only too well what the proponents of economic-bargaining models are at pains to theorize and verify empirically: that it was the right to fire workers (the managerial prerogative) that gave employers the upper hand in the relationship. The threat of job loss was sufficient menace to subdue most workers.

Figure 6.2 shows a time plot of the percentage of layoff requests presented by employers to the labor courts and fought by trade unions through some form of legal or collective action. After the peak in 1950, these figures were low throughout the 1950s, and even during the mid-1960s, despite the high number of layoff procedures in those years (see, in Chapter 8, the plots of various measures of layoffs, Figures 8.3, 8.4, and 8.5, pp. 324–5). The figures jumped in 1968, as labor militancy and solidarity were again on the rise. Throughout the 1970s, unions increased their efforts to limit employers' layoff prerogative. The 1970 Workers' Charter severely restricted the upper hand that employers held over their work forces, a true landmark in worker–employer relations.

A good indication of the unions' changing strength during the postwar period comes from a measure proposed by Tarantelli: the number of days that lapse between the expiration and renewal dates of collective agreements.[65] In Chapter 2, we saw that unfavorable labor-market conditions negatively affect workers' bargaining power and their propensity to strike. There is yet another way in which the labor market may affect workers' bargaining position in the Italian system of labor relations. Italian employers often refused to renew expiring contracts, or else they simply stalled the negotiations, leading to long delays before renewal of contracts. Thus, the longer the time that elapses between contract expiration and

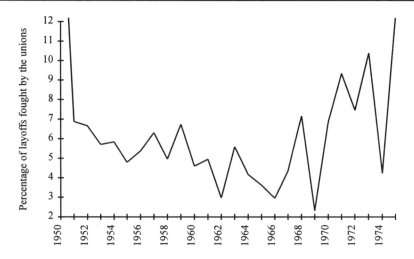

Figure 6.2. *Plot of the percentage of layoff procedures fought by the unions*

renewal, the lower the bargaining strength of the unions, for a quick contract renewal would indicate that unions had the bargaining power to demand and immediately receive a more favorable settlement. Timely contract renewals do not depend on labor-market conditions exclusively. They also reflect unions' organizational strength. A strong union will not let years go by without it having a collective contract, no matter how bad the labor market is. Tarantelli's measure is thus likely to reflect both labor-market and organizational effects.[66] The plots in Figure 6.3 of the numbers of days of both delayed and anticipated renewals provide a stark representation of the change in the power relationship between workers and employers between 1950 and 1977. The plots clearly show that workers faced an unfavorable balance of class power during the 1950s – with contract renewals typically delayed one, three, or even five years. Things gradually improved during the 1960s. But it was during the 1970s that the practice of delaying contract renewals almost disappeared. In fact, during that decade, contracts had a tendency to be renewed early (by a few months). Once again the plot of anticipated renewals shows the close correspondence between strike waves (1959–63 and 1968–72) and workers' ability to obtain quick settlements and concessions. The *autunno caldo* dealt a last, fatal blow to the employers' stalling practices of the 1950s and ushered in a new pattern of class relations.

The new power of the unions was symbolically displayed in the periodic demonstrations held throughout the country (but mostly in Rome, the center of political power), featuring hundreds of thousands of workers with hundreds of red flags, an imposing and certainly worrisome sight to the bourgeoisie. Not surprisingly, employers and the state sought to limit conflict and confine it within a more institutionalized framework. The 1975 *scala mobile* agreement between Confindustria (the private employers' association) and the three major unions

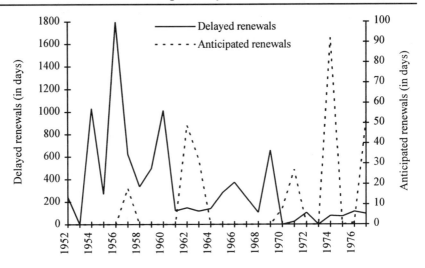

Figure 6.3. *Plots of Tarantelli's measures of workers' market power*

(CGIL, CISL, and UIL) marked a change in policy for both employers and the unions. Why the employers, particularly large-scale employers, would sign such a costly agreement we saw in Chapter 5 (i.e., to bring plant-level conflict down). In that chapter we also saw that the agreement proved to be a success for the employers. What we did not see was why the unions would sign that agreement. Why did they agree to give up a weapon that in years past had proved so formidable: strikes (*la lotta che paga*)? Let me now tackle that question in light of the political focus of this chapter.

The *scala mobile* agreement was both the last example of an old system of labor relations and the first example of a new system (Bordogna, 1985, p. 182). On the one hand, the agreement reflected the traditional union approach of dealing with employers via *bilateral bargaining* (unions versus employers) on issues of wages and cost of living (Bordogna, 1985, p. 183). On the other hand, the agreement marked a definite shift in the locus of bargaining from the *federal level* to the *confederal level* (Bordogna, 1985, p. 183). Whereas plant-level and industry-level bargaining (mostly in the hands of the unions' and employers' territorial and federal organizations) had prevailed during the first half of the 1970s, interindustry bargaining (in the hands of confederal unions) dominated the second half of the decade. It may have appeared that labor relations were shifting back to a paradigm more typical of the 1950s, given the unions' reliance on confederal bargaining in both periods. This was certainly true, at least for the level of bargaining. There was one important difference, however. In the 1950s, collective bargaining had been based on *bilateral agreements* between unions (at the confederal level: CGIL, CISL, and UIL) and employers (also at the confederal level: Confindustria). In the second half of the 1970s, *trilateral agreements* prevailed, involving unions, employers, and the state (Bordogna, 1985, p. 184). But if direct state involvement in labor relations was the distinguishing feature of the late 1970s, had the state not also intervened in labor relations during the 1960s, via the *conferenze triangolari*? Again, the answer is yes. But the *conferenze triangolari* of the 1960s had served only a consultative function for the Center-Left governments, more inclined than their predecessors to listen to the "social parts." In the trilateral agreements of the late 1970s, the state was neither spectator nor labor relations arbiter. The state participated in the bargaining process with resources of its own (fiscal policy, welfare, economic aid for firms and industrial sectors) (Bordogna, 1985, p. 184).

The bargaining rounds on the "cost of labor" (*costo del lavoro*) in the winter months of 1976–77 provide a typical example of the new framework of industrial relations.[67] The tripartite negotiations on the *costo del lavoro* were complex and protracted and resulted in an interconfederal agreement between the unions' and employers' associations, an agreement between the government and the unions, and proposals for one law and two law decrees (*decreti legge*). In the climate of economic stagnation of the time, the employers took the lion's share: a decrease in the total coverage of money wages against inflation provided by the *scala mobile*, and greater flexibility in the utilization of labor (regarding overtime, shift work, intraplant and interplant mobility, more stringent control over absenteeism, and elimination of five holidays from the calendar). Furthermore, certain indirect costs of labor (mostly welfare provisions, such as health and pensions) that had been paid by the employers were loaded onto the state (*fiscalizzazione degli oneri sociali*). Those obligations were to be financed by an increase in the value added tax.

The two proposed law decrees contained the following two provisions: (1) Firms could not take deductions on their tax returns for wages above the levels fixed in national, industrywide contract agreements. (2) Firms that signed plant-level agreements that contained wage provisions were not eligible for *fiscalizzazione degli oneri sociali*. The aim of those measures was drastic curtailment of plant-level bargaining. The measures did not pass, but the fact that they were even debated in Parliament marked a significant shift in the climate of labor relations from just five years earlier (Bordogna, 1985, p. 186).

In exchange for their moderation in economic demands, the unions obtained from the state a series of so-called contract laws (*leggi contratto*) that provided a series of guarantees for job expansion, particularly among youth (in 1977, law no. 285 on youth employment, *occupazione giovanile*), and industrial restructuring (again in 1977, law no. 675) (Giugni, 1982; Bordogna, 1985, p. 186).

The *scala mobile* agreement and subsequent agreements marked an overall change in union strategy, with the unions beginning to practice policies of self-restraint.[68] In February 1978, some 1,500 *delegati* and union cadres met at the EUR convention center in Rome for a national conference convened by the unitary federation (Federazione Unitaria) of the CGIL, CISL, and UIL confederations (Turone, 1984, pp. 497–501). The participants approved by a large majority (only 103 abstentions and 12 contrary votes) a new union strategy of moderation (to be known as *linea dell'EUR*, "the EUR line") in exchange for a larger voice in companies' investment decisions and participation in the formation of broader economic policy.[69] At the close of the decade, the Italian industrial-relations system was moving toward more centralized tripartite relations among employers, unions, and the state, along corporatist lines.[70] The participation of the Communist Party in the government seemed to provide labor with a guarantee that their short-term sacrifices would be rewarded with long-term gains. In any case, to further ensure that labor concessions would result in productive investments, unions increasingly pressed their demand that companies disclose their investment decisions to the unions (*diritti di informazione*) (Della Rocca and Negrelli, 1983). They pressed for a say in the firms' decision-making processes. As Luciano Lama put it in his interview with Massimo Riva,

> With wage increases and with labor contracts one does not modify social structures, while we can change them if the directions of investments change in quality and quantity.... Trade unions cannot really influence investment and employment decisions without participating in the overall management of the firm. (Riva, 1976, pp. 92, 120)

In conclusion, the ethnographic, historical, and statistical analyses of the costs of collective action have confirmed that the level of worker mobilization varied over time in relation to its cost and that costs were related to power: The cost of collective action was high in the 1950s, as working-class power was low; the costs were lowered during the 1960s and especially during the 1970s, as working-class power increased, at first in the labor market and later in the political arena. In light of these analyses, the answers to two questions raised in Chapter 5 are now clear. The questions: (1) Why did Italian unions accept the 1975 *scala mobile* agreement, with its potential for divisive effects on the working class? (2) Why did the unions agree to reduce the scope of plant-level bargaining, the form of bargaining that had earned the unions increased power (*la lotta che paga*)? The answers: During the mid-1970s, the unions were shifting their interest from the local level to the national level, from the labor market to the political market. The *scala mobile* agreement simply marked a convergence of interests toward more centralized bargaining, on the part of both the unions and the large-scale employers. It was that shift toward more centralized bargaining and direct involvement by the state in the deals that unions and employers cut that led to the unions' increasing reliance on classwide mobilization over more general issues (e.g., state investment in the South, employment guarantees) in the mid-1970s: Four large-scale strikes between October and December 1974, fourteen such strikes between January and April 1975, and another fourteen strikes throughout 1977 accounted for 86%, 74%, and 53% of total strikers in those years. As we saw in the preceding chapter, it is those outliers in the series for the number of strikers – outliers unexplained by the timing of industrywide collective contracts – that account for the poor performance of the contract variable in econometric models of the number of strikers (see Section 5.5, p. 168).

My analysis of political power has also put the 1950s arguments of a "withering away of strikes" and "embourgeoisement of the working class" in historical perspective. The "withering away of strikes" and the "embourgeoisement of the working class" during the 1950s had little to do with the ability of mature capitalism to quell the fires of class conflict. Repression, in the context of "recasting bourgeois Europe," provides a more plausible explanation. To be sure, repression of labor was not unique to the 1950s. Authorities had used both harsh and gloved forms of violence against labor throughout the postwar period. But the mix of repression and co-optation, carrot and stick, had changed over time, along with the political position of labor in the national power structure. The 1969 *autunno caldo* and the 1968–72 years of *conflittualità permanente* mark a watershed between those two eras. During the 1970s, repression by political authorities declined, and political mediation increased, at both the national and local levels (i.e., the "regions").[71] Closures and overtures, repression and facilitation by the upper classes toward the lower classes follow the swelling tide of mobilization, the conjunctural balance of class forces. Not very differently from surfing, the aim of the game for the elites is to ride the crest of the tide and move forward, while keeping afloat.

6.7. SHORT AND LONG TERM, ECONOMICS AND POLITICS: THE UNIONS' DILEMMAS

The historical analyses in this chapter have revealed a close connection between the economic and the political, between the industrial actions and political maneuvers of the Italian working class. Yet according to Giddens (1973, pp. 205–6) "the institutional separation of economic and political conflict is a fundamental basis of the capitalist state." Have I misinterpreted Italian postwar history? Or has the persistent strength of the Communist Party and the Marxist tradition in the Italian setting affected the way the economic and the political moves have been played out within the Italian society? Answers to these questions will require me to probe deeper into the arguments expounded in Section 4.9 (p. 134) concerning the Marxist approach to the problems of the economic and political organization of the working class and its economic and political actions.

Marxist thinkers at the dawn of the twentieth century increasingly insisted that it would be necessary to rely on a working-class party (particularly, in the form of a vanguard party) rather than on a union, on political organizations rather than on economic organizations, for revolutionary purposes. Why? Basically, because by the late 1800s, capitalism, contrary to Marx's dire prediction of its decline, had demonstrated considerable resilience and had enjoyed successes that hinted at the possibility of long-term prosperity, rather than immiseration, despite recurrences of deep economic crises. By the middle of the second half of the nineteenth century, Engels had already pointed out that capitalism had the economic ability to buy off the vanguard of the British working class ("the labour aristocracy")

(Lapides, 1987, pp. 123–33). In *Imperialism: The Last Phase of Capitalism*, Lenin used that same argument to explain workers' quiescence during the Victorian era. Industrial workers realized early on that with an expanding pie, it would be far easier to obtain economic concessions from the capitalists than to seize outright political power. As workers' economic struggles found capitalists more willing to compromise, often with "immediate, visible results" (Luxemburg, 1971, p. 84) a tendency developed for workers to concentrate on economic struggles, an arena in which they seemed to have a fighting chance, and to postpone political struggles into the future, thus implicitly or explicitly settling for a class compromise (opportunism).

The source of such opportunism was the simple perception that perhaps the interests of labor and capital were not totally incompatible after all. In his 1902 pamphlet *What Is to Be Done?* Lenin (1989, p. 98) had argued that there was an "irreconcilable antagonism of their [workers'] interest to the whole of the modern political and social system." Kautsky (1910, p. 189) echoed that sentiment: "The interests of the proletariat and the bourgeoisie are of so contrary a nature that in the long run they cannot be harmonized." But workers do not live in the long run; they must face the day-to-day problems of survival. And, in the short run, is it really true that employers' and workers' interests are necessarily fundamentally opposed? Consider what Giovanni Agnelli said in a 1983 interview with Arrigo Levi:

I believe that [unions and employers] have one main interest in common, the competitiveness of the enterprise, so that there remain large margins of income to distribute: one part, the largest, to employees; another part, which is minimum, to stockholders. . . . Both social parties share a common interest in the growth of the enterprise [because] this will allow workers to live better, to work more comfortably, to have more satisfying work hours.[72]

The argument is compelling. A company in which labor relations are in turmoil can easily lose market share and profitability. Ultimately, continuing losses will lead to downsizing or even bankruptcy (Hyman, 1989, p. 107), thus leaving the workers of that company without jobs. Under capitalism, although it is terrible to be exploited in one's job, it is no better to elude such exploitation by having no job. Under capitalism, a bankrupt firm is no good for either the capitalist or the workers. When industrial unrest is widely diffused and many companies experience troubles, then a whole country can come to the verge of bankruptcy.[73] Alighiero De Micheli, Confindustria president during 1955–61, put it succinctly in an interview with Piero Ottone:

"Saving" is a little creature with invisible and extra-sensitive antennas. At the first sign of danger, this creature abandons its natural function, that of investment. The economic situation is a double-edged sword in favor of or against communism. (quoted in Ottone, 1965, p. 63)

According to some immiseration theories (whether Marxist, vulgar Marxist, or Durkheimian), the bankruptcy of a country, as dismal as that state of affairs may be, can also open up new possibilities. It can lead to deep social transformations through a revolutionary process. Trotsky was a firm believer that crises offer opportunities, because they destroy the economic basis for working-class acquiescence. However, class struggle may be a necessary but not sufficient condition for a successful revolutionary outcome (Chile *docet*). Thus, high and protracted levels of class confrontation in a country may simply result in increased suffering for the workers of that country, without leading to permanent change.

Hence workers' and unions' dilemma: To kill or not to kill the goose that lays the golden eggs? The first strategy involves radicalizing the struggle, with all the uncertainties inherent in a revolutionary situation. The second strategy is no less problematic, for workers have no guarantee that capitalists will productively reinvest their profits, and even if they do, there is no guarantee that they will share the income from those investments.[74] Thus, unions face the predicament of having to press employers to share their profits, but without pressuring them to the extent of driving them out of business – a juggling act worthy of the best conjurors. In the words of the Italian Socialist politician Giorgio Ruffolo, "the unions must fear their strength as much as their weakness. The trade union paradox lies in the unions' capacity to destabilize a system on which they continue to depend, and which they cannot change, neither alone nor in the short run" (quoted in Lange et al., 1982, p. 165). It is in light of the trade-off between the present and the future that, under capitalism, workers' interests take on particularistic overtones, whereas those of entrepreneurs are more general ("what is good for General Motors is good for the country"). In an interesting twist of Marx's "revolutionary mission of the proletariat," in a letter addressed to the prime minister dated January 26, 1946, Confindustria president Angelo Costa wrote that

The entrepreneur is always projected into the future; labor, instead, and for obvious reasons, is preoccupied mostly with today: The former represents the propulsive and *revolutionary* element inside the factories; the latter is the conservative element. (quoted in De Carlini, 1972, p. 58; emphasis added)

Given the uncertainty of the outcome of revolutionary actions, and employers' greater willingness to give in to workers' economic demands, class compromise is likely to follow: Workers will consent to the continuation of capitalism as an institution, and capitalists will commit themselves to some rate of transformation of profits into wage increases and some rate of investment out of profit (Przeworski and Wallerstein, 1982, p. 137). But by accepting the terms of the profit–wages exchange, workers basically guarantee the persistence of capitalism (Przeworski, 1980–81). Workers consent to capitalism (and exploitation); capitalists consent to invest in order to enlarge the pie that lures workers into consent. Consent is not just a product of ideological manipulation (the "dominant-ideology thesis"). There are material bases for workers' consent.[75] Consent is bought with higher wages, the unions themselves becoming the workers' watchdogs. Lester commented as follows on the postwar labor–management settlement in the United States and the "productivity agreements":

Since 1950 no major strike has occurred in the soft coal industry, and the national union has been bearing down on any unauthorized strikes with fines and threat of expulsion of individual members. (Lester, 1958, p. 102)

Compromise, however, is not a blank check. It is neither automatic nor achieved once and for all. Not even the unions' fines and threats of expulsion could prevent American workers from going on strike when material benefits began to be eroded in the second half of the 1960s (Bowles et al., 1983, pp. 102–3). Without an occasional carrot, the material incentives for labor to continue its consent can dwindle, and the stick may have to be used to ensure the reproduction of capital (Bowles et al., 1983, pp. 105–13). Nevertheless, capitalism has, thus far, shown great (and, for the Marxists, unexpected) capacity for survival and growth, despite recurrent crises.

Well aware of the trap of opportunism, the CGIL, the Italian Communist union, tried every trick in the book to avoid falling prey. In the 1950s, it rejected plant-level bargaining, for fear of economism and of splitting the working class into the haves and have-nots, between workers who could wrest higher wages from more profitable firms and those who would be left behind. In the late 1960s and early 1970s, as the workers had reappropriated bargaining prerogatives at the plant level, the CGIL held high the *ultimate* political goal of the class via its reform strategy. Well aware of the uncertainties inherent in class compromise, in the middle and late 1970s the CGIL decided to make economic concessions to save some large-scale employers from bankruptcy, but in exchange it demanded some control over firms' investment decisions, and it demanded participation in the decision-making process for the country's economic policies.

Nevertheless, CGIL's policies throughout the period were somewhat ambiguous, if not outright hypocritical.[76] CGIL could maintain its "class purity" because labor contracts signed by any of the unions extended to all workers in the Italian system of industrial relations. As long as others (i.e., CISL and UIL) were there to do the dirty jobs of day-to-day bargaining and of extracting economic concessions from employers, all workers, including CGIL members, would enjoy the benefits of collective contracts. Furthermore, the official CGIL policy simply ignored the reality of shop-floor practice, where many of its militants and representatives were informally involved in a great deal of everyday bargaining in many Italian companies. Finally, the CGIL policy reproduced haves and have-nots at the employers' discretion, rather than at the union's demand. Again the CGIL maintained its ideal of class purity by letting the employers do the dirty job of splitting up the working class. The fact that, perhaps, that is precisely the employers' job did not justify giving them a free hand. The result was the *giungla retributiva*, the jungle of the Italian wage structure, and a decade of a highly repressive shop-floor climate. The fiction of CGIL's class purity was preserved at the cost of employment policies that were at best paternalistic and at worst repressive. The result was a weakened and demoralized working class. In 1976, Luciano Lama, while advocating the need for union involvement in firms' investment decisions and in directing the country's economic policy in exchange for concessions, declared that "we must participate in the policy making of the economy, yet refuse any form of institutionalization of this role . . . because the danger is a single trade union, and obligatory" (Riva, 1976, p. 124).

Whereas CGIL never wholeheartedly took the road of reformism and compromise, CISL never clearly eschewed the lure of class. During the 1968–72 strike waves, many of its shop-floor militants often were more radical in their choices of tactics and demands than were CGIL's workers. The title of a CISL metalworkers' union pamphlet of the time, *Per un sindacato di classe*, "For a class union," is a good case in point (FIM-CISL, 1972).

But if the economic organizations of the working class have severe limitations for revolutionary purposes, can the party ever *really* be ready for revolution? Caught in the dilemma of adventurism and revolutionary change, of losing not only the economic and political advantages already won but also the lives of hundreds and perhaps thousands of people in revolutionary bloodshed, even the political organization of the working class is likely to settle for class compromise. The stronger the position of the party in electoral politics, the more integrated into the polity it becomes, and the higher the stakes, as Trotsky well knew (Clarke and Clements, 1977, p. 77; Luxemburg, 1971, p. 39). Structural constraints within capitalist societies similar to those that impede unions also hinder working-class parties, particularly the imposition of short-term, bourgeois political rules (Kalecki, 1943; Offe and Wiesenthal, 1980, pp. 99, 101–3; see also Cohen and Rogers, 1983, pp. 47–87). Furthermore, the very structure of the capitalist state, with its reliance on private accumulation of capital for state funding, poses severe limitations for any attempted appropriation of the capitalist state for revolutionary purposes (Offe and Ronge, 1975; Block, 1977). Thus, both the unions and the party are forced to settle for only short-term gains in both the economic and political arenas. Consider Rosa Luxemburg's words:

> The parliamentary struggle, however, the counterpart of the trade union struggle, is equally with it, a fight conducted exclusively on the basis of the bourgeois social order. It is by its very nature political reform work, as that of the trade unions is economic reform work. It represents political work for the present, as trade unions represent economic work for the present. (Luxemburg, 1971, p. 80)

Class conflict in the form of strikes may be a necessary condition for revolution, but it is not sufficient. In fact, no revolution has ever resulted primarily from industrial conflict, not even from such potentially revolutionary contexts as the 1919–20 Red years and the 1969 *autunno caldo* in Italy or May 1968 in France.[77] The military breakdown and financial collapse of the state are important prerequisites for revolutionary outbreaks. Lenin, Bukharin, and Trotsky all maintained that large-scale wars among capitalist countries would accelerate political breakdown in those countries, leading to radical enlightenment of the masses under conditions of acute suffering.[78] In recent years, Skocpol (1979) has similarly argued that intrastate (class) conflict is a necessary but not sufficient condition for a successful revolution; unless there is also interstate conflict (wars), followed by the fiscal crisis of the state and collapse of the repressive apparatus of the state, class conflict will simply be crushed. The Italian experience in the postwar period, its position in the Western bloc, and its subordinate relationship to U.S. foreign policy do seem to support the view that the geopolitical position of a country severely constrains the revolutionary ferment among its working class, both in its manifestations and, even more so, in its final outcome.

Rightly or wrongly, the Italian PCI, the largest Communist party in the Western world, interpreted the balance of class forces in the immediate postwar period as unfavorable for a revolutionary outbreak in Italy. Given the presence of the occupation armies (American and British) still on Italian soil, the Yalta agreement whereby Italy fell into the Western sphere of influence, and the fact that the Soviet army was exhausted and in any case was not up to taking on the United States in a direct confrontation, in the late 1940s and early 1950s Togliatti took a very conciliatory stance in the political and social arenas. Thereafter, the PCI actively strove to make a bourgeois, representative democracy work. As the Italian political scientist Giorgio Galli (1975, p. 148) put it, "in almost thirty years of representative democracy in Italy, the PCI has tried to be helpful to the system with all its political choices." In abiding by the rules of the game, both the PCI and the Communist CGIL were implicated in the day-to-day bargaining process that kept the wheels of capitalism greased (Mann, 1973, p. 37).

Albeit with some wavering and wobbling, the PCI strategy, by and large, was to promote mobilization when workers did not want to hear of it and to contain it when spirits ran too high (Galli, 1975, p. 148). Time and again the PCI avoided direct confrontation with the bourgeoisie and its political representatives (the Christian Democrats). "The PCI was never too friendly with the social movements," wrote Pasquino (1985, p. 136). In Galli's (1975, p. 151) words, "the goal of the party always remained that of controlling the radicalization of class confrontations."[79] And the PCI took on that role repeatedly, with each major class confrontation of the postwar period: the 1945–48 period, as well as 1953–54, 1960–61, 1969–70, and 1976–79.[80] The PCI never used the mass-mobilization potential of the working class for the purpose of destabilizing the sociopolitical system embedded in the Constitution, nor did it ever try to use that potential to decisively propel the nation down the path of reformism (Galli, 1975, p. 124; Accornero, 1992). Instead, it advocated ill-defined concepts and strategies of "progressive democracy," an "Italian way to socialism," and, finally, *compromesso storico* (Galli, 1975, p. 162). The PCI relied on its network of militants and activists (200,000 in the 1950s, 80,000 in the 1960s, and 100,000 in the 1970s) to control all conflict (Galli, 1975, p. 166). In a party where, according to surveys, the majority of its militant base in the 1970s believed in the myth of the Soviet Union, and in "the Revolution," the party's directives for compromise were not always welcome or well understood.[81] In the 1970s, with the *compromesso storico* in full swing, the PCI strongly condemned leftist terrorism, organizing mass rallies against it and urging PCI supporters to ostracize terrorists in the workplaces. That strategy had rending consequences for its confused working-class base, accustomed to look for enemies on the right, rather than on the left. "The great majority of PCI members, despite the hammering campaign of the party leadership, remained clearly favorable to a government of the Left" (Pasquino, 1985, p. 161).

Given the uncertainty of their dilemma concerning wages versus profits, unions and the party are likely to settle for a strategy of moderate militancy: High militancy generates economic crisis; low militancy puts off the gains into a distant future (Przeworski, 1980, p. 43). Furthermore, they are likely to spend the resources of the movement within the parliamentary game. As Giovanni Agnelli reported in his interview with Arrigo Levi, "there is nothing strange anymore if Napolitano [Communist Party leader] goes out to dinner with one of the leaders of Confindustria or of the Bank of Italy" (Levi, 1983, p. 71). In the mid-1970s, *i signori dello sciopero* ("the strike lords"),[82] Lama, Carniti, and Benvenuto, came to dominate the media world; they became part of the power elite (Manghi, 1977, pp. 29, 78). Consider Manghi's scathing account:

In the auditorium, you still find "pathetic" militants who carry, well folded in their jackets, the paper of their party, residual testimony to great struggles, to publicly attest their political faith. At the presidency, every leader has his encyclopedic roll of newspapers, dignified by the technocratic yellow color of "Sole – 24 ore" [a financial paper owned by Confindustria and printed on yellow paper] and . . . the magazines that report the daring words of friends and foes. Sometimes, with a respectful shiver, you even find the exotic title of a French or English daily (we have not gotten to German yet). (Manghi, 1977, p. 76)

Thus, under capitalism, the employers' best strategy is quite clear. Cesare Romiti, chief executive officer of Fiat, put it plainly: Corporate management "must have a goal that comes before any other: make the company perform at its best, and have it making the highest possible profit" (quoted in Barca and Magnani, 1989, p. 14). Not so clear is what unions' and workers' best strategy should be: economic or political, aggressive or defensive economism, involved in collective bargaining in the economic market or in political exchange in the political arena. Caught in those dilemmas, has it turned out that the Italian unions' best strategy was to waffle – to try to have their cake and eat it too?[83]

6.8. ECONOMIC VERSUS ORGANIZATIONAL/POLITICAL MODELS OF STRIKES: SNYDER'S ARGUMENT ON ITALY

Quantitative strike research is plagued by two fundamental problems. First, different scholarly traditions have explored different causal aspects of strike activity. Whereas economists have, by and large, focused narrowly on the relationships between strikes and economic variables, sociologists and political scientists have focused on organizational and political variables. The second problem is worse: Such abundant scholarly production has led to little, if any, cumulation of knowledge. The literature reads like a collection of mathematical signs (positive, negative) and statistical significances. The findings vary widely from one author to another, reflecting differences in specifications of variables and choices of samples (time periods and countries).[84] Differences in empirical findings are rarely accounted for. The result has been a great deal of unexplained intertemporal and international variation in empirical findings. Attempts to integrate these two research traditions and to explain the discrepancies in findings have been quite rare.

Korpi, for instance, proposed a balance-of-power model that would integrate economic and political models in a unified theoretical framework. In Korpi's balance-of-power model, economic factors play significant roles in strike activity to the extent that those factors (particularly the level of unemployment) affect the current balance of power between workers and employers by improving the tactical position of labor (Korpi, 1974, p. 1577).[85] This model is similar to bargaining models. In Korpi's model, however, bargaining power is affected not only by short-term economic changes but also by long-term changes in the locus of conflict, caused by shifts in the political position of labor. Economic variables are central to bargaining models. Differences in power, as perhaps affected by economic conditions, form the core of Korpi's model.

Snyder (1974, 1975, 1977) similarly proposed a theoretical framework based on differences in institutional arrangements, in order to account for intertemporal and international differences in strikes, in particular economic versus organizational-political models. Snyder's argument is particularly interesting in the context of this book, because his theoretical argument depends heavily on Italy for empirical support. Furthermore, to date, it remains the only econometric work on Italian strikes available in English. Let us review the argument.

According to Snyder, strikes will be affected primarily by economic factors only in institutional contexts characterized by a highly unionized labor force and a well-institutionalized system of collective bargaining.[86] Organizational/political models, on the other hand, can best describe institutional settings of the opposite type. Economic-bargaining models imply rational economic calculations by the workers or the unions; they further imply that only economic factors enter into those calculations. In that type of institutional setting, workers act "rationally," calculating the economic costs and benefits of a strike. The labor market is the regulating mechanism for industrial conflict, because favorable changes in the position of workers in the labor market will improve their bargaining power and hence raise the level of conflict. The validity of these "implicit assumptions" is limited mostly to recent North American and northern European labor history. For countries such as France and Italy, or even the prewar United States, it is mostly political factors that figure prominently in workers' and trade unions' goals and calculations. Institutional arrangements in Italy, writes Snyder, are "still [sic] inconsistent with the assumptions underlying the bargaining approach and its economic models" (Snyder, 1975, pp. 272–4).

Snyder's findings, however, only partly support his arguments. Whereas the variables in the equations for the United States perform as expected, those for

Table 6.7. *Replication of Snyder's work*

Dependent variable:	Number of strikes for models 1 and 2 (logged values); number of strikers for models 3 and 4 (logged values)			
Agreggation level:	Economy; yearly series			
Sample period:	1947/1970 for model 1, 3 and 4; 1948/1970 for model 2			
Estimation method:	Almon polynomial distributed lags for all models (3rd degree polynomial, both-ends constraints, 6-year lag structure including contemporaneous effects); OLS for models 1, 3, and 4; GLS (Cochrane-Orcutt) for model 2			

	Model 1	Model 2	Model 3	Model 4
Constant	4.913*	6.272*	12.027*	12.218*
	(.828)	(1.333)	(1.174)	(.817)
Unionization rate	.143*	.047	.117	.103*
	(.053)	(.083)	(.075)	(.042)
Number of cabinet changes	-.097	-.082	-.174	-.167
	(.119)	(.107)	(.169)	(.162)
Election-year dummy	-.139	-.197	.404*	.402*
	(.131)	(.136)	(.186)	(.181)
Change in real wages (%)	-.004	-.013	.005	.004
	(.006)	(.011)	(.008)	(.007)
Gross national product	-8.69E-6**	2.97E-6*	1.48E-6	2.91E-6*
	(4.36E-6)	(1.12E-6)	(6.18E-6)	(8.43E-7)
Time trend	.222*		.027	
	(.080)		(.114)	
Adjusted R^2	.74	.68	.43	.47
Durbin-Watson	1.87	2.06	2.08	2.03

Note: Standard error in parentheses. **Significant at the .05 level; *significant at the .01 level.

Canada, France, and Italy do not.[87] For Italy, the percentage of the labor force unionized is the only significant variable for both prewar and postwar periods. Neither economic nor political variables seem to have had any effect on strike activity in Italy. On the one hand, the use of political dummy variables provides only crude approximations for underlying political processes. My econometric work at the beginning of this chapter fared no better. On the other hand, Snyder's work is plagued by serious methodological problems. In particular, two of the variables in Snyder's equation for Italy, time trend and GNP, are highly collinear ($r = .97$ for the Italian case).[88] To show how multicollinearity had affected Snyder's results, I reestimated Snyder's model with and without the time-trend variable.[89]

As can be seen from the four models estimated in Table 6.7, when time trend is entered into the model, the signs and significances of the GNP coefficients change dramatically as a result of multicollinearity. Thus, the poor performance of economic variables in the equations for the Italian case does not follow from Snyder's theoretical argument, but from a very basic problem of multicollinearity among the regressors, both being increasing functions of time (a classic case of "nonsense regression" due to the effects of a common-trend component).[90]

This is quite discouraging. A section that had started out with the intent of providing a broad theoretical framework that could account for empirical discrepancies in the literature ends up in the quicksand of further methodological problems. Unfortunately, Snyder's own findings (when properly corrected for multicollinearity) and the findings presented in this and the preceding chapters contradict Snyder's theoretical claims. The findings presented in Chapters 2 and 3 show how closely strike activity is related to the business cycle, even in the Italian case. The empirical results do not lend support to a view of Italian strikes in which economic factors played no role. Neither do they support an economic versus organizational/political model of strikes. The analyses in Chapter 4 confirm that organization had a significant effect on Italian strikes. Furthermore, the results in Chapter 5 show that the structure of collective bargaining shaped much of the temporal pattern of Italian strikes. Finally, in this chapter, I have shown that political processes were no less telling in determining the temporal patterns of Italian strikes. Thus, the statistical and historical analyses in this book show that not only economic factors but also organizational, institutional, and political factors contributed to shaping the empirically observable patterns of strikes in postwar Italy. The empirical evidence strongly supports an integrated model rather than a dichotomous model of strikes (economic vs. organizational/political). If anything, the question is: If all models seem to work in the Italian case, albeit at different times, under what conditions will one model prevail over another? This way, we are thrown back to Snyder's question, and still with no answer.

6.9. THE MICRO AND THE MACRO, THE ECONOMIC AND THE POLITICAL: MODES OF REGULATION OF LABOR

Bringing workers into the factories ("the Satanic mills"), breaking them in to the harsh discipline of industrial work, undoubtedly was not an easy task (Perrot, 1979; Thompson, 1967). Perhaps it indeed "required . . . a man of Napoleonic nerve and ambition to subdue the refractory tempers of work-people," as Andrew Ure emphatically wrote (quoted in Bendix, 1974, p. 59). But even with the workers safely in the factory, the problems of controlling them did not cease. Capitalists have developed both microlevel and macrolevel strategies in their attempts "to take care of labor." At the microlevel, the work of Edwards (1979) and Clawson (1980) described the variety of responses by capitalists to the problem of labor control within their enterprises, ranging from simple methods of control to technical and finally bureaucratic control.[91]

Although the use of firm-specific mechanisms to control workers is a universal characteristic of industrial capitalism, the organization of labor into unions forced capitalists to seek macrolevel solutions to the problems of regulating conflict and labor militancy, particularly the use of collective bargaining and political exchange (Pizzorno, 1977, 1978a, 1978b; Offe and Wiesenthal, 1980, pp. 106–8). In the context of ongoing collective bargaining, worker–employer relationships become less dependent on labor-market mechanisms.[92] As bargaining becomes institutionalized, each party comes to have some level of trust in the future behavior of the other. Workers moderate their demands in times of prosperity, because they feel confident that they can count on more benign treatment by the employers in times of hardship. Collective bargaining helps to smooth out the relationship involving wages, strikes, and unemployment over the vagaries of the business cycle.

In the context of ongoing political exchange, the labor market becomes even less important in labor relations. The state intervenes more and more frequently in all major industrial disputes. For a government concerned with consensus, social order is just as important in the upswing phase as in the downswing phase of the cycle. In the context of collective bargaining, workers exchange continuity in production (i.e., no strikes) for access to a greater share of resources. In the context of political exchange, consensus and social order are at stake. Corporatism is the most sophisticated form of political exchange, with its centralized decision-making process requiring consensus among the organized interests: capital, labor, and the state.

Which is the way of the future? Are the systems of industrial relations in advanced countries moving toward microlevel or macrolevel solutions to the problems of labor control, toward collective bargaining or political exchange? Which strike models will prevail, economic or political? According to Snyder, economic strike models, rather than organizational and political models, will prevail:

> To the extent that national labor relations systems move toward increased size and stability of union membership, institutionalization of collective bargaining and political integration of labor, the determination of strike fluctuations shifts from a primarily political to an economic process. (Snyder, 1975, p. 275)

A great deal of empirical evidence, however, seems to be stacked up against Snyder's prediction. For Ingham (1974, p. 57), on the basis of a comparative analysis of the United Kingdom and Scandinavia, the development of collective bargaining, if anything, reduces the dependence of industrial conflict on economic conditions. If strikes are no longer used as a bargaining strategy in highly institutionalized labor-relations systems, the pattern of strikes will be much less dependent on short-term and medium-term changes in bargaining power, that is, on variations in the state of the economy, the labor market in particular. According to Goetz-Girey (1965, p. 137), in France, (1) strikes were less sensitive to the fluctuations in the business cycle after World War II than during the period between the two world wars, and (2) noneconomic factors played greater roles in determining the pattern of strikes after 1945 than they did between the two wars. Cella (1979, p. 626), on the basis of the econometric evidence assembled in a collective comparative study, similarly concluded that economic models of strikes were the exception, rather than the rule, particularly after World War II. In fact, economic models seem to hold only for the United States. Pizzorno (1977, pp. 419–20) commented that

> Industrial relations are increasingly less limited to collective bargaining; political factors become more important everywhere, even if in different ways; they should not be considered

as exogenous factors, as imponderable forces that distort the economic equilibrium of the labor market, but rather as part themselves of a system of exchange, analogous to that prevailing under collective bargaining, even if different resources are exchanged.

My econometric findings in Chapter 5 (Table 5.12, p. 166) showed that the role of unemployment in determining strike patterns did not vanish when taking into account the institutionalization of collective bargaining.[93] Furthermore, the findings in this chapter seem to point to developments leading toward political, corporatist arrangements during the late 1970s in Italy. Thus, at least during the 1970s, the Italian system of industrial relations moved away from economic modes of regulation of labor toward more political arrangements. Yet the political *entente* between capital and labor was short-lived in Italy (Lange, 1987). Even microlevel, firm-level modes of regulation, once cast aside as paternalistic practices, have reappeared in the Italian factory world (see Streeck, 1984; Locke, 1990).

Perhaps both microlevel and macrolevel forms of labor control are unstable and historically specific (Offe and Wiesenthal, 1980, p. 106). The continuity of any mode of regulation of labor will depend on the degree of class struggle, the level and type of economic development, the ability of capitalism to provide material benefits, and the political position of labor in the power structure.[94] Ultimately, employers' reliance on one or another mode of regulation will depend on the balance of class forces. As these forces are always in precarious equilibrium, none of these forms of regulation will be stable over long periods of time. The retrenchment of capital in the 1980s away from collective bargaining in the United States and away from political exchange in Italy (and even in countries such as Sweden and Germany, where corporatist arrangements had been in place for decades) shows how precarious this equilibrium always is.[95]

6.10. THE POWER OF STATISTICS AND THE STATISTICS OF POWER

For some reason – perhaps because the variables we use to study the effects of political processes on strikes are too crude, or because our single-equation models are too simplistic, or, because the strike series are very vulnerable to outliers – nowhere else in this book has the power of statistics failed us to the same extent as in the study of power. Particularly for the short-term, political-crisis model, econometric coefficients often are insignificant and have unexpected signs. Should we take this setback as a methodological or theoretical failure? A failure of statistical modeling or a failure of the proposed theory of political crisis?

The trouble with much quantitative strike research is that it is typically void of any historical specificity; history operates only as a data warehouse. Statistical results are rarely discussed in relation to the unfolding of historical reality. Statistics tends to create a "historical reality" of its own based on the sign and significance of coefficients. Yet more than any of the numerous statistical tests we apply to our results, the real test of our time-series work should be comparison to history itself. There is a question we should always ask of our results, regardless of what the statistical tests say: Do the results make sense in light of history?

In light of the historical and ethnographic record, the econometric evidence presented at the beginning of this chapter certainly makes sense. That a redistributive, political-exchange model of industrial conflict should yield only marginally significant econometric results (see Table 6.1) is well in line with the historical reality of a main working-class party (the PCI) that never acquired stable and durable control of the executive branch in postwar Italy. During the 1970s, the politics of *compromesso storico* were short-lived. A decade earlier, during the 1960s, the broadly reformist program of the Center-Left governments failed when it became entangled in the quagmire of party politics and the Socialist Party was co-opted into the spoils system set up by the Christian Democrats. Yet the politics of *compromesso storico* were not without their effects on strikes.[96]

The shapes of strikes changed drastically between 1975 and 1978. Strikes during those years were shorter, on average, and less frequent, but also much larger than ever before. Strike shapes during those years were so uniform that not even the renewal of industrywide collective contracts in 1976 made any difference. In 1978, the number of hours lost to strikes per worker (8.1) reached a postwar low. One-third of the time lost was due to general strikes. Undoubtedly, the *scala mobile* agreement was largely responsible for the overall changes in the shapes of strikes after 1975. After all, strikes over wage issues represented the vast majority of strikes. Furthermore, most strikes were plant-level strikes. To the extent that the automatic adjustments of wages to offset inflation eliminated one of the main reasons for striking, it is no surprise that strike frequency declined. Less clear, however, is why that agreement would have contributed to increased strike sizes. It was the shift of bargaining to the centralized, confederal level, the PCI involvement in government responsibilities, and the political use of strikes that caused that increase. With the hegemonic working-class party (PCI) in the coalition government, conflict decreased, and political bargaining increased. After the years of permanent microconflict at the plant level and shop level in the early 1970s, conflict, at the close of the decade, took on the demonstrative characteristics of centralized general strikes under union control, aimed at bringing the weight of mass mobilization to bear upon the political system. The close ties of the PCI to one of the major unions (CGIL), and the latter's control over the network of *delegati*, constituted the basic mechanism for the management of conflict (Regini, 1980, p. 56).

The econometric estimates in Table 6.8 provide further evidence on how the politics of the *compromesso storico* affected strike activity: Use of a dummy variable for the 1975–78 period confirms that the new *scala mobile* brought down the numbers of both strikes and hours lost. Only the number of strikers increased. If the goal of Italy's large-scale employers was indeed to reduce the level of conflict, then the *scala mobile* agreement gave them exactly what they wanted. The econometric results also show that in 1978, the year the PCI joined a broad coalition government of national solidarity, all conflict indicators declined, not just

Table 6.8. *Testing the effect of the* compromesso storico

Dependent variable: Number of strikes for models 1 and 4; number of strikers for models 2 and 5; number of hours lost for models 3 and 6
Aggregation level: Industry; yearly series
Sample period: 1955/1978
Estimation method: GLS (Cochrane-Orcutt) for all models

	Model 1	Model 2	Model 3	Model 4	Model 5	Model 6
Constant	2,429.53*	378.96	34,712.12	3,043.21*	-457.16	61,553.66
	(383.23)	(1,434.77)	(43,153.05)	(635.09)	(1,220.43)	(44,330.27)
Unemployment rate	-227.36*	-273.91**	-11,645.50*	-215.19*	-240.02**	-11,598.01*
	(40.80)	(157.41)	(4,582.25)	(78.90)	(149.90)	(5,408.23)
Union membership	.87E-3*	.19E-2*	.42E-1*	.41E-3**	.24E-2*	.24E-1
	(.16E-3)	(.60)	(.18E-1)	(.23E-3)	(.43E-3)	(.16E-1)
Contract renewal	-6.75*	6.71	1,022.51*	-7.18*	4.68	995.62*
	(2.66)	(7.93)	(305.44)	(2.80)	(7.81)	(308.17)
D–1975/78	-1,285.55*	621.52	-42,425.03			
	(249.86)	(906.73)	(28,175.36)			
D–1978				-961.51*	-1,510.32	-22,285.77
				(442.55)	(1,105.20)	(42,502.12)
Adjusted R^2	.76	.52	.45	.44	.57	.40
Durbin-Watson	1.74	1.80	2.05	1.88	1.91	21.96

Note: Standard error in parentheses. **Significant at the .05 level; *significant at the .01 level.

the number of strikes. That would seem to be in line with the approach of political-exchange theories to the trend of strikes. Thus, the analyses in this section have extended the causal mechanisms that explain the changes in the overall shapes of strikes during the 1975–78 period beyond the restricted realm of industrial relations to that of politics. The *scala mobile* agreement was only the first step in a new union strategy toward self-restraint in the economic arena in exchange for political guarantees in the political arena. The *scala mobile* agreement in the economic market can be understood only in the context of changes in the political market and neo-corporatist developments in Italy.

If the long-term, redistributive political model of strikes stands up to the test of history, how does the short-term political model fare? Does it make sense, in light of Italian political history, that the results in Table 6.2 should show negative effects for political-crisis variables, contrary to expectations? Or are these results statistical artifacts? After all, throughout this book we have seen how different methodological problems can severely affect econometric results. In Section 2.3 (p. 33) we first saw how autocorrelation of the residuals can alter coefficient estimates. In Section 3.3.2 (p. 67) we ran into problems of reciprocal causation. In Section 4.5 (p. 106) I further explored problems of reciprocal causation and investigated a statistical game we often play: that of lagging variables until we obtain the expected results. In Section 5.3 (p. 153) we saw how these differences in lagged relationships reflect different underlying causal structures among variables. Furthermore, I probed into the effects of outliers (Section 5.5, p. 168).

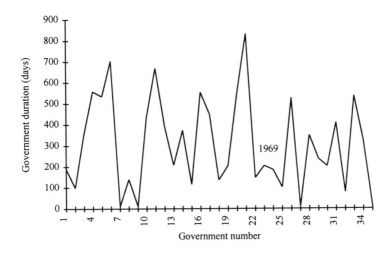

Figure 6.4. *Plot of the durations of governments between 1947 and 1980*

Finally, we saw the problems that temporal aggregation can create (Section 5.9, p. 185). In this chapter we have seen how econometric coefficients do not tell us at which frequency bands the relationships between variables are measured (Section 6.6.1, p. 213). We have just seen how Snyder's findings change dramatically when problems of multicollinearity are eliminated (Section 6.8, p. 237). The list of problems is long (and could be longer). Although I have always tried to test for potential statistical problems with the tools that the statistics discipline itself makes available, and, in any case, I have always checked the econometric results against the test of history, there appear to be plenty of reasons to take econometric results with a grain of salt. As usual, let us take refuge in exploratory analyses.

The plots of Figures 6.4, 6.5,[97] and 6.6 clearly show that government crises in Italy were routine occurrences throughout most of the postwar period (1947–87): 60% of postwar cabinets fell within one year of inception; only two cabinets (out of forty-two) lasted at least two years; cabinets had an average duration of less than eleven months, compared with a possible five-year duration (Battegazzorre, 1987, p. 293). But all three plots also show a peak in government instability during the period 1960–62, at the time of the first strike wave. And all three plots make it clear that in the decade after the 1969 *autunno caldo* the political situation became increasingly precarious, with a decline in the durations of governments (Figure 6.4) and increases in the durations (Figure 6.5) and number (Figure 6.6) of cabinet crises. The duration of cabinet crises almost tripled during the 1970s, indicating serious difficulties for the political parties in trying to form coalition governments (Battegazzorre, 1987, p. 304).

Did cabinet crises in Italy offer opportunities for changes in the political position of labor? Or did they rather reflect the instability of government coalitions under

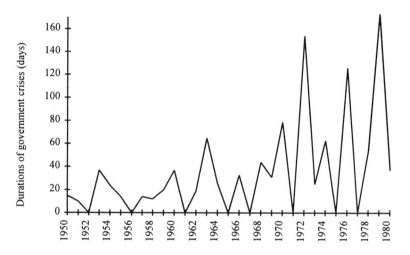

Figure 6.5. *Plot of the durations of government crises between 1947 and 1980*

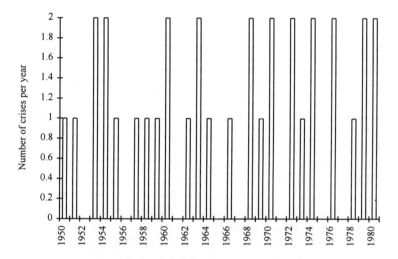

Figure 6.6. *Bar chart of number of government crises per year between 1950 and 1980*

conditions of structural political weakness? The historical record and the graphic plots examined in this chapter seem to support the second possibility: In the face of an increasingly powerful Left, with nowhere to go, government instability increased, particularly during the 1970s. The fact that routine cabinet crises rarely offered opportunities for change does not mean, however, that Italian governments were not vulnerable to the political demands of labor. On the contrary. Shorter and Tilly (1974, pp. 104–5) argued, for the French case, that governments often were the real intended targets of strikes. The centralization and politicization of French unions transformed strikes into lightning displays of working-class mobilization that targeted the government as much as the employers. The government, in other words, was present at many French strikes as a third, unnamed bargaining party. We have seen that the connection between the economic and the political was a characteristic of the Italian system of industrial relations as well. But for the larger, demonstrative types of strikes to be effective, for the workers' political demands to be heard, there must be a functioning government in office. During a government crisis, the period between the ouster of one cabinet and the formation of another, that simply was not the case. As a frustrated Italian banker put it, describing the cabinet crisis in the spring of 1970, "We're better off without a government. Workers don't strike and students don't protest when there is nobody in power to listen to them" (quoted in Allum, 1973, p. 241). The banker spoke from experience. As social scientists we are expected to validate people's assertions. Let me do that. And to avoid blurring effects due to temporal aggregation bias, let me use monthly data. After all, why should the effect of a cabinet crisis that lasted fifteen days show up when using yearly data? Furthermore, given the ambiguity of interpretation of regression coefficients – at which frequency band is the relationship between dependent and independent variable measured? – and the vulnerability of the econometric coefficients to outliers, let me rely on simple exploratory analyses.

Figure 6.7 shows a plot of the monthly numbers of strikers, with the months of political elections and of cabinet crisis clearly marked with vertical bars. By and large, it appears that during periods of cabinet crises, Italian unions restrained from mounting large-scale political protests. But if we observe the plot more closely, there appears to be a changing historical pattern: (1) During the 1950s, the unions never called large-scale strikes during the months of cabinet crises. (2) In the 1960s, at least four of the fouteen months invested by cabinet crises (July 1960, June and July 1964, November 1968) were characterized by high levels of workers involved in strikes. (3) In the 1970s, in five of the twenty-one months with a cabinet crisis of at least a few days' duration workers' mobilization soared (October and November 1974, January, February, and July 1976).

As for the vulnerability of Italian governments to pressures from below, there were only a handful of periods in which workers' mobilization may have possibly contributed to toppling governments, with high levels of workers' participation in collective actions immediately preceding a government's fall: In 1953–54 during the large-scale strikes for the *conglobamento* (i.e., the restructuring of wage scales), in July 1960 when strikes and demonstrations throughout the country brought down the Tambroni government, and then again in 1963 and 1976. In all other cases of cabinet crises mass mobilization does not appear to be particularly high in the months prior to a government's fall.

In summary, the graphical evidence of Figure 6.7 seems to point to the following: (1) empty governments meant empty streets: unions' displays of large-scale mobilization during cabinet crises were rare; (2) for all the unions' use of the

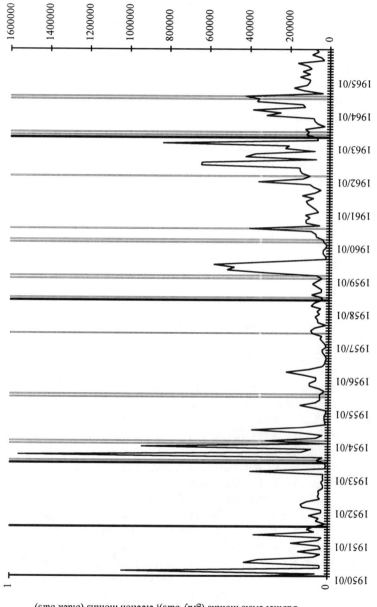

Figure 6.7. *Plot of monthly number of strikers (economic strikes)*

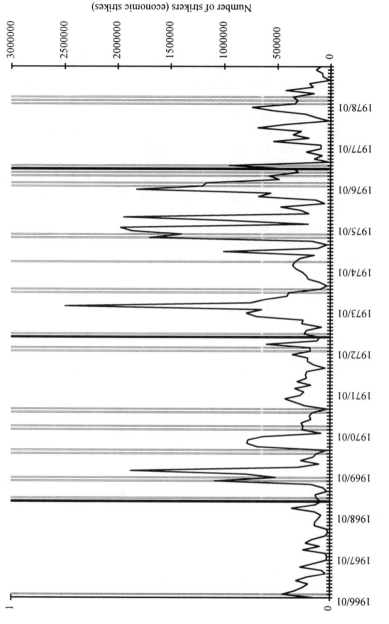

Figure 6.7. (continued) Plot of monthly number of strikers (economic strikes)

strike as a political weapon, governments did not seem to be particularly vulnerable to the repeated displays of mass mobilization; unions' ability to topple governments via collective action appears to be quite the exception (e.g., the Tambroni government in 1960).

However, even the use of such simple analyses on such disaggregated data is not without problems. First, if governments fall under pressure from below, those strikes are likely to be classified by ISTAT as "political" strikes. Unfortunately, as we have seen, those strikes were not recorded by ISTAT (see the appendix on data). The strike data that are available and that I have used in my multivariate work are thus likely to be inadequate to tease out the relationship between workers' mobilization strategies and political processes. Although it may be difficult in some cases to sort out the economic or political nature of a strike – and one might claim that all strikes are political, regardless of the immediate demands on which they focus – the failure to include "political" strikes in the official counts may well be an important reason why it is difficult to bring into sharper focus the relationship between short-term political processes and strike activity, *particularly when trade union actions were more politicized*, as during the mid-1970s (and that may be the reason why ISTAT began collecting separate data for economic and political strikes in 1975). The series of numbers of strikers is particularly likely to be distorted, because political strikes are typically large scale.[98] In 1975, however, ISTAT began recording political strikes separately. Even the use of these more appropriate data, however, come to our rescue only partially. The plot of the monthly numbers of workers involved in political strikes (Figure 6.8) confirms that the highest peaks of political mobilization of the working class occurred in months with no cabinet crisis. Yet, at least three (minor) peaks occurred during months of cabinet crises (March 1978, January and February 1979). Which brings me to consider the second problem.

The kind of strikes that lead to peaks in mobilization (as shown in the plots of Figure 6.7 and Figure 6.8) are likely to be 4- to 8-hour strikes involving as many as 20 million workers (such as the general strike of December 1977 encountered earlier). Just one of those strikes occurring the day before or after a cabinet crisis beginning or ending on a day other than the first or last day of the month would make it appear in the plots of Figure 6.7 and Figure 6.8 that months of cabinet crisis are characterized by high workers mobilization.[99] This is despite the fact that no large-scale strikes occurred for the entire duration of the crisis. Clearly, we need to work with even more disaggregated data. Unfortunately, ISTAT does not provide strike data with daily frequency. So, let me turn, one more time, to a daily reading of *Il Corriere della Sera* for each day of each of the 30 cabinet crises in the period 1950–78. What does that evidence say? Namely, two things.

First, by and large, Italian unions, particularly CGIL, CISL, and UIL, revoked even long-planned, large-scale strikes the moment a government crisis broke out. The *Corriere* recorded some 25 instances of large-scale strikes targeted to the state either as a political actor or as an employer (e.g., in teachers', doctors', and other state employees' strikes). In the vast majority of those cases, strikes were revoked with media news bulletins that read as follows:

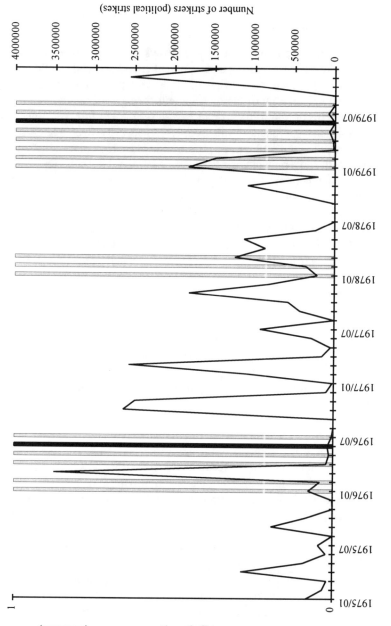

Figure 6.8. *Plot of monthly number of strikers (political strikes)*

Thursday, July 2, 1964 (p. 2)
"CGIL has decided to revoke the planned demonstration because the government fell and, therefore, an anti-government strike would make no sense."

The lack of a bargaining partner is the reason always given for why a large-scale strike "would make no sense" during a government crisis. But while calling off a strike seems to be the pattern, carrying out a strike within long and ongoing disputes is not completely out of the question either (e.g., dockers in a national strike during the crisis of May 1963, *Corriere della sera*, 5.18.1963, p. 2; medical doctors during the crisis of January 1966, Cds, 1.27.1966, p. 7). Even a large-scale general strike involving some 12 million industrial workers took place on October 17, 1974, despite the government crisis (Cds, 10.12.1974, p. 1). Again, on January 1, 1976, a 24-hour national strike of public employees and a 1-hour general solidarity strike of all salaried workers was confirmed because, in the unions' words, "a general strike is inevitable despite the government crisis" (Cds, 1.8.1976, pp. 1–2). The fact that both cases of large-scale strikes not revoked by the unions occurred in the mid-1970s would seem to confirm that the all-out political offensive of the unions in those years was directed as much against the political formula itself as against a specific government. But, even in those stormy years, on several occasions unions revoked large-scale strikes "to diffuse social tensions on the eve of the elections" (Cds, June 10, 1976, p. 1), or because, even in those years of relentless political pressure, "it would be crazy to have a general strike [without a government in office]" (Cds, 1.6.1978, p. 1, Cds, 1.9.1978, p. 2).

Second, only two of the many postwar governments fell under pressure from below: the 1960 Tambroni government and the 1970 Rumor government – an even smaller number than revealed by the graphical evidence of Figure 6.8. In fact, strictly speaking, of those two, only the Tambroni government was swept away by the high tide of mobilization, with its heavy toll of the dead and the wounded in the streets of Genoa, Reggio Calabria, Florence, and many other cities and even scuffles in Parliament between members of the opposition and conservative senators. The Rumor government, as many other Italian governments, fell in the midst of increasing friction among the members of the coalition. This time the issues were: the party composition of regional governments and the type of economic policies to be implemented as a way out of troubled times. But the final push came from labor. The Rumor government fell on the eve of a general strike for social reforms called by the unions for July 7, 1970. The coalition had split bitterly over its stance with the unions: Christian Democrats, Republicans, and Social Democrats wanted to take a hard line, while the Socialists were open to the unions' demands. The July 7, 1970 general strike was revoked by the unions, in line with what we just learned on the relationship between large-scale industrial conflict and government crises, but too late to bring the Rumor government back to life.

At last, the record is clear. The use of exploratory analyses on highly disaggregated data and even more so the daily reading of *Il Corriere della Sera* have cleared some of the ambiguities involved in pinning down the relationship between working class actions and political processes. Crude operationalization of political variables, the greater likelihood of outlying, influential observations when dealing with the series of number of strikers (or hours lost), the use of yearly data to study processes that are too brief (from a few days to a few weeks) to show any effect in longer time spans (a year), and the exclusion of politically motivated strikes from the data have made it very difficult to unravel the relationship between mass actions and political processes.[100]

But what with one twist after another, the record seems to be finally clear. If the power of multivariate statistics is frail, the simple statistics of power are strong and clear: (1) The use of the strike as a political weapon has a long tradition within the Italian working class. Unions have often made their voices heard through large-scale mobilization. (2) In the short run, periods of cabinet crisis were accompanied by working-class quiescence, particularly on the political front. The months in which there were cabinet crises and political elections were characterized by silence in the streets. The banker we met earlier in this section was right after all, which goes to show that statistical sophistication is a poor substitute for first-hand knowledge of one's data. (3) Yet, in at least one or two occasions, governments fell after short bouts of large-scale mobilization by the working class. (4) In the long run, political instability increased in Italy with each strike wave, particularly after the 1968–72 wave. Contrary to the political crisis models of Tilly and Snyder, and more in line with a Marxist view of class conflict as the motor of historical change, prolonged periods of political crisis (such as during the 1970s) seemed to follow, rather than precede, periods of increased class confrontation (such as during the 1968–72 strike wave).

If the purpose of our work is to find substantive explanations for historical processes, rather than to play statistical games, we should indeed be happy with the empirical findings obtained in this chapter on the relationship between political processes and strikes from the combined use of historical and ethnographic evidence, of multivariate and exploratory techniques. Perhaps, we should even be happy that the multivariate analyses failed us, because in the process of tracking down what went wrong with the statistical estimate of multivariate models we accumulated a great deal of knowledge about the substantive problem at hand. And that knowledge points to the disruptive power of strike waves. We have seen how the 1959–63 and 1968–72 strike waves greatly changed the economic and organizational capacities of the working class (and, reflexively, of the capitalist class) (Chapter 4) and the very system of industrial relations (Chapter 5). We have now learned that even the political capacities of the working class wax and wane with strike waves. Perhaps the time has come to take a closer look at the stuff of which strike waves are made.

6.11. THE FINISHED PICTURE?

With the 1975–78 strike shapes firmly in place, I have completed the puzzle. The empirical analyses and the theoretical arguments discussed in this book have accounted for all the pieces and have used all the theories. In fact, in the process of fitting together the original pieces that were assumed to comprise the puzzle, many more pieces of evidence, and many more theories than were originally at hand have turned up. These, too, have found their places in the puzzle.

The analysis of political power in this chapter has shown that the changes in the shapes of strikes in the period 1975–78 can be understood only in the context of the changes in the political position of labor in the national power structure (the PCI in particular). The forms of industrial conflict will change as challengers successfully stake claims to the distribution of political power, just as political-exchange theories would have it. But not always are challengers successful in altering the distribution of political power in their favor, and when they are not, repression is likely to be used to put down their mobilization efforts. That, indeed, was the case for the Italian working class during the 1950s and much of the 1960s.

The analysis of political power can finally allow me to answer the questions raised in Chapter 2 concerning the limits of a purely economic interpretation of Italian strikes. The first question: Why was it that in times of weak labor markets (such as the 1950s and mid-1960s), the Italian working class struck less often than would be predicted by a pure economic-bargaining model *(paradox of the génie d'un peuple)*? We now know the answer. There was more to the 1950s than unfavorable labor-market conditions. There was a political climate that was highly unfavorable to the Left. The structure of labor relations was paternalistic at best, and most likely very repressive and authoritarian, in a general political climate very unfavorable to the working class. That same repressive climate explains yet another paradox encountered in Chapters 3 and 4: the *paradox of large firms*. The largest firms, the ones that seemingly should have been easiest to organize, showed lower rates of unionization and lower strike propensities than did medium-size firms. We now know that it was the largest firms, particularly those working under the provisions of the Marshall Plan, that led the attack on labor in the early 1950s.

The second question: Why was it that during the 1970s, both unemployment and strikes went up *(paradox of the 1970s)*? That was contrary to the expectations derived from economic-bargaining models, as well as resource-mobilization models, to the extent that unfavorable labor-market conditions would be expected to reduce labor's stock of resources (i.e., job security and employment). The answer to this other question is more tentative, but it seems that Italian unions throughout the 1970s achieved an unprecedented degree of control over the labor market – the historical mechanism of control of conflict. After all, the 1970 Workers' Charter provided much stronger employment guarantees, and workers and unions took great advantage of it. That being true, it should not come as a surprise if conflict did not abate with rising levels of unemployment.

More generally, the analyses in this chapter have shown the roles that political factors can play in industrial conflict. The *paradox of small-scale production regions*, which we first encountered in Chapters 4 and 5 (small firms typically were outside of union control, and yet some regions based primarily on small-scale industrial production, e.g., Emilia Romagna, were also the most highly unionized in Italy) is explained by the existence of different political subcultures (Catholic and Socialist, White and Red areas). In particular, the presence of local governments favorable to labor (Red areas) gave labor access to organizational resources it did not have inside the workplace. Thus, the state can give and take away many of the organizational resources that classes use in the pursuit of their interests (Tilly, 1992, pp. 129, 139). Both the central and local governments provided different opportunities for different social classes at various times. The effects of structural economic conditions notwithstanding, the differences in the levels and forms of conflict in the 1950s and 1970s cannot be understood outside the broader political context of class relations that the state provided: the highly repressive centrist governments of the 1950s, the limits and opportunities inherent in the 1970 Workers' Charter, the corporatist policies of the late 1970s and early 1980s.

Contrary to the classic Marxist interpretation of the state, the analyses in this chapter have shown how the Christian Democrats pursued a strategy of their own, often fiercely opposed by organized capital. Those state-independent strategies shaped class relations in specific ways. Also contrary to a strand of classic Marxism, my analyses have confirmed the divisions within the capitalist class that emerged in Chapter 4: big business and small business, private and state-owned large-scale corporations, industrial capital and financial capital. So the working class was not the only class that was politically divided, with deep ideological and organizational cleavages running through it. The capitalist class was anything but monolithic, with different segments showing different political propensities toward the old and the new, expressing various political choices for conservatism or political stability (Farneti, 1970, pp. 187, 192, 194; Martinelli, 1978, pp. 43–6). Direct conflict among capitalists had erupted at various times, with more or less serious divisive consequences.

Finally, this chapter has explored the structural tendencies toward economism and opportunism in the trade-union movement under capitalism. The tendency toward economism is both rational and unstable. It is rational because as both employers and the state push toward a separation of economic and political struggles, and as workers realize that they stand a much better chance of success in the economic arena, it is only rational for unions to concentrate on those battles that they think they can win (i.e., economic struggles). It is unstable because concentration on economic struggles presupposes that capitalists can pay. Without prosperity, continuing cooperation by workers is much more problematic, and the outcome of the class compromise much less certain (hence Marxists' emphasis on economic crises).[101]

We have seen that the Italian working class in both its economic and political organizations has faced many, if not all, of the dilemmas that have confronted the Western working classes: short-term versus long-term goals, bread-and-butter unions versus class unions, cooperation versus opposition, acting in the labor market or in the political arena, in the government or in the opposition. Caught in the dilemma of these painful choices, the Italian Left neither completely compromised nor fully rejected. When it compromised, it did so with many misgivings and internal lacerations, and above all without the full consent of its working-class base. When it rejected, it never picked up on the rank-and-file willingness to engage in radical collective action. Taking for granted the geopolitical position of Italy in the Western bloc, the labor leadership spent the mobilization power of its base within the limits of the parliamentary game and the institutionalized framework of a system of industrial relations. Undoubtedly, Chile *docet*, but so does Cuba, less than 100 miles away from the coast of that same United States that so worried Togliatti and Berlinguer. History is full of opportunities missed, and others regrettably taken, with an occasional success. What is to be done?

7

Mobilization processes: the 1969 *autunno caldo*

> The massive strike waves ... march as exclamation marks in labor history ...
> Shorter and Tilly (1974, p. 104)

> The characteristic thing about [strike-wave] explosions is that they mark qualitative as well as quantitative changes.
> Hobsbawm (1964, p. 127)

7.1. CLEARLY AN OUTLIER: 1969

The year 1969 is clearly an outlier.[1] The plots reported in Chapter 1 of strike indicators (Figures 1.3, 1.4, and 1.5) and strike shapes (Figure 1.6) singled out that data point as an anomaly. The analyses of the regression residuals throughout this book have provided additional support. What caused the surge in strike activity in 1969? We have seen that the timing of the two major outbursts of industrial conflict in postwar Italy (1959–63, 1969–72) coincided with the timing of both the signing of industrywide collective agreements (1959, 1962, 1963, 1969, 1972) and favorable labor-market conditions (the nearly full levels of employment of the late 1950s and 1960s) (Halevi, 1972, p. 81; see also Bordogna and Provasi, 1979). In terms of my stated goal of fitting together all the pieces of the puzzle, following the clues provided by the available theories, this explanation could suffice. I could call off my investigative work.

But the theory of statistical outliers teaches us that there may be important lessons to be learned from them (Franzosi, 1994). In cross-sectional analyses, we typically throw out outliers, physically removing them from the sample. Because that is more difficult to do with time-series data, we are more likely to take a different route: ignore outliers, or deal with them via dummy variables. Whether we discard outliers, simply ignore them, or "dummy them out," from a substantive viewpoint the end result is the same: The model that we are fitting cannot fully explain some of the sample observations.[2] A good example is the experiment in which two different types of fertilizers are used on ten different adjacent plots of land. On measuring crop yields two clear outliers emerge. A social scientist would no doubt discard the two outliers, thus forgoing any chance of accomplishing what, after all, was the real purpose of the experiment: to find a high-yield fertilizer. In dismissing 1969, are we throwing out a high-yield fertilizer?

Why is 1969 an outlier? That is the basic question I will try to answer in this chapter. I will focus on both quantitative and qualitative aspects of the 1968–72 strike wave (with occasional forays into the 1959–63 strike wave), with special attention to the actors in the drama (workers, unions, employers, the state, the radical Left), and to the workers' tactics and demands. Given the lack of time-series statistics on actors, tactics, and demands, I will rely primarily on ethnographic evidence and oral history accounts. Occasionally, I will rely on the available quantitative data from survey research. However, I will not use the available quantitative data in the context of regression models. Nonetheless (because of that?), this strategy should provide a great deal of knowledge on the nature of large-scale workers' mobilization processes.

7.2. STRIKE WAVES AND CYCLES OF STRUGGLE

In 1969, the numbers of strikers and hours lost reached historical peaks, unprecedented in Italian labor history (see Figures 1.3, 1.4, and 1.5, pp. 4–5). The number of hours lost in 1969 was twice as high as the numbers for the two next highest years (1962 and 1973). Only the number of strikers continued to increase after 1969. In terms of the number of hours lost, the Italian *autunno caldo* represented the third largest mass movement in labor history for any country, after the 1968 "French May" and the 1926 general strike in England (Lumley, 1990, p. 167).

The statistical downside of such an explosion of conflict in one year is that this kind of outlier may also be an "influential" observation, that is, an observation that not only is far away from the center of the other observations in the space but also can severely affect the estimates.[3] Could all the econometric results involving the series for the number of hours lost reported in this book simply be statistical artifacts due to the exceptional value for 1969? Is the finished picture that has emerged from the puzzle that of a sand castle that will crumble as soon as it is completed? To answer these questions, let me respecify the models of number of hours lost previously estimated [equations (4.1), (5.4), (6.1), (6.2), and (6.3)] with the addition of a dummy variable for 1969:

$$H_t = \beta_0 + \beta_1 UN_t + \beta_2 UNION_t + \beta_3 \Delta W_{t-1} + \beta_4 D\text{-}1969_t + \epsilon_t \qquad (7.1)$$

$$H_t = \beta_0 + \beta_1 UN_t + \beta_2 UNION_t + \beta_3 \Delta W_{t-1} + \beta_4 CONTRACT_t + \beta_5 D\text{-}1969_t + \epsilon_t \qquad (7.2)$$

$$H_t = \beta_0 + \beta_1 UN_t + \beta_2 UNION_t + \beta_3 CONTRACT_t + \beta_4 WELF_t + \beta_5 D\text{-}1969_t + \epsilon_t \qquad (7.3)$$

$$H_t = \beta_0 + \beta_1 UN_t + \beta_2 UNION_t + \beta_3 CONTRACT_t + \beta_4 CRISIS_t + \beta_5 D\text{-}1969_t + \epsilon_t \qquad (7.4)$$

$$H_t = \beta_0 + \beta_1 UN_t + \beta_2 UNION_t + \beta_3 CONTRACT_t + \beta_4 LAY_t + \beta_5 D\text{-}1969_t + \epsilon_t \quad (7.5)$$

where H, the dependent variable, measures the number of hours lost, and, among the independent variables, UN measures the unemployment rate, ΔW_{t-i} measures lagged real blue-collar wages, $UNION$ measures the level of union membership (CGIL + CISL), $CONTRACT$ measures the percentage of workers subject to contract renewal, $WELF$ measures government welfare spending, $CRISIS$ measures the number of yearly cabinet crises, LAY measures either the number of workers laid off or the number of members of *commissioni interne* laid off, and $D\text{-}1969$ is a dummy variable taking on the value of 0 for all years except for 1969, when it takes on a value of 1. The expected signs for the coefficients are, as discussed in Chapters 4–6, negative for the unemployment rate, welfare spending, number of yearly cabinet crises, and layoffs, and positive for union membership, number of people subject to contract renewal, and the 1969 dummy.

Table 7.1 reports the econometric estimates of equations (7.1), (7.2), (7.3), (7.4), and (7.5). The estimates leave no doubt about the unusual level reached by the number of hours lost in 1969. The coefficient for the 1969 dummy is positive and significant in all models. The econometric results also highlight the effects of the 1969 outlier on the estimates. Most coefficients have achieved a higher level of statistical significance (at the 99% level, rather than at the 95% level or lower, as in the case of the wage coefficient; for direct comparisons, see Table 4.1, Table 5.14, Table 6.1, Table 6.2, and Table 6.6). But the most dramatic influence of the observation for 1969 is on the fitted values. The adjusted R^2 values jump from around .20 to around .80 and even .92, for increases exceeding threefold.

Thus, if the picture that has emerged is that of a castle, it is a castle of solid stone, and that is good news. The bad news is that the magnitude, sign, and significance of the 1969 dummy also clearly highlight the fact that an econometric model based on business-cycle, organizational, collective-bargaining, and political effects cannot explain the 1969 *autunno caldo*. Five chapters of statistical analyses have not succeeded in explaining what is probably the most striking characteristic of strikes: the explosions of conflict at a handful of historical moments.

Scholars have reserved special names for these momentous expressions of working-class protest and mobilization, to clearly set them apart from the routine conflict that arises out of everyday labor relations. Hobsbawm called them "strike explosions." Shorter and Tilly preferred the term "strike waves." Italian scholars use yet another term: "cycles of struggle."

According to Tilly, "A strike wave occurs when both the number of strikes and the number of strikers in a given year exceed the means of the previous five years by more than 50 percent" (Shorter and Tilly, 1974, pp. 106–7). That, like any other operational definition, has the disadvantage of being too dependent on the researcher's discretion. Why five years? Why 50%? In fact, according to that definition, 1969 would not qualify as a wave year, despite its historical peak in the number of hours lost. Furthermore, that definition tends to obscure the fact that

Table 7.1. Is 1969 an influential observation?

Dependent variable: Number of hours lost
Aggregation level: Industry; yearly series
Sample period: 1955/1978 for models 1 through 4; 1955/1975 for model 5
Estimation method: GLS (Cochrane-Orcutt) for all models

	Model 1 (7.1)	Model 2 (7.2)	Model 3 (7.3)	Model 4 (7.4)	Model 5 (7.5)
Constant	96,957.34*	75,790.41*	110,753.3*	57,488.00*	52,676.26*
	(26,531.38)	(25,785.46)	(37,044.46)	(24,639.04)	(18,242.01)
Unemployment rate	-12,425.81*	-12,375.39*	-13,879.81*	-10,332.99*	-10,668.62*
	(3,521.46)	(3,256.37)	(3,055.01)	(2,838.32)	(1,535.84)
Change in real wages$_{t-1}$ (%)	-2,313.58	-2,126.26	.47E-1*	.22E-1*	.33E-1*
	(1,778.11)	(1,516.76)	(.18E-1)	(.76E-2)	(.63E-2)
Union membership	.26E-1	.28E-1*	586.24*	545.41*	800.38*
	(.10E-1)	(.94E-2)	(217.53*)	(223.34)	(199.55)
Contract renewal		554.15*			
		(208.53)			
Welfare spending			-4,786.88		
			(3,290.35)		
Number of cabinet crises				7,103.48	
				(7,119.08)	
Workers laid off					-.65*
					(.28)
1969 dummy	166,945.4*	139,900.6*	153,781.4*	147,414.7*	131,353.0*
	(27,877.03)	(26,145.23)	(24,986.26)	(26,068.27)	(18,398.11)
Adjusted R^2	.71	.77	.81	.78	.92
Durbin-Watson	1.83	1.89	2.01	1.90	2.29

Note: Standard error in parentheses. **Significant at the .05 level; *significant at the .01 level.

explosions of strike activity often occur in cycles with longer durations than one year. Strike activity may peak during a wave year and remain at high levels for a few years to follow; yet none of those years may qualify as a wave year because of the mathematical properties of moving averages. Finally, the concept of a wave year, with its emphasis on a single leap in the level of conflict, misses out on the common and unifying characteristics of conflict during a wave year and its surrounding years: the actors, the themes, the tactics, and demands. These problems are all the more likely in an industrial-relations system (such as the Italian system) characterized by major contract renewals every three years. In this context, a wave year spurred by a round of contract renewals is likely to spill over into at least the next round, three years later. That was indeed the case for the two major cycles of conflict of the postwar period: 1959–63 and 1968–72. But then, after rejecting an operational definition à la Shorter and Tilly, what criterion do I propose for labeling the years 1959–63 and 1968–72 as strike waves? I am afraid I do not have a convincing answer. I have simply gone along with Italian labor scholarship that has identified these two sets of years as *cycles of struggle*, spanning across two consecutive rounds of contract renewals (Bordogna and Provasi, 1979, pp. 199, 230–9). I have then tried to show the distinctive character of those strike waves (particularly the 1968–72 wave) in terms of actors, actions, and demands.

For all its shortcomings, Shorter and Tilly's definition does have the advantage of emphasizing one of the major features of strike waves: the increase in the sheer magnitude of conflict. During wave years (i.e., years of particularly high strike activity), the characteristics of strikes are different from those in the surrounding years: Strikes tend to be longer; they involve a higher proportion of the work force, both at the plant level and at the industry level, and a greater number of establishments (Shorter and Tilly, 1974, pp. 142–6; Bordogna and Provasi, 1979). They also expand "into new industries, new regions, new classes of the population" (Hobsbawn, 1964, p. 127), an observation true for Italy as well. In Italy, the process of workers' mobilization in the period from 1968 to 1972 expanded from the metalworkers and the chemical workers to the traditionally more quiescent sectors, such as textiles, even reaching government employees and civil servants. It spread from the more industrialized and urbanized areas of the Northwest to the Northeast, to central Italy, and to the South, as well as from the large plants to the small plants. Even white-collar workers, particularly in large plants, showed unprecedented levels of militancy.

Strike activity during both strike waves soared. But of course, 1,000 strikes in a year may refer to 1,000 different plants averaging one strike each in the course of the year, or 100 plants with an average of ten strikes each per year. Increases in strike indicators may thus simply mean a higher average number of strikes in the same conflict-ridden firms by the same conflict-prone workers. For Italy, no official strike data are available on the number of plants on strike, and thus we have no way to gauge the diffusion process of strike waves. Nonetheless, there is plenty of evidence that points to the fact that large-scale workers' mobilization processes tended to expand gradually into previously quiescent areas. The plant-level data collected by Confindustria on the yearly elections for *commissioni interne* clearly

Table 7.2. *Frequency distribution of firms holding elections for* commissioni interne, *by year and firm size*

Number of employees	1958	1959	1960	1961	1962	1963
0–20	8	14	15	16	16	12
21–50	94	88	122	168	188	178
51–100	128	165	188	213	252	297
101–250	171	182	230	267	318	367
251–500	102	116	128	132	160	152
501–1,000	69	60	65	82	72	73
>1,000	39	39	42	42	41	45
Total	611	664	790	920	1,047	1,124

Source: Confindustria.

Table 7.3. *Percentage of firms with no strikes, by firm size and year*

	Number of employees					
	1–19	20–49	50–99	100–249	250–499	>500
1969	78.3	54.0	41.2	10.5	23.1	0
1972	70.0	57.1	31.8	20.7	8.3	0
1975	64.0	43.7	26.6	17.0	14.3	0

Source: Bergamaschi (1977b, pp. 260, 262, 264).

show that many firms were first drawn into the plant-based electoral process during the 1959–63 strike wave. Although plants of all sizes were affected by the mobilization process, it was among smaller plants, in particular, that the greatest expansion of the electoral process occurred (see Table 7.2). The data in Table 7.3, taken from a 1975 Federlombarda survey, show that the 1969 *autunno caldo* strikes mostly involved the larger firms. A culture of conflict, however, progressively spread over time across all firm sizes, affecting smaller firms as well.

Data on unionization show a similar diffusion process. During the 1968–72 strike wave, an Assolombarda survey of Lombardy firms showed that larger firms were unionized first (1968–72) and smaller firms were unionized somewhat later (1972–76) (Associazione Industriale Lombarda, 1983, pp. xii–xiv).[4] The Federlombarda data in Table 7.4 confirm that between 1972 and 1974, the process of unionization involved predominantly the smaller firms: The largest increases in both the numbers of workers and firms unionized occurred in the smaller firms (coincidentally for both measures, 15.9% in the 1–19 employee class size).[5] Plant-level data on unionization for the province of Turin (Table 7.5) bring into sharper focus the characteristics of the diffusion process: In terms of the number of firms newly unionized, the increase was greatest among smaller firms (unions had at least a foot in the door at larger firms); in terms of the number of workers, the expansion occurred in the large firms. This is well in line with the data on distribution of firms

Table 7.4. *Unionization by firm size and year (%)*

	Number of employees					
	1–19	20–49	50–99	100–249	250–499	>500
Work force unionized (%)						
1972	22.9	58.7	57.6	64.2	68.2	83.3
1974	38.8	70.5	64.8	72.6	76.8	86.2
Δ% points	15.9	11.8	7.2	8.4	8.6	2.9
Firms unionized (%)						
1972	25.0	66.0	94.4	92.9	100.0	100.0
1974	40.9	80.0	94.2	100.0	100.0	100.0
Δ% points	15.9	14.0	-0.2	7.1	0.0	0.0

Source: Bergamaschi (1977b, p. 258).

Table 7.5. *CGIL-FIOM union growth in the Turin province, in metalworking, by firm size (% values, 1971/1964)*

	Number of employees					
Level	10–50	50–100	100–250	250–500	500–1,000	>1,000
Workers	93.3	130.3	48.0	129.3	180.2	266.3
Firms	80.0	139.7	42.7	60.5	63.6	7.5

Source: Cavallo Perin (1980).

and the employment distribution by firm size presented in Chapter 3: There were, indeed, more workers to be won over to the movement among the larger firms, whereas there were more smaller firms than large yet to be unionized.

The available evidence leaves no doubt about the diffusion process of strike waves. It was not that the same workers from a few large plants were going on strike repeatedly. Rather, more and more factories were being drawn into the mobilization process, and more workers (and more different kinds of workers) were going on strike. But strike activity is only one of the many changes that occur during large-scale mobilization processes. The factory world during strike waves is seething with the ferment of strikes, workers' assemblies, rallies, meetings, unionization drives, and elections of workers' representatives. Indeed, more and more firms became unionized, and more and more factories took up new forms of workers' organizational structures (e.g., the *consigli di fabbrica*) during the two major cycles of struggle. But as important as the quantitative aspect of strike waves is – in fact, the very hallmark of a strike wave – no less important are the qualitative innovations (Hobsbawm, 1964, p. 127). Pizzorno (1974b, p. 9) wrote:

After 1968, the quantitative aspect may have seemed the new and characteristic element. But the novelty was mostly elsewhere. Certainly, the struggles were more intense and more widespread, but, above all, they took on forms and tactics that were at least partially new, and demands that often challenged traditional trade-union demands, or at least were highly innovative in comparison.

It is to the qualitative aspects of strike waves that I now turn my attention: the actors involved, the tactics they used, the claims they made.

7.3. THE SUPERMARKET AT FIAT MIRAFIORI: THE WORKERS

In those days [the 1969 *autunno caldo*] the gates of the Fiat Mirafiori plant had become a supermarket. They were all there: trade-union leaders, Communist Party leaders, young Marxist-Leninists dressed in red, policemen dressed in green, and so on. All in competition with street vendors waiting for the workers to come out, with their fruits, vegetables, T-shirts, and radios. All peddling their merchandise.[6]

Alfonso Natella, the Fiat worker who described that supermarket, clearly identified the actors involved in the 1968–72 strike wave: the employer (Fiat Mirafiori), the leaders of the "official" economic and political organizations of the working class (unions and the PCI), the unofficial radical Left (Marxist-Leninist students), the state (the police), and, of course, the workers. But with the exception of the street vendors, were those not the same actors that we have encountered throughout this book? Let us "zoom in" on the Mirafiori neighborhood in Turin and meet those actors in the 1968–72 strike wave to find out what was new and what was old in that apparently typical labor scene.

First the workers: There is ample evidence from the ethnographic material, workers' diaries, oral history, and historiography that in many plants the first to mobilize at the beginning of the cycle were the skilled, older workers, those with experience of past struggles, during the "glorious" 1940s, but also during the more recent 1959–63 cycle of struggles.[7] Those workers struck mostly offensively for higher wages and benefits, but also defensively, to protect themselves from the forces seeking to erode their skills.[8] Soon, however, in most factories, the leadership of the struggle shifted to the young, unskilled workers, who mostly had immigrated from the South.[9] They struck against the dehumanizing effects of combined Fordism and Taylorism: The increasing fragmentation of work on the assembly lines, the escalating pace of production, and the hierarchical organization of authority. Although for different reasons, the interests of unskilled and skilled workers coincided (Becchi Collidà and Negrelli, 1986, p. 162).

For many of the unskilled workers, particularly those who had entered factory life during the 1960s, that was their first experience with collective action. For others, involvement in industrial collective action was not new. Together with the skilled workers, they had participated in the previous cycle of struggles (1959–63). They had struck and marched side by side with the northern electromechanical workers in Milan in 1962.[10] During the 1962 *torrido luglio di Torino* ("Turin's torrid July") young southern immigrants had participated in the strikes at Fiat that had marked the beginning of a resurgence of conflict in the Italian working class.[11] In historical perspective, what happened at the Piazza Statuto in Turin defined the border between the old and the new. The new was the high rate of participation by Fiat workers (92%) in the strike of July 7, 1962, after eight years of quiescence. The old was that the UIL,[12] the night before the strike, had signed a separate agreement with Fiat management. Typically, in the past, that would have put an end to the strike. This time it did not. In the early afternoon, when the news of that signing spread, scores of angry workers marched toward the Piazza Statuto, where the UIL had its headquarters, and publicly tore up their union cards in protest. The police brutally attacked the demonstrators. The battle continued into the night, and for a few hours on Sunday, breaking out again, with renewed fury, on Monday (Lanzardo, 1979, pp. 11–21; Gianotti, 1979, p. 139). Hundreds of people were arrested. Century-old "agitator" theories were invoked by both the Right and the Left to explain what had happened (Lanzardo, 1979, pp. 36–71). At the trials, two-thirds of the defendants were young immigrant workers from the South (Turone, 1984, p. 290; Lanzardo, 1979, pp. 28–33). The hallmark of those strikes and battles, in fact, was "the angry participation of many young Southerners."[13] It was those unskilled Southern workers who were to take a leading role in the 1968–72 cycle of struggles. Let us try to meet them.

Let us join the ranks of the peddlers outside Mirafiori and similar Italian plants and wait for the workers at the end of their shifts, to interview them – figuratively, at least, because in reality we can rely on the interviews conducted by Isvet in 1971 among a national sample of 5,830 workers (De Masi and Fevola, 1974a). We can also rely on the 260 interviews of Alfa-Romeo workers at the Arese plant, near Milan, conducted by Cella and Reyneri's research team (Cella and Reyneri, 1974).

According to the Isvet data, even at the height of the strike wave, militancy was limited to a minority of the work force. It was mostly young, male blue-collar workers in the larger factories (particularly if state-owned and in the metalworking sector) who provided the core of militants (De Masi and Fevola, 1974a, pp. 779–97, 880).[14] Those at the militant core (involving perhaps no more than 25% of workers) (De Masi and Fevola, 1974a, pp. 780–1) were more likely than the rank and file to engage in collective actions, to favor demands for organizational and political changes (e.g., trade-union rights, reforms), to be union members taking active roles in union affairs (particularly the CGIL), and to view the Communist Party as the working-class party par excellence or to be a party member (De Masi and Fevola, 1974a, pp. 793, 795–6, 813, 850). The militant core were also more likely to come from the higher echelons of the blue-collar skill hierarchy.[15] Although unskilled workers were almost as likely as skilled workers to participate in strikes and mass meetings (Buratto et al., 1974, pp. 300, 303), they were not as likely to be union members or party members (De Masi and Fevola, 1974a, pp. 801, 840).[16]

As Table 7.6 shows, workers' participation decreased as the cost of actions increased (just as resource-mobilization theory would have it). Thus, workers were

Table 7.6. *Workers' participation in collective action*

	Never participate	Always participate
Trade union meetings	44[a]	19
Mass meetings inside the plant	19	44
Strike activity	33	30

[a]Percentage values.
Source: Buratto et al. (1974, pp. 298, 301, 303).

more likely "always" to attend mass meetings inside the plant (44%), because that was a legal right, as guaranteed by the Workers' Charter, and workers were paid for their time anyway. Strike participation came next, at 30%. Participation in union meetings (19% "always" attended) was a commitment beyond most workers, because it required, among other things, going to the union hall after working hours. Although most nonparticipants were clerical workers, an average of 30% of blue-collar workers were also nonparticipants. Low-Beer, in his study of the new working class in Italy, found similar results for technicians: the workers who were more likely to participate in all strikes were also more likely to be union members and party members and to come from a family background of political radicalism (Low-Beer, 1978, pp. 180–204).

The Alfa-Romeo survey focused sharply on the *operaio massa*, the militant unskilled worker to be found in the large-scale plants based on assembly-line technology. When compared with the skilled workers at Alfa, the *operaio massa* was much more likely to be a southern immigrant (65.5% vs. 34.5%), to have accepted work beneath his skill level in taking a job at Alfa-Romeo (68% vs. 28.3%), to have been a shift worker (77.8% vs. 26%), and to have a faster pace of production (68.3% vs. 30.3%) (Cella and Reyneri, 1974, pp. 52–4). The educational credentials of those two types of workers were also quite different: 60% of the unskilled workers had no more than five years of elementary education (6.8% did not complete elementary school), whereas 30.4% of skilled workers had completed elementary school (Cella and Reyneri, 1974, pp. 52–3). Half as many unskilled workers went on to junior and senior high school (24.3% vs. 50%; Reyneri and Tempia, 1974, p. 78).[17] Unskilled and skilled workers had similar rates of participation in strikes (Mangiarotti and Rossi, 1974, p. 146). Unskilled workers, however, tended to favor more radical and more damaging tactics, such as "stop-and-go" strikes or a form of picketing around the clocks where workers "punched in" (*blocco delle portinerie*). "In general, unskilled workers appear to be angrier" (Mangiarotti and Rossi, 1974, p. 146). Skilled workers were more likely to take active roles in plant-level organizational structures and in trade-union activities outside the plant, as well as to be union and party members (Mangiarotti and Rossi, 1974, pp. 139, 149). The *operaio massa*, however, was more than twice as likely to be a member of one of the "extra-parliamentary" groups (i.e., small radical groups on the far left without representation in Parliament). When coupled with his (mostly, but also her) preferences regarding strike tactics, that showed his/her lower enthusiasm for traditional working-class institutions and strategies.

Thus, at least one of the actors in our supermarket scenario (the worker) was only apparently the same as in past labor scenes. There was a new type of worker inside the Fiat Mirafiori plant, as in many other plants across the country: the unskilled worker, the *operaio massa*. That worker, the object of so much attention by so many peddlers, represented the shift in the class structure that I described in Chapter 3. That new worker was bringing to the industrial world new identities – personal (young, male, unmarried, and with little education), professional (a low level of skills, little or no experience with factory life), cultural (a southern peasant speaking a dialect different from that of the people around him), and political (unfamiliar with union and party politics).

7.4. THE TACTICS: "EVERYONE DID WHAT THEY WANTED"

The repertoire of available forms of labor actions is quite wide, ranging over individual and collective actions, unorganized and organized: limitation of one's output, sabotage, absenteeism, rallies, mass meetings, demonstrations, strikes (Kerr, 1954; Hyman, 1989, pp. 55–9). Strikes themselves come in a variety of forms: stop-and-go, work-to-the-rules, revolving (*sciopero a scacchiera* or *sciopero articolato*; the French *grève tournante*), sit-downs, slowdowns, and so forth.[18] Typically, employers and the state have succeeded in constraining workers and the unions to use only strike tactics that would be least damaging to production (e.g., an eight-hour strike declared days or weeks in advance). During strike waves, however, tactics become radicalized. Workers show a great deal of creativity in discovering or rediscovering those tactics that would hit employers the hardest at the lowest cost to workers, particularly revolving strikes, slowdowns, and blockade of incoming and outgoing goods.

Certainly, revolving strikes and slowdowns were not inventions of the *autunno caldo*. In fact, they had been quite common in the immediate postwar years, before disappearing during the 1950s in the new climate of repressive labor relations (e.g., Abbatecola, 1974, p. 37). Long forgotten labor scenes, not simply revolving strikes, reappeared with the 1959–63 strike wave. In 1960, thousands of electromechanical workers, on strike for the renewal of their collective contract, time and again paralyzed the city of Milan. Long columns of workers marched to the center of town from the industrial outskirts, carrying their red flags, banners, and signs, and introducing a novelty of the times: the use of whistles and drums, a cacophony of colors and sounds.[19] Those workers' rallies through the city had the effect of exporting labor conflict from the factories to society at large. Michelin workers on strike in Turin, on February 7, 1962, rallied downtown, marching through the streets of the historical district and on toward the railroad station. There the workers blocked traffic by lying on the streets and across the railroad tracks (Lanzardo, 1979, p. 87). Pickets became increasingly tough, and there were episodes of violence (Lanzardo, 1979, p. 84; Gallessi, 1981, p. 43). According to a worker at Siemens, a large Milan manufacturer of electric products, "in the morning, the few scabs that approached the entrances to the factory had to walk on a [noisy] carpet of morsels of dried bread . . . a 'red carpet' . . . under a shower of 5-lira coins that workers hurled at them" (quoted in Gallessi, 1981, p. 38). Vladimiro, a 31-year-old Michelin worker in Turin, recalled that "at the beginning, we organized many internal rallies that blocked machinery and everything; we didn't beat up workers; we only dragged away the most stubborn ones; for supervisors, however, it was a different story" (quoted in Lanzardo, 1979, p. 91). Workers vented the same anger toward scabs. Michele Dimanico recalled that "we beat up some scabs. . . . We picked up huge pieces of dirt that weighed several pounds and hurled them at the workers, screaming 'eat it, scab!' (quoted in Lanzardo, 1979, p. 109).

At Siemens, a variety of stop-and-go and revolving strikes were combined with an overtime ban to prevent management from rebuilding its stockpiles (Gallessi, 1981, p. 37; Bezza, 1981, p. 80). Ethnographic accounts of struggles in other plants described similar mixes of innovative strike tactics (e.g., at the Cotonifici Valle di Susa) (Mottura, 1961). At Siemens, Ercole Marelli, and other plants, workers, instead of walking out during a strike, adopted the practice of staying inside the factory and organizing rallies that marched through the departments to round up scabs.[20] Assolombarda, the powerful Milanese employers' association, protested loudly against the use of these new forms of struggle: "The presence of strikers inside the factory . . . has meant material prevention of work, using all means: from the usual threats to the siege of workers and the shutting off of electric current to stop all machines" (quoted in Gallessi, 1981, p. 43).

In many factories, workers in mass meetings collectively decided the most appropriate forms of struggle.[21] Most meetings were held outside the plants in workers' clubs or even in nearby cafes.[22] But there were also a few instances of the first mass meetings (*assemblee*) inside the plants during strikes or during lunch breaks, despite the fact that such meetings were illegal at the time (e.g., at the Magnadyne plant in S. Antonino, near Turin; see Pugno, 1961). The years of the "recession blackmail" in the mid-1960s had brought temporary peace to the factories. But when labor conflicts exploded again during the 1969 *autunno caldo*, their sheer number and the variety of their tactics startled employers, authorities, and the public.

Revolving strikes became the typical means of working-class protest. At first, strikes were rotated by department, by shift, or by hour, with short strikes of one or two hours' duration. As the strike wave progressed, revolving strikes became increasingly sophisticated and damaging, being organized by floor, or even by workers' identification numbers (odd or even) (Regalia, 1975b, p. 70).

To be effective, revolving strikes had to be planned on the basis of good knowledge of the production process. Workers would set up study groups to acquire that knowledge, and a network of activists would be formed (e.g., Regini, 1974, pp. 44, 49; Regalia, 1975b, p. 62). Those networks of activists played a crucial role in the struggles: They coordinated, they organized, they incited reluctant workers to action (Abbatecola, 1974, p. 79). The first shop-floor organizations (the CUB, *comitati unitari di base*, "unitary base committees," and the CdB, *comitati di base*, "base committees") in many plants were born of that need to coordinate complex strike tactics (Abbatecola, 1974, pp. 56–7; Reyneri, 1974a, p. 146; Avanguardia Operaia, 1971, 1973a). In the words of Cesare Cosi, Fiat worker,

Revolving strikes, like checkerboard strikes, sudden strikes, and strikes by alternate gangs within departments, required a high degree of knowledge of the production process. . . . In that phase, delegates and CI members would inspect departments in order to gather knowledge about the critical spots in the plant, where stockpiles were available and where a 100% worker participation was vital for the success of the strike. The general plans for the design of complex strike tactics came out of that work. (Polo, 1989, p. 155; see also p. 115)

The detailed knowledge of the production process that modern organization of production had taken away from the workers was being reappropriated by the workers in order to struggle more effectively.

Slowdowns (*autoriduzione dei tempi*) also became typical means of struggle, spreading from Pirelli and Candy to other plants (Regini, 1974, p. 81; Carabelli, 1974, p. 175). Slowdowns were particularly damaging, causing enormous production losses (Luppi, 1974, p. 67) and management opposed them vigorously (e.g., Regalia, 1975b, p. 76). As forms of protest against the rapid pace of production, slowdowns effectively offered a way for workers to set their own production pace (Regini, 1974, p. 54). In cases of revolving strikes, management often sent workers home without pay from departments not directly involved in the strikes (e.g., Luppi, 1974, p. 67), claiming that there was not enough work to keep them busy. Such pressure tactics had very divisive effects on shop-floor solidarity. By and large, workers' resistance somewhat reduced management's capacity to adopt those tactics, and by using slowdowns, workers did not even leave management the option of using them (Regini, 1974, p. 54).

Some forms of slowdowns and revolving strikes came close to sabotage. At the Autobianchi car plant in Milan (and also at Fiat, in Turin, and at other automobile plants), assembly-line workers would let every fifth or sixth chassis pass through the line without performing their assigned operations (*salto della scocca*) (and during the most intense periods of struggle, even one in every two chassis) (Luppi, 1974, p. 61). As one worker put it, "*Everyone did what they wanted*, one worker would put in a screw . . . another one wouldn't . . . the cars were all rejects" (quoted in Luppi, 1974, p. 61, emphasis added). Productivity at Autobianchi slowly declined from 133 chassis to 117, to 115, and even down to 106 (Luppi, 1974, p. 62). Things were not much better elsewhere. At Ignis, a large home-appliance manufacturer in Milan, a worker recalled that "Supervisors went crazy checking to see that refrigerators had all the screws . . . so that most of the time they had to be serviced. In some departments, production would pile up; in others there wasn't enough work" (quoted in Santi, 1974, p. 153).

Table 7.7. *Distribution of strike tactics adopted between 1969 and 1971, by firm size*

Tactic	Number of employees						Total
	51–100	101–250	251–500	501–1,000	1,001–5,000	>5,000	
Overtime ban	20.6[a]	25.6	33.0	37.1	52.4	53.3	35.0
Slowdown	6.1	7.8	16.8	21.7	24.7	46.3	17.3
Strike of all workers	79.4	85.2	92.1	92.6	93.7	91.4	88.3
Revolving strike[b]	11.0	16.7	30.2	45.0	61.6	80.7	35.8
Stop-and-go strike	26.2	34.6	49.1	46.5	65.8	78.0	46.7
Wildcat strike[c]	8.7	11.9	20.0	19.3	28.8	52.3	20.4
No conflict	11.7	7.3	2.1	1.0	0.7	0.4	4.6

[a] Percentage values.
[b] By department, by line, by gang, etc.
[c] Outside of union control.
Source: Buratto et al. (1974, p. 323).

Table 7.7 shows a frequency distribution of strike tactics by plant size, according to the 1971 Isvet survey (Buratto et al., 1974, p. 323). The data confirm the variety of strike tactics implemented during the 1968–72 strike wave. Nonetheless, the strike of all workers remained the most typical form of struggle (88.3%), followed by stop-and-go strikes (46.7%), overtime bans (35%), and revolving strikes (35.8%). The distribution by firm size shows that in larger plants, the mix of strike tactics was much more balanced across the available repertoire than in small factories, which seem to have relied predominantly on the strike by all workers. The work by Tarrow on the 1965–75 period in Italy, based on data collected from *Corriere della Sera*, the leading newspaper in Italy, similarly showed the wide range of collective actions during the strike wave (Tarrow, 1989a, pp. 186–92).

Workers' activities during the strikes were spirited both inside and outside the plants. Internal rallies moving from department to department, the hallmark of the "French May," became the most common means to round up scabs. Giovanni Falcone remembered those rallies at Fiat:

> When I heared them coming, the whistles, the tam-tam on the cans, I was happy. I would throw away my gloves and march along. . . . [We] would catch the scabs and place them in front of the rally. . . . It was the right thing to do to catch them, yank them out of the dumpsters where they hid, and put them right in front of the rally, kicking their butts. (Polo, 1989, p. 166)

Again, it was mostly the unskilled, southern workers who took the initiative. Nico Ciarciaglino, a Fiat worker, remembered that during the internal rallies, "There were rituals that were reminiscent of certain religious processions in the South: the appearance of a coffin, reserved for the capitalist, and for his lackeys" (Polo, 1989, p. 175).[23] As strike tactics became more damaging to production, violence often broke out. At the Candy factory, workers often threw furniture and equipment into the furnaces, in order to force the scabs to stop working (Regini, 1974, p. 57). At Fiat, Nazareno Bazzan remembered that

Anything could happen. In front of the main office building, Fiat had a series of flower pots, with geraniums and other flowers along the staircase: in one afternoon everything disappeared, vases flying all the way up through the third-floor windows. . . . Another time, on the same staircase, there was a real battle; 300 to 400 company guards participated; every ten seconds one of them flew down; it was a continuous coming and going of ambulances that took the injured away. (Polo, 1989, p. 104)

At Pirelli, the Milan-based tire manufacturer, strikers found out that trucks were bringing in tires from a Pirelli plant in Greece, whereupon they blocked the trucks, dumped the tires in the plant parking lot, and burned them, along with many company cars. Then they stormed the cafeteria reserved for clerical workers (a symbol of privilege) and smashed everything to pieces (Viale, 1978, p. 202). Roberto Sibona had similar recollections of the rallies through the Fiat offices in Turin: "We made a complete mess, we dirtied everything. The pink carpets of some offices were black after we went through them" (Polo, 1989, p. 190).

Strikers were particularly ruthless against clerical workers and management (Luppi, 1974, pp. 49, 140, 167–8; Regini, 1974, pp. 48, 58; Regalia, 1975b, p. 71). At the Fiat, Autobianchi, and Innocenti automobile plants, as at many other plants across the country, blue-collar workers often stormed the offices, sometimes breaking doors and desks, but most of the time only sampling some of the office privileges (Luppi, 1974, pp. 50–1, 77; Reyneri, 1974a, p. 139). Sibona recalled that during the office rallies at Fiat, "Many immigrants used the office telephones to call home, down South. 'We can talk at leisure, Agnelli [Fiat majority stockholder] is paying!' (Polo, 1989, pp. 190–1). At Autobianchi, workers burned the cars of two white-collar employees who had circumvented the picket line and gone in by climbing the factory walls (Luppi, 1974, p. 49; Reyneri, 1974a, p. 139). At GTE, workers would organize sit-ins in front of managers' offices; they would also search managers' cars (Regini, 1975, p. 180). Managers' windows were often stoned, and their offices stormed (Reyneri, 1974a, pp. 139, 147, 167–8; Regalia, 1975b, p. 71).

Not all plants experienced violence. At Falck, a Lombard metalworking plant, even the extreme forms of revolving strikes occurred, as union representatives proudly said, "without breaking a single window" (quoted in Beccalli, 1974, p. 175). The same was true for Redaelli, another Lombard metalworking plant, with a long tradition of Communist organization inside the plant (Beccalli, 1974). "We were always very good enemies" said a wistful director of personnel, speaking of a legendary Communist leader at Redaelli (quoted in Beccalli, 1974, p. 239).

Perhaps the resurgence in labor conflict took on the most violent overtones in those plants where repression and worker exploitation had been most harsh, and where labor organizations had been forced out of the plants during the 1950s (Giugni et al., 1976, p. 128; Low-Beer, 1978, p. 209). Both the 1971 and 1982

Isvet surveys of workers' attitudes confirmed a positive correlation between labor conflict and authoritarian/paternalistic management: Workers were much more likely to strike in firms that they perceived to be authoritarian, rather than democratic (De Masi and Fevola, 1974a, pp. 789–90, 849–50; De Masi et al., 1985, p. 530). In 1971, 41% of the most militant workers in the sample were employed in authoritarian firms, 32% in paternalistic firms, and only 14% in democratic firms (De Masi and Fevola, 1974a, p. 790).

During the 1968–72 strike wave, department-level meetings and plantwide mass meetings (*assemblee*) became the typical means of decision making,[24] and they were not always orderly. At Fiat, as Pasquale de Stefani recalled, "People just jumped on the tables in the cafeteria during lunch break, and that's how mass meetings started" (Polo, 1989, p. 134). But mass meetings provided a forum for workers to speak up, for common problems to be identified, for demands to be agreed upon, and sometimes for union leaders to listen, particularly in the general assemblies.[25] According to Roberto Sibona, a Fiat worker, "There was anger in the meetings . . . there were people who intervened just to scream out a few sentences, just to say 'Enough!' . . . just to say how pissed off they were" (Polo, 1989, p. 189).

Outside the plants, activities ranged from blockading incoming and outgoing goods to picketing, rallies, and obstructing access to roads, subways, and trains. The blockade of incoming and outgoing goods, more than any other strike tactic, helped to bring production to a grinding halt.[26] Faced with management's attempts to break such blockades, tough pickets, workers, and often students would stand vigil, particularly at night.

Rallies downtown and in neighboring towns, featuring the use of loudspeakers and distribution of leaflets, became common (Luppi, 1974, pp. 55, 63; Regini, 1975, p. 176). In the words of one of the participants, "We did not know what to do; we would go to the Valassina [main road] and stop cars; or we would sit at the factory gates and stop the bus; once we even stopped the tram in front of city hall" (quoted in Luppi, 1974, pp. 54–5).

To bring their protests to the attention of the public, striking workers set up tents in the main squares in the towns or in front of the factories. At Autobianchi and Candy, workers set up tents in front of the factories and held bonfires at night (Regini, 1974, p. 44; Luppi, 1974, p. 63). A tent in front of the Ignis plant, day and night, became a meeting place for workers, activists, and students – until Borghi, the owner of Ignis, bought the parcel of land where the tent was raised and kicked the workers out (Santi, 1974, p. 144).

7.5. THE DEMANDS: *VOGLIAMO TUTTO* ("WE WANT EVERYTHING")

For July 3, 1968, the unions in Turin had called a general strike to protest the housing situation in the city. On that day, the police charged into a rally of workers and students in front of the gates of the Fiat Mirafiori plant, and similar tactics were used downtown in Corso Traiano.[27] Barricades went up in the streets. All day and

Table 7.8. *Strike demands in plant-level bargaining (1970–71)*

	Agreements dealing with the demands			
	1970		1971	
Demand	No.	%	No.	%
Working hours	314	23.8	128	21.3
Health and environment	262	19.9	187	31.1
Work organization	113	8.5	60	10.0
Job classifications	389	29.5	337	56.1
Wage increases	1,146	87.0	447	74.5
Student workers	75	5.6	46	7.6
Trade union rights	51	3.8	134	22.3

Source: Cella (1976b, p. 197).

all night, clashes continued between the police and increasing numbers of students and workers. The news media shocked Italy the next morning with the words from a picket sign found on the battleground: *vogliamo tutto*, "we want everything" (Viale, 1978, pp. 164–5). Samuel Gompers, one of the founders of the American Federation of Labor, was once asked, What do workers want? He replied "More." Kornhauser (1954a, p. 77) echoed that when he wrote that "Basically industrial conflict arises from the persistent urge of working people to get more." During the strike waves in Italy, workers seemed to want not just more, but "everything." Demands took on radical overtones. Dreams of social change seemed close to becoming reality. Giampiero Carpo, Fiat worker, remembered that, "We wanted everything right away . . . the desire to change the world was the common thread to all" (Polo, 1989, p. 122). Shocking as the picket sign found at Corso Traiano may have been (the news media need their symbols), the workers' reality was a far cry from gaining "everything."

Table 7.8, which lists the demands covered by plant-level agreements in the metalworking industry in the Milan province, provides some evidence on workers' demands in the heat of the 1968–72 strike wave. The most notable thing is that workers' demands became increasingly diversified during the wave. In 1970, 87% of such agreements centered on wage issues; in 1971 the corresponding figure was 74.5%. Furthermore, in 1971, a much higher percentage of agreements concerned demands other than wages (56.1% concerned job classifications, compared with 29.5% for the preceding year; 31.1% involved health and work-environment issues, as compared with 19.9%; 22.3% pertained to trade-union rights, as compared with 3.8%).

Despite the diversification of strike demands, wage issues retained precedence throughout the cycle, as confirmed by both the number and percentage of agreements dealing with those issues. These figures, however, mask one of the most radical and innovative characteristics of the strike cycle: its egalitarian tendency. In 1967, percentage wage increases that varied with skill level were still

Table 7.9. *Wages by skill level in historical perspective*

Skill level	1959	1963	1959–63 (% change)	1966	1963–66 (% change)	1970	1966–70 (% change)
1st	125.4	132.0	(+6.6)	135.5	(+3.5)	127.5	(-8.0)
2nd	112.6	118.0	(+5.4)	121.0	(+3.0)	116.0	(-5.0)
3rd	106.6	111.0	(+4.4)	112.0	(+1.0)	109.0	(-3.0)
4th				107.0	(+0.5)	105.5	(-1.5)
4th women	103.0	106.5	(+3.5)				
5th[a]	100.0	100.0		100.0		100.0	
6th women	97.0						
7th women	89.0						

[a]The base is the 5th category (unskilled worker/hand laborer = 100).
Source: *Sindacato Moderno*, April–May 1970, p. 36, quoted by Cella (1976b, p. 174) and Regini and Reyneri (1971, p. 97).

typical. In 1968, the number of agreements with percentage increases was matched by the number that gave all workers increases by equal amounts. In 1969, egalitarian agreements predominated (Cella, 1976b, pp. 182–3). In 1970, among 1,316 plant agreements, 1,146 (87%) dealt with wage increases; of those, 817 (71.3%) specified wage increases equal for all, and only 26 (2.3%) specified percentage increases differentiated by skill level. In 1971, among 600 agreements, 447 (74.5%) dealt with wage increases; of those, 386 (86.4%) were egalitarian, and 24 (5.4%) were percentage increases (Cella, 1976b, p. 200). The data in Table 7.9, on the long-term trends for wages by skill level, confirm the tendency toward increasing pay differentiation across job categories over time, up to 1966.[28] Thereafter, egalitarian workers' demands began to reduce wage differentials.[29] During the strike wave, in a span of just a few years, wage differentials shrank across sectors and territories. In particular, the discrepancies between the wages of skilled and unskilled manual workers decreased in real terms (Dell'Aringa, 1976, p. 79).

An egalitarian tendency similar to that affecting wages also characterized bonuses. The 1967 plant-level agreements introduced the practice of flat bonuses for all skill levels. That practice became typical in the 1968 agreements: Of the 205 agreements that specified bonus increases, 154 either entirely eliminated or reduced differentials (Cella, 1976b, p. 182).

The increase in the number of agreements that dealt with job classification, organization of production, and health and environmental issues was certainly a novelty introduced by the strike wave. But the real novelty was the way those demands struck at the very heart of the capitalist organization of production, embodying workers' rejection of a Fordist and Tayloristic approach to work (Giugni et al., 1976, pp. 138–9). The monotony and the fatigue brought on by assembly-line work figured prominently in the complaints of line workers. As we saw in Chapter 3, during the 1960s, employers had increased the pace of assembly-line work through plant restructuring processes. According to an Autobianchi

Table 7.10. *Correlation coefficients between numbers of strikes, strikers, and hours lost and number of nonfatal work-related injuries (industry, 1950–I/1978–IV)*

	Strikes	Strikers	Hours lost
Work-related injuries	0.59	0.11	0.24

employee, "Workers really could not take those rhythms of production" (quoted in Luppi, 1974, p. 58; see also Bianchi et al., 1970, p. 17). In the late 1970s, when improved labor-market conditions gave workers a fighting chance, they struck back: "Every day we had a protest on the line; if it wasn't a half hour, it was an hour stoppage" (quoted in Luppi, 1974, p. 58) The assembly line (the "line") often became the target of workers' anger and violence. An Ignis worker recalled that "Workers would tear up the lines, cut them, bend them" (quoted in Santi, 1974, p. 147).

According to Hobsbawn, increases in work intensity and in the rhythms of production, although difficult to measure, are likely to have "an important connection" with labor activity, particularly during economic booms (Hobsbawn, 1964, pp. 136–7). Hobsbawn reported a positive relationship between the rate of nonfatal injuries (taken as a measure of change in work intensity) and trade-union expansion in 1889–91 in several British railway companies. Similarly, figures on changes in the pace of production during the second half of the nineteenth century in two northern French coalfields indicate that work intensity went hand in hand with increased labor activity (Hobsbawn, 1964, p. 137; see also Knowles, 1952, p. 187).

Table 7.10 shows the correlation coefficients between number of nonfatal work-related injuries and the number of strikes, strikers, and hours lost. Indeed, there was a positive relationship between labor unrest and the number of nonfatal work-related injuries, the relationship being particularly strong for strike frequency.[30] Even the plot in Figure 7.1 shows a close correspondence between the number of work-related injuries in industry and strike frequency (see the plot of Figure 1.3, p. 4), with major peaks in the 1960–63 and 1969–73 periods and troughs during the 1964–65 and 1974–75 recessions.[31]

On the one hand, these findings confirm the strong relationship involving the number of work-related injuries, the rate of economic growth, and the business cycle (the booms of 1960–63, 1969–73, and the busts of 1964–65, 1974–75) (Campiglio, 1973, 1976; d'Ambrosio and Biz, 1974). This is particularly clear when we compare the plot of the number of work-related injuries and the plot of the number of hours worked in manufacturing (Figure 7.1).[32] On the other hand, these findings illustrate the "seamy" side of expansion. As the pace of production picks up during expansion through overtime work and new hirings (often workers not accustomed to industrial work habits), workers are subjected to increasing stress and fatigue. As both workers and machines are pushed to the limits of their

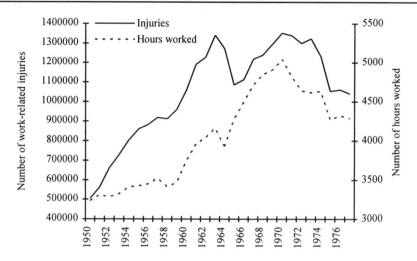

Figure 7.1. *Plots of the number of work-related injuries and of the number of hours worked in industry*

capacity, work-related injuries become much more likely. The discomfort and dissatisfaction that result from the increased pace of work lead to a flammable situation. When coupled with more favorable labor-market conditions, such a mixture is likely to explode in outbursts of industrial unrest.[33] Michele Dimanico, a 25-year-old worker at Fiat-Spa in 1959, reported that "After only five or six months, I had seen several work injuries – young men who lost their fingers because the rhythms were rather brutal. I never could keep up with the line. ... We all worked to the limits of our capacity" (quoted in Lanzardo, 1979, p. 105).

In the fall of 1968, workers at Candy, in a series of mass meetings, decided to take advantage of a 10% increase in the rate for piecework so as to work less instead of earning more (Regini, 1975, p. 48). Regressive work incentives were what conservatives had recommended at the beginning of the industrial revolution in England to get people to work ("Let them go hungry"). In 1747, John Smith, in *Memoirs of Wool*, wrote that, "We can fairly aver that a reduction of wages in the woolen manufacture would be a national blessing, and no real injury to the poor" (quoted in Thompson, 1963, p. 277). In the context of traditional work habits and standards of living, an increase in pay meant that workers could maintain their traditional way of life while doing less work (Thompson, 1967; Marglin, 1974, p. 92); and so they did. A concerned magistrate wrote in 1818 that "Some years ago [the weavers were] so extravagantly paid that by working three or four days in a week they could maintain themselves in a comparative state of luxury" (quoted in Thompson, 1963, p. 277). That workers should be willing to trade more money for less work in 1969, in the heart of consumeristic Milan, was a good indication that the pace of production had indeed become unbearable in many plants. The increase in the number of work-related injuries shows how speedups were fueled.

The time allotted for each worker operation and the determination of line speed rested in management's hands, but workers were ingenious in finding ways to monitor subtle increases in the speed of the assembly line. Luciano Parlanti, a Fiat worker, recounted how workers did it in his department:

A worker draws a mark on the floor at the point where, with the normal flow of the assembly line, the time assigned to perform his operation is up. Looking at the clock is forbidden. But with this method he can avoid working harder than he should, and the stopwatch guys can't cut time any longer. His fellow workers imitate him. (quoted in Viale, 1978, p. 182)

Many struggles in the 1968–72 period centered on the issues of line speed and organization of production. The slogan "a different way of building a car" became popular in those years. In many plants, workers succeeded in imposing a new work organization by "work group" (*isole*), partly based on elimination of line work through job enlargement and job enrichment. By and large, however, elimination of the jobs that posed the greatest health risks, reorganization of production, and implementation of new technologies were left in management's hands. Labor succeeded in imposing some changes, but management largely maintained control over the direction of change. Management often used that power to introduce new technologies and reorganize production in ways that would break the back of militancy (particularly, the homogeneous work group).[34]

Rejection of the capitalist organization of production was particularly strong among those workers operating in unsafe and unhealthy conditions. Against the long-standing practice of accepting higher wages to work in an unhealthy environment (*monetizzazione*, in the Italian labor jargon), there arose a new watchword: "Health is not a bargaining chip" (*la salute non si tratta*).[35] Workers, unions, and doctors began to set up study groups to better understand the issues involved (e.g., Milanaccio and Ricolfi, 1976).

Workers dealt another blow to the traditional organization of production in the factories when they began to reject the capitalist system of hierarchical classification of jobs. Against the traditional principle of individual promotions at the discretion of management, workers opposed the principle of "mass promotions" and "automatic promotions by seniority," outside of management's control. Dismissing skill as the guiding principle of job classifications, workers pushed for the abolition of job hierarchies altogether and for a single classification system common to manual and clerical workers and supervisors (*inquadramento unico*).[36] Thus, job-classification demands reflected the same egalitarian tendencies that characterized wage issues.

In 1967, plant-level agreements typically provided for individual (or small group) promotions from one category to the next. In 1968, "mass promotions" were already becoming numerous (in particular, there was a tendency to eliminate the fourth category, reserved for women). In 1969, many agreements abolished the fifth category altogether (sometimes even the fourth) (Cella, 1976b, pp. 183–4). Such demands became increasingly popular in 1970 and 1971. In 1970, among 1,316 agreements, 389 (29.5%) dealt with the issue of job classification; of those,

28% abolished the lowest category (fifth), and 15.7% abolished the fourth category (22.6% specified the classification of the fourth category as temporary); (on the Italian system of job classification see Table 3.12, p. 83). Of the 600 agreements in 1971, 337 (56.1%) dealt with job classification; of those, 55.5% abolished the fifth category, 20.8% abolished the fourth, and 36.8% classified the fourth as a temporary category (Cella, 1976b, p. 198). The data in Table 7.11 on the distribution of blue-collar workers among skill hierarchies in various Italian firms show that workers' struggles were successful, although, again, a far cry from the elimination of job hierarchies.[37]

The trend toward upgrading the labor force, if not in terms of actual skill content, at least in terms of nominal skill and pay level, is not simply due to the particular group of firms for which I could find published data. The Federlombarda survey of 358 Lombardy firms confirms that basic pattern for the textile and metalworking industries (Table 7.12). The percentage of skilled workers steadily increased in both sectors at every time point (1969, 1972, 1975) considered by the survey, and that for unskilled workers decreased. Dell'Aringa (1976, p. 71) similarly showed, on the basis of the Ministry of Labor survey data, that during the 1969–74 period the lower-level categories in industry slowly emptied out, while the top-level ones swelled (Table 7.13). Women did not fare as well as men. Their numbers increased mostly in the higher unskilled category (OC, *operai comuni*), a category in which the number of men declined.

In practice, the elimination of the lowest job categories and the mass promotions of workers into higher-level categories, without any change in the skill content of the jobs themselves, functioned as a surrogate mechanism to produce further wage increases (Villa, 1986, p. 188). Nonetheless, the egalitarian ideology expressed by the 1968–72 strike wave, with its combination of collective upgrading of skill levels and lump-sum wage increases across skill levels, resulted in a reduction of wage differentials across skill levels and in a narrower distribution of the work force (Dell'Aringa, 1976, p. 83).

The tendency toward a wider range of workers' demands revealed by the available data did not necessarily indicate a workers' "learning curve": It took time to break away from the traditional wage demands. It may actually have meant an employers' "learning curve": Organization of production under capitalism is in the hands of employers; it cannot be touched. Period. During the strike wave, workers began to put more diversified demands on the table, but the employers' refusal to deal with issues that would encroach on their prerogatives prevented such issues from being incorporated into collective contracts for some time. There is considerable evidence of that. The employers' initial refusal to deal, presumably premised on the assumption that the movement would lose steam with time, typically was followed by a softening of positions and willingness to deal, in light of continuing workers' mobilization.[38] But undoubtedly, workers also learned. A member of the Commissione Interna at Ignis put it well: "People are not born professors. It takes time. And in the meantime, what do we do? While we wait for the delegates to grow, while they learn the ropes . . . we [the old members of the

Table 7.11. Distribution of blue-collar workers by skill level and year in selected firms

Skill level	Autobianchi[a][b]			Ignis[c]			Italtel[d]		Dalmine[e]		Fiat[f]	
	1970	1972	1973	1966	1970	1973	1970	1975	1971	1972	1971	1972
1st and 2nd	–	–	–	14.0	6.0	4.0	–	–	–	–	–	–
1st super	.05	.1	.1	–	–	–	–	–	.62	1.20	–	–
1st	7.68	9.2	9.2	6.0	10.0	13.0	13.4	18.5	17.18	22.80	2.5	3.00
2nd	21.64	32.7	37.9	21.0	23.0	34.0	–	–	28.01	32.80	16.0	30.00
3rd super	12.52	19.5	15.9	44.0	42.0	49.0	–	–	52.56	41.50	–	–
3rd	53.27	38.5	36.9	15.0	19.0	–	15.8	57.1	.87	1.20	81.5	67.00
4th	4.84	–	–	–	–	–	70.8	24.4	.76	.50	–	–

[a] Percentage values in all columns of the table.
[b] Data from Luppi (1974, p. 101).
[c] Data from Santi (1974, p. 120).
[d] Data from Villa (1986, p. 320).
[e] Data from Negrelli (1989, p. 206).
[f] Fiat-Mirafiori (body department); data from Milanaccio and Ricolfi (1976, p. 76).

Table 7.12. *Distribution of work force in industry by skill level, sex, and year*

Skill level	Men			Women		
	1966	1969	1974	1966	1969	1974
OS[a]	16.3[b]	16.7	23.4	1.6	1.3	1.6
OQ	26.5	27.2	28.2	10.1	9.7	11.5
OC	16.9	17.7	15.8	6.2	7.1	9.6
MC	9.5	8.6	4.3	3.8	4.2	1.9

[a]OS, *operai specializzati* (skilled); OQ, *operai qualificati* (semiskilled); OC, *operai comuni* (unskilled); MC, *manovali comuni* (unskilled).
[b]Percentage values.
Source: Ministry of Labor data from Dell'Aringa (1976, p. 71).

Table 7.13. *Percentages of workers at various skill levels in the textile and metalworking industries, by year*

Industry	1969			1972			1975		
	UN[a]	SE	SK	UN	SE	SK	UN	SE	SK
Textile	41	41	20	39	40	22	38	37	24
Metalworking	35	35	27	29	37	31	26	39	34

[a]UN, unskilled; SE, semiskilled; SK, skilled.
Source: Bergamaschi (1977b, p. 255).

Commissione Interna] should organize, we should lead" (quoted in Santi, 1974, p. 151). Indeed, the strike wave began with traditional demands (Luppi, 1974, p. 48; Carabelli, 1974, p. 176; Reyneri, 1974a, p. 175). Those demands reflected the interests and needs of the workers first involved: mostly skilled workers. They pressed corporatist demands centered on issues of wage differentials, in order to reward their skills. They had no complaints of speedups, harsh supervision, or low pay. Their skills guaranteed them a minimum of independence, work autonomy, and higher pay. In fact, they had struck often to maintain those privileges. White-collar workers, when they occasionally did participate in strikes, similarly advanced demands that centered around the maintenance of privileges.

But as new actors, mostly unskilled southern workers on the assembly lines, became more involved in the struggles and began to take the lead, new demands came to the fore (Abbatecola, 1974, p. 60; Luppi, 1974, p. 76). It was in mass meetings inside the plants that workers voiced their anger, discovered common needs, explored the limits of their possibilities, made demands, and formulated contract proposals. A worker at Candy recalled that

> the period of the 1968 struggles was a disorderly, confused period. Sometimes we would stop working, before we even knew why. There was no organization in the movement. No. We would set up things in the meetings, a study group here, another one there. There was mind-boggling confusion. (quoted in Regini, 1974, p. 49)

The strike wave featured widespread rejection of the Tayloristic organization of production, capitalist job hierarchies, and traditional forms of factory discipline. It also brought rejection of authority relationships and paternalism (Bianchi et al., 1970, pp. 23–4). In a world where the "politics of production" had traditionally been upheld by authoritative relationships, defiance took on many faces. Pasquale De Stefani, a Fiat worker, gave it one face:

> I decided to get out of my subordinate condition. To make this clear to everyone, every morning, around eight o' clock, I would stop working for about twenty minutes and eat a sandwich. This may sound silly, but no one had ever done it before, certainly no one had done it so openly, right before the supervisors. (Polo, 1989, p. 130)

An anonymous Sicilian worker gave it another:

> I remember what happened to a Sicilian guy . . . who didn't speak any Italian; to a foreman who had asked him why he didn't speak Italian, he replied: 'But you, when you come to me, don't you speak the Piedmontese dialect?' That was his first act of rebellion. (quoted in Bulgarelli, 1978, p. 123)

To underscore their defiance of authority principles, workers often reversed their roles. As one of them recalled, "Four, five hundred workers would hunt down managers, pick one and tell him: 'From this moment you get the hell out of the plant, and you don't come back until we tell you'" (quoted in Regini, 1974, p. 68). At first, line supervisors were the targets of workers' protests against authority:

> Gabuto, the supervisor, had not understood that things were changing and had placed himself right in front of a rally going through his department, screaming, cursing, threatening, with his finger raised. In an instant, he was lifted up, his body passed from hand to hand. He flew like a ball above people's heads; like a torpedo, he was headed at an impressive speed toward the hot furnace. He got away by the skin of his teeth! (Pasquale De Stefani, in Polo, 1989, p. 135)

But slowly the workers' rejection of authority moved up the hierarchical ladder. From supervisors and department heads, to white-collar workers and management (but, at times, even skilled blue-collar workers) – "they all became class enemies" (Pasquale De Stefani and Roberto Sibona, in Polo, 1989, pp. 121, 191). As Roberto Sibona recalled, "Hunting for the bosses soon became a habit. Sometimes, we caught them and threw them out over the gates; other times we roped them up, stuck a red flag in their hands, and forced them to march along like that in front of the rally" (Polo, 1989, pp. 190–1). Episodes of both physical and psychological violence against bosses multiplied. In *Lotta Continua* one reads that "Managers not yet accustomed to being submissive [to workers] have often been forced to parade between two wings of enraged workers. On their bald heads, beaded with sweat drops and spit, the 5-lira coins hurled by the workers stick 'like confetti glittering in the sun.'"[39] One day, at Autobianchi, the car plant in Milan, workers dragged the director of personnel outside the building. As a worker recalled, for the duration of the strike (two hours), "He stayed there in the rain, among the workers, to take insults and spit. That was an incredible thing" (quoted in Luppi, 1974, pp. 50–1).

Authoritarian, repressive employer policies were not the only targets of workers' anger; paternalism, as well, came under attack. Many large-scale companies in Italy had, in years past, set up extensive welfare systems for their workers: kindergartens, schools, and resort facilities for employees' children, senior-citizen clubs, company housing, sports facilities, health-care clinics, preferential access to jobs for employees' sons and daughters.[40] Such welfare provisions often went hand in hand with company unionism (*sindacati gialli*) (Santi, 1974, p. 127) and with highly repressive methods in the workplace, particularly against the workers' vanguard – of such dichotomous elements, Italian capitalists had constructed their single system for "taking care" of labor.[41]

Even in 1970, a survey of Italian managers showed that the same managers who had a paternalistic view of class relations would not shy away from using repression in cases of conflict (Talamo, 1979, p. 66). An activist at Candy remembered one of the meetings between the workers and Mr. Fumagalli, the owner of the company, who called such meetings to try to uphold the myth of the great big family. On that occasion, the activist addressed Mr. Fumagalli: "Who was it that gave you the factory? You come here and tell us that we are a great big family, but you are the one who stashes away the millions, and people leave their hands in here" (quoted in Regini, 1974, p. 31).

The rhetoric of class came to tint the ideologies of class relations, even for the unions that traditionally had been more inclined to cooperation than to conflict, such as CISL (e.g., FIM-CISL, 1972). The crumbling of the old system of labor relations, based on a combination of paternalistic and repressive measures, is well symbolized by one of the first sparks of the struggles, at the Marzotto textile mills in the small town of Valdagno, on April 19, 1968: After a strike had erupted that morning, followed by all-out picketing, the police charged into the ranks of the workers. The workers were joined by students from the local high school and nearby University of Padua:

The statue of Count Gaetano Marzotto, founder of the industrial dynasty that owns the factory, the city, the valleys ... (houses, shops, social services, "everything" belongs to the employer) was knocked down by an angry crowd.... New times are coming. (Viale, 1978, p. 148; see also Foa, 1975, pp. 164–6; Lumley, 1990, p. 173)

The attacks on the authority structure (often with physical consequences) left many employers (particularly small employers) and managers frightened, disoriented, confused. The principle of traditional authority was sacred to them, the same principle that Confindustria president Angelo Costa had expounded to the Commissione Economica per l'Assemblea Costituente in 1946, in his argument against workers' control in the factories:

The principle of authority must be respected in any organization, whichever organization ... one cannot admit that he who is inferior in the hierarchy – hierarchy that is necessary to manage – could, for example, have a control function over those who are above him.... Such a control function would be detrimental to the principle of authority, because it is the superior who controls the inferior, never the inferior that controls the superior. (quoted in Pirzio Ammassari, 1976, pp. 50–1)

7.6. THE RADICAL LEFT

A few years before all of this happened, in 1967 and 1968, the student movement swept the country with a revolutionary wind that shocked the Italian middle and upper classes alike. After all, many of the young militants were the sons and daughters of the bourgeoisie. Beginning in 1967, and spreading in 1968 like wildfire, students occupied university after university, department after department (e.g., Trento, Venice, Milan, Turin, Genoa, Pisa, Rome, Naples) (Lumley, 1990, pp. 47–100; Tarrow, 1989a, pp. 143–67). Although labor was beginning to awaken here and there, but by and large was still quiescent, waiting for the 1969 renewals of their collective contracts (*appuntamento dei contratti*), 1968, *il sessantotto*, was the year of the students.

The organizational basis of the student movement was a loose structure of diverse groups, some with connections to the Communist Party, but others openly antagonistic to the PCI. The endless debates in their mass meetings were the closest they came to organization (Viale, 1978, p. 171):

1968 (*il sessantotto*) – at least in Italy – has neither newspapers nor free radios, books, journals through which to express itself. It circulates on the strength of the mimeographs, or even through oral communication in the mass meetings, in casual encounters, in trips with no destination. (Viale, 1978, p. 7)

The theoretical basis for the student movement was derived from the classic Marxist tradition (Lenin, but also Trotsky and Rosa Luxemburg), with additions from the scathing criticisms of contemporary capitalist societies voiced by Herbert Marcuse and other members of the Frankfurt School, as well as ideas from Chairman Mao's Cultural Revolution. "Mao-Marx-Marcuse" was spray painted in red on university walls. Particularly in the Cultural Revolution did the students claim to see fulfillment of Communism's great promise: egalitarianism and continuous challenge of authority relations (Lumley, 1990, pp. 109–42). Radical intellectuals operating on the left since the late 1950s (e.g., Potere Operaio) had identified the changes occurring in the class structure (*composizione di classe*), had theorized the relationship between class structure and class struggle, and had touted the key role of the working class in capitalist societies (*centralità operaia*).[42] They gave a name to the new, unskilled worker who occupied a central position in the class structure of advanced capitalism: *operaio massa* (the "mass worker"). They conducted surveys among workers to discover the needs of the mass worker.[43] They distributed leaflets, pamphlets, and periodicals to the workers at the factory gates. In a series of periodicals that made their appearance in the early 1960s, those groups initiated a lively debate on the left, often criticizing both unions and working-class parties (PSI and, in particular, PCI): for example, *Quaderni Rossi* in

1961 and *Quaderni Piacentini* in 1962, but also smaller, almost factory-based publications, such as the early *Classe Operaia* in Genoa, *Potere Operaio* in Milan and Porto Marghera, and *Gatto Selvaggio* in Turin, which later merged with the national *Classe Operaia* in 1964 (Gobbi, 1989, pp. 112, 115–6).[44] If the goal of those periodicals was to keep in touch with the working class, they were an absolute failure. As Gobbi recalled of *Quaderni Rossi*,

> All the articles were written in an esoteric-intellectual language: no worker was ever able to pick them up without having an impulse of repulsion for their total lack of intelligibility to nonexperts. The typical defect of intellectuals was even emphasized by the choice of the "workers' viewpoint." (Gobbi, 1989, p. 102)

But whether comprehensible or opaque to the workers, whether Leninist or anti-Leninist (emphasizing the need for tight organization among the vanguard revolutionaries, e.g., Avanguardia Operaia, or stressing reliance on the spontaneous revolutionary potential of the masses, e.g., Lotta Continua), these publications and the groups that backed them kept alive the language of revolutionary discourse on the left of the Communist Party from the 1960s onward.

Many students began to rally in front of the factory gates: the "young Marxist-Leninists dressed in red."[45] Those students brought to the workers' struggle experience from the student movement's battles with academic authorities and the police, a language of emancipation and freedom.[46] The November 7, 1969, issue of *Lotta Continua*, the journal of the homonymous extraparliamentary group, commented as follows:

> Workers are slowly freeing themselves. In the factories, they destroy authority . . . they shake off the taboos that have kept them enslaved. They discover that the power of capitalists is based on their consent; it is based on the fact that because of fear, ignorance, or indifference, workers have accepted, until now, as normal and even necessary something that, instead, they have the strength and power to destroy. The capitalist mode of production . . . is based, among other things, on the respect and fear that workers have for their supervisors and superiors. . . . The first victory of the class struggle in the factories is freedom from the fear of bosses.

For Lotta Continua, violence was seen to have a fundamental role in a revolutionary strategy:

> The masses must be ready to face up to any form of aggression by their enemies, *opposing violence to violence*. . . . The masses must learn to publicly try and punish their jailers, to organize military style. . . . The revolutionary party can be born only from these workers "wild" and "pissed off" who lead the internal rallies and shout in the mass meetings their resolve to turn everything upside down. (Bobbio, 1979, pp. 12, 40, 79)

Tarrow's data showed that the presence of those radical groups was associated with a maximum of disruptive effects during collective actions (Tarrow, 1989a, p. 186). The average amount of disruption caused by actions in which both students and workers participated was almost twice as high the average for actions in which workers participated alone (Tarrow, 1989a, p. 180).

The relationships between students and workers were not always easy.[47] As Pasquale De Stefani, a Fiat worker, put it, "It is hard [for a blue-collar worker] to accept that an employer's son will renounce his roots and come every morning at 5 a.m. to the factory gates, just because of ideals" (Polo, 1989, p. 138). On the other hand, Cesare Cosi, another Fiat worker saw it in a different light: "An old worker who for years had felt almost like an inferior being, all of a sudden had a young woman [student] taking interest in his life, telling him that he was the center of everything" (Polo, 1989, p. 152). For many workers, coming in contact with the student movement was an eye-opener. Giovanni Falcone, at Fiat, recalled that

> The leaflets [that students handed out] were very important, at least for me. I was a commuter and had no time to stop after work outside the gates to discuss things. I could understand them because they were written in a simple language, perhaps a little strained for those who wrote them, because I don't think that the students spoke like that at home ... but they made an effort to speak the language of the slave. (Polo, 1989, p. 165)

The young workers, particularly student-workers, provided the liaison between the inside and the outside world. They typically were more radical and closer to the extraparliamentary groups (Regini, 1975, p. 184). Nico Ciarciaglino, a Fiat worker, recalled that "The workers started using the students as their *writers*. They came out of the factory and said, 'Today this and that happened, write it all up.'" (Polo, 1989, p. 178). Romagnoli's 1971 survey of the *delegati* in eighty-five Milanese factories showed that some 15% of the delegates participated in the activities of extraparliamentary groups. Those delegates were mostly young, unskilled recent immigrants from the South (Romagnoli, 1973, pp. 56–7).

Clashes between union representatives and the new activists close to the radical extraparliamentary groups were quite frequent (e.g., Cacciari, 1969, p. 136). Whenever they were present in front of the factories, the students would urge the workers toward both radical tactics and radical demands.[48] Content analyses of the leaflets distributed at the Fiat automobile plant in Cassino between 1974 and 1977 by various organizations showed that conflict themes were prominent in 40.4% of the union leaflets, compared with 58.6% of the leaflets distributed by more radical organizations (e.g., Lotta Continua) (Bagnara and Diani, 1980). The unions tended to choose tactics that "show the strength, the unity, and the responsibility of workers" (quoted in Regini, 1975, p. 192). The young activists, particularly those aligned with extraparliamentary groups, rejected the unions' traditional tactics and demands (e.g., Regalia, 1975b, p. 70). Bagnara and Diani's data confirmed that the unions largely favored planned and traditional forms of strikes, rather than the more "spontaneous" and more damaging forms (84.7%, vs. 43.5% for more radical groups). Many of the workers' demands that composed the cornerstone of the 1968–72 strike wave (e.g., egalitarianism) were heralded by the radical Left. In the March 8, 1967, issue of *Potere Operaio*, one reads the following:

We demand that skill hierarchies (*qualifiche*) and wage differentials among workers be abolished. ... Skill hierarchies pit workers against workers, they turn them into each other's foes, they instill in them the petit bourgeois prejudice of "superiority" and individual egoism. ... To abolish them, on the contrary, means to affirm workers' solidarity; workers are all equal because they are all equally exploited. (quoted in Bobbio, 1979, p. 7)

The radical groups were particularly scornful of the unions' acceptance of the institutionalization of conflict, of no-strike clauses operative during the bargaining process:

According to these gentlemen [union leaders], the class struggle, like legal holidays, should be carried out only during certain days of the year, and they decide when. But we don't wait for anybody's permission. We struggle today because we have the strength to do so ... this struggle is important because it rejects the straightjacket of collective contracts. (quoted in Bobbio, 1979, pp. 34, 47–54)

According to a leaflet distributed to Pirelli workers by Lotta Continua, "We should not wait for Wednesday's bargaining meeting. Negotiations should not interrupt the struggle! We must strike the iron while it is hot!" (quoted in Cacciari, 1969, pp. 134–5).

The student movement and the extraparliamentary groups criticized both the unions and the Communist Party from the left. According to Giovanni Falcone, students' leaflets "criticized with clarity the tactics promoted by the unions and also their demands. It was this direct and explicit attack on the unions that grabbed the workers, already sold on having a head-on confrontation" (Polo, 1989, p. 166). The students accused the unions of continually trying to put out the fires when the flames raged too high, an action that the radicals scornfully called *pompieraggio*, "firemen's work" (Viale, 1978, p. 202). In the words of *Lotta Continua* (November 8, 1969):

Trade unions, born one hundred years ago as free associations of workers to defend themselves from employers, have become today, in all countries of the world, the main instrument in the hands of employers to maintain their control over the working class. (quoted in Viale, 1978, p. 211)

Manual workers have understood that they must organize their struggle on their own; they must make their own decisions, free themselves of the unions' control. Trade unions have lost their labor characteristics; they are official organizations, public offices like any other. We do not need trade unions; we need our own strengths. The Italian worker is of age and no longer needs the unions. (Bobbio, 1979, p. 33)

The task of the revolutionary vanguard was the "unveiling of the counterrevolutionary role of trade unions and political parties involved in parliamentary politics" (Avanguardia Operaia, 1972, p. 18). On the one hand, trade unions tried to limit the scope of the students' role, as well as the more radical influences, on "their" turf. Union and party leaders often scorned the young workers involved with extraparliamentary groups and students: "You follow the students because of the skirts," alluding to the young women in the student movement (quoted in Viale, 1978, p. 171). The radicalized workers retorted that "Trade unions, while they say that they want to lead the struggle, they are comfortable only when they break it up and sit down at the bargaining table," as recounted in a 1969 leaflet handed out at the Ignis factory (quoted in Santi, 1974, p. 144). On the other hand, in order to recapture the leadership of the movement, the unions tried to appropriate many of the themes, slogans, and tactics of the radical vanguard (an effort that was labeled *cavalcare la tigre*, "ride the tiger" of the movement).

The union and party leadership were not alone in finding it difficult to understand the "mass worker" and his tactics and demands. Even older PCI and CGIL workers were not eager to accept his reliance on radical tactics and demands. As Pasquale De Stefani said,

Many, in particular the Communist workers, could not see any possible relation with the external world, beyond the relationship with the party, and sometimes there were fistfights over these issues. Many times the discussion in front of gate 20 degenerated into a fight because of the prejudices against this new external reality, composed by and large by "daddy's boys." (Polo, 1989, p. 138)

The violence that the students were theorizing and advocating was completely extraneous to the PCI tradition. The traditional Communist worker took pride in his work (most were skilled workers). He took pride in having defended factory equipment against the Nazis, who dismantled entire factories and moved them to Germany toward the end of the war. He could not understand why workers would want to destroy the source of their own livelihood. In the words of a FIOM activist in the Falck works, the traditional Communist worker was one "who works on the machines, knows how to read and understands what he is reading. . . . A Communist trade union is a 'responsible' union. That's why FIOM does not support short and disruptive strikes" (quoted in Carabelli, 1974, pp. 128, 136). For such a party and such a union, made up of skilled, and mostly northern, workers, it was difficult to understand and justify the emotional charge, the anger, the disruptive violence of the newcomers, their "refusal of work" (*rifiuto del lavoro*, according to the "equation" +*soldi* = –*lavoro*, "more money = less work") (Castellano, 1980, p. 34; see also Viale, 1978, p. 208). Lotta Continua saw the role of the vanguard as "Damage production: Do away with material incentives that tend to involve workers in production growth, refuse economic and noneconomic divisions, refuse the rhythms of production, and unhealthy environmental conditions, work hours, shifts, etc." (quoted in *Avanguardia Operaia*, 1972, pp. 17–8; see also Viale, 1978, p. 208). As Pasquale De Stefani put it, "The PCI and the unions that in years past had the merit of keeping the fire alive under the ashes . . . did not fully appreciate the new" (Polo, 1989, p. 138). Lotta Continua, Avanguardia Operaia, and other radical extraparliamentary groups were behind many of the most radical experiments in grass-roots democracy that sprang up in

1968 in many northern factories (the CUB, in particular, *comitati unitari di base*) (*Avanguardia Operaia*, 1971, 1973a, 1973b, pp. 157–208). The hallmark of those experiments was an extension of democracy, a refusal to continue to vest decision-making power in the unions (*siamo tutti delegati*, "we are all delegates") (Bobbio, 1979, p. 33). The mass meetings involving students and workers were the main organizational assets of Lotta Continua, the basis of grass-roots democracy (*assemblea operai-studenti*) (Viale, 1978, p. 167; Bobbio, 1979, p. 31). Out of those meetings came the affirmation of demands that the radical Left had been urging for some time: (1) flat wage increases for all workers, regardless of skill level; (2) elimination of the skill hierarchy; (3) abolition of piece rates (Bobbio, 1979, p. 32). In 1970 came the slogan *prendiamoci la città*, ("Let's take the city"), which generalized the struggle from the factory to the outside world, stressing the need to extend the organizational form of the *assemblea operai-studenti* to the entire territory, with mass meetings among workers from different factories (Bobbio, 1979, pp. 75–87):[49] "The discovery by the working class of the necessity to unhinge not only Agnelli's factory [Fiat] but also the social factory . . . to extend the attack from the factory to society, will become the fundamental working-class task" (Castellano, 1980, pp. 58, 67).

Thus, it is in the context of that seething climate of groups, people, and ideas that we must understand the "spontaneous" quality of the struggles of 1968 and of the *autunno caldo*: the workers' rejection of traditional union tactics and demands – in fact, their repudiation of unions and party organizations themselves, as they came to embrace the egalitarian demands of the movement.[50] It is probably fair to say that without the student movement and the radical critique by the extreme Left, the 1968–72 strike wave would not have taken such a radical course. As Viale (1978, p. 177) wrote: "The projection of relations of production on society at large would not have occurred without the encounter [of the labor movement] with the student movement."

That the egalitarian demands of the mass worker best represented his own interest there is no doubt. Being at the bottom of a highly stratified system of job classification, it was in his interest to eliminate that system. He could not wait for individual promotions (unlikely, anyway) from one job level to the next; he was pushing for immediate change, and for mass promotions. Neither could he afford to wait to improve his standard of living via the slow process of percentage wage increases; he pushed for lump-sum increases equal for all. That living conditions were very hard, particularly in some cities (e.g., Turin), can explain his demands for improved housing and transportation. That he should be concerned to increase the efforts toward development of the South is also understandable, because he had left the South, probably just a few years earlier, on his quest for a job. That he should dream of a new and better way of making cars or refrigerators or television sets reflects the physical and psychological stress of the assembly line, where he most often worked.

That the radical Left, not only the groups that came out of the student movement but also the veterans of earlier groups operating in the late 1950s and early 1960s, played a fundamental role in anticipating, amplifying, and generalizing the demands and needs of the *operaio massa* there is little doubt. That the official working-class organizations (unions and party) had to scramble both to catch up and keep up there also is little doubt. It was all too easy to place the blame for the massive mobilization on the radical Left, particularly the extraparliamentary groups that led the most radical actions (the old agitator theory again). Agnelli declared that: "Terrorism had been responsible for the radicalization of conflict: The Turin Red Brigades. They threatened supervisors and managers, and at night they shot in the legs those who had not obeyed" (Levi, 1983, p. 72).[51]

Perhaps the fact that intellectuals were also present in large numbers in the Italian unions enabled the unions to face up to the need for change and, in fact, after some initial confusion, to lead in making changes (Giugni et al., 1976, p. 133). But certainly the interactions among radical intellectuals and students and the *operaio massa* can explain the limited ways in which, by himself, "the unskilled worker involved in mass production was the *portatore* [bearer and bringer] of a blueprint for social change of his own" (Accornero, 1992, p. 59). The egalitarian demands of the movement, the rejection of the very logic of capitalist organization of production, the violence and the rejection of authority relations, the view of traditional labor organizations as instruments of control *over* rather than *for* the working class, the extension of the democratic decision-making process, and the refusal to continue to delegate authority to the traditional unions – in other words, the characteristic features of the *autunno caldo* – all must be understood in the context of this radical tradition on the left operating in Italy throughout the postwar period.

7.7. STRUCTURE AND CULTURE

Within the theoretical framework that I have adopted, disciplinary boundaries become blurred. The economists' business cycle becomes a *political* business cycle; economic relations disguised by the "invisible hand" become quite visible as social and political relations. The framework forces us to look beyond the economic motivations of individual capitalists (i.e., profit) into the political interests of the class as a whole. Within this framework, the business cycle is as much a consequence as a cause of class conflict. As we have seen, the same dialectic relationship characterizes organization and conflict. Marxist and resource-mobilization theories of collective action share the view that mobilization rests on the availability of resources. It is organization that maximizes the available resources. In Chapter 4, I embraced this approach to organization, viewing conflict as the outcome of both opportunities (favorable business cycle) and resources (organization). This chapter has added a new dimension to the study of conflict: reasons. The unskilled worker had plenty of gripes about his work, his employer, and society. This chapter has also confirmed the reciprocal relationship between organization and conflict: organization as both a cause and a consequence of conflict. For one thing, most strikes were outside of union control. As Perrot (1974,

p. 424) said of early French strikers, "41% of the strikes studied here do not have any trace [of organization], by and large, sudden strikes, brief hay fires with no time" to develop an organization. That held true not only for the heyday of working-class organization. The majority of strikes, even during the period considered in this book, still were outside of union control: brief stoppages in a department, sudden workers' responses (a work accident posing serious health risks for the workers, the announcement of a pay cut, a dismissal, a layoff) in which there was no time to contact outside unions. The circumstances of factory life required immediate responses. The extensive work of the Donovan Commission in England showed similar patterns in British strikes (see also the work by Batstone et al., 1978, 1979). The spreading of "unofficial" strikes in the late 1960s and 1970s, even in Sweden, with its tight union control over grass-roots activities, showed that much conflict occurred outside the realm of formal organization (Korpi, 1981). Most importantly, much of the 1968–72 strike wave in Italy was in the hands of informal organizations, based on networks of activists and on the solidarity of work groups.

Marxist thinkers have been well aware of the dialectic nature of conflict and organization. In the words of Rosa Luxemburg (1971, p. 66),

The overestimate and the false estimate of the role of organizations in the class struggle of the proletariat is generally reinforced by the underestimate of the unorganized proletarian mass and of their political maturity.

The work of social historians adds credibility to that statement:

In the case of organized strikes – which constitute the majority of strikes (59%) – strikes come before the organization; the strike produces its forms; the union itself is often nothing but its creation, born through and for the strike, living of its success, dying of its defeat. (Perrot, 1974, p. 424)

The strike, even when it flares up spontaneously . . . seeks the organization; better yet it expresses it or promotes it. . . . The struggle will also create the labor leaders who will lead it and who, afterward, will often take on leading roles in the plant or outside of it when employers' reactions will have forced them out. (Merli, 1972, pp. 511–12)

Innovation comes from unorganized, "spontaneous" strikes, wrote Merli (1972, p. 511), to which Perrot echoed, "the push forward comes not from a nonexistent, central organization, but from below" (Perrot, 1974, p. 499). But "below" is not an empty slot. Workers showed both great ingenuity and creativity in the course of the *autunno caldo* and subsequent struggles. As Fiat worker Roberto Sibona recalled,

In early 1969, every day there was a gang on strike, but without involving the other workers, who could continue work regardless of the strike. . . . Because of the way work was organized . . . a gang strike had little chance of extending to the whole shop. For this reason, an internal form of organization was born in order to coordinate and develop the individual gang struggles that in 1969 had sprung up like mushrooms. (Polo, 1989, p. 192)

Indeed, the most ingenious tactics, the most radical demands, and the most democratic and innovative forms of representation and shop-floor organization during the 1968–72 cycle of struggle were formulated and implemented in precisely those plants where the union presence had been weakest. Certainly the mass defiance of authority that was at the heart of the *autunno caldo*, the angry tiger that ran wild through the country in those days, did not result from any challenge mounted by formal organizations of labor. At best, it can be said that the unions had their wits about them sufficiently to try to ride the tiger. As Piven and Cloward (1979, p. 5) wrote, "Defiance does not usually characterize the activities of formal organizations," and in the case of postwar Italy, that was true even of organizations formally committed to a revolutionary ideology.[52] The defiance began with people like Pasquale De Stefani, who stopped work during normal working hours, sat down, read *l'Unità*, and ate a sandwich right in front of his supervisors.

Organization breeds institutionalization, and institutionalization means an end to violence, a decline in conflict, a channeling of protest according to a set of rules, at certain times, in certain ways, under certain circumstances, over certain issues, *come le feste comandate* (like calendar holidays). With a helping hand from the state (via the Workers' Charter) and, in many cases, from employers, by 1970–71 the unions had regained control over the movement. They were already spending in the institutional arena the assets that had been won in noninstitutionalized struggles. Certainly the growth of formal organizations during the 1970s, with their new leaders and strategies, both inside and outside the factories, was the result of those bitter grass-roots struggles, often begun as protest movements against the unions as much as against the employers. Both the economic and political capacities of the working class increased in the 1970s as the unions and the PCI rode the crest of the 1968–72 strike wave.

"Below," at the grass roots, we find not only the workers and their creative ingenuity but also at the beginning of the 1968–72 strike wave, radical extraparliamentary groups. Many of those groups encouraged the workers to take spontaneous actions (*gruppi spontaneisti*), much along the lines touted by Rosa Luxemburg. Though suspicious of the entrenched Leninist conception of organization (e.g., Lotta Continua), those groups brought to the workers a great deal of organization. They provided some basic leadership: They encouraged innovative tactics, they amplified themes, and they developed slogans. Those groups brought to the workers' movement their experience of grass-roots democracy (based on mass meetings, *assemblee*), developed during the course of their struggles against academic authorities, as well as their experience in organizing mass rallies and in fighting the police. Many of the slogans, tactics, and issues developed by those groups came to be incorporated into official union policy in the years following. Organization must be viewed in the context of formal and informal structures, material and symbolic resources, as a process of organic interaction between workers and intellectuals.

Indeed, militants and revolutionaries do not materialize out of thin air. The preceding section has described the seething ferment of people and ideas that surrounded the 1969 *autunno caldo*. Structural characteristics no doubt play important roles. They do have a great deal to say about *where* conflict will arise (in which settings: town or country, large plant or small plant, agriculture or services), *who* the actors will be (peasants, skilled or unskilled factory workers, technicians, clerical workers), and *when* conflict will erupt (at the height of the business cycle, at the height of a "long wave"). Structural factors will also help determine the issues involved and the tactics used (the *why* and the *how*). In the Italian context, skilled factory workers on maintenance tasks were relatively unconcerned with problems of supervision or restricted mobility. Their trade put them above close supervision; their work tasks required mobility. Their fears mostly concerned the erosion of skills, the basis for their privileged position. For the unskilled workers on the assembly line, the relentless repetitiveness and monotony of their work, the close supervision, the fatigue, the stress, and the low pay created sufficient grievances for radical actions.

Structures define the realm of possibilities. But within the constraints of structural determination, much of the specific content of any conflict situation will be shaped by the available patterns of cultural responses. The legacy of past struggles, the available organizational assets, the cultural and ideological frameworks for interpreting social relations, and particularly the availability of radical models will shape the tactics, the issues, and the overall tone of the struggle (*within* or *about* the rules of the game). Models of behavior must be available for people to follow. If we were to ignore that, then much of the context of the 1969 *autunno caldo* – what made it specifically Italian and different from the events in France in May 1968 or the 1926 general strike in England, the other two major labor confrontations in world history[53] – would make no sense. We have seen how many of the working-class ritualistic actions of the 1968–72 strike wave embodied the cultural traditions of southern immigrant workers. The official labor movement, the unions and the parties, in their efforts to achieve bourgeois, or at least middle-class respectability as they maneuvered to gain access to power, usurped the content and style of those struggles. Through a selective process of adoption of some of the more radical tactics and issues (*cavalcare la tigre*), and rejection of others, traditional working-class organizations (unions and parties) ultimately reaped the benefits of that long struggle, despite the fact that at the beginning, they, almost as much as the employers, had been regarded as targets of the workers' protests.

Workers in many factories, in setting up their own organizational structures (e.g., the CUB) against the will of the unions and with more militant goals,[54] showed great ingenuity in devising ways to reappropriate that knowledge of the factory world that capitalist practices had taken away from them. Their dream was to profoundly change the relations of power in capitalist enterprises, to redesign factory work. Members of radical, extraparliamentary groups and students were out in front of the factory gates, not at all factories, to be sure, but at enough key factories to introduce many workers to the language of radicalism, a sense of the possibility of making a clean break with the past, a sense of self-worth (*centralità del lavoro*), and a theoretical framework within which to interpret their lives, within which to make the larger connections between factory life and the outside world. Intellectuals close to the unions had also kept up a tradition of radicalism. A Marxist culture prevailed, with a flourishing press of papers, journals, and factory leaflets. Undoubtedly, as Calhoun (1982, p. 49) said, "culture is not autonomous; it is part of a broader social formation."[55] To neglect the role of the radical culture would be not only to forget at least part of the historical reality of what happened during and after the 1968–72 strike wave, what distinguished that wave and made it historically unique, but also to forget the legacy of an Italian who had thought long and hard about the organic relationship between radical intellectuals and mass movements: Antonio Gramsci.

7.8. THE LIMITS OF PARTICIPATION

In this chapter we saw how the *autunno caldo* and the strike wave that followed galloped from sector to sector, from larger firms to smaller firms, from city to country. In an attempt to meet the participants of the wave, we stopped at the factory gates. There we met the *operaio massa*. There, we came face to face with the young radicals of the student movement, "daddy's boys and girls," who embraced the cause of the working class. Workers and students shared their dreams with us, and their anger. We took note of the violence. And with that, we took note of some of the little acts of ordinary daily heroism: the anonymous activist at the Candy large-appliance plant who rebuked his employer, Mr. Fumagalli, with these words: "Who was it that gave you the factory? You come here and tell us that we are a great big family, but you are the one who stashes away the millions, and people leave their hands in here" (quoted in Regini, 1974, p. 31); Pasquale De Stefani, Fiat worker, who challenged his boss and "every morning, around eight o' clock ... would stop working for about twenty minutes and eat a sandwich" (Polo, 1989, p. 130). Step by step, we followed the wave as it unfolded through time and space, as it swelled along its path.

For Marxists the swelling of mobilization is the prime catalyst in the process of class formation. Marx himself provided the basic framework for an understanding of that process in a famous passage:

Economic conditions had first transformed the mass of the people of the country into workers. The domination of capital has created for this mass a common situation, common interests. This mass is thus already a class as against capital, but not yet for itself. In the struggle ... this mass becomes united, and constitutes itself as a class for itself. (Lapides, 1987, p. 34)

According to that model, the process of class formation involves the transition from a class in itself to a class for itself, from an objective class to a subjective and conscious class. It involves not only the creation of objective positions in society (class "in itself") but also, and foremost, the process of acquisition of class consciousness and the organization of the interests of the class in various forms and agencies (labor unions, working-class political parties, etc.) (class "for itself"). For Marx and for many Marxists after him, the class struggle occupied a key role in that process. To the extent that the workers recognize themselves in the course of their struggles, class conflict shapes the very process of class formation. Thus, for Rosa Luxemburg (1971, pp. 36, 38, 64), classes are formed in the course of struggle. The levels of both the economic and political organizations of the working class increase in the wake of mass struggles. Those organizational capacities then determine the level and form of the next round of struggles. Przeworski (1977, pp. 370–2) similarly argued that "objective positions are not prior to class struggles . . . classes are an effect of struggles. . . . Classes are not a datum prior to the history of concrete struggles. . . . Classes are organized and disorganized as outcomes of continuous struggles." For E. P. Thompson (1978, p. 149), "Class . . . is inseparable from the notion of 'class struggle'. . . . Class struggle is the prior, as well as the more universal concept."

Class formation is a never-ending process. Classes and class consciousness, in this historical sense, are not static entities achieved once and for all. As E. P. Thompson (1963, p. 10) wrote, "Consciousness of class arises in the same way in different times and places, but never in just the same way." In this process of the continual making and remaking of a class, one may wonder if a class is ever *really* made. As the class structure is in a constant state of change and turmoil, is a class ever really conscious?[56] More specifically, was the Italian working class class conscious, at the moment of its highest peak of mobilization in history? To answer that question we will have to look at various indicators: rates of participation in collective actions, imageries of class, political affiliations, and organizational structures.

For one thing, even at the height of mobilization, the strike wave did not sweep uniformly through the country; the movement did not involve all workers. Far from it. Large geographic areas were left untouched, particularly where peasant workers were predominant, with their problems of identification with an industrial proletariat and their individualistic attachment to the land and the community.[57] Not only many regions but also many economic sectors remained relatively quiescent. Most strike activity was confined to the industrial sector (in 1969, 62% of all strikes, 63% of all strikers, and 77% of all hours lost). Within the industrial sector, the strike movement was particularly strong in metalworking (in 1969, 32% of strikes in industry, 46% of strikers, and 67% of hours lost). Within the metalworking sector, workers in smaller plants, where a good portion of the Italian working class was concentrated, were mostly spectators, rather than participants. But even in larger plants, not everyone participated.

In most firms, participation of technical and clerical workers remained low.[58] Furthermore, white-collar workers often struck in defense of old privileges[59] or even against blue-collar workers on the side of management.[60] In most settings, blue-collar workers had to resort to tough picketing and internal rallies to get white-collar workers out of their offices.[61] Survey research confirms the lower rates of participation of clerical workers highlighted by the handful of available case studies. According to the 1971 Isvet survey (Table 7.14), clerical workers, particularly those classified in the highest positions, were much less likely than blue-collar workers to participate in various forms of collective action. Confindustria survey data on absenteeism for 1972, the first year of the survey, confirm that the rates of time lost due to strikes was 1.57 for blue-collar workers and 0.49 for white-collar workers and technicians (Confederazione Generale dell'Industria Italiana, 1974).[62]

But even the participation of blue-collar workers was far from high. The same 1971 Isvet survey indicates that approximately only (or fully?) 30% of the workers *always* participated in strikes (Table 7.14).[63] Among them, women had slightly lower rates of participation (Table 7.15). The Confindustria survey, based on a sample of smaller firms, reveals a much wider gap in participation rates between men and women (1.76 vs. 0.97). The Confindustria data also reveal that the gap was much higher in "traditional" settings (e.g., 1.60 for men vs. 0.08 for women in the South and 1.70 vs. 1.08 in the "industrial triangle" of the Northwest; 1.91 vs. 0.73 in factories with 51 to 250 employees and 2.38 vs. 2.07, almost identical rates, in the largest factories).

According to the Isvet survey, the core of militant workers, the vanguard who participated in all strikes, mass meetings, and demonstrations, who were also union members and members of the Communist Party (still fewer belonged to the more radical, extra-parliamentary groups), was only (fully?) 20% of the industrial workers. Only that minority of workers had a coherent class vision of work and societal relations; the rest, the bulk of the working class, had a fragmented consciousness and viewed work relations only partially in class terms (70%) (De Masi and Fevola, 1974a, p. 788). Paradoxically, survey research indicates that it was skilled workers who were more likely to constitute the vanguard core, although it was among the *operaio massa* that one was more likely to find the few workers who belonged to the more radical groups.

Electoral returns show that the working class was even more divided at the polls. The Italian Communist Party at the time of the 1968–72 strike wave was essentially a party of blue-collar workers (Barbagli and Corbetta, 1978; Farneti, 1983, p. 125), but not all blue-collar workers were electoral supporters of the Communist Party. The presence of two distinct political subcultures (the Socialist and the Catholic) in different regions divided the political allegiances of the working class. In the Northeast, such as Veneto, a Catholic subculture was dominant (White regions, *regioni bianche*). In central Italy (particularly in Emilia Romagna, Tuscany, and Umbria), the Socialist subculture prevailed (Red regions, *regioni rosse*).[64] The 1978 election was an exception to the rule, with blue-collar support for the Communist Party rising to 45%, compared with 25% for the Christian Democrats, but in prior elections the difference had been much narrower, with around 20–30% of blue-collar workers casting their ballots for each party (Farneti, 1983, p. 131). During the 1968–78 decade, 40% of Communist Party votes came from blue-collar

Table 7.14. *Rates of participation in collective action of blue-collar and white-collar workers*

Participation	Trade-union meetings			Plant-level assemblies			Strikes		
	BC^a	WC		BC^a	WC		BC^a	WC	
		A^b	B^c		A^b	B^c		A^b	B^c
Always	20.8^d	10.3	3.7	48.1	23.7	15.3	33.7	14.7	6.1
Often	13.3	7.6	8.0	19.1	14.7	11.7	15.0	9.7	3.1
Sometimes	24.1	19.7	20.9	16.6	21.8	30.7	21.9	22.5	21.5
Never	41.4	62.0	65.6	16.0	39.4	40.5	29.1	53.0	67.5

[a] All blue-collar workers.
[b] White-collar workers in the 3rd and 2nd (lowest) skill levels.
[c] White-collar workers in the 1st and 1st super (highest) skill levels.
[d] Percentage values.
Source: Buratto et al. (1974, pp. 298, 300, 303).

Table 7.15. *Rates of participation in collective action of male and female blue-collar workers*

Participation[a]	Trade-union meetings		Plant-level assemblies		Strikes	
	Female	Male	Female	Male	Female	Male
Always	17.5	20.0	43.6	44.5	28.9	31.1
Often	9.6	13.8	16.1	19.3	11.1	15.1
Sometimes	21.9	24.2	17.9	17.6	23.3	21.2
Never	50.4	41.5	22.1	18.2	31.8	32.3

[a] Percentage values.
Source: Buratto et al. (1974, pp. 299, 301, 304).

workers, as did 40% of Socialist Party votes (a party that had renounced any revolutionary goals since at least the years of the *centro-sinistra* governments), and 30% of Social Democrat votes (Farneti, 1983, p. 125).

Workers were similarly divided in their allegiances to specific unions, each union being rooted in different political traditions. For all the talk, the high-level meetings, and the pressure from below to achieve trade-union unity, the economic organizations of the working class (CGIL, CISL, UIL) remained divided in their party affiliations and in their strategies.

In summary, workers' rates of participation in collective action, their overall imageries of class, and their allegiances to different class organizations in both the economic and political arenas point to a somewhat fragmented class. In appears that there never was a politically united working class, a conscious working class, even at the height of the mobilization ferment. Perhaps one could marvel that such a momentous mobilization process as the 1968–72 strike wave was in the hands of only 20–30% of the industrial working class in the larger metalworking and chemical plants. Perhaps what is marvelous is that there were so many. After all, Koenker and Rosenberg (1989, pp. 299–329) show that there was limited worker involvement in strike activity even during the Russian Revolution – in 1917, Russian strikes were mostly in the hands of vanguards of skilled workers.

Whether we look at the glass as half full or half empty, certainly, the student leaflets of the time proclaimed that the moment for a revolutionary outcome was close at hand. Commenting on the resurgence of conflict at Fiat Mirafiori, Viale wrote that "The Turin experience shows that a revolutionary process has been set off" (quoted in Bobbio, 1979, p. 40). Many of the workers, particularly those close to the student movement, harbored visions of imminent revolutionary triumph. Viewed in that light, then both the Italian Communist Party, the largest Communist party in the West at the time, and the workers' mobilization movement were failures. The party, despite its name and stated goals, failed to seize the moment. In fact, throughout the postwar period, the party never really wanted to seize the moment (Farneti, 1983, p. 158). As for the workers, many of them primed to a high state of militancy and treasuring the class imagery of changed social relations, they took on the employers and took on the police, but never mounted a more global challenge to the state. Instead, the unions, the party, and the movement became bogged down in the quagmire of party politics and administrative inefficiency and resistance, looking to achieve social reforms by playing the parliamentary game (Carrieri and Donolo, 1986, pp. 97–118). Indeed, when viewed against that yardstick, both the unions and the party, both the economic and political wings, may have failed. With all that in mind, the outcome of the 1968–72 strike wave, despite all the economic and political gains obtained, must have seemed a dismal failure to those who dreamed of social revolution. The analysis of that failure thus brings us back to Chapter 6 and to the limitations of revolutionary initiatives in capitalist societies. If it did not happen in Italy, with the strongest Communist Party in the West, with its tradition of working-class militancy, with its highly politicized unions, with its counter-hegemonic culture of revolutionary discourse, then can it ever happen anywhere in the West?

7.9. STRIKE WAVES: POLITICAL OR ECONOMIC EXPLANATIONS?

The analyses in this chapter have made clear the characteristics (the actors, the actions, the demands, the individual and collective acts of defiance and challenge to authority relations, the violence) and the temporal dynamics of strike waves. We got a glimpse of the thousand little events that made up the "big" event of 1969 and surrounding years. But for all the descriptive power of the pages of this chapter, the causes of such momentous outbreaks of conflict remain elusive.

For Piven and Cloward, "Sudden hardship, rather than rising expectations, is probably the more important precondition for mass turmoil" (Piven and Cloward, 1979, p. 9). We have already seen in Chapter 4 that economic hardship theories of strikes do not fare well as explanations of Italian strike waves. We may not know much about the causes of workers' mobilization, but we do know this: In Italy, the two strike waves of the postwar period had immediate causes in the renewals of major collective contracts (metalworking, in particular) under favorable labor-market conditions. Piven and Cloward, however, provide a more general explanation of mass disruption movements as the results of simultaneous occurrences of different social dislocations (Piven and Cloward, 1979, pp. 7, 8, 14). With specific reference to the late 1960s movement of protest in Italy, Tarrow similarly wrote that mass movements were more likely to erupt when there occurred "Major transitions to new productive processes, international division of labour and internal power relations" (Tarrow, 1989a, p. 49). These explanations, unfortunately, by providing a list of different economic and political causes, leave unresolved the problem of pinning down precisely the causes of strike waves and of disentangling the causal relationships among various social processes. For example, what are the specific mechanisms that link the international division of labor to national mobilization movements? The explanatory power of an interpretative model may be lost in causal explanations that tend to become too vague in their aspirations to be omni-comprehensive.

Shorter and Tilly were more specific about the timing of strike waves. For them, "The timing of strike waves depends largely on the timing of political crisis" (Shorter and Tilly, 1974, p. 105):

> We do not intend to say that political crises cause strike waves to happen; instead, it seems more sensible to claim that politics constitute an important kind of precondition for the eruption of large-scale workers' movements. . . . We are pointing to a sense of political crisis as a prime factor in bringing a large number of men together for collective action.

Tarrow shares this interpretation. With reference to "protest cycles," which broadly include social and labor-movement forms of collective action, Tarrow (1989b, p. 49) commented that "Protest cycles arise when the political opportunity structure expands for a number of groups at the same time, in the presence of deep grievances and increasing solidarity." Thus, for Tarrow, both "deep grievances" (as suggested by relative-deprivation theories) and "increasing solidarity" (as suggested by resource-mobilization theories) are important preconditions for cycles of protest. Groups must have both reasons to do battle and resources with which to struggle (as in Marxist theories). But they must also have opportunities (Tilly, 1978), and such opportunities arise within the "political-opportunity structure."[65]

A "political" interpretation of the events of the 1969 *autunno caldo* could account for the unusual character of much strike activity during that year and subsequent years. More generally, a "political" interpretation of strike waves resonates well with the deeply political nature of Italian strikes: the often direct and explicit involvement of the state as a target of protest, the involvement of radical Marxist groups in the management of many strikes, the highly political nature of the unions (in their rhetoric and language of class, in their ties with political parties, in their continued use of the strike as a political weapon). Unfortunately, there are several problems with a political explanation of strike waves: First, during the period 1950–78, there were thirty distinct incidences of political crises, as reflected in the premature fall of a government; but there were only two strike waves during that same period. Furthermore, the painstaking empirical work that I carried out in Chapter 6 in order to disentangle the relationship between workers' militancy and cabinet crises showed that, if anything, Italian unions moderated their militancy for the duration of a crisis, often revoking or postponing long-planned strikes: No sense striking if there is no government to listen to one's demands.

The reader who endured Chapter 6 may question such a narrow interpretation of political crises and of the opening of political opportunities for labor (i.e., cabinet crises). After all, I argued there that government crises never presented genuine opportunities for deep political change in Italy. Rather, they reflected the structural instability of government coalitions within the postwar political formula. If I relax my criteria and adopt a broader view of political change, it turns out that there were, indeed, two major shifts in the political position of labor in the national power structure: *centro sinistra*, and *compromesso storico* and *unità nazionale*. The number of these broader political crises is remarkably identical to the number of strike waves. The problem, however, is that political change seems to have followed rather than preceded strike waves. As I showed in the preceding chapter, the *centro sinistra* came shortly after the 1959–63 strike wave and the politics of *compromesso storico* and the government of *unità nazionale* came a few years after the 1968–72 strike wave.

Third, if strike waves are mainly related to national politics, how do we account for the fact that many strike waves seem to have occurred at approximately the same time in different countries?[66]

But in rejecting a political explanation of strike waves, are we left with the business-cycle explanation? A business-cycle interpretation of strike waves is particularly appealing. First, to the extent that changes in the state of the labor market directly affect the bargaining position of labor and power relations between classes (i.e., class capacities), the business cycle affects the level of industrial conflict: When the cycle is on the upswing, the number of strikes soars. Second, the two major strike waves of the postwar period in Italy indeed occurred at intersections between renewals of major collective contracts and favorable labor-market conditions. Third, a business-cycle interpretation seems to account for broader aspects of working-class mobilization processes. Business-cycle effects are generally significant in statistical models of both unionization and strikes, and surges in union membership go hand in hand with the outbursts of conflict typical of strike waves. As Goetz-Girey (1965, pp. 146–7) put it,

> The fundamental movements that cause strikes are often the same as those that cause union growth. When we observe a correlation between union growth and strike activity, that does not necessarily mean that union growth is at the root of increases in strike activity. Rather, the same causes, in particular, industrialization and economic cycles, affect both union growth and strike activity.

There is a major problem, however, with a business-cycle interpretation of strike waves. There were seven complete business cycles in Italy between May 1945 and December 1977, as we saw in Chapter 3 (Table 3.9, p. 75), but there were only two distinct strike waves during the same period. There were only eleven strike waves in the period between 1890 and 1960 in France (Shorter and Tilly, 1974, p. 143), and even fewer in Italy, partly because of the long tenure of the Fascist regime, during which strikes were forbidden (Bordogna and Provasi, 1979). Yet there were many more business cycles than that during the same period. Clearly, there is no correspondence between business cycles and cycles of struggle or strike waves. Although a business-cycle interpretation of strikes may well explain part of the fluctuation in the levels of strike activity, as the econometric findings presented in Chapters 2 and 3 indicate, it leaves unexplained these major upsurges of industrial conflict.

Yet, despite the failure of business cycles to explain the occurrence of strike waves, the historical record and much of the empirical evidence presented in this book point to the close connection between strike waves and the economy. In particular, the two periods of postwar economic expansion in the late 1950s–early 1960s and late 1960s remarkably coincide with the timing of the two postwar cycles of struggles (see the plots of numbers of strikes, strikers, and hours lost, Figures 1.3, 1.4, and 1.5, pp. 4–5, and the plots of ISCO cyclical indicator, Figure 3.2, p. 61, of capacity utilization, Figure 3.3, p. 61, of hours worked in manufacturing industry and of work-related injuries in industry, Figure 7.1, p. 276).

My trouble now is this: Having excluded both political explanations and business-cycle and economic-hardship explanations for strike waves, are we left without any explanation? This is not a good predicament to find myself in at the end of the book. Perhaps, the fact that there are as many strike waves as cycles of economic expansion and of shifts in the political position of labor in the power structure is pure coincidence. Perhaps, the fact that political change followed the periods of intense working-class mobilization is merely a reflection of a very restrictive conception of time and causation. But the connection between the economic and the political, between class conflict and the economic and political organization of capitalist societies may also provide clues to finally find an answer to the question: What causes strike waves? One thing is clear: In order to find an answer to that question I need to drag the reader into further investigative work.

8

Countermobilization processes: reactions by the state and employers to strike waves

The action effects of the mobilization drive of one unit depend considerably on the degree to which this drive triggers *counter-mobilizations* in other units in the same system or situation, which seek to neutralize the new power of the mobilizing unit or to block its intended self-changes . . . this is the case with mobilization; the mobilization of a unit frequently does trigger the mobilization of opponents.
Etzioni (1968, pp. 412–13)

The great wave-year mobilizations . . . were invariably rewarded with some kind of legislative success, the ultimate touchstone of the value of political action.
Shorter and Tilly (1974, p. 145)

It would be tedious in the extreme to take the reader along every inch of the road travelled by the main currents of the fear . . . It is however possible to convey in reasonably clear terms how these currents moved across the country.
Lefebvre (1973, p. 171)

8.1. SWITCHING SIDES: THE VIEW FROM ABOVE

Mobilization of a group is likely to lead to countermobilizations by other groups. In the case of industrial conflict both political and economic elites may respond. And if the telltale signs of the magnitude of a mobilization process are the speed and extent of the elites' responses, then the 1968–72 strike wave was a momentous process. Political elites reacted quickly, in some cases repressing but mostly facilitating those official, large-scale organizations (i.e., unions) that could control conflict. In the case of industrial conflict, political elites could also remain aloof from the movement, letting social classes deal with their problems on their own. Prime Minister Giolitti adopted such a hands-off strategy during the 1919–20 "red years" (*biennio rosso*). That strategy proved fatal to both Giolitti and the working class, and that may have been an important reason why the Italian state never followed such a policy in the postwar period. The *memoria storica* (historical memory) lingers on, not only for the working class.

Italian capitalists, unable to count on an authoritative response by the state to the *autunno caldo* (in fact, confronted with the state's facilitative response that strengthened labor's position) pondered long and hard on how to deal with the problems that the changing balance of class forces had created in their factories. As labor defensively entrenched to protect its gains, employers faced rising labor costs and increasing *rigidities* constraining their use of labor. The issue of *labor mobility* (the freedom to fire workers and move them around inside the plant) became the employers' battle cry.

This chapter will trace the basic elements of the state's response to workers' mobilization: repression of the most radical fringes of the movement and reward of the organizations. This chapter will also tell the story of how employers attempted to regain control of their factories and how they ultimately succeeded. Basically, employers tried both to get rid of the most militant vanguard of workers (via layoffs and transfers) and to decrease the weight of labor in the mix of the factors of production (capital, labor, and raw materials). Furthermore, because large factories had become sites of ongoing conflict and labor rigidities, employers turned to small factories for labor peace and flexibility. Finally, while individual employers were busy trying to recapture control of their firms, using a variety of short-term and long-term, soft and hard measures, they were also trying to develop a collective response to the changed climate of class relations.[1]

The account of the state's and employers' strategies in response to labor mobilization tells a fascinating tale of how the class struggle affects the path of history.

8.2. STATE RESPONSES

The world of politics reacts quickly to mobilization from below.[2] Each strike wave in Italy brought out conservative political reactions. In 1960, following the resurgence of class conflict in the preceding year, the most conservative wing of the Christian Democrat Party (DC) formed a new coalition government, with crucial votes from the right-wing monarchic and Fascist parties. In the summer of 1964, in the midst of negotiations for the formation of the Moro *centro–sinistra* government (involving DC, PSI, PRI and PSDI), right-wing conservative forces headed by General De Lorenzo[3] were plotting a coup d'etat (Turone, 1984, pp. 309–12). Again, in December 1970, Fascist forces and elements of the bourgeoisie mounted an abortive coup d'etat, led by Junio Valerio Borghese (Turone, 1984, pp. 427–8).[4] Black (Fascist) terrorism soared in the years immediately after the *autunno caldo*.

But aside from such obscure political maneuvering at the margins between the most reactionary political and economic forces, repression by police and the courts was a more typical response. At the end of the 1969 *autunno caldo* on January 27, 1970, the minister of the interior, Franco Restivo, reported to the Senate that in the months of September–December 1969, labor conflicts had resulted in 8,396 criminal charges. A total of 14,036 offenses had been prosecuted: 235 charges for personal injuries, 179 for property damage and disruption, 4 for unlawful restraint, 124 for illegal possession of firearms and explosives, 1,712 for personal violence, 1,610 for railroad blocks, 29 for threats to the security of public transportation,

3,325 for trespass on factory premises and public buildings, 1,376 for interruption of public services (Miata et al., 1970, p. 3). Brutal police assaults against workers who were on strike and police raids into factories on strike with mounting tolls of wounded and killed were almost daily occurrences. Two trade-union pamphlets, *14000 denunce* (Borgomeo and Forbice, 1970) and *Repressione!* (Miata et al., 1970), gave detailed accounts of the events and a chronology of both police and court reactions to the increasing of conflict.

The state's use of the stick at times of such high levels of labor conflict often was tempered by simultaneously offering the carrot. While the police were busy battering students and workers across the country and the courts were clogged with cases relating to the *autunno caldo*, the Italian Parliament was nervously debating a proposed law to bring conflict within a legal framework. That new labor law, law no. 300, better known as the Workers' Charter, which had been in parliamentary committees for many years as part of the *centro-sinistra* package, was hastily passed in May 1970. We have encountered that law many times in this book. We have already seen how effective it was in restructuring labor relations, as it provided, for the first time, a package of plant-level legal guarantees for workers and unions.

The highly disruptive characteristics of the 1969 *autunno caldo*, with its radicalization of demands and tactics and its mass defiance of authority relations, seem to qualify that strike wave as one of the typical "mass disruption" movements that Piven and Cloward (1979) described. The fact that the strike movement forced authorities to make concessions lends further credibility to Piven and Cloward's characterization. From the state, the workers obtained the new legal framework that strengthened workers' and unions' bargaining position in the workplaces. In particular, the Workers' Charter extended labor's "citizenship" rights in the economic arena (not just the political arena), in firms employing more than 15 workes: the rights to plant-level organizations, to plant-level bargaining, to hold assemblies inside the plant, and to appeal employers' decisions to transfer and fire workers. There was another way in which the 1969 *autunno caldo* closely resembled Piven and Cloward's model for mass disruption movements. The concessions by political authorities were aimed at bringing the movement into a more institutionalized framework. It was because of the guarantees to the "official" unions sanctioned in the law that the extraparliamentary Left renamed the Workers' Charter the "Unions' Charter" or, worse yet, the "Employers' Charter" (Comitato di Difesa e di Lotta Contro la Repressione, 1970). The charter strengthened the unions, while at the same time clipping the wings of the movement. The law empowered the unions to become the watchdogs over labor, particularly to monitor against the most radical fringes of the movement. Little by little, as we saw in Chapter 7, the unions did indeed succeed in bridling the movement, translating the disruptive power of the movement into organizational growth. In a stormy process of rejection of some tactics and demands, and appropriation of others, of isolation and co-optation of leaders, the unions tamed the tiger. The research by Tarrow on the protest movements in Italy showed that the peak of mobilization lasted from

1967 to 1969. After that date, conflict, although remaining at high and even increasing levels, took on more traditional and less disruptive forms under the institutional control of the official union organizations (Tarrow, 1989a, pp. 81–2). As Piven and Cloward said, "Concessions are rarely unincumbered. If they are given at all, they are usually part and parcel of measures to integrate the movement into normal political channels and to absorb its leaders into stable institutional roles" (Piven and Cloward, 1979, p. 32). Thus, although authorities may empower official organizations, they mainly are responding to the disruptive vanguard of a movement (Piven and Cloward, 1979, p. xxi). As the movement swells, elites respond, "And one of their responses is to cultivate those lower-class organizations which begin to emerge in such periods, for they have little to fear from organizations, especially organizations which come to depend upon them for support" (Piven and Cloward, 1979, p. xxii).

Thus, again, short-term success must be evaluated in the context of long-term failure. If the dream of many of the participants in the strike wave (*i sessantottini*, "the generation of 1968") was a social revolution, involving deep structural transformations of social, political, and production relationships, that dream was frustrated. But for all the limitations and ambiguities surrounding the explicit intention of the Workers' Charter to curb conflict, the law did provide labor with basic means to fight back against the tidal wave of employers' reactions.

To understand how extensively the Workers' Charter facilitated labor's efforts to redress an unfavorable balance of class forces, let us take a closer look at the unions' use of the law. An empirical investigation directed by Treu (1975, 1976b), involving 4,317 cases of appeals to the labor courts on the basis of the Workers' Charter in 57 provinces between 1970 and 1973, showed that unions tended to appeal to the charter in situations of structural weakness (small firms[5], White provinces).[6] The charter gave workers in smaller firms, the ones where the trade-union presence was weaker and labor relations were more paternalistic and repressive, a powerful legal instrument to fight their employers. The frequency of appeals to the labor courts under the provisions of the charter was much higher for workers in newly unionized firms and smaller firms (Melucci and Rositi, 1975, pp. 152, 158). Unions also were more likely to win in those situations.[7] In White provinces, the unions used the charter to impose on reluctant employers the new balance of power via (defensive and offensive) political demands (Melucci and Rositi, 1975, p. 169).

No doubt, the charter helped to institutionalize a new system of labor relations in which unions became legitimate actors in the firms with specific rights under the law. By 1973, after just three years, the charter had partly achieved its goals. The frequency of appeals to the labor courts over traditional issues increased, whereas that of political issues decreased (Melucci, 1975, p. 262). Political issues were prominent in actions lodged against firms newly unionized under conditions of strong resistance from emloyers. Furthermore, the frequency with which individual workers invoked the law kept increasing while that for trade unions kept declining (Melucci, 1975, p. 261). Because unions tended to appeal to the charter in

Table 8.1. *Involvement of the Ministry of Labor in labor disputes*

Agency	1966	1967	1968	1969	1970
Ministry of Labor	1	2	1	7	8
Provincial or regional labor office	2	2	4	13	7
With personal involvement of the minister	–	–	–	18[a]	22[b]

[a] Acted in 18 of 39 cases submitted.
[b] Acted in 22 of 77 cases submitted.
Source: Giugni et al. (1976, pp. 197–8).

situations of structural weakness,[8] the decline in the unions' use of the charter, as unions rather than as individual workers, signified the institutionalization of the unions in the new system of industrial relations. Furthermore, a follow-up study by Treu showed that appeals to the charter and its labor courts became increasingly extensive over time. If we set the number of labor cases brought before the courts under the charter at 100 in 1970, the index would have the following temporal pattern: 1970 = 100, 1973 = 112, 1974 = 226 and around 170 thereafter. The incidence of individual labor cases involving social-welfare provisions was even higher: 1970 = 100, 1973 = 150, 1974 = 382, 1975 = 470, 1977 = 347 (Treu, 1984, p. 503).

During the 1968–72 strike wave, the state also took a much more active role in mediating conflict. The data in Table 8.1, compiled by the Interdisciplinary Study Committee set up in 1970 in the government Institute for Economic Planning (ISPE, Istituto di Studi per la Programmazione Economica), chaired by Gino Giugni, show that the Ministry of Labor became increasingly involved directly in labor disputes during the strike wave (Giugni et al., 1976, pp. 197–8). Ministerial involvement took on a variety of forms and occurred at various levels (provincial labor offices, regional labor offices, Labor Ministry, and the minister personally). The intervention of the ministry was not simply one of mediation and arbitration. Labor ministers co-signed agreements, suggested their own proposals for resolving the dispute,[9] used the power and influence of the ministry to coax and pressure the parties into a settlement, and publicly chastised reluctant parties in the news media. "The Red minister," Carlo Donat Cattin, a Christian Democrat, shocked conservatives and moderates alike by often speaking out against employers.

The neo-Marxist literature of the 1970s on the nature of the capitalist state highlighted the structural constraints on state policies designed to promote a business climate favorable to private capitalist investment and accumulation (Offe and Ronge, 1975; Block, 1977). That ultimately meant keeping the level of class conflict down.[10] For instance, the Bank of Italy pursued deflationary ("cooling") policies after each strike wave. The drastic increases in interest rates and the cost of money imposed by the Bank of Italy in 1963 brought about a sudden, deep recession in 1964, characterized by a drastic fall in the level of employment, even in heavily industrialized regions such as Lombardy.[11] The Left accused the government of "blackmailing labor" (*ricatto congiunturale*) via an engineered recession. Many employers, as well, protested loudly, accusing the government of having brought the *miracolo economico* to a halt. During the boom years, many firms had financed their expansion with money borrowed from the banks. When the cost of money soared and the demand for goods declined, many overexposed employers folded, and they blamed the government. But the most enlightened capitalists understood the purpose of the government's monetary policies.[12] The class struggle often calls for drastic sacrifices within the upper class itself, the Meiji restoration in Japan being a good case in point. No doubt, the end result was a sharp decline in the level of labor militancy, which had reached unprecedented highs during the 1959–63 rounds of contract renewals. The government played the deflationary trump again in 1970, but with less success, because of greater union organizational strength (Valli, 1976, p. 83; Salvati, 1984, p. 120). The fluctuation-devaluation of the lira in February 1973 by the Bank of Italy allowed employers to pass on to consumers the burden for the high wage increases obtained by workers in preceding years.

In conclusion, the Italian state appears to have reacted quickly to each strike wave, with the aim of reducing conflict. In 1963, when the balance of class forces was clearly in favor of the capitalist class, mostly repressive measures were applied. In 1969, with labor in a much stronger position, with conflict at much higher levels, more disruptive and more diffused than a few years earlier, the state quickly tried to extend greater rights to workers on the shop floor and, more broadly, incorporate labor into the political framework of the state. Concessions, however, went hand in hand with antilabor measures, for the authorities again applied the same monetary policies that had proved successful in 1963. Nor did those concessions lead to any decrease in police repression of workers' and students' protests. State repression was not limited to any particular decade, but the mixture of hard and soft repressive measures was more balanced in the wake of the second strike wave. The working class had won that for itself on the field of battle.

8.3. THE LONG AFTERMATH

From the state, workers obtained certain basic rights that extended citizenship in the economic sphere. From their employers, industrial workers wrested the highest wage increases in the postwar period (Figure 5.12, p. 184). As shocking as the *autunno caldo* had been, as painfully damaging to the traditional conceptions of authority in the workplace, the employers hoped that with the passage of the Workers' Charter in 1970 and the signing of costly contracts in that same year they had put all that behind them. French employers had that good fortune in the wake of May of 1968. But that was not to be for the Italian employers. What *Fortune* magazine had said of the costly 1948 and 1950 contracts that General Motors had signed with the United Auto Workers could not be said in the case of Fiat or other Italian companies: "GM may have paid a billion for peace [but] it got a bargain. General Motors has regained control over . . . the crucial management function" (Bowles et al., 1983, p. 74). The 1969 *autunno caldo* dragged on for several more autumns, accumulating gains for the workers: greater union control in the areas of layoffs, internal transfers, and promotion criteria, abolition of or strict limitations on incentives and the piecework system, effective shortening of the workweek, reductions in the pace of production, elimination of the most unhealthy and dangerous jobs, and redesign of production processes to make work more meaningful. During the 1969–74 period, yearly wage increases were greater than in any previous year since the 1950s (Dell'Aringa, 1976, p. 51). As Giovanni Agnelli put it,

> In 1968–69, with the *autunno caldo*, we were not disappointed by the brutality of protest, but by the fact that after the shock there was no change. In 1968, in Paris, a half-revolution occurred; but three weeks later the Gaullist march took place in the Champs-Elysées. Instead, we experienced a continuous loss of managerial authority until the march of the 40,000 in Turin in 1980. For us, then, the lack of equilibrium between management and unions inside the factories lasted ten to twelve years. That cost us dearly. It was very expensive for employers. (Levi, 1983, p. 9)

Indeed, not only Fiat's authority structure but also those of many Italian firms came out of the experience of the years of *conflittualità permanente* almost completely shattered.[13] In a national survey, 90% of corporate managers believed that their authority had suffered a major setback (Derossi, 1982, p. 101).

The atmosphere changed drastically inside Italian factories. Paternalism[14] and authoritarianism (the carrot and the stick), the two pillars of the employers' approach to labor relations throughout the 1950s and 1960s, gave way to more democratic forms of labor relations. The rhythms of production became less intense. As Roberto Sibona recalled,

> Fatigue was greatly diminished; I never experienced again rhythms of production as high as before. In some departments, you worked half an hour and went on break for half an hour; in our department, from some 600 engines a day we went down to 400. . . . The gains had been so significant that we had the sensation of holding the plant in our hands. (Polo, 1989, p. 194)

Roberto Sibona's account reflects more than just the situation at Fiat. True to the unions' slogan *lavorare meno per lavorare tutti*,[15] the number of working hours stipulated in the collective contracts and overtime hours kept declining (Barca and Magnani, 1989, p. 35). During the three-year period between 1971 and 1973, the total number of hours worked in manufacturing industries declined 4.3% in 1971, 4.4% the following year, and 2.0% in 1973 (Barca and Magnani, 1989, pp. 35–7) (see Figure 7.1, p. 276). Those declines were not due to any shrinking of the labor force. In fact, even per-capita hours worked declined at the following yearly rate: 3.3% in 1971, 3.4%, and 4.1%. By 1974, industrial workers, substantially the same in number as in 1970, had achieved a per-capita reduction in work time of 11.3% (Barca and Magnani, 1989, p. 36).

Unions, fearful of an employers' backlash that would use layoffs and internal mobility as means to break the back of militancy (and there is considerable evidence to substantiate their fears), took an increasingly defensive stance. Symbolic of that strategy was the unions' slogan during the second half of the 1970s: *la scala mobile non si tocca!* ("don't touch the wage escalator agreement!"). In the context of the new balance of class forces, layoffs in the large firms became virtually impossible. Even internal mobility (workers' transfers) were subject to a continual process of negotiation, renegotiation, and sometimes conflict.

From the employers' viewpoint, those labor victories translated into so many encroachments on managerial prerogatives, so many *rigidities* restricting their use of labor. The employers' ability to use the carrot and the stick as means to maintain factory discipline and productivity had been severely limited because of increased workers' power inside the factories, deriving from the more democratic legal framework established by the Workers' Charter. Many of the traditional inducements (e.g., promotions) had been brought under union and workers' control; on the steel industry, see Villa (1986, pp. 182–202). The length of service in any skill level and the conditions for promotion were all specified in both national and plant-level contracts, severely curtailing the despotic power supervisors had formerly held. The individual piece rate as a form of incentive disappeared, swept away by the tide of protest. Automatic mechanisms for wage increases (e.g., seniority and *scala mobile*) became the most important items in determining wages.[16] High rates of absenteeism and union freezes on overtime meant that employers could meet peak demand only by maintaining larger numbers of full-time workers. As Guido Carli discouragingly put it at the time of his presidency of Confindustria,

We are in the situation we are in because we combined the worst of two systems: we have taken responsibilities away from the entrepreneur without, however, eliminating him; we have paved the road to state intervention without, however, planning it. We have corrupted both socialism and capitalism at the same time. We could not have done worse. (Scalfari, 1977, pp. 68–9)

Higher labor costs, declining profits, increasing rigidities in the use of the work force, permanent microlevel conflict, continual bargaining at several levels (interconfederal, confederal, territory, group, plant, department), often over the same issues, loss of "managerial prerogatives," collapse of the firm's authority structure: That's how the employers saw the *autunno caldo* and its long aftermath – labor's most epic years.

8.4. THE GREAT FEAR: FROM PATERNALISM TO PERSONNEL MANAGEMENT

Large-scale mobilization is always worrisome to public authorities and the upper classes, regardless of the location of conflict: the streets, poor neighborhoods, the schools. When conflict arises right inside their factories, however, it is much more difficult for the upper classes to escape it or ignore it. For the industrial upper class, 1969 came as a severe shock, a traumatic experience. The higher cost of labor and the continual disruptions of production did not frighten them as much as the complete breakdown of authority. A worker at Candy put it very well:

This is what really bugs management: the collapse of the whole authority system. They complain to us not so much because productivity is low, but because in the assembling department people just lie down on the lines. . . . It is the authority system; in the factory one is supposed to work, one is supposed to hold a certain demeanor; if this crumbles it is a big blow to them. (quoted in Regini, 1974, p. 51)

All of the available surveys of employers' attitudes agreed on one point: 1969 was a "traumatic experience" for many entrepreneurs. Small and first-generation entrepreneurs, particularly when located in smaller, rural communities, experienced "rage, shame, and frustration" with the onset of the strikes, the plant occupations, the rallies through the village, the pickets, banners, and signs in front of their houses – in a word, the public exposure of their troubles before the community (Martinelli, 1978, pp. 32, 57; Associazione Industriale Lombarda, 1983):

The only event that really crushed me and resulted in a crisis of conscience was 1968, for the difficulties in communicating with workers and finding common ground, and for the feeling of impotence that came with it. (quoted in Martinelli, 1978, p. 58)

The words of that small entrepreneur from Lombardy capture well the way many employers experienced the "hot autumn." In one survey, the words most commonly used by 663 corporate managers to describe their reactions were "bewilderment," "dismay," and "panic" (Derossi, 1982, p. 106). Many of those managers said they had suffered psychological trauma (Derossi, 1982, p. 102).

Feeling themselves under siege, some entrepreneurs "packed their suitcases and left for Brazil" (quoted in Martinelli, 1978, p. 31). Others, "overcome with discouragement, took their money abroad, not for speculative reasons, but for fear," as a demoralized entrepreneur confessed in an interview (quoted in Martinelli, 1978, p. 29).[17] Indeed, it is noteworthy that the timing of the two major waves of illegal export of capital from Italy coincided with the two major waves of industrial conflict and their related political events (e.g., the formation of a Center-Left government in 1962).[18] As Vicarelli, an economist for the Bank of Italy, wrote,

The Italian experience of the past decade [the 1960s] witnessed the extraordinary growth of a particular type of outflow of capital: the illegal export of bills. In the 1960–69 period, out of a total gross outflow of 19,000 million dollars, 44% took the form of export of bills. This figure provides only an idea of the average dimension of the phenomenon that in certain periods, particularly in 1962–64 and in 1968–69, achieved particularly high peaks. (Vicarelli, 1970, p. 322)

Some entrepreneurs left the country; others, less fearful but still cautious, stashed their money away in the safe havens of Swiss banks. But the vast majority stayed. In the scathing words of one employer, "Those who run away with family and suitcases are not entrepreneurs" (quoted in Martinelli, 1978, p. 24). That majority who remained began to look for ways to recoup their losses. Later in this chapter, I will analyze the ways in which Italian employers organized their counteroffensive, both inside and outside their firms. But before doing that, I would like to understand why Italian employers were so completely unprepared for the events of 1969, why their surprise and shock were so traumatic. To understand that situation, we need to analyze the employers' attitudes toward labor, attitudes with roots going far back in history. Let us consider what the Stanford Research Institute had to say. The institute was called in by the Italian Parliament in 1950 to study the state of the Italian metalworking industry. On the basis of a survey of some 120 firms, the Stanford team concluded in its final report that

[Italian] management is guided by the idea that since it has the property right in physical plant facilities, it has absolute power to control all aspects of plant operation. . . . Too little regard is held by management groups for the mental attitude of workers. . . . This attitude is basically one of aloof condescension. . . . In return for paternalistic welfare benefits, management has been able to win a considerable measure of filial gratitude from the workers. (CISIM, 1952, pp. 268–9)

Back then, in 1950, labor relations were based primarily on a mixture of paternalism and authoritarianism. Not even the larger firms had modern personnel departments specifically devoted to personnel management. There had been no need for any of that under the protective umbrella of the Fascist regime. In the words of the Stanford Research Institute,

The management function of "industrial relations" . . . requires wider application throughout Italy. It includes the treatment of workers as associates in an enterprise, and recognizes the important contributions they can make in its success or failure. This attitude may be difficult to adopt by a management trained under a regime which promoted the idea that workers are wards of the state, and that they must be controlled by regulation rather than negotiation. . . . Labor–management relations are so poor as to prejudice any real cooperative endeavor. (CISIM, 1952, pp. 39, 67)

Italian workers could not have agreed more strongly with that last statement. In the report by ACLI (1953), the Italian Association of Christian Workers, one reads that

[We] workers treat our dogs much better. Employers should treat us better, too! [p. 31]

Human relations are not human. We have gone back to the times of slavery. The watchword is "production," "production." [p. 22]

That was in the 1950s, the decade of "repressive development," to give it Salvati's term. But surely things would eventually change. And things did indeed change, as we saw in Chapter 6. Yet even in 1976, many employers still explained their shock over 1969 in the same terms (quoted in Martinelli, 1978, pp. 58, 60): "For me, the company is a big family," "I treated them [workers] like my own children." Paternalism dies hard; 71.8% of employers interviewed by Bonazzi et al. (1972, p. 361) favored a paternalistic approach to labor relations. Employers whose firms totaled lower sales (<50 million lire) were much more likely to hold paternalistic views (81.0%, compared with 50.3% in firms with sales ranging between 201 and 500 million lire). Of course, paternalism is never just about parental love. Consider one more time the report of the Stanford Research Institute:

Frequently, management has acted like a parent in withholding these benefits when a worker has been recalcitrant or undisciplined . . . Management has not been like a parent in helping labor to mature, to reach a state where it can share in the family councils, to provide for its own welfare, and to contribute its initiative to the family harmony. (CISIM, 1952, pp. 268–9)

Thus, paternalism and authoritarianism often went hand in hand. The relationship between paternalistic employers and their workers was like the relationship between father and son depicted by Gavino Ledda in his novel *Padre Padrone*: a relationship of despotic and heavy-handed authoritarianism. Interestingly enough, the same small-scale employers in the survey by Bonazzi and associates were almost twice as likely as large-scale entrepreneurs (52.4% vs. 29.1%) to attribute changes in productivity to workers' willingness or reluctance to work, rather than to organizational factors (Bonazzi et al., 1972, p. 358). That paternalism and repression often went together was confirmed by a 1971–72 survey of 663 corporate managers: The same managers who embraced a paternalistic approach to class relations were quite willing to support the use of repressive measures to quell conflict (Talamo, 1979, p. 66).

Employers' paternalistic and authoritarian attitudes, as might be expected, were accompanied by antiunion attitudes. In the mid-1960s, in one of the first surveys of employers to be found in the literature, 51% of the employers interviewed rejected the concept of unions altogether (Farneti, 1970, p. 134). The figure was 62% among smaller entrepreneurs, as compared with 37% among larger ones. Furthermore, 73% of the interviewees believed that unions did not serve workers' "real" interests (Farneti, 1970, p. 131). Again, employers in larger firms (managers, in particular) were more likely to view trade unions as serving the workers' interests (63% vs. 38%) (Farneti, 1970, pp. 131–2). Regardless of firm size, the UIL was viewed as the lesser of the union evils (28%), followed by CISL; CGIL trailed at 6% (Farneti, 1970, p. 134).

Not surprisingly, given their attitudes, many employers turned increasingly toward the right wing of the political spectrum as the mobilization tide of the *autunno caldo* engulfed them. Talamo's survey of a sample of Italian managers showed that most managers favored either a repressive (41%) or a paternalistic (35%) response to the escalation in conflict. Only 24% of the managers interviewed called for greater worker participation in their firms' decision-making processes (Talamo, 1979, p. 109).[19] Managers favored a strong state and the use of force to restore law and order. They expressed their views (Talamo, 1979, p. 118) in these terms: "Impose order, even it means using force." "If violence goes outside of the factory, we need the machine gun: We should have avoided the *autunno caldo* with tanks and armored divisions." "Only the colonels can restore the proper way of viewing things."

The self-made man, the founder of his company, was particularly upset by the new state of affairs.[20] Founders were more likely to perceive labor relations as conflict-ridden and to view strikes negatively (Farneti, 1970, pp. 125, 141). On Thursday, March 12, 1970, one reads on the front page of *Il Corriere della Sera*, Italy's quality paper:

Serious incident in front of a factory in the Vicenza province.
Father and son open fire on strikers: ten wounded. A small entrepreneur and his son opened fire on a group of workers who were demonstrating in front of their factory during a textile workers' strike. Ten men, including two trade union representatives, were wounded. The entrepreneur and his son were arrested by the carabinieri.

The textile entrepreneur, himself a former factory worker, was later to declare in court: "I got scared and lost my head."[21] Rare as this episode may be (although by no means unique[22]), it does bear witness to the passions of the long *autunno caldo* and to the sentiments of small-scale employers.

Heirs and managers, and even the better-educated founders, were more liberal.[23] They accepted the idea of change and the sharing of authority (Martinelli, 1978, p. 40). They were less likely "to lose their heads." They were less involved emotionally in their confrontation with labor, more pragmatic and realistic about the interests of the other party. They were more likely to view labor relations in terms of "antagonistic cooperation." As one of those employers put it, "Trade unions and employers are two opposing forces, and we must fight each other . . . but this struggle must result in the common good" (quoted in Martinelli, 1978, p. 62). As would be expected, founders were more likely to be encountered in small firms, and managers in large firms – once again linking small firms to a more conservative approach to labor relations.[24]

Certainly, as we saw in Chapters 4 and 5, the wide territorial dispersion of small firms made it more rational for unions to spend their scarce organizational resources in the larger firms. But the analyses in this chapter have revealed another dimension to the problem of organizing small firms: Employers' opposition to unionization drives was much more intense in smaller firms.[25] Regalia's 1981 survey of *consigli di fabbrica* showed that management in small firms was much more likely to view them as nuisances (54% vs. 10%), whereas 53% (vs. 23%) of large-firm management viewed them as useful (Regalia, 1984a, p. 304). Some of the small-firm delegates put it quite succinctly (quoted in Regalia, 1984a):

If he [the employer] could, he would have us up against the wall. The delegate is a thorn, the black sheep of the factory. And the employer tries to stir up other workers against us. [p. 305]

The delegates are the employers' ball-busters. Without the delegates they would do as they pleased. [p. 305]

Not surprisingly, labor relations in smaller firms, even those that had accepted workers' representation, were more likely to be antagonistic. In smaller firms, delegates were twice as likely (29% vs. 14%) as their large-firm counterparts to express antagonism toward the employer (Regalia, 1984a, p. 122). The available evidence shows that meetings between delegates and management/employers were fewer in smaller firms.[26]

As paternalism was slow to die and survived well into the 1960s and beyond, the management function of labor relations had no easy time in being born. For many years, the experiment in modern labor relations carried out at Olivetti remained a distant object of curiosity, rather than an example for others to follow. In the early 1970s, most large firms finally did set up personnel departments. The concepts of labor relations, industrial relations, personnel management, and human resources were novelties to Italian firms, when they were belatedly "discovered" in the early 1970s. Even then, modern labor relations remained confined to the larger firms. On the basis of a survey of small entrepreneurs, Martinelli concluded that in many smaller firms, even in the mid-1970s, "There did not exist a system of industrial relations, but rather a system of personal relations" (Martinelli, 1978, p. 59). A 1983 Assolombarda survey confirmed that, still in the 1980s, management of labor relations in many small firms was rather casual, marked with the stamp of chance and expediency (Associazione Industriale Lombarda, 1983, p. 49) – and that survey included only unionized firms!

Indeed, labor relations were not high on the list of employers' priorities. A Federlombarda survey showed that large employers were much more likely than smaller ones (75% vs. 17.2%) to participate in managerial courses. Even for employers with larger firms, however, a course in industrial relations occupied the last place on a long list of courses they would have liked to attend if they had had a choice (1.6% of preferences vs. 46.1% for managerial courses, the top choice) (Urbani, 1977a, p. 412). The same survey showed that 20.4% of employers had no contacts with trade unions and 41.6% had only occasional contacts (Martinelli, 1977, pp. 330, 355). Not surprisingly, an absence of any plant-level organizational structure and a shop-floor climate of peaceful labor relations were correlated with the low rates of contact with unions (Martinelli, 1977, pp. 331, 355, 356). Conflict breeds interaction, and interaction, even under conflict situations, seems to breed reciprocal understanding. In many surveys of employers, the most positive opinions about unions and labor relations were expressed by precisely those employers whose firms were also more likely to be conflict-ridden (Martinelli, 1977, p. 333; Trigilia, 1986, p. 232).[27]

If the first strikes in their factories had been traumatic for many Italian employers, the Workers' Charter must have seemed the last straw. By providing greater protection for the workers and the unions, by extending to workers and unions some rights of citizenship within the firm, the law was seen as a trespass on traditional "managerial prerogatives." The employers' old tricks could no longer succeed under the new law. "The charter is a crime" howled a small entrepreneur (quoted in Martinelli, 1978, p. 63). To be sure, not all employers felt that way. Thus, to the above ultraconservative, a more open-minded entrepreneur replied that "The Workers' Charter sanctions sacred principles, such as the workers' dignity."[28]

But whether for or against the charter, most employers blamed the new law for many of the problems they faced in their factories: absenteeism, strikes, labor's inflexibility, lack of motivation. In a survey of the largest industrialists in the country, 91% of the respondents believed that the Workers' Charter had caused an increase in plant-level bargaining, and 98% believed that it had resulted in higher levels of absenteeism (Martinelli et al., 1981, p. 106). More generally, employers viewed the charter as tilting too far to the left the power relationships that once had been too far to the right. As one employer put it, "Until ten years ago the employer had absolute discretionary power over the worker, while now the opposite is true" (quoted in Martinelli, 1978, p. 64). Again, small employers were more likely to view the charter negatively. The 1983 Federmeccanica survey of employers regarding the state of labor relations in their firms showed that 40% of small employers (as compared with 23% of large ones) agreed with the statement that industrial relations would improve if the charter were abolished (Mortillaro, 1984, p. 200). Furthermore, some 80% of the surveyed employers had no faith in the impartiality of labor judges (Mortillaro, 1983, p. 184).

Scared, angry, humiliated, confused, and unsure of whose side the state was on, it is no surprise that Italian employers searched desperately for a way out, both inside and outside their plants. At stake was their very survival as a class.

8.5. COLLECTIVE RESPONSES: REAFFIRMING *LA CENTRALITÀ DELL'IMPRESA*

On February 20, 1970, Confindustria made public the final report of a commission Confindustria itself had set up in 1969 to investigate the role of the employers' association and to suggest possible organizational changes, the so-called *Rapporto Pirelli,* after the head of the commission, Leopoldo Pirelli, the Milan-based tire manufacturer (Pirzio Ammassari, 1976, pp. 130–3; Lanzalaco, 1990, pp. 167–71). The Pirelli report called for an ideological break with the past, away from stubborn opposition to labor, toward a new one featuring dialogue and openness with labor. The leadership role in Confindustria was passing from the hands of an old-fashioned, conservative, and sternly antilabor capitalist faction composed of small-scale employers, operating in a competitive domestic market, into the hands of those who led the multinational oligopolies that had grown during the postwar period (e.g., Fiat, Pirelli, Olivetti). Within a short time, most of the old guard, both in Confindustria itself and in the territorial associations, had been replaced (Pirzio Ammassari, 1976, p. 138; Lanzalaco, 1990, p. 172).

The new Confindustria leadership embraced Giovanni Agnelli's vision of a new, broadly political role for Confindustria (Pirzio Ammassari, 1976, p. 142). Consistent with Agnelli's view, some decentralization of functions, particularly of bargaining functions, was implemented. On December 11, 1971, a new industrial association was created, Federmeccanica, the federation of mechanical, engineering, metalworking and heavy-machinery industries. The main purpose of the new, tough-minded organization was to carry out the collective-bargaining function. Consistent with Agnelli's view, also, the ideology of class relations changed. Rather than opposition and conflict, the new ideology stressed commonality of interests and cooperation. That new vision was further developed when Giovanni Agnelli himself took the presidency of Confindustria in 1973. In a series of interviews, Agnelli hammered home his position (Pirzio Ammassari, 1976, pp. 182–8). He invited his fellow entrepreneurs to take a more active role in the cultural and political life of the country. He thundered against the hoarding of unproductive capital, whether in state or private hands. He advocated the need for efficiency and predictability. He stressed the community of interests between labor and capital. The struggle with labor shifted to the ideological realm. To the leftist slogan of "workers' centrality" (*centralità operaia*), the employers' ideological offensive opposed the motto of "firm's centrality" (*centralità dell'impresa*).

In a 1973 interview with *Il Corriere della Sera*, after an unsuccessful strike at Fiat, Giovanni Agnelli declared that "We prefer to have a strong union. It is better for everyone. [The risk otherwise is that there will be a return to] a disorderly protest in the hands of radical groups" (quoted in Pirzio Ammassari, 1976, p. 182). Still in 1983, at a time when Italian unions were declining, Giovanni Agnelli declared in his long interview with Arrigo Levi that

In my opinion, a union must be strong, first and foremost. . . . Unions are necessary because they represent the needs of workers, in the interest of enterprise growth. . . . A strong and representative union is useful; rather, it is necessary. . . . Unions represent workers, but also, yes, to some extent they reconcile workers to their work. . . . Now, unions are troubled: this is their lowest moment.[29] And this is no good for us. (Levi, 1983, pp. 64–70, passim)

Agnelli's words reveal a drastic change in tone compared with employers' rigid anti-union attitudes in the 1950s and 1960s. What really scared big business was the possibility of a repetition of the 1969 *autunno caldo*, when workers' violence often broke out not only in opposition to the employers but also in open challenge to the unions, in highly disruptive forms and over highly radical issues (Talamo, 1979, pp. 96–108).

Of course, employers and managers had their own view of what a union should be: A union should be apolitical, first and foremost; it should be "representative" (meaning that it should abide by bourgeois democratic rules of decision making); it should be "responsible" (meaning that it should not press demands that are incompatible with the profitability of the firm); finally, as Agnelli put it, "It should interpret the *real* needs of the workers, which are those involving the growth of the enterprise, . . . so that workers can live better, can work more comfortably, can have better working hours" (Levi, 1983, pp. 69–71; Talamo, 1979, pp. 105–8). In that respect, the answers that some 663 Italian managers provided in a survey conducted in 1971–72 were quite telling. At a time when managerial authority was at its lowest in the factories, under attack from highly radicalized groups, any attempt to allow the unsanctioned, extraparliamentary groups on the extreme left to become involved in labor relations was viewed by those managers as an absolute evil. It was those groups that had dangerously fused together economic and political demands: "Trade unions have been surpassed on the left by radical groups." "Obsessed by fears of being surpassed on the left, unions are forced to put forward ever more radical demands in order to justify themselves," managers complained (quoted in Talamo, 1979, p. 106). In that climate, the employers and managers (especially in large factories) came to see the trade unions (adversaries, bitter foes only a few years earlier) as allies.[30]

In an interview with the weekly *Espresso* on November 19, 1972, Agnelli appealed to labor for a common struggle against unproductive capital:

National product is divided into profits and salaries. I am stating absolutely elementary things. Besides profits and salaries there are rents. We learned these distinctions in school. Unfortunately, along the way, we forgot them. Rents remunerate unproductive social groups. . . . My impression is that in Italy today the weight of unproductive, parasitic rents has expanded in a pathological way. Since salaries cannot be shrunk in a democratic society, profits must take a cut. This is the disease that plagues us and against which we must absolutely react. (Pirzio Ammassari, 1976, p. 157; Provasi, 1976, p. 289)

A few years later, Guido Carli, former governor of the Bank of Italy and Agnelli's successor as president of Confindustria, expressed that same ideology of a coincidence of interests between labor and capital in a modern industrial society that can facilitate efficiency and planning against both the unproductive rents going to some capitalists and the bureaucratic red tape that chokes the state (the strings, *lacci e lacciuoli* in Carli's famous expression, that strangle the economy) (Scalfari, 1977):

The interest [of the manufacturing bourgeoisie] consists, above all, in a hard and relentless fight against all forms of parasitism, of inefficiency, of unproductive rent, of normlessness that are suffocating not only the country's economic life but also its moral life. The manufacturing bourgeoisie for many years did not realize that *that was its real enemy*. Now, they have. . . . Industrial workers, technicians, the productive middle class, farmers: *those are the allies*. (Scalfari, 1977, pp. 121–2; emphasis added)

As capitalists tried to rally labor to their side, the parallel with the changes in capitalist ideology that had occurred in England at the time of the Anti-Corn-Law League was impressive (Bendix, 1974, pp. 99–116).

The anxious horde of small employers closed ranks behind the strong leadership of Agnelli and Carli. After so much talk about exploitation, surplus value, repression, and paternalism, finally someone was putting the spotlight back on the innovative capacities of Schumpeter's entrepreneurial hero. In the words of some of those heroes, "The Agnelli presidency shook the waters by reaffirming the socio-political role of the entrepreneur"; "Today when we talk, people listen, while just a few years ago it was not easy to get our point across" (quoted in Martinelli, 1978, pp. 51–2, 33). Mostly, the hero prided himself on his contribution to the economic development of the country. He took center stage and did not tire of telling his success story, fashioned of hard work ["a company created from nothing through incredibly hard work" (quoted in Martinelli, 1978, p. 37)], ingenuity, and creative capacities *against all odds*: a state that had done nothing to help him export his product, but in fact had done everything possible to throw sticks through the spokes of his fast-spinning wheels, a banking system that had rolled out the red carpet for even bankrupt large-scale employers, but had forced him (*him*, so busy with work!) to wait around for hours, days, months to get credit for his blossoming firm, not to mention the unfair competition from state-owned conglomerates with their easy access to bank loans, and finally the unions, surely infiltrated by a bunch of Redheads, strangling him with their unreasonable demands. All of that, *Siur Brambilla*[31] did not like.

A battery of employers' surveys during the 1970s and 1980s, most financed directly by employers' associations, bore witness to the changes in attitudes, the opening of doors that formerly were closed.[32] As two small employers confessed in one of those surveys (quoted in Martinelli, 1978, pp. 23–4),

> We only thought about work; that was our mistake, a mistake we are now paying for; we stayed inside our firms, more or less egoistically; but the entrepreneur must be involved in politics, must go outside the firm.

> The fundamental mistake of the entrepreneur goes back to the 1950s and the first half of the 1960s when his only thoughts were for production and company growth, in isolation from the outer social context.[33]

But those surveys also revealed the enduring conservative attitudes among employers and the limits of employers' support for Agnelli's policies of compromise with labor. Small employers did not like Agnelli's friendly entente with the unions. Agnelli's policy of compromise was beneficial only for large-scale employers, not for him, the entrepreneurial hero pressed on all sides by intraclass and interclass conflicts (Martinelli, 1978, p. 53). The 1975 Federlombarda survey showed that employers were much more likely to favor employer participation over union participation in the formulation of government policies (Urbani, 1977a, p. 389): Only 13% of employers interviewed favored a decision-making role for trade unions in the elaboration of policies of national interest; 60.7% favored a consulting role; and 26.3% were against any union involvement in national political affairs (Martinelli, 1977, p. 332; Urbani, 1977a, p. 388). Again, the distribution was linked to firm size, smaller employers being the least favorable to a policy-making role for the unions (Martinelli, 1977, p. 332).[34] On the other hand, almost all employers (96.9%) believed that employer associations should be involved in the country's decision-making process. Just as the politics of *compromesso storico* had not found widespread support among the working-class base of the Communist Party, the parallel politics of corporatist arrangements did not find widespread support among Confindustria's members, who were mostly small-scale entrepreneurs. Given such little enthusiasm on all sides, it is no surprise that the *compromesso* failed in both the political and economic arenas.

8.6. CONVERGING INTERESTS: INQUADRAMENTO UNICO (*MOBILITÀ INTERNA*)

Nowhere can the convergence of interests between unions and employers (at least large-scale employers) be better seen than in the *inquadramento unico* (the "unified

Table 8.2. *Skill-grading system: the old and the new*

New system (IU)	Old system	
	Manual workers [a]	Clerical workers
I	MC (5th), OC2 (4th)	3rd B
II	OC1 (3rd)	3rd A
III	OQ (2nd)	3rd A
IV	OS (1st), CS2	2nd
V	OSP (1st super), CS1	2nd Super
V super		1st
VI		1st Super
VII		

[a]MC, *manovale comune* (unskilled); OC, *operaio comune di prima (di seconda)* (unskilled); OQ, *operaio qualificato* (semiskilled); OS, *operaio specializzato* (skilled); CS, *categoria speciale di prima (di seconda)* (skilled); OSP, *operaio specializzato provetto* (skilled).
Source: Speranza (1977, p. 217); Graziosi (1979, p. 25).

skill–classification system"). *The inquadramento unico* (IU) classified both manual and clerical workers in a single hierarchy of skills. The IU was introduced in some state-owned steel firms after prolonged bargaining and struggles during the 1970–72 period.[35] In 1972, the metalworkers' unions made the IU the cornerstone of their proposal for renewal of their collective contract.

As Table 8.2 shows, in the traditional system of skill classification, manual and clerical workers had been organized into two separate grading systems. In the new system, manual and clerical workers shared at least some of the positions in the grading structure, although manual workers tended to occupy the bottom part of the structure, and clerical workers the top part.[36] Furthermore, the new system reversed the traditional scale: The lowest numbers corresponded to the lowest skill categories. Finally, the new system eliminated some of the skill categories, lumping them together, and changed the wage scale slightly in favor of skilled manual workers and unskilled clerical workers: The distance between the lowest and highest blue-collar levels grew from 32 points in the old system to 35.2, and that between the lowest and highest clerical levels shrank.[37]

In the traditional system of job classification (*sistema delle qualifiche*) the task that a worker was assigned was the basis for the worker's classification in a skill level, independently of the worker's particular skills. The task determined the skill level and, as a consequence, the wage level. Under the IU, the skill level of the worker, as measured by the number of jobs that he or she had mastered in an established system of job rotation, was the basis for the worker's classification in the skill hierarchy, regardless of the particular task the worker currently performed (Del Lungo, 1976). According to the 1973 metalworkers' collective contract, "the [IU] system will be based on the recognition and valorization of the workers' professional capacities . . . [based on] the following provisions: (a) training courses; (b) job enrichment and job enlargement; (c) job rotation."

The acquisition of skills (*professionalità*) was the basis for skill upgrading. Skill upgrading was a reward for *professionalità*, a meritocratic and individual reward, rather than an automatic and collective promotion (Graziosi, 1979, pp. 35–7). Job rotation was the main mechanism for the acquiring of new skills (Graziosi, 1979, p. 35). Thus, job rotation reintroduced labor mobility on the shop floor, after years of rigidity and inflexibility.

A proper application of the IU agreement would have required the introduction of job rotation on an extensive scale and a complete redesign of the organization of the production process. In some large Italian factories the IU did indeed result in reorganization of production such that work groups (*unità operative*) had the prime responsibility for coordinating their labor processes. At Olivetti and Alfa-Romeo, the assembly lines were dismantled, and the production process was organized around work groups (*isole*) (Graziosi, 1979, p. 136). Similarly, in the steel industry, workers were organized into autonomous groups. But, in most Italian factories, work groups were implemented only on a limited and experimental basis. The IU, by and large, amounted to very little change in the organization of the production process (Segatori and Torresini, 1977, p. 26). There was a tendency for firms simply to rely on automatic mechanisms without changing the real skill content of a job or the organization of production (Segatori and Torresini, 1979, pp. 18, 23). In most firms, management simply transferred the old system into the new classification system, literally applying the equivalence scheme of Table 8.2 (Segatori and Torresini, 1979, p. 74). At Fiat, job enlargement and rotation involved 80% of skilled workers, but only 50% of the unskilled (Becchi Collidà and Negrelli, 1986, p. 174). Thus, the trade-union goal of upgrading the real skill content in jobs was only partly met.

The fact that the IU did not extensively transform the organization of production did not mean that the IU was without consequences. The first visible effect of the IU, and certainly the one most advertised by employers, was a tendency toward upgrading (Dell'Aringa, 1976, p. 71). Furthermore, there was a tendency to bunch workers in a couple of grade levels (three for heavy-machinery firms, four and five for steel). In time, the lowest two levels became almost empty (Villa, 1986: 188; Segatori and Torresini, 1979, p. 67; Speranza, 1977). The data in Table 8.3, from different sources, all confirm how, over time, the skill hierarchy became increasingly topheavy, with workers concentrated mostly in two grades only (four and five in the steel industry, and three and four in other sectors) (Accornero and Carmignani, 1978a, p. 116; Villa, 1986, p. 188). As would be expected, the IU and the concentration of the work force at the top resulted in higher labor costs (Villa, 1986, pp. 191–2).

A less visible effect (or a less widely advertised effect) was that the IU offered management the possibility of transferring workers from job to job, after years of frozen labor mobility (Pipan and Salerni, 1975, p. 39). Through the IU, employers finally regained control over internal mobility in the workplace. Furthermore, in firms where the authority structure had collapsed, employers were able to unload

Table 8.3. *Distribution of blue-collar workers by skill level in metalworking industry*

Survey	Skill level[a]				
	1	2	3	4	5
Ministry of Labor 1971[b]	1.9	26.4	–[c]	36.1	28.5
1974	3.3	19.2		40.5	35.7
1977	2.3	15.8		32.3	48.4
Ministry of Labor 1971[d]	7.6	27.9	–[c]	38.2	20.4
1974	5.1	26.4		40.1	24.4
1977	3.0	21.2		43.0	29.9
Federmeccanica 1972[e]	10.5	37.5	34.2	16.0	1.8
1974	1.3	31.6	41.1	18.9	7.1
1976	0.9	13.5	49.8	24.4	11.4
IRI machinery firms 1974[f]	1.7	23.4	43.4	26.9	4.6
1975	0.8	11.9	49.3	26.9	11.1
1976	1.1	6.4	51.1	29.3	12.1
Parliament 1976[g]	0.4	7.9	46.8	29.6	15.3
FLM Milan 1975[h]	1.3	13.6	46.3	24.8	14.0
FLM Bologna 1975	0.4	20.8	38.6	25.6	14.6
FLM Varese 1975	0.4	12.7	43.9	25.3	16.7
FLM Lecco 1976	0.1	6.5	43.6	30.8	19.0

[a] Levels: 1 and 2 (unskilled workers), 3 (semiskilled), 4 (skilled), 5 (highly skilled).
[b] Sample of firms assembled by the Ministry of Labor (steel industry).
[c] Level 3 is included in level 2.
[d] Sample of firms assembled by the Ministry of Labor (manufacturing industries).
[e] Sample of firms belonging to Federmeccanica.
[f] State-owned heavy-machinery firms belonging to IRI.
[g] Sample of firms assembled by a parliamentary commission.
[h] Samples of firms in the respective provinces assembled by the metalworkers' union (FLM).
Sources: For Ministry of Labor data, see Villa (1986, p. 354); for Federmeccanica, Parliament, and FLM data, see Accornero and Carmignani (1978b, p. 116); for data on IRI firms, see Segatori and Torresini (1979, p. 71).

the responsibility of labor control, placing that burden directly on the work group (Graziosi, 1979, p. 143; Villa, 1986, p. 200).[38] In many firms, the workers' delegates had to decide who would and who would not be rotated (Bulgarelli, 1978, pp. 121). Inevitably, rotation would favor some workers and alienate others.[39] Many delegates resigned under such pressure. In other firms, the members of the *esecutivo* were viewed by workers and delegates as the counterparts with whom to bargain, rather than management (Vento, 1980). Workers often regarded the delegates as substitutes for the old bosses (a great advantage for management, if unions did their policing work). The employers' reassertion of control over internal mobility was the final blow to highly militant groups, for internal mobility broke up the homogeneous work group, the basis for solidarity and militancy.[40]

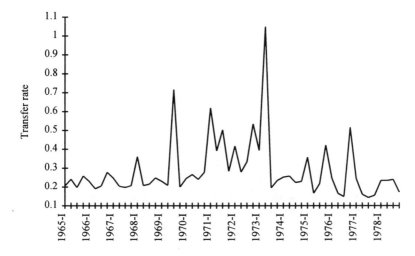

Figure 8.1. *Plot of transfer rate (1965–I/1977–IV)*

Interviews with a handful of radicals at Fiat (Bulgarelli, 1978, pp. 121–5) clearly reveal the stuff of which solidarity is fashioned: mutual trust developed through common struggles (knowing who can be depended on and who cannot, knowing who has stood up to the bosses, knowing who will fill in so that a co-worker can take a break), the heated political debates at the cafeteria ("the cafeteria is very important for the formation of the group"), and perhaps, at least for the young and unmarried, social interaction outside the plant (soccer games, etc.). A handful of tightly knit workers can mobilize a whole department. But when the company starts moving those workers around, it can break the back of militancy,[41] and when it does that continually and in a systematic way, the company can take control of "the politics of production," the everyday struggles over quality and quantity on the shop floor. Workers often reacted to disruptions of factory life and the breakup of solidarity via individual absenteeism ("calling in sick"), rather than via collective action (Bulgarelli, 1978, pp. 127, 133).

The plot of quarterly transfer rates during the period between 1965 and 1978 (Figure 8.1) does, indeed, confirm a peak in transfer rates in 1973 at the time of the first implementation of the IU. But the plot also reveals bouts of transfers, in part, related to seasonality (e.g., the first quarters of 1975, 1976, and 1977) and, in part, related to higher levels of strike activity (e.g., the peak in the fall of 1969). That there is more behind workers' transfer rates than purely economic reasons is made even more clear by the plot of monthly transfer rates during the period 1958–64 (Figure 8.2). The number of transfers shot up in early 1962 and kept at high levels throughout the year as employers (private employers, in particular) defensively retrenched against labor for the renewal of collective contracts. That story I have already told in Chapters 3 and 5 (it is part of the *paradox of the 1962 and 1966*

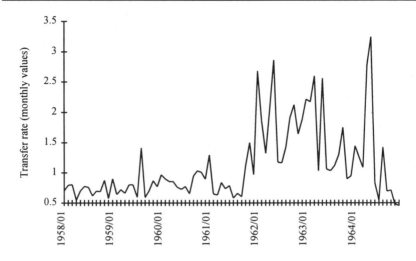

Figure 8.2. *Plot of transfer rate (1958–01/1964–12)*

strike shapes). But once again, the plots reveal the close connection between workers' and employers' class strategies (in this case, strikes and transfers).

Although the metalworkers' unions had proposed and pushed for the IU, the IU represented a convergence of different interests: unions, employers, and workers.[42] It emphasized the need for bargaining at more centralized levels, an opinion shared by firms, unions, and the state. It did so without sacrificing workers' interests or humiliating the workers. In fact, it gave workers an egalitarian banner under which to rally (Pipan and Salerni, 1975, p. 104).

To the trade unions the IU offered the possibility of regaining the initiative in worker–employer relationships, which during the strike wave often had been directly in the hands of militant workers. The increasingly technical nature of the issues involved meant more committees, more formal meetings (Pipan and Salerni, 1975, p. 44). Most delegates were not technically competent to deal with the problems involved (Vento, 1980), leaving it for the members of the *esecutivo* and of the outside unions to take up the task. Bargaining power began to slip through the fingers of small groups, coming to rest in the hands of territorial unions and union "technical experts" (Pipan and Salerni, 1975, pp. 104–5).[43]

Employers shared the unions' desire to limit plant-level bargaining and to regain organizational control over the bargaining process (Pipan and Salerni, 1975, pp. 116–20).[44] Furthermore, job rotation gave employers a free hand in regard to internal mobility. Although it cost them a higher wage bill (because of the general upgrading of skill), employers found in the IU a solution to the problems of rigidity and inflexibility that had limited their use of the work force.

As for the workers, surveys seem to indicate that they did not quite understand the whole thing (Pipan and Salerni, 1975, pp. 113–6). Nonetheless, workers embraced the IU proposals for ideological reasons: The proposals squared with the egalitarian stance of the 1968–72 strike wave. More specifically, the parity between blue-collar and white-collar work, between manual and mental work, had been a long standing demand by the Left.[45] Furthermore, workers, particularly lower manual and clerical workers, saw in the IU a way to obtain collective skill upgrading (i.e., a disguised wage demand) (Pipan and Salerni, 1975, pp. 115–6; Segatori and Torresini, 1979, p. 19). Skilled workers and supervisors were less happy, despite the widening wage gap between the lowest and highest levels of manual work under the new system. They felt that workers with greatly inferior credentials were edging ever closer to their skill and wage levels. After all, most manual workers came to be classified in the top skill levels and many semiskilled workers were mass promoted to the top level. Despite the emphasis on *professionalità*, in practice, the employers' reliance on automatic mechanisms for skill upgrading further undermined the role of skill in the conception of blue-collar work.[46]

8.7. HOUSECLEANING (*MOBILITÀ ESTERNA*)[47]

The 1969 *autunno caldo* had been a severe shock to all employers. A few packed their suitcases and left; many stayed but took the precautionary measure of stashing their money away. But most simply continued their work, trying to stem the tidal wave of workers' mobilization, and one of their first reactions was to break up the wave front by firing the most militant workers (*le teste calde*, "the hotheads"). Firing a few, carefully selected workers here and there throughout the plant could go a long way toward quelling the fires. Even more so than intershop and interplant transfers, layoffs "break up the continuity of organizations and men" (Perrot, 1974, p. 433). As the 1952 report compiled by ACLI of Milan (the Christian Association of Italian Workers) on labor conditions inside the factories put it,

With the layoff of four activists, the employer has reached his goal: You will not find another worker who will have the guts, that is the right word, to be a member of the Commissione Interna. (ACLI, 1953, p. 22)

All three members of the Commissione Interna were fired . . . No one wants to try to set it up again for fear of receiving the same treatment. (ACLI, 1953, p. 30)

That was true not only in the 1950s. The 1983 Assolombarda report on the state of labor relations in Milanese firms showed how a handful of layoffs could rid a plant of troubles for years to come: No one would want the job of union representative on the shop floor (Associazione Industriale Lombarda, 1983, pp. 59, 68). Indeed, we saw in Chapter 6 that the coefficient of a layoff variable in an econometric model has negative and significant effects on both the number of strikes and the number of strikers (see Table 6.6, p. 223). The plots of Figures 8.3 and 8.4 bring the relationship into sharper focus: Italian employers increased their use of layoffs during or right after both the 1959–63 and 1969–72 strike waves. The different measures of layoffs collected by Confindustria increased in the early 1960s and

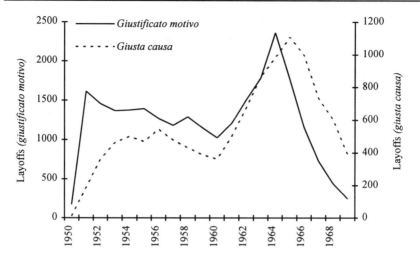

Figure 8.3. *Plots of the numbers of individual layoffs for* giustificato motivo *and* giusta causa

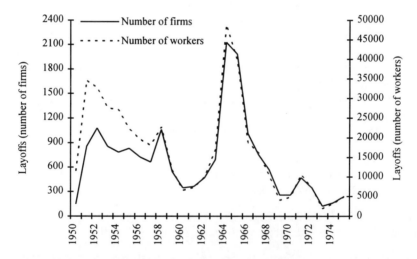

Figure 8.4. *Plots of the numbers of workers laid off and firms requesting layoffs*

1970s in remarkable correspondence with the increase in labor militancy.[48] The plots make it clear how Italian employers brought conflict down in the mid-1960s: It is no surprise that the unions would speak of *ricatto congiunturale* ("recession blackmailing").

The surge in layoffs in 1970 is even clearer when considering Ministry of Labor data (Figure 8.5).[49] Labor economist Carlo Dell'Aringa (1979a, p. 187) thus commented on the high rate of layoffs in 1971:

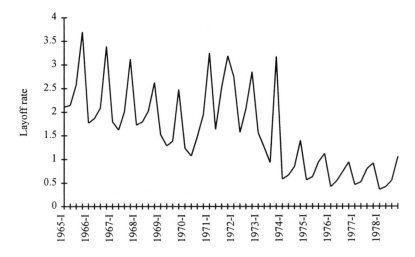

Figure 8.5. *Plot of layoff rate (1965–I/1978–IV)*

In 1971, compared to 1970, hirings remained more or less constant around 31%, while the number of layoffs increased from 10.7% to 18.1%. The possibility comes to mind that that phenomenon was at least partially an employers' reaction to the labor-market tensions of those years. The possibility is that, particularly in 1971, but partly also in 1972, layoffs were used by employers in order to acquire (or reacquire) greater power in the ongoing labor disputes, and not merely in order to adjust employment levels.

The plots of various measures of layoffs not only reveal the remarkable temporal correspondence between strike waves and increases in the employers' use of layoffs.[50] They also confirm the increasing rigidity of the Italian labor market: "Who is in is in, and who is out is out" (Reyneri, 1989a, p. 137).[51] Over time, the employers' use of the layoff became a less viable option for labor control, as revealed by the declining trend of the plots. Consistent with the long-term decline in employers' use of layoffs, the surge in the number of layoffs after the *autunno caldo* (Figure 8.5) was much smaller than that after the 1959–63 strike wave (Figure 8.4), despite the much higher levels of conflict reached during and after the *autunno caldo*. Indeed, the new climate of labor relations made it increasingly hard for employers to fire workers, whether for economic or political reasons.

Faced with the possibility of never being able to fire or lay off any new workers they might hire, employers reacted with a freeze on hiring. Between 1970 and 1975, the rate of blue-collar hiring in manufacturing declined steadily (Bulgarelli, 1978, pp. 10, 23). Between 1965 and 1976, worker turnover in industry (i.e., people losing one job and getting another) fell from 34.3% (as a percentage of total employment) to 17.4% (Dell'Aringa, 1979a, p. 118).

The comparative data in Table 8.4 provide a stark indication of the rigidity of the Italian labor market by the mid-1970s (Dell'Aringa, 1979a, p. 129). The data

Table 8.4. *People looking for job by reason (April 1975)*

	Italy	Germany	France	Belgium	Netherlands	U.K.
Dismissals	23.1	62.3	43.2	69.4	65.5	34.9
Quits	4.6	9.0	19.1	6.7	16.1	22.2
Looking for first job	61.8	12.9	14.3	21.8	11.1	6.4
Other[a]	10.5	15.8	23.4	2.1	7.3	36.5
Total	100.0	100.0	100.0	100.0	100.0	100.0

[a] End of self-employment, of temporary employment, etc.
Source: EEC, *Labour Force Sample Survey*, 1975 (Dell'Aringa, 1979, p. 129).

show that employers in Belgium, Germany, and the Netherlands were three times as likely as those in Italy to fire workers, and those in France and the United Kingdom were almost twice as likely. The number of people looking for a first job was, on average, six times as high in Italy as elsewhere. Finally, given the difficulties of reentering the labor market, people were much less likely to resign their jobs in Italy than elsewhere. The larger firms, in particular, by the mid-1970s had become ossified mammoths, with labor mobility severely restricted: Yearly layoff rates averaged 7.7% of the work force in firms employing 10–49 workers, compared with 4.6% in firms of size 50–99, 4.0% in firms of size 100–199, 2.7% in firms of size 200–499, 1.0% in firms of size 500–999, and 1.1% in larger firms (Dell'Aringa, 1979a, p. 125).

A disaggregated analysis of unemployment figures further highlights the changed structure of the labor market. An unemployment indicator is basically a composite made up of two categories: (1) people who have lost their jobs and are looking for new jobs and (2) people who are looking for their first jobs (e.g., youth). A disaggregated analysis of unemployment using these two components shows that the number of people looking for new jobs after having lost their previous jobs continually declined during the postwar period and reached a record low of 1% of the labor force in 1980 (Reyneri, 1989a, p. 360). On the other hand, the number of people looking for their first jobs continually grew, particularly during the 1970s. It was that component of unemployment that led to the "unemployment explosion" of the late 1970s and 1980s (Reyneri, 1989a, p. 360). Thus, the increasing unemployment rates of the 1970s did not really show a situation of growing instability in workers' jobs. Rather, unemployment was a measure of the increasing difficulties of young people (and women) attempting to enter the primary labor market. But the gainfully employed continued to enjoy considerable privileges. And the unions entrenched to defend those privileges.

It is that (temporarily) successful retrenchment of powerful unions along defensive lines and their control over labor-market mechanisms that can explain the poor performance of economic-bargaining models (e.g., the Ashenfelter and Johnson model) during the 1970s *(paradox of the 1970s)*.[52] The solution to the *paradox of the 1970s* that I entertained at the end of Chapter 6 (unions' increased power to regulate the labor market) was thus uncharacteristically (for this book) correct. The French historian Michelle Perrot (1968, p. 120) has reminded us that "there are people behind numbers." Nowhere is that reminder more appropriate than in the case of unemployment. Had I bothered, in Chapter 2, to take a closer look at the people who were unemployed in the 1970s, I probably would have been alerted to a basic change in the structure of unemployment. Once again, the statistical paraphernalia that surrounded the econometric estimation of the Ashenfelter and Johnson model turns out to be a poor substitute for firsthand knowledge of the data. For all my emphasis on exploratory statistical work, I did not do all my homework in Chapter 2. I apparently preach better than I practice. Furthermore, had I bothered, in Chapter 2, to look beyond economic history and into labor and political history, I might sooner have found the answer to the *paradox of the 1970s*.

Needless to say, employers missed no occasion to thunder against the rigidity of the labor market and to return to the same point: *mobilità*.

It is necessary to give industry the indispensable margin of action, allowing labor turnover, which means, without any false veils, . . . accept the *duty* to close unproductive activities, the *duty* to open new activities, the *right* to declare bankruptcy and fire workers.[53]

In order to properly function, the firm must be free to aggregate capital and labor in the quantity and quality that the entrepreneur deems most appropriate.[54]

Mobility is the only way toward economic recovery.[55]

We cannot solve the firms problems if these cannot eliminate superfluous jobs and move a worker even within the same productive unit.[56]

But in the mid-1970s the time had not come for the unions to give up their control over the labor market, nor for employers simply to take it. The *cassa integrazione guadagni* (CIG) provided a temporary solution to the problem of external mobility. As the Milan *pretore*, Canosa, wrote, the CIG is "a typical expression of a situation of stalemate in the class struggle" (quoted in Bulgarelli, 1978, p. 14). Under the CIG, excess industrial workers, instead of being dismissed, were temporarily "suspended." Workers under the CIG did not go to work, but legally they continued to be employed by their firms and to draw nearly their full salaries. Between 1968 and 1976, the applications of the CIG became more and more extensive (Reyneri, 1989a, p. 381).[57] The 1975 *scala mobile* agreement widened the coverage of the *cassa integrazione guadagni* (CIG), providing further job security for workers. A 1976 law allowed CIG status to be extended to workers even after their employers had gone out of business (Barbano, 1987). The CIG increasingly came to operate as a social shock-absorber against layoffs.[58] The plot of Figure 8.6 shows that the number of hours covered by the CIG increased during the 1970s, providing large-scale employers an instrument with which to regulate external mobility, often times with the collusion of unions and workers who would continue receiving their wages and perhaps even drawing a second salary from employment in the flourishing underground economy.[59]

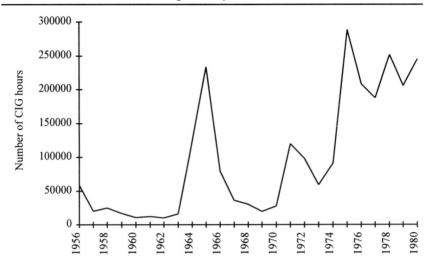

Figure 8.6. *Plot of number of hours covered by* cassa integrazione guadagni

8.8. MACHINES DON'T STRIKE

Layoffs and the threat of layoffs are powerful weapons in the hands of employers. Under capitalism workers' need to sell their labor power makes them particularly dependent on the employer's willingness to buy that power. Employers know that all too well. In the 1983 Federmeccanica survey of metalworking employers, the interviewees listed "workers' fear of losing their jobs" as the number-one reason for the improvement in the climate of labor relations in the early 1980s (Mortillaro, 1984, p. 137). But the use of the "layoff stick" does not always work. Under conditions of nearly full employment, the threat of layoff loses much of its bite. Skilled workers, of course, are always protected because their skills are in short supply. Finally, the political climate and the balance of class forces may make a recourse to layoffs unwise or simply impossible. All of those factors were operative in Italy during or after 1969. Although employers did use layoffs, even in the early 1970s, that use was limited. In its absence, they tried hard to reorganize production via technological innovation and investment in new equipment. At the very least, new machines gave employers a legitimate excuse (even under political conditions unfavorable to capital) to move workers around, as the plots of transfer rates in the preceding section show. Moving workers around provided an opportunity to break up homogeneous work groups, the breeding ground for solidarity and militant attitudes. Consider this worker's explanation for the low levels of conflict at an Ignis plant during the 1960s: "At the Cassinetta plant, the physical layout of machinery was subverted every year from top to bottom. Up until 1968, it never happened that workers coming back from summer vacations would find the same layout" (Santi, 1974, p. 117).

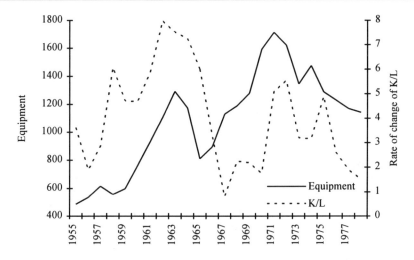

Figure 8.7. *Plots of investment in industrial equipment and rate of change of capital-to-labor ratio (K/L)*

The plot of the capital-to-labor ratio (K/L) in Figure 8.7 shows how industrial conflict provided a strong incentive for capitalists to substitute the factors of production; indeed, the slope of the K/L line sharply increases in conjunction with both the 1959–63 and 1968–72 strike waves. The plot of investment in industrial equipment in the same Figure 8.7 is just as revealing of the relationship between strike waves and investment decisions.[60] Again, the two highest peaks in equipment investment correspond very closely to the timing of the 1959–63 and 1968–72 strike waves. Of course, these plots may simply reveal the close connection between capital investment and economic growth (e.g., the years of *miracolo economico* in the late 1950s and early 1960s). In that case, the relationship between investment decisions and labor militancy may be altogether spurious – both conflict and investment being the product of a healthy and expanding economy. However, peaks in investment levels came after the peaks in labor militancy, particularly after the *autunno caldo*. As Barca and Magnani (1989, p. 122) wrote, "Big firms tried hard to react to the higher costs of labor, to the increased rigidities in the use of labor, and the higher cost of raw materials by raising the intensity of the other factor of production: fixed capital."

Fixed capital in the aftermath of the *autunno caldo* consisted mainly in an extensive deployment of machinery of traditional design and conception. The social organization of production remained unchanged, along basic Tayloristic and Fordistic lines. It was simply more of what was already there, as employers were shifting the mix of the factors of production, lowering the input of labor and raising that of capital (Heimler and Milana, 1982). Even though the new machinery that they were able to purchase and the technology they were able to access may not have been at the cutting edge of scientific development, a good indicator of the fact

Table 8.5. *Ratio between borrowed and internally generated capital, by firm size and year*

Firm size	1968	1969	1970	1971
Medium-size firms	1.87	1.97	2.41	3.00
Large firms	2.84	3.04	3.14	3.26

Source: Fondazione Giovanni Agnelli (1973, p. 121).

that technological investment played a key role in employers' strategy against labor was that they were ready to go heavily into debt for it. Firm indebtedness to financial institutions as a means to finance investment jumped from 33.9% in 1970 to 50.5% in 1973 (Barca and Magnani, 1989, p. 34). Firms' levels of indebtedness remained at those record highs until the end of 1977, declining to 40% in 1980 (Barca and Magnani, 1989, p. 49). The data in Table 8.5 show that the ratio between borrowed capital and internally generated capital worsened for larger firms[61] during the 1968–71 period, from 1.87 in 1968 to 3.0 in 1971, for a 60.4% increase, compared with a 14.8% increase for medium-size firms, from 2.84 to 3.26.[62] By 1971, profits for larger firms were at half their levels for 1968, and losses were five times as high; for medium-size firms, profits were 11% higher than they had been in 1968, and losses were only 28% higher (Fondazione Giovanni Agnelli, 1973, p. 122) (for a plot of firm profits, see Figure 3.9, p. 91).

Pressed on one side by labor and on the other by competing capitalists, employers dreamed of flexibility, against both labor and capital (interclass and intraclass conflict). The story of the large-scale manufacturers' search for flexibility inside their plants, rather than outside, is worth telling.

8.8.1. Experimenting with new technologies

In the early 1970s, Fiat began experimenting with the use of robots in the production process (Becchi Collidà and Negrelli, 1986, pp. 210–42). The workers and the unions had been pushing the company for the elimination of the most dangerous and unhealthy jobs (recall their motto *la salute non si tratta*, "Health is not a bargaining issue"), and it was a commendable decision for Fiat to try to meet those demands. But Fiat had reasons of its own to want to meet that challenge.[63] Like all Italian companies in those troubled times, Fiat had experienced the collapse of its authority structure and control over the production process. It had compelling reasons to push technological innovation because of the opportunities that would provide for reorganizing production and moving workers around, or perhaps firing some (particularly militant workers, such as those in the painting, assembling, and welding departments).

Experimentation with technological innovation began at Fiat in 1972 with the introduction of sixteen robots in welding, and twenty-three more in assembling in 1974 (Becchi Collidà and Negrelli, 1986, p. 214). Vulnerability of the assembly lines was also decreased. Long lines were broken up into shorter segments, and intermediate stockpiles (*polmoni*, "breathing lungs") were introduced in order to reduce the dependence of the entire line on a rigid synchronization of operations.[64] The end result of those innovations was a more flexible system; its new features included limited capabilities for the production of different models on a single assembly line and an increased ability to deal with bottlenecks along the line. It was in 1977, however, that Fiat pushed forward toward the development of a completely automated plant. The Robogate system, introduced in 1978 at the Rivalta plant (in Turin) and Cassino (in central Italy), was the result of years of experimentation with robots, conveyor machines, and microcomputers.

Behind the design of that highly complex and expensive system was Fiat's dream of total flexibility, as best laid out in a Fiat memorandum (Becchi Collidà and Negrelli, 1986, p. 218): (1) flexibility in the reutilization of the equipment at the end of production of a particular car model; (2) flexibility in using the system to produce different car models at the same time; (3) improvement of workers' quality of life inside the factory.[65] As the third point in that Fiat memorandum, we would have expected to find "flexibility against labor." That, of course, would have been politically unwise. But it does strike one as odd that Fiat should have mentioned, instead, the quality of workers' lives as an objective, because Fiat management had designed the Robogate system without any consultation with unions or workers – and perhaps with good reason. After all, Fiat engineers had designed the most sophisticated and automated production system in the world, at that time, in the social context of high and increasing unemployment. In the caustic words of Federico Butera, "Almost no one measures the effect of the content of work on the workers' well-being, while instead even the amount of grease consumed is measured with absolute precision" (quoted in Sabel, 1982, p. 213). But Fiat's management had single-mindedly followed its dream of total flexibility against labor and the market. The Robogate system fulfilled that dream, of robots that keep on working without ever complaining about fumes, noise, or fatigue, that never strike, and that work as well on one model as on another, with only a split-second notice, and without any need for retooling.[66] Robogate was an expensive system, requiring years of investment before and even after its introduction. But for Fiat, the end result of total flexibility against both consumers' and workers' whims was well worth the price (Locke and Negrelli, 1989, p. 69). Interestingly enough, subsequent Fiat plant designs (e.g., Mirafiori, Termoli 3), introduced at a time when labor unrest had plummeted to 1950s levels, incorporated only part of the flexibility achieved at Rivalta and Cassino.[67]

Fiat, of course, was not alone in its drive to find new technologies that would fulfil Agnelli's dreams of total flexibility. When a strike wave sweeps through an entire country, in fact, through the entire capitalist world economy, then many companies will lean hard on their research departments and many employers will share the same dream. There is a good deal of evidence in support of the fact that technological innovations come in long waves, out of employers' collective dreams (e.g., Hartman and Wheeler, 1979; Mandel, 1980).

8.9. SMALL PLANTS DON'T STRIKE

Machines don't strike. And, certainly, at least at times of high labor militancy, employers must dream of factories in which production goes on by machines, with no workers on the floor. But in the early 1970s, machines by themselves could not carry out production – not yet, anyway. Workers were still needed, and workers could strike. Not all of them, however. In Chapter 3, in fact, we saw that workers in small plants did not strike. Furthermore, in Chapter 4, we saw that small plants were mostly outside of union control, both in practice and under the law: The provisions of the 1970 Workers' Charter applied only to firms with more than fifteen workers. Finally, in Chapter 5, we saw that plant-level bargaining, often beset by high levels and militant forms of collective action, was mostly a characteristic of larger plants. In cases in which plant-level bargaining was used in smaller firms, contract clauses tended to be more standardized, and provisions less likely to encroach on managerial prerogatives. Giubilato's analysis of a subsample of plant-level agreements in 36 firms in the size classes of 30–40, 150–200, and more than 300 workers, from a population of 1,223 firms that signed plant-level agreements in the period 1979–81 in Veneto, showed that workers' control over the organization of production (*organizzazione del lavoro*) was not a bargaining issue in smaller firms (Giubilato, 1982; Castegnaro, 1983). Those findings were confirmed by both the Giovani Imprenditori and Assolombarda studies of small and medium-size firms: Workers' control over the organization of production was never a bargaining issue (Pastorino and Ragazzoni, 1980, p. 55; Associazione Industriale Lombarda, 1983, p. xx).

Not only workers in smaller firms had not pushed demands centered on the control over the organization of production, but also employers in smaller firms had been able to resist the tidal wave of skill upgrading of the work force that had hit the larger firms. All of the available survey research shows that in the 1970s, workers in larger firms tended to be classified toward the top grades; the opposite was true in smaller firms. Small firms employing fewer than ten workers disproportionately tended to classify workers, particularly younger workers and women, in the unskilled category (Bagnasco and Trigilia, 1984, pp. 156, 160). Furthermore, whereas only a handful of workers in the larger firms were classified in the apprentice category (which was below even the unskilled category), the percentage of apprentices was quite high in small firms.[68] Turnover was high[69] in small firms, and thus small employers avoided paying the higher wages due to seniority wage increases (Centro Studi Federlibro, 1974, p. 136). At the opposite end, the percentage of skilled workers was linearly and positively related to firm size.[70]

The distribution of skills in the smaller firms, skewed toward the lower grades, resulted in a per capita wage bill much lower than that for large firms. Furthermore, small firms had been more successful in avoiding both collective-contract provisions and the unions' egalitarian wage policies. Bonus payments under the table were quite typical in those firms (Brusco, 1975, p. 22). The most highly specialized craft firms, often operating with fewer than ten workers, employed both highly skilled workers, who made twice as much money as their factory counterparts, and unskilled workers, who made only one-third of what they could have made in a factory.[71]

The absence of unions and of plant-level bargaining, the lower wages, and the greater possibilities for evading contract provisions (not to mention social security payments and taxes) in small plants were all excellent reasons for beleaguered entrepreneurs to want to keep plant size down. But perhaps even more important in the 1970s was the small employers' greater flexibility in the use of the work force. Survey data showed that internal mobility was not a problem for small firms (Associazione Industriale Lombarda, 1983, pp. xx, 107). Workers would pitch in to cover for absent co-workers whether it was their regular job assignment or not (Pastorino and Ragazzoni, 1980, p. 30). What were pilot programs in larger firms (job rotation, job enrichment, job enlargement, i.e., the worker's ability to perform a variety of tasks) were part and parcel of everyday life in the smaller firms, their very strategy of survival.

Official skill grading in smaller firms had little to do with the type of technology used or the real level of skill needed to do the job. Rather, it reflected the structural weakness of the organization of the workers in smaller firms and their (and the unions') inability to push for a more favorable classification of the work force (Brusco, 1975, pp. 15–18). In fact, the acquisition of real skills and the ability to master a trade in the old craft tradition were much more widespread in smaller firms (Bagnasco and Trigilia, 1984, pp. 162–3). Workers seem to have been aware of the greater diversity of the work itself in small firms: 81.5% of workers in firms with fewer than ten employees judged their work as "interesting," as compared with 70.9% of workers in larger firms (Bagnasco and Trigilia, 1984, p. 186).

But if that aspect of life in the small firms was positive, others were not. Overtime work was typical, if not the rule, in smaller firms (Brusco, 1975, p. 20; Pastorino and Ragazzoni, 1980, p. 95). Working on Saturday and even Sunday was not uncommon. Peak demand was met with long stretches, sometimes even a few months, of seven-day workweeks (Bagnasco and Trigilia, 1984, p. 171). Consider Giovanni Agnelli's characterization of the smaller entrepreneurs:

These are people who demand a lot from themselves; it is quite logical that they should be as demanding of their employees in terms of work discipline; these are people who don't kid around with strikes, although they are rather generous with wages. As employers they expect a great deal from their workers, overtime on Saturdays and, perhaps, even on Sundays. (Levi, 1983, p. 15)

In summary, through a variety of mechanisms (an absence of plant-level contracts calling for automatic skill upgrading of the work force, combined with the use of individual bonuses, under-the-table bonuses, and evasion of the provisions of national contracts), small firms in the 1970s avoided the massive skill upgrading forced on larger firms by the introduction of the IU and the flattening of the wage curve due to the unions' egalitarian policies.[72]

Given those variations in the climate of labor relations in firms of different sizes, it was to be expected that Italian employers in the early 1970s would seek out flexibility where it could be found: in the small firms. In some cases, desperate employers with 100–200 workers would close down their plants when the problems of labor relations became overwhelming. Then they would reorganize production in perhaps a dozen small productive units (each with 10–15 workers), rehiring their most trusted workers (Associazione Industriale Lombarda, 1983, pp. 51–2). Sometimes employers facing that same kind of pressure would ask the workers of a highly militant, homogeneous work group to set themselves up as a cooperative, with the promise of contracting out to them the work that they currently were doing inside the plant (Centro Studi Federlibro, 1974). In any case, larger firms increasingly subcontracted to outside firms part of the production previously carried out internally: *decentramento produttivo*.

There is considerable evidence regarding the diffusion of *decentramento produttivo* during the 1970s and 1980s.[73] Surveys conducted in Bologna in 1972, 1975, and 1977, in Modena in 1974, and in Reggio Emilia in 1976 showed that in the metalworking industry, around 40% of total production was contracted out, with peaks close to 50% in some sectors (e.g., motorcycles).[74] At the Morini motorcycle plant in Bologna, only the camshaft and the engine were produced in-house; everything else was contracted out (frame, shock absorbers, breaks, fuel tank, handlebars, wheels, gearbox). Almost the entire motorcycle was produced by subcontractors for in-house final assembly (Brusco, 1982, p. 172). Some 70% of the metalworking firms in the 1983 Federmeccanica survey on the state of labor relations subcontracted part of the production process (Mortillaro, 1984, p. 116). Although 40% of firms contracted out less than 10% of their production, some 30% of the firms subcontracted more.

Once Italian employers learned the administrative skills required to decentralize, further decentralization became easy for them, and they came to rely on it extensively (Brusco, 1975, pp. 30–41). Thus, decentralized production became characteristic of both large and small firms. According to the Bergamo FLM data, 12.5% of firms in even the size class with 1–9 employees decentralized production that could have been carried out in-house; that number was 66.7% for firms employing more than 100 workers.[75]

As large firms facing the pressures of conflict-ridden labor relations increasingly farmed out production, small firms flourished. As we saw in Chapter 3, the data from the industrial census showed that the 1970s were characterized by an economic boom among smaller firms (particularly those with 1–20 workers) and by stagnation among larger firms, which declined in terms of both number of units (Table 3.13, p. 85) and average size (Table 3.14, p. 85). In summarizing his analysis of the underground economy Italian labor economist Bruno Contini[76] commented as follows:

It seems to be an undisputed fact that in Italy, one of the determining elements of plant size is workers' capacity to control the organization of the labor process. The causal model is:

Table 8.6. *Percentage change in blue-collar employment by firm size and period*

Period	Number of employees					
	1-19	20–49	50–99	100–249	250–499	500–999
1969–75	+99.9	+4.6	-3.2	+.1	-1.1	-4.3
1972–75	+23.4	-.2	+4.0	+6.1	+.8	+3.5

Source: Bergamaschi (1977b, p. 253).

high workers' control over the organization of production and small plant size leading to decentralization of production.

Brusco (1975, p. 58), on the basis of an analysis of smaller firms in the Lombardy province of Bergamo, similarly concluded that "The tendency toward decentralized production, which speeded up in the late 1960s, can only be explained in terms of an employers' strategy to resist a strong working-class offensive."

Revealing though the census data may be of an economic boom among smaller firms during the 1970s, the decade-long span of the census survey tends to blur the connection between strike waves and *decentramento produttivo*. The data collected by Federlombarda in a sample survey of member firms confirmed the census findings that in the period between 1969 and 1975, Lombardy, the most industrialized region in Italy, suffered a decline in employment in firms with more than 250 employees (Bergamaschi, 1977a, p. 253). It was in firms with fewer than 20 workers that employment showed spectacular growth (+99.9%) (Table 8.6). Employment in firms of all other sizes showed either minor growth or decline. However, the Federlombarda data showed that most of the growth in smaller firms and most of the decline in all others occurred in the three years following the *autunno caldo* (i.e., during the years of *conflittualità permanente*). The dramatic variations in the structure of firms in the period 1969–72 reflect Italian employers' all-out attempts to regain control over production and competitiveness. The observations that the growth in smaller firms slowed down (23.4% growth vs. 99.95%) during later years, between 1973 and 1975, and that even larger firms all showed positive growth in those years confirm that by 1973, Italian employers were well on their way to success in their struggle against labor.

8.10. AGAINST THE MARKET AND LABOR: THE EMPLOYERS' DREAM OF TOTAL FLEXIBILITY

The *autunno caldo* and the following years of *conflittualità permanente* go a long way toward explaining the great reshaping of the Italian industrial structure during the 1970s (*decentramento produttivo*, the growth in the number of smaller firms, the general reduction in the size of larger firms). But other historical processes were pushing in that direction as well (Pennacchi, 1980; Brusco, 1982; Sabel, 1982, pp. 194–209). In particular, specialization of market demand was revealing the inflexibility and limitations of Fordism-Taylorism as a form of production.

The great advantage of Fordism was that it could produce large volumes of goods at low cost for mass markets (Aglietta, 1979, pp. 116–21; Sabel, 1982, pp. 32–6, 194–231). Production was based on highly specialized machines designed to perform very specific tasks. Tasks were arranged as successive operations along mechanically moved assembly lines where the product was transported from one station to the next. Given the minute division of labor necessary for that technology, basically unskilled workers could carry out the production process. Only a few skilled workers were needed for maintenance and other specialized tasks. But the great advantage of Fordism was later to prove its greatest disadvantage: The system was very rigid, inflexible. Also, the system was very vulnerable. Any bottleneck along the line, whether caused by machines or workers, would stop the entire line. Both American employers during the sit-down strikes of the 1930s and Italian owners of large-scale factories during the 1969 *autunno caldo* painfully discovered their vulnerability to work stoppages.

The system was vulnerable not only to dissatisfied labor but also to the changeable preferences of consumers. Specialized machines could perform at high speed and with high precision those tasks for which they had been designed, but they could do no more. With the introduction of any new model, the assembly line would have to be disassembled, its layout redesigned, and the machines either substituted or retooled. The result was periodic downtime for retooling, and that was extremely costly. Profitability depended on the presence of a mass market of consumers capable of absorbing volume production, but it also required that consumer demand be stable over time, at least over the time required to recoup the high investment costs of the specialized equipment and the assembly line. It was also necessary that consumer demand be for a standard, undifferentiated product. As Ford put it, he could offer to the consumer his famous "Model T, painted any color so long as it was black" (quoted in Sabel, 1982, p. 168).

But consumers eventually came to expect cars in the colors of their choosing, with two or four doors, with engine sizes that would best suit their needs, with or without air bags, with or without antilock brakes, with plastic or velvet interiors in various colors. When consumers demand an industrial product that is custom-made (and are willing to pay a premium for the luxury of choice), then a rigid technology will not suffice, no matter how inexpensively it can turn out its goods. Decentralized production, on the other hand, offers precisely what is needed: the flexibility to adjust to highly volatile demand and the capacity to give consumers precisely what they want.

Paradoxically, the emergence of Fordism and assembly-line technology created a market for standardized inexpensive goods, but it also led to a higher standard of living, which allowed people to differentiate their tastes. Decentralized production allowed employers to meet the challenge of flexibility, and once in place, decentralized production tended to sustain its pace, to replicate itself: First, once employers learned the organizational skills involved in subcontracting, the practice became easier and more widespread (Brusco, 1975, p. 38). Second, once consumers became accustomed to tailor-made, customized products, they would accept nothing less, not only in their shirts, suits, and shoes but also in their motorcycles, cars, refrigerators, and furniture. In the 1980s, the *griffe*, the designer's signature, became an obsession for Italian consumers.

When the world's market demand changed during the late 1970s and 1980s, the Italian economy already had in place a flexible system of production, set up over the course of the protracted struggle between capital and labor, and based on small firms, linked together through mutual subcontracting practices. The solutions to problems of both labor relations and market competition (interclass and intraclass conflict) had converged to reward that highly flexible system of specialized production.[77] The success story of small firms in Italy (particularly when compared with the dismal performance of larger firms) prompted a flurry of enthusiastic literature. The PMIs (*piccola-media industria*, the small and medium industries) became "in" even with the unions and the Communist Party, which previously had focused on the big firms, the strongholds of labor (*aree forti*).[78] The unions began setting aside their old prejudices against small firms, best expressed by the equation *small firm = big exploitation*.[79] Thus, when the unions adopted minimum firm size as a criterion for including firms in a survey sample, they kept that minimum high enough so as to hide the reality of the underworld of the smaller productive units.[80] Alternatively, when they did not set lower limits for the parameter of firm size, they would present statistical findings in ways that lumped small firms within larger aggregates (e.g., 1–100).

Unions were, indeed, hard-pressed to dispel the dismal picture of labor relations in smaller firms. Even when there was no union presence in small firms, unions argued, that should not be read as a complete lack of union protection for the workers in smaller firms. Italian unions provided such free services as fiscal, insurance, and legal assistance to their members.[81] In larger firms, such services were available to union members directly inside the plants. Because that was more difficult in smaller plants, territorial unions provided the services (Squarzon, 1990).[82] The more precarious position of workers in smaller firms and the greater difficulties of unions in penetrating those firms forced unions to shift their strategy in smaller firms away from collective protection and toward individual protection, based on court appeals under the Workers' Charter (Cagnato, 1981; Castegnaro, 1983). In that way, no worker in Italy was left completely without support, either individually or collectively.

That strategy seems quite rational, given the cost of organizing workers in smaller firms, and given the higher percentage of victories in labor-court proceedings for individual workers than for trade unions, particularly in smaller firms. But, unions (and scholars) claimed, labor relations were *more complex* in small firms. The argument was: not only is there individual and collective union protection in small firms, but also there is collective bargaining as well as individual bargaining, in which an individual or a handful of skilled individuals could fare much better on their own than through collective bargaining (Trigilia,

1986; Perulli and Trigilia, 1990). In light of the record uncovered here, that view appears to be overly optimistic.

And so it was that "small is beautiful" came in vogue. PMIs were in. During the decade from 1970 to 1980 it was the firms employing 10–20 workers whose number increased the most (+61.8%), followed by firms with 6–9 workers (+47%). The number of firms with 20–49 workers grew less rapidly (+19.2%), and firms of all other sizes either declined, as in the larger sizes, or grew slightly (around 5%) (Barca and Magnani, 1989, p. 195). The miracle of the smaller firms was the miracle of a size class that had been outside the influence of the unions and outside the scope of most empirical research. Perhaps it is worth citing Castegnaro's warning:

Researchers, by choice or for lack of systematic availability of data on plant-level agreements, tend to focus on the larger firms. There exists a sort of convergence between the cognitive interests of researchers and the organizational interests of local unions that systematically produces analyses that overestimate the extent of bargaining. (Castegnaro, 1983, p. 195)

If that was true for plant-level bargaining, it was also true for unionization figures and other labor-relations indicators. And if that was true for union-sponsored research, one cannot be too optimistic about finding out the real state of labor relations in small firms from research funded by employers – the main sponsors, with trade unions, of labor-relations research in Italy.[83]

8.11. THE PUZZLE IS COMPLETE

The analyses in Chapter 7 focused on the characteristics of strike waves, on their nature as direct challenges to existing economic, social, and political relations. Strike waves are no ordinary events. But what makes them special is not so much the unusual characteristics of the thousand little events that make up the "big one," such as the 1969 *autunno caldo*; rather, what makes them special are the effects strike waves can have on the course of history, their ability to potentially transform those very structures that brought them to the fore of history in the first place. The analyses of this chapter have made that point quite clear. Indeed, it was the nature of the responses by the state and employers and the changes they brought about that marked strike waves as the motors of sociopolitical change.

The 1969 *autunno caldo*, in particular, had deep and long-lasting effects. New plant-level organizational structures and figures emerged, such as factory councils and workers' delegates. Union membership grew manyfold. In fact, the entire organizational structure, the bureaucratic apparatus, and the overall strategy of the unions changed. The two-tier bargaining structure (at the industry level and at the plant level) that so clearly shaped the temporal dynamic of Italian strikes for years to come was consolidated during the 1968–72 strike wave. Perhaps most importantly, the 1968–72 wave affected the political organization of the Italian working class. Communist Party membership grew steadily during the 1970s, and the party also scored a series of electoral victories, gaining up to 30% of the votes. In 1978, it joined in a short-lived coalition government of "national solidarity." The overall balance of class forces shifted in the workers' favor during the 1970s.[84]

But if the effects of strike waves are indeed deeply political, their causes are most likely economic. Economic? Did I not reject at the end of Chapter 7 both a political explanation and an economic explanation of strike waves? To be precise, what I rejected there was a business-cycle explanation of strike waves, not all possibility of an economic explanation. I rejected an explanation based on short-term cycles of economic activity. As we saw in Chapter 3, however, scholars working within a broad Marxist framework have argued for the existence of long-term economic cycles.[85] Unlike the business cycle, which is only a few years in duration, a long cycle will span several decades. Perhaps it is to these cycles that we must turn our attention in search of an explanation.

Several authors have linked the long-term fluctuations in strike activity to the Kondratieff cycle, a regular economic cycle of some fifty-years' duration, the so-called *long wave* described by the Russian economist Kondratieff (1935). Mandel (1980, pp. 37–61), for instance, argued that major waves of class struggle and long waves of economic growth go together. Cronin (1980) showed how strike waves and long waves went together in the British historical experience. Screpanti (1987) provided comparative evidence based on five countries (France, Germany, Italy, the United States, and the United Kingdom) and three strike indicators (frequency, size, and duration). Screpanti concluded that "Major upheavals tend to explode around the upper turning points of the long cycles."[86]

Mandel (1980, pp. 37–61) specified the causal mechanisms relating strike waves and long economic cycles: In European countries over the past century, when labor-market conditions favorable to workers occurred at the peak of a long phase of prosperity, that led to large-scale eruptions of industrial conflict. The high levels of workers' militancy forced employers to seek and implement "radical" technological innovations. There is evidence to suggest that technological innovation occurred in spurts linked to the initial phase of the downswing periods of the Kondratieff cycle (e.g., Hartman and Wheeler, 1979). The commercial and widespread application of technological innovations ultimately led to radical changes in the organization of production. Needless to say, these new forms of organization of production eliminated the kinds of workers who had been central in the previous form of organization of production and who had been most active in the previous struggles. The economy then entered into a new phase characterized by a new, "specific technology, radically different from the previous one . . . [and] centered around a specific type of machine system . . . [which], in turn, presupposes a specific form of organization of the labor process" (Mandel, 1980, pp. 42–3).[87] In each phase, a specific type of worker occupied a central position in the production process. It was that worker who became most involved in the struggles as each phase reached maturity.

An explanation of strike waves based on the long waves of the economy is particularly appealing, for several reasons. Such a theory can account for the approximate concurrence of the major strike waves that cut across different countries in the Western world: 1840s, 1880s, 1920s, 1960s. Each occurred at the height of a specific phase of capitalist development, and that helps to pin down the main actors involved in the conflict during a given strike wave: the workers who were most central to the predominant form of organization of production. With specific reference to the Italian case, the theory helps to answer the question of why there was a strike wave in 1969. It was because the 1960s were the peak years in the long postwar economic growth of capitalist economies (not only in Italy) characterized by a specific technical mode of factory production (i.e., Fordism).[88] It was that technical mode of production that gave the Italian 1968–72 strike wave its peculiar characteristics: the *operaio massa* as the main actor, the egalitarian demands, the strike tactics centered on the assembly line. Most importantly, the analyses in this chapter have highlighted the fact that strike waves impose on employers tremendous incentives to find alternative forms of organization of production, much along Mandel's line.

For all its appeal, there are several problems with a Kondratieff's explanation of strike waves. First, the strict periodicity of the long waves (regular intervals of fifty years' duration) has been hotly contested. Even theories broadly conceived within a Marxist framework (the American social-structure-of-accumulation theory and the French regulation theory) that support the existence of long cycles of economic activity have rejected the notion of periodicity. Yet, as we saw in Chapter 3, both theories would clearly link each economic phase to particular forms of production. Those forms are never purely technical. They represent various combinations of technical and sociopolitical processes. A crisis represents a structural failure in that combination. The way out of a crisis requires solutions in both the technical and the sociopolitical spheres. For both theories, the class struggle is the main ingredient in a crisis situation. But whereas the structure-of-accumulation theory sees the class struggle as the cause of the crisis, the regulation theory sees it as an accompanying effect, with the causes being rooted within the mode of capitalist accumulation itself. The analyses presented in this book show how the class struggle and the wider economic, social, and political processes go together, just as those theories hypothesize. A crisis requires a settlement at both the political level and the economic level. That much is clear from the Italian experience of the 1970s, with its drawn-out search for a new class compromise and a new settlement of class relations. The Italian case, however, seems to lend support to the social-structure-of-accumulation theory, to the extent that the heightened levels of class confrontation during the 1968–72 strike wave seem to have jolted the system into change.

Second, if these cycles, whether periodic or nonperiodic, have a duration of several decades, why did the two great strike waves in Italian postwar history (1959–63 and 1968–72) occur less than ten years apart? Does that not seem more like the length of the regular business cycle? The criticism is well taken. However, central to the notion of economic long cycles (particularly in the social-structure-of-accumulation or regime-of-accumulation approach), are both the technical mode of production and the sociopolitical institutions that favor accumulation. The same social processes and technical mode of production obtained during both the 1959–63 and 1968–72 strike waves. Factory life was dominated by a combination of Fordism and Taylorism. During the 1960s, that type of organization of production came to full maturity. Furthermore, the institutional (economic and political) mechanisms for conflict regulation were the same. The 1959–63 strike wave was simply a foreshadowing of events to come. The continuity of historical events was interrupted by the somewhat artificial recession of 1964–66. Screpanti, in his comparative analysis of strike waves and long waves, concluded that although major strike waves occur at the peak of the Kondratieff cycle, minor ripples occur at the trough of the cycle (defensive conflicts) and along the way during the expansion phase.

Finally, how can I build an argument about strike waves based on only one data point (i.e., 1969)? Is this not an extreme case of "small N's and big conclusions"? (Lieberson, 1991). This, too, is a well-taken criticism. The N is small to start with. To the extent that the long waves are linked to the development of the *industrial* capitalist mode of production, and given that the process of industrialization did not involve most countries until the middle of the nineteenth century, we have only a handful of data points available.[89] In this chapter, I have simply focused even more narrowly on just one of these data points. Again, I believe that the analyses presented in this book leave no doubt about the connections among historically specific sociotechnical modes of production, changes in the class structure, and the central positions that certain actors occupy in the prevailing sociotechnical organization of production and, as a consequence, in the class structure. The analyses, I believe, have clearly shown the roles that those central actors play in the struggles that erupt when a particular mode of production comes to maturity. There seems to be ample evidence to substantiate the basic mechanisms that link long cycles of economic activity and strike waves, at least for one of a handful of historical occurrences of such processes. As for the other occurrences, I have mostly relied on comparative evidence taken from the available literature.

In conclusion, the analyses in this chapter have allowed me to answer the question of the causes of strike waves. Having rejected in Chapter 7 both a political explanation and a business-cycle explanation for strike waves, in this chapter I have proposed a broader political-economic explanation, based on specific modes of production, and on the structures (or regimes) of accumulation. Characteristic of those structures is the interplay between economic institutions and broader sociopolitical institutions. A regime of accumulation (e.g., the postwar Fordist regime) thrives through the combined workings of different institutions. Throughout this book, we have indeed seen that in order to understand class conflict, we have to understand not only its economic basis but also the wider sociopolitical context.

In summary, in light of the analyses of this chapter it was no mere historical accident that Italy experienced two bouts of economic expansion in the postwar period (albeit along a single long-term upswing cycle), two strike waves, and two favorable shifts in the political position of the working class. Neither was it merely a result of a very narrow conception of time and causality that both instances of political change (*centro-sinistra*, and *compromesso storico* and *unità nazionale*) followed the two periods of heightened class confrontation. Indeed, changes in the social relations of production bring about changes in the balance of class forces. When that balance tilts to the workers' favor, workers will use their more favorable bargaining position to exact concessions from employers via collective mobilization. As those concessions may ultimately cut into the profitability of firms and the ability of capital to reproduce itself, a way out of the crisis may ultimately require a "political" solution. That solution may not always be favorable to the working class, but when it is, it will involve a more equitable distribution of political (and not just economic) resources. Again, the economic and the political spheres of society appear to be tightly interwoven: The clues that at the end of the last chapter may have seemed like a desperate and last-minute attempt to salvage a book from failure turned out to be fruitful after all.

The analyses have also allowed me to answer another question posed in Chapter 6. What caused the change in the political position of labor in the national power structure during the 1970s? That change was caused by working-class mobilization and widespread conflict. Strike waves and cycles bring about changes in the forms of institutionalization of conflict (bargaining structure), in class capacities (in terms of the membership and organization of working-class institutions – unions and parties), and in the overall distribution of power in capitalist societies. Even the economic structure of a capitalist society is radically transformed by the class struggle, strike waves, in particular. Indeed, it would be impossible to understand such momentous mobilization processes as strike waves without understanding the actions of the employers and the state.

Thus, events such as the 1969 *autunno caldo* and the strike wave that accompanied it are set within a structural context that explains their location in time and space, but, in their turn, these events appear to be deeply transformative of those structures. But if strike waves produce changes in the economic, organizational, institutional, and political spheres, then conflict is not just a dependent variable. Rather, conflict would appear to be the main independent variable in a web of wider relations. But that would reverse the entire causal structure on which this book has thus far rested: strikes as the result of a set of economic, organizational, institutional, and political *determinants*. Conflict, our *dependent* variable through several chapters, seems to have become the *independent* variable. Statistical causality is a poor excuse for the complexity of historical reality. The causal direction of the arguments, from economic, organizational, institutional, and political factors to conflict, has taken a sudden and unexpected turn. Where does this leave us? What is the picture in the puzzle?

9

The picture in the puzzle

The organisation arises as product of the struggle ... organisations ... are ... born from the mass strike ... from the whirlwind and the storm, out of the fire and glow of the mass strike and the street fighting rise again, like Venus from the foam, fresh, young, powerful, buoyant trade unions. ... In the midst of the struggle the work of organisation is being more widely extended.

Rosa Luxemburg (1971, pp. 64, 36, 38)

Class struggle, which is itself structurally limited and selected by various social structures, simultaneously reshapes those structures. ... Class struggle is intrinsically a process of transformation of structures, and thus the very process which sets limits on class struggle is at the same time transformed by the struggles so limited. ... Organizational capacities are objects of class struggle. ... The organizational capacity of the working class to engage in struggle is itself transformed by class struggle.

Wright (1979, pp. 21, 105)

In history, as elsewhere, the causes cannot be assumed. They are to be looked for.

Bloch (1953, p. 197)

9.1. UNEXPECTED FINDINGS, ONE MORE TIME: CLASS CONFLICT AS THE *INDEPENDENT* VARIABLE

Just when we thought that we had it all wrapped up, with a pat solution for the temporal dynamics of Italian strikes in the postwar period, the reversal of the causal reading at the end of Chapter 8 (strikes as the cause, rather than the effect, of economic, organizational, institutional, and political factors) has brought in a new twist. *Conflict*: The demon that I tried to exorcise through several chapters of countless statistical analyses, through patient reconstruction of the historical record, through a sympathetic ear for the words of many of the participants, through careful mapping of causal arguments, is back, and back with a vengeance, with the passion and anger of the participants, with all the disruptive power of massed numbers (not those of statistics, but those of mobilization). Of conflict, I would have expected no less. To be sure, this is not the conflict embodied in your everyday, run-of-the-mill strike, but rather strike waves, those momentous insurgencies of working-class protest that "March as exclamation marks in labor history" (Shorter and Tilly, 1974, p. 104). And we did see that strike waves can be very disruptive.

For one thing, strike waves transform the very nature of working-class organizations. We saw in Chapter 4 how unionization and the expansion of working-class organizational resources seem to have followed intense periods of industrial conflict, strike waves in particular. Furthermore, not only did union membership increase, but also the union personnel changed as a consequence of the two major postwar outbursts of industrial conflict. The very organizational structure of unions changed in the aftermath of those two strike waves. After the 1959–63 strike wave, the federal level (e.g., metalworkers, textile workers) took over the confederal level, which had dominated the labor-relations scene during the 1950s. The 1969 *autunno caldo* brought out new plant-level organizational structures. Strike waves, however, affect not only the organization of labor but also that of employers. As we saw in both Chapters 4 and 8, the *autunno caldo* swept away much of the old apparatus of Confindustria and of the territorial associations and brought out new organizational structures (e.g., the creation of new industrial associations, such as Federmeccanica) and a complete turnaround in ideologies and strategies of class relations.

The political organization of the working class and its political position in the national power structure also changed with both strike waves, as we saw in Chapter 6. In 1962, after a couple of years of unprecedented levels of conflict, the Socialists were brought into a coalition government (*centro sinistra*), for the first time since the Popular Front government of 1947.[1] The 1968–72 strike wave set in motion a long-term shift in the political position of the Italian working class that eventually brought the Communists into a coalition government. Labor involvement in political institutions increased after each strike wave, particularly after the *autunno caldo*. A survey conducted in Lombardy on the extent of the union presence in public institutions revealed that in the six-year period between 1968 and 1974, the number of institutions in which unions had a presence doubled with respect to the number reached between 1900 and 1968 (Ferrari, 1979, p. 56).[2] Unions were not very successful in reaching the "control room," that is, the governing bodies of the institutions in which they participated (in fact, in only 20% of the cases) (Ferrari, 1979, p. 65). But again, 75% of the cases in which unions did have a presence in governing bodies arose after 1968 (Ferrari, 1979, p. 94).[3]

In Chapter 5 we saw that along with organizational and political changes, strike waves also brought about changes in the forms of institutionalization of conflict. The 1959–63 strike wave resulted in more decentralized, industrywide bargaining (*contrattazione articolata*). The 1969 *autunno caldo* extended the practice of plant-level bargaining. Thus, if it is true that the bargaining structure helps to explain the prevailing patterns of conflict in postwar Italy, it is also true that changes in the bargaining structure itself came about only through conflict and were the results of changing power relations (Korpi, 1974).

Finally, in Chapter 8 we saw how even economic structures, the invisible hand of the market, were deeply shaped and transformed by specific historical actors.

The business cycle itself can be viewed as a product of class conflict, as the by-product of employers' actions and state actions aimed at curbing labor militancy by thwarting workers' bargaining power in the labor market (Kalecki, 1943, Soskice, 1978). Both workers and employers strategically maximize their bargaining positions with respect to the business cycle. Employers, however, are in a far better position to take advantage of economic conditions, because they control directly or indirectly the levers of the economy (e.g., by controlling the types and the locations of investments, credits, interest rates, economic policies, etc.). Italian unions argued that the short and abrupt 1964 recession had been deliberately brought about by the monetary policies of the Bank of Italy in order to curb the high levels of labor militancy that had surfaced during the previous rounds of contract renewals. In any case, the tremendous growth in the number of small firms during the 1970s and 1980s, Italy's economic miracle of the 1980s, was in large part the result of the employers' attempts to find an area in which they would have flexibility in their use of the work force. Workers' successful struggles in the early 1970s had tilted power relations in larger firms in the workers' favor. Employers' use of the work force in the larger firms had become increasingly "rigid" (obviously, that is, from the employers' viewpoint): overtime bans, restrictions on layoffs and the use of internal mobility, workers' control over the organization of production, greater levels of absenteeism and conflict, disruption of production schedules due to continuous bargaining (at all levels: sector, group, firm, department, homogeneous work group), and conflict. The absence of a union presence to provide protection in the smaller firms assured employers the upper hand in those settings, more freedom in their "flexible" use of the work force.

9.2. SUMMING UP WHAT WE KNOW (FIRM EMPIRICAL GROUNDS)

My analyses of strike waves bring out broad and unsettling questions about the nature of industrial conflict. The empirically observable reciprocal causation between conflict and what I have considered to be the *determinants* of conflict throughout this book – namely, economic, organizational, institutional, and political processes – poses challenging theoretical problems. But reciprocal causation is hardly the only empirical finding in this book that has theoretical implications whose significance I have barely touched upon. Driven by the task of fitting together into a coherent picture the pieces of empirical evidence, I have overlooked some of the theoretical questions that my empirical findings have been uncovering. Let me highlight those findings and the theoretical problems they pose.

The most surprising empirical finding is that all of the factors considered (economic, organizational, institutional, and political) seem to have contributed to determining the temporal patterns of strikes in postwar Italy. Thus, when unemployment went up, the number of strikes went down. Union organizational strength and strike activity – the number of strikers, in particular – went hand in hand. The two-tier bargaining structure (industry-level and plant-level contracts) and the three-year duration of collective contracts explained the empirically observable three-year cycle of strike indicators and the one-year lag in the peaks for the number of strikes and number of workers involved. Finally, power relationships highly unfavorable to the working class in both the economic and political arenas explained the low levels of mobilization during the 1950s. Shifts in the political position of labor during the 1970s changed the locus of conflict from the economic to the political arena. And that sharply modified the shapes of strikes (particularly in the 1975–78 period).

The finding that various social processes (and therefore different theoretical approaches, particularly business-cycle, resource-mobilization, collective-bargaining, and political-exchange theories) seem to have provided plausible explanations for various parts of the data is somewhat bewildering. On the one hand, we are rather accustomed to playing off theories against one another. If all these theories are partially right, we are deprived of the cathartic resolution of finding out who is right and who is wrong, the good guys and the bad guys, good and evil. But most importantly, that finding demonstrates that there are limits to each of these theories. Each theory is limited because it cannot, by itself, account for all the evidence. In the metaphor of this book, each theory allows me to fit only a limited number of the pieces of the puzzle. A general explanation of strikes probably would require pulling these different theories together. Which raises the question: How can we combine such different theories in a coherent framework?

Another important finding of this book is that strikes are multiple-actor, multiple-action phenomena. Strikes are workers' strategic responses to (or anticipation of) the actions of other social actors. Strikes – strike waves in particular – provide the nexus for the strategic interactions among organized actors. Classes and the state strategically interact in the pursuit of their interests. But other actors, as well, are key participants in the process of national class struggles. We have seen, for instance, how the hegemonic influence of the United States in Italian affairs severely constrained the outcome of Italian struggles. On the one hand, this points to the limitations of strikes as means to achieve revolutionary change. On the other, it points to the capitalist world-system and to the set of states actively involved in maintaining that system and severely constraining the possibilities for different paths of national development.

Finally, there is little doubt that conflict is a cyclical phenomenon. Industrial conflict is characterized by both short-term and long-term movements, periodic and nonperiodic movements (with regular and irregular patterns over time). Short-term, seasonal cycles create a busy jigsaw pattern around the edges of a regular, three-year cycle induced by collective bargaining. Both of these periodic cycles fluctuate around longer, nonperiodic movements induced by the business cycle. Every few years, depending on the length of a particular business cycle, strikes flare up during booms and die out during busts. Finally, regular minor seasonal ripples and institutional cycles, as well as irregular business-cycle movements, follow the lines of a yet longer cycle, the strike waves, related to the long-term swings of the capitalist world economy. Recent work on the new social movements (e.g.,

Koopmans, 1993; Snow and Benford, 1992) and Tarrow's (1989a) work on the relationship between the labor movement and other social movements in Italy have shown that the same cyclical behavior that characterizes strikes characterizes other forms of protest.

Strike waves are the nexus of the strategic interaction between workers, employers, and the state. The financial and legitimation crisis provoked by strike waves requires solutions at *both* the economic and political levels. Reactions by employers and the state to strike waves set the terms of class relations for years to come. As a strike wave unfolds, and the power of mass mobilization tilts the balance of class forces to the workers' favor, employers scramble to stem the tide of mobilization and to regain their margins of power. And among the things employers try is to shift the mix of the factors of production away from labor and toward fixed capital. Not only machines don't strike, but the introduction of new machines and new technologies provides opportunities to reorganize production with an eye to breaking up networks of solidarity and militancy. Thus, technical decisions have not only social motivations, but also social consequences. The changes that employers introduce in the organizational forms and in the technical mode of production in their reaction to heightened levels of class confrontation ultimately displace militant actors central to a given form of organization of production (e.g., assembly line). Such changes eliminate old working-class figures from the shop floor and bring out new ones. New workers are forced into long-term processes of self-identification and organization. In Italy, the skilled workers who had been involved in the struggles of the late 1940s and the 1959–63 strike wave were replaced by a new historical actor of the late 1960s and 1970s: the *operaio massa* ("mass worker"). But the process of accelerated industrial restructuring throughout the 1970s displaced that working-class figure, in turn, from a central role in the production process (Accornero, 1981; Rieser, 1981).

Given the disruptive power and the revolutionary threat of strike waves, and their relation to other social movements that tends to radicalize a whole generation ("the revolutionary generation"), these momentous expressions of working-class mobilization tend to be deliberately eliminated from public discourse. From the Right (and sometimes, paradoxically, from the Left as well), the class struggle and its potential for revolutionary change are exorcised through countless theories of "the labor aristocracy," "the withering away of strikes," "the end of ideology," "the embourgeoisement of the working class," in fact, the very "end of the working class." In that way, social theories, as well, swing around the long waves of conflict.

The problem with the withering-away-of-strikes theories is that they regard as trend what in reality is cycle, although of a longer wavelength.[4] Theories of the withering away of strikes are based on a remarkably narrow temporal window. Industrial conflict is a cyclical phenomenon, where cycles of a few months' duration overlap longer ones, some of a few years' duration, some lasting a few decades. At every downturn, we rejoice for the withering away of strikes; at every upturn, we brace for revolution. Thus, along the cycles of conflict, "up and down the long roller coaster"[5] ride and swing our theoretical explanations for historical reality, with theories of labor aristocracy joining hands with theories of embourgeoisement.[6] Industrial conflict (strikes) appears to be an endemic feature of capitalist, industrial societies. Even recent historical work on national experiences of class formation has shown the universal presence of unions and of industrial conflict in capitalist societies (Zolberg, 1986, p. 398). This is in spite of the basic anticonvergence approach of much of that scholarship.[7] The arguments on strike trends reviewed in Chapter 6 left no doubt about strikes being a permanent feature of capitalist societies. Those arguments also highlighted the possible conditions for a long-term decline of strikes: on the one hand, long-term prosperity; on the other, political exchange. In the climate of worldwide increases in class confrontations in the 1960s and early 1970s, withering-away arguments smelled of ideology ("dominant" ideology) and fell into disrepute. But at the opposite end of the political spectrum, and for different reasons, Przeworski, Offe, Wiesenthal, and others, echoing Marxist arguments from the turn of the century, argued that indeed long-term prosperity is a precondition for consensus (i.e., for low levels of conflict).

There is a powerful metaphor that best captures the notion that industrial conflict is cyclical: Gramsci's imagery of *war of movement* and *war of position*. According to that metaphor, the labor movement proceeds by sudden giant leaps forward, when the movement breaks through enemy lines and scores dazzling victories. Then come the times of retrenchment, the times for digging in to withstand the tide of counterattacks, the times for stout defense of the positions conquered. At those times, most likely terrain will be lost, but when it is conquered it is measured in inches rather than in miles. The war of movement involves the masses. Its touchstone is collective action. The 1969 *autunno caldo* and the entire 1968–72 strike wave provide a good example of a war of movement. Within a few years (arguably, in fact, within a few months), the Italian labor movement won what it had been unable to win in two decades of constant skirmishes: the Workers' Charter, union representation at the plant level, increased power for both the unions and the Italian Communist Party. The strike wave swept away in its tidal swell several decades of paternalistic (at best) and repressive labor relations and ushered in a new era. The 1970s were the long years of management of the ground won in 1969. And the movement kept growing, although growing while declining, to use Manghi's expression.

Thus, a book that opened with "This book tells a story" seems to be ending on an ambiguous note. So what is the story? This unsettling ending of my "story" is well in line with the narrative framework of the book. After all, any story worth the telling is not without its red herrings, false clues, seemingly pat solutions, and final twists. But if that works well for fiction, how does it fit with a "scientific" explanation of strikes? Can our theories of strikes accept the reversal of the causal order? Can the theories account for this dialectic process? In light of these questions, it appears that the puzzle of fitting together pieces of empirical evidence has turned into the puzzle of fitting pieces of theoretical explanations.

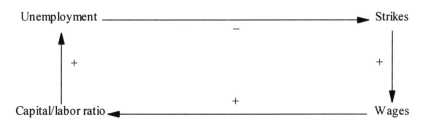

Figure 9.1. *Causal structure of an economic model of strikes*

9.3. SUMMING UP WHAT WE DON'T KNOW (THEORETICAL PUZZLES AND TENTATIVE SOLUTIONS)

This book has provided ample evidence that economic, organizational, institutional, and political factors all contribute to shape the patterns of industrial conflict at any given historical juncture. The interplay of these *determinants* is constantly changing, and these determinants of conflict themselves change as a consequence of conflict. The dialectic nature of conflict and the reciprocal causation between strikes and independent variables, and among independent variables, are at the heart of the model of strikes that emerges from the analyses provided in this book. These analyses make it clear that historical processes do not unfold in an additive, linear fashion, that causation does not go in one direction only, that we cannot simply look at industrial conflict as the "dependent" variable and at economic, organizational, institutional, and political factors as the "independent" variables, that industrial conflict itself (particularly such momentous outbursts of working-class protest as strike waves) produces effects in the economic, organizational, institutional, and political spheres, subverting established relationships and setting up new ones. More generally, the class struggle shapes the very process of class formation: the structural composition of classes, and of the working class in particular, and the organizational forms and agencies for the articulation of its interests. Strikes, strike waves in particular, provide the melting pot for classes.

Whether Marxist or non-Marxist, a "general" theory of strikes must be able to address those issues. It must be able to account for the simultaneous interplay of various social processes (economic, organizational, institutional, and political). Furthermore, it must be able to explain (1) the cyclical nature of strikes and (2) the occurrence of strike waves; finally, (3) it must link specific forms of conflict to specific kinds of actors, that is, link class conflict to the underlying class structure. How would our theories of strikes approach those issues?

Let me start with economic theory. The economic-bargaining theory of strikes specifies that unemployment has a negative effect on strikes (see the model in Figure 9.1). But if economists were to explore the broad causal chain in which unemployment and strikes are enmeshed, they would find that strikes may result in higher wages. Capitalists confronted with higher labor costs may decide to shift

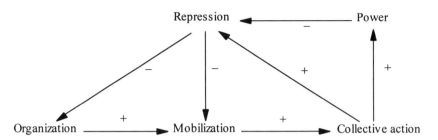

Figure 9.2. *Causal structure of a power model of strikes*

the mix of the factors of production (capital, labor, raw materials, energy), reducing the input of labor in order to keep production costs down. That may mean using more capital, more raw materials, or more energy.[8] The end result, however, may be a reduction of the labor factor. If, at any given time, only a handful of capitalists are faced with this decision, their individual choices will not affect the overall level of unemployment. But when most capitalists are faced with this decision at the same time, such as during strike waves, individual decisions may lead to higher levels of unemploy-ment. As production becomes, for instance, more capital-intensive, companies will start shedding excess labor. The rise in unemployment will then bring conflict down, just as bargaining theories of strikes would predict. Equilibrium is brought back into the system. Thus, an account of the reciprocal causal mechanisms that link strikes and the state of the labor market is certainly in the theoretical tool bag of neoclassical economics.

Similarly, as we saw in Chapters 4 and 6, resource-mobilization theories look at collective action as the result of organization and mobilization (see the model of Figure 9.2 modified from Tilly, 1974, p. 216). However, mobilization is not an end in itself. Mobilization of a group is aimed at obtaining an allocation of the available resources (be they economic, symbolic, political, or others) more favorable to the group. Resource-mobilization theories view the outcome of mobilization in terms of power (Tilly, 1974, 1978, pp. 98–142). Mobilization changes a group's power. Unfortunately, mobilization of a challenging group is likely to lead to counter-mobilization of the challenged group, perhaps leading to the use of repression against the challenging group. Repression can ultimately lead to the demobilization of the challenging group. If the mobilization is successful, however, the group will have increased its power. The group will then wield that power to obtain a more favorable distribution of resources. If that is the aim of mobilization, the acquisition of power will ultimately tail off into demobilization. Thus, either via repression or following a favorable redistribution of resources, any grab for power will ultimately lead to the demobilization of a challenging group, bringing the system back to its state of equilibrium (Figure 9.2). Again, the Italian postwar experience shows that labor mobilization led to both outcomes for the power grab: Repression during the 1950s, and a more favorable distribution of resources during the 1970s.

Within the resource-mobilization/political-power model, one can easily incorporate bargaining-structure and political-exchange arguments. After all, the bargaining structure is nothing but a form of institutionalization of labor (e.g., at the national level or at the plant level), an intervening variable between power and mobilization. Similarly, political-exchange theories are concerned with different forms of management of the power that results from mobilization (e.g., short or long term, in the economic or political market).

The fact that complexity can be added to the theoretical models of strikes encountered in this book (beyond the narrow focus that problems of statistical specification and estimation force upon us) does not mean that we always do so. Particularly when crossing the boundary between economic and political models, disciplinary parochialism and specialization keep scholars focused on specific societal spheres, on specific sets of variables. Political-exchange theories should be best equipped to bridge the gap between economic and political models; after all, the shift between economic and political action is at the heart of their theoretical concerns. Even these theories, however, tend to focus on the political side of the exchange. Indeed, the *paradox of the 1970s* can be explained precisely by the fact that a purely economic model of society does not have much to say about political power and the state (aside from its tax, monetary, and spending policies). But in fact, the changed nature of the broad power relations between classes during the 1970s and the unions' greater control over labor-market mechanisms changed the traditional relationship between unemployment and strikes (at least in the short run). Perhaps there is no escape from academic specialization and the professionalization of science. But certainly, one unfortunate outcome of these combined processes is that theories of strikes rooted in different academic disciplines have largely ignored one another.

Contrary to the narrow focus of mainstream social theories upon specific societal spheres and processes (economic, organizational, institutional, political), Marxism has always promoted its all-encompassing view of social relations as the hallmark of its theory of society and history. As Lukacs (1971, p. 21) wrote, "It is not the primacy of economic motives in historical explanation that constitutes the difference between Marxism and bourgeois thought, but the point of view of totality." Furthermore, as a social theory, Marxist theory is both dialectic and dynamic: It can account for the simultaneous interplay of various actors on the stage of history, and it allows for the introduction of change into the system. The causal model of Figure 9.3, borrowed and modified from Wright (1979, pp. 15–29, 104, 165, 223; see also Tilly, 1978, p. 43), makes this quite clear. In a simplified and schematic way, the model embeds the class struggle (read "strikes" in this context) in a set of three other social processes and structures: organization of accumulation, political/economic organization, and class structure.

The model provides two main types of relationships (or modes of determination): Limitation and transformation.[9] Thus, for instance, throughout this book, we have seen how the economic and political organization of the working class has affected ("limited," in the language of the model) workers' capacity to mobilize

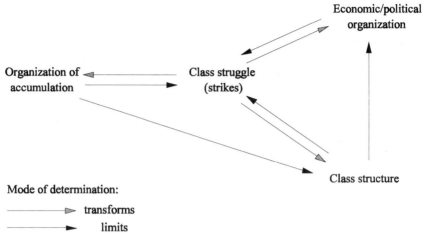

Figure 9.3. *Causal structure of a power model of strikes*

("class struggle"). The traditional lack of union representation within the factories, the poverty of Italian unions' financial resources, and the deep divisions along political lines had resulted in a pattern of conflict characterized by brief instances of micro-level conflict, centered around a single department and the members of a single union. Highly centralized bargaining at the national level further explains the handful of very large strikes (of the "general strike" type). It was the distorting effects of those few outliers on the average sizes of strikes that prompted Ross and Hartman to marvel that "Italian rates of participation have been fantastically high" (Ross and Hartman, 1960, p. 121). The institutionalization of conflict in the economic arena (e.g., bargaining structure) further limited the outcome; in fact, it "selected" certain years as peak years, it "selected" different strike indicators for different peak years.[10] Thus, the years of industrywide contract renewals were characterized by strikes of large size and low frequency, whereas the years of plant-level contract renewals were characterized by the opposite pattern of small size and high frequency. The class structure similarly "limited" the class struggle. The shift from an agricultural to an industrial and finally to a service work force over the 1950–78 period explains the decline in the importance of agricultural struggles and the recent rise of white-collar conflict in the service sector. Finally, the different forms of organization of production make available different repertoires of collective action, involving different types of actors, with different demands. Thus, the changes in Italy's productive structure during the 1950s and 1960s reviewed in Chapter 3 toward a Fordist mode of production brought to the fore of Italian labor history the *operaio massa*, the protagonist of the *autunno caldo*.

Not only are the analyses provided in this book concerning the limitations that different social structures put on strikes compatible with the Marxist model of Figure 9.3, but also my analysis of the transformative nature of conflict is similarly broadly compatible with a Marxist approach. The empirical analyses and the theoretical arguments on strike waves presented in Chapter 8 clearly point to the "transformative" nature of conflict (Hyman, 1975, p. 185). As I summarized at the beginning of this chapter, both the 1959–63 and 1968–72 strike waves brought about sweeping changes in the political position of labor, in the types of working-class organization, in the very forms of capitalist accumulation and organization of production, and, ultimately, in the class structure itself.

As capitalists continually transform the very class composition of labor through the implementation of new technologies and through the reorganization of production,[11] the forms of working-class organization, the forms of the struggle, and the very historical actors involved in the struggle change from one cycle of struggles to the next. Those processes only accelerate in the aftermath of strike waves and cycles, ultimately leading to the displacement of the actors involved in the struggle[12] of the preceding wave. In other words, the class struggle perpetually destroys and re-creates the class structure, and not just the structure of the working class.[13] The capitalist class itself is in a constant state of flux. The "engineered recession" of 1964, to take care of the increased levels of conflict during the 1959–63 strike wave, not only shrank the size of the working class but also eliminated a fraction of the capitalist class, via the increased number of bankruptcies. Processes of capitalist concentration designed to better deal with problems of both intraclass conflict and interclass conflict also cyclically recompose the capitalist class. On the other hand, the tremendous increase in the processes of decentralized production that followed the 1968–72 strike wave brought the flowering of a healthy class of small entrepreneurs. In their turn, changes in the class structure will force changes in the forms of consciousness, in a process known as class formation (see Section 7.8, p. 293).[14]

No doubt, Marxist theory seems to be able to account for much of the empirical evidence that I have accumulated in this book and to provide an overall theoretical framework for many of my arguments. To wholeheartedly and acritically embrace this framework, however, is to forget (1) that Marxists, by and large, have had little to say about strikes and (2) that many of the elements that would contribute to a Marxist theory of strikes often contradict one another. First, despite the central position of the "class struggle" in the Marxist theory of history, Marxists have not produced a coherent theory of strikes. For Marxists, the aim of the class struggle is the revolutionary overthrow of capitalist social relations (Elster, 1985, pp. 371–97). In view of the danger of falling into the trap of economism, classic Marxist thinkers often have regarded the everyday skirmishes between capital and labor with some suspicion. Nonetheless, the Marxist literature, from Marx and Engels to Kautsky, Rosa Luxemburg, and Lenin, has filled many pages with important remarks on strikes, on their relationship to political struggle, on the economic and political wings of the working class. From that scattered material, one must derive the elements of a Marxist theory of strikes, as I have teased out in this book.

Second, many of the elements of a Marxist theory of strikes often contradict one another. For instance, different Marxist traditions lead to different predictions about the timing of widespread class struggle. Immiseration theories link class conflict to the deterioration of material conditions, perhaps in conjunction with favorable circumstances in the international arena. Conversely, crisis theories link increased levels of class confrontation to the end of the upswing phase of the long-term cycle of accumulation. Among crisis theories, some view the cycle as having a fixed and predetermined length (e.g., Kondratieff), and others make the length of the cycle historically contingent. Within this last approach, the class struggle may play a fundamental role in reversing the long phase of prosperity (e.g., the U.S. social structure of accumulation theories) or may simply be a by-product of worsening economic conditions due to the internal dynamics of the accumulation process (e.g., the French regulation school). The analyses in this book strongly point to a relationship between strike explosions and long-term prosperity; they also provide some evidence in favor of a fundamental role for conflict in bringing about structural changes in the economy. Elsewhere, the process of change may well be less closely tied to the class struggle. Certainly, intraclass conflict (capitalist competition) is a powerful enough mechanism for change, and once change starts somewhere in the capitalist world economy, other countries must follow suit. As Lee Iacocca, Chrysler's chairman of the board, emphatically put it, "In this business, you either lead, follow, or get out of the way."

Contrary to the classic Marxist view,[15] the analyses herein have revealed varied interests within both the capitalist class and the working class. We have seen how divisions between the majority of small-scale Italian entrepreneurs, with their conservative view of industrial relations, and the large-scale employers, with their modernizing, neocapitalist vision of rationality and efficiency, have tinted class relations in postwar Italy. Similarly, within the working class, differences in the interests of the skilled and the unskilled, manual workers and clerical workers, have shaped union strategies. Furthermore, we have seen the contradictory nature of workers' interests (not always so fundamentally opposed to those of capital, as emphasized by the classic tradition). Finally, the state itself, again contrary to the classic Marxist view ("The executive of the modern state is nothing but a committee to manage the common affairs of the whole bourgeoisie," reads *The Communist Manifesto*), often appears to be pursuing a strategic logic that is not always consistent with the aims of the capitalist class. And that is not surprising. After all, if the capitalist class itself is internally divided into different segments with somewhat different interests, which specific class interests should the state "manage"?[16] Many similar examples could be cited (and this book does provide many). Thus, just as there is no single unified mainstream theory of strikes, there is no coherent Marxist theory of strikes. To propose a Marxist theory of strikes implies a process of selection among the often competing and contradictory positions within a broad theoretical framework, with one element in common: an emphasis on classes and on the political economy of social relations.

One thing is clear from the theoretical and empirical analyses of this book: Strikes can be understood only within a broader theoretical framework. We have seen that specific theories can be quite successful at times in explaining part of the historical variation in strike activity. Nonetheless, the complete picture can be grasped only through the goggles of a theoretical framework that can account for the simultaneous interplay of the various factors at work. Working within the Marxist paradigm would require a process of selection among and integration of often antithetic explanations. Working within a non-Marxist paradigm would involve building bridges between models often parochially and narrowly housed in disciplinary academic turfs.[17] Furthermore, it would require stretching the limits of the ideological premises of the paradigm. With the notable exception of Schumpeter's work, long-term economic cycles are not part and parcel of neoclassical economists' theoretical tool bag, neither is the relationship between class structure and class conflict. Again, with the notable exception of Dahrendorf, that remains uncharted terrain in mainstream sociology.

9.4. LOOKING INTO THE CRYSTAL BALL: VENTURING PREDICTIONS FROM THE MODEL

Throughout this book, I have consistently put my econometric results to the test of history: Statistical findings had to be true to the historical record before they could be true to the battery of statistical tests to which I subjected them. Testing a historical theory against the past, however, may seem like a form of methodological cheating; after all, we can always propose the theoretical framework that best fits history (i.e., choose that theory that best fits the data – and we have seen that there are plenty of theories in our sociological practice to make this game possible). The ultimate test of a historical theory should really be whether the theory can stand up to the future: What is the predictive power of a theory? More specifically, what is the predictive power of the theory of strikes that I painfully put together in the preceding section?

The theory of statistical forecasting teaches us that there are several methods available for forecasting, both qualitative and quantitative, short- and long-term, univariate and multivariate, in the time and frequency domains (Makridakis and Wheelwright, 1978). One thing is common to all these methods: They use past behavior to predict future behavior, past patterns to predict future patterns. Knowledge of those patterns is therefore fundamental to any ability to forecast. Univariate models of forecasting go to great pains to tease out the "temporal components" of a time series (trend, and periodic and nonperiodic, short-, medium- and long-term cycles). Forecasting basically involves projecting those components into the future. In a sense, then, univariate models are blind. They can predict only patterns that have already manifested themselves in the past. Their view of the future is that there will be more of the same of what happened in the past. Yet history involves both continuity and change. Social processes unfold in innovative ways, often disruptive of past behavior.

Forecasting models that are based on a simple rule of extending past patterns into the future do not fare well in the face of structural change. Structural models would be more appropriate, because historical change is the result of a convergence of social processes and of their interaction. In this book we have seen many examples of change resulting from the interaction of social processes: the defeat of the Left in the 1950s, the emergence of "articulated bargaining" in the early 1960s, the two periods of economic boom in 1959–62 and 1968–69, and the *compromesso storico* strategy.

In economic forecasting, interestingly enough, univariate models fare better than multivariate models in terms of forecasting power.[18] Once again, the complexity of mapping causal structures in multivariate, multiequation models renders the structural approach less reliable as a forecasting tool (leaving the question of development costs aside). Typically, multivariate forecasts are supplemented and corrected by the qualitative forecast of a panel of experts.

In the case of strikes, a multivariate model would require quantitative measurements of all the relevant variables: economic, organizational, institutional, and political. That would mean measuring the American influence in Italian domestic affairs, the levels of employer and state repression, the influence of the radical Left in the 1968–72 strike wave, and so on. We have seen that such a project would be doomed to failure, at least at the current level of quantification of social indicators. Thus, to forecast future strike patterns, I have to approach the problem using a mixture of quantitative univariate forecasting and qualitative expert opinions. I can call on the various scholars that we have encountered in this book for their expert opinions.

First, let me approach the problem from the viewpoint of quantitative univariate forecasting. The time-series work on the temporal components of strikes discussed in Chapter 1 would provide the basic forecasting model:[19] (1) periodic seasonal and three-year cycles (out of phase for the number of strikes and the number of strikers); (2) nonperiodic cycles. Forecasts based on periodic cycles are fairly straightforward. If the number of hours lost was down in August, we can reasonably expect it to be down again next August. If the number of strikes was up this year, we *know* it is going to be up again in three years. If the number of strikes will be up next year, then the number of strikers will be down. Forecasting for irregular cycles in a series simply on the basis of past values would not be as easy. But if those cycles were sufficiently similar to each other in terms of length, a forecast would not be too far off the mark.

Certainly, bringing in knowledge about the structural determinants of the various temporal components would make forecasting more informed and more reliable. For instance, the analyses in Chapters 2 and 3 revealed that nonperiodic cycles are related to the business cycle. Knowledge about the timing of the next boom or bust (assuming that economists in fact have that knowledge) would allow us to predict strike behavior. We would know that strike frequency would go down with the next recession and that, perhaps, strike duration would go up. Again, the analyses of Chapter 5 revealed that the timing of contract renewals and the level (plant or industry) of negotiations determine the three-year cycle in strike indicators. That knowledge would certainly allow us to improve our predictive power, particularly if renewal dates were not perfectly periodic. Such a forecasting model should allow us to make sense of some bewildering statements not uncommon during the 1970s in the economic sections of Italian dailies: "The last figures published by ISTAT on strike activity show a considerable increase in the number of strikers over the previous two years. The number of strikes, *however*, was at a minimum." In light of the bargaining-structure arguments, the *"however"* should rather read "as expected." Predictions based on our political models are more problematic. Basically, that derives from the fact that there is less agreement among scholars on the basic relationships. One could make safe bets predicting a decline in labor militancy *during* cabinet crises. In the context of a political use of the strike weapon, Why strike if there is no one in government to listen? One could also feel safe in betting on a long-term decline in strike activity when labor-oriented social democratic parties take secure, long-term control of the executive branch. The presence of labor-friendly governments in power will then foster neocorporatist arrangements among unions, employer organizations, and the state. Betting on the outcome of labor relations under short-term, labor-oriented governments is riskier. On the one hand, labor may take advantage of the presence of a friendly government, seeing that as a good time to challenge employers. Alternatively, it may reduce conflict in order not to embarrass the friendly government, particularly if that government rewards labor's restraint by implementing pro-labor welfare policies. Again, Italian labor never enjoyed a friendly government in power long enough to establish a precedent for behavior. However, extrapolating from the behavior of the Italian Communist Party in its relations with both labor and social movements, one could expect that given a coalition government with the Communists in it, there would be a decrease in the frequency of strikes and perhaps an increase in the average size of strikes used as weapons of mass mobilization. After all, that is what happened during the years 1975–78 when the Communist Party came close to sharing government responsibilities.

Finally, I believe that I can confidently predict a resurgence of conflict (and not just in Italy, but across the capitalist world) around the year 2010. Or could it be 2005 or 2015? Odd that I should feel confident in making a prediction based on only one data point (the 1969 *autunno caldo*) from a single country – a case of really "small N's and big conclusions!" (Lieberson, 1991). However, I believe that the panel of experts who contributed their opinions to the making of this prediction (Kondratieff, Aglietta, Boyer, Mandel, Screpanti, Cronin, Reich, Gordon, Edwards) also provided corroborating evidence on the existence of waves of conflict at 40- to 50-year intervals. Certainly the assumption of strict periodicity of economic crises and related strike waves is untenable, which cautions me about setting an exact date for the next strike wave. But I have little doubt about the resurgence of conflict. In fact, I can even venture to guess the type of worker who will play a key role in the next wave. The *operaio massa* of the *autunno caldo* is out of the picture. Robots are now standing along the assembly lines (at least those that are still around) in modern factories, and robots don't strike, which is an important reason for them being there in the first place. So who will be the next "bearer of conflict," as the Italian labor literature refers to the worker who is central to a particular type of sociotechnical organization of production? The theory of strikes proposed in this chapter suggests the answer: Look at the class structure. In which direction is it changing? Who are the actors who are increasingly occupying a central position in this structure? Service-sector workers are becoming increasingly predominant. Thus, the "bearer of conflict" probably will come from there – odd as that may sound, because the typical service worker (white-collar and female) has traditionally been less strike-prone than blue-collar males. The available evidence, however, does indicate increasing militancy among workers in the service sector (bank employees, teachers, nurses, and doctors).[20]

These attempts to look into the crystal ball are based on the simplifying assumption of ceteris paribus, that is, of unchanging relations between variables. Thus, we could safely have predicted that if 1977 was a year of plant-level bargaining, the number of strikes was going to be high. That, however, assumes that the state of the labor market has no effect on the relationship. In fact, if the unemployment rate in 1977 was high, then the number of strikes would be low, even under conditions of plant-level bargaining. But simultaneous changes in the political arena can further complicate the picture. That was indeed the case in Italy in the 1970s, when the labor market ceased to operate as a mechanism for regulating conflict, because political exchange was taking up that role.

Thus, unfortunately, the assumption of ceteris paribus is untenable. In the real world of history, ceteris are never paribus, things are never the same. If the reader walks away from this book with one certainty, it must be this: Strikes and the social processes that are related to strikes are in a constant state of flux and change. Undoubtedly, structural knowledge about interrelationships between variables would improve the power of our forecasting. On many of those relationships we have a reasonable amount of knowledge: for instance, on the interplay between the business cycle and collective bargaining. We know that the tempo of collective bargaining imparts a periodic pattern to strikes. We also know that in times of recession, employers tend to postpone the renewal of collective agreements. The interaction between the business cycle and collective bargaining may thus blur perceptions of the periodicity of industrial conflict. But other elements in the forecasting equations are not as easily predictable. For instance, national class relations do not exist in a vacuum. What other nation-states do will affect the limits and possibilities of national paths. Few in the generation of *i sessantottini* hailing "Mao, Marx, Marcuse" would have predicted the collapse of the Soviet Empire, the spread of capitalist enterprises in Mao's own China, the disappearance of such glorious symbols as the hammer and sickle. The tension between the unique and the recurrent, the contingent and the permanent, between event and structure plays itself out in history (see the excellent discussion by Le Roy Ladurie, 1979, pp. 111–32).

Furthermore, even when considering the combined effects of economic, organizational, institutional, and political factors, a great deal is left out. The precise effects on industrial conflict of the personality of a Togliatti, Valletta, or

Berlinguer perhaps we will never be able to gauge. What would have happened to the course of history had the 1976 electoral results been reversed, with the Communist Party at 38.9% of the votes and the Christian Democrats at 33.8%?

Thus, predictions based on our simplified models may be no more than futile exercises. We may, indeed, do better by looking into a crystal ball. Nonetheless, what turn did Italian history take in the 1980s and early 1990s? Did the course of history during those years conform to the basic picture in the puzzle? To answer these questions, let me turn to history, one last time.

9.5. THE TEST OF HISTORY, ONE LAST TIME: THE 1980S

In October 1979, Fiat fired 61 workers accused of violence and terrorism.[21] Amid protests, reciprocal blaming, and denials, the dispute dragged on in court. A few months later, in June 1980, Umberto Agnelli, Fiat vice-president and chairman of the board, announced a plan to lay off 15,000 excess workers. Fiat's intentions were then clear. Workers replied with a volley of radical strikes: shop-level strikes, tough pickets blocking the entrances, attempts to occupy some plants. Berlinguer, secretary general of the Communist Party, speaking in late September to a crowd at the gates of the Fiat Mirafiori plant in Turin, shocked the conservatives when he expressed the party's support, even for a factory occupation, if it came to that. On October 14, 1980, some 40,000 skilled manual workers, clerical workers, and supervisors marched through the streets of Turin in protest against the strike (the so-called *marcia dei quarantamila*).

If Berlinguer's speech was a shock to the employers, the antistrike, antiunion march came as a shock to the unions. The unions accused Fiat of having organized the march. They belittled the march and tried to minimize the reported participation of manual workers in it. But regardless of Fiat's involvement and the number of manual workers who actually participated, that march signaled the end point of a decade of increasing difficulties brought on by egalitarian union policies.

Certainly the status of supervisors in large factories had deteriorated during the 1970s (Villa, 1986, pp. 190–1; Segatori and Torresini, 1979, pp. 46–7, 55). In many firms, supervisory roles had lost much of their power and importance in the production process. Either technological developments and automated processes or the organization of production in semi-autonomous work groups had reduced the need for coordination and control. In any case, the development of collective bargaining had severely eroded the discretionary power of the supervisor, a power that had once been absolute. Workers' careers had become less dependent on the supervisor's evaluation, having come to be determined by union-controlled automatic mechanisms of seniority. Similarly, wage incentives and productivity bonuses had fallen under union control. The employers' carrot had wilted, their stick had become blunt. With the collapse of the firm's authority structure, warnings, suspensions, and fines had fallen into disuse. In fact, many supervisors had been harassed and publicly humiliated. Many had been the targets of violence.

As the supervisors' position on the shop floor had deteriorated, clerical and skilled workers had fared no better. At Fiat, between 1969 and 1980, the wages of manual workers had increased more than those of clerical workers (+37.8% vs. +12.2%) (Becchi Collidà and Negrelli, 1986, p. 170). Differentials between the highest manual level (the 5th) and the intermediate clerical level (the 7th) went from 171–230 in 1969 to 129–187 in 1974 and to 127–167 in 1980. Among blue-collar workers, the reduction had been less drastic. Nonetheless, the difference between the 3rd and 5th levels went from 107–125 in 1969 to 107–129 in 1974 and to 106–121 in 1980. That did not happen only at Fiat. As we saw in the preceding two chapters, the flattening of wage and skill differentials was a general characteristic in many industries in the 1970s. Many forces had pushed in that direction.

Unions' demands for flat wage increases across skill levels and for collective skill upgrading had become increasingly widespread during the 1970s. The 1973 *inquadramento unico*, the single grading scale for manual and clerical workers and intermediate supervisory people, further narrowed skill and wage gaps (particularly between manual and clerical workers). The new mechanisms of wage adjustment against inflation introduced with the 1975 *scala mobile* agreement further undermined the positions of both skilled and clerical workers: Salaries for those at the lower levels of manual work had more extensive coverage against inflation than did the salaries of skilled and, especially, clerical workers.

Not surprisingly, the available survey evidence – the 1971 survey of Milan Alfa-Romeo workers and the 1971 and 1980 Isvet surveys – reveals lower levels of support for egalitarian policies among skilled workers.[22] Even in 1987, a survey of workers belonging to the CISL union found that 59.6% of skilled workers (41.4% of unskilled workers) believed that skill was not sufficiently rewarded (La Valle, 1987).[23] Even more telling than skilled workers' attitudes were their actions. In many firms, skilled and clerical workers protested the unions' egalitarian policies, even at the height of the 1968–72 mobilization (e.g., at Candy, a manufacturer of household appliances; Regini, 1974, p. 66). The introduction in 1973 of the *inquadramento unico* in the metalworking industry had resulted in many instances of conflict among workers (Villa, 1986, p. 187; La Valle, 1987). In many firms, the most skilled workers, while threatening to resign, demanded and obtained higher wages (Associazione Industriale Lombarda, 1983, p. 187). Other skilled workers, dissatisfied with the compression of the wage and skill hierarchies, simply left the large firms to set up their own shops in the climate of *decentramento produttivo*, illustrating the convergence of interests and collusion between entrepreneurs trying to regain control over production and craftsmen trying to regain control over wages and skills (Sabel, 1982, p. 221).[24]

For a while, Italian unions were able to contain dissent. On the one hand, they appealed to ideological themes of egalitarianism, reviling particularistic demands ("corporatist" demands, in the language of Italian unions). After all, the skilled segment of the working class was more highly unionized and more involved in union politics than the rest of the class. On the other hand, the risk of fragmenting the working class remained latent so long as there was enough to be gained for everyone. Although wage differentials between unskilled and skilled workers had been narrowing, wages in the early 1970s had increased for all, skilled and clerical workers included.[25]

But when wages began to be eroded by inflation, when unions began to regain control over the mobilization potential of the mass workers during the years of the *compromesso storico*, and, later, when the extensive industrial restructuring of the early 1980s and the massive layoffs and recourse to the *cassa integrazione guadagni* considerably reduced workers' bargaining power at the plant level, the egalitarian system broke down, leaving a fragmented and divided class. As Barca and Magnani noted with regard to the 1975 *scala mobile* agreement, while Confindustria seems, ex post, to have achieved its goals, the long-term effects for the unions were quite negative (Barca and Magnani, 1989, p. 44). The *marcia dei quarantamila* made that quite clear. The march rudely awoke the leaders of organized labor from the dreams of social transformation that, for a decade, some of them may have held or, more simply, from the dreams of greater participation to power that certainly most of them had held. They awoke only to face a long nightmare: For a decade, Italian unions had embraced the needs of the *operaio massa* as representative of *the needs of the class*. They had developed their whole strategy around that working-class figure (e.g., egalitarianism, mass promotions to higher skill grades, job enrichment). For a decade, the unions had desperately clung to the idea of defending a class structure that they must have believed to be immutable. And though union membership had been growing during the 1970s, the power of unions had started showing alarming signs of decline (Manghi, 1977). Throughout the decade, the employers (often with the unions' help) had slowly succeeded in their efforts to eliminate the *operaio massa*, or at least to reduce the importance of the *operaio massa* in the labor process, and consequently in the class structure. The Italian labor movement in the 1980s found itself in the position of having to redefine its strategies, of trying to put together the pieces of a fragmented working class that had changed profoundly without the unions even noticing it. Giovanni Agnelli put it well in his 1983 interview with Arrigo Levi:

If you go visit an auto plant, you will find huge pavilions with seven, eight machines, two white-coated men, and a computer. The "original sin" of the assembly line . . . is a thing of the past. Those who do not live the factory life have not realized this yet. *Even trade unions are behind in their demands; they continue to advance requests that are completely out-of-date.* (Levi, 1983, p. 91; emphasis added)

Some twenty years earlier, Lanzardo and Vetere, in *Quaderni Rossi*, had expressed similar doubts about the unions' ability to understand change:

Capitalist rationalization is a continuous process, with more or less intense phases; daily, it modifies the relationship between workers and machines, between worker and worker; daily, it crushes traditional forms of labor organizations, it poses and reposes the terms of the struggle in a continuous renewal of the conditions. . . . But labor organizations do not see in capitalist technological change the political instrument of subordination of the working class and of the very economic and political organizations of the class . . . they become aware of the effects of restructuring only at the moment when its phases have become an integral and irreversible part of a new situation. (Lanzardo and Vetere, 1965, p. 56)

The rhetoric of protest in 1980 and the violence of those struggles (in a last defense) exposed the reality of a wounded giant coming to grips with defeat, frustrated at having been cheated of its power, of having made perhaps an irreparable strategic mistake. The *operaio massa* was gone, either unemployed or lost in the world of decentralized production that unions could not reach.

The struggle over layoffs at Fiat in the fall of 1980 raged for 35 days. It was clear to everyone that a loss there would mark the beginning of the end for labor across the country, not just at Fiat. And labor lost that fight. Throughout the postwar period, events at Fiat often foreshadowed the fortunes and misfortunes of Italian labor as a whole. And just as in the 1950s, Fiat's layoffs in 1980 broadcast the signal for widespread attacks on labor. The 1981–82 Assolombarda survey (Associazione Industriale Lombarda, 1983) on the state of labor relations in Milanese firms highlighted the range of employers' practices. Warnings and fines against workers found their way back into the factory world (pp. 61, 65, 143). Absentee workers were encouraged, with special bonuses, to resign (p. 61). Harassment of union representatives, particularly in smaller firms, became more common (pp. 47, 54, 59). Individual productivity bonuses and bonuses linked to workers' attendance records were introduced, in order to discourage absenteeism (pp. 60, 116, 189). Against the prevailing norms, individual wage inducements and skill upgrading were reintroduced (in 40.8% of the firms, particularly larger firms) (pp. 184–5) (Table 9.1). Corrado Squarzon's analysis of *Cesos* yearly survey data on the state of industrial relations shows a clear trend during the 1980s (increasing over time and by firm size) in the use of wage incentives (Table 9.2). According to Squarzon (1989b, p. 38), the reintroduction of wage incentives (individual and collective) gave employers greater flexibility in the use of workers' wages. Dell'Aringa and Lucifora's (1994, p. 37) analyses of aggregated wage data similarly show an increase in wage differentials in the 1980s and 1990s mainly due to employers' use of individual incentives outside union control.

Half of the larger firms and a quarter of the smaller firms in the Assolombarda survey had fired workers for absenteeism (Associazione Industriale Lombarda, 1983, p. 115). Indeed, the use of layoffs became, one more time, the most effective tool for labor control. In only one or two years, Italian employers had succeeded in an area in which they had been failing for over a decade: They finally regained the use of *mobilità esterna*. For employers, greater flexibility in the structure of wages went hand in hand with greater flexibility in the use of the work force.[26] Within a few years, between 1980 and 1985, industrial employment declined 29.3% in firms with more than 500 workers. In the next three years, the decline slowed down, but it further reduced the work force by another 6% (Barca and Magnani, 1989, p. 130). Overall, between 1977 and 1986, the work force in the

Table 9.1. *Percentage of firms with egalitarian wage increases, by firm size*

	Number of employees	
Type of wage increases	16–99	100–250
Increases equal for all	81.2	27.3
Increases different by skill level	18.8	72.7

Source: Associazione Industriale Lombarda (1983, p. 185).

Table 9.2. *Percentage of firm-level contracts characterized by wage incentives, by year and firm size*

	Year		
Number of employees	1984–85	1985–86	1987
20–99	7.3	18.3	21.1
100–499	14.9	25.7	23.9
500 or more	30.6	26.3	32.1

Source: Data from CESOS, *Osservatorio sulla contrattazione aziendale*, Squarzon (1989b, p. 43).

manufacturing industries shrank by 13%, and that was without counting the large number of workers under the *cassa integrazione guadagni* (CIG) (Figure 9.4). Whereas in the 1970s the number of CIG hours had oscillated around 100 million per year, in 1981 it reached 300 million, and 600 million in 1984, equivalent to some 300,000 workers (Reyneri, 1989a, p. 357); 1984 was the year of maximum use of the CIG. Larger firms were the heavy users of the CIG.[27] The unemployment rate jumped from 5.9% in 1975 to 12% in 1987 and higher (Figure 9.4). Overall unemployment figures, however, can hide varied realities. First, it was people looking for their first jobs who bore the brunt of unemployment (with a peak of 57% of total unemployment in 1983).[28] Youths, in particular, found it increasingly difficult to land stable jobs in the primary labor market. The South, as well, experienced staggering levels of unemployment, at around 20%, compared with 5% in Lombardy.

The process of industrial restructuring in the late 1970s and early 1980s produced extensive changes in the class structure. In 1970, industrial workers accounted for half of all salaried workers.[29] In that year, the Italian working class was at its peak, both numerically and in terms of its mobilization power. By 1975, the share of industrial workers had declined to 46%. In 1987, that figure had gone down further to 38%. While employment in industry declined, it picked up in services, particularly public services (Reyneri, 1989a, p. 371). In 1975, service employment represented 44% of total employment. In 1987, it took the lead, with 57% of total employment.

Figure 9.4. *Plots of unemployment rate and numbers of hours of* cassa integrazione guadagni

Not surprisingly, after the "great fear" that accompanied the 1969 *autunno caldo*, Italian employers during the 1980s felt that they could finally sit back, relax, and enjoy. According to a survey conducted in 1966–67, entrepreneurs, by and large, believed that they wielded more power in Italian society than did the unions (Farneti, 1970, p. 185). The 1969 *autunno caldo* certainly shook that confidence, as we saw in Chapter 8. By the mid-1970s, however, employers had regained it. Scores of employer surveys made that point quite clear.[30] According to a Federlombarda survey in 1975, employers viewed the state of labor relations in their firms quite positively, with 14.5% of employers seeing relations as excellent, 60.5% as good, and 19.3% as mediocre (Urbani, 1977a, p. 397). Only a handful of employers viewed labor relations as either terrible (0.3%) or difficult (4.6%). And things only got better. Giovanni Agnelli, in his interview with Arrigo Levi, commented that "Manual workers do not consider capitalists as exploiters any longer.... Today the shop-floor climate is very normal" (Levi, 1983, pp. 64, 72). According to a 1983 Federmeccanica survey, only 20% of the employers believed that the labor-relations climate in the 1970s was better than in the 1960s. But only 15% of the same interviewees believed that the current state of labor relations was unsatisfactory (Mortillaro, 1984, pp. 127–8). Things were particularly good in the smaller firms (<100 workers): 61% of small employers (vs. 43% of the larger ones) were likely to view labor relations in their firms more positively (Mortillaro, 1984, p. 139).

Italian employers had good reason to be confident. The total number of hours worked in the larger firms grew at a rate of 0.7% per year in the first half of the 1980s, and even faster in later years (Barca and Magnani, 1989, p. 133). The cost of labor decreased (Barca and Magnani, 1989, p. 134): 73% of the employers in the

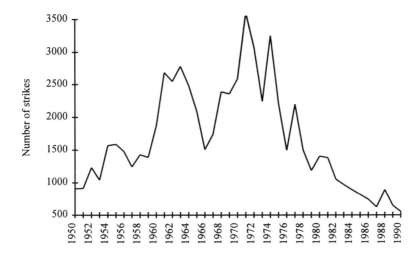

Figure 9.5. *Plot of the number of strikes in industry*

1983 Federmeccanica survey acknowledged having greater flexibility in their use of the work force (e.g., shift work, overtime, internal mobility), improved relations between supervisors and workers (77%), a slowdown in plant-level bargaining (73%), reduced participation in strikes (55%), an increase in individual output (74%), and a reduction in absenteeism (99%) (Mortillaro, 1984, pp. 130–1). The structure of collective bargaining survived intact, with its three-year cycle and two bargaining levels, but with labor on the defensive, collective bargaining lost much of its vitality. With the balance of class forces in the factories once again clearly in the employers' favor, employers abandoned their once-steadfast opposition to plant-level bargaining, and in fact pushed for plant-level bargaining. Interestingly enough, despite such an optimistic picture, according to the 1983 Federmeccanica survey, disciplinary actions against workers did not decrease (in 73% of the cases) (Mortillaro, 1984, p. 131).

With the continuing decline of the industrial labor force and the massive layoffs of factory workers, particularly in the larger firms, traditionally the most strike-prone, came a rapid decline in strike activity in the industrial sector (see Figures 9.5, 9.6, and 9.7). After the mobilization years of the 1968–72 strike wave, industrial conflict in the 1980s fell to the rock-bottom levels not seen since the 1950s. Union membership followed suit (Figure 9.8). Only in the service sector did conflict increase during the 1980s (Franzosi, 1992).

If Italian employers had good reason to sit back and relax, they also had good reason to enjoy. In the mid-1980s, Italy experienced remarkable economic growth, although at the slower pace of the 1980s – the years of the downswing phase of the long postwar cycle (Figure 9.9).

It is an easy game to describe in the late 1990s what happened in the 1980s. Worse yet, it may be a classic example of trimming the theory to fit the data in such

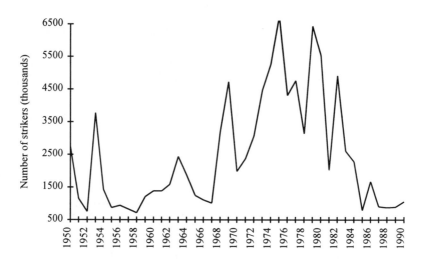

Figure 9.6. *Plot of the number of strikers in industry*

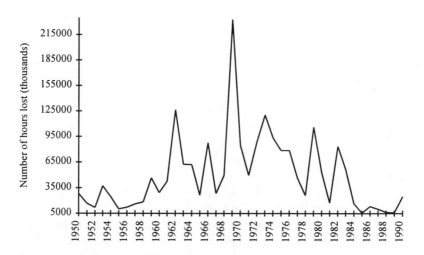

Figure 9.7. *Plot of the number of hours lost in industry*

a way that neither holds any surprise. I have frowned on such practices too many times throughout this book for me to begin playing such games at the very end. Nonetheless, for what it is worth, I will highlight the theoretical implications of the course that history took in the 1980s. First, when viewed in a longer historical perspective, the rise and demise of industrial conflict during the postwar period clearly stand out. What may have seemed to be a trend toward ever-increasing levels of conflict in the mid-1970s was only a peak in a long-term cycle of conflict.

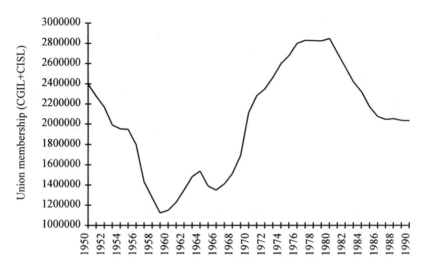

Figure 9.8. *Plot of union membership in industry (CGIL + CISL)*

When coupled with the structural changes in Western economies (the plot of GNP growth in Figure 9.9 gives a clear picture of the long-term decline in the rate of growth typical of the late 1970s and 1980s), these trends of strikes (and unionization) seem to provide strong support for crisis theories (the social structure of accumulation theory, in particular, at least for the Italian case). The temporal pattern of working-class mobilization (as measured by either strikes or unionization) does seem to describe long cycles, broadly related to specific sociotechnical forms of organization of production. Peaks in mobilization occur during the latter part of the upswing phase of prosperity. Ripples in the contour of the mobilization curve can occur during the long upswing phase of the cycle, as workers begin testing against employers the strength that prosperity is bringing their way (as in the 1959–63 strike wave in Italy). They can also occur during the long downswing, as workers mount a heroic (and mostly vain) defense against employers' encroachment upon the positions workers conquered during the period of prosperity (as in the 1980 peak). No doubt, political factors (such as government crises, international events, the passing of new laws) can sometimes provide opportunities for working-class mobilization, but ultimately the temporal pattern of strikes closely follows the long-term ups and downs of capitalist economies, as they impress their tempo on the shifting class structure of our societies, as they bring to life on the stage of history the actors that act in the economic and political arenas in the pursuit of their interests.

Indeed, many noneconomic elements of the post-1969 settlement have the characteristics envisioned by crisis theories. The way out of the crisis broadly involved new forms of class compromise. During the "long 1970s," with the balance of class forces tilted in the workers' favor, new overtures toward labor were tested, and new political alliances were hammered out. But if one of the

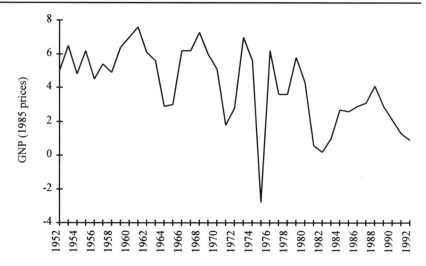

Figure 9.9. *Plot of GNP growth*

conditions for corporatism and political exchange is stable and durable participation by a major labor party in a country's governance, then that movement faltered in Italy no sooner than it had begun (e.g., Korpi and Shalev, 1980; for Italy, see Regini, 1981, 1983). The politics of the *compromesso storico* by the Communist Party died in 1979 with the assassination of Aldo Moro. The Communist Party never made it back into a coalition government. With the party out of the government, the corporatist overtures ended. The Italian state continued to play an active role in industrial relations, but labor's input in the governance of the economy remained marginal (Lange, 1987).

We were surprised by the disruptive power of the 1968–72 strike wave, the sweeping changes it wrought in the political position of labor inside and outside the factories. When viewed in historical perspective, what is perhaps surprising is how little things ultimately changed. The fines, the warnings, the layoffs, the productivity bonuses, the speedups, the overtime, the lower purchasing power of wages, the lower benefits, and the *managerial prerogatives* all made their way back into the Italian factory world. The Communist Party abandoned the *compromesso storico* for its more traditional role as the opposition. Ultimately, it even abandoned its name and its symbols. If the Italian unions during the long 1970s rode the tiger of the mobilization movement, ultimately tamed it, and cashed in on institutional rewards, the Italian capitalists rode the tiger of both the mobilization movement and the unions' strategies and ultimately won – until the next wave.

9.6. LOOKING BACK, LOOKING FORTH: THE 1969 *AUTUNNO CALDO* IN HISTORICAL PERSPECTIVE

The analyses of the preceding section show that, by and large, the theoretical model that I developed in this book and that I outlined more closely in this chapter stands up against the test of history. Yet, one more time, the test of history seems to bring out paradoxical conclusions.

On the one hand, throughout the book, and in particular at the end of the last chapter and at the beginning of this chapter, I have argued that strike waves have a deeply transformative character. I provided a great deal of evidence on how the *autunno caldo* and the strike wave that followed it changed the organizational capacities of the Italian working class and its institutionalization in the political and economic spheres, and the very structure of the Italian economy. On the other hand, the historical analysis of the 1980s show that in the longer perspective of a few decades after the wave . . . nothing seems to have *really* changed. For all the traumas of 1969 on all the protagonists, for all the changes set in motion by the *autunno caldo* and consolidated during the 1970s, the Italian economy during the 1980s showed the same slowdown in growth rates of other capitalist economies, and Italian politics slowly moved to the Right, again embarking a path similar to that of other nation states that had *not* experienced the *autunno caldo*. While these results are well in line with a cyclical view of strike waves,[31] they are harder to reconcile with a view of strike waves as motors of socio-political change. If events (e.g., the 1969 *autunno caldo*) are truly capable of transforming the structures that bring them to the fore of history, why should those same events periodically creep back up on the stage of history under similar structural conditions? How can strike waves follow cyclical temporal patterns, and, at the same time, deeply subvert and transform those very structures of which they are a product? How are we to understand the relationship between events and structures, between the enduring nature of structures and the changing nature of events? I can take two different approaches to those questions (Le Roy Ladurie, 1979, pp. 111–31).

The first approach requires us to firmly situate an event in its historical time, looking both backward and forward in time, before and after an event, at both causes and consequences of an event. An eye on the causes of an event will identify the uniqueness of the event and will link a specific event to specific outcomes. An eye on the consequences will determine the historical importance, the weight of particular events and their transformative capacities. In part, that is what I have done in this book. On the one hand, looking backward, I carefully traced the structural conditions that brought about the 1969 *autunno caldo*. In Chapter 3, I outlined the changes in the Italian industrial structure and its social and technical organization. I outlined the corresponding changes in the composition of the labor force and, more generally, in the class structure. In Chapter 8, I extended the analyses beyond Italy, setting the temporal location of the 1968–72 strike wave at the height of a long phase of international postwar expansion of capitalist economies and in the spatial context of similar flares of working class militancy in other countries. Pushing further back in time, I took occasional glimpses at other historical peaks in working-class insurgency, such as the 1919–20 *biennio rosso*, similarly located at the height of another long phase of international economic expansion, and similarly accompanied by working-class insurgencies in other countries. On the other hand, looking forward in time, in Chapter 8 I focused on state and employers' responses to the *autunno caldo*. It is those responses that deeply changed the organizational, institutional, political, and economic structure of Italian society.

Looking back and forth in time away from the *autunno caldo*, however, constantly shifts our perspective on that event. Looking back, the *autunno caldo* appears as just another strike wave, as there have been and more will be in history; the emphasis is on historical continuity. Looking forth, the *autunno caldo* appears as a creative demiurge, as a forger of historical change; the emphasis is on discontinuity and break. Yet when pushing our gaze further into the future, into the 1980s and beyond, we find, as we did in the last section, that employers regained much of the terrain lost in both the political and economic arenas, and that the sweeping changes favorable to the working class introduced in the wake of the *autunno caldo* were slowly encroached upon and reabsorbed. One more time the emphasis is on continuity, rather than change. Thus, the further we step away from the temporal location of an event, the more likely we are to downplay the transformative role of events in history – well, at least, of one such event, the 1969 *autunno caldo*.

But, there is a second and even simpler way of approaching the question of the historical relevance of events and the role they play in history. Basically, the relevance of an event depends upon our answer to the question: Would the course of history have changed in the way it did *without* the occurrence of a particular event? More specifically, Did the 1968–72 strike wave change the course of Italian history just as outlined in this book? Would the organizational, institutional, political, and economic changes that came after the *autunno caldo* have occurred *without* the *autunno caldo*? And more generally, Would the course of world history be the same without the occurrence of the French Revolution, the Russian Revolution, or the American War of Independence? Were all these occurrences epiphenomenal representations of, perhaps, the long-term (very long-term) development of capitalism? North and Fogel have taken this counterfactual approach to history (for a lengthy discussion, see Le Roy Ladurie, 1979, pp. 111–31). They have stretched their historical imagination to a history where some momentous events traditionally thought of as having radically influenced the course of history did not occur (e.g., the War of Independence or the development of the railroad system in U.S. history). Interestingly enough, the answer that Fogel's (1964) and North's counterfactual history provides is: No, the course of history would not have changed significantly had those events not occurred. In view of the fact that countries that did not experience the trauma of the *autunno caldo* followed similar socio-economic paths to that of Italy during the 1980s and 1990s, the temptation is to answer: No, when viewed in a longer historical perspective, the *autunno caldo* did not *really* change the course of Italian history. Embracing that view of events and of the *autunno caldo* is not to deny the deep changes that took place in the aftermath of the 1968–72 strike wave. After all, I went to great length to document those changes (and this time, *The Puzzle* is really complete with no more twists and red herrings). Neither is it to deny the array of possible solutions available at any given time (e.g., the fascist or the social-democratic path to the problem of labor control in the 1920s and '30s). Rather, it is to focus scholarly attention on the need to consider different temporalities – different time spans, each moving with different rythms and different historical tempos – in the study of historical processes.

Indeed, as Braudel has shown (1980, pp. 25–54, 64–82, 91–104, 177–218), in order to understand the unfolding of historical processes we need to think not just in terms of events versus structures, of the constantly changing versus the never changing (Le Roy Ladurie's "history that stands still," 1981, p. 1), but also of the conjunctural, of the short- to medium-run changes that events can and do introduce on the scene of history. We measure the temporal span of structures in centuries (if not millenia); we measure events at the much faster rhythm of minutes, hours, days, and months. Conjunctures unfold over decades. It is in the time frame of conjunctures that the changes brought about by the 1969 *autunno caldo* fall. In an event-driven view of history, the emphasis is on the unique and the nonrepeatable. In a structure-driven view of history, the emphasis is on regularities, patterns, repetitions, and sequences, with occasional disruptions and discontinuities conjuncturally introduced by events of particular significance. Attention to the conjunctural level, perhaps, provides an escape from the predicament of a choice between the determinism of *l'histoire structurelle*, where structures engulf within their slow movements even the most eventful of events, and the randomness of *l'histoire événementielle* that beats at the fast drum of daily events. But one thing is clear: Understanding events implies thinking of history in terms of different temporalities (structures, conjunctures, and events), different times spans, from the very short term, to the long term, from the immediate, to the distant past and future. Again, in part, this is what I have done in this book. My shortest time span has been the seasonal rhythm of strikes (with rare glimpses at day-to-day relationships), followed by the two-to-three-year cycle of the rhythm of collective bargaining, up to the years-long cycles imparted by the business cycles, and to the decades-long rhythm imparted by the economic long waves. Charles Tilly's (e.g., 1986) monumental work on forms of contention in the European scene over the last several hundred years has shown that a proper understanding of strikes requires that we locate this form of contention within an even much longer time frame: that of the centuries-long repertoires of collective actions, of the transition from a traditional moral economy to an industrial economy (see Section 4.4, p. 101, in this book).

In the structural, long-term perspective, events, however momentous in the context of their own times, appear as much more insignificant things. Closeness to an event will make that event look bigger that it may actually be, more unique than the undoubted uniqueness and historical nonrepeatability of the actors and actions involved will warrant. But as we place more and more distance between us and an event, we may be able to see the event as part of a larger chain of events, bearing a close resemblance to each other, disseminated like a trail of bread crumbs along the path of history. The momentous (and tragic) revolt of the *Nu-Pieds* of Normandy in 1639 so magisterially described by Mousnier (1970, pp. 87–113) is but one of several hundred peasants' revolts against an overburdening state and an encroaching capitalist economy between the fourteenth and the seventeenth centuries. Even the French revolution appears on the scene of history in 1789 along with many other such *bourgeois* revolutions in the nineteenth century, that decreed the final political demise of the aristocracy and the ascendance of the bourgeoisie. Similarly, the Italian 1969 *autunno caldo* was preceded a year earlier by the French *May*, and by other, albeit less momentous, labor insurgencies across the industrialized world during the 1960s.

When viewed in the perspective of the long term, strike waves lose their characteristics as unique and distinct events, as events capable of changing the course of history. Rather, they appear as simply accompanying the major turns in the historical unfolding of long-term processes of capitalist accumulation, as these processes follow their own internal logic of development. For all the innovative characteristics of strike waves (the actors, the actions, the tactics, the demands), for all their momentous consequences (the responses they bring out from the political and economic elites, the changes in the organizational, institutional, economic, and political structures), strike waves themselves seem to follow predictable patterns. Rather than being freak and random occurrences that come to disrupt the even and long-term rhythm of structures setting them along entirely new historical paths, the role of strike waves appears to be built into the genetic code of long-term structures. Strike waves mark periods of transition along the long-term path of structures often in ways no less dramatic, no less worrisome, no less traumatic, than, let us say, puberty or menopause are in the life course, but, nonetheless, no less predictable.

Unfortunately, such a long-term view of history vastly reduces the historical role of the hustle and bustle of daily events, even when, taken together, such daily events amount to the *autunno caldo* or, perhaps even to the French or Russian revolutions. In Le Roy Ladurie's (1981, p. 23) words: "Seen in a very long-term perspective like this, the system takes on a fatalistic quality: Revolts against it make little impression." Unfortunately, when viewed in that same long-term perspective, the role of strike waves as motors of socio-political change is also vastly reduced, because the class struggle itself appears as an epiphenomenal manifestation of much deeper structural forces that cyclically push strike waves on the stage of history. In this perspective, I may have to revise the interpretation that I provided in Chapter 8 (see Section 8.11, p. 340) of the Italian evidence on the crisis of the 1970s. There, I argued that the Italian evidence seemed to support the American "social structure of accumulation" perspective on the crisis, with its emphasis on class conflict, rather than the French "regulation" perspective, with its emphasis on the internal logic of capitalist accumulation. And thus, I still find myself in the need of having to refit some pieces of the puzzle, despite my earlier promises to the contrary and only a few pages away from the end of the book.

9.7. WHICH ROAD TO THE PAST? METHODOLOGICAL DILEMMAS

My reflections upon the broader theoretical and historical implications of my work (of our social scientific work) inevitably lead me to other reflections that I have partly entertained throughout the book: on the methods we use in the study of historical processes. On the one hand, econometric techniques and econometric modeling provide powerful tools for exploring relationships among variables. On the other hand, it is all too easy to mistake statistical modeling for scientific rigor. The mathematics, the equations, the statistics, the numbers, all make it seem so objective, so impersonal, so value free, in a word, so scientific. The criteria for the inclusion or exclusion of a variable, for the acceptance or rejection of a model lie outside the researcher's personal values and beliefs; rather they are given by objective statistical criteria of significance and insignificance. They are printed on tables that everyone can check. In their turn, the mathematical and statistical models, the tests, the numbers, the tables translate into easy replicability of results – the hallmark of science, to keep charlatans and impostors at bay. Causality, as well, is less of a subjective construction, less of an esoteric, if not altogether *ad hoc*, process than in qualitative work. Causality is built into those very statistical models. And those models allow rigorous testing of carefully laid out theoretical hypotheses. Objectivity, replicability, causality, and hypothesis testing: isn't that what science should be all about? Perhaps. But there is much rhetoric in those arguments.

Even introductory statistics texts warn the reader of the limits and dangers of basing one's decisions of acceptance or rejection of hypotheses on standard levels of significance (10%, 5%, and 1%) (e.g., Moore and McCabe, 1993, pp. 472–7; see also McCloskey, 1985, pp. 154–73). For one thing, the presence of outliers can drastically change the statistical significance of results. Second, in reality, there is no sharp distinction between "significance" and "insignificance," only varying levels of confidence in the likelihood of certain statistical results which increase steadily from 0 to 100. It was mostly a matter of convenience (and of personal experience as a seasoned statistician) for Sir R.A. Fisher to set the levels of confidence at the *standard* levels. But those levels became codified and they are still enforced today when the practical reasons for their use have diminished vastly. So much so that scientific papers that present results that do not achieve the standard levels of significance have a hard time making it into the journals (only 8 articles out of 294 in psychology journals; see Sterling, 1959; Skipper, Guenther, and Nass, 1967).

As for causality, on the one hand, the difficulties involved in the statistical specification and estimation of multiple-equation econometric models capable of capturing the complex causal structure of historical processes produce models that, by and large, only mimic that complexity.[32] The nature of history, with its complex criss-crossing of different factors operating at different temporalities, force us to adopt toy models before which, unfortunately, we fall to our knees in adoration as if they were the true Gods. On the other hand, even introductory statistical texts warn us in big letters that statistical models are merely correlational, rather than causal (again, see, Moore and McCabe, 1993, pp. 173, 197–204, 715). It is unfortunate that we quickly forget those early lessons. No better example of this problem I know that the one I found in the strike literature itself. As we have seen, in strike models a measure of strikes is typically made to be dependent upon the levels of unemployment, union membership, and wages (e.g., Ashenfelter and Johnson, 1969). Yet, the relationships among strikes, unionization, and wages are hopelessly intertwined. So much so that, whereas strike models treat the number of strikes as the dependent variable, with unionization and wages as the independent variables, union growth models and wage determination models simply reverse the causal order, treating the rate of change of union density and money wages as the "dependent" variables with a measure of strike activity among the regressors. Some authors have reaped the benefits of this inherent ambiguity in the causal structure of econometric models by publishing three different papers, each focused on a different dependent variable out of the pool of the same three basic variables (e.g., Ashenfelter and Johnson, 1969, on strike models; Ashenfelter and Pencavel, 1969, on union growth models; Ashenfelter, Johnson, and Pencavel, 1972, on wage determination models). In these papers, the only variable that always appears as an "independent" variable in the three models is the business cycle (namely, unemployment rate). Yet, even the business cycle itself is entangled in this web of multiple causation. As I argued in Chapter 8, the level and the intensity of the class struggle can bring about deep structural changes in underlying economic conditions (e.g., the short 1964–66 recession or the changes in the productive structure of the early 1970s – flexible specialization).

As for hypothesis testing, true enough, statistical models require scientists to be very clear about what they are testing. But that promises more than it can deliver. In our statistical work, we run hundreds of equations, adding and deleting variables, adding and deleting cases, transforming variables, and changing sample periods. At the end, some results go one way and others go the other way. At the end, to make sense of this contradictory evidence, to impose order on chaos we simply recur to our theoretical framework (or, alternatively, to our personal values). And thus theory, that same theory in the name of which we run all those models supposedly to provide an *independent* test for the theory, becomes the main guiding criterion for the organization and interpretation of a historical reality that is very reluctant to be nicely fitted into the pigeonholes of theoretical constructs (Elton, 1967, p. 36). But there is yet another danger. Exclusive reliance on econometric methods for empirical testing of a theory produces a mind-set in which only data that can be expressed in time-series form constitute adequate empirical evidence. What cannot be tested statistically is left out. What is left out is forgotten. What is forgotten is irrelevant and unimportant. Such an approach to the puzzle of strikes would not have taken me much beyond a handful of negative and positive coefficients. I would never have been able to tease out the strategic interactions among workers, employers, and the state. The 1969 *autunno caldo* would have remained a statistical problem of outliers, easily taken care of by dummy variables. Employers' reactions to the strike wave, as well as the sweeping changes in the very structure of the Italian economy, would have remained hidden behind the invisible hand of the market. I would have come out relatively empty-handed had I stopped at the multivariate analyses presented at the beginning of each chapter. Worse yet, I would have been somewhat off target. Much of what I have learned about the roles of organization and politics has come from a very simple use of the available historical record. We ignore a great deal of information when we focus exclusively on high-powered techniques. For example, quantitative data may be available, but not at the aggregation level or for the sample period at which the model is being tested. Also, three data points (e.g., 1974, 1975, and 1977; see section 5.5, p. 169) can have a great deal to tell us about the unfolding of historical processes, if we are only willing to listen.

In the frantic pursuit of ever more powerful methods, we have lost the archeologist's and the historian's pleasure of savoring the detail, of milking a data point for the last bit of information it holds. By letting the computer do the work, we may have ceased to do ours. Under the worst scenario, the use of the computer and of sophisticated methodologies may just distort reality (and we have seen many cases of that in this book). Under more optimistic scenarios, "The computer . . . [will only tell us] what everyone knew in the first place . . . What matters is not so much the machine as the questions one asks it" (Le Roy Ladurie, 1979, p. 3; see also Elton, 1967, pp. 30–9). Or, in Carlo Ginzburg's (1979, p. 276) disillusioned words:

The quantitative and anti-anthropocentric approach of the sciences of nature from Galileo on has placed human sciences in an unpleasant dilemma; they must either adopt a weak scientific standard so as to be able to attain significant results, or adopt a strong scientific standard to attain results of no great importance.

Are we inextricably caught in the dilemma between powerful methods that may distort reality under the worst scenario or lead to trivial and banal answers in the best of cases, and weak methods that bite off more than they can chew? The approach that I adopted in this book perhaps holds the promise of a simple way out of that dilemma. Whether I fulfilled that promise I let the reader be the judge. But to remind the reader, that approach does not simply consist of grabbing whatever evidence is available and then applying to it the most appropriate method (which I did). Rather, the approach involves bringing into the open what powerful methods cannot account for, going inside the regression black box, endlessly cross-examining the evidence, and pursuing the unexplained rather than the explained, because in that process we learn a great deal about the object of our study, and at the end that is what should really count: We drop hypotheses that do not seem to help, we entertain new hypotheses that come from the clues of our work, we seek new data, we apply new methods, until it all seems to fit. Hopefully, the questions we ask and the answers we find will make that lengthy process worthwhile.

But for all this jargon of scientific discourse, a frank and honest recognition of the partly rhetorical foundations of scientific work would lead to a healthier view of our research practices – not rhetoric as falsehood and deception, but rhetoric as the old art of persuasion (McCloskey, 1985, pp. 27–30). In this view, statistics is but one of the basic means by which we try to persuade others in scientific discourse (McCloskey, 1985, pp. 54–7, 70–2). How can we not be but full of admiration for those who have mastered techniques that require years of training?

Mathematical/statistical virtuosity adds to the mystique of the scientist as someone doing things out of the ordinary. It is a proof of credentials and expertise on the part of the scientist; it adds credibility to the scientist's competence; it places the necessary distance between the scientist and the audience; it predisposes audiences to accept arguments. We, as quantitative social scientists, certainly do not go around telling people (or even avowing to ourselves for that matter) of the selective process involved in the scientific enterprise. In fact, we are not even expected or encouraged to do so. Reviewers and editors (should I assume readers, as well?) want to see our results, not how we got there. And yet, the road we take to get there has so much to say about what we will find there (on the different roads to the past, see the arguments in the beautiful essays by Fogel and Elton, 1983).

And statistics, of course, is not the only trick of persuasion up the scientist's sleeve. Indeed, in this book, I have run the gammut of rhetorical devices: from the heavy use of statistics – 19 equations, 60 graphs, 91 tables, within an ironic (albeit occasionally sarcastic) view of our statistical work – and the recourse to a bounty of different types of empirical evidence – quantitative, historical and ethnographic narrative, the findings of survey and content analysis research – to back up my arguments, to my reliance on quotations (some 490, count them!) and authoritative citations (some 35 pages!), the involvement of the reader in the trying task of searching for a solution to the puzzle of strikes – the pat solutions, the false steps, the twists and turns, the constant fitting and refitting of the pieces – not to mention the involvement of the reader in the emotional world of the protagonists, down to the very metaphor of the puzzle adopted to embed scientific discourse in the narrative framework typical of a mystery story. All to give the impression of competence, the impression that no stone was left unturned, that, indeed, the solution provided to the puzzle, is *the* solution. And yet, what is that solution? For all the passion and determination that has animated this book, I seem to have lost that committment to fitting the puzzle of Italian strikes right at the very end: I waver in my solution to the theoretical puzzle – I basically leave it up to the reader to choose the "right" theory – I waver in my view of the role of class conflict in history, finally, I waver in my view of powerful statistical methods in the study of historical processes. Perhaps, I was not up to the task that I had set up for myself. As the puzzle became more and more complex, as its fitting required jumping ever higher theoretical, historical, and methodological hurdles, I simply lost control of the individual pieces and, worse yet, I lost sight of the overall picture. Perhaps, I never had a vision of that overall picture. Perhaps, I got carried away by my own metaphor of *the puzzle*. As I floated above time and science, trying to shed the passions that animate both the historical actors we study and us as scientists, or, better yet, trying to feel those passions as deeply as I could, in the unbearable lightness of poetry I simply lost touch with reality. Or, did that reality scare me? Perhaps, it is time for the reader to do some of the work and put together her/his own puzzle. If interested, the reader can even clarify for herself/himself some of those doubts about my vision of history, of theory, of methodology, and, last but not least, about my personal values. In this quest, the reader can trace the trail of clues that I have left behind. But this work of exegesis is hardly worth the reader's time. After all, we reserve such work for the classics of the past. The solution lies elsewhere: in a different view of science.

Indeed, a view of science as rhetorical discourse in a community of scholars would free us all of the many ambiguities involved in our research practices, it would not require us to hide our professional insecurities behind the verbiage and pomp of "scientific" discourse. This, of course, may end up rescaling scientists to human dimensions, down from the image of heroes that we have constructed for ourselves. But take heart, fellow social scientists! Discovering ourselves as humans may not be such terrible outcome. At the end of scene 13 of the play *Life of Galileo*, by Bertold Brecht (1972, pp. 84–5), Galileo returns, "unrecognizably changed," from his trial with the Inquisition. The big bell of the St. Mark's church in Rome rings gravely as it is publicly announced that Galileo has abjured his doctrine that the earth rotates around the sun. Andrea, a pupil disappointed at the *maestro*, screams in anger: "Unhappy the land that has no heroes! . . . Have you saved your precious skin? I feel sick." To which Galileo replies: "No. Unhappy the land that needs a hero."

Epilogue

Lo duca e io per quel cammino ascoso
intrammo a ritornar nel chiaro mondo;
e sanza cura d'alcun riposo,

salimmo su, el primo e io secondo,
tanto ch'i vidi de le cose belle
che porta 'l ciel, per un pertugio tondo.

E quindi uscimmo a riveder le stelle.

(My guide [Virgil] and I started our journey back to the world of light through that hidden tunnel; and caring not for rest, we climbed up, he first and I second, until I saw up above, through the round opening, those beautiful things that the sky holds [stars]. And then we emerged to see the stars again.)
Dante (Inferno, Canto XXXIV)

Modernism promises knowledge free from doubt, free from metaphysics, morals, and personal conviction. What it is able to deliver renames as scientific methodology the scientist's and especially the economic scientist's metaphysics, morals, and personal convictions. It cannot deliver what it promises.
McCloskey (1985, p. 16)

We usually take the side of the underdog [but] there is no position from which sociological research can be done that is not biased in one or another way.... We can never avoid taking sides. So we are left with the question of whether taking sides means that some distortion is introduced into our work so great as to make it useless. ... Our problem is to make sure that, whatever point of view we take, our research meets the standards of good scientific work, that our unavoidable sympathies do not render our results invalid. ... Whatever side we are on, we must use our techniques impartially enough that a belief to which we are especially sympathetic could be proved untrue. We must always inspect our work carefully enough to know whether our techniques and theories are open enough to allow that possibility. ... We take sides as our personal and political commitments dictate, use our theoretical and technical resources to avoid the distortions that might introduce into our work, limit our conclusions carefully, recognize the hierarchy of credibility for what it is, and field as best we can the accusations and doubts that will surely be our fate.
Becker (1967, pp. 244–7, passim)

Appendix: the data

Everything that man says or writes, everything that he makes, everything that he touches can and ought to teach us about him.

Bloch (1953, p. 66)

Anything is evidence which is used as evidence . . . Question and evidence . . . are correlative. Anything is evidence which enables you to answer your question – the question you are asking now. . . . nothing is evidence except in relation to some definite question.

Collingwood (1956, pp. 280–1)

There is no need to choose between the qualitative and the quantitative evidence: an intelligent rhetoric of economic history would give privilege to neither.

McCloskey (1985, p. 45)

In this book I have relied on many different forms of empirical evidence, from quantitative to qualitative. I have used two types of quantitative data: time-series and cross-sectional. Most cross-sectional data came from surveys of workers, union representatives, employers, and firms. Some quantitative data came from content analysis of text sources (e.g. newspapers). Qualitative data came from newspapers, case studies, workers' diaries, oral histories, interviews with workers, union leaders, and employers. I list here at least the main sources in the firm belief that they *all* provide empirical evidence. More generally, however, I have to admit that I ransacked the library shelves, extensively using books and articles as empirical evidence. What Collingwood (1956, p. 278) wrote for historians applies to sociologists as well:

So, however much testimony he has, his zeal as an historian makes him want more. But if he has a large amount of testimony, it becomes so difficult to manipulate and work up into a convincing narrative that, speaking as a mere weak mortal, he wishes he had less. . . . historians who brush the dilemma aside . . . are only confessing that in their own professional practice they do not find that it troubles them, because they work to such a low standard of scientific cogency that their consciences become anaesthetized.

As for myself, I never balked at the sheer amount of evidence. If anything, I kept searching for more, and until the very end. But all too aware of being "a mere weak mortal," I simply postponed "the very end."

TIME-SERIES DATA

Labor disputes

The Istituto Centrale di Statistica (ISTAT) has published data on strikes (or "labor conflicts," as they are defined by ISTAT) since November 1948. ISTAT publishes three different strike indicators: Number of strikes, number of strikers, and number of hours lost. In 1955, ISTAT started publishing strike data by region, by cause, and by scope (plant-level strikes, sectorwide strikes, or strikes involving several industrial sectors; unfortunately, in 1975, ISTAT stopped publishing strike data by scope). In 1975, ISTAT started collecting and reporting industrial disputes that were extraneous to the work relationship strictly defined (e.g., conflicts over issues of government economic policies, national or international events). These conflicts had been previously excluded from recording. Starting in 1965, ISTAT has published the number of hours lost by classes (i.e., the distribution of strikes involving less than 500 hours lost, between 501 and 1,000, etc.). In 1976, ISTAT began publishing strike data by classes to strike size, i.e., the distribution of strikes involving less than 10 workers, between 10 and 50 workers, between 50 and 100, etc.. Monthly strike data are published in *Bollettino mensile di statistica*. Yearly data can be found in *Annuario statistico italiano* and *Annuario di statistiche del lavoro* (where some monthly data are also published). The number of hours lost by province can be found in *Annuario di statistiche provinciali* from 1959 until 1972, when the publication was cancelled.

Until 1954 a strike for ISTAT was any labor dispute between employers and employees that led to an interruption of normal working activities, whether from strike or lockout, for a duration of at least one working day or, if of shorter duration, of parts of several consecutive days. Starting in 1955, labor conflicts included all temporary work stoppages of any duration, even a few minutes. "Political" strikes dealing with fiscal and economic policies or with national and international events were never included. After 1975 these types of strikes have been recorded separately. In any case, ISTAT's definition of strikes excludes those forms of industrial conflict that do not lead to even temporary interruptions of work, such as noncollaboration, slowdowns, etc. Furthermore, in ISTAT's definition, the unit of collection is not the individual work stoppage but the set of work stoppages dealing with the same issue.

Definitions do make a difference.[1] According to Korpi (1981, p. 75), for instance, British definitions leave out the great majority of strikes, indeed, something on the order of 90% of all strike occurrences. Similarly, Kuhn (1961, p. 194) argues that a change in the data-collection procedures in the mid-1950s by the U.S. Department of Labor increased the number of strikes reported by an estimated 5%. As for Italy, it is likely that all strike measures prior to 1975 may have been biased downward. Typically, demonstrative strikes are large-scale nationwide strikes that may involve, for just a handful of hours (sometimes even minutes), millions of workers throughout the country. The fact that such strikes were excluded from the counts will have biased the measures of number of strikers and number of hours lost.[2] The extent of the bias depends on the frequency and average duration of these disputes. The exclusion of smaller strikes from the records in the years immediately following the war is likely to have resulted in considerable underestimation of the number of strikes.

The organization of data collection can further compound problems. In Italy, the collection of strike data is organized by ISTAT, the government Central Statistical Office. But data collection itself is carried out by local police departments (*questure*). ISTAT provides standard data collection forms and handles and publishes the data collected by police departments. Obviously, police departments will record a strike only when they are informed by the company or by the workers or unions. If the company reports the strike, it may underestimate workers' involvement (to embarrass the union). The company may even prefer not to report a strike in order to promote a public image of harmonious labor relations.[3] Giulio Calosso, a Fiat worker, reported the following in an interview:

One time, three serious accidents happened in twenty four hours.... When I went in with my shift, I ... went to the engineer [manager] with all the workers and said: "We would like to protest because three workers have been injured and you did nothing.... " He said that if the workers went on strike, they would have offended the injured (!) ... [but] when the workers [still] wanted to go on strike, he sent them all home with a permit, so that the strike would not go on record. (quoted in Accornero and Rieser, 1981, pp. 122–3)

Alternatively, management may exaggerate the scope of the conflict in order to justify future retaliatory actions and/or police or government intervention. Union-reported figures, on the other hand, are more likely to overestimate strike figures. When police departments themselves estimate the figures, these can be little more than guesswork.[4]

The number of strikes is likely always to be underestimated. The majority of strikes are short, sudden shop-level stoppages. Field research has repeatedly shown that this type of strike is rarely recorded in most countries (Turner, Clack, and Roberts, 1967; Korpi, 1978, 1981; Batstone et al., 1978). For instance, Turner (1969) reported that in England in the motor industry and coal mining, approximately 80% and 30%, respectively, of all work stoppages, as recorded by the firms themselves, never made it into the official statistics. For the United States, Kuhn argues that "Short strikes are much more likely to go underreported" (Kuhn, 1961, p. 194; Edwards, 1981, pp. 306–13). On the basis of a sample survey among metalworking firms in Sweden, Korpi (1981, p. 73) estimated an annual average of 1.8 unreported strikes per 10,000 workers, and a figure at least three times higher if all forms of collective actions were included. Salerni (1980), in a case study of industrial conflict at the Alfa-Romeo plant in Pomigliano d'Arco in southern Italy (Alfasud), reported strike data for the years 1973, 1974, and 1975. A direct comparison of the Salerni and ISTAT data (Table A.1) allows one to make

Table A.1. *Measuring the extent of bias in Italian strike data*

		1973	1974	1975
Alfasud[a]	Number of strikes	569	1452	1521
	Number of hours lost	813,353	1,527,766	549,670
Italy[b]	Number of strikes	3769	5174	3568
	Number of hours lost	163,935,000	136,267,000	181,381,000
Campania[b]	Number of strikes	509	587	389
	Number of hours lost	7,386,000	5,772,000	7,962,000
Naples[b]	Number of hours lost[c]	4,375,000	3,254,000	3,623,000

[a] Data from Salerni (1980, p. 222).
[b] Data from ISTAT.
[c] Number of strikes not available at the provincial level.

a good estimate of the extent of bias in Italian strike data. According to these data, Alfasud contributed, by itself, 15% of all Italian strikes in 1973, 28% in 1974, and 43% (i.e., almost half) in 1975. In fact, in 1973, Alfasud, by itself, was struck slightly more often than the rest of the entire region in which the plant is located (Campania), more than twice as often in 1974, and almost four times as often in 1975! Although Salerni's data could be exaggerated, it is much more likely that official statistics grossly underestimated strike frequency.[5]

Most countries publish raw counts of the numbers of strikes, strikers, and hours lost.[6] In the strike literature, however, proportions, rather than raw counts, have often been used: frequency, size, duration, and volume (Franzosi, 1980, 1985). The frequency of strikes measures the number of strikes per thousand employed workers, the size measures the number of strikers per strike, and the duration measures the number of hours lost per striker. The product of these three measures gives the volume of strikes, which is nothing but the number of hours lost deflated by employment, i.e., the average number of hours lost per employed worker.

It has often been argued that standardized indicators (e.g., frequency, rather than the number of strikes) have the advantage over raw counts that they take into consideration the "population at risk." That is true, particularly for long time series. However, the problem with standardized indicators is that different deflating procedures have been used (e.g., total civilian labor force, nonagricultural labor force, unionized labor force, employment figures) leading to an unnecessary proliferation of strike indicators that stand in the way of comparability of findings (see Stern, 1978). Furthermore, standardized measures, such as frequency or volume, where labor force figures appear in the denominator, have been used in the context of multivariate regression analysis as "dependent" variables. The appearance among the regressors of such variables as unemployment or unionization rates which also contain, by definition, labor force figures in the denominator, builds into the model potential artificial correlations between "dependent" and "independent" variables (see Stern, 1978; on the ratio-variable debate, see Fuguitt and Lieberson, 1974; Schuessler, 1974; Long, 1979).

For these reasons, I have preferred to report here only the results obtained using raw counts (numbers of strikes, strikers, and hours lost) rather than standardized measures (strike frequency, size, duration, or volume).[7]

Employment and unemployment

Statistical collection of labor-force data through sample surveys is quite recent. The first surveys date back to the 1940s in the United States. From there, in the postwar period, they spread to other countries, including Italy.

In Italy, the first national survey dates to September 1952 and was carried out by ISTAT. Later surveys were conducted in May 1954, May 1955, April 1956, May and November 1957, and October 1958. Starting in 1959, the survey became quarterly, and it is normally conducted in January, April, July, and October. In January 1977, a new series of quarterly surveys was started. The new survey is so different from the previous one as to make any comparison with the earlier results difficult (see ISTAT, 1978a, 1979a). Furthermore, with the new series, data on sectoral unemployment (industry, agriculture, and tertiary sectors) are no longer available. Recently, however, ISTAT made the two series continuous. The unemployment rate is given by the ratio between (1) the unemployed and the people looking for their first jobs and (2) the total labor force.

For the quarterly analyses involving sample periods prior to 1959 (1954 for yearly analyses), in place of the ISTAT unemployment rate, I used the *uffici di collocamento* data, published every month by the Labor Department. These data have been available since the prewar years. They provide the number of people registered in employment offices (*uffici di collocamento*). I used the numbers of registered workers in the first and second classes (i.e., the number of currently unemployed but formerly employed workers looking for jobs, and the number of workers looking for their first jobs (for an assessment of the reliability of employment and unemployment data in Italy, Malfatti, 1972).

Layoffs

I used two different types of data on layoffs, biannual data collected and published until recent years by Confindustria (see Confederazione Generale dell'Industria Italiana, *Annuario*, various years) and data on the rates of labor turnover, published by the Labor Department (see Ministero del Lavoro e della Previdenza Sociale, *Rassegna di statistiche del lavoro*, various quarters).

Confindustria data were collected through questionnaires mailed out to member firms. The data distinguish between layoffs for reduction of personnel (number of firms requesting layoffs, number of workers involved, and number of cases accompanied by strike activity) and various forms of individual dismissals, including members of *commissioni interne*). Data on turnover rates, particularly on layoff rates per thousand workers, are collected by the Labor Department through sample surveys. The survey, started in December 1946, collects a variety of information on employment in industry. In 1965, the survey became quarterly instead of monthly and was based on a sample of 55,000 plants instead of the previous 17,000 plants. At the same time, the survey adopted ISTAT 1959 classification of industries in place of the previous one used by the Labor Department, based on forty-three sectors. Since 1977, only those productive units with more than fifty employees have been surveyed; before then, all units with more than ten workers were sampled (five for the construction industry). The Labor Department has provided data on turnover rates only since January 1958. The rates are given by the ratio between the number of entrances or exits for each cause (new hirings, dismissals) and the average number of workers during the month or quarter.

Index of industrial production

After the wartime interruption in the publication of the old industrial-production indices in base 1928 = 100, ISTAT began the publication of a new series of indices in base 1938 = 100. The indices, divided by categories, classes, and branches of industry, are weighted averages of elementary indices. Starting in September 1953, the indices in base 1953 = 100 replaced the old indices. In the following decades, several indices in different base years were published in order to include larger numbers of branches of industry, categories, and products: the indices in base 1966 = 100 from January 1967 until January 1973 and the indices in base 1970 = 100 from January 1971 (see ISTAT, 1957a, 1967a, 1976a). ISTAT did not link the four series (base 1938 = 100, 1953 = 100, 1966 = 100, and 1970 = 100). I constructed a continuous series in base 1970 = 100 for the entire period and for the index of industrial production in the manufacturing industry by dividing the annual averages of the indices in the two different bases. This gave me the following set of link coefficients: 1938–53, .6648; 1953–66, .3448; 1966–70, .8076. I multiplied the values of the original series by these coefficients in order to transform all series in the same base, 1970 = 100.

Gross national product at market prices

A yearly series of data on gross national product (GNP) has been available for many decades. However, in 1978, ISTAT revised the series for the 1975–78 period in order to correct for an underestimate in the level of economic activity due to the underground economy. The changes introduced were of such significance as to make the revised series noncomparable with the previous one (see ISTAT, 1978b). Subsequently, ISTAT extended the revised series back to the 1960–74 period. Quarterly series of national accounts, including GNP figures in 1970 prices, have been made available for the 1954–75 period (Da Empoli, Siesto, and Antonello,

1979). For GNP data for the 1980s, I used the Prometeia elaboration of ISTAT data.

Labor share of national income

ISTAT data on national accounts provide information on the total wage bill by branch of economic activity. I obtained the labor share of national income as the ratio to GNP of that total for the entire economy. As mentioned earlier, ISTAT revised national income figures for the 1960–78 period. I used the new series of total wages for salaried workers and GNP for the 1960–78 period (see ISTAT, 1979b). I extended the series back to 1954 using the data published by Da Empoli et al. (1979).

Bank of Italy index of capacity utilization

The index of capacity utilization is considered as the most sensitive business-cycle indicator. The index measures the current level of utilization of installations in a sector as a percentage of a sector's maximum capacity. Thus, the index can vary between 0 to 100. It is based on the method of peak-to-peak interpolation of industrial-production indices (Klein and Summers, 1966; Klein and Preston, 1967).

ISCO cyclical indicator

The cyclical indicator published by ISCO (Istituto Italiano per lo Studio della Congiuntura) is a composite business-cycle indicator. The ISCO index is based on twenty-seven economic series of the type proposed by Burns and Mitchell (1947). For the index, see ISCO, *Congiuntura Italiana, Rassegna Mensile.*

Index of minimum contractual wages

The index of minimum contractual wages is published by ISTAT for several branches and classes of economic activity for blue- and white-collar workers with and without family allowances. I used the index for blue-collar workers in manufacturing industries, including family allowances. The index provides a measure of the variations in minimum wages introduced by national or provincial collective labor contracts. Until 1967, the index in base 1938 = 100 was based on daily wage rates. It measured variations in gross base pay, including social-security benefits paid by the workers, increases due to the *scala mobile,* and other items such as cafeteria benefits, clothing benefits, etc. It did not include compensations for vacation time, holidays, the "thirteenth" monthly pay (Christmas bonus), or variations in the number of weekly working hours. After 1967, a new index in base 1966 = 100 was published. The new wage rate refers to the hour for blue-collar workers and to the month for white-collar workers. The index in base 1966 = 100 included the pay items of the old index and compensation for vacation time, holidays, and thirteenth monthly pay (see ISTAT, 1968a, 1968b). Since 1976, the index has been published in base 1975 = 100. ISTAT provided link coefficients with the previous series, although it warned that "From a strictly logical viewpoint the series (base 1966 = 100 and base 1975 = 100) are not perfectly comparable in relation to the changes introduced" (ISTAT, 1976b, p. 263, 1977).

I transformed all three series (base 1938 = 100, from January 1950 to December 1966, base 1966 = 100 from January 1967 to December 1975, and base 1975 = 100 from January 1976 to December 1978) in base 1966 = 100. In order to link the series 1966 = 100 and 1975 = 100, I used the link coefficients provided by ISTAT (3.26135 for blue-collar workers in the manufacturing industry, including family allowances). I obtained the coefficient to link the series 1938 = 100 and 1966 = 100 by dividing the annual averages of the indices in the two different bases (0.6943 for blue-collar workers in the manufacturing industry, including family allowances). I aggregated the indices for the metal and mechanical sectors in base 1938 = 100 with a weighted average in order to link the series with the aggregate index in base 1966 = 100. As weights I used the employment figures in the two sectors taken from ISTAT's (1942) industrial census data.[8]

Cost of living

Two different consumer price indices are available for the postwar period in Italy: for the nation as a whole and for blue-collar and white-collar families (formerly called index of cost of living). I used the consumer price indices for blue- and white-collar workers, and in particular the national general index, which is the weighted average for five different consumer items: food (including tobacco), clothing, electricity and fuel, housing, and various goods and services. Both price series have been modified several times during the postwar period in order to keep up with the variations in consumer items and with the changing structure of wages (base 1938 = 100 until December 1962, base 1961 = 100 until December 1965, base 1966 = 100 until December 1970, base 1970 = 100 until December 1976, and base 1976 = 100 until December 1978) (see ISTAT, 1957b, 1967b, 1971, 1978c). ISTAT published a complete series of consumer price indices for blue- and white-collar households, providing the link coefficients between series in different bases (ISTAT, 1978d).

Number of work-related injuries

The Istituto Nazionale per l'Assicurazione contro gli Infortuni sul Lavoro (INAIL) publishes quarterly data on work injuries in Italy. I used the series on number of injuries in industry, which in the INAIL classification includes manufacturing industries, construction, electricity, gas and water, and other minor industries (e.g., animal and fish breeding, transports).

The data refer to the number of injuries reported until December 31 of the year when the work accidents occurred (*per competenza*, as INAIL calls them) (see

INAIL, *Notiziario Statistico*, various issues). I used the number of work injuries *denunciati per competenza* at the end of each quarter. Quarterly data do not coincide with the total number of injuries reported at the end of the year or even several years later, because INAIL continuously and retroactively updated the data. I tried to use the most recently published data.

Cassa integrazione guadagni

The *cassa integrazione guadagni* (CIG) provides an income to those workers laid off temporarily. CIG works similarly to unemployment benefits, which in Italy are very low (Miscione, 1978). However, from a strictly formal and legal viewpoint, workers in the *cassa integrazione* with zero hours are still employed workers and are not unemployed. The data refer to the total number of hours allowed for *cassa integrazione guadagni ordinaria* and *straordinaria*, as collected and published each quarter by sector and region by INPS (Istituto Nazionale di Previdenza Sociale). I took the data from Confindustria's *Rassegna di statistiche del lavoro*.

Percentage of blue-collar workers subject to contract renewal

The indicator is based on forty-two manufacturing sectors (on this indicator, see Tarantelli, 1976). I took the expiration and renewal dates for the various sectors from Alinari (1979) and from *Relazione sull'attività confederale* (various issues) of the Confederazione Generale dell'Industria Italiana. I took quarterly data on sectoral employment from *Rassegna di statistiche del lavoro*, Ministero del Lavoro e della Previdenza Sociale.

I considered an industrial sector to be "under contract renewal" for all quarters included between the contract expiration and renewal dates. This presumes that before the expiration of the old contract, no strikes were declared. If that is true for most cases, it is also true that (particularly under favorable labor-market conditions) anticipatory strikes often occurred (e.g., in 1962 for the metalworkers).

Union membership and unionization rate

Yearly data on union membership and unionization rates for CGIL and CISL come from Romagnoli and Rossi (1980). Unfortunately there are no reliable figures for the third major Italian union UIL for earlier periods. Santi (1988) updated Romagnoli and Rossi's data for the period 1977-86 (including UIL membership data; unionization data by unions is not available in Santi, 1988, but in Santi, 1987). Unionization data for later periods can be found in the yearly reports *Le relazioni sindacali in Italia* by CESOS, Centro di Studi Sociali e Sindacali. Given the slight differences between Romagnoli and Rossi's and Santi's data for CGIL and CISL, I computed link coefficients between the two series (dividing Romagnoli and Rossi's CGIL and CISL figures for 1977 by Santi's 1977 figures and then multiplying Santi's post-1977 figures for CGIL and CISL by these two coefficients – 0.990816 for CGIL and 0.985556 for CISL).

PCI membership

Communist Party membership was taken from Barbagli and Corbetta (1978).

Dates of national political elections

June 7, 1953; May 25, 1958; April 28, 1963; May 19, 1968; May 7, 1972; June 20, 1976; June 3, 1979; June 26, 1983; June 14, 1987.

Government crises

Beginning date	Ending date	Duration (in days)[9]
1.12.50	1.27.50	15
7.16.51	7.26.51	10
6.29.53	7.16.53	17
7.28.53	8.17.53	20
1.5.54	1.18.54	13
1.30.54	2.10.54	11
6.22.55	7.6.55	14
5.6.57	5.19.57	13
6.19.58	7.1.58	12
1.26.59	2.15.59	20
2.24.60	3.25.60	30
7.19.60	7.26.60	7
2.2.62	2.21.62	19
5.16.63	6.21.63	36
11.5.63	12.4.63	29
6.26.64	7.22.64	26
1.21.66	2.23.66	33
6.5.68	6.24.68	19
11.19.68	12.12.68	23
7.5.69	8.5.69	31
2.7.70	3.27.70	48
7.6.70	8.6.70	31
1.15.72	2.17.72	33
2.26.72	6.26.72	121
6.12.73	7.7.73	25
3.2.74	3.14.74	12
10.3.74	11.23.74	51

Beginning date	Ending date	Duration (in days)
1.7.76	2.12.76	36
4.30.76	7.29.76	90
1.16.78	3.11.78	54
1.31.79	3.20.79	48
3.31.79	8.4.79	126
3.19.80	4.4.80	16
9.27.80	10.18.80	21
5.26.81	6.28.81	33
8.7.82	8.23.82	16
11.13.82	12.1.82	18

SURVEYS OF WORKERS, UNION REPRESENTATIVES, EMPLOYERS, AND FIRMS

ACLI (Associazioni Cristiani Lavoratori Italiani) (ACLI, 1953): A *cahiers de doleances* against employers collected through the locals of the Association of Italian Christian Workers in the early 1950s.

Alfa-Romeo workers' survey (Cella and Reyneri, 1974): A survey of 236 Alfa Romeo workers at the Arese and Portello plants near Milan (190 unskilled and 46 skilled workers).

Assolombarda (Associazione Industriale Lombarda) 1958–62 surveys on labor turnover (various years): A survey conducted yearly by the Lombard employers' association among member firms on labor turnover.

Assolombarda (Associazione Industriale Lombarda) 1953–57 and 1963–67 surveys on absenteeism (various years): A survey conducted yearly by the Lombard employers' association among member firms on workers' absenteeism.

Assolombarda (Associazione Industriale Lombarda) 1981–82 survey (Associazione Industriale Lombarda, 1983): A survey of the state of labor relations conducted among a sample of 177 member firms employing less than 250 workers.

Bagnasco and Trigilia's 1982–83 survey (Bagnasco and Trigilia, 1984; Trigilia, 1986): A research survey in the area of Bassano del Grappa, in Veneto, based on interviews of 380 blue-collar workers, 100 employers, and 200 members of the middle class.

Bagnasco and Trigilia's 1982–83 survey (Bagnasco and Trigilia, 1985; Trigilia, 1986): A research survey (parallel to the one conducted by the same authors in the area of Bassano del Grappa, in Veneto) in the area of Valdelsa, in Tuscany, based on interviews of 380 blue-collar workers, 100 employers, and 200 members of the middle class.

Bonazzi, Bagnasco, and Casillo 1969 survey of Salerno entrepreneurs (Bonazzi et al., 1972): A survey of employers from the southern province of Salerno. The sample of 202 industrial firms included 88 firms with more than 40 employees and 114 with less than 40 employees. Interviews were conducted in the fall of 1969.

Cesos (Osservatorio Cesos) (Camonico, 1986; Squarzon, 1989b, 1990): Yearly surveys among a national sample of firms on the state of industrial relations. Sample size varies by year, ranging from a few to several hundred firms.

CGIL survey (Baccalini et al., 1981): Survey of delegates to the congresses of territorial unions in Lombardy.

CISIM (Commissione indagini e Studi sull'Industria Meccanica) 1951 survey (CISIM, 1952): Approximately 120 metalworking plants visited and inspected by the Stanford Research Institute to assess the state of the metalworking industry in Italy.

CISL 1972–73 survey (Cella, 1973): A survey conducted December 1972–January 1973 among CISL Lombardy metalworking-union cadres.

CISL (Milan) 1987 survey (La Valle, 1987): A survey conducted in 1987 among 585 union members of Milan CISL.

Commissione Parlamentare d'Inchiesta sulle Condizioni dei Lavoratori in Italia 1956 survey (1958a, 1958b, 1958c): Survey of 195 manufacturing firms directly inspected by members of the 1956 Commissione Parlamentare, with testimony collected from several thousand workers.

Confindustria's surveys on absenteeism (Confederazione Generale dell'Industria Italiana) (1972 to present): Yearly surveys conducted by the private employers' association among a sample of member firms on workers' absenteeism. Data published in *Rassegna di statistiche del lavoro*.

Confindustria 1970 survey (Confederazione Generale dell'Industria Italiana, 1973): A survey conducted by Confindustria in 1970 on consigli di fabbrica (Cdf) among a sample of its member firms.

Confindustria-Censis national survey of entrepreneurs (Confindustria-Censis, 1989): A survey of a national sample of 964 entrepreneurs operating in both industrial and service sectors. Firms in the industrial sector had a minimum of twenty employees. Interviews were carried out in 1988.

Farneti's 1966–67 survey of entrepreneurs (Farneti, 1970): The survey was carried out among 179 entrepreneurs from Piedmont in 1966–67 via questionnaire. Firms were classified by size as follows: small, 50–100; regular, 101–250; medium, 251–500; medium large, 501–1,000; large, >1,000.

Federlombarda's 1975 survey (Federazione Regionale fra le Associazioni Industriali della Lombardia, 1977): A survey based on a sample of 358 member firms distributed in the following size classes: 1–19, 20–49, 50–99, 100–249, 250–499, >500. To the personal questions asked of the employers, only 172 employers answered (42% of the sample).

Federmeccanica 1983 and 1984 surveys (Mortillaro, 1984, 1986): National surveys of metalworking firms belonging to Federmeccanica on the state of labor relations. The 1983 survey was based on a sample of 150 firms employing more than 20 workers. Questionnaires were given directly to employers and/or managers (139 responses). The 1984 survey was based on 164 firms. All results are presented also by firm size (0–100, 101–500, >500).

FLM (Bergamo) 1972 survey (FLM di Bergamo, 1975): Survey of 389 firms with a total of 39,000 employees by the Bergamo FLM, through interviews with the members of *Consigli di fabbrica* (Cdf) or single workers for the smaller firms. Interviews were conducted by trade-union representatives in September 1972 (Brusco, 1975, pp. 10, 13). The size distribution of firms was as follows: 29.1% had 1–9 employees; 38.8% had 10–49 employees; 14.4% had 50–99 employees; 11.8% had 100–249 employees; 3.9% had 250–499 employees; 2.1% had more than 499 employees (FLM di Bergamo, 1975, p. 204).

FLM (Bologna) 1975 survey (Maestrali, 1979): A 1975 survey of 452 metalworking firms in the province of Bologna distributed in the following size classes: 0–49, 50–99, 100–249, 250–499, 500–999, >1,000.

FULC (Federazione Unitaria Lavoratori Chimici) 1978–79 survey (Vento, 1980): A national survey of 60 chemical-sector firms (including ceramic, plastic, rubber, pharmaceutical, and chemical proper) employing some 35,000 workers. The survey collected the answers of the members of Consigli di Fabbrica to a questionnaire.

Giovani Imprenditori's survey (1978?) (Pastorino and Ragazzoni, 1980): Survey commissioned by Giovani Imprenditori and carried out by the Scuola di Formazione Superiore of Genoa covering 43 small and medium-size firms employing between 30 and 300 employees and located in eight provinces of northern and central/southern Italy. Date of survey not given (presumably 1978).

Giubilato's 1981 survey of Veneto firms (Giubilato, 1982; Castegnaro, 1983): A research survey on the diffusion of plant-level bargaining among Veneto firms with more than 20 employees between 1979 and 1981: 1,223 firms (for a total of 1,296 agreements) and 450 firms involved in territory bargaining.

IDOM (Impresa Domani) 1976 survey (Bratina and Martinelli, 1978): A survey of 72 entrepreneurs of small and medium-size firms located in Lombardy, Emilia Romagna, and Veneto.

IRES (Istituto de Ricerche Economiche e Sociali) Lombardia 1987, 1988, 1989 surveys (Ronchi, 1990): Yearly surveys conducted by Ires Lombardia in 1987, 1988, and 1989 among Lombardy manufacturing firms in the following size classes: 50–99, 100–499, and >500.

Isvet 1971 survey (Buratto, De Santis, and Ventrella, 1974): A national survey of workers' attitudes conducted among a sample of 5,830 workers across 653 firms each employing more than 50 workers. Another 1,617 workers were interviewed in 145 state-owned firms.

Isvet 1982 survey (De Masi et al., 1985): A national survey of workers' attitudes on a sample of 3,500 workers from 266 firms with more than 50 workers.

Regalia's 1981 survey (Regalia, 1984a): In 1981, Ida Regalia conducted a survey of 63 firms with *consigli di fabbrica*. Regalia classified the firms as small (100–200 employees), medium (200–999), and large (>1,000).

Romagnoli's 1970 and 1972 surveys (Romagnoli, 1971, 1973, 1976): The 1970 survey involved a sample of 429 firms operating in the province of Milan in the mechanic, chemical, textile, and printing sectors. The 1972 survey involved a sample of 85 firms chosen from among the 230 firms with new plant-level organizational structures in the 1970 sample.

1971–72 survey of managers (Talamo, 1979; Derossi, 1982): A survey of 663 managers of 50 manufacturing firms carried out in 1971–72. The firms with total revenues in 1970 of more than 10 billion lire, were taken from Mediobanca's publication *Le principali società italiane*.

1973 survey of Liguria entrepreneurs (Guerci, 1975): A survey of 263 Liguria firms with employment ranging between 10 and 250 employees. The survey was carried out in 1973.

CONTENT ANALYSIS DATA

Bagnara and Diani (1980). Content analysis of the leaflets distributed at the Fiat automobile plant in Cassino between 1974 and 1977 by various organizations (e.g. CGIL, CISL, UIL, Lotta Continua).

Tarrow (1989a). Content analysis of *Il Corriere della sera*, Milan quality paper, from January 1, 1966 to Decemeber 31, 1973. 4,980 protest events of all kinds were recorded from some 20,000 newspaper articles originally scanned (Tarrow, 1989a, pp. 30, 360).

From *Il Corriere della sera* I collected data on strikes for every day of each of the 30 political crises during the period 1950–1978.[10]

ETHNOGRAPHIC MATERIAL

Workers' diaries (Accornero, 1959, 1973; see also Accornero and Rieser, 1981; Accornero et al., 1960; Pugno and Garavini, 1974); worker interviews and oral history (Lanzardo, 1979; Polo, 1989); interviews with employers (Ottone, 1965; Levi, 1983; Scalfari, 1977) and union leaders (Riva, 1976).

CASE STUDIES

I relied on two types of case studies, either of strikes or of specific firms. Pizzorno's (1974–75) monumental research on the 1968–72 strike wave based on 11 firms belong to the first category, along with Bianchi et al. (1970), Giugni et al. (1976), Cacciari (1969), Gianotti (1979), Salerni (1980), Bezza (1981), Gallessi (1981), and Mattina (1981). The work by Milanaccio and Ricolfi (1976), Becchi Collidà and Negrelli (1986), Locke and Negrelli (1989) on Fiat, belong to the second category.

Notes

Preface

1. For a very empathetic account of the hidden injuries of class, see Sennett and Cobb, 1973.

Chapter 1   The puzzle box

1. Ross and Hartman (1960; p.121); see also Shorter and Tilly (1974).
2. I will rely on these three strike indicators for all the empirical analyses throughout the book. In the strike literature, however, other indicators have often been used: frequency, size, and duration; see Franzosi (1980, 1985). See the Appendix on data for a discussion of strike indicators and for the reasons behind my choice of indicators.
3. On the shape of strikes, see Shorter and Tilly (1971, 1974; pp. 51–8).
4. On these strike indicators see the Appendix on data.
5. I show the shape starting in 1954, because new employment series are available only from that year (see the Appendix on data).
6. For a detailed description of strike activity in the 1960s, see Accornero (1971).
7. See Shorter and Tilly (1974; pp. 318–31) for international comparisons.
8. On the shapes of strikes prior to World War II, see Bordogna and Provasi (1979).
9. For a review of the literature, see Franzosi (1985, 1989b); see also Shalev (1980).
10. For example, see Ashenfelter and Johnson (1969).
11. Particularly, "Useless Durkheim" (Tilly, 1981).
12. For a review, see Jenkins (1983).
13. For a notable exception, see Hyman (1971, 1975, 1989); see also Mandel (1980; pp. 37–61. On the relationship between strikes and the business cycle from a Marxist perspective, see Boddy and Crotty (1975). On the relationship between strike waves and long-term economic cycles, see Screpanti (1987), Aglietta (1979), Cronin (1980), Bowles, Gordon, and Weisskopf (1983), Boyer (1987). See also Przeworski and Wallerstein (1982).
14. Korpi (1974; 1978, in particular pp. 31–54); see also Kaufman (1982; p. 489).
15. For example, see Luxemburg (1971; pp. 9–43), in particular; see also Brecher (1972); see also Gouldner's (1954) classic.
16. On the availability of strike data at the international level, see Fisher (1973).
17. For example, see Stearns (1968), Shorter and Tilly (1974), Perrot (1974), Griffin, Wallace, and Rubin (1986).
18. See, however, Shorter and Tilly (1974) and Cronin (1979, 1980). See also Tarrow's work (1989a) on Italy.
19. van Dijk (1972); for a specific application to news schemata, see van Dijk (1986); on some of these issues, see Agger (1989).
20. Using the econometric package TSP (Time Series Processor), I enclosed all my statistical procedures (e.g., correlations, regressions) within two sets of FORTRAN

DO-loop statements, varying the starting and ending points of the sampling period systematically, and keeping the size of the minimum sample (typically, at least twelve observations) fixed. Fabio Manzetti, a colleague at Confindustria, properly labeled the method the yo-yo.
21. On these issues, see the articles in the special issue "Temporality, Events, and Explanation in Historical Sociology." *Sociological Methods and Research*, Vol. 20, No. 4, 1992; see also Abbott (1991).
22. For example, the monumental work directed by Pizzorno (1974–5), on the 1968–72 strike wave.
23. I use the term "ethnography" in a very broad sense, as field research, oral history, workers' diaries, and interviews.
24. On the relationship between history and sociology, see Abbott (1991) and Tilly (1981).

Chapter 2 Labor-market conditions and bargaining power

1. The sample period starts in 1959 because reliable quarterly survey data on unemployment are not available before those data. Employment-office (Ufficio di Collocamento) data on unemployment are available for earlier periods. These data, however, have much lower reliability than ISTAT survey data (on unemployment statistics in Italy, see Malfatti, 1972). See the Appendix for data sources and descriptions.
2. A distributed lag structure simply means that the statistical relationship between an independent and a dependent variable (in this case, real wages and number of strikes) is not restricted to a particular time (whether contemporaneous at time t, or lagged at time t-1, t-2, or other); rather, the relationship is distributed over several preceding n time periods that together constitute the lag structure. Basically, the Almon estimating technique assumes that the coefficients of the distributed lag structure lie on a polynomial of low order p, where $p \leq n$ (Almon, 1965). Unfortunately, the Almon technique does not suggest any statistical criteria for choosing either the correct order of the polynomial or the correct length of the lag structure.
3. For a detailed treatment of the controversy and for the results of these preliminary analyses, see Franzosi (1981).
4. See Cochrane and Orcutt (1969); see also Johnston (1972). In order to avoid local minima, I also searched over the whole set (-1,+1) of possible ρ values for the one that would yield the minimum standard error of the transformed equation (Hildreth and Lu, 1960). The econometric package that I used, TSP, did not allow me to estimate an Almon structure with maximum-likelihood (ML) estimation procedures (on ML, see Beach and MacKinnon, 1978). Although Cochrane-Orcutt and ML estimates are asymptotically equivalent, they may present substantial small-sample differences (Rao and Griliches, 1969). I should add, however, that I obtained equivalent results when I applied the three different methods to equations that did not require the Almon procedure for their estimation. That is why I reported only Cochrane-Orcutt estimates throughout the book.
5. Given that the number of strikes S is affected by moving seasonality (Franzosi, 1980), I also estimated some alternative seasonal specifications. To allow for moving seasonality, I followed Cowden's suggestions (Cowden, 1942; Lovell, 1963; Stephenson and Farr, 1972) and regressed S in the following way:

$$x_{tm} = \sum S_{tm}(a_{0m} + a_{1m}t + \ldots + a_{dm}t^n) + C_{tm} \text{ where, } S_{tm} = 1 \text{ in season } m, \text{ and } 0 \text{ otherwise.}$$

The best results, obtained applying the Cochrane-Orcutt procedure, without end-point constraints, for a value of $n = 1$, are as follows:

Table N.2.1. *Strike frequency model with moving seasonality*

Dependent variable: Number of strikes
Aggregation level: Manufacturing industry; quarterly series
Sample period: 1959–I/1978–IV
Estimation method: GLS (Cochrane-Orcutt)

$S_t =$ 477.81*C + 127.87*D_{1t} − 2.02**$D_{1t}T_t$ + 128.67*D_{2t} − 2.46$D_{2t}T_t$
(142.47) (57.66) (1.09) (41.72) (.93)

− 9.47D_{3t} − 2.21*$D_{3t}T_t$ − 34.33 UN_t + 251.64*R_{t-i}
(39.77) (.88) (22.39) (53.57)

Adjusted $R^2 = .81$ Durbin-Watson = 1.76 Wallis = 2.46

Note: Standard error in parentheses. **, significant at the .05 level; *, significant at the .01 level.

and where C = constant, D_1= 1st-quarter dummy, D_2 = 2nd-quarter dummy, D_3 = 3rd-quarter dummy, T = trend, UN = unemployment rate, R = % change in real wages.

The results confirm a moving seasonal pattern for number of strikes. However, the magnitudes and signs of the coefficients of unemployment and wages do not change significantly, when compared with those of Table 2.1. It should be noted, though, that the more than 50% increase in the standard error makes the unemployment variable insignificant at the usual acceptance levels. This would seem to support Mayhew's argument, since a correct specification of the seasonal pattern makes the unemployment variable insignificant. To the extent that seasonal movements in strike activity are induced by seasonal variations in unemployment, it should not come as a surprise if a correct specification of the seasonal model leaves the unemployment-rate coefficient insignificant. In fact, a correctly specified seasonal model picks up that portion of total seasonal variability in strike frequency previously explained by seasonality in unemployment, leaving the unemployment coefficient to measure only cyclical, medium-term effects on strikes. I also tried to deseasonalize the number of strikes with the X11 method, before regressing it on unemployment and wages. I was unable, though, to totally eliminate seasonality using this deseasonalization procedure, as confirmed by the autocorrelation function and by the significance of the seasonal dummies of the deseasonalized series. Given, also, the distorting effects of seasonal adjustment procedures on the relationship among variables (Nerlove, 1964; Wallis, 1974), in other than seasonal frequency bands, I preferred not to take this approach.
6. For a general critique of the model, see Shalev (1980).
7. Gramm (1986); on the relationship between microlevel hypotheses and macrolevel data in strike models, see Stern (1978), Mayhew (1979), and Edwards (1981, p. 64).
8. Unions, for instance, focus on consumer price indices, income taxes, real wage changes, and wage differentials between industries, whereas employers focus on production prices, profits, and labor productivity.
9. See Shalev (1980) and Kaufman (1981) for the United States and Swidinsky and Vanderkamp (1982) for Canada. See also Mauro (1982) and Gramm (1987).
10. See also Aminzade (1980, p. 76).
11. According to Granger (1976), the predominant causes of seasonality in economic time series belong to the following three broad categories:
    Calendar: The dates of certain holidays, such as Christmas and Easter, have direct consequences on many time series, particularly those related to production. Even the

mere month-to-month differences in numbers of working days can induce seasonal movements in flow variables (import, production, etc.). Interestingly enough, according to the International Bureau of Labour, the introduction of a national holiday and the elimination of a working day result in a more severe loss of production than do all strikes taken together (Troiani, 1978, pp. 162–4).

Context: The institutional context comprises causes that belong to the organizational structure of modern societies (e.g., the system of vacation in schools and industry, the payment of dividends). Employment series are affected by these causes.

Weather: Climatic, seasonal changes have strong effects on agricultural production, construction, transportation, industries based on tourism, etc.

12. For the United States, see Yoder (1938) and Griffin (1939); for the United Kingdom, see Knowles (1952); for Italy, during the 1950s, see Melotti (1964).
13. For an example in industry, see Regini (1974, p. 24).
14. The problem of omitted variables also includes, as a special case, an incorrect specification of the functional form of the relationship between dependent and independent variables. Suppose, in fact, that a linear relationship is specified when the "true" relationship is quadratic. The x^2 term will then be contained in the disturbance component, and if there is any serial correlation in the X values, there will be serial correlation in the error term also. In order to check for misspecification of the functional form, I took several steps. First, I performed exploratory data analysis; specifically, I made various scatter plots between all variables involved, in order to find an initial suitable functional form (Anscombe, 1973). In general, my variables presented no evidence of nonlinearity. Second, when in doubt, I carried out the analyses using different functional forms and transformations of the original data, in order to try to make the relationship more clearly linear (on data transformation as a way of checking the accuracy of the assumed functional form and of obtaining linearity, see Bartlett, 1947; Hoerl, 1954; Tukey, 1957; Box and Tidwell, 1962). In no case, however, could I reject the linearity assumption. Finally, I used scatter plots of the residuals against the fitted values. I also used scatter plots of the residuals against each independent variable to assess the importance of nonlinearity, if any, for the ith independent variable and to choose the appropriate transformation. In multivariate regression, partial effects of the remaining K variables make this type of plot less useful (Draper and Smith, 1966, p. 91; Anscombe, 1973; see also Anscombe and Tukey, 1963; Larsen and McCleary, 1972). Again, I did not find any evidence of nonlinearity among the variables. For all these reasons, I feel confident in saying that low Durbin-Watson statistics have to be taken, in this case, more as an indication of the omission of relevant variables, rather than as misspecification of the functional form.
15. Granger and Newbold (1974) and Plosser and Schwert (1978) suggest that first differences should be taken prior to using trended variables in a regression model. Trend is in fact one of the main causes of autocorrelation and nonsense regressions, and first-differencing is a good method for eliminating it (on differencing as a method of trend elimination, see Tintner, 1940; see also Durbin, 1962). But, after all, the Cochrane-Orcutt procedure is based on a transformation of the variables, which is equivalent to taking first differences, for values of the first-order serial correlation coefficient ρ close to 1, as in this case.
16. Phillips (1958); see also Boyer (1979).
17. See, for all, Santomero and Seater (1978).
18. The number of strikes reached its postwar peak in 1970, as did strike frequency in 1971, number of hours lost in 1969, and duration in 1972.
19. A plot of the observed and estimated values obtained from model 4 in Table 2.1 would in fact show that the underestimates and overestimates of the model disappear when applying the Cochrane-Orcutt procedure.

20. Statistical tests of stability of the structural parameters work in the following way (e.g., Chow, 1960; see also Brown, Durbin, and Evans, 1975). Estimate the Ashenfelter and Johnson model of equation (2.2) on two sub-samples (I used the two periods from 1959–I to 1968–IV and from 1969–I to 1978–IV). Construct the following F ratio:

$$F = \frac{(A - B - C)/p}{(B + C)n2p}$$

where: A is the sum of squares of the residuals from the regression estimated over the whole sample (1959–I/1978–IV), with n observations and n-p degrees of freedom, B is the sum of squared residuals obtained from the first half of the period (1959–I/1968–IV) with $n/2$ observations and $n/2$-p degrees of freedom, and C is the sum of the squared residuals obtained from the second half of the period (1969–I/1978–IV), with $n/2$ observations and $n/2$-p degrees of freedom. Under the null hypothesis that both groups of observations belong to the same regression model, the computed F would be distributed as an F $(p, n$-$2p)$. In this case, A=494043 and $B+C$=375270 and $F(8, 62)$=2.45. Since this value of F exceeds the tabulated value (even if only marginally), I cannot accept the null hypothesis that the estimates of the two linear regressions come from the same structural relation.

21. In this and in the following analyses I report only the results obtained using the Almon technique without end-point constraints. As we have already seen, with end-point constraints the results only improve, even if, perhaps, for artificial reasons.

22. Quarterly survey data are not available prior to 1959. On unemployment statistics in Italy and their reliability, see the Appendix.

23. I omitted from the specifications the wage variable, because (1) I was mainly interested in labor-market effects and (2) during the 1950s there does not seem to have been a strong relationship between strikes and wages. In fact, collective agreements often did not get renewed for several years in a row (Dore, 1976).

24. For a general view of Italian postwar economic development, see Daneo (1975) for the immediate postwar years; see also De Cecco (1972), Fuà (1973), D'Antonio (1973), Valli (1976, latest edition 1981), Nardozzi (1980), Salvati (1984), and Graziani (1979, latest edition 1992). For an easy introduction in English, see Allen and Stevenson (1974).

25. The British economy experienced a similar mid-decade downturn.

26. According to the data assembled by the Commissione Parlamentare d'Inchiesta sulle Condizioni dei Lavoratori in Italia (1958c, p. 164) via a survey of 3,382 industrial workers, only 21.67% of the 1,192 workers hired after January 1, 1950, were hired outside the Ufficio di Collocamento. This figure, however, is somewhat misleading. The vast majority of workers (60.24%) were hired with requests *ad personam*. All a worker hired through private channels had to do was to register with the Ufficio di Collocamento. The high and increasing numbers of injunctions and fines against employers by inspectors from the Ministry of Labor for breaking Collocamento rules confirm the widespread reliance on private channels (1958a, p. 126). Injunctions: 13,526 (1951), 19,813 (1953). Fines: 8,315 (1951), 11,474 (1955). A 1983 Federmeccanica survey of metalworking firms showed that 70% of employers attached little or no importance to the Ufficio di Collocamento (Mortillaro, 1984, p. 123).

27. For example, see Regalia (1975a, p. 36), Reyneri (1974a, pp. 121, 124), Abbatecola (1974, p. 38), Regini (1975, p. 162), and Villa (1986, p. 182).

28. As Ascoli (1979, pp. 52–3) points out, this massive migration from the South to the North of Italy and to other European countries was related to the defeat, at the end of 1958, of the southern agricultural laborers on the issue of agricultural reform.

29. The same Assolombarda survey of turnover rates provides a good indicator of the poor quality of jobs at the lowest grade level. During the years of the economic miracle, as

the labor market provided plenty of opportunities for employment, workers classified in the lowest skill grade increasingly quit their jobs (1959–62)

<250 12.0 21.0 31.9 52.5
>250 7.1 19.6 26.6 46.2

Quit rates were somewhat lower in the larger firms. Perhaps Pasquale's mother-in-law was right about working conditions in the larger firms.

30. For Milan, see Paci (1973, pp. 66–9); for Turin, see Fofi (1975, p. 42).
31. Some authors have argued that the labor-market situation during the beginning years of the 1960s did not really reflect full employment, but, more simply, a saturation of chronic underemployment conditions (e.g., Salvati, 1984, p. 62).
32. The term "padrone" is used by the Left in place of "employer."
33. See the significant title by Giugni et al. (1976): *Gli anni della conflittualità permanente* (The years of permanent conflict).
34. Bank of Italy, *Relazione annuale*, 1992; on public debt in Italy, see Graziani (1988).
35. Montgomery (1979, p. 94); see also Hobsbawm (1964, p. 126); for Italy, see Procacci (1970), and Merli (1972); see also Lay and Pesante (1974).

Chapter 3 When do workers strike? How the economy matters

1. On labor force statistics, see the Appendix.
2. For price indices, see Hansen, 1921; Griffin, 1939; Yoder, 1938; Knowles, 1952; de Wasseige, 1952; Goetz-Girey, 1965; Andreani, 1968; Skeels, 1971; Perrot, 1974; Sapsford, 1975; Bordogna and Provasi, 1979; for wage indices, see Yoder 1938; Griffin, 1939; Jurkat and Jurkat, 1949; Knowles, 1952; de Wasseige, 1952; Andreani, 1968; Perrot, 1974; for values of imported raw materials, Andreani, 1968; Perrot, 1974; for industrial production, Jurkat and Jurkat, 1949; Knowles, 1952; de Wasseige, 1952; Goetz-Girey, 1965; Andreani, 1968; Skeels, 1971; Mayhew, 1979; Bordogna and Provasi, 1979; for composite cyclical indicators, see Jurkat and Jurkat, 1949; Rees, 1952; Weintraub, 1966; for GNP, see Gomberg, 1944; Goetz-Girey, 1965; Vanderkamp, 1970; Skeels, 1971; Mayhew, 1979; Bordogna and Provasi, 1979.
3. Knowles (1952, p. 146); see also Forcheimer (1948), Skeels (1971), and Walsh (1975).
4. For more detailed information on data and their sources, see the Appendix.
5. Plosser and Schwert (1978); see also Granger and Newbold (1974).
6. Actually, given that I am using quarterly series, I detrended via fourth-differencing.
7. For example, see Andreani (1968, p. 136), Goetz-Girey (1965, p. 133), Turner et al. (1967, p. 111), Knowles (1952, p. 153ff.), Kennan (1985), and Harrison and Stewart (1989).
8. As one would expect, given the close correspondence between the trends for the numbers of strikers and hours lost, the relationship between capacity utilization and number of hours lost does not differ much from that for the number of strikers (plots not reported for brevity).
9. Spectral analysis allows us to isolate the components of a time series and therefore determine the period (i.e., the length) of possible periodic fluctuations present in the series. According to this method, the variance of a time series can be imagined as the sum of the variances of the different frequencies in which a time series can be decomposed, where the frequency is the number of cycles per unit time, or the number of times the cycle goes through a given period. The period, therefore, is the inverse of frequency (e.g., with monthly observations, a frequency of 0.25 corresponds to a period of four months and measures a seasonal cycle).

The distribution of variance with frequency is defined as the "power spectrum," and it is given by the Fourier transform of the autocovariance function. This last function measures the correlation between the values of a time series and the lagged values of the same time series, as a function of the lag k. Because the autocovariance function depends on the unit of measurement in which the series is expressed, it is often more convenient to work with the autocorrelation function, or the normalized autocovariance function, with a range between -1 and +1, like a normal correlation coefficient.

The autocovariance function is defined only for stationary processes with constant mean and variance. However, one can transform nonstationary series into stationary series: With the difference method, one can obtain stationarity in the mean, whereas with an appropriate transformation (e.g., the logarithmic transformation), one can obtain stationarity in the variance. On transformations to achieve stationarity in the mean, see Tintner (1940), Anderson (1971, pp. 30–91), Granger and Newbold (1977, pp. 303–17), and Nelson (1973, p. 569). For a survey of the literature on power transformations, such as the logarithmic transformation, see Franzosi (1994). Because the series S (number of strikes), W (number of strikers), and H (number of hours lost) are nonstationary in both mean and variance, I estimated the autocorrelation function and the power spectrum using first differences of the log values of the original series.

On spectral analysis, see Jenkins and Watts (1968). For a treatment of spectral analysis applied to economic time series, see Granger and Hatanaka (1964) and Granger and Newbold (1977); see also Fuller (1976). On the autocovariance and autocorrelation functions, see Box and Jenkins (1970). For an easier treatment of the time-domain approach, see Nelson (1973). For a more general introduction to the specific properties of time series data and different methods of analysis, see Kendall (1973). For a comparative analysis of different time-domain approaches – econometric and ARIMA – and spectral approaches, see Chatfield (1975) and Granger and Newbold (1977).

10. I focused on capacity utilization because the other two economic indicators (industrial production and composite business cycle) are affected by trend. However, the plots of detrended values for the industrial-production index and the composite business-cycle indicator (not reported here) show remarkable similarity to the plot of capacity utilization.

11. The shorter the recording interval for the data, the more negative the relationship between strikes and production will be. In fact, lost production due to strikes may in time be recovered, and sometimes even overshot, by means of higher work intensity and overtime before and after the strike. The lost output due to strikes that shows up, say, with monthly recordings may not appear the same within a quarter, once the economy has had enough time to recover from and make up for the negative effects of strikes (Knowles, 1952; de Wasseige, 1952).

Temporal and sectoral aggregation problems are such that not all strikes will put a dent in macroeconomic production series. Conversely, not all dents in production series are caused by strikes. Lost time due to strikes is only one of the determinants of capacity utilization. Certainly, no one would argue that the short but severe 1975 recession, when capacity utilization reached its postwar minimum as a result of the second "oil shock," was caused by the high levels of conflict, in terms of worker participation and lost time due to strikes, during that same year.

12. Because spectral analysis works best with stationary series (i.e., series without a significant trend), I detrended all series via first-differencing. This way, we don't have to worry about trend, and we can focus on the cyclical behavior of the series.

13. The *period* is the inverse of *frequency*. Thus a frequency of .0312 gives a period of 32 months (1/.0312 = 32.05).

14. After all, when using bivariate relations there is always the danger of dealing with correlations that tend to wither away, once other explanatory variables are brought into the picture.

15. On the Almon technique, see the discussion in Chapter 2, Section 2.3. in particular.
16. I did not have access to simultaneous estimating methods with autocorrelated errors (Fair, 1970). In order to avoid serial correlation problems due to trend, I detrended the model by taking fourth differences of the values of the relevant variables (on differencing as a way of detrending, see Tintner, 1940).
17. Granger (1966) showed that the typical spectral shape of trended macroeconomic series concentrates most of the power of the series (i.e., of the variability to be explained) at the low frequencies that generate long-term movements of the series. If we take these out by way of detrending, we are, in effect, left with a lot less to be explained, whether in terms of spectral power in the frequency domain or adjusted R^2 in the time domain.
18. I used the X11 decomposition method to isolate nonperiodic cycles. The X11 deseasonalization method was developed at the Bureau of the Census by Shiskin, Young, and Musgrave (1965), and it is based on the method of weighted moving averages (Kallek, 1976). For more details, see Franzosi (1980).
19. For similar conclusions based on the U.S. case, see Kaufman (1981, p. 352).
20. On the interindustry propensity to strike, see Kerr and Siegel (1954); on the relationship between class structure and class consciousness, see Wright and Shin (1988).
21. On agricultural conflict see Lana (1972); On service-sector conflict, see Marchese (1972), Accornero (1985), Pipan (1989), and Franzosi (1992).
22. Approximately 80% of the work force in the food-processing, shoe, textile, woodworking, and construction industries work in firms with less than 50 employees; 65% of the work force in the metalworking, chemical, and rubber industries work in larger firms (with more than 100 employees) (Graziani, 1976, pp. 201–2).
23. For example, for the United States, see Kerr and Siegel (1954) and Edwards (1981, pp. 96–116, 151–61, 189–211). For France, see Shorter and Tilly (1974, pp. 194–235). For Italy, see Bordogna and Provasi (1979, pp. 224–39) and Troiani (1978, pp. 84–106).
24. For a general introduction to the development of Italian industry, see Romeo (1961) and Castronovo (1980).
25. For instance, at Necchi, a manufacturer of sewing machines in Pavia, between 1953 and 1958, universal machines increased about 10% in number, whereas the number of single-purpose machines more than doubled (Grassini, 1969, p. 254).
26. Around 1910, Henry Ford began experimenting with various ways to improve the efficiency of automobile production in his shop. Within a three-year period, Ford had put together his assembly line (on the history of the assembly line, see Gartman, 1979). It does not really matter that the assembly-line type of production had previously been used in sixteenth-century Venetian shipyards, nor that the meat-packing industry in Chicago had relied on it for a few decades before Ford came up with his own version. Nor does it matter that since the beginning of the industrial revolution, solutions to bottlenecks in production (particularly labor's "rigidities") have been based on combinations of technical and organizational innovations (Marglin, 1974; Stone, 1974; Lazonick, 1978, 1979). The fact remains that it was in the automobile industry that the assembly line came of age. From there, it spread rapidly to other manufacturing industries, soon to become the symbol of mass production itself. The assembly line embodied within the very technical organization of production what Frederick Taylor had been preaching since the late 1880s: a scientific organization of production, based on an extreme division of labor. On the drive toward rationalization and standardization before Taylor, see Nelson (1975). On Frederick Taylor, see Nelson (1980), Clawson (1980, pp. 167–253), Braverman (1974, pp. 85–138), and Edwards (1979). The combination of Fordism and Taylorism was to dominate the factory world for decades to come. On the term "Fordism" see Aglietta (1979, pp. 116–29), Boyer (1987), and Sabel (1982, pp. 194–231).

27. Available cross-national data on productivity shows the following behavior:

Table N.3.1. *Cross-national productivity indices*

	BG[a]	DK	FR	WG	ITALY	NT	NW	SW	UK	USA
1955	169	150	180	168	190	164	224	197	176	203
1960	191	182	216	208	229	192	263	224	193	217

[a]BG Belgium, DK, Denmark, FR France, WG, West Germany, NT Netherlands, NW Norway, SW Sweden, UK United Kingdom.
Source: Farneti (1970, p. 124).

28. The French "regulation" school first developed the concept of Fordism; see Aglietta (1979, pp. 116–30); see also Sabel (1982, pp. 194–231).
29. On the process of "rationalization" of the organization of factory production in the 1960s and the struggles that accompanied that process, see Lanzardo and Vetere (1965); for an analysis of the Olivetti case, see Alquati (1963).
30. A 1978 survey by Giovani Imprenditori of a sample of forty-three firms with 30 to 200 employees found no instances of an assembly line among firms of that size (Pastorino and Ragazzoni, 1980, pp. 108, 110). For an empirical assessment of the technological level of development in smaller firms, see Brusco (1975).
31. Blauner divided production technology into four basic types: craft technology, with little mechanization and standardization (e.g., printing industry); machine-tending technology, highly mechanized and standardized (e.g., textiles); assembly-line technology (auto industry); process or continuous-flow technology, where the production process is carried out automatically (e.g., chemical industry).
32. Alienation is defined by Blauner in psychological terms as "a quality of personal experience which results from specific kinds of social arrangements." For Marxists, alienation is an ontological characteristic. "Alienation" refers to the long historical process of loss of control over both the means of production and the labor process by formerly independent producers. On this concept, see Ollman (1971); on the historical process, see Braverman (1974), Edwards (1979), Clawson (1980), Gordon, Edwards, and Reich (1982).
33. Woodward divided production technologies into eleven categories, ranging in complexity from unit and small-batch production to process production. Woodward believed that firms with similar production systems tended to have similar organizational structures and that there was a particular form of organization most appropriate to each technical situation. More complex technologies were associated with an increase in the levels of management, tighter control by the chief executive, a smaller proportion of turnover allocated to labor costs, and a high ratio of managers, supervisors, clerical and administrative staff, and indirect workers (maintenance staff) compared with direct producers.

In process technology, wages are relatively higher, given the high capital-to-labor ratio; production is organized around smaller working groups, and individual workers have greater latitude for decision making. For Woodward, this contributes to better industrial relations. Woodward pointed to similarities between small-batch production and process production that enhance labor relations. In both there is a tendency for management to be flexible and to delegate authority and responsibility. Communication usually is verbal and the atmosphere is pleasant and easygoing compared with the more formal procedures in large-batch production and mass production.

34. Mallet was not alone in his criticisms of Blauner's and Woodward's work. Against technological arguments, Gallie (1978) argued that cultural and institutional effects are more important in determining the prevailing levels of conflict. On the basis of a comparative analysis of British and French oil refineries using the same kind of process technology, Gallie concluded that the different rates of conflict in the two countries could be explained only by different cultural, institutional, and political structures (Gallie, 1978, p. 295).
35. On the new working class in Italy, see Low-Beer (1978).
36. *Operaio specializzato, operaio qualificato, manovale specializzato, manovale comune* – a system known as *sistema delle qualifiche* (Cella, 1976b, p. 170).
37. A 1975 Federlombarda survey of a sample of Lombardy firms showed that in firms with 500 to 999 employees, the percentages of unskilled workers were 68.6% in 1969, 78.1 in 1972, and 81.5% in 1975, as compared with an average of 30% in smaller firms (Bergamaschi, 1977a, p. 255).
38. During the postwar period, economists have increasingly challenged the neoclassical model of a labor market regulated by competition and of a hierarchy of jobs based on skills. Rather, the labor market has been seen as segmented (horizontally and vertically) in impermeable layers, with competition occurring within rather than across layers (for a quick summary of the theories, see Villa, 1986, pp. 5–27; see also, Edwards, Reich, and Gordon, 1975). Furthermore, larger firms operate a sort of internal labor market that provides employees with opportunities for advancement up a career ladder by restricting the entry of outsiders (for Italy, see Paci, 1973, p. 152).

    Labor economists Doeringer and Piore (1971) systematized the various approaches to noncompetitive labor markets in the unified framework of a dual labor-market theory. The theory views the labor market as basically characterized by two distinct sectors governed by very different rules: the primary sector and the secondary sector. The primary sector is characterized by high wages, stability of employment, career opportunities, and better working conditions. It is made up mostly of the larger firms, with their high levels of investment, productivity, and growth. Workers in the secondary sector are not nearly as privileged: Their wages are lower, their job tenure much more precarious, and their working conditions far worse. The world of the secondary market is mostly the world of the smaller plants operating under competitive conditions and always on the brink of failure. It is the world of obsolete technologies and stagnant work organization.

    To some extent, the experience of the 1980s has challenged this view of a progressive primary market and a backward secondary market. On the one hand, the crisis of international capitalism has proved the primary-market firms to be vulnerable. Plant closing and relocation, and loss of jobs and reduction of wages have accompanied the restructuring of even conglomerate giants. On the other hand, secondary-market firms have shown surprising vitality and flexibility (for Italy, see Bagnasco, 1977; Sabel, 1982; Regini, 1988; Regini and Sabel, 1989; Barca and Magnani, 1989). The second "economic miracle" of the *Terza Italia* during the late 1970s and 1980s in the face of stagnant oligopolies was the product of such small-scale production.

    But even the view of a primary market as a locus of skills may have been overstated. The general tendency of capitalism to reduce the skill content of any job is accentuated in the large firms, particularly where production is based on a combination of Fordism and Taylorism (Braverman, 1974; Marglin, 1974). Furthermore, there are career opportunities in the large firms only because the work force is widely distributed across an extensive hierarchy of jobs.
39. Despite the internal labor market, for the individual worker the market has a strong element of uncertainty: 20% of all job changes among the workers surveyed by Blackburn and Mann (1979) were involuntary.

40. One should not exaggerate workers' gullibility. According to a 1971 Isvet survey of workers' attitudes, 67.5% of unskilled workers answered "no" to the question: "In your firm, are there real career prospects for you?" Even most skilled and semiskilled workers (60.9%) answered "no" to the same question (Buratto et al., 1974, p. 219).
41. Blackburn and Mann (1979, p. 280); see also Reyneri and Tempia (1974).
42. Thus, in Italy in the 1970s, the labor market became increasingly rigid, as unions pushed for and obtained guarantees of job security and stability. The labor market became impermeable to both youth and women. Similarly, competitive struggles to maintain wage and skill differentials among workers differently situated in the occupational structure were not uncommon in postwar Italy, even during the 1970s, despite the strong egalitarian tendencies of the period (for some examples, see Reyneri, 1974a, pp. 145, 175; Abbatecola, 1974, p. 44; Villa, 1986, p. 187; Tarrow, 1989a, p. 91).
43. Notwithstanding unions' and workers' interest in the creation of new job categories, one should remember that workers and unions operate in the context of overall societal power relations that are unfavorable to them. They work within the constraints imposed by a system of hierarchy and control that has been the hallmark of capitalism from its beginning. In fact, according to some, the capitalist division of labor and hierarchy are what justify the capitalist's very existence (Marglin, 1974). Furthermore, control over promotions from one category to the next rests firmly in the employer's hands.
44. Speranza (1977, p. 208) wrote that "Trade union policies until 1970 were oriented toward a continuous growth of skill levels."
45. On the overall class structure in Italy and on the structuring of the working class, see the excellent volume edited by Paci (1978) and its extensive bibliography.
46. For comparative data, see Valli (1976, pp. 14–5) and Jalla (1974, pp. 4, 13).
47. Still in 1980, *Fortune* magazine (August 10, 1981) listed only 11 Italian corporations (2 of which were foreign owned) among the Fortune 500; compared with 121 Japanese corporations, 88 British, 62 German, 42 French, 32 Canadian, 26 Swedish, 13 Swiss.
48. Firm size is measured by the entropic mean (on firm size in Italy, see Jalla, 1974; Valcamonici, 1977, pp. 181–92; Barca and Magnani, 1989, p. 196). Given m size classes, the entropic mean is defined as:

$$Mean = exp(\sum_{j=1}^{m} L_j/L \times log(L_j/N_j))$$

"where L_j and L represent the number of workers in the jth class and in the entire sector, respectively, and N_j represents the number of plants. The average size of each class L_j/N_j contributes to the mean value in proportion to the contribution of the class to total employment" (Valcamonici, 1977, p. 181; Barca and Magnani, 1989, p. 196).
49. More disaggregated data in the 6–100 size class provide further evidence on the types of firms that contributed to the economic miracle of the *Terza Italia*. The most rapid growth came in the 10–19 employees size class:

Table N.3.2. *Distribution of Italian plants by size (6–99 employees)*

Size	Number of productive units			Number of employees		
	1971	1981	% change	1971	1981	% change
6–9	39,685	58,318	47.0	286,296	422,730	47.7
10–19	32,848	53,132	61.8	439,969	703,827	60.0
20–49	21,892	26,086	19.2	666,851	780,723	17.1
50–99	7,977	8,385	5.11	550,685	575,992	4.6

Source: (Barca and Magnani, 1989, p. 195).

50. There has been no empirical work on the relationship between plant size and strike activity in Italy. For other countries, the available evidence on the effects of plant size confirms a greater likelihood of radicalism in larger industrial settings (e.g, Cleland, 1955; Cass, 1957; Shorey, 1975, 1976; Prais, 1978; Churnside and Creigh, 1981). For a discussion of the broader relationship between unit size and industrial relations, see Ingham (1967, 1969, 1970). On the relationships among plant or firm size, unionization, and industrial and regional characteristics, see Kerr and Siegel (1954), Britt and Galle (1972), Shorter and Tilly (1974), and Stern (1976).

    On the basis of microlevel data published by the U.K. Department of Employment in its gazette, Prais (1978) concluded (1) that the likelihood of a plant being strike-free decreases with size, (2) that strike frequency is almost directly proportional to the size of the plant, and (3) that the number of working days lost per plant rises nearly proportionally with the square of plant size.

    Shorey (1976, p. 359) tested the hypotheses of a positive causal relationship between plant size and industrial conflict, and a negative relationship between firm size and industrial conflict. The empirical evidence, based on macrolevel interindustry strike frequencies and average sectoral plant and firm sizes in the United Kingdom, however, provided only partial support for those hypotheses: The coefficients of plant-size and firm-size variables had the correct signs but they were insignificant. According to Shorey, the multicollinearity between the two measures does not allow proper testing of the separate effects of plant size and firm size on strike frequency.

51. According to the Isvet survey, other important predictors were background characteristics (age, sex) and work characteristics (e.g., skill level).

52. See De Masi and Fevola (1974a, p. 803); see also De Masi et al. (1985, pp. 527–8). In small plants employing 50–100 workers, 50.3% of workers "never" participated in external trade-union meetings (33.5% in establishments with 251–500 workers), 30.7% "never" participated in mass meetings inside the plant (around 11% in plants with 250–1,000 workers), and 42.5% "never" engaged in collective action (29.5% in plants with 251–500 workers).

53. According to a 1980 Isvet survey of workers' attitudes, as plant size increased, the propensity for individual conflict decreased, while collective conflict increased (De Masi et al., 1985, pp. 527–8).

54. The predominance of face-to-face relationships in smaller work settings, as well as identifications and loyalties based on *community* rather than on *society*, helps to explain workers' behavioral differences in the two settings. However, one should not forget that in smaller work settings, workers are less "protected" by both the unions and the law. The 1971 Isvet survey of workers' attitudes revealed that fear of layoffs and insecurities about their jobs declined linearly with plant size (De Masi and Fevola, 1974a, p. 655).

55. Absenteeism includes time lost due to strikes, as well as time lost due to a variety of medical reasons.

56. It is more difficult to assess the impact of production technology on industrial conflict, because no microlevel data are available to link plant-level technology and strikes. Indirectly, however, Blauner and Woodward's arguments on the effects of process technology do not seem to hold. In Italy, the metalworking sector, with its prevalence of assembly-line technology, and the chemical sector, with its prevalence of process technology, were the most strike-prone industries in the postwar period.

57. Many smaller surveys conducted during the 1970s and 1980s provided ample evidence that smaller plants were less likely to have strikes. For example, see Giovani Imprenditori's national survey (Pastorino and Ragazzoni, 1980, p. 92), the Assolombarda survey of Milanese firms (Associazione Industriale Lombarda, 1983, p. 139), and Giubilato's survey among small firms in Veneto (Giubilato, 1982), as well

as Bagnasco and Trigilia (1984, p. 240) and Trigilia (1986, p. 193) for a survey of the White and Red districts of Bassano del Grappa and Valdelsa.
58. For an empirical investigation of the relationship between strikes and the business cycle from a Marxist perspective, see Boddy and Crotty (1975).
59. "Political" because capitalists have a political interest, as a class, in maintaining unemployment at a level that will not threaten their hegemonic political position.
60. For a review of several positions on the issue, see Colletti and Napoleoni (1970).
61. In Lenin's famous words, a revolution occurs: "1) When it is impossible for the ruling classes to maintain their rule without any change; . . . For a revolution to take place, it is usually insufficient for the lower classes to not to want to live in the old way; it is also necessary that the upper classes should be unable to live in the old way. 2) When the suffering and want of the oppressed class have grown more acute than usual. 3) When, as a result of the above causes, there is a considerable increase in the activity of the masses, who . . . in turbulent times, are drawn both by all the circumstances of the crisis, and by the upper classes themselves into independent historical action. . . . The totality of these objective changes is called a revolutionary situation" (Harding, 1983, p. 37).
62. For a summary of various Marxist theories of crisis and cycles, see Kotz (1987, 1990); for a more comprehensive treatment, see Goldstein (1988). On the differences between business-cycle crises and capitalist crises, see Wright (1979, p. 125), Gordon (1980, p. 20), and Boyer (1987, p. 16).
63. Namely, infrastructural investment in transportation systems, communication systems, and systems for supply of raw materials.
64. Among non-Marxist economists, Schumpeter (1939) argued for the existence of long waves in capitalist economies. For both Schumpeter and Kondratieff, changes within economic institutions were the sole causes of long-term cyclical fluctuations of capitalist economies. For Schumpeter, however, it was the rhythm of technological innovation that ultimately determined long waves. Furthermore, for both of them, the waves were seen as regular and predictable (Kotz, 1987, p. 19).
65. For a summary of various Marxist theories of crisis and cycles, see Kotz (1987, 1990). On the social-structure-of-accumulation theory, see Gordon (1978, 1980), Gordon et al. (1982), and Bowles et al. (1983). On the "regulation" theory, see Aglietta (1979), Boyer (1987), and Lipietz (1987).
66. Referred to as a social structure of accumulation, or a mode of regulation. A social structure of accumulation is composed of all noneconomic institutions that are indispensable for capitalist accumulation and that form a coherent whole at any given historical conjuncture: the structure for supply of raw materials, the structure of the family, the structure of labor management, the structure of administrative management, the network of consumer demand, and the means of finance and access to capital, but also the state.
67. Too many conflicting actors (class, class segments, the state) are at work, each protecting its own narrow interests, to permit precise prediction of the outcome of these struggles (Kotz, 1987, p. 24).
68. For example, Sylos-Labini (1975). For an introduction to studies of the Italian class structure, see Paci (1978).

Chapter 4 Organizational resources and collective action

1. Davies (1969, p. 690); see also Feierabend and Feierabend (1966).
2. For example, see the first chapter of De Masi and Fevola (1974b, pp. 51–72), but also see De Masi and Fevola (1974a, p. 851), where the whole process of class conflict and

the formation of class capacities (unionization and politicization) is seen as the result of the *frustration* of needs.
3. See, for example, the shapes of Italian strikes during the 1966 recession (Figure 1.6, pp. 8–9); on industrial conflict and mass media, see Glasgow University Media Group (1976).
4. The prediction of bargaining models is that strike frequency will decrease with unemployment, i.e., economic models hypothesize an inverse negative relationship between unemployment and strike frequency. However, during recession, the frequency of defensive strikes could go up. The number of defensive strikes over employment issues normally tends to represent a minor proportion of all strikes. In Italy it stayed around 10% until the late 1960s and further decreased during the next decade. But that percentage almost doubled during the 1964–65 and 1974–75 recessions. It is quite conceivable that during periods of prolonged recession, the proportion of defensive strikes could become even higher. Consider the correlation coefficients reported below between unemployment and strike indicators by cause (offensive, wage issues; defensive, against layoffs) over the period for which such data were available.

Table N.4.1. *Correlation coefficients between unemployment rate and numbers of strikes, strikers, and hours lost, by cause (1959–II/1975–IV) (economywide data, first-differenced values)*

	Strikes for higher wages			Strikes against layoffs		
	S^a	W	H	S	W	H
Unemployment rate	-.26	-.01	-.04	.27	.02	.11

$^a S$, number of strikes; W, number of strikers; H, number of hours lost.

As one would expect on the basis of the economic-bargaining arguments, the worsening of workers' position in the labor market, as measured by high rates of unemployment, leads to a decrease in the number of offensive strikes, but to an increase in the number of defensive strikes, particularly against layoffs. The correlation coefficients also show that the duration of labor disputes increases when workers strike to protect their jobs threatened by recession. Given that defensive strikes are positively related to unemployment, as the correlations show, this fact could reverse, from positive to negative, the relationship between the number of strikes and unemployment. Econometric results for the United States (Romagnoli, 1979) show that in the 1930s, during the Great Depression, strike activity increased with increasing unemployment. Those findings shed some light on the hardship-versus-prosperity debate: Given a prolonged recessionary period, strike frequency could go up at the same time as unemployment.
5. See Tilly (1975, pp. 483–555), Tilly (1978, pp. 16–24). For a review, see Jenkins (1983). As Tilly (1978, p. 48) wrote, "That will be the general attitude of the analyses to follow: doggedly anti-Durkheimian, resolutely pro-Marxian, but sometimes indulgent to Weber and sometimes reliant on Mill."
6. Tilly (1978, p. 153); see also Tarrow (1989a), Aminzade (1980, 1981, 1984), and Ingham (1974, p. 36).
7. For this critique, see Snyder (1975).
8. See Shorter and Tilly (1971, 1974), Tilly, Tilly, and Tilly (1975), Britt and Galle (1974), Snyder (1974, 1975, 1977), Hibbs (1976, 1978), Crouch and Pizzorno (1978), Cella (1979), and Korpi and Shalev (1980). It goes without saying that a reactive

collective action implies proactive practices and claims: Peasants in food riots resist the encroachment of capitalist agriculture; in tax rebellions they resist the encroachment of an expanding state; in machine breaking they resist the encroachment of factory production. Now, capitalist agriculture, the state, and factory production introduce practices and claims on people's resources that are new, extraneous to traditional social relations. However, despite people's reactive protest – and there was a lot of it – the state did succeed in imposing ever more taxes, the enclosure movement did expel the people from the land, and machines and factory production did strip craftsmen of their traditional skills and autonomy.

9. On repertoires of collective action, see Tilly (1978, pp. 151–9). The notion of a repertoire of collective actions implies that at any given time, the array of collective actions available to a population is surprisingly limited (Tilly, 1978, p. 151) – surprising, given the innumerable ways in which people could, in principle, deploy their resources in pursuit of common ends, and given the many ways in which real groups have pursued their common ends at one time or another. A population's repertoire of collective actions generally includes only a handful of alternatives. Repertoires change slowly, and they last over long periods of time, indeed centuries (Tilly, 1978, p. 151).

10. Not all forms of collective action are either reactive or proactive. Many are simply competitive (e.g., village fights, in the traditional repertoire; sports events in the modern repertoire) (Tilly, 1978).

11. That traditional ideology based on reciprocity has been practiced by some entrepreneurs even in modern times, in small settings, where face-to-face relationships still prevail; see Edwards (1979) on simple control. Newby (1979) would describe that kind of relationship as paternalistic. As a system for social control, paternalism is highly dependent on the presence of several conditions: (1) face-to-face relationships; (2) small, closed communities; (3) a highly stratified, dualistic society; and (4) an absence of any alternatives (both ideological and practical) for the individuals involved in this kind of relationship at the lower end.

12. Urbanization has affected strikes by creating the conditions necessary for effective collective action. Urban centers, with their greater opportunities for internal communication, became the centers of the working-class struggle. Industrialization has continually modified modes of production, subverting acquired patterns of social stratification and of work organization (Touraine, 1955, 1966). As we saw in Chapter 3, industrialization has increased the number and average size of industrial establishments and their geographic concentration, leading to higher strike propensities. Industrialization has also shifted the distribution of the labor force among different productive sectors. The distribution of the labor force in different age groups and economic sectors is likely to result in different strike propensities. See, among others, Bordogna and Provasi (1979, pp. 192–3), Kerr and Siegel (1954), Edwards (1981, pp. 96–133, 151–61, 189–211), and Shorter and Tilly (1974, pp. 195–201).

13. Historically, these organizations have taken many forms: the strike committees hastily set up during the nineteenth century to carry on negotiations during strikes in the absence of more permanent organizational structures (such a committee would die with the strike); the art and craft societies, or labor associations along professional lines; the leagues of resistance formed with the main goal of collecting strike funds; the mutual-aid societies, truly the first forms of modern worker organizations; trade unions and labor parties. On temporary, strike-related forms of organizations, see Perrot (1974, pp. 426–8); on the first forms of organizations in Italy, see Rigola (1947), Abrate (1967), Merli (1972, pp. 513, 581–837), Procacci (1970), and Tilly (1992, pp. 100–22, 180–207). Incidentally, it should be noted that strike committees were not just characteristic of the distant past or of settings where there were no organizational

structures. On the contrary. Strike committees often were set up during the periods of increased conflict even in 1969 and 1970; for many examples, see the ethnographic work of Pizzorno (1974–75).
14. See Shorter and Tilly (1974, pp. 89–188); see also Procacci (1970, p. 66), Merli (1972, pp. 549–58), and De Santis (1979, pp. 45–6, 48–9). It does not seem, however, according to Shorter and Tilly, that trade unions, during strikes, could marshall a higher percentage of workers from the same establishment (Shorter and Tilly, 1974, p. 189). Beccalli (1971) noted that often trade unions do not exist in small firms in Italy. The data from the two Isvet workers' surveys confirm that. According to Beccalli, however, when unions had gained entrance to a factory, they tended to unionize a higher percentage of workers than in large firms, where they were always present. If that is true, we would expect that, at least in the case of small firms, the presence of an organization would enable a union to call out on strike a higher percentage of workers from a given establishment, since it could count on a broader membership. Another way to say this is that in smaller plants, where face-to-face interpersonal worker-employer relationships prevail, the fewer strikes are more likely to be all-or-none propositions. The 1971 Isvet survey also confirmed that workers in small firms, much more so than those in large firms, perceived that the most effective form of struggle was the strike of all workers (De Masi, 1972, p. 129; De Masi and Fevola, 1974a, pp. 894–6).
15. Louise Tilly (1992, p. 179) thus summarized her findings based on an analysis of several case studies: "Organizational success predicted effective collective action, and such success favored the winner in the next period of struggle."
16. See Zolberg (1986, p. 398); on theories of convergence, see Aron (1967), Kerr, et al. (1960), and Kerr (1983).
17. In France, only during the years between 1890 and 1900, was unionization inversely related to the number of successful strikes. For all other periods, particularly after World War I, the percentages of strikes ending with an acceptable compromise, if not success, increased (Shorter and Tilly, 1974, pp. 82–191).
18. See, on this point, Hobsbawm (1968, p. 41) and De Santis (1979, p. 32).
19. In more recent times, as during the 1968 outbreak of industrial conflict, trade unions, whenever present to channel workers' demands, contributed to rein in workers' anger which sometimes tended to erupt in acts of violence (Regalia, Regini, and Reyneri, 1978, p. 8; Pizzorno et al., 1978, p. 66).
20. For a critique of the union-membership indicator, see Reyneri (1973); on this indicator for Italy, see Bordogna and Provasi (1979, p. 274).
21. With both variables, I adopted a lagged specification in order to ward off a possible simultaneous-equation bias deriving from reciprocal, contemporaneous effects. In fact, the presumption that either the wage variable or the union variables are exogenous may be untenable. The relationship between strikes and wages is affected by reciprocal causation (Hines, 1968; Ward and Zis, 1974). As for the relationship between strike activity and unionization, Goetz-Girey (1965, pp. 146–7) hypothesized circular, rather than unidirectional, causation. Even in the specifications of recent econometric models of union growth and strike frequency, the same variables (i.e., unionization and strikes) appear in both models, alternatively as dependent or independent variables (Hines, 1964; Ashenfelter and Pencavel, 1969; Bain and Elsheikh, 1976; Romagnoli and Rossi, 1980).
22. The adjusted R^2 for all the equations in the matrices show a clearly linear pattern: They worsen from left to right, from top to bottom, i.e., the best fit is found in the upper left corner of each matrix, the worst in the lower right corner.
23. CISL membership for the 1956–59 period showed highly erratic behavior, with wild fluctuations, positive at first and then negative (1956, 23.1%; 1957, -29.7%; 1958,

26.9%; 1959, -29.6%; those were the highest values between 1950 and 1978, if we exclude 1970). CISL did not suffer the dramatic decrease of CGIL membership.
24. In the period between 1945 and 1969, the *commissioni interne* (CI) were the only workers' representative bodies at the plant level. The CI have a long history in the Italian labor movement. They were first set up in 1906 (Romagnoli and Della Rocca, 1989, p. 114). They were reorganized in 1943 after their prohibition by the Fascist regime, and they were further disciplined by three agreements among CGIL, CISL, UIL, and Confindustria in 1947, 1953, and 1966. Formally, the CI were never part of the trade-union organizational structure. They were workers' representative bodies inside the plant, regardless of union affiliation. In reality, the CI increasingly came to operate as links between the union's base and its leadership. Most CI members belonged to one of the unions and acted as collectors of union dues. On paper, the CI enjoyed a wide range of union prerogatives: They performed collective-bargaining functions, they could post memos and distribute trade-union press around the factory, they could call mass meetings, they had their own offices inside the plants, their members could move freely about the factory, and they enjoyed company time for trade-union activities (Romagnoli and Della Rocca, 1989, p. 114). They acted as workers' representatives in cases of labor-management disputes. In the authoritarian and/or paternalistic labor-relations climate in which most of them operated, reality often was quite distant from what was stated in the agreements.
25. On the limitations of this last indicator, see Cella (1976a); on the history of *commissioni interne*, see Neufeld (1954), Accornero (1974), Baglioni (1971), Treu (1971), and Romagnoli and Della Rocca (1989).
26. The different magnitudes of the coefficients obtained using the absolute level of membership or unionization rate could mean that part of the effect of membership is due to labor-force growth.
27. On the history of the Italian labor movement, see Rigola (1947), Horowitz (1963), Manacorda (1953), La Palombara (1957), Spriano (1958, 1964), Gradilone (1959), Neufeld (1961), Procacci (1970), Weitz (1975), Peschiera (1976, 1979, 1982), and Turone (1984).
28. On the struggles of the immediate postwar period, see Marino (1991).
29. Filippelli (1989, p. 155; see also pp. 45, 54–5, 57, 72, 75); on U.S. involvement with Italian labor, see Migone (1974).
30. On the organizational aspects of Italian unions, see Romagnoli and Della Rocca (1989) and Della Rocca (1974).
31. The names for the horizontal unions vary with each confederation (e.g., at the lower level, Camera del Lavoro Territoriale for CGIL, Unione Sindacale Territoriale for CISL, and Unione Camerale Territoriale for UIL) (Cella and Treu, 1989a, p. 91).
32. Despite their poor overall records, the Ssa had a positive effect on the Italian industrial-relations system. The 1970 Workers' Charter sanctioned in law the principle of union representative bodies in the plant, in the form of *rappresentanze sindacali aziendali* (plant-level union representative bodies), or Rsa.
33. For a summary of the positions on the relationships between political parties and unions, see Alquati (1974).
34. Workers' preference for union unity has been borne out over the years by countless surveys. Still, in 1987, when the 1970s hopes for unity had definitely vanished, the 585 interviews conducted by the Milan CISL on a sample of its members confirmed that union members viewed trade-union unity, rather than competition, as the unions' best strategy (79.2% vs. 20.8%) (La Valle, 1987). Yet, faced with the political rifts, Italian unions were not able to forge unity, despite popular demand.
35. On mass meetings, see Regalia (1975a). According to the survey data analyzed by Celadin (1974, p. 178), delegates had available from their employers an average of 96

hours for meetings. Of 4,211 delegates, 138 enjoyed either part-time or full-time paid *distacco sindacale*, i.e., they were not involved in production, and they earned company salaries for trade-union activities.

36. The literature on the *the comitati unitari di base*, the *consigli di fabbrica* and the *delegati* is vast. On the *the comitati unitari di base*, see Bellasi and Pellicciari (1972), Avanguardia Operaia (1971, 1973a). On the *consigli di fabbrica* and *delegati*, see Aglietta et al. (1970), Albanese et al. (1973), Censi et al. (1973), Romagnoli (1971, 1973, 1976), Salvarani and Bonifazi (1973), Accornero and Cardulli (1974), Celadin (1974), D'Agostino (1974), Forbice and Chiaberge (1974), Milanaccio et al. (1978), Maestrali (1979), Vento (1980), Baccalini (1981), Regalia (1984a), Mershon (1986, 1989), Squarzon (1989a).

37. That was particularly true for the beginning of the delegate movement. Later, the unions took the lead in the movement. Particularly in smaller firms, the delegate movement resulted from penetration by outside unions, rather than an internal process, as in larger firms (Vento, 1980).

38. The *consigli* (councils) had a long tradition in the Italian labor movement. They dated back to the revolutionary ferment of the "Red years" (1919–20) and the factory-occupation movement of the summer of 1920. From Turin, where the factory occupation began, Gramsci (1954, pp. 34–48, 123–7, 131–5, 176–86, in particular) theorized about the experience in *L'Ordine Nuovo*. The experience of the councils was repeated toward the end of World War II, with the name of *consigli di gestione* (plant-operation councils); see Neufeld (1954, pp. 20–30), Lanzardo (1976), and Forbice and Chiaberge (1974, pp. 19–32); see also the essays in the volume edited by Ganapini et al. (1978). The *consigli di gestione* were set up, mostly in northern factories, by Communist workers, with high hopes of real workers' control inside the factories. Some five hundred councils were operating by the summer of 1946. In the postwar anti-Communist climate, the councils were disbanded by 1948. As Neufeld (1954, p. 30), not a very sympathetic writer, put it, "By 1947 and 1948, despite propaganda, furor, demonstrations, plant violence, and strikes, the game was lost." The radical Left in Italy rediscovered the *esperienza consigliare* during the 1960s (e.g., see the articles that appeared in the Marxist journal *Problemi del socialismo*).

39. At a later stage, in some instances, larger groups were formed, in order to reduce the power of certain homogeneous groups.

40. Albanese, Liuzzi, and Perella (1973) reported a somewhat lower number (22 workers per delegate).

41. Celadin (1974, p. 175) reported 800 executive members for 4,211 delegates, i.e., an average of 20% of the members of the *consiglio di fabbrica* were also members of the executive.

42. Celadin (1974, p. 178) reported that the principle of revoking the mandate was recognized in most firms where Cdf were present (105 of 117 in her sample), although it was rarely used (in 17 firms).

43. The unions adopted the *delegati* as their official shop-floor representatives in a 1972 agreement.

44. Romagnoli (1973, p. 48). See also the empirical research conducted by Gallino and Barbano (1962).

45. For these data, see Regalia (1978, p. 224).

46. Romagnoli (1976, p. 116) reported that by the end of 1970, 429 industrial firms in the Milan province had set up new workers' representative forms (either Rsa or Cdf) in the metalworking, chemical, textile, and print sectors. Although that figure represented only 5% of all the firms in the four sectors, it encompassed 33.1% of all workers (Romagnoli, 1976, p. 117). That compares with 70% of firms that still had CI at the end of 1969 (Romagnoli, 1976. p. 138).

47. The Rsa survived in settings where unions were weaker, such as in small plants and in the South. According to a 1975 Federlombarda survey, 65% of the firms had Rsa, and 38.4% had Cdf (only 10% of small firms, but 93% of the larger ones) (Bergamaschi, 1977b, pp. 232, 256). Surprisingly, the CI survived in 22.1% of the firms, particularly smaller firms. Perhaps no one informed them of the changes that had taken place in the forms of representation. Another 1975 survey of 452 metalworking firms in the province of Bologna showed that, among 223 smaller firms (1–49 workers), 147 had Cdf and 65 had Rsa (only 10 of the larger firms, with 50 workers, had Rsa) (Maestrali, 1979, p. 35). Similarly, a survey of 60 chemical-sector firms (including ceramics, plastics, rubber, pharmaceuticals, and chemicals proper) conducted between 1978 and 1979 by *Fulc* (Federazione Unitaria Lavoratori Chimici) showed that the Rsa survived, particularly in the South (Vento, 1980, p. 52). Both the 1983 and 1984 Federmeccanica surveys showed that the Rsa survived well into the 1980s, particularly in smaller firms. In the 1983 survey, 34.3% of metalworking firms had the Rsa (Mortillaro, 1984, p. 129), compared with 38% in the 1984 survey (Mortillaro, 1986, p. 161).
48. On the diffusion of the Cdf, see Regalia (1978, pp. 223–35); see also *Quaderni di rassegna sindacale*, No. 51, where these data are also found. In central Italy and in the South, the figures were much lower, less than 10% of those for the North. A survey conducted by Confindustria among member firms confirmed the higher incidence of the Cdf in the North (Confederazione Generale dell'Industria Italiana, 1973); for a summary of the Confindustria findings, see also Regalia (1978, p. 227).
49. Formally, the delegates were representatives of the workers, rather than the unions. However, there was a tendency to view the delegates as representatives of particular unions, rather than of all the workers (Vento, 1980). Furthermore, delegates came to take on many of the functions connected with membership drives, once typical of the old *commissioni interne* (e.g., distribution of union membership forms and cards, recruiting), particularly in larger firms (Squarzon, 1990).
50. For a quick introduction to the organization of Italian employers, see Becchi Collidà (1989); for English-language works, see Martinelli and Treu (1984) and Chiesi and Martinelli (1989). For a broader treatment, with particular emphasis on Confindustria, see Lanzalaco (1990). On Confindustria, see Pirzio Ammassari (1976). On Confindustria, Intersind, and Confagricoltura, see Collidà et al. (1972). On the Italian bourgeoisie, see Martinelli et al. (1981). On the state bourgeoisie, see Mutti and Segatti (1977), Galli and Nannei (1976), and Scalfari and Turani (1975). On interest groups, including Confindustria, see La Palombara (1964).
51. On the power of Confindustria, see Martinelli et al. (1981, pp. 241–6); see also La Palombara (1964, pp. 252–305).
52. Although in Italy labor organizations were similarly organized along both territorial and sectoral associations, in comparative perspective that mirroring was less than perfect (Lanzalaco, 1990, pp. 59–81).
53. For these data, see Pirzio Ammassari (1976, p. 28).
54. In 1980, the organization had grown to 80,600 firms, with a total of 2,700,000 employees; for these data, see Martinelli and Treu (1984, pp. 271–2); for later data, see Becchi Collidà (1989, p. 135).
55. See Pirzio Ammassari (1976), Martinelli et al. (1981), and Lanzalaco (1990, p. 165).
56. For another example, see Mattina (1991, p. 304).
57. For several examples, see Pirzio Ammassari (1976, pp. 50, 55, 57–9).
58. See Martinelli et al. (1981, p. 259). On employers' political beliefs and support, see Farneti (1970), Martinelli (1977), Martinelli et al. (1981, pp. 63–138), and Urbani (1977a,b); for managers, see Talamo (1979, pp. 133–65).
59. The "line" of *rapporti interni* was to deal with Confindustria membership and with the other *lines* within the organization. *Rapporti esterni* were to deal with political

institutions and mass media. *Rapporti economici* were to develop the economic policies of Confindustria. *Rapporti sindacali* were to deal with labor and unions.

60. In particular, it was not until 1984 that the problem of the "dual membership" of Confindustria member firms was solved in a major organizational overhaul (Lanzalaco, 1990, pp. 175–85).
61. The first change that the *Riforma Pirelli* brought was, indeed, the suppression from Article 3 of the Confindustria charter of the expression "The Confederation is apolitical" (Pirzio Ammassari, 1976, p. 137).
62. For these data, see Pirzio Ammassari (1976, p. 143).
63. On the relationship between union membership and strike waves, see Shorter and Tilly (1974) and Cronin (1979, p. 105).
64. Union membership is a more stable indicator than conflict itself. The procedures of canceling membership in a union could make it difficult, or at least unpleasant, for a worker to do so. On the basis of the data collected by the Osservatorio Cesos on the state of industrial relations in 1987, Squarzon (1990) showed that in most firms, union members had to withdraw their membership via a written statement, or else membership would be automatically renewed. In only 16.8% of some 400 firms examined was membership canceled at the beginning of the year for all workers and a new membership drive started; and those typically were cases in which the unions had reason to believe that they would stand to gain from a new drive. Interestingly enough, many union members rejected the practice of automatic renewal. According to a 1987 survey of 585 Milan CISL members, 33.1% believed that membership should not be renewed automatically (La Valle, 1987).
65. Resistant smoothers are built by successive applications of simple smoothers. The smoother used here is based on running medians, where each data value in the original series is replaced by the median of the n data values immediately before and after it (in this case, n had a value of 4 in the first pass, then 2, 5, and 3). The result obtained was then followed by "hanning," i.e., a running average computed as $y_t = .25x_{t-1} + .5x_t + .25x_{t+1}$. Running medians, with respect to the more traditional moving averages used in time-series work, take on the properties of greater resistance typical of medians (for the properties of these smoothers, see Velleman, 1980).
66. The same is true for the series of numbers of strikes and hours lost.
67. Typically, a wage measure and a business-cycle measure (unemployment rate or GNP) are added to the unionization model. On union-growth models, see Hines (1964), Ashenfelter and Pencavel (1969), and Bain and Elsheikh (1976); for Italy, see Romagnoli and Rossi (1980) and La Valle (1989).
68. The empirical evidence is based on plots of three-year moving averages for unionization data and strike indicators.
69. The empirical evidence is based on plots of the number of hours lost in strike activity and the percentage changes in union levels.
70. What is meant by "small," "medium-size," and "large" firms is somewhat historically dependent. It reflects the unions' ability to penetrate the Italian industrial structure. This ability has varied historically.
71. The relatively large number of firms in which the CI were present, however, gives a somewhat misleading picture of the conditions under which the CI were forced to operate in most firms throughout the 1950s and 1960s. Some 40% of the firms inspected by the Commissione Parlamentare did not grant time off to CI members. All other firms granted time off on request, only in exceptional cases or not at all (Commissione Parlamentare, 1958b, p. 96). Mobility of CI members was highly restricted or altogether forbidden (1958b, p. 100). In only 13% of the firms were union meetings held during regular working hours; that brought attendance down, particularly for women with family responsibilities (1958b, p. 106). In 84% of the firms inspected,

relationships between management and the CI were found to be strained (1958b, p. 144).
72. Although there was some year-to-year variation in the number of voting firms, the changes certainly were not such as to alter the basic picture.
73. Massimo Pagani at Confindustria has repeatedly pointed out to me that smaller firms were much less likely to respond to Confindustria's questionaires. However, Farneti's survey of employers in the province of Turin confirm that the CI were much less likely to be found in smaller firms, particularly firms still in the hands of their founders (Farneti, 1970, p. 129). Regardless of firm size, firms not controlled by a family were also more likely to have the CI (Farneti, 1970, pp. 129–30, 137).
74. The metalworking sector (with 41.3% of factories having the Cdf) and the chemical sector (37.3%) were the most active in the Cdf movement. That was in line with the highly militant stance of both metal and chemical workers, in terms of both strike activity and unionization levels. On the diffusion of the Cdf, see Regalia (1978, pp. 223–35); see also *Quaderni di rassegna sindacale*, No. 51, where these data can be found.
75. In practice, as we have seen, both the CI and Cdf came to be closely connected to the union movement.
76. The data refer only to FIOM, the CGIL category union for the metalworking sector. However, the data do provide some idea of union strength in one of the most industrialized (and militant) Italian provinces.
77. This figure partly reflects the low unionization levels at Fiat (8.4% in 1971), Turin's largest firm. Even excluding Fiat, unionization among the largest firms would be 24.1% (Cavallo Perin, 1980, p. 179).
78. CI, Cdf or Coordinamento di Fabbrica.
79. The yearly surveys of Lombardy manufacturing firms conducted by *Ires* Lombardia in 1987, 1988, and 1989 confirmed the widespread diffusion of forms of workers' representation at the plant level in all size classes considered (50–99, 100–499, >500). They also confirmed that only a handful of firms in the 50–99 size class were without workers' organizational structures (Ronchi, 1990).
80. In Regalia's study, a firm was classified as small if it had 100–200 employees. Other available studies confirmed that smaller firms were characterized by fewer levels and forms of workers' organizations (Squarzon, 1989a; Maestrali, 1979).
81. See Maestrali (1979); for similar empirical findings, see Regalia (1984a), Squarzon (1989a), and Ronchi (1990).
82. In some large firms, delegates would perform full-time trade-union activities for a decade or more (Vento, 1980; Regalia, 1984a); the handful of members of the executive tended to monopolize those privileges. For one whose alternative might be a lifetime of assembly-line work, becoming a delegate might seem quite an opportunity. Yet, interestingly enough, delegates in larger firms were more likely to cite "ideological" reasons as the main reasons for their union involvement (86% vs. 53% in smaller firms) (Regalia, 1984a, p. 122).
83. In the Turin case analyzed by Cavallo Perin, among firms with 10–50 employees there were 1,375 firms out of 1,519 without any union presence, and some 30,000 workers without any contact with unions – a bleak picture for most firms and workers, but not such a bad situation (actually better than that for larger firms) for the unionized small firms.
84. See Associazione Industriale Lombarda (1983, pp. 73–5); see also Vento (1980) and Amoretti (1981).
85. Informal interviews with union personnel confirmed that in smaller firms, with fewer than 50 workers, trade-union structures virtually did not exist (Biagi, 1976, p. 398). In a book written by the research unit of the Verona Federlibro, the union federation of

typographers, one reads that "Cdf and plant-level bargaining are working-class instruments rarely found in smaller firms. . . . Cdf and plant-level bargaining are problems that leave small firms unscathed. . . . We all know all too well that small firms are rarely involved even in strikes for the renewal of their collective contracts" (Centro Studi Federlibro, 1974, pp. 101–4, passim).

86. God helps those who help themselves.
87. According to Dahrendorf (1959, p. 244), "Marx showed himself a consistent philosopher but a poor sociologist when he tried to ridicule such 'partial results' and the operation of trade unions (i.e., industrial conflict, as distinct from political class conflict) in general." I find no evidence in Marx's writings of "ridicule" against trade unions and against "partial results." Although Marx always tenaciously held (as did subsequent Marxists) to the inseparability of economic and political struggles, Marx never ridiculed economic struggles per se. Quite the contrary, as some of his passionate writings attest. What Marx did ridicule was an exclusive emphasis on purely economic struggles. But Marx never ridiculed or rejected the short-term gains stemming from economic struggles. Even when unsuccessful, strikes and the organization of workers' economic interests around trade unions serve a positive function. Kautsky (1910, p. 92) expressed the Marxist approach in a pungent way: "We by no means imply that all struggles on the part of the exploited against their present sufferings are useless within the framework of the existing social order. Nor do we claim that they should patiently endure all the ill-treatment and all the forms of exploitation which the capitalist system may decree to them. . . ."
88. For a good and quick summary of various Marxist positions on trade unionism, see Hyman (1971); on Marx and Engels, see Lapides (1987).
89. Lukacs (1988, pp. 74–6) expressed a similar dichotomy between "real" consciousness and "psychological" consciousness.
90. Trotsky, however, had not lost all hope that there would be a revolutionary role for the unions. He wrote that "Revolutionary work in the trade unions, performed intelligently and systematically, may yield decisive results in a comparatively short time" (quoted in Clarke and Clements, 1977, p. 79). Lenin wrote that "As schools of war, the unions are unexcelled" (quoted in Clarke and Clements, 1977, p. 40).
91. If the goal of organization is revolutionary overthrow of capitalism, the lack of revolutionary success by national working classes in the West has left recent Marxists with the problem of explaining why the revolution has not happened. From the point of view of organization, Offe and Wiesenthal (1980) argued that workers face much greater difficulties than do capitalists. For one thing, unions are secondary organizers for labor. The capitalist firm itself is the primary organizer (Offe and Wiesenthal, 1980, p. 72). Second, whereas capital is liquid and is under the unified command of the capitalist, labor is physically separated in discrete individuals (1980, pp. 73–4). Third, capitalists can count on three different forms of collective action: the firm itself, informal cooperation (e.g., blacklisting of workers), and the employers' association. Labor has only one form: the union (1980, p. 75). Capitalists are fewer in number and can pursue their interests individually without any need to consult other capitalists (1980, p. 91); they have a clearer view of their interests [on capitalists' class consciousness, see Whitt (1979–80) and Useem (1979–80, 1982); on class consciousness in the Italian capitalist class, see the excellent essay by Martinelli (1978, pp. 43–6)] and greater resources (Offe and Wiesenthal, 1980, p. 78). Their interests are seen as being more legitimate and are generally accepted and supported in the general culture and the dominant ideology (Offe and Wiesenthal, 1980, p. 91). Capitalists' interests are also protected by the state, via constitutional guarantees to private property and limits on workers' organizational forms and actions (Offe and Wiesenthal, 1980, p. 91; see also Offe and Ronge, 1975; Block, 1977; Przeworski, 1977, p. 373).

92. There is yet another way to show the close relationship between the PCI and strike activity. On the basis of a cross-sectional analysis of strike data by region and province, Troiani (1978, pp. 107–34) concluded that the level of industrialization in a region is a very good predictor of strike rates. It can certainly explain why Piedmont and Lombardy, the two most industrialized Italian regions, were the most strike-prone regions. However, only the fact that Tuscany and Emilia Romagna were "Red regions," i.e., under local Communist administrations, can explain why Tuscany had the highest number of hours lost per 1,000 workers or why Emilia Romagna had the highest participation (on the arbitration role of regions in industrial conflict, see Regalia, 1984b).
93. On the separation between economic struggles and political struggles, see Lukacs (1988), Dahrendorf (1956, pp. 268–9), Moorhouse (1973), and Offe and Wiesenthal (1980, p. 99). For Rosa Luxemburg there was no such thing as economic struggles versus political struggles. Often, struggles that start in the terrain of economic demands spill over into the political terrain (Luxemburg, 1971, p. 47). Conversely, political actions often break up into economic strikes (Luxemburg, 1971, p. 48). "The political struggle is the periodic fertilization of the soil for the economic struggle" (Luxemburg 1971, p. 49). "There are not two different class struggles of the working class, an economic and a political one, but only one class struggle" (Luxemburg 1971, p. 79). "The trade union struggle embraces the immediate interests, and the Social Democratic struggle the future interests, of the labor movement" (Luxemburg, 1971, p. 80). Each page of Rosa Luxemburg's essay *The Mass Strike* is a negation of the separation of political and economic struggles. Luxemburg correctly perceived that such separation and the independence of each represented success for the combined state and employer policies. It is the "Artificial product of the Parliamentarian period, even if historically determined" (Luxemburg, 1971, p. 79). In a revolutionary situation, no such distinction exists; in fact, the boundaries between the two forms of action are swept away (Luxemburg, 1971, p. 79).
94. Employers, however, often "punished" political strikes, fearful of a highly politicized and radicalized working class. In Accornero's diary we read that "Management posts a memorandum, no. 1375: 'Work stoppages for non economic reasons, or at least for reasons not relating to the job, constitute disciplinary breaks'" (Accornero and Rieser, 1981, p. 205).
95. Only 34% of the *delegati* surveyed in 1971 by Romagnoli (1973, p. 53) also belonged to a party.
96. The *consigli generali* were the highest decision-making bodies between congresses. The *comitati direttivi* carried out the decisions made by the *consigli generali* and congresses (Biagioni et al., 1980, p. 172).
97. Some 57% belonged to the PCI, and 22% to the PSI (Biagioni et al., 1980, p. 174). The data refer to national category unions, provincial unions, regional category federations, local *camere del lavoro*, and regional CGIL branches (Biagioni et al., 1980, p. 174).
98. 63% were PCI members, and 24% belonged to the PSI (Biagioni et al., 1980, p. 175).
99. Between the first and fifth legislatures, i.e., between 1948 and 1969 (when trade unions declared it incompatible to hold both union and party leadership roles), 68 CGIL leaders (representing 4.36%, 5.25%, 4.03%, 2.70%, and 1.27% of all representatives in each legislature) and 54 CISL leaders had also been members of Parliament. The participation of union leaders in Parliament had several characteristics. First, for both CGIL and CISL, most of those representatives served in the 1950s. Second, it was mostly high-level union leaders who held political positions. Third, the average length of stay in Parliament for union leaders was lower than the overall average. Fourth, the Parliamentary experience was the result of a political career within the party, rather than within the union. Fifth, union leaders in Parliament confined their activities mostly

to their areas of expertise, such as labor committees (*commissione lavoro*), and labor issues. Sixth, CGIL members of Parliament were mostly from the PCI (17 from the Socialist Party). All CISL members who served in Parliament were Christian Democrats (except for one who was a Social Democrat). When union leaders were not directly involved in politics, they tended to actively and officially support and campaign for party candidates (Feltrin, 1991, p. 341).
100. Formally, the system of *cinghia di trasmissione* between party and union was abandoned in 1956 at the eighth PCI congress, although in practice the system continued for years (Ferrante, 1982, p. 683).
101. A good indication of the difficulties that unions encountered in organizing smaller firms was the fact that in smaller firms, workers typically all belonged to the same union. It was too costly and too difficult for different unions to try to unionize in a small firm (Associazione Industriale Lombarda, 1983, p. 78).
102. See Associazione Industriale Lombarda (1983). The likelihood of no intervention from outside union representatives was 8% in large firms and 47% in small ones (Regalia, 1984a, p. 268). Not surprisingly, given the more sporadic contacts with union representatives, delegates from small firms were less likely than were delegates from larger firms to participate in union activities outside their firms (28% vs. 56%; Regalia, 1984a, p. 272).

Chapter 5 The structure of collective bargaining

1. For a general introduction to the Italian system of industrial relations, see Cella and Treu (1989b) and Baglioni (1989). On the Italian bargaining structure, see Merli Brandini (1971), Giugni (1957, 1965, 1971, 1976), Dore (1976), Valcavi (1987) and Cella and Treu (1989a). For an analysis of the main collective category and plant agreements, see Veneziani (1978); see also the yearly volumes *Movimento sindacale e contrattazione collettiva*, published by Franco Angeli (Drago et al., 1971; Guidi et al., 1976), Bellardi et al. (1978), and Bellardi and Pisani (1978). On plant-level bargaining, see Ammassari and Scaiola (1962), CGIL (1969), Guidi and Cermigna (1970), Drago (1971), Guidi et al. (1972, 1973, 1974), and Porrello (1979).
2. In Italy, this level of bargaining is also called interconfederal, because it involves all major confederations of labor at the same time.
3. During the 1950s, and for many production sectors even during later decades, most collective contracts had a two-year duration (Guidi et al., 1974, p. 85). But during the 1960s and 1970s, collective contracts typically ran for three years, with contemporaneous expirations of several contracts in a given year.
4. This statement does not have universal validity. In Germany and Sweden unions pushed for highly centralized bargaining and high wage increases. As Streeck (1984, pp. 304–5) wrote: "The bankruptcy of marginal firms was seen not just as inevitable but as an entirely desirable result of centralized bargaining." But Italian unions, CGIL in particular, never accepted that principle.
5. After more debating and more labor struggles, Confindustria finally signed the agreement on February 8, 1963.
6. Guidi et al. (1974, p. 384); see also Ammassari and Scaiola (1962).
7. On the "creeping May" (*Maggio strisciante*), see Reyneri (1978); for a comparison of the French "May" and Italian *autunno caldo*, see Gigliobianco and Salvati (1980), Salvati (1983), and Lange, Ross, and Vannicelli (1982); on the years of "permanent conflict," see Giugni et al. (1976).
8. Milanaccio et al. (1978); see also Regalia's significant title *Eletti e abbandonati* (1984a), "Elected and abandoned."

9. The so-called reforms, *riforme*; see Cella and Treu (1983, p. 104) and Accornero (1992).
10. The agreement became fully operational on January 2, 1977. On the history and technical aspects of wage escalators in Italy, see Mariani (1957, 1975, 1979), Robotti (1973), and Somaini (1989).
11. In 1983, in an interview with Arrigo Levi, Agnelli reiterated that point: "Those agreements [the 1975 *scala mobile* agreement] must be evaluated in the context of the times. At that time, we thought that a decrease in strike activity was the goal to reach; those agreements were signed in order to reduce conflict. It was clear that with the increase in the cost of living, workers would obtain wage adjustments, one way or another; we thought that if workers obtained wage adjustments automatically conflict would have gone down" (Levi, 1983, p. 103).
12. For Fiat, see Becchi Collidà and Negrelli (1986, p. 178).
13. Again, for Fiat, see Becchi Collidà and Negrelli (1986, p. 184).
14. Confindustria data on absenteeism confirm the greater loss of time due to strikes during years of national contract renewals. The few available firm-level data also confirm that, as shown by the Fiat and Pirelli data reported in the table below.

Table N.5.1. *Absenteeism data for Fiat and Pirelli (1969–81)*

Firm	1969	1970	1971	1972	1973	1974	1975
Fiat	133^{*ab}	28	22	30	65^*	52	28
Pirelli	102	73	44^*	35	63	65^*	47

	1976	1977	1978	1979	1980	1981
Fiat	56^*	49	13	75^*	115	–
Pirelli	20	30^*	21	26	45^*	14

[a] Number of hours per worker.
[b] Figures for years of national contract renewals are marked with asterisks. Fiat workers fell under the metalworkers' contract; Pirelli workers fell under the chemical-workers' contract. The dates for the two contracts differ.
Source: For Fiat, Becchi Collidà and Negrelli (1986, p. 171); for Pirelli, Negrelli (1982, p. 491).

The data for Fiat and Pirelli, however, also confirm that no year was a conflict-free year for large Italian firms during the 1970s, particularly in the first half of the decade.

15. For Fiat, see Becchi Collidà and Negrelli (1986, p. 164).
16. See, however, Bordogna (1985, p. 183) and Somaini (1989).
17. Kornhauser et al. (1954, p. 12); Kornhauser (1954b, p. 524); see also Dahrendorf (1959, p. 277).
18. See Clegg (1976), chap. 6 in particular. According to Bean (1985, p. 92), Clegg's bargaining theory does not hold in cross-national perspective: When one controls for other variables (e.g., unemployment, profits, real wages), collective bargaining is no longer a significant predictor of strike patterns.
19. See also Olson (1968) for a behavioral theory of large latent groups.
20. The data on the number of plant agreements have serious shortcomings. First, both of the available series are quite short; one covers the 1969–72 period, with yearly observations, and the quarterly Confindustria series is based on a survey among member firms that began in 1979–I. Second, even for the sample periods covered, the low response rates (30–40% for the Confindustria survey) raise serious questions about

the reliability of the information published. In any case, both series are likely to have been highly underestimated, because most plant-level bargaining escaped the control of central organizations, whether labor's or employers' organizations. Finally, the data are highly aggregated, both over time (trade-union data show only yearly observations) and across sectors (Confindustria data were published at the manufacturing level exclusively). Confindustria data, though, being based on a periodic quarterly sample, can provide an invaluable and unique source of information on plant-level bargaining. For my purposes, however, these shortcomings are less telling, because the bias is likely to be constant over time, and I am interested in the patterns of plant agreements between categorywide contract expiration dates.

21. See Glasgow University Media Group (1976).
22. The plot also shows a declining role for large-scale strikes during the 1980s.
23. Mershon (1986, p. 2) described the process of plant-level bargaining quite well: "During the spring and summer of 1980, union leaders and managers in a large Milanese metalworking factory negotiated the renewal of their firm's collective contract. From the presentation of contract proposals in March to the signature of the new three-year contract in July, about 120 hours of strikes and almost 200 stoppages took place. The conflict responded to the rhythm of bargaining. The workplace union leaders first backed up their requests by coordinating an overtime ban, and then moved to several 4-hour and 2-hour strikes. As contract negotiations progressed – or, rather, failed to do so – the workplace leaders reduced strike duration and rotated the stoppages throughout the plant. Various work units carried out brief strikes (60, 30, or 15 minutes long) at different times of day."
24. Bean, who challenged the cross-national validity of Clegg's theory, recognized that the theory might hold for individual countries (Bean, 1985, p. 92).
25. See also Mershon (1986, pp. 2–3).
26. See also Moro (1980).
27. The residuals from the estimates for all other models show the same basic pattern.
28. In fact, the t statistic, the measure used to evaluate the statistical significance of econometric coefficients, is negatively affected by the magnitude of the variance of the coefficient, given that the variance appears in the denominator of the t statistic.
29. See the Appendix regarding data.
30. See Shalev (1980) and Kaufman (1981) for the United States; see Swidinsky and Vanderkamp (1982) for Canada; see also Mauro (1982) and Gramm (1987).
31. Or of hours lost, for that matter, given the high correlation between the two series.
32. In my yearly models, as a contract variable I use the percentage of workers subject to contract renewal, as proposed by Tarantelli (1976) and applied by Alinari (1979). I used my own work to update Alinari's data for the 1978 observation. In my quarterly models, I constructed the variable from basic data on employment and contract expirations (see the Appendix).
33. Data on the distribution of strikes by size, i.e., by number of strikers, are not available prior to 1976 (see Appendix on data).
34. We could modify the dependent variable in two ways: (1) use the monthly series for the number of strikers, cut peaks above the value of a 12-month trimmed mean, and recompute the yearly total; (2) use the yearly values and subtract the values of the largest strikes, as provided by the data on the distribution of strikes by number of strikers and by number of hours lost. Unfortunately, the first approach is somewhat crude; the second runs into problems of data availability. Data for categorywide and intercategory strikes are available only for the years 1955 through 1975. Data on the distribution of strikes by size (that could be used to estimate the weight of largest strikes) are available since 1965 for number of hours lost, and from 1976 for number of strikers.

35. I subtracted from the number of strikers in 1974 and 1975 the values of the largest strikes, as provided by the data on the distribution of strikes by number of strikers and by number of hours lost. Following this procedure, I obtained the values of 2106 and 4053 (instead of 5264 and 6755).
36. See Freedman's beautiful article (1991).
37. On newspapers as sources of socio-historical data, see Franzosi (1987).
38. To this, one should add an estimated 104 agreements that did not require direct trade-union involvement.
39. The number of workers excluded from plant-level bargaining would be even higher if one considered firms employing 1–19 workers. Cagnato (1981) argued that above the 100–employee mark, the presence of trade unions in Veneto was "quite high." The most serious problems of union penetration were found in firms with fewer than 50 workers. Among the collective agreements available for size classes, those for firms with fewer than 50 employees composed only 20–25%. This number is quite small when compared with the weight of this size class in the distribution of firms by size.
40. 411 firms and 384 agreements.
41. 1,163 firms and 691 agreements.
42. None of the firms employing more than 1,000 workers, and 23% of small firms employing 100–200 workers, used plant-level bargaining.
43. Even in industry, however, direct bargaining between employers and workers outside of workers' representative bodies and/or trade unions was quite diffused (31.1% of firms). According to the Federmeccanica 1984 survey, 18% of firms with fewer than 100 employees signed plant-level contracts in 1983, as compared with 34% of firms with more than 500 employees (Mortillaro, 1986, p. 204).
44. As measured by the number of different contract clauses.
45. Most small-firm agreements were stipulated on standardized forms.
46. An average of 7 clauses for firms in the 30–40 size class, 9 in the 150–200 class, and 11 for firms with more than 300 employees (Giubilato, 1982; Castegnaro, 1983; Cagnato, 1981).
47. See Camonico (1986). On the higher likelihood of small firm militancy during firm crisis, see Associazione Industriale Lombarda (1983).
48. For the electoral process: 88% vs. 18% for firms with more than 1,000 employees (Regalia, 1984a, p. 58). For delegates' meetings: 79% vs. 0% (Regalia, 1984a, p. 183). The Cdf in smaller firms were much more likely never to meet (29% vs. 4%) (Regalia, 1984a, p. 176). General assemblies were more typical in smaller firms (Regalia, 1984a, p. 64). Oral communication also was more typical: 80% vs. 15% (Regalia, 1984a, p. 203). For channels of communication with the unions: 67% vs. 14% (Regalia, 1984a, p. 275).
49. See Squarzon (1989a, 1990). For similar findings based on the yearly surveys of Lombard firms, see Ronchi (1990). Introducing their own ideological bias, the researchers of the Scuola di Formazione Superiore di Genova, on the basis of their analysis of labor relations in small firms (1–300 employees), concluded that "trade union strategy is characterized by *realism*, without any of the ideological bents that characterize union strategy in larger firms" (Pastorino and Ragazzoni, 1980, p. 90). "Realism" in smaller firms appears to have been related to the union's acceptance of the greater power of management, while ideology in larger firms was perhaps the result of an opposite structure of power relations. The Assolombarda survey of member firms confirmed the greater informality and flexibility of labor relations in smaller firms (Associazione Industriale Lombarda, 1983, pp. 86–7, 153).
50. See Associazione Industriale Lombarda (1983, p. 158). On the involvement of unions and of employers' associations in the bargaining process, see the 1983 and 1984 Federmeccanica surveys (Mortillaro, 1984, p. 167; 1986, pp. 208–9).

51. Associazione Industriale Lombarda (1983, pp. xvii, 132). On the use of the overtime ban, see also CISL Milano (1975b). In years past, such forms of conflict as revolving strikes and blockade of incoming and outgoing goods had not been uncommon even among smaller firms (Associazione Industriale Lombarda 1983, pp. xvii–xviii).
52. The evasion rate was higher (29%) in firms with financial problems. Because smaller firms tended to carry out plant-level bargaining at times of company crises, the evasion rate for smaller firms was likely to be much higher than average.
53. Brusco (1975, p. 15). See also Dell'Aringa (1976, pp. 62–3). On the greater wage differentials in smaller firms, see Centro Studi Federlibro (1974, p. 142).
54. Barca and Magnani (1989, p. 132); see also the data provided by Bagnasco and Trigilia (1984, p. 170).
55. Namely, widespread evasion of social security and insurance payments, salaries below the levels fixed by national contracts, unpaid overtime, lack of adequate workers' facilities (e.g., cafeteria, bathrooms), and widespread use of domestic labor at subsistence wages.
56. For example, Chamberlain and Metzger Schilling (1954) and Fisher (1973).
57. To avoid problems of seasonality, the series has been put through a fourth-differencing filter.
58. Kornhauser et al. (1954, p. 8) wrote that "the number of man-days lost because of unemployment in the single year 1933 was more than five times as great as the loss from all strikes from 1927 up to the present time [1954]."
59. See also Bianchi, Dugo, and Martinelli (1972).
60. Italian employers often complained that the Workers' Charter, the 1970 labor law, gave workers excessive opportunities to be absent from work, because it prohibited employers from conducting private investigations into employees' health when they called in sick (Pagani, 1973, p. 22). Furthermore, for illnesses lasting less than three days, no medical justification was required.
61. On Italian absenteeism surveys, see Pagani (1973).
62. There are three peaks in the curve of contractual minimum wages that do not correspond to a contract renewal: 1974–1, 1975–2, and 1977–2. Each of these three points, however, reflects provisions of delayed wage increases included in the 1973 and 1976 contracts.
63. Bordogna and Provasi (1979) reported similar findings, interpreted, though, as the result of mobilization (*la lotta che paga*): the more you strike, the more you get, and the more you get, the more you strike.
64. The first metalworkers' collective contract of the postwar period was signed on June 25, 1948, expiring on March 31, 1950, and renewable every two years. From that date, we go to the renewal of June 21, 1956, expiring on December 31, 1963, and then to the renewals of October 23, 1959 (expiration date October 22, 1962), February 17, 1963 (October 31, 1965), December 15, 1966 (December 31, 1969), December 21, 1969 (December 31, 1972), April 19, 1973 (December 31, 1976), and January 5, 1976 (January 1, 1979).
65. On unions' changing power in the 1950s versus the 1970s, and on the relationship between economic and political effects, see Pizzorno (1973, pp. 117–20; 1977); see also Accornero (1976).

Chapter 6 Class power, politics, and conflict

1. There are several facets to these arguments: class structure, institutionalization of conflict, economic prosperity. According to the class-structure argument, the class structure of industrial society has become more fragmented, rather than polarized.

Ownership and control have separated, leading to a capitalism without capitalists. Skills have increasingly been differentiated (Dahrendorf, 1959, pp. 36–71, 246). The proliferation of white-collar occupations has increased the size of the middle class. At the same time, the blue-collar working class has been shrinking. The economic importance of such sectors as mining and shipping, the traditional strongholds of working-class militancy, has declined (Kerr and Siegel, 1954).

According to the economic-prosperity argument, the postwar boom years brought higher living standards to the working class. During prosperity, Levitt argued, particularly after several uninterrupted years of prosperity, workers are likely to incur long-term financial obligations for housing and durable consumer goods, thereby becoming more dependent on weekly paychecks – all the more so because the decline of the extended family and the support network that it provided has made one-income workers financially more vulnerable and dependent on a continuous cash flow. "The prospect of a strike of even two weeks' duration can be frightening to a debt-burdened worker." For Levitt, mature prosperity can mean only one thing: a decline in strike activity (Levitt, 1953a,b, 1954; see also Goldner, 1953; Blitz, 1954).

More generally, during prosperity, the working class takes on standards of living and patterns of behavior that are typical of the white-collar middle class (the so-called embourgeoisement of the working class; see Golthorpe et al., 1968, in particular, the Introduction). The working class is increasingly defined by patterns of consumption rather than by patterns of production (Dahrendorf, 1959, p. 273). Even in their political orientations, blue-collar workers have become more "like" middle-class white-collar workers. More often than not, they cast their votes for conservative parties; on political conservatism in the working class, see Lipset (1981). As blue-collar workers "converge" toward middle-class values, the clash between the Left and the Right declines, slowly bringing about the "end of ideology." On the "end of ideology," see Bell (1960) and Lipset (1981, pp. 524–65); see also the summary of the debate (Waxman, 1969); on the convergence theory, see Aron (1967) and Kerr et al. (1960); for a return to the thesis, see Kerr (1983).

Contrary to Marxist predictions of long-term immiseration of industrial working classes, capitalism has shown a great capacity to produce (ever-increasing) prosperity and wealth. In a general climate of class cooperation, rather than confrontation, procedures for conflict management and resolution have spread and have become more accepted; see the essays by Harbison, Kornahuser, Ross, and Dubin in Kornhauser et al. (1954). Prosperity and the institutional mechanisms for conflict resolution and collective bargaining have brought about industrial peace, rather than conflict (Dahrendorf, 1959, pp. 257–79; Kornhauser, 1954b, pp. 524–5; Ross, 1954, p. 532. The end result has been "the withering away of the strike, the virtual disappearance of industrial conflict in numerous countries where collective bargaining is still practiced" (Ross and Hartman, 1960, p. 6).

Similarly, according to Kerr et al. (1960, pp. 208–9), workers' protests peak during the early phases of industrialization and decline thereafter. Again, contrary to the classic Marxist argument, the critical period for industrialization is during the early phase rather than the late phase. For Lester (1958), the long-term decline in labor militancy must be associated with the changes in goals and strategies of labor unions. As unions "mature," they bring workers' discontent into peaceful channels (Lester, 1958, p. 17). To the extent that unions in advanced capitalist societies have become the official voice of labor, the "channel and administrative agency for worker protest," a change in union strategy toward a more accommodative approach to labor relations will bring conflict down (Lester, 1958, p. 14). According to Lester, both internal processes (e.g., centralization and political-machine control) (1958, p. 107) and external process (e.g., increases in workers' living standard) (1958, p. 30) have led to the long-term

"maturity" of unions. According to Lester, it is very doubtful that the direction will reverse "in the foreseeable future" (1958, p. 110).
2. Levitt himself, however, conceded that in the short run, the correlation between strike frequency and the business cycle is positive, while still maintaining that the long-term relationship is negative (Levitt, 1953b; see also Edwards, 1981, p. 148).
3. With the notable exceptions of the United States and Canada, whose post-World War II strike shapes continued to be remarkably similar to their prewar shapes.
4. On the concept of political exchange, see Pizzorno (1977, 1978a, 1978b; see also Offe and Wiesenthal (1980, pp. 106–8).
5. For example, Hibbs (1976), Paldman and Pedersen (1982); for the United States, see Skeels (1971, 1982) and Kaufman (1982).
6. For example, Pencavel (1970) found that in the United Kingdom, the presence of the Labour Party in power or the presence of government income policies had a negative effect on the number of strikes. For the United States, Skeels (1971, 1982) systematically studied the effects of different political indicators (party in power in the House of Representatives, party of the president, and a dummy variable for the presidential-election year) on different measures of strike activity. The indicator for the congressional party in power was significant in all equations involving some measure of the number of workers as a dependent variable (Democrats in power leads to a higher incidence of strikes). The party of the president, on the other hand, seemed to significantly affect only the number of strikes (Democratic presidencies lead to higher strike frequencies). The presidential-election-year dummy did not prove significant. Snyder (1975) used the percentage of Democrats in Congress and the party of the president for the United States, and an election-year dummy and the yearly number of cabinet changes for France and Italy. For the United States, see also Edwards (1981, pp. 79–81).
7. According to Santagata, inflation tends to slow down in the months preceding elections, while both industrial production and the monetary base tend to expand (Santagata, 1981, pp. 277–8). The relationship between strike activity and the electoral cycle is less clear. The three-year cycle of collective bargaining tends to blur the effect of the political/business cycle.
8. There may be several reasons for this. The choice of variable could be responsible. Santagata uses the number of hours lost as a measure of strike activity, while Snyder uses the number of strikes and strikers. Yet, given the high correlation between number of strikers and of hours lost (Franzosi, 1980), I would expect a much more similar behavior between these two variables. The choice of methodology of data analysis, as well, could account for the discrepancy. Snyder uses econometric work; Santagata uses more descriptive techniques.
9. For some general treatments of Italian postwar political history, see Kogan (1966, 1981), Mammarella (1966, 1975, 1990) and La Palombara (1964, 1966). For a discussion of the overall political system, particularly in historical perspective, see Allum (1973) and La Palombara (1987).
10. The MSI received 8.7% of the votes (its highest postwar share) in 1972, at a time of increasing working-class strength.
11. Farneti (1983, p. 29). On the host of Italian parties, see Farneti (1983, pp. 35–46). On the polarization of the Italian party system, despite the multiplicity of parties, see Sartori (1982).
12. On U.S. influence on Italian postwar politics, see Faenza and Fini (1976), Leonardi and Platt (1977), Leonardi (1978), and Quartararo (1986); with specific reference to U.S. involvement in Italian labor affairs, see Migone (1974) and Filippelli (1989).
13. On the Marshall Plan, see Gimbel (1978), Hogan (1991), and Maier (1991b); on American policies toward Europe during the cold war, see Maier (1978, 1991b).

14. "Offshore aid" means the orders for military products (e.g., ammunition, parts) placed abroad by the U.S. government (Migone, 1974, pp. 244–6).
15. In a 1983 interview, Giovanni Agnelli said that "there have been two extremes [in labor relations at Fiat]. The first extreme occurred at the time of the U.S. ambassador to Rome, Clare Luce, the time of the Marshall Pan, of the military orders, of American will to keep Communist control out of the factories that received those orders and financial assistance" (Levi, 1983, p. 8).
16. A *clientela* relationship, in La Palombara's words (1964, pp. 252–305).
17. Direct participation in politics by the Italian bourgeoisie was always negligible. Nonetheless, contacts between entrepreneurs and politicians were not uncommon. According to the 1975 Federlombarda survey, a small percentage of employers (22.9%) admitted to some contacts with politicians. But whereas only 16.9% of employers with fewer than 20 workers had "political contacts," the percentage linearly increased to 20.1% in the 20–49 size class, 24.3% in the 50–99 class, 25% in the 100–249 class, and 40% in the 250–500 class (Martinelli, 1977, p. 328; see also Urbani, 1977a, p. 393). There seems to be some truth to the lament of a small entrepreneur: "In large firms, economic power translates directly into political power; this does not happen in small firms" (quoted in Martinelli, 1978, p. 43). Three-quarters of employers with more than 500 employees had political contacts (Urbani, 1977b).
18. For several examples, see Mutti and Segatti (1977, pp. 108–9) and Provasi (1976, p. 91 ff.).
19. As the Left of the DC was gaining power inside the party, Confindustria's opposition to the DC grew. In the mid-1950s, Confindustria withdrew its unilateral support for the DC and shifted to the right, to the Liberal Party. It even made an unsuccessful attempt at a broader political coalition of employers (Confintesa), based on an alliance between Confindustria and Confcommercio (Mattina, 1991, pp. 299–307; Martinelli, 1978, p. 50). In the intentions of its promoters, Confintesa was to influence the vote in the 1956 administrative and 1958 political elections toward the right. Notwithstanding the Confintesa experiment and some right-wing maneuvering by a small fraction of the capitalist class, particularly financial capital, the available evidence shows that throughout the postwar period, Italian entrepreneurs expressed, as a class, pro-government and pro-stability political choices (Farneti, 1970, pp. 188–9). The political choices of Italian entrepreneurs went to the DC and, in a smaller proportion, to the Liberal Party (PLI) (Farneti, 1970, pp. 188–9; see also Bagnasco and Trigilia, 1984, p. 224).
20. IRI and ENI were the largest of several state-owned corporations that operated in Italy during the postwar period. EFIM (Ente Partecipazioni e Finanziamenti Industria Manifatturiera) was created in 1967 on the ashes of another corporation created in 1962, FIM (Fondo per il Finanziamento dell'Industria Meccanica). EFIM dealt with ailing firms, operating mostly in the South. EGAM (Ente Autonomo di Gestione per le Aziende Minerarie) was originally set up for mining industries, but later it became involved in metalworking industries. GEPI (Società di Gestioni e Partecipazioni Industriali) was created in 1971 to deal with ailing industries in need of temporary restructuring. Restructured companies would then be returned to the private sector.
21. For a brief introduction to the history of ENI and IRI, see Becchi Collidà (1976); see also Allen and Stevenson (1974, pp. 217–66).
22. For a cross-national, comparative analysis of state capitalism, see Shonfield (1965).
23. Martinelli et al. (1981, p. 261); for more data, see Martinelli et al. (1981, pp. 207–25).
24. In the 1954 Vanoni Plan, the DC, for the first time, had indicated the need for economic planning. The Vanoni Plan was not really a plan, but simply an indication of future trends in economic development in Italy (La Palombara, 1966, p. 59).
25. The coalition was formed by DC, PSDI, and PRI.

26. In order to gain further independence from Confindustria, the DC further expanded and "conquered" the Italian credit system, which provided the DC with leverage over small entrepreneurs (Martinelli, 1978, p. 51).
27. To be fair, Italian employers not only should admit their responsibility in crushing the reform movement in the 1960s, with all that followed, but also should appreciate the positive role that, at least throughout the 1950s and 1960s, state-owned companies played in Italy's economic development. On these issues, see Shonfield (1974) and Forte (1974). For one thing, approximately one-third of Italy's total yearly capital investment came from state-owned conglomerates. Second, that investment typically was countercyclical, expanding when private capital contracted, and contracting when private capital expanded. Investment in state-owned companies acted as a stimulus to keep up demand. Third, state conglomerates contributed to raising the technological level of production. They typically operated in capital-intensive ways. Fourth, state firms invested mainly in the South. Finally, those conglomerates often expanded, against the advice of their top-level management, to bail out ailing private firms (e.g., ENI in textiles and food processing). Public firms had always been under a great deal of pressure to intervene. Otherwise, bankrupt private companies would have fallen prey of multinational corporations operating in Italy.
28. Eventually, in 1964, the left wing of the PSI formed a new party (PSIUP, Partito Socialista di Unita Proletaria). PSIUP was critical of the PSI involvement in Center-Left governments. Such governments, PSIUP argued, could serve only one function: to split the working class.
29. La Palombara (1966, p. 148); on the Italian approach to planning and trade-union responses, see also Valli (1970).
30. Accornero (1981, 1992, pp. 171–212); Regini (1981, pp. 119–48); Carrieri and Donolo (1986, pp. 73–118).
31. See Accornero (1981). On the "reforms," see the issue of *Quaderni di rassegna sindacale*, "Sindacati e riforme," 1972, no. 36.
32. For some quantitative measures of the political and legislative impacts of PCI government participation, see Cazzola (1982).
33. On the social bases of voting, see Dogan (1963), Radi (1975, p. 97), Sani (1978), Beyme (1985, p. 291), and Corbetta et al. (1988).
34. The DC drew very heavily from people for whom the Catholic religion was a regular practice.
35. For a historical analysis of voting patterns in the two areas, see Trigilia (1986, pp. 149–66).
36. For a historical analysis, see Trigilia (1986, pp. 43–131).
37. Indeed, the Red regions were the PCI training ground for an impressive and unmatched organizational machinery, based on the party's control over (1) local governments, (2) the extensive cooperative movement, and (3) the CGIL union (Sartori, 1982, pp. 17–8). On the PCI's organizational strength, see Barbagli and Corbetta (1978, 1980); also see the collection of articles edited by Ilardi and Accornero (1982) and the collection edited by Accornero, Mannheimer, and Sebastiani (1983), particularly the article by Fausto Anderlini on the PCI in Red and White regions.
38. Or, in the case of the White area, knit by the church with the active support of the Christian Democrat Party. Political preferences in the two areas seemed to indicate that culture overrode even material interests, as manifested by people's positions in the class structure. Interestingly enough, however, a comparison of voting behaviors in the two areas showed that, in the long run, material interests won out. In the White district of Bassano, it was mostly people at the bottom of the class structure (i.e., industrial workers) who changed their votes (presumably from the DC to the PCI). In the Red district of Valdelsa, it was mostly people at the top of the class structure (i.e., artisans

and entrepreneurs) who changed their votes (presumably from the PCI to more conservative parties); for the data, see Trigilia (1986, pp. 302–4).
39. For extensive empirical evidence on this point, see Romagnoli and Rossi (1980, pp. 95–124); see also Fasol (1980) and Castegnaro (1980). On union strategies in Red and White areas, see two issues of *Prospettiva sindacale* (no. 37 in 1980 and no. 41 in 1981) entirely dedicated to the topic. See also Bagnasco and Trigilia (1984, p. 217) for the White district of Bassano del Grappa, where industrial workers, particularly in smaller firms, predominantly joined the CISL union and voted for the DC. See also Bagnasco and Trigilia (1985), for the Red district of Valdelsa, and see Trigilia (1986, p. 229) for comparative data.
40. For comparative data, see Trigilia (1986, pp. 190–1). Unionization data by firm size in the industrial districts of Bassano del Grappa and Valdelsa studied by Bagnasco and Trigilia showed much higher rates for the Red Valdelsa (see Table 6.3).
41. Bagnasco and Trigilia's work showed that employers in the White area of Bassano were less likely than their counterparts in the Red area of Valdelsa to have regular meetings with the unions (Trigilia, 1986, p. 233). The 1975 Federlombarda survey of Lombardy firms similarly showed that the province of Bergamo (a White province) was much more likely to be characterized by lack of employer contacts with the unions than was any other province (Martinelli, 1977, 330–1).
42. It was through its control over local governments (communes and regions) that the PCI acquired its reputation for efficient management of public resources. A 1975 survey directed by Sartori on the political attitudes of Italians showed that the majority of people interviewed believed the DC to be an "old" party, "corrupted" and "inefficient" (Marradi, 1978). The opinions expressed on the PCI were exactly the opposite. Yet even many who expressed negative opinions of the DC and positive opinions of the PCI candidly admitted to having been and continuing to be DC voters. Fear of change would seem to be at the basis of political conservatism in the face of such negative views of the leading government party. As a young saleswoman put it, "they [DC politicians] are crooks. But I am afraid of change. The DC is OK for me." Or, in the words of a retired unskilled worker, "The DC has been at the helm for a long time. Therefore, it inspires trust" (Marradi, 1978, p. 69).
43. More generally, on the role of the "region" in arbitrating labor disputes, see Regalia (1984b).
44. The Christian Democratic governments of the White area were less likely to intervene directly in education and child-care programs. Rather, they funneled public funds into church organizations that provided those services.
45. On labor relations in the Red textile district of Prato, see Trigilia (1989).
46. The value is lower (42%) in the Valdelsa area (Trigilia, 1986, p. 222).
47. On the subordination of small firms to large firms, see Brusco (1975, pp. 30–41).
48. Many were also the same Communist workers laid off throughout the 1950s during Fiat purges of the Left. Agnelli did not mention those.
49. See Della Rocca (1976, pp. 613–14). For several examples of police brutality in the early 1960s in Turin, see Lanzardo (1979); on different techniques of policing industrial disputes, see Geary (1985).
50. The *consigli di gestione* (plant-operation councils) were set up, mostly in northern factories, by Communist workers with high hopes of real workers' control inside the factories (Neufeld, 1954, pp. 20–30; Lanzardo, 1976). Some 500 councils were active by the summer of 1946. As Neufeld (1954, p. 30), not a very sympathetic writer, put it, "by 1947 and 1948, despite propaganda, furor, demonstrations, plant violence, and strikes, the game was lost."
51. See Reyneri (1974a, pp. 1221, 124; 1989a, pp. 377–9), Regalia (1975b, p. 36), Abbatecola (1974, p. 38), Regini (1975, p. 162), and Villa (1986, p. 182).

52. In the words of a worker in a Milanese metalworking firm in 1952, the employer "distributes envelopes (antistrike envelopes, as we call them), and beautiful the motivation written on the envelope: 'For your dedication to work and production, the firm *offers* the sum of . . . lire.'" (ACLI, 1953, p. 40).
53. For example, the Stella Rossa (Red Star) shop at Fiat (Accornero, 1959); for examples in other plants, see Reyneri (1974a, p. 124), Regalia (1975b, p. 35), and Abbatecola (1974, p. 38).
54. See Perrot (1974, p. 505). For an appraisal of women's militancy see Purcell (1979). ISTAT did not provide strike data by sex or type of worker (manual or clerical). All available survey evidence for Italy, however, points to lower rates of strike participation by women in manual occupations and by clerical workers (in particular, see the yearly surveys on absenteeism by Assolombarda and Confindustria). Even during the *autunno caldo* and following years, participation by women and clerical workers in strikes was lower, as confirmed by ethnographic evidence (Pizzorno, 1974–75). More specific surveys, such as the Assolombarda 1983 survey on the state of labor relations, also show, for instance, lower participation by clerical workers (Associazione Industriale Lombarda, 1983, p. 140).

Low, also, was both female and clerical workers' union involvement. Already in the 1950s, the Commissione Parlamentare d'Inchiesta sulle Condizioni dei Lavoratori in Italia noted that women were less likely to participate to union meetings. In only 13% of the firms inspected by the commission were union meetings held during regular working hours. That fact, the commission notes in its final report, brought attendance down, particularly for women who had family responsibilities after work (Commissione Parlamentare d'Inchiesta sulle Condizioni dei Lavoratori in Italia, 1958b, p. 106).

A 1978–79 survey of chemical workers showed that white-collar workers were less willing to serve as delegates and that women were underrepresented (Vento, 1980). Similarly, according to Regalia's survey of *consigli di fabbrica* (Cdf), women and clerical workers were much more likely to have no representation in the Cdf (Regalia, 1984a, p. 91). Women's underrepresentation in workers' organizational structures was even more noticeable in economic sectors that were highly feminized (e.g., textiles, food processing). According to the 1983 Assolombarda survey of labor relations, clerical workers in smaller firms were not unionized (Associazione Industriale Lombarda, 1983, p. 81; see also, Pastorino and Ragazzoni, 1980, p. 90). Only in factories with more than 100 employees were there some unionized clerical workers. In fact, when clerical workers were involved in trade-union affairs in smaller firms, blue-collar workers often accused them of being the employers' spies (Associazione Industriale Lombarda, 1983, p. 81).

Finally, both the 1971 and 1982 Isvet surveys of workers' attitudes confirmed the lower rates of participation in collective action and trade-union activities for both women and clerical workers.
55. The "collaboration" bonuses were granted during the 1950s in many Italian companies to those workers who were not members of the Communist Party nor of the Communist CGIL union and did not participate in strikes.
56. For a discussion of the sample, see Biagi (1976, p. 387).
57. For the Dozzo diaries, see Accornero et al. (1960); also see Pugno and Garavini (1974); for Accornero's diaries, see Accornero (1959, 1973); also see Accornero and Rieser (1981); see also Accornero et al. (1960).
58. Fines and disciplinary measures were not restricted to the 1950s. Given the balance of class forces, they probably were worse then. But the survey conducted by Assolombarda in 1983 and the 1983 and 1984 Federmeccanica surveys showed how widespread fines and disciplinary measures were even in the early 1980s (Associazione Industriale Lombarda, 1983, p. 65; Mortillaro, 1984, pp. 171–2; 1986, pp. 195–9).

59. Unfortunately, Skeels did not explain why the two effects (unemployment and layoffs) should be kept separate, nor did he present empirical evidence on the effects of layoffs.
60. For a detailed description of the use of layoffs and transfers at Fiat during the 1950s and their impact on militancy, see Gianotti (1979).
61. ACLI (1953). See also the material assembled by the Commissione Parlamentare d'Inchiesta sulle Condizioni dei Lavoratori in Italia (1958a, 1958b, 1958c).
62. The commission of inquiry, made up of senators and deputies, was set up in early 1955. Interviews with workers and trade-union and employer representatives were concluded in two years of work. The results were published in two separate parts: *Relazione della Commissione Parlamentare d'Inchiesta sulle Condizioni del Lavoratori in Italia*, in 12 volumes. Rome: Segretariati Generali della Camera dei deputati e del Senato della Repubblica, 1958–60. On the commission of inquiry, see Addario (1976).
63. See Reyneri (1987, p. 160). I translated Reyneri's original Italian text, which literally reads "Italian unions never had a really 'friendly government' in power," rather than using the translation in the English edition which reads "Italian unions never sought to foster a truly friendly government of the Left" (Reyneri, 1989b, p. 135). The meanings are quite different. The Italian original is closer to historical reality.
64. The institutions that unions "occupied" were involved in a variety of tasks: social welfare, price control, approval of a variety of licenses (e.g., a stall in a public market), preparation of merit lists of candidates in public competitions, arbitration, planning, etc.
65. See Tarantelli (1976) and Alinari (1979).
66. Whereas union membership and unionization rate measure the absolute degree of labor's organizational strength, the Tarantelli indicator is more likely to measure relative union strength – relative to other social actors, employers in particular, because promptness in contract renewal depends not only on unions' strength but also on employers' resistance.
67. On the cost of labor negotiation, see Bordogna (1985, pp. 184–6). The negotiation continued with various intermediate agreements until the January 22, 1983, agreement, the so-called *lodo Scotti*, from the name of the minister of labor who concluded the agreement. On the 1983 agreement, see Bordogna (1985, pp. 188–91), Carrieri and Donolo (1986, pp. 127–32), and Regini (1985, pp. 22–6).
68. See Regini (1980, p. 55) and Lange and Vannicelli (1982, pp. 142–80). On the effects of the new strategy at the plant level, see Roccella (1982).
69. For an in-depth analysis of the EUR line, see Lange and Vannicelli (1982, pp. 165–80); see also Regini (1980, p. 49). On union control over investment, see the issue of *Quaderni di rassegna sindacale*, no. 62–3, 1976; see also Della Rocca and Negrelli (1983).
70. On corporatism in Italy, see Lange and Vannicelli (1982, pp. 165–80), Regini (1980, 1981, pp. 167–88, 1982, 1983, 1984, 1985), Bordogna (1985), Giugni (1985), Carrieri and Donolo (1986), Lange and Regini (1989), Lange (1979, 1987), and Cella (1989b).
71. On the political mediation of the regions, see Fidanza and Treu (1976) and Regalia (1984a). For recent data on political mediation in the early 1980s, see the 1984 Federmeccanica survey of metalworking firms (Mortillaro, 1986, p. 209).
72. Levi (1983, pp. 66, 69). As Chancellor Helmut Schmidt of Germany put it, "The profits of enterprises today are the investments of tomorrow, and the investments of tomorrow are the employment of the day after" (quoted in Przeworski, 1980–81, p. 133; Przeworski and Wallerstein, 1982, p. 216).
73. To some extent, that was indeed the experience of the Italian economy during the 1970s, with the devaluation/fluctuation of the currency, the International Monetary Fund (IMF) loan, the increasing loss of firm profitability, and high levels of indebtedness.

74. As Marx wrote, "It is altogether too naive to suggest that if the total product of labor rises, the three classes among whom it is to be shared will share equally in that growth. If profit were to rise by 20%, the workers would have to strike to obtain a 2% rise in wages" (Lapides, 1987, p. 183).
75. As Gramsci (1971, p. 161) wrote, "Undoubtedly the fact of hegemony presupposes that ... the leading group should make sacrifices of an economic-corporate kind. But there is also no doubt that such sacrifices and such a compromise cannot touch the essential; for though hegemony is ethical-political, it must also be economic, must necessarily be based on the decisive function exercised by the leading group in the decisive nucleus of economic activity."
76. See also Accornero (1992, pp. 201–4).
77. On the role of strikes in the Russian revolution see Koenker and Rosenberg, 1989.
78. For Lenin's position, see Harding (1983, pp. 36–7).
79. Farneti similarly wrote that "Since 1953 ... the policy of the Communist Party has been that of diffusing tension" (1976, p. 97).
80. Galli (1975, p. 173). For the appeasing role of the PCI in various episodes, see Mauro (1973, pp. 48–54) on land-occupation movements by southern peasants; on the insurgency in Milan for the dismissal of the leftist prefect Ettore Troilo, see Turone (1984, pp. 132–3); on the attempted assassination of PCI leader Palmiro Togliatti, see Turone (1984, pp. 145–7), Marino (1991, pp. 13–28), and Galli (1975, p. 153); for protests over the 1953 "swindle bill" (*legge truffa*), see Galli (1975, p. 156); on the 1960 revolt of Genoese workers against the Tambroni government, see Turone (1984, p. 265); for the 1962 clashes at *Piazza Statuto*, see Lanzardo (1979, p. 163); for Fiat, see Viale (1978, pp. 203–4, 231), Gobbi (1989, p. 115), and Polo (1989, p. 193).
81. See the survey data analyzed by Farneti (1985, pp. 154–61).
82. See the title of Giorgio Bocca's book (1980).
83. On the "choices for labor" in Italy and trade union dilemmas, see Regini (1981), Lange and Vannicelli (1982, pp. 163–5), Carrieri and Donolo (1986), Chiesi and Martinelli (1989), Cella (1989a, 1989b), and Accornero (1992); see also the interview with Luciano Lama, CGIL secretary general (Riva, 1976, pp. 90, 92, 110, 114, 120, 122, 124).
84. For example, Ashenfelter and Johnson (1969) said that passage of the Landrum-Griffin Act in 1959 significantly increased strike activity, by 88 strikes per quarter. Kaufman (1982), on the other hand, found that the Landrum-Griffin Act had a negative effect on the number of strikes, but a positive effect on the number of strikers.
85. Korpi (1974, 1978, pp. 31–54). See also Kaufman (1982, p. 489).
86. By "institutionalization of collective bargaining," Snyder means (1) parties' willingness to negotiate with each other, (2) bargaining leading to contract agreements, and (3) contracts being honored by both parties (Snyder, 1975, p. 265).
87. In the postwar equation for the United States, the two economic variables are significant, as expected; in the prewar equation, only the organizational/political variables are significant, supporting the hypothesis of institutional change. For a critique of Snyder's work on Canada (Snyder, 1977), see Smith (1979). On the United States, see Edwards (1981, pp. 52–4, 67, 79–81). For France, neither model is appropriate. Economic variables are insignificant for both prewar and postwar periods. Among the organizational/political variables, the unionization variable is significant only for the prewar period, the number of cabinet changes is insignificant for both periods, and the election-year variable, although significant in both periods, has the wrong sign in the postwar equation.
88. For instance, Snyder specified the relationship among wages and strikes and strikers as a six-year moving average of percentage changes in real wages. Snyder adopted that same specification for all three countries (France, Italy, United States). Yet if

institutional arrangements played such a fundamental role in strike activity, as Snyder claimed, then how could the same lag structure fit equally well industrial relations systems that Snyder himself placed at opposite poles (France and Italy vs. the United States)? The extent of collective bargaining, the level at which bargaining was held (e.g., centralized vs. decentralized), the duration of collective contracts, and the existence of automatic cost-of-living adjustment clauses all mediated the relationship between strikes and wages.

Furthermore, Snyder used product-market (GNP) rather than labor-market variables for his French and Italian equations. As argued in Chapter 3, the statistical relationship between industrial production and strikes is affected by reciprocal causation. After all, hours lost in strike activity, as the term itself suggests, are hours lost from productive activity; the larger the number of strike hours, the more likely it will be that strike activity will have a negative effect on production, particularly in the presence of a union overtime ban after strikes. The shorter the sample period analyzed and the more disaggregated the unit of observation (economy as a whole, single economic sector, plant), the more likely it will be that production and strike activity will be negatively related. However, Snyder's reliance on highly aggregated data (yearly and economy-wide) should have attenuated the effects of reciprocal causation. Whereas the bulk of strike activity was concentrated in the manufacturing sector, that sector accounted for less than half of GNP. Even more puzzling is the fact that, contrary to the expectations deriving from the foregoing argument, Snyder reported a negative coefficient for the effect of GNP on the number of strikes and a positive coefficient for the effect of GNP on the number of workers involved.

89. For the estimates, I used the data published in Snyder's dissertation (1974). There may be slight differences between my estimates and Snyder's estimates, despite my use of Snyder's data. First, Snyder did not specify which kind of GLS procedure he used to correct for autocorrelation in his equation for the number of strikes (Hildreth-Lu, Cochrane-Orcutt, Beach-MacKinnon, etc.) (Johnston, 1972; Beach and MacKinnon, 1978); however, as the value of the Durbin-Watson statistic does not indicate the need to correct for autocorrelation, I used the OLS method. Furthermore, Snyder did not specify the degree of the polynomial nor whether or not he applied end-point constraints; I was best able to approach his results using a third-degree polynomial and imposing constraints on both.

90. On these issues, see Granger and Newbold (1974) and Plosser and Schwert (1978). I suspect that problems of multicollinearity may also have affected Snyder's French equations, given that Snyder also used GNP in those equations.

91. Burawoy (1985) argued that working-class politics and radicalism are shaped by "factory regimes," the overall politics of production, as determined by the labor process and the political apparatus of production within the firm. Four factors determine "factory regimes": market forces, the degree of workers' dependence on wages, the labor process, and the state. The production process lies at the heart of working-class radicalism, decisively shaping working-class politics.

92. Under individual bargaining, what counts is the position of the single worker in the labor market. The labor market provides the mechanism for regulating worker-employer relationships.

93. Many of the scholarly "certainties" about corporatist arrangements that were seen in the 1970s as the future of labor relations in industrialized nations have faded in recent years (particularly with respect to Italy). But Snyder's own certainty about the ability of economic models of strikes to describe the future of labor relations rested on even frailer grounds.

94. With respect to collective bargaining, Harbison (1954, p. 279) wrote that "the dominance of collective bargaining as a method for resolving conflict is logically, if

not exclusively, associated with a society which is capable of sustaining economic prosperity and maintaining quite high levels of employment."
95. Crouch (1978), Streeck (1994); for Italy, see Carrieri and Donolo (1986, pp. 145–7).
96. On the characteristics of strikes during the years of the *compromesso storico*, see Perulli (1982).
97. For the correspondence between government number and year, see the appendix on data.
98. To get an idea of the characteristics of economic and political strikes, I report below data for the numbers of strikes, strikers, and hours lost for the years 1975–82 for the two types of strikes. The data clearly show that political strikes were rare in comparison with their economic counterparts. They numbered in the tens rather than in the thousands. In many years, that handful of political strikes accounted for as many strikers as did the thousands of economic strikes, if not more. But even in the years when the number of strikers was higher for political strikes than for economic strikes (e.g., 1977, 1978, 1981), the average duration for political strikes was much shorter. The data confirm that, by and large, political strikes were rare, large, and brief displays of working-class strength, typical "demonstrative" strikes. They also confirm the vulnerability of the series for the number of strikers to potential outliers: A handful of large-scale strikes can make a dramatic difference in this series.

Table N.6.1. *Economic and political strikes*

		1975	1976	1977	1978	1979	1980	1981	1982
Strikes	Economic	3,568	2,667	3,259	2,465	1,979	2,224	2,176	1,741
	Political	33	39	49	14	21	14	28	6
Strikers	Economic	10,717	6,974	6,434	4,347	10,521	7,428	3,567	7,490
	Political	3,392	4,924	7,369	4,427	5,717	6,397	4,660	2,993
Hours lost	Economic	181,381	131,711	78,767	49,032	164,914	75,214	42,802	114,889
	Political	8,943	45,932	37,196	22,207	27,799	39,987	30,889	15,051

Source: ISTAT, *Annuario Statistico Italiano*, various issues.

99. Only one cabinet crisis during the period under consideration began on the last day of the month, April 30, 1976.
100. Unfortunately, the econometric requirement to use data at the same level of aggregation for all variables in the model, and the lack of more disaggregated (monthly) data on other independent variables (e.g., unemployment rate, union membership), forces us to work at a level of aggregation that in light of the exploratory analyses is clearly inadequate for the study of many political processes.
101. Streeck (1984), however, argued that during economic crises workers may be even more divided than during prosperity, reducing the prospects for solidarity.

Chapter 7 Mobilization processes: the 1969 autunno caldo

1. For a quick description in English of the events surrounding the 1969 *autunno caldo*, see Lumley (1990, pp. 167–269); see also Regalia et al. (1978).
2. Leaving problems of statistical influence aside (Franzosi, 1994).
3. Be these estimates, the coefficients, a linear combination of these coefficients, their variance, the fitted values, etc. (see Franzosi, 1994, and Belsley et al., 1980, p. 11).

4. The Assolombarda research, directed by Ponterollo, had an odd research design. In 43.5% of the firms in the sample, employers were interviewed; in the rest of the firms, trade-union representatives were interviewed. In smaller firms, interviews with trade-union representatives were predominant. For the textile sector, interviews with trade-union representatives were all conducted on the basis of a structured questionnaire; for all other sectors (i.e., metalworking) the questionnaire was open-ended. Results were sometimes reported systematically (e.g., "35% of the firms . . . "); most typically, however, they were reported superficially (e.g., "Most firms . . .," "Some entrepreneurs . . ."). Despite all of that, the picture of the state of industrial relations that emerged from the research was quite dismal; all the more so if we keep in mind that the sample included only unionized firms.
5. The data refer to male workers. Data for female workers show no appreciable differences. Unfortunately, there is no way for me to aggregate the data across sex, because most firms would unionize both men and women, but some would unionize only one or the other, depending on the composition of the work force. Needless to say, I do not have information on the sex composition of the work force by firm. That probably is why these data are slightly different from Bergamaschi's data (1977b, p. 256).
6. Quoted in Viale (1978, p. 172); see Nanni Balestrini's novel, *Vogliamo tutto* (1971).
7. See Giuliani and Pecora (1970), Luppi (1974, p. 50), Reyneri (1974a, pp. 139, 143), Beccalli (1974, p. 249), Abbatecola (1974, pp. 45, 51), Giugni et al. (1976, pp. 128–9).
8. For a good analysis of the tensions surrounding the craftsman's position, his ambiguous attitude toward the mass of unskilled workers, his wavering loyalties among craft, unskilled workers, and even management, his dogged defense of craft skills against encroachment, and ultimately his contradictory political role within the working class, caught between the "labour aristocracy"and revolutionary leadership, see Sabel (1982, pp. 167–79).
9. See the collections of Fiat workers' memories in Polo (1989), Reyneri (1974a, p. 146), Luppi (1974, p. 75), and Abbatecola (1974, pp. 56–7).
10. On these struggles, see Bezza (1981).
11. Turone (1984, p. 288). For an extensive reconstruction of events from different perspectives, see Lanzardo (1979).
12. UIL was the smaller of the three unions, but the one that had struck an alliance with Fiat management. In exchange for controlling workers' militancy, UIL obtained union privileges on the shop floor. In 1961, at the plant-level elections of the Commissione Interna, UIL and Sida (the company union) together obtained 63% of the votes (Turone, 1984, p. 289; Becchi Collidà and Negrelli, 1986, p. 160).
13. Turone (1984, p. 291); see also Gianotti (1979, p. 140); for some oral history accounts of those events, see Lanzardo (1979, pp. 101–204).
14. On the basis of several questionnaire items, De Masi and Fevola (1974a, p. 781) computed a composite index of militancy ranging from zero, for the least-conflict-prone worker, to five.
15. That finding was also confirmed by the 1981 Isvet survey (De Masi et al., 1985).
16. Unfortunately, the published Isvet results lump together *manovali* and *operai comuni* in one category of unskilled workers, and *operai qualificati* and *operai specializzati*. Most likely, aggregation blurs more significant differences between the extremes of the skill hierarchy. The interviews conducted by the Milan CISL with a sample of its members in 1987 (585 interviews) confirmed that unionized unskilled workers were less likely than skilled workers to participate in trade-union meetings (35.7% vs. 50.6%) or strike activity (24.8% vs. 44.7%) (La Valle, 1987).
17. The background characteristics of the *operaio massa* were similar in the 1971 Isvet survey in terms both of educational credentials (De Masi and Fevola, 1974c, pp. 258–9) and geographic origin (De Masi and Fevola, 1974c, p. 267).

18. For Italy, see Melotti (1964), Del Turco (1970), and Sartori (1973); see also Dubois (1978).
19. Gallessi (1981, pp. 37–42, passim); Bezza (1981, pp. 80–1). On the use of whistles in Turin during the 1962 strikes, see Lanzardo (1979, p. 86).
20. Gallessi (1981, pp. 46–7); Regalia (1975b, p. 39); see Lanzardo (1979, p. 85) for similar practices in Turin.
21. See Lanzardo (1979, pp. 84–95) for the 1962 Lancia and Michelin strikes in Turin.
22. On cafes as meeting points in Turin, see Pugno (1961) and Lanzardo (1979, p. 108).
23. The use of symbolic and expressive forms of protest became quite widespread during the strike wave, with effigies of political figures and industrialists being publicly burned (Tarrow, 1989a, p. 189). Such expressive forms of protest had been typical in times past, in such forms of collective action as *charivari* (Tilly, 1978, pp. 144–5). According to a high-level manager, "The boss's coffin was paraded amid red flags; *it was not funny at all*" (quoted in Derossi, 1982, p. 105).
24. See Luppi (1974, pp. 55, 77), Beccalli (1974, p. 151), Carabelli (1974, p. 249), and Regini (1974, pp. 174, 179).
25. Most often, however, union representatives used the mass meetings simply to pass on decisions taken elsewhere. On mass meetings, see Pugno (1961), Beccalli (1974, p. 151), Carabelli (1974, p. 179), Regalia (1975a), Treu (1971, pp. 126–34), and Tarrow (1989a, p. 189).
26. See Luppi (1974, pp. 63, 78), Reyneri (1974a, pp. 147, 167), Regini (1974, pp. 44, 57, 61), Beccalli (1974, p. 174), and Regalia (1975a, pp. 70, 180).
27. For a detailed description of the events, see Castellano (1980, pp. 37–40).
28. Dell'Aringa (1976, p. 31). In 1969, egalitarian demands tended to reduce wage differentials (Cella, 1976b, p. 173).
29. On egalitarianism, see Giugni et al. (1976, p. 139), Dell'Aringa (1976, pp. 31–3, 52), Accornero and Carmignani (1978b), Dell'Aringa and Lucifora (1994).
30. Quarterly estimates using the Ashenfelter and Johnson model, with the addition of a variable of number of work-related injuries, yielded, as expected, a negative and significant coefficient for the unemployment rate and a positive (although insignificant) coefficient for work-related injuries.
31. The correspondence between the plot for the number of industrial work-related injuries and that for equipment investment is impressive. Basically, this confirms the two peaks in Italy's economic miracle in the early and late 1960s.
32. Given that work-related injuries follow very closely the business cycle, the effect of number of nonfatal work injuries on strikes is mainly indirect, mediated through the state of economic conditions. In this sense, the number of work-related injuries constitutes only a good proxy for the business cycle. Work injuries, however, particularly if severe, may also have direct effects, since they often lead to immediate, spontaneous protests and walkouts on the part of fellow workers.
33. Italian scholars have repeatedly pointed out how the work pace greatly intensified during the 1960s and how that was a common grievance at the onset of the 1968–72 strike wave (Pizzorno, 1974–75; Bianchi et al., 1970; Giugni et al., 1976). For the increases in the rhythm of production and work accidents in the late 1940s and early 1950s, see Onofri (1955, pp. 70–96).
34. For example, for Fiat, see Milanaccio and Ricolfi (1976, pp. 95–9).
35. The extent of the refusal to bargain over health and hazard issues should not be exaggerated. In fact, the practice of company bonuses to compensate for those issues continued to be widespread among Italian companies (Giugni et al., 1976, p. 179).
36. See Regini and Reyneri (1971, pp. 71–91), Cella (1976b, pp. 178, 182), and Giugni et al. (1976, pp. 139–40); on the characteristics of *inquadramento unico* and on its effects, see Del Lungo (1976).

37. For further evidence on the changes in skill hierarchies during the years of the strike wave, see Villa (1986, pp. 318–22).
38. On managers' "cautious" approach to increased militancy, and on the mix of repressive, paternalistic, and democratic strategies, see Talamo (1979, p. 116); for that cycle at Fiat, see Milanaccio and Ricolfi (1976, pp. 90–4).
39. For a description of those practices as seen by the "victims," see the interviews with high-level corporate managers (Derossi, 1982, p. 105).
40. For Ignis, see Santi (1974, pp. 124, 127); for Falck, see Carabelli (1974, p. 118) and Neufeld (1954, p. 42–4); on welfare capitalism, see Edwards (1979, p. 91–7).
41. For some examples, see, for Ignis, Santi (1974, p. 129); for Falck, see Carabelli (1974, pp. 118–19).
42. Viale (1978, pp. 176–93). On the role of Potere Operaio in the student movement, see Bobbio (1979, pp. 6–26).
43. For some examples at Fiat, see De Palma, Riser, and Salvadori (1965); for Olivetti, see Carrara (1965) and Viale (1978, pp. 181–2); on the use of the *inchiesta operaia* (survey of workers), see the papers by Panzieri, Rieser, and Lanzardo in issue no. 5 of *Quaderni rossi*, 1965.
44. On the radical press, see Gobbi (1989, pp. 77–116); see also Bobbio (1979, pp. 6–9, 29); for an anthology of the later texts of *La Classe* and *Potere Operaio*, see Castellano (1980, pp. 25–82); see also Lumley (1990, pp. 33–41); on the factory-based political journals, see Ferraris (1965).
45. Many of these students were actually anti-Leninists, in particular, Lotta Continua with its antiorganizational overtones and its emphasis on spontaneous action. Students had first appeared at some of the factory gates in the early 1960s (e.g., Gallessi, 1981, pp. 45, 47), but it was in 1967 and in the following years that their presence became continuous and significant; for many examples, see Luppi (1974, pp. 55, 65), Reyneri (1974a, pp. 140, 148), Regini (1974, pp. 44, 55, 58), Santi (1974, pp. 137, 138), and Regalia (1975b, p. 60).
46. Both the student movement and the feminist movement contributed to the discourse on emancipation.
47. For the encounter of students and workers at Fiat Mirafiori, see Bobbio (1979, pp. 27–35); on the relationship between the unions and the extraparliamentary groups, see Antoniazzi (1969), Foa (1969), and Donini (1972).
48. For example, rent strikes or fare strikes on public transportation, proletarian expropriations, such as shoplifting (Reyneri, 1974a, p. 148; Regalia, 1975b, p. 73; Regini, 1975, p. 184).
49. The unions, after adopting the measures of *delegati* and *consigli di fabbrica*, tried to extend the experience of territory-based networks of militants through the *consigli di zona* (Forbice and Chiaberge, 1974, pp. 157–230). Again, I should stress the historical continuity of experience of radical organizational forms. The *consigli di zona* had been active in the mid-1940s along with the *consigli di gestione* (Landarzo, 1976; Forbice and Chiaberge, 1974, pp. 19–32).
50. On the effects of those groups on egalitarian workers' demands, see Regini and Reyneri (1971, pp. 73–84). For a critical analysis of the spontaneity of Lotta Continua, see *Avanguardia Operaia* (1972).
51. Many Italian managers similarly interpreted the upsurge of conflict (Talamo, 1979, pp. 100, 105).
52. The abandonment of revolutionary politics was not simply a matter of the leaders "selling out" for self interest, rather than pursuing the workers' interests; that thesis was expounded by Michels with his "iron law of oligarchy" (Michels, 1966). As we saw in Chapter 7, there were strong pressures toward "opportunism" and class compromise, regardless of the goodwill and intentions of labor leaders.

53. In terms of hours lost, see Lumley (1990, p. 167).
54. The antiunion character of the struggles was particularly strong at Fiat and Pirelli; for Pirelli, see Cacciari (1969), Beccalli (1973); in general, see Giugni et al. (1976, p. 143).
55. E. P. Thompson's work is the best example of work that emphasizes the role of culture, perhaps over and above that of structure itself (Thompson, 1963). See also the excellent discussion of the role of culture by Calhoun (1982, pp. 34–59, 204–40).
56. In light of the lack of revolutionary consciousness in the West, several authors compiled listings of obstacles and difficulties on the path toward class consciousness. According to Ollman (1972) nine steps of increasing difficulties stand in the way. In Mann's (1973) scheme the steps are only four: Class identity, i.e., the definition of oneself as part of the working class, class opposition, i.e., the perception that capitalists constitute an enduring opponent to oneself, class totality, i.e., the awareness that the class structure defines one's total situation, and, finally, alternative society, i.e., the conception of a different society.
57. Masiero (1974). On the peasant worker, see Sabel (1982, pp. 132–6).
58. For example, for Autobianchi, see Luppi (1974, pp. 50–51, 75); for Innocenti, see Reyneri (1974a, p. 145); for Candy, see Regini (1974, p. 33). When technicians and white-collar workers participated on the side of workers, they often provided vanguard leadership for the movement, see Lumley (1990, pp. 197–204). On the basis of an in-depth analysis of two Milanese factories (GTE and Sit-Siemens), Low-Beer (1978) found evidence of radicalism in tactics and demands among technicians and white-collar workers in those firms, providing support for Mallet's "new-working-class" thesis. However, Low-Beer's assessment of the role of technical and clerical workers in the strike wave is quite exaggerated. In fact, it was only at Sit-Siemens and GTE, the two firms studied by Low-Beer, that Pizzorno's research team found widespread evidence of white-collar participation and, in fact, leadership (for Sit-Siemens, see Regalia, 1975a, pp. 58–62; for GTE, see Regini, 1975, pp. 167, 169).
59. For example, for Dalmine, see Abbatecola (1974, p. 44); for Innocenti, see Reyneri (1974a, p. 145).
60. For Candy, see Regini (1974, p. 68).
61. For Autobianchi, see Luppi (1974, p. 49); for Candy, see Regini (1974, pp. 48, 58); for Magneti Marelli, see Reyneri (1974b, p. 43); for Ercole Marelli, see Dolci (1974, p. 144); for Fiat, see Polo (1989, p. 190).
62. Confindustria data also confirm the great deal of variation in strike rates across sectors (from 0.50 among blue-collar workers in food processing to 2.09 in metalworking) and across factories of different sizes (from 1.55 among blue-collar workers in plants employing between 51 and 250 workers to 2.34 in plants with more than 1,000 workers).
63. See Buratto et al. (1974, p. 303), Cella and Reyneri (1974), and Low-Beer (1978).
64. The South was politically unstable; the Northwest had traditionally been on the left.
65. See Tarrow (1989b, pp. 34–5); again, not unlike Marxist theories (Calhoun, 1982, pp. 222–33). Political-opportunity structures are characterized by their (1) degree of openness of the polity (especially regarding the presence or absence of repression), (2) stability or instability of political alignments (which may lead to the inclusion of previously excluded groups into the polity), (3) presence or absence of allies and support groups, and (4) elite fragmentation (Tarrow, 1989b, pp. 34–5).
66. For example, 1893 in both France and Italy, 1899 in France, 1896–97 in Italy, 1906 in France and 1907–08 in Italy, 1919–20 in both countries, 1968 in France, and 1968–72 in Italy. See Shorter and Tilly (1974) and Bordogna and Provasi (1979); for France, see Shorter and Tilly (1974, p. 107); for the United Kingdom, see Cronin (1979, p. 39); for the United States, see Edwards (1981, pp. 28–9); for a comparative analysis of strike waves across countries, see Screpanti (1987); see also Boll, 1985.

Chapter 8 Countermobilization processes: reactions by the state and employers to strike waves

1. Employers' collective responses to strike waves have a long history. Stearns, for instance, showed how the rise of French labor organizations and increased strike activity toward the end of the nineteenth century brought about counterorganizations and various collective defense mechanisms on the part of French employers (Stearns, 1968). No less common, around the same time in Italy, were employers' coalitions designed to break down strikes and workers' organizations, leagues of resistance in particular (Spriano, 1958, 1964; De Santis, 1979; Merli, 1972, pp. 535–41).
2. For a comparative analysis of the role of the state in postwar Western European countries, see Crouch (1978). For an in-depth, historical analysis of the relationship between the state and the unions, see Macdonald (1960) for the United Kingdom, and see the beautiful work by Tomlins (1985) for the United States.
3. A general of *carabinieri*, the paramilitary police.
4. In the summer of 1991, the Italian press revealed the existence throughout the postwar period of detailed anti-Communist plans linked to NATO (the "Gladio" plan).
5. One should keep in mind, however, that the Workers' Charter did not apply to firms with fewer than 15 employees.
6. According to Treu's research findings, unions tended to rely less on the new legal instrument in factories and geographic areas where they were strong. In those cases, unions preferred to solve their problems directly through collective action, rather than seeking the mediation of a third party (the judiciary system), with all the uncertainties involved.
7. See Melucci and Rositi (1975, p. 174). The 1984 Federmeccanica survey on the state of labor relations confirmed that labor-court sentences on the basis of the Workers' Charter were more likely to be favorable to workers in smaller firms (33%, vs. 22% in larger firms) and favorable to employers in larger firms (17% vs. 39%) (Mortillaro, 1986, p. 212).
8. Research on political mediation by public authorities (at the regional level, in particular) similarly showed that unions were more likely to invoke the mediation at the regional level in situations of structural weakness, particularly cases of plant closings (Martinelli, 1976). Otherwise, unions preferred to solve their problems directly via collective action.
9. For several examples of intervention of the Ministry of Labor, see Giugni et al. (1976, pp. 189–208).
10. For example, via unemployment (Kalecki, 1943) or via selective economic incentives to maintain a pluralistic class structure; see Berger (1974), Pizzorno (1974a), and Weiss (1984).
11. Valli (1976, p. 80); see also D'Antonio (1973) and Soskice (1978).
12. On the attitudes of Italian capitalists during the 1964 crisis, see the interviews assembled by Ottone (1965).
13. On the collapse of authority structure at Fiat, see Becchi Collidà and Negrelli (1986, p. 165).
14. Welfare capitalism, as Edwards (1979, pp. 91–7) called it.
15. "To work less in order that all may work" – the strategy of reducing the workweek and eliminating overtime in order to force employers to hire new workers.
16. Villa's data on the distribution of the work force in several steel companies, by length of service and skill levels, showed that workers with longer service were bunched up at the top of the skill hierarchy (Villa, 1986, pp. 324–5).
17. To be sure, there are several possible causes for capital flight from one country to another: (1) fiscal, due to the capitalists' search for tax havens, (2) short-term

speculative, due to the difference between internal and external interest rates, or between immediate or delayed exchange of domestic currency versus foreign currencies, and (3) long-term speculative, related to portfolio and direct investments abroad by multinational firms. "Expectation of economic and political crisis" is also often listed by economists among the causes of capital flights; unfortunately, though, "economic theory is not well equipped to deal with these issues," and the argument is dropped altogether (Vicarelli, 1970, p. 325).

18. Because of that, Salvati (1984, pp. 89–97) called the entire 1963–69 period "the strike of capital," as opposed to "the strike of labor" during the 1969–73 period. In fact, the period of "strike of capital" was characterized by the absurd paradox of a country that exported abroad both capital ("mostly illegally") and labor (350,000 people) (Salvati, 1984, pp. 93–4). The high level of strike activity, the much talk about economic planning (the Papi government commission on planning), the coming to power of the Socialists within the *centro-sinistra* government coalition in February 1962, and the nationalization of electric companies at the end of 1962 all contributed to generate a climate of "Red scare" in a capitalist class composed mostly of small, first-generation entrepreneurs. The 1969 *autunno caldo* must have been seen as the beginning of a full-fledged revolution.

19. Repressive responses were more likely among managers, particularly high-level managers, in firms based on traditional technology, located in the South, and characterized by previous low levels of conflict and paternalistic labor relations.

20. Many Italian employers' surveys, from Farneti onward, adopted Bendix's seminal classification of entrepreneurs: founders, heirs, and managers (Farneti, 1970; Arvati, 1975; Martinelli, 1977; Urbani, 1977a).

21. *Corriere della Sera*, Friday, March 13, 1970.

22. For other similar episodes, see Miata et al., 1970, pp. 71–2, 73–4, 86–7.

23. The available surveys showed that Italian employers had higher-than-average levels of education (Farneti, 1970, p. 79; Arvati, 1975, pp. 82–92; Martinelli, 1977, pp. 323, 349; Urbani, 1977a, p. 380). The educational level among entrepreneurs linearly increased with firm size, from elementary school and junior high school in firms with 1–19 employees to a college degree in the larger firms (>100 employees) (Martinelli, 1977, pp. 323, 349; Urbani, 1977a, p. 380). Managers had higher educational credentials, and so did heirs. Education typically was related to more liberal attitudes.

24. On the distribution of founders and managers by firm size, see the surveys of Piedmontese entrepreneurs (Farneti, 1970, p. 42), of Liguria entrepreneurs (Arvati, 1975, p. 108), and of Salerno entrepreneurs (Bonazzi et al., 1972, p. 318). Bagnasco and Trigilia's comparative study (1984, 1985) of two industrial districts also showed that small entrepreneurs were more likely than larger ones to view labor relations in their firms negatively, despite the fact the workers struck much less often in smaller firms (Trigilia, 1986, p. 232).

25. Except for the very large firms, particularly the ones working under the Marshall Plan, in the 1950s and 1960s, as we saw in Chapter 7.

26. 23% less frequent in small firms, vs. 4% in larger firms (Regalia, 1984a, p. 223). Regular meetings were more typical of the larger firms (52% vs. 23%) (Regalia, 1984a, p. 223). For similar evidence, see Squarzon (1989a) and Ronchi (1990).

27. In the Federlombarda survey, employers in firms characterized by new forms of workers' representation (notably, *consigli di fabbrica*) were more likely to express positive opinions on unions. Educated employers also were more likely to be positive (Martinelli, 1977, p. 333). Both new forms of workers' representation and educated employers were more likely to be found in larger plants. Those plants also were the most conflict-ridden plants. Nevertheless, employers in these plants expressed a more positive evaluation of unions.

28. For an analysis of employers' reactions to the charter, see Martinelli (1978, pp. 63–8).
29. As of 1983. The lowest moment was yet to come.
30. Of course, on condition that they would behave within reason; Talamo (1979, p. 106). According to a 1984 Federmeccanica survey, 81% of employers and managers in the metalworking industry believed that unions were useful for the management of labor inside the plant (Mortillaro, 1986, p. 191). That number, however, was linearly related to plant size: 71% of respondents in firms with less than 100 employees, 84% of respondents in the 101–500 size class, and 89% of respondents in larger plants. Incidentally, that Italian employers in the early 1970s should have viewed unions favorably in the midst of the highest levels of conflict in Italian labor history only seems to confirm the skeptical views of the revolutionary potential of unions outlined in Chapter 7, paradoxically, even of unions, such as the Italian ones, that had maintained the language and rhetoric of class.
31. The typical generic name for the Lombardy entrepreneur.
32. To my knowledge, the first systematic survey of employers' attitudes was by Farneti (1970), with interviews conducted in 1966–67. Many more followed, by Bonazzi et al. (1972), Federindustria Liguria (Guerci, 1975), IDOM (Bratina and Martinelli, 1978), Federazione Regionale fra le Associazioni Industriali dalla Lombardia, 1977, Giovani Imprenditori (Pastorino and Ragazzoni, 1980), and Confindustria Censis (1989). See also Bagnasco and Trigilia's research in the industrial districts of Bassano del Grappa and Valdelsa (Bagnasco and Trigilia, 1984, 1985; Trigilia, 1986).
33. Even in 1988, however, 20.7% of entrepreneurs denied any social role for entrepreneurs (Confindustria-Censis, 1989, pp. 77–8). The figure was around 40% for entrepreneurs with only an elementary school diploma (typically small entrepreneurs), and only 16% for those with college degrees.
34. The 1983 Federmeccanica survey confirmed that employers were not very willing to share their power. Only 10% of the employers interviewed would have been willing to seek unions' collaboration at the cost of sharing some power, in order to get out of an economic crisis (Mortillaro, 1984, p. 202).
35. For instance, Italsider, 1970, Dalmine and Breda Siderurgica, 1971, and later at Terni, Asgen, Ansaldo Meccanica Nucleare, and CMI; see Speranza (1977) and Segatori and Torresini (1979 p. 18). For an in-depth analysis of the Italsider–Bagnoli experience, see Pipan and Salerni (1975, pp. 70–9) and Segatori and Torresini (1979, pp. 39–64).
36. The V skill level remained a ceiling for blue-collar workers.
37. Dell'Aringa (1976, pp. 66–7, 81–3); Pipan and Salerni (1975, p. 106); Segatori and Torresini (1979, p. 18).
38. The actual outcome in each firm reflected the diverse interests represented in the firm: whether technical engineers or personnel officers controlled change, the level of class struggle between workers and management, the level of intraclass struggle among workers over the terms of the distribution of the work force in the skill levels.
39. When the company set the rotation system, it often did so with "political" criteria. At FIAT, the firm tended to not move around the most loyal workers, but kept moving the most militant ones (Bulgarelli, 1978, p. 120). Sometimes, internal mobility was used to prevent a worker from being upgraded to a higher skill level. A certain number of continuous months on a job were necessary in order to be eligible for promotion (Bulgarelli, 1978, p. 119).
40. Pipan and Salerni (1975, p. 119); Bulgarelli (1978, pp. 66, 115–6, 125–6); Viale (1978, p. 246); Graziosi (1979, p. 37).
41. Management often took groups of militants from two departments and exchanged them, mixing them with loyal workers.
42. It was precisely for its compatibility with the basic egalitarian values expressed by the 1968–72 strike wave that the *inquadramento unico* (IU) may have seemed like a

workers' demand (Pipan and Salerni, 1975, p. 96). The official union line was that the IU was a synthesis of the issues in the 1968–72 strike wave, the culmination of workers' struggles for equality (e.g., Speranza, 1977, p. 214). But as Pipan and Salerni argued, the IU was a contract demand elaborated by the unions and sold to the workers, independently of any push from the state, employers, or workers (Pipan and Salerni, 1975, pp. 95–7) – so much so that the origins of the IU dated back to the 1966 metalworkers' contract, when it did not pass.

43. Pipan and Salerni (1975, p. 107) summarized the unions' interest in the IU in the following four points: (1) centralize plant-level bargaining; (2) limit the cost of the renewal without losing the movement; (3) consolidate the national level of bargaining; (4) set a new equilibrium between the old (skilled workers) and the new (unskilled workers) in the union organization itself. CISL–FIM (in particular, the Milan FIM) supported the unskilled workers' demands for equality; CGIL–FIOM supported the skilled workers' line (Pipan and Salerni, 1975, pp. 107–12).

44. Small and medium firms opposed the IU. They had nothing to gain from it, as they could already count on all the mobility they needed (Pipan and Salerni, 1975, p. 115).

45. Incidentally, parity between manual and clerical workers was only partially achieved in the 1973 metalworkers' contract (Pipan and Salerni, 1975, p. 114).

46. Segatori and Torresini (1979, pp. 20, 23, 46, 70); for an analysis of the views of foremen, see Segatori and Torresini (1979, pp. 46–7, 55).

47. *Mobilità esterna* or external mobility, i.e., layoffs.

48. The increase in the number of layoffs was not due simply to the 1964–67 recession. In fact, layoffs increased much earlier than labor market conditions and the overall state of the economy worsened (toward the end of 1963). The unemployment rate continued to decrease until the end of 1963. Capacity utilization, after the decrease in 1960–IV and 1961–I due to strike activity, attained a historical peak in 1961–IV. Despite another trough in 1963–I, again related to strike activity, capacity utilization remained at historically high levels until the end of 1963.

49. On employers' reactions to the *autunno caldo*, see Borgomeo and Forbice (1970), Miata et al. (1970), and Treu (1972).

50. Incidentally, the negative trend in the various measures of layoffs underscores the limits of the interpretation of the econometric coefficients of the layoff variable that I offered in Chapter 6 (Table 6.6, p. 225). Do those coefficients really say that the higher the number of layoffs in one year, the lower the level of strike activity, however measured? Or, in light of the negative trend for various measures of layoffs and the positive trend for the various measures of strike activity, do the econometric coefficients simply say that in the long run, layoffs went down, while strike activity went up? Or do they say that both strikes and layoffs increased at two historical moments, but because layoffs increased after strikes, the relationship is negative? Again, in econometric models, we have only one coefficient to measure relationships that potentially can be different at different frequency bands. In this book, I have dealt with the problems that arise from the use of trended variables by eliminating trend via first or fourth differencing. In recent years, the theory of econometrics has pursued that line of inquiry making available tests of integration for series in a model characterized by different trends (see the collections of seminal contributions in Engle and Granger, 1991; see also Charemza and Deadman, 1992, pp. 116–71).

51. On the relationship between workers' layoffs and the Workers' Charter, see Lazerson (1988).

52. See Reyneri (1989a, p. 360). For a provocative analysis of unemployment in the late 1970s and 1980s, see Accornero and Carmignani (1986).

53. De Benedetti, Olivetti's chairman of the board, at a conference in 1976 (Bulgarelli, 1978, p. 19).

54. *Il Sole 24 Ore*, a newspaper owned by Confindustria (Bulgarelli, 1978, p. 19).
55. De Benedetti, in an article in *La Stampa*, a newspaper owned by the Agnelli family (Bulgarelli, 1978, p. 21).
56. *Il Sole 24 Ore* (Bulgarelli, 1978, p. 31).
57. That was the so-called *cassa integrazione guadagni ordinaria* (ordinary CIG).
58. The new 1975 CIG agreement between the unions and Confindustria, and law no.164 of the same year, extended the application and the wage coverage of CIG and shifted onto the state the burden of cost. The 1975 CIG agreement and law implemented four main points: (1) Workers under CIG would get 80% of gross salary and 93% of net salary. (2) The cost of CIG was shifted mostly onto the state, which would provide 20 billion lire per year. (3) All firms would contribute 1% or .75% of their total wage bill, depending on firm size (>50 workers, <50); furthermore, firms that used CIG would pay an extra 8% (4% for smaller firms) during the periods CIG was in use. (4) Firms undergoing restructuring could use CIG for an unlimited time (Bulgarelli, 1978, p. 13).

    Big business was behind the CIG agreement and the *scala mobile* agreement. Small firms were hostile to the new CIG agreement. After all, they had no problems with mobility, internal or external, and yet they would have to pay the .75% (Bulgarelli, 1978, p. 17). Once again, that emphasized the rift between big business and small business in Italy.
59. Incidentally, the plot of the number of hours covered by CIG (Figure 8.6) also confirms the depth of the recession caused by the restrictive monetary and fiscal policies of the 1970s (Valli, 1976, p. 84).
60. For those data, see Barca and Magnani (1989, p. 149). The data refer to medium and large plants (with more than 200 employees in manufacturing industries excluding clothing, leather and shoes, and woodworking) (Barca and Magnani, 1989, p. 148).
61. In the Fondazione's study, large firms were defined as operating on budgets above 500 million lire; medium-size firms had budgets between 100 and 500 million lire.
62. The initial higher levels among indebtedness in 1968 of medium-size firms, as compared with large firms, confirm the well-known difficulties of smaller firms in self-financing.
63. Regardless of the good or bad intentions of individual capitalists, the bottom line was always profitability (Sabel, 1982, p. 213; Villa, 1986. p. 195).
64. See also Graziosi (1979, pp. 119–22).
65. The introduction of robots was a general characteristic of large Italian manufacturing complexes seeking to achieve greater flexibility (Barca and Magnani, 1989, p. 126).
66. On the technical properties of the Robogate system, see Becchi Collidà and Negrelli (1986, pp. 215–20).
67. Namely, the use of robots installed along a more traditional assembly line; see Becchi Collidà and Negrelli (1986, p. 220) and Locke and Negrelli (1989, p. 70).
68. Bagnasco and Trigilia (1984. p. 160) found that in the area of Bassano, none of the work force was classified in the apprentice category; 3.0% were apprentices in the firms with 51–200 employees, compared with 7.9% in firms with 11–50 employees, and 18.5% in the very small firms employing fewer than 10 people. Brusco (1975, p. 214) found that in the Bergamo area, close to 50% of workers in firms with 1–9 employees were classified as apprentices. On that issue, see also Centro Studi Federlibro (1974, p. 164).
69. That was particularly true for younger workers and women. Close to 50% of the firms surveyed by Giovani Imprenditori had rates of labor turnover between 9% and 14% (Pastorino and Ragazzoni, 1980, pp. 97–8).
70. In Bagnasco and Trigilia's study (1984, p. 160) of Bassano, the percentages of skilled workers by firm size were as follows: 6.2%, <10; 14.6%, 11–50, 13.4%, 51–200; 19.3%, >200. For similar findings in the Bergamo area, see Brusco (1975, p. 214).

71. For some evidence of that uneven distribution of wages in small firms, see Bagnasco and Trigilia (1984, p. 170). It should also be noted that many of the unskilled workers would not have been able to find jobs in larger factories (because they were recent immigrants, because they did not have minimum educational credentials, because they were not mobile, especially married women, and because there were no large factories in the area). Thus, productive decentralization expanded wage relations and provided new opportunities for income (Brusco, 1982).
72. According to the 1984 Federmeccanica survey, large firms were more likely to comply with the unions' egalitarian policies of collective skill upgrading: 89% of large firms (>500 workers) never promoted workers on an individual basis, and 55% of smaller firms (<100) never did (Mortillaro, 1986, p. 199).
73. See, in particular, Brusco (1975) and Fuà (1976).
74. For a review of those surveys, see Capecchi (1978, p. 51).
75. Brusco (1975, pp. 38, 225); see also Capecchi (1978, p. 51) and Mortillaro (1984, p. 116).
76. Contini (1979, p. 86); see also Valcamonici (1977, p. 174) and Barca and Magnani (1989).
77. On the European employers' strategies in search of labor market flexibility in the 1970s and 1980s, see Boyer (1988).
78. As a sign of the changing attitude of the Left toward small firms, see the symposium jointly organized in Milan in 1974 by the Gramsci Institute and Cespe, the Communist Party research institute, on the issue of small and medium firms in the Italian economy (Istituto Gramsci and Cespe, 1975).
79. See the significant title *Piccola azienda, grande sfruttamento*, by Centro Studi Federlibro (1974).
80. For example, in Beccalli's study, firms were classified as small (<500 employees), medium (500–1,000), and large (>1,000) (Beccalli, 1971, p. 98). In Romagnoli's study, firms were classified as small (15–499 employees), small-medium (500–999), medium-large (1,000–2,999), and large (>3,000) (Romagnoli, 1971, p. 61).
81. Those services were highly emphasized during unionization drives. The increase in union membership among the elderly during the 1970s and 1980s was due to the expansion of union services.
82. According to a 1985 survey of 585 members of the Milan CISL union, 60% of the members had used those services (77% satisfactorily), particularly assistance in individual disputes with employers (La Valle, 1987).
83. To be sure, not all of the small firms in the area of decentralized production were sweatshops. Many were backyard operations using equipment often owned by larger capitalists, and the family members, particularly peasant families, worked long hours; for examples, see Pastorino and Ragazzoni (1980, p.109). But others relied on equipment almost as sophisticated as the equipment found in the large factories, particularly computers and numerical-control equipment. The Bergamo FLM survey showed that although smaller firms (1–10 employees) were much more likely to be characterized by manual technology, they were far from being sites of backward technology (Brusco, 1975, pp. 54–5; 1982). In fact, according to a union analysis of the printing industry in the Verona area, smaller firms, having been born more recently, were more likely to have the latest technologies (Centro Studi Federlibro, 1974, 125–88). A study commissioned by Giovani Imprenditori on a sample of 43 firms with 30–200 employees similarly found some cases of small firms using numerical-control machines and no cases of firms using the assembly line (Pastorino and Ragazzoni, 1980, pp. 108, 110). A 1983 Federmeccanica survey provided information on production technologies used by firms in three size classes (0–100, 101–500, >500 employees). Thus, the Federmeccanica data did not allow me to assess the

technological level of small firms (1–20, 1–50). However, according to the survey, 9% of the firms in the 1–100 size class used robots in their production processes (compared with18% in the larger size class); 48% (vs. 45%) used automatic numerical-control machines, and 24% (vs. 27%) used computer-regulated technologies (Mortillaro, 1984, p. 121; 1986, pp. 174–6).

Thus, although we did see plenty of evidence in Chapter 6 in support of the Doeringer and Piore (1971) claim about secondary labor markets characterized by lower wages (although not uniformly for all wage categories) and poorer benefits, there was little evidence in favor of Doeringer and Piore's other claim of the secondary market characterized by slow growth, low productivity, and obsolete technology. During the 1970s, the area of decentralized production in Italy (particularly Bagnasco's *Terza Italia*) was the most vital part of the economy.

Conventional wisdom has it that smaller firms are structurally weaker; small entrepreneurs cannot afford to be generous with their workers, as they eke out a meager living, always on the brink of bankruptcy. A 1972 yearly report by the Unione Regionale delle Camere di Commercio del Veneto best expressed that view: "Craft firms are characterized by low levels of capital investment per worker and a clear prevalence of the human factor. When the cost of labor increases, it is difficult to recover in terms of productivity; furthermore, the levels of in-house financing are generally limited" (Centro Studi Federlibro, 1974, p. 63). That may well be, and the higher rate of bankruptcies among small businesses would seem to confirm that view. But certainly, small entrepreneurs, regardless of whether or not they could afford to be generous, could get away with not being generous. In fact, one thing is clear: by and large, those firms were outside of union control. The vitality of those firms was based on their flexible use of the work force and their ability to hire and fire in response to the vagaries of the market, to pay lower- and higher-than-contracted wages, and to avoid social security payments (often in collusion with the workers themselves, e.g., in the case of workers under the CIG from larger firms or retired workers).

84. According to Piven and Cloward (1979, p. 9), it is precisely the characteristics (mass disruption) and the effects (concessions and institutionalization) of mass mobilization that constitute the most salient aspects of mobilization. Contrary to Piven and Cloward's view of such movements, however, the Italian 1968–72 strike wave was at least partly in the hands of powerful, formal labor organizations (the unions, the Communist Party). But in agreement with Piven and Cloward's interpretation, much of the original disruption caused by the movement did not arise from those formal organizations, but from organizations that were at the periphery of the labor movement (e.g., extraparliamentary groups) or that were born during the struggle (e.g., CUB).
85. For a summary of the various "long-wave" positions, see Kotz (1987, 1990); for a lengthier treatment, see Goldstein (1988).
86. Screpanti (1987, p. 111); for further comparative evidence see Boll (1985).
87. According to Mandel (1980), technological innovation is characterized by a cyclical pattern closely related to both the Kondratieff cycle and strike cycle. On the long waves of technological innovation, see Hartman and Wheeler (1979); for periodizations similar to Mandel's four stages of the historical forms of organization of production (craft, machinist, assembly line, continuous flow), see Touraine (1955, 1966). On the relationships involving mode of production in the workplace, forms of labor control, and forms of working-class organization and struggle, see Foster (1974) and Burawoy (1984).
88. On Fordism as a sociotechnical mode of production, see Aglietta (1979), Lipietz (1987), and Sabel (1982).
89. For a comparative evaluation of the views on long waves for different authors, see Kotz (1987).

Chapter 9   The picture in the puzzle

1. On the history of *centro-sinistra*, the government coalition that included the Socialist Party, see Tamburrano (1971); see also Kogan (1966) and Salvati (1976, pp. 241–9).
2. The union presence in public institutions in Italy has a long history, dating as far back as the beginning of the twentieth century (e.g., management of workers' retirement funds, price control, labor-market control); for a brief history, see Roccella (1979) and Ferrari (1979, pp. 55–7).
3. Not surprisingly, 17% of the union personnel felt that the public body in which they were involved was absolutely irrelevant (another 9.4%, rarely relevant) (Ferrari, 1979, p. 76). What is surprising, instead, is the fact that 50.6% of the union personnel involved reported that their unions never inquired about the outcome of their work in those institutions (Ferrari, 1979, p. 93). There appears to have been both a great disinterest on the part of the unions as organizations in their presence in public institutions and great personal commitment by the individuals involved (Ferrari, 1979, p. 102).
4. To better understand the relationship between trend and cycle, let me borrow an example from meteorology. Suppose we have minute-by-minute recordings of temperatures between 1 a.m. and 1 p.m. for a summer day, with the data showing an increasing trend from 50 to 100 degrees Fahrenheit. If one were to regard those increases as a long-term trend, by 10 a.m. one would be inclined to recommend one's soul to the Lord, to perform a rain dance, or to dig a cool cave in the backyard, depending on one's inclination. No one, however, mistakes daily temperature cycles for trends. Neither does anyone make that mistake in considering the rising daily temperatures between the months of March and July, because we are all familiar with seasonal cycles. Even these seasonal patterns are part and parcel of longer temperature cycles (the interglacial periods). To mistake daily temperatures for seasonal temperatures or, worse yet, for glacial temperatures would be to look at temperature through a very restricted time window.
5. See Gordon's "Up and Down the Long Roller Coaster" (1978).
6. As Dahrendorf (1959, pp. 253–4) wrote, "For the emergence of social conflicts the standard of living of their participants is in principle irrelevant, for conflicts are ultimately generated by relations of authority, i.e., by the differentiation of dominating and subjected groups. Even if every worker owns a car, a house, and whatever other comforts of civilization there are, the root of industrial class conflict is not only not eliminated, but hardly touched. . . . Social conflict is as universal as the relations of authority and imperatively coordinated associations, for it is the distribution of authority that provides the basis and cause of its occurrence."
7. On convergence, see Aron (1967) and Kerr et al. (1960); see also Kerr's recent return to the argument (Kerr, 1983).
8. For an analysis of the changing optimal mix of the factors of production for Italian employers, see Heimler and Milana (1982).
9. A social process "limits" another social process by constraining the array of possible outcomes, by making certain outcomes more or less likely than others. For instance, large-scale Communist parties, as forms of the political organization of the working class, have a very low probability of being associated with primitive forms of capital accumulation. Similarly, land-occupation movements, as forms of class struggle, cannot exist unless the peasantry occupies relevant positions in the class structure. "Transformation" refers to the capacity of a social process to change another one. It is this particular mode of determination that brings about change in the system. Thus, the class struggle transforms both the organization of production and the class structure.

Think, for instance, of the limiting case in which a successful revolution subverts existing social relations of production, sets up new ones, and changes the class structure (e.g., by eliminating certain classes).
10. On "selection" as a form of double limitation, see Wright (1979, 17–18).
11. On the relationship involving the mode of production in the workplace, factory regimes, and forms of organizations and struggles, see Foster (1974), Hanagan (1980), and Burawoy (1984, 1985).
12. The "bearers of conflict," as Italian scholars on the left refer to them.
13. On the relationship between class structure and class conflict, see Hyman's (1978) excellent essay.
14. On class formation, see the collection of essays in Katznelson and Zolberg (1986); see also Kocka (1983).
15. Rather than the *classic* view, perhaps one should talk about a vulgar or popularized version of classes, particularly in conservative scholarship. Although it is true that Marx proposed a dichotomous view of classes in his political writings (e.g., *The Communist Manifesto*), the treatment of the nuances of intraclass interests and alliances transpires from Marx's own more historical work (e.g., *The Eighteenth Brumaire of Louis Bonaparte*, *The Class Struggle in France*).
16. On Marxist theories of the state, see Poulantzas (1969), Offe (1975), Offe and Ronge (1975), Block (1977), Jessop (1982).
17. As we saw in Chapter 6, Korpi (1974) attempted to link economic and political models in his "balance of power" model, where a variety of social factors (economic, institutional, or political) can change the overall balance of power between classes.
18. The accuracy of forecasting depends on the length of the historical series (how far back we have information), the length of the forecast horizon (how far ahead we want to predict the future), and the forecasting method.
19. For the analyses, see Franzosi (1980).
20. For the Italian case, see Franzosi (1992).
21. On the crucial events at Fiat between 1979 and 1980, see Becchi Collidà and Negrelli (1986, pp. 167–75) and Mattina (1981).
22. On the Alfa-Romeo survey see Mangiarotti and Rossi (1974, pp. 128, 131, 135); on the Isvet surveys see Buratto et al. (1974, p. 210) and De Masi et al. (1985, p. 815).
23. Given the greater adherence of unionized workers to union policies, the rift likely would be much larger among nonunionized workers.
24. *Decentramento produttivo* further split the Italian working class: between those employed in the primary and secondary labor markets, between those who had job guarantees and higher wages and those who could not even enter the market. Furthermore, in the secondary market, a handful of skilled workers got paid twice as much as their fellow factory workers, but most took home only one-third (Brusco, 1982, p. 174; Sabel, 1982, p. 228).
25. Similarly, the flourishing of the underground economy was viewed positively by even those workers who fared worse in that system (e.g., older immigrant women, or worker-peasants). The worsening of economic conditions probably would leave those people without jobs and no possibility of finding jobs in the primary market, because of their skill and demographic characteristics (Brusco, 1982, p. 175).
26. For an introduction to the state of Italian labor relations during the years of "flexible specialization," see Wolleb (1988), and Negrelli and Santi (1990); for a comparative analysis of labor relations in the 1980s, see Baglioni and Crouch (1990); for a general treatment of the problem of labor-market flexibility, see Boyer (1988).
27. Among firms with more than 500 workers, an average of three times as many workers in CIG with respect to firms with 20–99 workers (Barca and Magnani, 1989, p. 131).

28. It was that component of unemployment that led to the "unemployment explosion" of the late 1970s and 1980s (Reyneri, 1989a, p. 360).
29. For the figures in this paragraph, see Reyneri (1989a, pp. 370–1).
30. Worker surveys, as well, confirmed the changed balance of class forces. In Bagnasco and Trigilia's study (1984, pp. 217, 237), the majority of workers believed that trade-union strength and ability to protect workers' interests had diminished in recent years (from around 40% to 25%).
31. On the other hand, I have argued that strikes are cyclical phenomena, going up and down with the business cycle, the structure of collective bargaining, and the political position of labor in the power structure. I have argued that even strike waves, the most momentous manifestations of working-class protest, appear to be recurrent phenomena, the product of the structural unfolding of industrialized capitalist economies. We encounter strike waves somewhat equally spaced at some fifty-year intervals. Every fifty years, we encounter workers willing to engage in collective actions, giving social scientists good material to ponder over "the free rider problem." Every fifty odd years, we encounter an increasing number of workers willing to pluck up their courage for little individual acts of daily heroism. It is then that an anonymous activist at the Candy large-appliance plant would rebuke his employer, Mr. Fumagalli, with these words: "Who was it that gave you the factory? You come here and tell us that we are a great big family, but you are the one who stashes away the millions, and people leave their hands in here" (quoted in Regini, 1974, p. 31). It is then that Pasquale De Stefani, a Fiat worker, would challenge his boss and "every morning, around eight o' clock . . . would stop working for about twenty minutes and eat a sandwich" (Polo, 1989, p. 130).
32. First, data may not be available consistently for all series over the entire sample period under consideration (e.g., for Italy, strike data are available for the period 1950–78, unemployment-rate data for the 1959–78 period, and layoff data for the 1954–72 period). The econometric requirement that model estimation be done in such a way that each variable in the model is measured over the same sample period may shorten the sample period to the point that the available number of observations will be too small to provide efficient parameter estimates.

Second, data may be available for different variables at different levels of aggregation (monthly, quarterly, yearly, biannually). Statistical estimation of a fully specified model (i.e., with all the variables included in the model) would require using data at the highest level of aggregation. On the one hand, that would further reduce the available sample size. Yearly observations over a ten-year period would provide a sample size of 10 observations; with quarterly observations over the same time period, the sample size would be 40. On the other hand, that would result in loss of information. Nothing could be said about short-term, seasonal behavior on the basis of yearly data. Loss of empirical information may have theoretical consequences if the model prescribes a level of aggregation (e.g., quarterly) lower than that afforded by the available data (e.g., yearly). Typically, we solve the problem of sample size and estimation efficiency by estimating our models over sample periods as long as possible. The problem with that solution is that history is just as much about change as it is about continuity. A good historical analysis needs to identify the points of break and change. We need to identify the historical periods in which given relations hold.

Third, data may not be available at all for some relevant variables. The abundant scholarly production of strike research dealing with labor-market or business-cycle effects on strike activity has depended, to a large extent, on the ready availability of macroeconomic series since early days. But noneconomic factors are also at work – perhaps not as readily quantifiable, but nonetheless present. For instance, resource-mobilization models claim that repression reduces the likelihood of collective action (e.g., strikes), because repression raises the cost of collective action (Tilly, 1978, p.

100). Yet, given the difficulties of collecting empirical evidence, strike models rarely include measures of repression.

The more complex the model (e.g., multiple-equation models), the larger the number of variables involved, and the greater the difficulty of assembling a data set with the proper (i.e., theoretically relevant) level of aggregation, sample period, and variables.

Appendix

1. On these issues, see Turner (1969); on the more general issue of the reliability of strike data, see Benetti and Regini (1976), Shalev's brilliant piece (1978), and Franzosi (1985).
2. It will also bias all the indicators derived from the number of strikers and number of hours lost: size, volume, and duration.
3. This is particularly true if management is negotiating the company's sale (e.g., Reyneri, 1974a, p. 163); on the social definition of strikes, see Batstone et al. (1978).
4. For an assessment of the reliability of strike data, see Shalev's (1978) brilliant piece; see also Franzosi (1985).
5. There is also another reason why the two series differ. Salerni's data refer to the number of individual work stoppages. As I pointed out, ISTAT's data refer to the number of conflicts, each conflict aggregating all work stoppages over the same issue.
6. On the availability of international strike data, see Fisher (1973).
7. For a comparative exploratory analysis of standardized and unstandardized strike indicators in postwar Italy, see Franzosi (1980).
8. For a critique of the various sources of wages in Italy, see Malfatti and Mariani (1972).
9. Including the day of the beginning of the crisis and excluding the ending day. Data on the beginning date of Italian governments are reported in Beyme (1985, pp. 394–5). However, there are many inaccuracies with Beyme's data.
10. On newspapers as sources of socio-historical data, see Franzosi (1987).

Bibliography

Abbatecola, Giuseppe. 1974. "Dalmine." Pp. 25–105, in Alessandro Pizzorno (ed.), *Lotte operaie e sindacato in Italia: 1968–1972, Dalmine, Falck, Redaelli*. Bologna: Il Mulino.
Abbott, Andrew. 1991. "History and Sociology: The Lost Synthesis." *Social Science History*, Vol. 15, No. 2, pp. 201–38.
Abrate, Mario. 1967. *La lotta sindacale nella industrializzazione in Italia 1906–1926*. Milan: Franco Angeli.
Accornero, Aris. 1959. *Fiat confino. Storia dell'Ors*. Milan: Avanti!
    1971. "Le lotte operaie negli anni '60." *Quaderni di rassegna sindacale*, Vol. 9, No. 31/32, pp. 113–38.
    1973. *Gli anni '50 in fabbrica, con un diario di Commissione Interna*. Bari: De Donato.
    1974. "Le strutture di base negli anni '50." *Quaderni di rassegna sindacale*, Vol. 12, No. 49, pp. 84–121.
    1976. "Per una nuova fase di studi sul movimento sindacale." Pp. 1–108, in Aris Accornero (ed.), *Movimento sindacale e società italiana*. Milan: Feltrinelli.
    1981. "Sindacato e rivoluzione sociale." *Laboratorio politico, Il sindacato nella crisi*, Vol. 1, No. 4, pp. 5–34.
    1985. "La 'terziarizzazione' del conflitto e i suoi effetti." Pp. 275–341, in Gian Primo Cella and Marino Regini (eds.), *Il conflitto industriale in Italia. Stato della ricerca e ipotesi sulle tendenze*. Bologna: Il Mulino.
    1992. *La parabola del sindacato*. Bologna: Il Mulino.
Accornero, Aris, Giovanni Alasia, Giuseppe Dozzo, and Domenico Tarizzo. 1960. *La scatola di cemento*. Rome: Editori Riuniti.
Accornero, Aris, and Alessandro Cardulli. 1974. "1970. La spinta dell'autunno: delegati e riforme." *Quaderni di rassegna sindacale*, Vol. 12, No. 51, pp. 11–43.
Accornero, Aris, and Fabrizio Carmignani. 1978a. "Classe operaia e modificazioni nella struttura sociale." Pp. 49–103, in Gabriella Pinnarò (ed.), *L'Italia socio-economica, 1976–77*. Rome: Editori Riuniti.
    1978b. "La 'giungla' delle retribuzioni." Pp. 104–33, in Gabriella Pinnarò (ed.), *L'Italia socio-economica, 1976-77*. Rome: Editori Riuniti.
    1986. *I paradossi della disoccupazione*. Bologna: Il Mulino.
Accornero, Aris, Renato Mannheimer, and Chiara Sebastiani (eds.). 1983. *L'identità comunista. I militanti, le strutture, la cultura del PCI*. Rome: Editori Riuniti.
Accornero, Aris, and Vittorio Rieser. 1981. *Il mestiere dell'avanguardia. Riedizione di "FIAT confino" di Aris Accornero*. Bari: De Donato.
ACLI. 1953. *La classe lavoratrice si difende*. Milan: Associazioni Cristiani Lavoratori Italiani.
Addario, Nicolò. 1976. *Inchiesta sulla condizione dei lavoratori in fabbrica (1955)*. Turin: Einaudi.

Agger, Ben. 1989. *Reading Science: A Literary, Political, and Sociological Analysis.* Dix Hills, N.Y.: General Hall, Inc.

Aglietta, Michel. 1979. *A Theory of Capitalist Regulation: The U.S. Experience.* London: Verso.

Aglietta, Roberto, Giuseppe Bianchi, and Pietro Merli Brandini. 1970. *I delegati operai.* Rome: Edizioni Coines

Aguet, Jean Pierre. 1954. *Contributions à l'histoire du mouvement ouvrier français: Les grèves sous la monarchie de Juillet (1830–1847).* Geneva: Droz.

Alasia, Franco, and Danilo Montaldi. 1960. *Milano, Corea – Inchiesta sugli immigrati.* Milan: Feltrinelli.

Albanese, L., Fernando Liuzzi, and Alessandro Perella. 1973. *I consigli di fabbrica.* Rome: Editori Riuniti.

Alberoni, Francesco, and Guido Baglioni. 1965. *L'integrazione dell'immigrato nella società industriale.* Bologna: Il Mulino.

Alinari, Luigi. 1979. "Il ruolo economico del sindacato in Italia: 1943–1978." Unpublished thesis, Facoltà di Scienze Politiche, University of Florence.

Allen, Kevin, and Andrew Stevenson. 1974. *An Introduction to the Italian Economy.* London: Martin Robertson.

Allum, P. A. 1973. *Italy. Republic Without Government?* New York: Norton.

Almon, Shirley. 1965. "The Distributed Lag Between Capital Appropriations and Expenditures." *Econometrica*, Vol. 33, No. 1, pp. 178–96.

Alquati, Romano. 1963. "Composizione del capitale e forza lavoro all'Olivetti." *Quaderni Rossi*, Vol. No. 3, pp. 119–85.

1974. *Sindacato e partito.* Turin: Stampatori Università.

Aminzade, Ronald. 1980. "French Strike Development and Class Struggle. The Development of the Strike in Mid-Nineteenth-Century Toulouse." *Social Science History*, Vol. 4, No. 1, pp. 57–79.

1981. *Class, Politics, and Early Industrial Capitalism. A Study of Mid-Nineteenth-Century Toulouse, France.* Albany: State University of New York Press.

1984. "Capitalist Industrialization and Patterns of Industrial Protest: A Comparative Urban Study of Nineteenth-Century France." *American Sociological Review*, Vol. 49, No. 4, pp. 437–53.

Ammassari, Giuseppe, and Gianni Scaiola. 1962. "La contrattazione integrativa aziendale nel 1961." *Nuovo osservatore*, No. 2, pp. 149–62.

Amoretti, Aldo. 1981. "Problemi organizzativi del sindacato tessile," *Quaderni di rassegna sindacale*, Vol. 19, No. 88, pp. 63–78.

Anderson, T. W. 1971. *The Statistical Analysis of Time Series.* New York: Wiley.

Andreani, Edgard. 1968. *Grèves et fluctuations: la France de 1890 a 1914.* Paris: Editions Cujas.

Anscombe, F. J. 1973. "Graphs in Statistical Analysis." *The American Statistician*, Vol. 27, No. 1, pp. 17–21.

Anscombe, F. J., and John Tukey. 1963. "The Examination and Analysis of Residuals." *Technometrics*, Vol. 5, No. 2, pp. 141–60.

Antoniazzi, Sandro. 1969. "Sindacati e contestazione." *Problemi del socialismo*, Vol. 11, No. 41, pp. 671–82.

Aron, Raymond. 1967. *18 Lectures on Industrial Society.* London: Weidenfeld & Nicolson.

Arvati, Paolo. 1975. "Formazione e struttura dell'imprenditorialità." Pp. 79–113, in Carlo Maria Guerci (ed.), *La piccola e media impresa. Il caso della Liguria.* Milan: Franco Angeli.

Ascoli, Ugo. 1979. *Movimenti migratori in Italia.* Bologna: Il Mulino.

Ashenfelter, Orley, and George E. Johnson. 1969. "Bargaining Theory, Trade Unions and Industrial Strike Activity." *American Economic Review*, Vol. 59, No. 40, pp. 35–49.

Ashenfelter, Orley, George E. Johnson, and John H. Pencavel. 1972. "Trade Unions and the Rate of Change of Money Wages in United States Manufacturing Industry." *Review of Economic Studies*, Vol. 39, No. 1, pp. 27–54.
Ashenfelter, Orley, and John H. Pencavel. 1969. "American Trade Union Growth: 1900–1960." *Quarterly Journal of Economics*, Vol. 83, pp. 434–48.
Asor Rosa, Alberto. 1968. "Movimenti di lotta e partiti," *Problemi del socialismo*, Vol. 10, No. 28–9, pp. 268–78.
Associazione Industriale Lombarda (Assolombarda). 1958. *L'assenteismo da lavoro. Cinque anni di rilevazione fra gli operai dell'industria milanese.* Milan: AIL.
  1960. *Il ricambio del lavoro nel 1958.* Milan: AIL.
  1961. *Il ricambio del lavoro nel 1959.* Milan: AIL.
  1962. *Il ricambio del lavoro nel 1960.* Milan: AIL.
  1963. *Il ricambio del lavoro nel 1961.* Milan: AIL.
  1964. *Il ricambio del lavoro nelle industrie Milanesi. Risultati del 1961. Riepilogo del quinquennio 1958–1962.* Milan: AIL.
  1983. *Le relazioni industriali nelle piccole e medie imprese milanesi.* Milan: AIL.
Avanguardia Operaia. 1971. *I CUB: tre anni di lotte e di esperienze.* (Quaderni di Avanguardia Operaia, No. 4). Milan: Sapere Edizioni.
  1972. *Lotta Continua: lo spontaneismo dal mito delle masse al mito dell'organizzazione.* (Quaderni di Avanguardia Operaia, No. 5). Milan: Sapere Edizioni.
  1973a. *I Comitati Unitari di Base: origini, sviluppi, prospettive.* (Quaderni di Avanguardia Operaia, No. 6). Milan: Sapere Edizioni.
  1973b. *La configurazione della sinistra rivoluzionaria e la linea dei Marxisti-Leninisti.* (Quaderni di Avanguardia Operaia, No. 7, Part 2). Milan: Sapere Edizioni.
Baccalini, Franco, Stefano Draghi, Renata Semenza, and Sandro Sironi. 1981. "Composizione della struttura dirigente e valutazione sul ruolo e sul funzionamento dell'organizzazione sindacale – Una ricerca sui delegati ai Congressi territoriali della CGIL lombardia," *Bollettino di ricerca.* Milan: CGIL IRES Lombardia.
Baccetti, Carlo. 1987. "Memoria storica e continuità elettorale. Una zona rossa nella Toscana rossa." *Italia contemporanea*, No. 167, pp. 7–30.
Baglioni, Guido. 1963. "Rapporto fra livelli di contrattazione e grado di sindacalizzazione dei lavoratori." *Studi di sociologia*, Vol. 1, No. 1, pp. 51–7.
  1966. *Il conflitto industriale e l'azione del sindacato.* Bologna: Il Mulino.
  1971. "Sindacati e rappresentanze di fabbrica." *Quaderni di rassegna sindacale*, No. 31–2, pp. 75–93.
  1989. "Il sistema di relazioni industriali in Italia: caratteri ed evoluzione storica." Pp. 17–46, in Gian Primo Cella, and Tiziano Treu (eds.), *Relazioni industriali. Manuale per l'analisi dell'esperienza italiana.* Bologna: Il Mulino.
Baglioni, Guido, and Colin Crouch (eds.). 1990. *European Industrial Relations. The Challenge of Flexibility.* Newbury Park, CA.: SAGE.
Bagnara, Sebastiano, and Marco Diani. 1980. "Conflittualità e microconflittualità in una fabbrica del Sud." Technical report, Institute of Psychology, CNR, Rome. (also in) 1980. *Quaderni di rassegna sindacale*, Vol. 18, No. 84–5, pp. 158–72.
Bagnasco, Arnaldo. 1977. *Tre Italie. La problematica territoriale dello sviluppo italiano.* Bologna: Il Mulino.
Bagnasco, Arnaldo, and Carlo Trigilia. 1984. *Società e politica nelle aree di piccola impresa. Il caso di Bassano.* Venice: Arsenale Editrice.
  1985. *Società e politica nelle aree di piccola impresa. Il caso della Valdelsa.* Milan: Franco Angeli.
Bain, George S., and Farouk Elsheikh. 1976. *Union Growth and the Business Cycle.* Oxford: Blackwell.
Balestrini, Nanni. 1971. *Vogliamo tutto.* Milan: Feltrinelli.

Barbagli, Marzio, and Piergiorgio Corbetta. 1978. "Partito e movimento: aspetti e rinnovamento del PCI." *Inchiesta*, Vol. 8, No. 31, pp. 3–46.
  1980. "L'elettorato, l'organizzazione del PCI e i movimenti." *Il Mulino*, Vol. 29, No. 3, pp. 467–90.
Barbano, Filippo (ed.). 1987. *L'ombra del lavoro. Profili di operai in Cassa Integrazione*. Milan: Franco Angeli.
Barca, Fabrizio, and Marco Magnani. 1989. *L'industria tra capitale e lavoro. Piccole e grandi imprese dall'autunno caldo alla ristrutturazione*. Bologna: Il Mulino.
Bartlett, M. S. 1947. "The Use of Transformations." *Biometrics*, Vol. 3, No. 1, pp. 39–52.
Batstone, Eric, Ian Boraston, and Stephen Frenkel. 1978. *The Social Organization of Strikes*. Oxford: Blackwell.
  1979. *Shop Stewards in Action*. Oxford: Blackwell.
Battaglia, Filippo. 1971. "I dirigenti sindacali: alcuni dati." *Rassegna italiana di sociologia*, Vol. 12, No. 2, pp. 355–67.
Battegazzorre, Francesco. 1987. "L'instabilità di governo in Italia." *Rivista italiana di scienza politica*, Vol. 17, No. 2, pp. 285–317.
Beach, Charles M., and James G. MacKinnon. 1978. "A Maximum Likelihood Procedure for Regression with Autocorrelated Errors." *Econometrica*, Vol. 46, pp. 51–8.
Bean, R. 1985. *Comparative Industrial Relations. An Introduction to Cross-National Perspectives*. New York: St. Martin's Press.
Beccalli, Bianca. 1971. "Scioperi e organizzazione sindacale: Milano 1950–1970." *Rassegna italiana di sociologia*, Vol. 12, No. 1, pp. 83–120.
  1973. "Lotte alla Pirelli," *Quaderni Piacentini*, Vol. 12, No. 50, pp. 178–85.
  1974. "Redaelli." Pp. 211–84, in Alessandro Pizzorno (ed.), *Lotte operaie e sindacato in Italia: 1968–1972, Dalmine, Falck, Redaelli*. Bologna: Il Mulino.
Becchi Collidà, Ada. 1976. "La formazione dell'imprenditorialità pubblica: i gruppi dirigenti delle partecipazioni statali." Pp. 595–625, in Aris Accornero (ed.), *Problemi del movimento sindacale in Italia 1943–1973*. Milan: Feltrinelli.
  1989. "Le associazioni imprenditoriali." Pp. 135–54, in Gian Primo Cella and Tiziano Treu (eds.), *Relazioni industriali. Manuale per l'analisi dell'esperienza italiana*. Bologna: Il Mulino.
Becchi Collidà, Ada, and Serafino Negrelli. 1986. *La transizione nell'industria e nelle relazioni industriali: l'auto e il caso Fiat*. Milan: Franco Angeli.
Bechelloni, Giovanni. 1968. Pp. 205–48, in Mattei Dogan and Orazio Maria Petracca (eds.), *Partiti politici e strutture sociali in Italia*. Milan: Comunità.
Becker, Howard. 1967. "Whose Side Are We On?" *Social Problems*, No. 14, pp. 239–47.
Bell, Daniel. 1960. *The End of Ideology; On the Exhaustion of Political Ideas in the Fifties*. New York: Free Press.
Bellardi, Lauralba, Angela Groppi, Francesco Liso, and Elena Pisani (eds.). 1978. *Sindacati e contrattazione collettiva in Italia nel 1972–74*. Milan: Franco Angeli.
Bellardi, Lauralba, and Elena Pisani. 1978. *Sindacati e contrattazione collettiva in Italia nel 1975*. Milan: Franco Angeli.
Bellasi, Pietro, and Giovanni Pellicciari. 1972. "I Comitati Unitari di Base: Autogestione delle lotte e sociologia della partecipazione." Pp. 501–22, in Pietro Bellasi, Michele La Rosa, and Giovanni Pellicciari (eds.), *Fabbrica e società. Autogestione e partecipazione operaia in Europa*. Milan: Franco Angeli.
Belsley, A. David, Edwin Kuh, and Roy E. Welsch. 1980. *Regression Diagnostics. Identifying Influential Data and Sources of Collinearity*. New York: Wiley.
Bendix, Reinhard. 1974. *Work and Authority in Industry, Ideologies of Management in the Course of Industrialization*. Berkeley: University of California Press.

Benetti, Maurizio, and Marino Regini. 1976. "Confronti temporali e spaziali sui conflitti di lavoro." Pp. 35–85, in Pietro Alessandrini (ed.), *Conflittualità e aspetti normativi del lavoro*. Bologna: Il Mulino.
Bergamaschi, Tullia Myriam. 1977a. "Organizzazione della produzione." Pp. 165–96, in Federazione Regionale fra le Associazioni Industriali della Lombardia (ed.), *La piccola e media industria in Lombardia, Vol. 1, Relazione generale. Rapporti del gruppo di lavoro. Indagine campionaria*. Milan: Edizioni Industriali.
1977b. "Occupazione e sindacato." Pp. 225–67, in Federazione Regionale fra le Associazioni Industriali della Lombardia (ed.), *La piccola e media industria in Lombardia, Vol. 1, Relazione generale. Rapporti del gruppo di lavoro. Indagine campionaria*. Milan: Edizioni Industriali.
Berger, Suzanne. 1974. "Uso politico e sopravvivenza dei ceti in declino." Pp. 291–313, in Fabio Luca Cavazza and Stephen R. Graubard (eds.), *Il caso italiano*. Milan: Garzanti.
Berlinguer, Enrico. 1973a. "Imperialismo e coesistenza alla luce dei fatti cileni," *Rinascita*, September 28, Vol. 30, No. 38, pp. 3–4.
1973b. "Via democratica e violenza reazionaria," *Rinascita*, October 5, Vol. 30, No. 39, pp. 3–4.
1973c. "Alleanze sociali e schieramenti politici," *Rinascita*, October 12, Vol. 30, No. 40, pp. 3–5.
Bertaux, Daniel. 1981. *Biography and Society: The Life History Approach in the Social Sciences*. Beverly Hills: Sage.
Beyme, Klaus von. 1985. *Political Parties in Western Democracies*. Aldershot, England: Gower.
Bezza, Bruno. 1981. "L'esperienza contrattuale della lotta degli elettromeccanici." Pp. 71–118, in Bruno Bezza, Stefano Datola, and Roberto Gallessi (eds.), *Le lotte degli elettromeccanici*. Milan: Franco Angeli.
Biagi, Marco. 1976. "Sindacato, Statuto dei lavoratori e piccole imprese." Pp. 375–408, in Tiziano Treu (ed.), *Sindacato e magistratura nei conflitti di lavoro, Vol. 2. Lo statuto dei lavoratori: prassi sindacali e motivazioni dei giudici*. Bologna: Il Mulino.
Biagioni, Eligio, Stefania Palmieri, and Tatiana Pipan. 1980. *Indagine sul sindacato*. Rome: Editrice Sindacale Italiana.
Bianchi, Giuseppe, and Mario D'Ambrosio. 1970. "L'evoluzione della qualificazione del lavoro in Italia dal 1951 al 1968" *Quaderni ISRIL*, Vol. 1, No. 2.
Bianchi, Giuseppe, Antonella Dugo, and Umberto Martinelli, 1972. *Assenteismo, orario di lavoro e scioperi nell'industria italiana*. Milan: Franco Angeli.
Bianchi, Giuseppe, Franco Frigo, Pietro Merli Brandini, Alberto Merolla, and Mariuccia Musazzi-Cella. 1970. *Grande impresa e conflitto industriale. Ricerca su quattro casi di conflitto sindacale: FIAT, Pirelli, Mazotto, Italcantieri*. Rome: Coines.
Bishop, Robert. 1964. "A Zeuthen-Hicks Theory of Bargaining." *Econometrica*, Vol. 32, No. 3, pp. 410–7.
Blackburn, Robin, and Michael Mann. 1979. *The Working Class in the Labour Market*. London: Macmillan.
Blauner, Robert. 1964. *Alienation and Freedom*. University of Chicago Press.
Blitz, Rudolph. 1954. "Prosperity versus Strikes Reconsidered." *Industrial and Labor Relations Review*, Vol. 7, No. 4, pp. 449–51.
Bloch, Marc. 1953. *The Historian's Craft*. New York: Vintage Books.
Block, Fred. 1977. "The Ruling Class Does Not Rule." *Socialist Review*, Vol. 7, pp. 6–28.
Bobbio, Luigi. 1979. *Lotta Continua. Storia di una organizzazione rivoluzionaria*. Rome: Savelli; reprinted in 1988 as *Storia di Lotta Continua*. Milan: Feltrinelli.
Bocca, Giorgio. 1980. *I signori dello sciopero*. Milan: Longanesi.

Boddy, Raford, and James Crotty. 1975. "Class Conflict and Macro-Policy: The Political Business Cycle." *Review of Radical Political Economics*, Vol. 7, No. 1, pp. 1–17.

Boll, Friedhelm. 1985. "International Strike Waves: A Critical Assessment." Pp. 78–99, in Wolfgang J. Mommsen and Hans-Gerhard Husung (eds.), *The Development of Trade Unionism in Great Britain and Germany, 1880–1914*. London: Allen & Unwin.

Bonazzi, Giuseppe, Arnaldo Bagnasco, and Salvatore Casillo. 1972. *L'organizzazione della marginalità. Industria e potere politico in una provincia meridionale*. Turin: LI/ED L'impresa Edizioni.

Bordogna, Lorenzo. 1985. "Tendenze neo-corporatiste e trasformazioni del conflitto industriale. L'esperienza negli anni Settanta e primi anni Ottanta." Pp. 173–202, in Gian Primo Cella and Marino Regini (eds.), *Il conflitto industriale in Italia. Stato della ricerca e ipotesi sulle tendenze*. Bologna: Il Mulino.

Bordogna, Lorenzo, and Giancarlo Provasi. 1979. "Il movimento degli scioperi in Italia (1881–1973)." Pp. 169–304, in Gian Primo Cella (ed.), *Il movimento degli scioperi nel XX secolo*. Bologna: Il Mulino.

Borgomeo, L., and Aldo Forbice (eds.). 1970. *14000 denunce*. Rome: Stasind.

Bowles, Samuel, David Gordon, and Thomas Weisskopf. 1983. *Beyond the Wasteland: A Democratic Alternative to Economic Decline*. Garden City, N.Y.: Anchor Press/Doubleday.

Box, George, and Gwilym Jenkins. 1970. *Time Series Analysis. Forecasting and Control*. San Francisco: Holden-Day.

Box, George E. P., and Paul W. Tidwell. 1962. "Transformation of the Independent Variables." *Technometrics*, Vol. 4, No. 4, pp. 531–50.

Boyer, Robert. 1979. "Wage Formation in Historical Perspective: The French Experience." *Cambridge Journal of Economics*, Vol. 3, pp. 99–118.

1987. *Technical Change and the Theory of Regulation*. Paris: CEPREMAP, No. 8707.

1988. *The Search for Labour Market Flexibility. The European Economies in Transition*. Oxford: Clarendon Press.

Bratina, Darko, and Alberto Martinelli. 1978. *Gli imprenditori e la crisi. Ricerca sull'imprenditorialità a cura dell'IDOM – Impresa Domani*. Bologna: Il Mulino.

Braudel, Fernand. 1980. *On History*. University of Chicago Press.

Braverman, Harry. 1974. *Labor and Monopoly Capital: The Degradation of Work in the Twentieth Century*. New York: Monthly Review Press.

Brecher, Jeremy. 1972. *Strike!* Boston: South End Press.

Brecht, Bertolt. 1972. *Collected Plays*. Vol. 5. New York: Pantheon.

Brentano, Dominique. 1975. *Storie di vita e di violenza*. Bologna: Il Mulino.

Britt, David W., and Omer Galle. 1972. "Industrial Conflict and Unionization." *American Sociological Review*, Vol. 37, pp. 46–57.

1974. "Structural Antecedents of the Shape of Strikes: A Comparative Analysis." *American Sociological Review*, Vol. 39, No. 5, pp. 642–51.

Brown, R. L., J. Durbin, and J. H. Evans. 1975. "Techniques for Testing the Constancy of Regression Relationships over Time." *Journal of the Royal Statistical Society*, Series B, Vol. 37, No. 2, pp. 149–92.

Brusco, Sebastiano. 1975. "Organizzazione del lavoro e decentramento produttivo nel settore metalmeccanico." Pp. 9–67, in FLM di Bergamo (ed.), *Sindacato e piccola impresa. Strategia del capitale e azione sindacale nel decentramento produttivo*. Bari: De Donato.

1982. "The Emilian Model: Productive Decentralisation and Social Integration." *Cambridge Journal of Economics*, Vol. 6, No. 2, pp. 167–84.

Bulgarelli, Aviana. 1978. *Crisi e mobilità operaia*. Milan: Mazzotta.

Buratto, Fabio, Gustavo De Santis, and Anna Maria Ventrella (eds.). 1974. *I lavoratori nell'industria italiana. Volume II: Appendici*. Milan: Franco Angeli.

Burawoy, Michael. 1984. "Karl Marx and the Satanic Mills: Factory Politics under Early Capitalism in England, the United States and Russia." *American Journal of Sociology*, Vol. 90, No. 2, pp. 247–82.
  1985. *The Politics of Production*. London: Verso.
Burns, Arthur, and Wensley C. Mitchell. 1947. *Measuring Business Cycles*. New York: National Bureau of Economic Research.
Cacciari, Massimo (ed.). 1969. *Ciclo capitalistico e lotte operaie. Montedison, Pirelli, Fiat 1968*. Padua: Marsilio.
Cagnato, Alberto. 1981. "Azione sindacale e piccola impresa nel Veneto," *Prospettiva sindacale*, Vol. 12, No. 41, pp. 63–70.
Caleffi, Giuseppe, and Marco Mietto. 1980. "La CGIL dal dopoguerra alla fine degli anni '60," *Prospettiva sindacale*, Vol. 11, No. 37, pp. 5–12.
Calhoun, Craig. 1982. *The Question of Class Struggle*. University of Chicago Press.
Camonico, Marina. 1986. "La contrattazione aziendale nel biennio della concertazione. Primi risultati dell'Osservatorio CESOS," *Prospettiva sindacale*, Vol. 17, No. 60, pp. 132–45.
Campiglio, Luigi. 1973. "La dinamica degli infortuni sul lavoro nel periodo 1951–1970." *Rivista internazionale di scienze sociali*, Vol. 81, pp. 134–65.
  1976. *Lavoro salariato e nocività*. Bari: De Donato.
Canteri, Celestino. 1964. *Immigrati a Torino*. Milan: Edizioni Avanti!
Capecchi, Vittorio. 1978. "Sviluppo economico emiliano, ruolo dell'industria metalmeccanica, problema del Mezzogiorno." Pp. 9–113, in Vittorio Capecchi et al. (eds.), *La piccola impresa nell'economia italiana. Politica del lavoro e proposte per il Mezzogiorno nell'iniziativa del sindacato*. Bari: De Donato.
Carabelli, Giuliana. 1974. "Falck Unione." Pp. 109–208, in Alessandro Pizzorno (ed.), *Lotte operaie e sindacato in Italia: 1968–1972, Dalmine, Falck, Redaelli*. Bologna: Il Mulino.
Caracciolo, Alberto. 1969. "Il processo d'industrializzazione." Pp. 96–186, in Giorgio Fuà (ed.), *Lo sviluppo economico in Italia, Vol. 3, Studi di settore e documentazione di base*. Milan: Franco Angeli.
Carocci, Giovanni. 1960. *Inchiesta alla Fiat*. Florence: Parenti.
Carrara, Mario. 1965. "L'inchiesta alla Olivetti nel 1961." *Quaderni Rossi*, No. 5, pp. 256–69.
Carrieri, Mimmo, and Carlo Donolo. 1986. *Il mestiere politico del sindacato*. Rome: Editori Riuniti.
Cass, Millard. 1957. "The Relationship of Size of Firm and Strike Activity." *Monthly Labor Review*, Vol. 80, No. 11, pp. 1330–4.
Castegnaro, Alessandro. 1980. "Una provincia del Nord a prevalenza CGIL." Pp. 47–88, in Guido Romagnoli (ed.), *La sindacalizzazione tra ideologia e pratica. Il caso italiano, 1950/1977. Volume 2*. Rome: Edizioni Lavoro.
  1983. "Modelli di azione sindacale decentrata nel Veneto," *Prospettiva sindacale*, Vol. 14, No. 49, pp. 186–224.
Castellano, Lucio. 1980. *Aut. Op. La storia e i documenti: da Potere operaio all'Autonomia organizzata*. Rome: Savelli.
Castronovo, Valerio. 1980. *L'industria italiana dall'800 a oggi*. Milan: Mondadori.
Cavalli, Luciano. 1964. *Gli immigrati meridionali e la società ligure*. Milan: Franco Angeli.
Cavallo Perin, Maria Cristina. 1980. "Analisi quantitativa della sindacalizzazione dei metalmeccanici a Torino (1961–71)." *Quaderni di rassegna sindacale*, Vol. 18, No. 82, pp. 171–87.
Cazzola, Franco. 1982. "La solidarietà nazionale dalla parte del Parlamento." *Laboratorio politico, Il compromesso storico*, Vol. 2, No. 2–3, pp. 182–210.

Celadin, Anna. 1974. "Delegati e Consigli: una rilevazione a Milano," *Quaderni di rassegna sindacale*, Vol. 12, No. 49, pp. 170–9.
Cella, Gian Primo. 1973. "La composizione sociale e politica degli apparati sindacali metalmeccanici della Lombardia." *Prospettiva sindacale*, Vol. 4, No. 10, pp. 7–23.
    1976a. "Sindacato e politica organizzativa negli anni '50." *Quaderni di rassegna sindacale*, Vol. 14, No. 59–60, pp. 114–36.
    1976b. *Divisione del lavoro e iniziativa operaia*. Bari: De Donato.
    (ed.). 1979. *Il movimento degli scioperi nel XX secolo*. Bologna: Il Mulino.
    1989a. *La solidarietà possibile*. Rome: Edizioni Lavoro.
    1989b. "Criteria of Regulation in Italian Industrial Relations: A Case of Weak Institutions." Pp. 167–86, in Peter Lange and Marino Regini (eds.), *State, Market, and Social Regulation. New Perspectives on Italy*. Cambridge University Press.
Cella, Gian Primo, and Emilio Reyneri. 1974. "Il contributo della ricerca all'analisi della composizione della classe operaia." Pp. 33–58, in *Classe. Quaderni sulla condizione e sulla lotta operaia. Quaderno No. 8. L'operaio massa nello sviluppo capitalistico*. Bari: Dedalo Libri.
Cella, Gian Primo, and Tiziano Treu. 1982. "National Trade Union Movements." Pp. 166–89, in R. Blanplain (ed.), *Comparative Labour Law and Industrial Relations*. Dordrecht: Kluwer.
    1983. "Italia. La crisi economica e la trasformazione delle relazioni industriali." Pp. 101–22, in Tiziano Treu (ed.), *Crisi economica e mutamenti politici nell'area mediterranea. Problemi e prospettive delle relazioni industriali*. Rome: Edizioni Lavoro.
    1989a. "La contrattazione collettiva." Pp. 157–218, in Gian Primo Cella and Tiziano Treu (eds.), *Relazioni industriali. Manuale per l'analisi dell'esperienza italiana*. Bologna: Il Mulino.
    (eds.). 1989b. *Relazioni industriali. Manuale per l'analisi dell'esperienza italiana*. Bologna: Il Mulino.
Censi, G., N. de Pamphilis, A. Fasola, G. Fassio, A. La Porta, G. Mantovani, M. Polverari, M. Ricceri, and S. Scaiola. 1973. *Delegati e consigli di fabbrica in Italia*. Milan: Franco Angeli.
Centro Studi Federlibro, FIM, SISM-CISL di Verona. 1974. *Piccola Azienda, grande sfruttamento. Note sul decentramento produttivo*. Verona: Bertani.
CESOS-CISL (Centro Studi Sociali e Sindacali) and IRES-CGIL (Istituto di Ricerche Economiche e Sociali). 1982. *Sindacalisti in parlamento 1. CISL*. Rome: Edizioni Lavoro.
    1984. *Sindacalisti in parlamento 2. CGIL*. Rome: Edizioni Lavoro.
    1986. *Sindacalisti in parlamento 3. Le attività non legislative (1948–1968)*. Rome: Edizioni Lavoro.
CGIL. 1953. "Come si vive nelle fabbriche." *Notiziario*, No. 21, pp. 595–602.
    1969. *La contrattazione aziendale e di gruppo nel 1968*. Documentazione, No. 9.
Chamberlain, Neil W., and Jane Metzger Schilling. 1954. *The Impact of Strikes. Their Social and Economic Costs*. New York: Harper & Brothers.
Charemza, W. Wojciech, and Derek F. Deadman. 1992. *New Directions in Econometric Practice. General to Specific Modelling, Cointegration and Vector Autoregression*. Brookfield, VM : Edward Elgar.
Chatfield, Christopher. 1975. *The Analysis of Time Series: Theory and Practice*. London: Chapman & Hall.
Chiesi, Antonio, and Alberto Martinelli. 1989. "The Representation of Business Interests as a Mechanism of Social Regulation." Pp. 187–216, in Peter Lange and Marino Regini (eds.), *State, Market, and Social Regulation. New Perspectives on Italy*. Cambridge University Press.

Chomsky, Noam. 1968. *Language and Mind*. New York: Harcourt Brace Jovanovich.
Chow, Gregory C. 1960. "Tests of Equality Between Sets of Coefficients in Two Linear Regressions." *Econometrica*, Vol. 28, No. 3, pp. 591–605.
Churnside, R. J., and S. W. Creigh. 1981. "Strike Activity and Plant Size: A Note." *Journal of the Royal Statistical Society*, Series A, Vol. 144, part 1, pp. 104–11.
Cicero. 1962. *Orator*. (with an English translation by H. M. Hubbell). Cambridge, Mass.: Harvard University Press.
CISIM (Commissione Indagini e Studi sull'Industria Meccanica. Gruppo di consulenza dello Stanford Research Institute, Stanford, California). 1952. *Economic and Industrial Problems of the Italian Mechanical Industries*. Tivoli: Arti Grafiche A. Chicca.
CISL Milano (Ufficio Studi). 1975a. "La sindacalizzazione CISL in provincia di Milano (1960–1973)," *Prospettiva sindacale*, Vol. VI, No. 1, pp. 100–20.
    1975b. "La Contrattazione aziendale in provincia di Milano nel 1974," *Prospettiva sindacale*, Vol. VI, No. 2, pp. 90–127.
Clark, Colin. 1940. *The Conditions of Economic Progress*. London: Macmillan.
Clarke, Tom, and Laurie Clements (eds.). 1977. *Trade Unions Under Capitalism*. Glasgow: Fontana.
Clawson, Dan. 1980. *Bureaucracy and the Labor Process, The Transformation of U.S. Industry, 1860–1920*. New York: Monthly Review Press.
Clegg, Hugh A. 1976. *Trade Unionism Under Collective Bargaining*. Oxford: Blackwell.
Cleland, Sherill. 1955. *The Influence of Plant Size on Industrial Relations*. Princeton University Press.
Cochrane, D., and G. Orcutt. 1949. "Applications of Least-Squares Regressions to Relationships Containing Auto-Correlated Error Terms." *Journal of the American Statistical Association*, Vol. 44, pp. 32–61.
Cohen, Joshua, and Joel Rogers. 1983. *On Democracy*. New York: Penguin Books.
Coi, Salvatore. 1979. "Sindacati in Italia: iscritti, apparato, finanziamento." *Il Mulino*, Vol. 28, No. 262, pp. 201–42.
Colasanti, Giuseppe. 1982. "Partito comunista, sindacato e conflitto in Italia 1949–1977: analisi empirica." Pp. 79–99, in Giuseppe Colasanti and Luca Perrone (eds.), *Scioperi e movimenti collettivi*. Proceedings of the Conference "I conflitti di lavoro." Dipartimento di Sociologia e di Scienza della Politica, Università della Calabria, 7–8 March 1980. Rome: Casa del libro editrice.
Colletti, Lucio, and Claudio Napoleoni (eds.). 1970. *Il futuro del capitalismo. Crollo o sviluppo?* Bari: Laterza.
Collidà, Ada, Lucio De Carlini, Gianfranco Mossetto, and Renzo Stefanelli. 1972. *La politica del padronato italiano dalla ricostruzione all'autunno caldo*. Bari: De Donato.
Collingwood, R. G. 1956. *The Idea of History*. Oxford University Press.
Comitato di Difesa e di Lotta Contro la Repressione. 1970. "Uno Statuto per padroni e sindacati." *Quaderni Piacentini*, No. 42, pp. 75–82.
Commissione Parlamentare d'Inchiesta sulle Condizioni dei Lavoratori in Italia. 1958a. Vol. 3, *Legislazione protettiva del lavoro. Osservanza delle norme protettive del lavoro*. Rome: Camera dei Deputati e Senato della Repubblica.
    1958b. Vol. VI, *Le Commissioni Interne*. Rome: Camera dei Deputati e Senato della Repubblica.
    1958c. Vol. XV, *Condizioni di vita del lavoratore. Risultati dell'indagine statistica sugli aspetti aziendali ed extra-aziendali*. Rome: Camera dei Deputati e Senato della Repubblica.
Confederazione Generale dell'Industria Italiana (Confindustria). (Various monthly issues). *Rassegna di statistiche del lavoro*. Rome: CGII.

(Various annual issues). *Relazione sull'attività confederale.* Rome: CGII.
(Various annual issues). *Annuario.* Rome: CGII.
1973. *Le rappresentanze dei lavoratori in fabbrica.* (October). Rome: CGII.
1974. "I tassi di gravità dell'assenteismo dal lavoro nell'anno 1972." *Rassegna di statistiche del lavoro. Supplemento.* Pp. 63–70. Rome: CGII.
Confindustria-Censis. 1989. *Gli imprenditori. Cultura e comportamenti associativi.* Rome: Il Sole 24 Ore Libri.
Contini, Bruno. 1979. *Lo sviluppo di un'economia parallela.* Milan: Comunità.
Corbetta, Piergiorgio, Arturo Parisi, and Hans Schadee. 1988. *Elezioni in Italia.* Bologna: Il Mulino.
Cosi, Dante, and Francesco Pugliese. 1977. *I modelli organizzatori degli enti pubblici.* Milan: Franco Angeli.
Cousineau, Jean-Michel, and Robert Lacroix. 1976. "Activité economiqué, inflation et activité de grève." *Relations industrielles,* Vol. 31, pp. 341–57.
   1986. "Imperfect Information and Strikes: An Analysis of Canadian Experience, 1967–1982." *Industrial and Labor Relations,* Vol. 39, No. 3, pp. 377–87.
Cowden, Dudley J. 1942. "Moving Seasonal Indexes." *Journal of the American Statistical Association,* Vol. 37, pp. 523–4.
Cronin, James E. 1979. *Industrial Conflict in Modern Britain.* London: Croom Helm.
   1980. "Stages, Cycles and Insurgencies: The Economics of Unrest." Pp. 101–18, in T. K. Hopkins and I. Wallerstein. (eds.), *Processes of the World-System.* Beverly Hills: Sage.
Crouch, Colin. 1978. "The Changing Role of the State in Industrial Relations in Western Europe." Pp. 197–220, in Colin Crouch and Alessandro Pizzorno (eds.), *The Resurgence of Class Conflict in Western Europe Since 1968. Volume 2. Comparative Analyses.* New York: Holmes & Meier.
Crouch, Colin, and Alessandro Pizzorno (eds.). 1978. *The Resurgence of Class Conflict in Western Europe Since 1968.* New York: Holmes & Meier.
Crouzel, Adrien. 1887. *Etude historique, économique, juridique sur les coalitions et les grèves dans l'industrie.* Paris: A. Rousseau.
Da Empoli, Domenico, Vincenzo Siesto, and Paola Antonello. 1979. *Finanza pubblica e contabilita nazionale in base trimestrale (1954–1975).* Padova: Cedam.
D'Agostini, Fabrizio. 1974. *La condizione operaia e i Consigli di Fabbrica.* Rome: Editori Riuniti.
Dahrendorf, Ralf. 1959. *Class and Class Conflict in Industrial Society.* Stanford University Press.
d'Ambrosio, Mario. 1972. "Piccole e medie imprese ai rinnovi contrattuali del 1972." *Quaderni ISRIL.*
d'Ambrosio, Mario, and Giovanni Biz. 1974. "Gli infortuni sul lavoro: analisi settoriale e regionale del fenomeno, confronti internazionali, individuazione delle cause e proposte di intervento" (mimeograph). Rome: Istituto di studi sulle relazioni industriali.
Daneo, Camillo. 1975. *La politica economica della ricostruzione (1945–1949).* Turin: Einaudi.
D'Antonio, Mariano. 1973. *Sviluppo e crisi del capitalismo italiano 1951–1972.* Rome: De Donato.
Davies, James C. 1969. "The J-Curve of Rising and Declining Satisfactions as a Cause of Some Great Revolutions and a Contained Rebellion." Pp. 690–730, in Hugh Davis Graham and Ted Robert Gurr (eds.), *Violence in America: Historical and Comparative Perspectives.* New York: FA Praeger.

De Carlini, Lucio. 1972. "La Confindustria." Pp. 53–82, in Ada Collidà, Lucio De Carlini, Gianfranco Mossetto, and Renzo Stefanelli (eds.), *La politica del padronato italiano: dalla ricostruzione all "autunno caldo."* Bari: De Donato.
De Cecco, Marcello. 1972. "Una interpretazione ricardiana della dinamica della forza-lavoro in Italia nel decennio 1959–69." *Note economiche*, Vol. 5, No. 1, pp. 76–120.
Della Porta, Donatella, and Maurizio Rossi. 1985. "I terrorismi in Italia tra il 1969 e il 1982." Pp. 418–56, in Gianfranco Pasquino (ed.), *Il sistema politico italiano*. Bologna: Il Mulino.
Dell'Aringa, Carlo. 1976. *Egualitarismo e sindacato. L'evoluzione dei differenziali retributivi nell'industria italiana*. Milan: Vita e pensiero (Pubblicazioni dell'Università Cattolica).
   1979a. *Distribuzione del reddito e mobilità del lavoro*. Milan: Giuffrè.
   (ed.). 1979b. *Rapporto sulla manodopera. Parte I*. Rome: CNEL.
Dell'Aringa, Carlo, and Claudio Lucifora. 1994. "Egualitarismo e sindacato: vent'anni dopo." *Lavoro e relazioni industriali*, Vol. 1, No. 1, pp. 3–41.
Della Rocca, Giuseppe. 1974. "L'evoluzione delle strutture di categoria." *Quaderni di rassegna sindacale*, Vol. 12, No. 49, pp. 59–83.
   1976. "L'offensiva politica degli imprenditori nelle fabbriche." Pp. 609–38, in Aris Accornero (ed.), *Problemi del movimento sindacale in Italia 1943–1973*. Annali Feltrinelli. Milan: Feltrinelli.
   1978. "Una analisi sull'organizzazione del sindacato in Italia: il funzionario e l'operatore." Pp. 45–93, in Giovanni Gasparini (ed.), *Sindacato e organizzazione*. Milan: Franco Angeli.
   1981. "L'organizzazione del sindacato agli inizi degli anni '80." *Laboratorio politico, Il sindacato nella crisi*, Vol. 1, No. 4, pp. 131–51.
Della Rocca, Giuseppe, and Serafino Negrelli. 1983. "Diritti di informazione ed evoluzione della contrattazione aziendale (1969–1981)." *Giornale di diritto del lavoro e di relazioni industriali*, Vol. 5, No. 19, pp. 549–79.
Del Lungo, Silvano. 1976. "Esperienze organizzative in alcune aziende metalmeccaniche a partecipazione statale." *Quaderni di sociologia*, Vol. 25, No. 2–3, pp. 225–62.
Del Turco, Ottaviano. 1970. "Una tipologia delle forme di lotta oggi in Italia." *Quaderni di rassegna sindacale*, Vol. 8, No. 25, p. 62–9.
De Masi, Domenico. 1972. "Un'indagine sull'atteggiamento dei lavoratori: consenso e propensione alle forme di lotta." *Quaderni di rassegna sindacale*, Vol. 10, No. 38, pp. 116–31.
De Masi, Domenico, Fabio Buratto, Alfio Cascioli, Gustavo De Santis, Renzo Raimondi, Filippo Vacirca, and Anna Maria Ventrella. 1985. *Il lavoratore post-industriale. La condizione e l'azione dei lavoratori nell'industria italiana*. Milan: Franco Angeli.
De Masi, Domenico, and Giuseppe Fevola. 1974a. *I lavoratori nell'industria italiana. Volume I: Rapporto generale. Tomo III: Classe e conflitti*. Milan: Franco Angeli.
   1974b. *I lavoratori nell'industria italiana. Volume I: Rapporto generale. Tomo I: Basi teoriche e contesto strutturale*. Milan: Franco Angeli.
   1974c. *I lavoratori nell'industria italiana. Volume I: Rapporto generale. Tomo II: Uomini e organizzazione*. Milan: Franco Angeli.
Demier, Francis. 1982. "Les ouvriers de Rouen parlent à un economiste en juillet 1848." *Le mouvement social*, Vol. 2, pp. 3–31.
Dente, Bruno, and Gloria Regonini. 1989. "Politics and Policies in Italy." Pp. 51–80, in Peter Lange and Marino Regini (eds.), *State, Market, and Social Regulation. New Perspectives on Italy*. Cambridge University Press.
De Palma, Dino, Vittorio Rieser, and Edda Salvadori. 1965. "L'inchiesta alla FIAT nel 1960–61." *Quaderni Rossi*, No. 5, pp. 214–55.

Derossi, Flavia. 1982. *The Technocratic Illusion. A Study of Managerial Power in Italy.* Armonk, N.Y.: M. E. Sharpe, Inc.
De Santis, Gustavo. 1979. *Il ricorso allo sciopero. Contributi per una storia del movimento sindacale in Italia.* Milan: Franco Angeli.
De Ste. Croix, G.E.M. 1981. *The Class Struggle in the Ancient Greek World: From the Archaic Age to the Arab Conquests.* Ithaca, N.Y.: Cornell University Press.
de Wasseige, Yves. 1952. "La grève. Phénomène économique et sociologique. Étude inductive des conflicts du travail en Belgique de 1920 à 1940." *Bullettin de l'Institut de Reserches Économiques et Sociales.* Louvain, Vol. XVIII, pp. 663–724.
Doeringer, Peter, and Michael Piore. 1971. *Internal Labor Markets and Manpower Analysis.* Lexington, Mass.: Heath.
Dogan, Mattei. 1963. "La stratificazione sociale dei suffragi." Pp. 407–74, in Alberto Spreafico and Joseph La Palombara (eds.), *Elezioni e comportamento politico in Italia.* Milan: Comunità.
Dolci, Luigi. 1974. "Ercole Marelli." Pp. 127–86, in Alessandro Pizzorno (ed.), *Lotte operaie e sindacato in Italia: 1968–1972, Vol. 3, Magneti Marelli e Ercole Marelli.* Bologna: Il Mulino.
Donini, Antonio. 1972. "Gli extraparlamentari e il sindacato." *Quaderni di rassegna sindacale*, Vol. 10, No. 33–4, pp. 105–21.
Dore, Lorenzo. 1976. *La contrattazione nell'industria (1945–1976).* Proposte No. 36–7. Rome: Editrice Sindacale Italiana.
Drago, Francesco. 1971. *La contrattazione integrativa aziendale e di gruppo nel 1970.* Rome: Edizione Stasind.
Drago, Francesco, Giambarba Eugenio, Eugenio Guidi, Alberto La Porta, Gianni Salvarani, Domenico Valcavi, and Gianni Vinay. 1971. *Movimento sindacale e contrattazione collettiva 1945–1970.* Milan: Franco Angeli.
Draper, N. R., and H. Smith. 1966. *Applied Regression Analysis.* New York: Wiley.
Dubin, Robert. 1954. "Prospects of Industrial Conflict – A Prediction." Pp. 527–30, in Arthur Kornhauser, Robert Dubin, and Arthur Ross (eds.), *Industrial Conflict.* New York: McGraw-Hill.
Dubois, Pierre. 1978. "New Forms of Industrial Conflict 1960–1974." Pp. 1–34, in Colin Crouch and Alessandro Pizzorno (eds.), *The Resurgence of Class Conflict in Western Europe Since 1968.* New York: Holmes & Meier.
Durbin, J. 1962. "Trend Elimination by Moving-Average and Variate-Difference Filters." *Bulletin de l'Institut International de Statistique*, Vol. 39, pp. 131–41.
Edwards, P.K. 1981. *Strikes in the United States 1881–1974.* Oxford: Blackwell.
Edwards, Richard. 1979. *Contested Terrain.* New York: Basic Books.
Edwards, Richard, Michael Reich, and David M. Gordon (eds.). 1975. *Labor Market Segmentation.* Lexington, Mass.: Heath.
Elster, Jon. 1985. *Making Sense of Marx.* Cambridge University Press.
Elton, G.R. 1967. *The Practice of History.* Sidney University Press.
Engle, R.F., and C.W.J. Granger (eds.). 1991. *Long-Run Economic Relationships. Readings in Cointegration.* Oxford University Press.
Etzioni, Amitai. 1968. *The Active Society.* New York: Free Press.
Faenza, Roberto, and Marco Fini. 1976. *Gli americani in Italia.* Milan: Feltrinelli.
Fair, Ray C. 1970. "The Estimation of Simultaneous Equation Models with Lagged Endogenous Variables and First Order Serially Correlated Errors." *Econometrica*, Vol. 38, No. 3, pp. 507–16.
Farneti, Paolo. 1970. *Imprenditori e società.* Turin: LI/ED L'impresa Edizioni.
    1976. "I partiti politici e il sistema di potere." Pp. 61–104, Valerio Castronovo (ed.), *L'Italia contemporanea, 1945–1975.* Turin: Einaudi.
    1983. *Il sistema dei partiti in Italia (1946–1979).* Bologna: Il Mulino.

1985. *The Italian Party System (1945–1980)*. London: Frances Pinter.
Fasol, Rino. 1980. "Una provincia del Nord a prevalenza CISL." Pp. 15–46, in Guido Romagnoli (ed.), *La sindacalizzazione tra ideologia e pratica. Il caso italiano, 1950/1977. Volume 2*. Rome: Edizioni Lavoro.
Federazione Regionale fra le Associazioni Industriali della Lombardia (Federlombarda). 1977. *La piccola e media industria in Lombardia, Vol. 1, Relazione generale. Rapporti del gruppo di lavoro. Indagine campionaria. Vol. 2, Relazioni del Comitato Scientifico*. Milan: Edizioni Industriali.
Feierabend, Ivo K., and Rosalind Feierabend. 1966. "Aggressive Behaviors Within Politics, 1948–1962: A Cross-National Study." *Journal of Conflict Resolution*, Vol. 10, pp. 249–71.
Feltrin, Paolo. 1991. "Partiti e sindacati: simbiosi o dominio?" Pp. 293–366, in Leonardo Morlino (ed.), *Costruire la democrazia*. Bologna: Il Mulino.
Ferrante, Gianni. 1982. "Interscambio di dirigenti tra partito e sindacato." Pp. 673–91, in Massimo Ilardi and Aris Accornero (eds.), *Il partito comunista italiano. Struttura e storia dell'organizzazione (1921/1979)*. Milan: Feltrinelli.
Ferrari, Giuseppe. 1979. "La presenza dei sindacati negli organismi pubblici lombardi." Pp. 48–138, in Tiziano Treu, Massimo Roccella, and Giuseppe Ferrari (eds.), *Sindacalisti nelle istituzioni*. Rome: Edizioni Lavoro.
Ferraris, Pino. 1965. "Giornali politici nelle fabbriche del Biellese." *Quaderni Rossi*, No. 5, pp. 31–48.
Fidanza, Mirko, and Tiziano Treu (eds.). 1976. *La mediazione della regione nei conflitti di lavoro: l'esperienza lombarda*. Bologna: Il Mulino.
Filippelli, Ronald. 1989. *American Labor and Postwar Italy, 1943–1953*. Stanford University Press.
FIM-CISL. 1972. *Per un sindacato di classe. Lotte di fabbrica, lotte sociali sull'organizzazione*. Milan: Sapere Edizioni.
Fisher, Malcolm. 1973. *Measurement of Labour Disputes and Their Economic Effects*. Paris: OECD.
FLM di Bergamo (ed.). 1975. *Sindacato e piccola impresa. Strategia del capitale e azione sindacale nel decentramento produttivo*. Bari: De Donato.
Foa, Vittorio. 1969. "Note sui gruppi estremisti e le lotte sindacali." *Problemi del socialismo*, Vol. 11, No. 41, pp. 658–70.
——— (ed.). 1975. *Sindacati e lotte operaie (1943–1973)*. Turin: Loescher.
Fofi, Goffredo. 1975. *L'immigrazione meridionale a Torino*. Milan: Feltrinelli.
Fogel, Robert William. 1964. *Railroads and American Economic Growth. Essays in Econometric History*. Baltimore: Johns Hopkins University Press.
Fogel, Robert William, and G.R. Elton. 1983. *Which Road to the Past? Two Views of History*. New Haven: Yale University Press.
Fondazione Giovanni Agnelli. 1973. *Il sistema imprenditoriale italiano. Rapporto di ricerca*. Turin: Fondazione Giovanni Agnelli.
Forbice, Aldo, and Riccardo Chiaberge. 1974. *Il sindacato dei consigli*. Verona: Bertani.
Forcheimer, K. 1948. "Some International Aspects of the Strike Movement." *Bulletin of the Oxford Institute of Statistics*, Vol. 10, pp. 9–24.
Forte, Francesco. 1974. "L'impresa: grande, piccola, pubblica, privata." Pp. 338–67, in Fabio Luca Cavazza and Stephen R. Graubard (eds.), *Il caso italiano*. Milan: Garzanti.
Foster, John. 1974. *Class Struggle and the Industrial Revolution*. London: Weidenfeld & Nicolson.
Franzosi, Roberto. 1980. "Strikes in Italy: Exploratory Data Analysis." *Rivista di politica economica*, Vol. 70, pp. 73–122.

1981. "La conflittualità in Italia tra ciclo economico e contrattazione collettiva." *Rassegna italiana di sociologia*, Vol. 22, No. 4, pp. 533–75.

1985. "Cent'anni di dati e di ricerche sugli scioperi: una rassegna critica dei metodi e dei limiti della ricerca quantitativa sul conflitto industriale." Pp. 21–54, in Gian Primo Cella and Marino Regini (eds.), *Il conflitto industriale in Italia. Stato della ricerca e ipotesi sulle tendenze*. Bologna: Il Mulino.

1987. "The Press as a Source of Socio-Historical Data: Issues in the Methodology of Data Collection from Newspapers." *Historical Methods*, Vol. 20, No. 1, Pp. 5–16.

1989a. "From Words to Numbers: A Generalized and Linguistics-based Coding Procedure for Collecting Textual Data." Pp. 263–98, in Clifford Clogg (ed.), *Sociological Methodology, 1989*. Oxford: Blackwell.

1989b. "One Hundred Years of Strike Statistics. Methodological and Theoretical Issues in Quantitative Strike Research." *Industrial and Labor Relations Review*, Vol. 42, No. 3, pp. 34–63.

1992. "Toward a Model of Conflict in the Service Sector. Some Empirical Evidence from the Italian Case (1986/1987)." Pp. 7–34, in Gian Primo Cella (ed.), *Il conflitto. La trasformazione. La prevenzione. Il controllo*. Turin: Giappichelli Editore.

1994. "Outside and Inside the Regression 'Black Box:' From Exploratory to Interior Data Analysis." *Quality and Quantity*, Vol. 28, pp. 21–53.

Freedman, David. 1991. "Statistical Models and Shoe Leather." Pp. 291–313, in Peter V. Marsden (ed.), *Sociological Methodology, 1991*. London: Basil Blackwell.

Fuà, Giorgio. 1973. "Cicli e tendenze di fondo dell'economia italiana nell'ultimo ventennio." *Rassegna economica* (Banco di Napoli), Vol. 37, No. 5, pp. 1163–98.

1976. *Occupazione e capacità produttive. La realtà italiana*. Bologna: Il Mulino.

Fuguitt, Glenn V., and Stanley Lieberson. 1974. "Correlation of Ratios or Difference Scores Having Common Terms." Pp. 128–44, in Herbert L. Costner (ed.), *Sociological Methodology, 1973–1974*. San Francisco: Jossey-Bass.

Fuller, Wayne. 1976. *Introduction to Statistical Time Series*. New York: Wiley.

Gallessi, Roberto. 1981. "Presupposti e sviluppi della lotta degli elettromeccanici." Pp. 13–70, in Bruno Bezza, Stefano Datola, and Roberto Gallessi (eds.), *Le lotte degli elettromeccanici*. Milan: Franco Angeli.

Galli, Giorgio (ed.). 1968. *Il comportamento elettorale in Italia*. Bologna: Il Mulino.

1975. *Dal bipartitismo imprefetto alla possibile alternativa*. Bologna: Il Mulino.

Galli, Giorgio, and Alessandra Nannei. 1976. *Il capitalismo assistenziale*. Milan: Sugar.

Gallie, Duncan. 1978. *In Search of the New Working Class*. Cambridge University Press.

Gallino, Luciano, and Filippo Barbano. 1962. "Commissioni interne e progresso tecnico." in Franco Momigliano (ed.), 2 Vols., *Lavoratori e sindacati di fronte alle trasformazioni del processo produttivo*. Milan: Feltrinelli.

Gamson, William. 1975. *The Strategy of Social Protest*. Homewood, Ill.: The Dorsey Press.

Ganapini, Luigi, Martino Pozzobon, Roberto Mari, Febo Guizzi, Ettore Santi, and Giulio Sapelli. 1978. *La ricostruzione nella grande industria*. Bari: De Donato.

Gartman, David. 1979. "Origins of the Assembly Line and Capitalist Control of Work at Ford." Pp. 193–205, in Andrew Zimbalist (ed.), *Case Studies on the Labor Process*. New York: Monthly Review Press.

Geary, Roger. 1985. *Policing Industrial Disputes: 1893 to 1985*. Cambridge University Press.

Gianotti, Renzo. 1979. *Trent'anni di lotte alla FIAT (1948–1978)*. Bari: De Donato.

Giddens, Anthony. 1973. *The Class Structure of the Advanced Societies*. London: Hutchinson.

Gigliobianco, Alfredo, and Michele Salvati. 1980. *Il maggio francese e l'autunno caldo: la risposta di due borghesie*. Bologna: Il Mulino.

Gimbel, John. 1978. "The Origins of the Marshall Plan." Pp. 143–78, in Charles S. Maier (ed.), *The Origins of the Cold War and Contemporary Europe*. New York: New Viewpoints.

Ginzburg, Carlo. 1979. "Roots of a Scientific Paradigm." *Theory and Society*, Vol. 7, No. 3, pp. 273–88.

Giubilato, M. 1982. "La contrattazione aziendale nel Veneto," *Quaderni Veneti*, No. 4.

Giugni, Gino. 1957. "Bargaining Units and Labor Organisation in Italy." *Industrial and Labor Relations Review*, Vol. 10, pp. 424–39.

    1964. *Evoluzione della contrattazione collettiva nelle industrie siderurgiche e minerarie 1953–1963*. Milan: Giuffrè.

    1965. "Recent Developments in Collective Bargaining in Italy." *International Labor Review*, Vol. 91, pp. 273–91.

    1971. "Recent Trends in Collective Bargaining in Italy." *International Labor Review*, Vol. 104, pp. 307–28.

    1976. "La nascita della contrattazione articolata." *Quaderni di rassegna sindacale*, Vol. 14, No. 59/60, pp. 154–70.

    1982. "Il diritto del lavoro negli anni '80," *Giornale di diritto del lavoro e relazioni industriali*, Vol. 4, No. 15, pp. 373–410.

    1985. "Concertazione sociale e sistema politico in Italia," *Giornale di diritto del lavoro e di relazioni industriali*, Vol. 7, No. 25, pp. 53–64.

Giugni, Gino, Enzo Bartocci, Marcello De Cecco, Renzo Frinolli Puzzilli, Edoardo Ghera, Francesco Liso, Massimo Paci, Roberto Pessi, and Bruno Veneziani. 1976. *Gli anni della conflittualità permanente*. Rome: Franco Angeli.

Giuliani, Roberto, and Giulio Pecora. 1970. "Ricognizione sulle nuove forme della lotta operaia." *La critica sociologica*, No. 15, pp. 94–124.

Glasgow University Media Group. 1976. *Bad News*. London: Routledge & Kegan Paul.

Gobbi, Romolo. 1989. *Com'eri bella, classe operaia*. Milan: Longanesi.

Goetz-Girey, Robert. 1965. *Le mouvement des grèves en France*. Paris: Editions Sirey.

Goldner, William. 1953. "Strikes and Prosperity." *Industrial and Labor Relations Review*, Vol. 6, No. 4, pp. 579–81.

Goldstein, Joshua S. 1988. *Long Cycles. Prosperity and War in the Modern Age*. New Haven: Yale University Press.

Golthorpe, John, David Lockwood, Frank Bechhofer, and Jennifer Platt. 1968. *The Affluent Worker: Industrial Attitudes and Behaviours*. Cambridge University Press.

Gomberg, Eugene L. 1944. "Strikes and Lock-Outs in Great Britain." *Quarterly Journal of Economics*, Vol. 59, pp. 92–106.

Gordon, David M. 1978. "Up and Down the Long Roller Coaster." Pp. 22–35, in Union for Radical Political Economics (ed.), *Capitalism in Crisis*. New York: Union for Radical Political Economics.

    1980. "Stages of Accumulation and Long Economic Cycles." Pp. 9–45, in Terence K. Hopkins and Immanuel Wallerstein (eds.), *Processes of the World-System*. Beverly Hills: Sage.

Gordon, David M., Richard Edwards, and Michael Reich. 1982. *Segmented Work, Divided Workers*. Cambridge University Press.

Gorrieri, Ennio. 1973. *La giungla retributiva*. Bologna: Il Mulino.

Gouldner, Alvin. 1954. *Wildcat Strike: A Study in Worker-Management Relationships*. Yellowsprings, Ohio: Antioch University Press.

Gradilone, Alfredo. 1959. *Storia del sindacalismo*. Milan: Giuffrè.

Gramm, Cynthia L. 1986. "The Determinants of Strike Incidence and Severity: A Micro-Level Study." *Industrial and Labor Relations Review*, Vol. 39, No. 3, pp. 361–76.

1987. "New Measures of the Propensity to Strike During Contract Negotiations, 1971–1980." *Industrial and Labor Relations Review*, Vol. 40, No. 3, pp. 406–17.
Gramsci, Antonio. 1954. *L'Ordine Nuovo. 1919–1920*. Turin: Einaudi.
1971. *Prison Notebooks. Selections*. New York: International Publishers.
Granger, C. W. 1966. "The Typical Spectral Shape of an Economic Variable." *Econometrica*, Vol. 34, No. 1, pp. 150–61.
1976. "Seasonality: Causation, Interpretation and Implications." Paper presented at the Bureau of the Census Conference on Seasonal Analysis of Economic Time Series, Washington D.C., September 9–10.
Granger, C. W., and M. Hatanaka. 1964. *Spectral Analysis of Economic Time Series*. Princeton University Press.
Granger, C. W., and Paul Newbold. 1974. "Spurious Regressions in Econometrics." *Journal of Econometrics*, Vol. 2, No. 2, pp. 111–20.
1977. *Forecasting Economic Time Series*. New York: Academic Press.
Grassini, Franco. 1969. "Il progresso tecnico nell'industria dopo la seconda guerra mondiale." Pp. 274–314, in Giorgio Fuà (ed.), *Lo sviluppo economico in Italia, Vol. 3, Studi di settore e documentazione di base*. Milan: Franco Angeli.
Graziani, Augusto. 1976. "Lo sviluppo di un'economia aperta." Pp. 189–215, Mario Centorrino (ed.), *Consumi sociali e sviluppo economico in Italia, 1960–1975*. Rome: Coines.
1979. *L'economia italiana dal 1945 a oggi*. Bologna: Il Mulino.
(ed.). 1988. *La spirale del debito pubblico*. Bologna: Il Mulino.
Graziosi, Andrea. 1979. *La ristrutturazione nelle grandi fabbriche, 1973–1976*. Milan: Feltrinelli.
Griffin, John I. 1939. *Strikes: A Study in Quantitative Economics*. New York: Columbia University Press.
Griffin, Larry, Michael Wallace, and Beth Rubin. 1986. "Capitalism and Labor Organization," *American Sociological Review*, Vol. 51, No. 2, pp. 147–67.
Gruppi di studio sulla formazione extra-legislativa del diritto del lavoro delle Università di Bari e Bologna. 1968. *I licenziamenti nell'industria italiana*. Bologna: Il Mulino.
Guala, Chito. 1975. "Imprenditore e contesto sociopolitico: atteggiamenti e comportamenti." Pp. 115–43, in Carlo Maria Guerci (ed.), *La piccola e media impresa. Il caso della Liguria*. Milan: Franco Angeli.
Guerci, Carlo Maria. 1975. *La piccola e media impresa. Il caso della Liguria*. Milan: Franco Angeli.
Guidetti Serra, Bianca. 1984. *Le schedature FIAT. Cronaca di un processo e altre cronache*. Turin: Rosenberg & Sellier.
Guidi, Eugenio, and Enzo Cermigna. 1970. *La contrattazione integrativa aziendale e di gruppo nel 1969*. Documentazione, No. 11. Rome: SEUSI.
Guidi, Eugenio, Domenico Valcavi, Gianni Salvarani, Eugenio Giambarba, Alberto La Porta, Francesco Drago, and Gianni Vinay. 1974. *Movimento sindacale e contrattazione collettiva – 1945–1973*. Milan: Franco Angeli.
Guidi, Eugenio, Domenico Valcavi, Gianni Salvarani, Eugenio Giambarba, Alberto La Porta, Francesco Drago, and Gianni Vinay. 1976. *Movimento sindacale e contrattazione collettiva – 1945–1975*. Milan: Franco Angeli.
Guidi, Eugenio, Domenico Valcavi, Gianni Salvarani, and Alberto La Porta. 1972. *La contrattazione integrativa aziendale e di gruppo nel 1971*. Rome: SEUSI.
Guidi, Eugenio, Domenico Valcavi, Gianni Salvarani, Alberto La Porta, Eugenio Giambarba, Luigi Di Vezza, Alberto Bonifazi, Mario Sepi. 1973. *Gli sviluppi della contrattazione aziendale nel 1972*. Rome: SEUSI.

Gurr, Ted Robert. 1969. "A Comparative Study of Civil Strike." Pp. 572–631, in Hugh Davis Graham and Ted Robert Gurr (eds.), *Violence in America: Historical and Comparative Perspectives*. New York: FA Praeger.
 1970. *Why Men Rebel*. Princeton University Press.
Halevi, Joseph. 1972. "Evoluzione ed effetti degli scioperi negli ultimi vent'anni." *Quaderni di rassegna sindacale*, Vol. 10, No. 38, pp. 79–115.
Hanagan, Michael. 1980. *The Logic of Solidarity: Artisans and Industrial Workers in Three French Towns, 1871–1914*. Urbana: University of Illinois Press.
Hansen, Alvin. 1921. "Cycles of Strikes." *American Economic Review*, Vol. 11, No. 4, pp. 616–21.
Harbison, Frederick H. 1954. "Collective Bargaining and American Capitalism." Pp. 270–9, in Arthur Kornhauser, Robert Dubin, and Arthur Ross (eds.), *Industrial Conflict*. New York: McGraw-Hill.
Harding, Neil. 1983. *Lenin's Political Thought*, Atlantic Highlands, N.J.: Humanities Press.
Hardy, Thomas. 1978. *Tess of d'Urbevilles*. New York: St Martin's Press.
Harrison, Alan, and Mark Stewart. 1989. "Cyclical Fluctuations in Strike Durations." *American Economic Review*, Vol. 79, No. 4, pp. 827–41.
Harsanyi, John C. 1956. "Approaches to the Bargaining Problem Before and After the Theory of Games: A Critical Discussion of Zeuthen's, Hicks' and Nash's Theories." *Econometrica*, Vol. 24, No. 2, pp. 155–62.
Hartman, Raymond, and David Wheeler. 1979. "Schumpeterian Waves of Innovation and Infrastructure Development in Great Britain and the United States: The Kondratieff Cycle Revisited." *Research in Economic History*, Vol. 4, pp. 37–85.
Heimler, Alberto, and Carlo Milana. 1982. *Prezzi relativi, ridistribuzione e produttività*. Bologna: Il Mulino.
Hibbs, Douglas Jr. 1976. "Industrial Conflict in Advanced Industrial Societies." *American Political Science Review*, Vol. 70, No. 4, pp. 1033–58.
 1978. "On the Political Economy of Long Run Trends in Strike Activity." *British Journal of Political Science*, Vol. 8, No. 2, pp. 153–75.
Hicks, J. R. 1932. *The Theory of Wages*. London: Macmillan and Company.
 1974. *The Crisis in Keynesian Economic*. New York: Basic Books.
Hildreth, C., and J. Y. Lu. 1980. "Demand Relations with Autocorrelated Disturbances." Research bulletin No. 276, Michigan State University Agricultural Experiment Station.
Hilton, Rodney. 1977. *Bond Men Made Free. Medieval Peasant Movements and the English Rising of 1381*. London: Methuen.
Hines, A. G. 1964. "Trade Unions and Wage Inflation in the United Kingdom 1893–1961." *Review of Economic Studies*, Vol. 31, pp. 222–52.
 1968. "Unemployment and the Rate of Change of Money Wages in the United Kingdom, 1862–1963." *Review of Economics and Statistics*. Vol. 50, pp. 60–7.
Hobsbawn, Eric. 1964. *Labouring Men*. New York: Basic Books.
Hoerl, Arthur E. Jr. 1954. "Fitting Curves to Data." Pp. 20–77, in John Perry (ed.), *Chemical Business Handbook*. New York: McGraw-Hill.
Hogan, Michael. 1991. "The Marshall Plan." Pp. 203–40, in Charles Maier (ed). 1991. *The Cold War in Europe*. New York: Markus Wiener Publishing.
Horowitz, Daniel. 1963. *The Italian Labor Movement*. Cambridge, Mass.: Harvard University Press.
Hyman, Richard. 1971. *Marxism and the Sociology of Trade Unionism*. London: Pluto Press.
 1975. *Industrial Relations. A Marxist Introduction*. London: Macmillan .
 1978. "Occupational Structure, Collective Organisation and Industrial Militancy." Pp. 35–70, in Colin Crouch and Alessandro Pizzorno (eds.), *The Resurgence of Class*

Conflict in Western Europe Since 1968. Volume 2. Comparative Analyses. New York: Holmes & Meier.
1989. *Strikes*. London: Macmillan.
Ilardi, Massimo, and Aris Accornero (eds.). 1982. *Il partito comunista italiano. Struttura e storia dell'organizzaione (1921/1979)*. Milan: Feltrinelli.
Ingham, Geoffrey. 1967. "Organizational Size, Orientation to Work and Industrial Behavior." *Sociology*, Vol. 1, No. 3, pp. 239–58.
1969. "Plant Size: Political Attitudes and Behavior," *Sociological Review*, Vol. 17, pp. 235–49.
1970. *Size of Industrial Organization and Work Behavior*. Cambridge University Press.
1974. *Strikes and Industrial Conflict*. London: Macmillan.
IRSI (Istituto di ricerche sui problemi dello stato e delle istituzioni). 1981. *Il sindacato nello stato*. Rome: Edizioni Lavoro.
ISCO. 1985. *Congiuntura italiana. Rassegna mensile*. Rome: ISCO.
(Various monthly issues). *Congiuntura italiana. Rassegna mensile*. Rome: ISCO.
Istituto centrale di statistica (ISTAT). (Various monthly issues). *Bollettino mensile di statistica*. Rome: ISTAT.
(Various annual issues). *Annuario statistico italiano*. Rome: ISTAT.
(Various annual issues). *Annuario di statistiche del lavoro*. Rome: ISTAT.
(Various annual issues). *Annuario di statistiche provinciali*. Rome: ISTAT.
1942. *Censimento industriale e commerciale 1937–40. Prima serie: risultati generali. Vol. 1: Industrie. Parte 1: Esercizi, addetti, forza motrice*. Rome: Tipografia F. Failli.
1957a. "Numeri indici della produzione industriale, base 1963 = 100." *Metodi e norme*, Series A, No. 1.
1957b. "Numeri indici dei prezzi, base 1953 = 100." *Metodi e norme*, No. 2, Series A.
1967a. "Numeri indici della produzione industriale, base 1966 = 100." *Metodi e norme*, Series A, No. 7.
1967b. "Numeri indici dei prezzi base,1966 = 100." *Metodi e norme*, No. 6, Series A.
1968a. "Numeri indici dei tassi delle retribuzioni minime contrattuali, base 1966 = 100." *Supplemento straordinario al bollettino mensile di statistica*, No. 3.
1968b. "Numeri indici dei tassi delle retribuzioni minime contrattuali, base 1966 = 100." *Metodi e norme*, No. 9, Series A.
1971. "Numeri indici dei prezzi, base 1970 = 100." *Metodi e norme*, No. 12, Series A.
1976a. "Numeri indici della produzione industriale, base 1970 = 100." *Metodi e norme*, Series A, No. 14.
1976b. *Appendici al bollettino mensile di statistica*, September.
1977. *Appendici al bollettino mensile di statistica*, February.
1978a. "Rilevazioni campionaria della forza di lavoro." *Metodi e norme*, Series A, No. 15.
1978b. *Relazione generale sulla situazione del paese*. Appendice 2.
1978c. "Numeri indici dei prezzi, base 1976 = 100." *Metodi e norme*, No. 16, Series A.
1978d. "Indici dei prezzi al consumo per le famiglie di operai e impiegati (già indici del costo della vita), 1861–1977." *Collana di informazioni*, Vol. 2, No. 2.
1979a. "Una metodologia di raccordo per le serie statistiche sulle forze di lavoro." *Note e relazioni*, No. 56.
1979b. "Conti economici nazionali 1960–78, Nuova serie, Dati sommari." *Collana di informazioni*, Vol. 3, No. 6.
1986. *Sommario di statistiche storiche, 1926–1985*. Rome: Istituto centrale di statistica.
Istituto Gramsci, and Cespe. 1975. *La piccola e media industria nella crisi dell'economia italiana. Atti del convegno tenuto a Milano 4-5-6 novembre 1974*, 2 vols. Rome: Editori Riuniti.

Istituto Nazionale per l'Assicurazione contro gli Infortuni sul Lavoro (INAIL). (Various quarterly issues). *Notiziario Statistico.* Rome: INAIL.
Jalla, E. 1974. "La struttura dimensionale dell'industria manifatturiera italiana secondo i censimenti 1961 e 1971: analisi regionale." *Contributi di ricerca n. 3 sul sistema imprenditoriale italiano.* Turin: Fondazione G. Agnelli.
Jackson, Dudley, H. A. Turner, and Frank Wilkinson. 1972. *Do Trade Unions Cause Inflation? Two Studies: with a Theoretical Introduction and Policy Conclusion.* Cambridge University Press.
Jenkins, Craig. J. 1983. "Resource Mobilization Theory and the Study of Social Movements." *Annual Review of Sociology,* Vol. 9, pp. 527–53.
Jenkins, Gwilym, and Donald Watts. 1968. *Spectral Analysis and Its Applications.* San Francisco: Holden Day.
Jessop, Bob. 1982. *The Capitalist State.* New York: New York University Press.
Johnston, J. 1972. *Econometric Methods.* New York: McGraw-Hill.
Jurkat, Ernest H., and Dorothy B. Jurkat. 1949. "Economic Fluctuations of Strikes." *Industrial and Labor Relations Review,* Vol. 2, No. 4, pp. 527–45.
Kalecki, Michael. 1943. "Political Aspects of Full Employment." *Political Quarterly,* Vol. 14, No. 4, pp. 322–31.
Kallek, Shirley. 1976. "An Overview of the Objectives and Framework of Seasonal Adjustment." Paper presented at the Bureau of the Census Conference on Seasonal Analysis of Economic Time Series, Washington, D.C., September 9–10.
Katznelson, Ira, and Aristide Zolberg. 1986. *Working-Class Formation.* Princeton University Press.
Kaufman, Bruce. 1981. "Bargaining Theory, Inflation, and Cyclical Strike Activity in Manufacturing." *Industrial and Labor Relations Review,* Vol. 34, No. 3, pp. 333–55.
 1982. "The Determinants of Strikes in the United States, 1900–1977." *Industrial and Labor Relations Review,* Vol. 35, No. 4, pp. 491–503.
Kautsky, Karl. 1910. *The Class Struggle (Erfurt Program).* Chicago: Charles H. Kerr & Co.
Kendall, Sir Maurice. 1973. *Time-Series.* London: Charles Griffin & Co.
Kennan, John. 1985. "The Duration of Contract Strikes in U.S. Manufacturing." *Journal of Econometrics,* Vol. 28, No. 1, pp. 5–28.
Kerr, Clark. 1954. "Industrial Conflict and Its Mediation." *American Journal of Sociology,* Vol. 60, No. 3, pp. 230–45.
 1983. *The Future of Industrial Societies. Convergence or Continuing Diversity.* Cambridge, Mass.: Harvard University Press.
Kerr, Clark, John T. Dunlop, Frederick H. Harbison, and Charles A. Myers. 1960. *Industrialism and Industrial Man.* Cambridge, Mass.: Harvard University Press.
Kerr, Clark, and Abraham Siegel. 1954. "The Interindustry Propensity to Strike. An International Comparison." Pp. 189–212, in Arthur Kornhauser, Robert Dubin, and Arthur Ross (eds.), *Industrial Conflict.* New York: McGraw-Hill.
Kintsch, Walter, and Teun van Dijk. 1978. "Toward a Model of Text Comprehension and Production," *Psychological Review,* Vol. 85, No. 5, pp. 363–94.
Klein, Lawrence R., and R. S. Preston. 1967. "Some New Results in the Measurement of Capacity Utilization." *American Economic Review,* Vol. 57, No. 1, pp. 34–58.
Klein, Lawrence R., and Robert Summers. 1966. *The Wharton Index of Capacity Utilization.* Studies in Quantitative Economics No. 1. Department of Economics. Wharton School of Finance and Commerce. University of Pennsylvania.
Knowles, Kenneth G. J. C. 1952. *Strikes – A Study in Industrial Conflict.* Oxford: Blackwell.
Kocka, Jürgen. 1980. *White Collar Workers in America, 1890–1940.* Beverly Hills: Sage.
 1983. "Class Formation, Interest Articulation, and Public Policy: The Origins of the German White-Collar Class in the Late Nineteenth and Early Twentieth Centuries."

Pp. 63–82, in Suzanne Berger (ed.), *Organizing Interests in Western Europe.* Cambridge University Press.

Koenker, Diane P., and William G. Rosenberg. 1989. *Strikes and Revolution in Russia, 1917.* Princeton University Press.

Kogan, Norman. 1966. *A Political History of Postwar Italy.* New York: Praeger.

　1981. *A Political History of Postwar Italy. From the Old to the New Center-Left.* New York: Praeger.

Kondratieff, N.D. 1935. "The Long Waves in Economic Life." *Review of Economic Statistics,* Vol. 17, No. 6, pp. 105–15; reprinted in 1979 in *Review,* Vol. 2, No. 4, pp. 519–62.

Koopmans, Ruud. 1993. "The Dynamics of Protest Waves: West Germany, 1965 to 1989." *American Sociological Review,* Vol. 58, No. 5, pp. 637–58.

Kornhauser, Arthur. 1954a. "Human Motivations Underlying Industrial Conflict." Pp. 62–85, in Arthur Kornhauser, Robert Dubin, and Arthur Ross (eds.), *Industrial Conflict.* New York: McGraw-Hill.

　1954b. "The Undetermined Future of Industrial Conflict." Pp. 519–26, in Arthur Kornhauser, Robert Dubin, and Arthur Ross (eds.), *Industrial Conflict.* New York: McGraw-Hill.

Kornhauser, Arthur, Robert Dubin, and Arthur Ross (eds.). 1954. *Industrial Conflict.* New York: McGraw-Hill.

Korpi, Walter. 1974. "Conflict, Power and Relative Deprivation." *American Political Science Review,* Vol. 68, No. 4, pp. 1569–78.

　1978. *The Working Class in Welfare Capitalism.* London: Routledge & Kegan Paul.

　1981. "Unofficial Strikes in Sweeden." *British Journal of Industrial Relations,* Vol. 19, No. 1, pp. 66–86.

Korpi, Walter, and Michael Shalev. 1980. "Strikes, Power and Politics in the Western Nations, 1900–1976." Pp. 301–34, in Maurice Zeitlin (ed.), *Political Power and Social Theory,* Vol. 1. Greenwich, Conn.: JAI Press.

Kotz, David M. 1987. "Long Waves and Social Structures of Accumulation: A Critique and Reinterpretation." *Review of Radical Political Economics,* Vol. 19, No. 4, pp. 16–38.

　1990. "A Comparative Analysis of the Theory of Regulation and the Social Structure of Accumulation Theory." *Science and Society,* Vol. 54, No. 1, pp. 5–28.

Kuhn, James. 1961. *Bargaining in Grievance Settlement.* New York: Columbia University Press.

Lana, Angelo. 1972. "Bilancio ed esperienze decennali delle forme di lotta in agricoltura." *Quaderni di rassegna sindacale,* Vol. 10, No. 38, pp. 33–48.

Lange, Peter. 1979. "Il PCI e i possibili esiti della crisi italiana." Pp. 657–718, in Luigi Graziano and Sidney Tarrow (eds.), *La crisi italiana.* Turin: Einaudi.

　1987. "La crisi della concertazione sociale in Italia." *Giornale di diritto del lavoro e di relazioni industriali,* Vol. 9, No. 33, pp. 61–75.

Lange, Peter, and Marino Regini (eds.). 1989. *State, Market, and Social Regulation. New Perspectives on Italy.* Cambridge University Press.

Lange, Peter, George Ross, and Maurizio Vannicelli. 1982. *Unions, Change, and Crisis: French and Italian Union Strategy and the Political Economy, 1945–1980.* London: Allen & Unwin.

Lange, Peter, and Maurizio Vannicelli. 1982. "Strategy Under Stress: The Italian Union Movement and the Italian Crisis." Pp. 95–206, in Peter Lange, George Ross, and Maurizio Vannicelli (eds.), *Unions, Change, and Crisis: French and Italian Union Strategy and the Political Economy, 1945–1980.* London: Allen & Unwin.

Lanzalaco, Luca. 1990. *Dall'impresa all'associazione: le organizzazioni degli imprenditori. La Confindustria in prospettiva comparata.* Milan: Franco Angeli.

Lanzardo, Dario. 1979. *La rivolta di Piazza Statuto. Torino, Luglio 1962.* Milan: Feltrinelli.

Lanzardo, Liliana. 1976. "I consigli di gestione nella strategia della collaborazione." Pp. 325–66, in Accornero Aris (ed.), *Problemi del movimento sindacale in Italia 1943–1973*. Annali Feltrinelli. Milan: Feltrinelli.
Lanzardo, Liliana, and Massimo Vetere. 1965. "Interventi politici contro la razionalizzazione capitalistica," *Quaderni Rossi*, No. 6, pp. 46–140.
La Palombara, Joseph. 1957. *The Italian Labor Movement: Problems and Prospects*. Ithaca, N.Y.: Cornell University Press.
  1964. *Interest Groups in Italian Politics*. Princeton University Press.
  1966. *Italy: The Politics of Planning*. Syracuse University Press.
  1987. *Democracy Italian Style*. New Haven: Yale University Press.
Lapides, Kenneth (ed.). 1987. *Marx and Engels on the Trade Unions*. New York: Praeger.
Larsen, Wayne A., and Susan J. McCleary. 1972. "The Use of Partial Residual Plots in Regression Analysis." *Technometrics*, Vol. 14, No. 3, pp. 781–90.
La Valle, Davide. 1987. "La CISL di Milano attraverso i suoi iscritti," *Prospettiva sindacale*, Vol. 18, No. 65, pp. 133–70.
  1989. "Esiste un ciclo della partecipazione sindacale? Osservazioni sulla esperienza italiana." *Quaderni di sociologia*, Vol. 34, No. 12, pp. 33–66.
Lay, Adriana, Dora Marucco, and Maria Luisa Pesante. 1973. "Classe operaia e scioperi: ipotesi per il periodo 1880–1923." *Quaderni storici*, Vol. 8, No. 22, pp. 87–147.
Lay, Adriana, and Maria Luisa Pesante. 1974. "Ciclo economico e lotte operaie in Europa 1880–1920," *Rivista di storia contemporanea*, Vol. 3, No. 3.
Lazerson, Mark. 1988. "Labor Conflicts Within the Structure of the Law: Dismissals Under the Italian Workers' Charter in Two Plants." *International Journal of the Sociology of Law*, Vol. 16, pp. 31–50.
Lazonick, William. 1978. "The Subjugation of Labor to Capital: The Rise of the Capitalist System," *Review of Radical Political Economics*, Vol. 10, No. 1, pp. 1–31.
  1979. "Industrial Relations and Technical Change: The Case of the Self-Acting Mule," *Cambridge Journal of Economics*, Vol. 3, pp. 231–62.
Lefebvre, Georges. 1973. *The Great Fear of 1789. Rural Panic in Revolutionary France*. New York: Pantheon Books.
Lenin, Vladimir. 1989. *What Is to Be Done?* London: Penguin Books (1st ed. 1902).
Leonardi, Robert. 1978. "Gli Stati Uniti e il compromesso storico." *Il Mulino*, Vol. 27, pp. 370–90.
Leonardi, Robert, and Alan A. Platt. 1977. "La politica estera americana nei confronti della sinistra italiana." *Il Mulino*, Vol. 26, pp. 546–73.
Le Roy Ladurie, Emmanuel. 1979. *The Territory of the Historian*. University of Chicago Press.
  1981. *The Mind and Method of the Historian*. University of Chicago Press.
Lester, Richard A. 1958. *As Unions Mature*. Princeton University Press.
Levi, Arrigo. 1983. *Giovanni Agnelli. Intervista sul capitalismo moderno*. Bari: Laterza.
Levitt, Theodore. 1953a. "Prosperity versus Strikes." *Industrial and Labor Relations Review*, Vol. 6, No. 2, pp. 220–6.
  1953b. "Reply to Goldner." *Industrial and Labor Relations Review*, Vol. 6, No. 4, pp. 579–81.
  1954. "Reply to Blitz." *Industrial and Labor Relations Review*, Vol. 7, No. 4, pp. 462–5.
Lieberson, Stanley. 1991. "Small N's and Big Conclusions: An Examination of the Reasoning in Comparative Studies Based on a Small Number of Cases." *Social Forces*, Vol. 70, No. 2, pp. 307–32.
Lipietz, Alain. 1987. *Mirages and Miracles: The Crisis of Global Fordism*. London: Verso.
Lipset, Seymour Martin. 1981. *Political Man: The Social Bases of Politics*. Baltimore: Johns Hopkins University Press.

Locke, Richard. 1990. "The Resurgence of the Local Union: Industrial Restructuring and Industrial Relations in Italy." *Politics and Society*, Vol. 18, No. 3, pp. 347–79.

Locke, Richard, and Serafino Negrelli. 1989. "Il caso Fiat Auto." Pp. 61–95, in Marino Regini and Charles Sabel (eds.), *Strategie di riaggiustamento industriale*. Bologna: Il Mulino.

Long, Susan. 1979. "The Continuing Debate Over the Use of Ratio Variables: Facts and Fiction." Pp. 37–67, in Karl Schuessler (ed.), *Sociological Methodology, 1980*. San Francisco: Jossey Bass.

Lovell, Michael C. 1963. "Seasonal Adjustment of Economic Time Series and Multiple Regression Analysis." *Journal of the American Statistical Association*, Vol. 58, No. 304, pp. 993–1010.

Low-Beer, John. 1978. *Protest and Participation. The New Working Class in Italy*. Cambridge University Press.

Ludtke, Alf. 1979. "The Role of State Violence in the Period of Transition to Industrial Capitalism: The Example of Prussia from 1815 to 1848." *Social History*, Vol. 4, No. 2, pp. 175–222.

Lukacs, Georg. 1971. *History and Class Consciousness*. Cambridge, Mass.: MIT Press.

Lumley, Robert. 1990. *States of Emergency: Cultures of Revolt in Italy from 1968 to 1978*. London: Verso.

Luppi, Laura. 1974. "Autobianchi." Pp. 31–112, in Alessandro Pizzorno (ed.), *Lotte operaie e sindacato in Italia: 1968–1972, Vol. 1, Autobianchi e Innocenti*. Bologna: Il Mulino.

Luxemburg, Rosa. 1971. *The Mass Strike, The Political Party and the Trade Unions*. New York: Harper & Row, (1st ed. 1906).

Macdonald, D. F. 1960. *The State and the Trade Unions*. London: Macmillan.

Maestrali, Alcssandro. 1979. "Il sindacato e i delegati nell'industria metalmeccanica in provincia di Bologna." Pp. 21–47, in Giuseppe Della Rocca (ed.), *Potere e democrazia nel sindacato*. Rome: Edizioni lavoro.

Maier, Charles (ed.). 1978. *The Origins of the Cold War and Contemporary Europe*. New York: New Viewpoints.

1991a. "The Politics of Productivity: Foundations of American International Economic Policy After World War II." Pp. 169–202, in Charles Maier (ed.), *The Cold War in Europe*. New York: Markus Wiener Publishing.

1991b. *The Cold War in Europe*. New York: Markus Wiener Publishing.

Makridakis, Spyros, and Steven Wheelwright. 1978. *Forecasting Methods and Applications*. New York: Wiley.

Malfatti, Eugenia. 1972. "Le statistiche della occupazione e della disoccupazione in Italia." Pp. 355–465, in Francesco Ferrari, Francesco Forte, Francesco Indovina, Eugenia Malfatti, and Isidoro Franco Mariani (eds.), *Analisi metodologica delle statistiche economiche in Italia*. Milan: Comunità.

Malfatti, Eugenia, and Isidoro Franco Mariani. 1972. "Le statistiche salariali in Italia." Pp. 123–354, in Francesco Ferrari, Francesco Forte, Francesco Indovina, Eugenia Malfatti, and Isidoro Franco Mariani (eds.), *Analisi metodologica delle statistiche economiche in Italia*. Milan: Comunità.

Mallet, Serge. 1965. "Socialism and the New Working Class." *International Socialist Journal*, Vol. 2, No. 8, pp. 152–72.

1975. *The New Working Class*. Nottingham: Bertrand Russell Peace Foundation for Spokesmen Books.

Mammarella, Giuseppe. 1966. *Italy After Fascism. A Political History. 1943–1965*. Notre Dame, Ind.: University of Notre Dame Press.

1975. *L'Italia dopo il fascismo: 1943–1973*. Bologna: Il Mulino.

1990. *L'Italia contemporanea. 1943–1989*. Bologna: Il Mulino.

Manacorda, Gastone. 1953. *Il movimento operaio italiano attraverso i suoi congressi (1853–1892)*. Rome: Edizioni Rinascita.
Mandel, Ernest. 1980. *Long Waves in Capitalist Development*. Cambridge University Press.
Manghi, Bruno. 1977. *Declinare crescendo*. Bologna: Il Mulino.
Mangiarotti, Gabriella, and Giovanna Rossi. 1974. "Atteggiamenti e comportamenti rivendicativi." Pp. 115–52, in *Classe. Quaderni sulla condizione e sulla lotta operaia Quaderno No. 8. L'operaio massa nello sviluppo capitalistico*. Bari: Dedalo Libri.
Mann, Michael. 1973. *Consciousness and Action among the Western Working Class*. Atlantic Highlands, N.J.: Humanities Press.
March, Lucien. 1911. "Mouvements du commerce et du credit. Mouvement ouvrier en relation avec le mouvement des prix." *Bulletin de la Statistique generale de la France*. October, pp. 188–222.
—— 1913. "Grèves, grévistes et variations de prix." *Revenue d'Economie politique*, Vol. 27, pp. 113–5.
Marchese, Carlo. 1972. "Bilancio ed esperienze decennali delle forme di lotta nei pubblici servizi." *Quaderni di rassegna sindacale*, Vol. 10, No. 38, pp. 59–78.
Marglin, Stephen A. 1974. "What Do Bosses Do? The Origins and Functions of Hierarchy in Capitalist Production." *Review of Radical Political Economics*, Vol. 6, No. 2, pp. 60–92.
Mariani, Franco Isidoro. 1957. "La revisione della scala mobile dei salari." *Rassegna di statistiche del lavoro*, No. 1, pp. 3–20.
—— 1975. "Gli aspetti tecnici della riforma dell'indennità di contingenza." *Rassegna di statistiche del lavoro (Supplemento)*, pp. 12–28.
—— 1979. "Promemoria sulla scala mobile." *Rivista di politica economica*, Vol. 69, No. 11, pp. 1289–1300.
Marino, Giuseppe Carlo. 1991. *Guerra fredda e conflitto sociale in Italia. 1947–1953*. Caltanisetta–Rome: Salvatore Sciascia Editore.
Marradi, Alberto. 1978. "Immagini di massa della DC e del PCI." Pp. 66–103, in Alberto Martinelli and Gianfranco Pasquino (eds.), *La politica nell'Italia che cambia*. Milan: Feltrinelli.
Martinelli, Alberto. 1976. "Conflitti di lavoro e mediazione della regione Lombardia: il punto di vista sindacale." Pp. 9–48, in Mirko Fidanza and Tiziano Treu (eds.), *La mediazione della regione nei conflitti di lavoro: l'esperienza lombarda*. Bologna: Il Mulino.
—— 1977. "Una prima indagine sugli atteggiamenti imprenditoriali nella piccola e media industria lombarda." Pp. 311–58, in Federazione Regionale fra le Associazioni Industriali della Lombardia (ed.), *La piccola e media industria in Lombardia, Vol. 2, Relazioni del Comitato Scientifico*. Milan: Edizioni Industriali.
—— 1978. "La cultura economico-politica e ideologica degli imprenditori." Pp. 15–71, in Darko Bratina and Alberto Martinelli (eds.), *Gli imprenditori e la crisi. Ricerca sull'imprenditorialità a cura dell'IDOM – Impresa Domani*. Bologna: Il Mulino.
Martinelli, Alberto, Antonio Chiesi, and Nando Dalla Chiesa. 1981. *I grandi imprenditori italiani. Profilo sociale della classe dirigente economica*. Milan: Feltrinelli.
Martinelli, Alberto, and Tiziano Treu. 1984. "Employers Assosiations in Italy." Pp. 264–93, in John Windmuller and Alan Gladstone (eds.), *Employers Associations and Industrial Relations. A Comparative Study*. Oxford: Clarendon Press.
Masiero, Attilio. 1974. "Dall'operaio di mestiere all'operaio massa. Modello di sviluppo, organizzazione del lavoro e coscienza operaia nel Vicentino." Pp. 271–340, in *Classe. Quaderni sulla condizione e sulla lotta operaia. Quaderno No. 8. L'operaio massa nello sviluppo capitalistico*. Bari: Dedalo Libri.
Mattina, Enzo. 1981. *FIAT e sindacati negli anni '80*. Milan: Rizzoli Editore.

Mattina, Liborio. 1991. *Gli industriali e la democrazia. La Confindustria nella formazione dell'Italia repubblicana*. Bologna: Il Mulino.
Mauro, Martin J. 1982. "Strikes as a Result of Imperfect Information." *Industrial and Labor Relations Review*, Vol. 35, No. 4, pp. 522–38.
Mauro, Vincenzo. 1973. *Lotte dei contadini in Calabria. Testimonianze sulle lotte dei braccianti negli anni 1944–1954*. Milan: Sapere Edizioni.
Mayhew, K. 1979. "Economists and Strikes." *Oxford Bulletin of Economics and Statistics*, Vol. 41, No. 1, pp. 1–19.
McCloskey, N. Donald. 1985. *The Rhetoric of Economics*. Madison: University of Wisconsin Press.
Meldolesi, Luca. 1972. *Disoccupazione ed esercito industriale di riserva in Italia*. Bari: Laterza.
Melotti, Umberto. 1964. *Lo sciopero*. Milan: La Culturale.
Melucci, Alberto. 1975. "Una rassegna ragionata dei dati." Pp. 223–310, in Tiziano Treu (ed.), *Sindacato e magistratura nei conflitti di lavoro. Vol. 1. L'uso politico dello Statuto dei Lavoratori*. Bologna: Il Mulino.
Melucci, Alberto, and Franco Rositi. 1975. "L'ambivalenza istituzionale: sindacato e magistratura nell'applicazione dello statuto dei lavoratori." Pp. 129–200, in Tiziano Treu (ed.), *Sindacato e magistratura nei conflitti di lavoro. Vol. 1. L'uso politico dello Statuto dei Lavoratori*. Bologna: Il Mulino.
Merli, Stefano. 1972. *Proletariato di fabbrica e capitalismo industriale*. Florence: La nuova Italia.
Merli Brandini, Pietro. 1971. "Sindacati e struttura contrattuale." *Il sindacato in Italia 1960–70*, Quaderni di rassegna sindacale, Vol. 9, No. 31/32, pp. 62–74.
Mershon, Carol A. 1986. *The Micropolitics of Union Action: Industrial Conflict in Italian Factories*. Unpublished Ph.D. dissertation. Yale University.
  1989. "Between Workers and Union: Factory Councils in Italy." *Comparative Politics*, Vol. 21, No. 2, pp. 215–35.
Miata, Ernesto, Pasquale Nonno, Alberto Bonifazi, and Riccardo Corato (eds.), 1970. *Repressione!* Rome: Tindalo.
Michels, Robert. 1966. *Political Parties*. New York: Free Press (1st ed. 1915).
Migone, Gian Giacomo. 1974. "Stati Uniti, FIAT e repressione antioperaia negli anni cinquanta," *Rivista di storia contemporanea*, Vol. 2, pp. 232–81.
Milanaccio, Alfredo, Giampiero Boggio, Lucio Ceccarelli, Giovanna Cuminatto, Sergio Freilone, Fabio Fucci, Vincenzo Gallo, Tommaso Panero, Armando Pomatto, and Franco Sburlati. 1978. *La partecipazione subalterna. Una ricerca con cinque consigli di fabbrica*. Turin: Einaudi.
Milanaccio, Alfredo, and Luca Ricolfi. 1976. *Lotte operaie e ambiente di lavoro. Mirafiori 1968–1974*. Turin: Einaudi.
Mills, C. Wright. 1959. *The Sociological Imagination*. Oxford University Press.
Ministero del Lavoro e della Previdenza Sociale. (Various quarterly issues). *Rassegna di statistiche del lavoro*. Rome: MLPS.
Miscione, Michele. 1978. *Cassa integrazione e tutela della disoccupazione*. Napoli: Jovene.
Moni, Adolfo. 1980. "Le aziende tessili nella zona pratese," *Quaderni di rassegna sindacale*, Vol. 18, No. 86–87, pp. 92–5.
Montgomery, David. 1979. *Workers' Control in America: Studies in History of Work, Technology and Labor Struggles*. Cambridge University Press.
Moore, Barrington. 1978. *Injustice. The Social Bases of Obedience and Revolt*. White Plains, N.Y.: M.E. Sharpe.
Moore, David S., and George P. McCabe. 1993. *Introduction to the Practice of Statistics*. New York: W.H. Freeman and Company.

Moorhouse, H. 1973. "The Political Incorporation of the British Working Class: An Interpretation." *Sociology*, Vol. 7, pp. 341–59.
Morisi, Massimo, and Cetti Vacante. 1981. "L'esperienza parlamentare della CGIL e della CISL," *Laboratorio politico, Il sindacato nella crisi*, Vol. 1, No. 4, pp. 152–73.
Moro, Carlo. 1980. "La contrattazione aziendale in Lombardia (1979–80)." *Quaderni di rassegna sindacale*, Vol. 18, No. 84–85, pp. 134–52.
Mortillaro, Felice. 1984. *Sindacati e no. Primo rapporto della Federmeccanica sulle relazioni industriali.* Milano: Edizioni del Sole 24 Ore.
  1986. *Aspettando il robot. Secondo rapporto della Federmeccanica sulle relazioni industriali.* Milano: Edizioni del Sole 24 Ore.
Mottura, Giovanni. 1961. "Cronaca delle lotte ai Cotonifici Valle di Susa." *Quaderni Rossi*, No. 1, Lotte operaie nello sviluppo capitalistico. Reprinted in 1970 by Milan: Sapere Edizioni.
Mousnier, Roland. 1970. *Peasant Uprisings in Seventeenth–Century France, Russia, and China.* New York: Harper & Row.
Mutti, Antonio, and Paolo Segatti. 1977. *La borghesia di stato. Struttura e funzioni dell'impresa pubblica in Italia.* Milan: Mazzotta.
Nardozzi, Gian Giacomo (ed.). 1980. *I difficili anni '70.* Milan: Etas Libri.
Nash, John F. Jr. 1950. "The Bargaining Problem." *Econometrica*, Vol. 18, No. 2, pp. 155–62.
Negrelli, Serafino. 1982. "La Pirelli dopo l'autunno caldo. Studi di un caso," *Giornale di diritto del lavoro e di relazioni industriali*, Vol. 4, No. 15, pp. 485–516.
  1989. "Il caso Italtel." Pp. 171–206, in Marino Regini and Charles F. Sabel (eds.), *Strategie di riaggiustamento industriale.* Bologna: Il Mulino.
Negrelli, Serafino, and Ettore Santi. 1990. "Industrial Relations in Italy." Pp. 154–98, in Guido Baglioni and Colin Crouch (eds.), *European Industrial Relations. The Challenge of Flexibility.* Newbury Park, CA.: SAGE.
Nelson, Daniel. 1975. *Managers and Workers, Origins of the New Factory System in the United States, 1880–1920.* Madison: University of Wisconsin Press.
  1980. *Frederick W. Taylor and the Rise of Scientific Management.* Madison: University of Wisconsin Press.
Nelson, R. Charles. 1973. *Applied Time Series Analysis for Managerial Forecasting.* San Francisco: Holden Day.
Nerlove, Marc. 1964. "Spectral Analysis of Seasonal Adjustment Procedures." *Econometrica*, Vol. 32, No. 3, pp. 241–86.
Neufeld, Maurice F. 1954. *Labor Unions and National Politics in Italian Industrial Plants – A Study of the Development and Functions of Grievance Committees in Italy.* Ithaca, N.Y.: Cornell University Press.
  1961. *Italy: School for Awakening Countries. The Italian Labor Movement in Its Political, Social and Economic Setting from 1800 to 1960.* Ithaca, N.Y.: Cornell University Press.
Newby, Howard. 1979. *The Deferential Worker.* Harmondsworth, U.K.: Penguin.
Nordhaus, William. 1975. "The Political Business Cycle." *Review of Economic Studies*, Vol. 42, No. 2, pp. 169–90.
Obershall, Anthony. 1973. *Social Conflict and Social Movements.* Englewood Cliffs, N.J.: Prentice-Hall.
Offe, Claus. 1975. "The Theory of the Capitalist State and the Problem of Policy Formation." Pp. 125–44, in Leon Lindberg, Robert Alford, Colin Crouch, and Claus Offe (eds.), *Stress and Contradiction in Modern Capitalism.* Boston: Lexington Books.
Offe, Claus, and Volker Ronge. 1975. "Theses on the Theory of the State." *New German Critique*, No. 6, pp. 137–47.

Offe, Claus, and Helmut Wiesenthal, "Two Logics of Collective Action: Theoretical Notes on Social Class and Organizational Form." Pp. 67–116, in Maurice Zeitlin, (ed.), *Political Power and Social Theory*, Vol. 1, 1980, Greenwich, Conn.: JAI Press.

Ollman, Bertell. 1971. *Alienation, Marx's Conception of Man in Capitalist Society*. Cambridge University Press.

1972. "Toward Class Consciousness in the Working Class," *Politics and Society*, Vol. 3, No. 3, pp. 1–24.

Olson, Mancur Jr. 1968. *The Logic of Collective Action*. New York: Schocken Books.

Onofri, Fabrizio. 1955. *La condizione operaia in Italia*. Rome: Editori Riuniti.

Ottone, Piero. 1965. *Gli industriali si confessano*. Florence: Vallecchi Editore.

Paci, Massimo. 1973. *Mercato del lavoro e classi sociali in Italia*. Bologna: Il Mulino.

(ed.). 1978. *Capitalismo e classi sociali in Italia*. Bologna: Il Mulino.

Pagani, Massimo. 1973. "Il Concetto e la misura dell'assenteismo dal lavoro." *Rassegna di statistiche del lavoro (Supplemento 2)*, pp. 22–41.

Palanca, Vaifra. 1979. "Dinamica dello sviluppo nelle province italiane 1963–76." *Congiuntura sociale*, No. 3, pp. 1–26.

1983. "La geografia del disagio sociale: Italia 1971–81," *Politica ed economia*, Vol. 14, No. 9, pp. 40–8.

Paldman, Martin, and Peder Pedersen. 1982. "The Macroeconomic Strike Model: A Study of Seventeen Countries, 1948–1975." *Industrial and Labor Relations Review*, Vol. 35, No. 4, pp. 504–21.

Pasquino, Gianfranco. 1985. "Il partito comunista nel sistema politico italiano." Pp. 128–69, Gianfranco Pasquino (ed.), *Il sistema politico italiano*. Bologna: Il Mulino.

Pastorino, Silvana, and Alessandro Ragazzoni. 1980. "I contenuti della ricerca." Pp. 27–154, in Valeria Maione, Silvana Pastorino, Alessandro Ragazzoni, Gianni Tamburri, and Vittorio Traverso (eds.), *Vivere in fabbrica. Ricerca dei Giovani Imprenditori sull'organizzazione del lavoro nella piccola e media impresa*. Rome: CEDIS.

Pencavel, John H. 1970. "An Investigation into Industrial Strike Activity in Britain." *Econometrica*, Vol. 37, No. 147, pp. 239–56.

Pennacchi, Laura. 1980. "Decentramento Produttivo o Divisione del Lavoro?" *Politica ed economia*, Vol. 11, No. 2, pp. 33–40.

Perrone, Luca. 1983. "Positional Power and Propensity to Strike," *Politics and Society*, Vol. 12, pp. 231–61.

1984. "Positional Power, Strikes, and Wages," *American Sociological Review*, Vol. 49, pp. 412–21.

Perrot, Michelle. 1968. "Grèves, grévistes et conjoncture. Vieux problem, travaux neufs." *Le mouvement social*, No. 63, pp. 109–24.

1974. *Les ouvriers en grève (France 1871–1890)*. Paris: Mouton.

1979. "The Three Ages of Industrial Discipline in Nineteenth-Century France." Pp. 149–68, John M. Merriman (ed.), *Consciousness and Class Experience in Nineteenth-Century Europe*. New York: Holmes & Meier.

Perulli, Paolo. 1982. "Il conflitto del compromesso." *Laboratorio politico, Il compromesso storico*, Vol. 2, No. 2–3, pp. 290–300.

Perulli, Paolo, and Carlo Trigilia. 1990. "Organizzazione degli interessi e relazioni industriali nelle aree di piccola impresa." Pp. 73–88, in Paolo Perulli (ed.), *Le relazioni industriali nella piccola impresa*. Milan: Franco Angeli.

Peschiera, Filippo (ed.). 1976. *Sindacato, industria e stato nel dopoguerra. Storia delle relazioni industriali in Italia dal 1943 al 1948*. Florence: Le Monnier.

1979. *Sindacato, industria e stato negli anni del centrismo. Storia delle relazioni industriali in Italia dal 1948 al 1958*. 2 vols. Florence: Le Monnier.

1982. *Sindacato industria e stato nel centrosinistra. Storia delle relazioni industriali in Italia dal 1958 al 1971*. Florence: Le Monnier.
Phillips, A. W. 1958. "The Relation Between Unemployment and the Rate of Change of Money Wage Rates in the United Kingdom, 1861–1957." *Economica*, New Series, Vol. 25, No. 100, pp. 283–99.
Pipan, Tatiana. 1989. *Sciopero contro l'utente*. Turin: Bollati Boringhieri.
Pipan, Tatiana, and Dario Salerni. 1975. *Il sindacato come soggetto di equilibrio*. Milan: Feltrinelli.
Pirzio Ammassari, Gloria. 1976. *La politica della Confindustria*. Naples: Liguori.
Piven, Frances Fox, and Richard A. Cloward. 1979. *Poor People's Movements. Why They Succeed, How They Fail*. New York: Vintage Books.
Pizzorno, Alessandro. 1973. "I sindacati nel sistema politico italiano: aspetti storici." Pp. 117–46, in Paolo Farneti (ed.) *Il sistema politico italiano*. Bologna: Il Mulino.
 1974a. "I ceti medi nel meccanismo del consenso." Pp. 314–37, in Fabio Luca Cavazza and Stephen R. Graubard (eds.), *Il caso italiano*. Milan: Garzanti.
 1974b. "Introduzione." Pp. 7–27, in Laura Luppi and Emilio Reyneri, *Autobianchi e Innocenti*, Vol. 1, Pizzorno, Alessandro (ed.), *Lotte operaie e sindacato in Italia: 1968v1972*. Bologna: Il Mulino.
 (ed.). 1974–75. *Lotte operaie e sindacato in Italia: 1968–1972*, 6 vols. Bologna: Il Mulino.
 1977. "Fra azione di classe e sistemi corporativi. Osservazioni comparate sulle rappresentanze del lavoro nei paesi capitalistici avanzati." Pp. 949–86, in Aris Accornerno (ed.), *Movimento sindacale e societa italiana*. Milan: Feltrinelli.
 1978a. "Political Exchange and Collective Identity in Industrial Conflict." Pp. 277–98, in Colin Crouch and Alessandro Pizzorno (eds.), *The Resurgence of Class Conflict in Western Europe Since 1968. Volume 2. Comparative Analyses*. New York: Holmes & Meier.
 1978b. "Le due logiche dell'azione di classe." Pp. 7–45, in Alessandro Pizzorno, Emilio Reyneri, Marino Regini, and Ida Regalia (eds.), *Lotte operaie e sindacato: il ciclo 1968–1972 in Italia*. Bologna: Il Mulino.
Pizzorno, Alessandro, Emilio Reyneri, Marino Regini, and Ida Regalia. 1978. *Lotte operaie e sindacato: il ciclo 1968–1972 in Italia*. Bologna: Il Mulino.
Plosser, Charles I., and G. William Schwert. 1978. "Money, Income and Sunspots: Measuring Economic Relationships and the Effects of Differencing." *Journal of Monetary Economics*, Vol. 4, No. 4, pp. 637–60.
Polo, Gabriele (ed.). 1989. *I tamburi di Mirafiore. Testimonianze operaie attorno all'autunno caldo alla FIAT*. Turin: Cric Editore.
Porrello, Antonio. 1979. *Politica sindacale e contrattazione aziendale in provincia di Treviso nel triennio 1976–1978*. Treviso: SIT.
Poulantzas, Nicos. 1969. "The Problem of the Capitalist State." *New Left Review*, Vol. 58, pp. 67–78.
Prais, S. J. 1978. "The Strike-Proneness of Large Plants in Britain." *Journal of the Royal Statistical Society*. Series A, Vol. 141, part 3, pp. 368–84.
Procacci, Giuliano. 1970. *La lotta di classe in Italia agli inizi del secolo XX*. Turin: Einaudi.
Prospettiva sindacale. 1980. *Il sindacato in una regione rossa*. Vol. 11, No. 37.
 1981. *Il sindacato in una regione bianca*. Vol. 12, No. 41.
Provasi, Giancarlo. 1976. *Borghesia industriale e Democrazia Cristiana. Sviluppo economico e mediazione politica dalla Ricostruzione agli anni '70*. Bari: De Donato.
Przeworski, Adam. 1977. "Proletariat into a Class: The Process of Class Formation from Karl Kautsky's 'The Class Struggle' to Recent Controversies." *Politics and Society*, Vol. 4, pp. 343–401.

1980. "Material Bases of Consent. Economics and Politics in a Hegemonic System." *Political Power and Social Theory*. Vol. 1, pp. 21–66.

1980–1981. "Material Interests, Class Compromise, and the Transition to Socialism." *Politics and Society*, Vol. 10, pp. 125–53.

Przeworski, Adam, and Michael Wallerstein. 1982. "The Structure of Class Conflict in Democratic Capitalist Societies." *American Political Science Review*, Vol. 76, No. 2, pp. 215–38.

Pugno, Emilio. 1961. "Assemblee operaie e sindacato," *Quaderni Rossi*, No. 1, pp. 111–4, Lotte operaie nello sviluppo capitalistico; reprinted in 1970 by Milan: Sapere Edizioni.

Pugno, Emilio, and Sergio Garavini. 1974. *Gli anni duri alla FIAT. La resistenza sindacale e la ripresa*. Turin: Einaudi.

Purcell, Kate. 1979. "Militancy and Acquiescence Amongst Women Workers." Pp. 112–31, in Sandra Burman (ed.), *Fit Work for Women*. New York: St. Martin's Press.

Quartararo, Rosaria. 1986. *Italia e Stati Uniti. Gli anni difficili (1945–1952)*. Naples: Edizioni Scientifiche Italiane.

Radi, Luciano. 1975. *Partiti e classi sociali in Italia*. Turin: SEI.

Rao, P., and Z. Griliches. 1969. "Small Sample Properties of Several Two-Stage Regression Methods in the Context of Auto-Correlated Errors." *Journal of the American Statistical Association*, Vol. 64, pp. 253–72.

Reder, Melvin W., and George R. Neumann. 1980. "Conflict and Contract: The Case of Strikes." *Journal of Political Economy*, Vol. 88, No. 5, pp. 867–86.

Rees, Albert. 1952. "Industrial Conflict and Business Fluctuations." *Journal of Political Economy*, Vol. 60, No. 5, pp. 371–82.

Regalia, Ida. 1975a. Gli strumenti d'informazione del sindacato: le assemblee, *Quaderni di rassegna sindacale*, Vol. 13, No. 56–7, pp. 103–12.

1975b. "Sit-Siemens." Pp. 25–136, in Alessandro Pizzorno (ed.), *Lotte operaie e sindacato in Italia: 1968–1972, Vol. 4, Sit-Siemens e GTE*. Bologna: Il Mulino.

1978. "Rappresentanza operaia e sindacato: Mutamento di un sistema di relazioni industriali." Pp. 179–290, in Alessandro Pizzorno, Emilio Reyneri, Marino Regini, and Ida Regalia (eds.), *Lotte operaie e sindacato: il ciclo 1968–1972 in Italia*. Bologna: Il Mulino.

1984a. *Eletti e abbandonati. Modelli e stili di rappresentanza in fabbrica*. Bologna: Il Mulino.

1984b. "La mediazione della regione nei conflitti di lavoro come fattore di riequilibrio delle relazioni industriali," *Prospettiva sindacale*, Vol. 15, No. 54, pp. 137–73.

Regalia, Ida, Marino Regini, and Emilio Reyneri. 1978. "Labour Conflicts and Industrial Relations in Italy." Pp. 101–58, in Colin Crouch and Alessandro Pizzorno (eds.), *The Resurgence of Class Conflict in Western Europe Since 1968. Volume 1. National Studies*. New York: Holmes & Meier.

Regini, Marino. 1974. "Candy." Pp. 23–110, in Alessandro Pizzorno (ed.), *Lotte operaie e sindacato in Italia: 1968–1972, Vol. 2, Candy e Ignis (IRE)*, Bologna: Il Mulino.

1975. "GTE." Pp. 153–219, in Alessandro Pizzorno (ed.), *Lotte operaie e sindacato in Italia: 1968–1972, Vol. 4, Sit-Siemens e GTE*. Bologna: Il Mulino.

1980. "Labour Unions, Industrial Action and Politics." Pp. 49–66, in Peter Lange and Sidney Tarrow (eds.), *Italy in Transition, Conflict and Consensus*. London: Frank Cass.

1981. *I dilemmi del sindacato. Conflitto e partecipazione negli anni settanta e ottanta*. Bologna: Il Mulino.

1982. "Changing Relationships Between Labour and the State in Italy: Towards a Neo-Corporatist System?" Pp. 109–32, in Gerhard Lehmbruch and Philippe C. Schmitter (eds.), *Patterns of Corporatist Policy-Making*. London: Sage.

1983. "Le condizioni dello scambio politico. Nascita e declino della concertazione in Italia e Gran Bretagna." *Stato e mercato*, No. 9, pp. 353–84.

1984. "I tentativi italiani di 'patto sociale' a cavallo degli anni '80." *Il Mulino*, Vol. 33, No. 2, pp. 291–304.

1985. "Relazioni industriali e sistema politico: l'evoluzione recente e le prospettive degli anni '80." Pp. 15–42, in Mimmo Carrieri and Paolo Perulli (eds.), *Il teorema sindacale*. Bologna: Il Mulino.

(ed.). 1988. *La sfida della flessibilità*. Milan: Franco Angeli.

Regini, Marino, and Emilio Reyneri. 1971. *Lotte operaie e organizzazione del lavoro*. Padua: Marsilio.

Regini, Marino, and Charles Sabel (eds.). 1989. *Strategie di riaggiustamento industriale*. Bologna: Il Mulino.

Reyneri, Emilio. 1973. "I livelli di sindacalizzazione della forza lavoro industriale in Italia." *Rassegna italiana di sociologia*, Vol. 14, No. 3, pp. 361–94.

1974a. "Innocenti." Pp. 115–209, in Alessandro Pizzorno (ed.), *Lotte operaie e sindacato in Italia: 1968–1972, Vol. 1, Autobianchi e Innocenti*. Bologna: Il Mulino.

1974b. "Magneti Marelli." Pp. 23–123, in Alessandro Pizzorno (ed.), *Lotte operaie e sindacato in Italia: 1968–1972, Vol. 3, Magneti Marelli e Ercole Marelli*. Bologna: Il Mulino.

1978. *Il "Maggio strisciante:" l'inizio della mobilitazione operaia*. Pp. 49–107, in Alessandro Pizzorno, Emilio Reyneri, Marino Regini, and Ida Regalia (eds.), *Lotte operaie e sindacato: il ciclo 1968–1972 in Italia*. Bologna: Il Mulino.

1987. "Il mercato del lavoro italiano tra controllo statale e regolazione sociale." Pp. 151–76, Peter Lange and Marino Regini (eds.), *Stato e regolazione sociale. Nuove prospettive sul caso italiano*. Bologna: Il Mulino.

1989a. "Mercato e politiche del lavoro." Pp. 345–88, in Gian Primo Cella and Tiziano Treu (eds.), *Relazioni industriali. Manuale per l'analisi dell'esperienza italiana*. Bologna: Il Mulino.

1989b. "The Italian Labor Market: Between State Control and Social Regulation." Pp. 129–46, in Peter Lange and Marino Regini (eds.), *State, Market, and Social Regulation. New Perspectives on Italy*. Cambridge University Press.

Reyneri, Emilio, and Anna Tempia. 1974. "Le caratteristiche sociali e professionali." Pp. 59–94, in *Classe. Quaderni sulla condizione e sulla lotta operaia. Quaderno No. 8. L'operaio massa nello sviluppo capitalistico*. Bari: Dedalo Libri.

Rieser, Vittorio. 1981. "Sindacato e composizione di classe." *Laboratorio politico, Il sindacato nella crisi*, Vol. 1, No. 4, July–August, pp. 56–73.

Rigola, Rinaldo. 1947. *Storia del movimento operaio italiano*. Milan: Edizioni Domus.

Rist, Charles. 1907. "La progression des grèves en France et sa valeur symptomatique." *Revue d'Economie Politique*, Vol. 21, pp. 161–93.

1912. "Relations entre les variations annuelles du chomage, des grèves et des prix." *Revue d'Economie politique*, Vol. 26, pp. 748–58.

Riva, Massimo (ed.). 1976. *Luciano Lama. Intervista sul sindacato*. Bari: Laterza.

Robotti, Lorenzo. 1973. "Incidenza dell'indennità di contingenza nella dinamica salariale in Italia, 1951–70." *Rassegna di statistiche del lavoro (Supplemento 1)*, pp. 7–21.

Roccella, Massimo. 1979. "Sindacato e poteri pubblici: Il quadro istituzionale." Pp. 19–47, in Tiziano Treu, Massimo Roccella, and Giuseppe Ferrari (eds.), *Sindacalisti nelle istituzioni*. Rome: Edizioni Lavoro.

1982. "La composizione dei conflitti di lavoro nella grande impresa: il caso dell'Alfa Romeo di Arese," *Giornale di diritto del lavoro e di relazioni industriali*, Vol. 4, No. 14, pp. 251–73.

Rollier, Matteo, and Tullia Piccoli. 1978. "Note preliminari per una indagine organizzativa sulla federazione lavoratori metalmeccanici di Torino." Pp. 129–40, in Giovanni Gasparini (ed.), *Sindacato e Organizzazione*. Milan: Franco Angeli.

Romagnoli, Guido. 1971. "Delegati e sindacato: dialettica o integrazione?" *Prospettiva sindacale*, Vol. 2, No. 2, pp. 17–104.

———. 1973. "Democrazia di base e organizzazione di classe nell'esperienza dei consigli," *Prospettiva sindacale*, Vol. 4, No. 1, pp. 1–75.

———. 1976. *Consigli di fabbrica e democrazia sindacale*. Milan: Mazzotta.

———. 1979. "Il movimento degli scioperi negli Stati Uniti d'America (1900–1970)." Pp. 451–82, in Gian Primo Cella (ed.), *Il movimento degli scioperi nel XX secolo*. Bologna: Il Mulino.

Romagnoli, Guido, and Giuseppe Della Rocca. 1989. "Il sindacato." Pp. 85–134, in Gian Primo Cella and Tiziano Treu (eds.), *Relazioni industriali. Manuale per l'analisi dell'esperienza italiana*. Bologna: Il Mulino.

Romagnoli, Guido, and Maurizio Rossi. 1980. "La sindacalizzazione in Italia fra ciclo economico, conflitto e facilitazioni istituzionali." Pp. 43–174, in Guido Romagnoli (ed.), *La sindacalizzazione tra ideologia e pratica. Il caso italiano, 1950/1977. Volume 1*. Rome: Edizioni Lavoro.

Romeo, Rosario. 1961. *Breve storia della grande industria in Italia*. Rocca San Casciano: Cappelli.

Ronchi, Rossella. 1990. "Le strutture di rappresentanza in azienda. Alcune tendenze nella realtà lombarda," *Prospettiva sindacale*, Vol. XXI, No. 78, pp. 175–84.

Ross, Arthur H. 1954. "Concluding Observations." Pp. 531–3, in Arthur Kornhauser, Robert Dubin, and Arthur Ross (eds.), *Industrial Conflict*. New York: McGraw-Hill.

Ross, Arthur H., and Paul T. Hartman. 1960. *Changing Patterns of Industrial Conflict*. New York: Wiley.

Rubery, Jill. 1978. "Structured Labour Markets, Worker Organization and Low Pay," *Cambridge Journal of Economics*, Vol. 2, No. 1, pp. 17–36.

Sabel, Charles. 1982. *Work and Politics. The Division of Labor in Industry*. Cambridge University Press.

Salerni, Dario. 1980. *Sindacato e forza lavoro all'Alfasud. Un caso anomalo di conflittualità industriale*. Turin: Einaudi.

Salvarani, Gianni, and Alberto Bonifazi. 1973. *Le nuove strutture del sindacato*. Milan: Franco Angeli.

Salvati, Michele. 1976. "L'origine della crisi in corso." Pp. 216–58, in Mario Centorrino (ed.), *Consumi sociali e sviluppo economico in Italia, 1960–1975*. Rome: Coines.

———. 1983. "May 1968 and the Hot Autumn of 1969: The Responses of Two Ruling Classes." Pp. 331–66, in Suzanne Berger (ed.), *Organizing Interests in Western Europe*. Cambridge University Press.

———. 1984. *Economia e politica in Italia dal dopoguerra a oggi*. Milan: Garzanti.

Sani, Giacomo. 1978. "La composizione degli elettorati comunista e democristiano." Pp. 104–23, in Alberto Martinelli and Gianfranco Pasquino, *La politica nell'Italia che cambia*. Milan: Feltrinelli.

Santagata, Walter. 1981. "Ciclo politico-economico: il caso italiano, 1953–1979." *Stato e mercato*, Vol. 1, No. 2, pp. 257–99.

Santi, Ettore. 1974. "Ignis (IRE)." Pp. 113–209, in Alessandro Pizzorno (ed.), *Lotte operaie e sindacato in Italia: 1968–1972, Vol. 2, Candy e Ignis (IRE)*, Bologna: Il Mulino.

———. 1987. "Un decennio di sindacalizzazione (1977–1986)," CISL, Segreteria Organizzativa Confederale-CESOS (Centrodi Studi Sociali e Sindacali) (mimeograph).

———. 1988. "Un decennio di sindacalizzazione (1977–1986)," *Quaderni di Sociologia*, Vol. 34, No. 11, pp. 61–98.

Santomero, Anthony M., and John J. Seater. 1978. "The Inflation–Unemployment Trade-off: A Critique of the Literature." *Journal of Economic Literature*, Vol. 16, pp. 499–544.
Sapelli, Giulio. 1976. "Appunti per una storia dell'organizzazione scientifica del lavoro in Italia." *Quaderni di sociologia*, Vol. 25, No. 2–3, pp. 154–71.
Sapsford, D. 1975. "A Time Series Analysis of U.K. Industrial Disputes." *Industrial Relations*, Vol. 14, No. 2, pp. 242–9.
Sartori, Giovanni. 1973. "Il potere del lavoro nella società post-pacificata (un futuribile sindacale)." *Rivista italiana di scienza politica*, Vol. 3, No. 1, pp. 31–82.
―――. 1982. "Bipartitismo imperfetto o pluralismo polarizzato?" Pp. 7–44, in Giovanni Sartori, *Teoria dei partiti e caso italiano*. Milan: Sugarco Edizioni.
Scalfari, Eugenio. 1977. *Guido Carli. Intervista sul capitalismo italiano*. Bari: Laterza.
Scalfari, Eugenio, and Giuseppe Turani. 1975. *Razza padrona. Storia della borghesia di stato*. Milan: Feltrinelli.
Schmidt, Peter, and Roger N. Waud. 1973. "The Almon Lag Technique and the Monetary Versus Fiscal Policy Debate." *Journal of the American Statistics Association*, Vol. 68, No. 341, pp. 11–9.
Schuessler, Karl. 1974. "Analysis of Ratio Variables: Opportunities and Pitfalls." *American Journal of Sociology*, Vol. 80, No. 2, pp. 379–96.
Schumpeter, Joseph. 1939. *Business Cycles. A Theoretical, Historical, and Statistical Analysis of the Capitalist Process*. New York: McGraw-Hill.
Sclavi, Gastone. 1971. "La contrattazione aziendale come punto di forza." *Quaderni di rassegna sindacale*, Vol. 9, No. 31–32, pp. 168–84.
Screpanti, Ernesto. 1987. "Long Cycles in Strike Activity: An Empirical Investigation." *British Journal of Industrial Relations*. Vol. 25, No. 1. pp. 99–124.
Sebastiani, Chiara. 1982. "Il ceto politico del compromesso storico." *Laboratorio politico, Il compromesso storico*, Vol. 2, No. 2–3, pp. 211–40.
Segatori, Roberto, and Daniela Torresini. 1979. *La professionalità difficile. Nascita e sviluppo dell'inquadramento unico*. Rome: CEDIS.
Sellier, Francois. 1960. "Cohesion syndacale et niveau de negotiation." *Sociologie du travail*, Vol. 12, No. 4, pp. 289–99.
Sennett, Richard, and Jonathan Cobb. 1973. *The Hidden Injuries of Class*. New York: Vintage Books.
Shalev, Michael. 1978. "Lies, Damned Lies and Strike Statistics: The Measurement of Trends in Industrial Conflicts." Pp. 1–20, in Colin Crouch and Alessandro Pizzorno (eds.), *The Resurgence of Class Conflict in Western Europe Since 1968. Volume 1. National Studies*. New York: Holmes & Meier.
―――. 1980. "Trade Unionism and Economic Analysis: The Case of Industrial Conflict." *Journal of Labor Research*, Vol. 1, No. 1, pp. 133–73.
Sherman, Howard. 1979. "A Marxist Theory of the Business Cycle." *Review of Radical Political Economics*, Vol. 11, No. 1, pp. 1–23.
Shiskin, J. A., H. Young, and J. C. Musgrave. 1965. "The XII Variant of the Census Method II Seasonal Adjustment Program." Technical paper No. 15, Bureau of the Census, Washington, D.C.
Shonfield, Andrew. 1965. *Modern Capitalism: The Changing Balance of Public and Private Power*. Oxford University Press.
―――. 1974. "L'impresa pubblica: modello internazionale o specialità locale?" Pp. 269–90, in Fabio Luca Cavazza and Stephen R. Graubard (eds.), *Il caso italiano*. Milan: Garzanti.
Shorey, John. 1975. "The Size of the Work Unit and Strike Incidence." *Journal of Industrial Economics*, Vol. 23, pp. 175–88.

Shorter, Edward, and Charles Tilly. 1971. "The Shape of Strikes in France 1830–1960." *Comparative Studies in Society and History*, Vol. 13, pp. 60–86.
   1974. *Strikes in France, 1830–1968*. Cambridge University Press.
Sims, Christopher A. 1972. "Money, Income and Causality." *American Economic Review*, Vol. 52, No. 4, pp. 540–52.
Skeels, Jack W. 1971. "Measures of United States Strike Activity." *Industrial and Labor Relations Review*, Vol. 24, No. 4, pp. 515–25.
   1982. "The Economic and Organizational Basis of Early United States Strikes, 1900–1948." *Industrial and Labor Relations Review*, Vol. 35, No. 4, pp. 491–503.
Skipper, J.K, A.L. Guenther, and G. Nass. 1967. "The Sacredeness of 0.05: A Note Concerning the Uses of Statistical Levels of Significance in Social Sciences," *American Sociologist*, Vol. 1, pp. 16–8.
Skocpol, Theda. 1979. *States and Social Revolutions. A Comparative Analysis of France, Russia, and China*. Cambridge University Press.
Smith, M. R. 1979. "Institutional Setting and Industrial Conflict in Quebec." *American Journal of Sociology*, Vol. 85, No. 1, pp. 109–34.
Snow, David A., and Robert D. Benford. 1992. "Master Frames and Cycles of Protest." Pp. 133–55, in Aldon D. Morris and Carol McClurg Mueller (eds.), *Frontiers in Social Movement Theory*. New Haven: Yale University Press.
Snyder, David. 1974. "Determinants of Industrial Conflict: Historical Models of Strikes in France, Italy and the United States." Unpublished Ph.D. dissertation, University of Michigan.
   1975. "Institutional Setting and Industrial Conflict: Comparative Analysis of France, Italy and the United States." *American Sociological Review*, Vol. 40, No. 3, pp. 259–78.
   1977. "Early North American Strikes: A Reinterpretation." *Industrial and Labor Relations Review*, Vol. 30, No. 3, pp. 325–41.
Snyder, David, and William R. Kelly. 1976. "Industrial Violence in Italy, 1878–1902." *American Journal of Sociology*, Vol. 82, No. 1, pp. 131–62.
Somaini, Eugenio. 1989. "Politica salariale e politica economica." Pp. 307–44, in Gian Primo Cella and Tiziano Treu (eds.), *Relazioni industriali. Manuale per l'analisi dell'esperienza italiana*. Bologna: Il Mulino.
Soskice, David. 1978. "Strike Waves and Wage Explosions, 1968–1970: An Economic Interpretation." Pp. 221–46, in Colin Crouch and Alessandro Pizzorno (eds.), *The Resurgence of Class Conflict in Western Europe Since 1968. Volume 2. Comparative Analyses*. New York: Holmes & Meier.
Speranza, Lorenzo. 1977. "L'evoluzione dell'assetto delle qualifiche," *Quaderni di rassegna sindacale*, Vol. 15, No. 64–65, pp. 208–26.
Spriano, Paolo. 1958. *Socialismo e classe operaia a Torino dal 1892 al 1913*. Turin: Einaudi.
   1964. *L'occupazione delle fabbriche. Settembre 1920*. Turin: Einaudi.
Squarzon, Corrado. 1989a. "I consigli dei delegati vent'anni dopo," *Prospettiva sindacale*, Vol. 20, No. 73–74, pp. 151–71.
   1989b. "Gli incentivi salariali nella contrattazione collettiva." Pp. 37–65, in Gian Primo Cella (ed.), *Il ritorno degli incentivi. Una ricerca Asap-Cesos sulle retribuzioni ad incentivo nelle relazioni industriali italiane*. Milan: Franco Angeli.
   1990. "Tesseramento e proselitismo: soggetti e procedure a livello di fabbrica." *Prospettiva sindacale*, Vol. 20, No. 77, pp. 193–212.
Stearns, Peter. 1968. "Against the Strike Threat: Employer Policy Toward Labor Agitation in France, 1900–1914." *Journal of Modern History*, Vol. 40, No. 4, pp. 474–500.
Stern, Robert N. 1976. "Intermetropolitan Patterns of Strike Frequency." *Industrial and Labor Relations Review*, Vol. 29, No. 2, pp. 218–35.

1978. "Methodological Issues in Quantitative Strike Analysis." *Industrial Relations*, Vol. 17, No. 1, pp. 32–42.
Stephenson, James A., and Helen T. Farr. 1972. "Seasonal Adjustment of Economic Data by Application of the General Linear Statistical Model." *Journal of the American Statistical Association*, Vol. 67, No. 337, pp. 37–45.
Sterling, T.D. 1959. "Publication Decisions and their Possible Effects on Inferences Drawn from Tests of Significance – or Vice Versa." *Journal of the American Statistical Association*, Vol. 54, pp. 30–4.
Stone, Katherine. 1974. "The Origins of Job Structures in the Steel Industry," *Review of Radical Political Economics*, Vol. 6, No. 2, pp. 61–97.
Streeck, Wolfgang. 1984. "Neo-Corporatist Industrial Relations and the Economic Crisis in West Germany." Pp. 291–314, in John H. Golthorpe (ed.), *Order and Conflict in Contemporary Capitalism*. Oxford: Clarendon Press.
Swidinsky, Robert, and John Vanderkamp. 1982. "A Micro-econometric Analysis of Strike Activity in Canada." *Journal of Labor Research*, Vol. 3, No. 4, pp. 455–71.
Sylos-Labini, Paolo. 1975. *Saggio sulle classi sociali in Italia*. Bari: Laterza.
 1977. *Sindacati, inflazione e produttività*. Bari: Laterza.
Talamo, Magda. 1979. *I dirigenti industriali in Italia*. Turin: Einaudi.
Tamburrano, Giuseppe. 1971. *Storia e cronaca del Centro-Sinistra*. Milan: Feltrinelli.
Tarantelli, Ezio. 1976. "Mercato del lavoro, rinnovi contrattuali e politica economica." Pp. 205–70, *Crisi economica e condizionamenti internazionali dell'Italia*. Proceedings of a conference promoted by Cespe, Rome, Teatro Eliseo, March 15–17, 1976. Rome: Editori Riuniti.
Tarrow, Sidney. 1989a. *Democracy and Disorder. Protest and Politics in Italy, 1965–1975*. Oxford: Clarendon Press.
 1989b. *Struggle, Politics, and Reform: Collective Action, Social Movement, and Cycles of Protest*. Western Societies Program occasional paper No. 21, Center for International Studies, Cornell University.
Thomas, J. J., and Kenneth F. Wallis. 1971. "Seasonal Variation in Regression Analysis." *Journal of the Royal Statistical Society*, Series A, Vol. 134, Part 1, pp. 57–72.
Thompson, E. P. 1963. *The Making of the English Working Class*. London: Vintage.
 1967. "Time, Work-Discipline, and Industrial Capitalism," *Past and Present*, Vol. 38, pp. 56–97.
 1971. "The Moral Economy of the English Crowd in the Eighteenth Century." *Past and Present*, Vol. 50, pp. 76–136.
 1978. "Eighteenth-Century English Society: Class Struggle Without Class?" *Social History*, Vol. 2, pp. 133–66.
Tilly, Charles. 1974. "Do Communities Act?" *Sociological Inquiry*, Vol. 43, No. 3–4, pp. 209–40.
 1975. "Revolutions and Collective Violence." Pp. 483–555, in Fred Greenstein and Nelson Polsby (eds.), *Handbook of Political Science. Macro-political Theory, Vol. 3*. Reading, Mass.: Addison-Wesley.
 1978. *From Mobilization to Revolution*. Reading, Mass.: Addison-Wesley.
 1981. *As Sociology Meets History*. New York: Academic Press.
 1986. *The Contentious French*. Cambridge, Mass.: Harvard University Press.
Tilly, Charles, Louise Tilly, and Richard Tilly. 1975. *The Rebellious Century 1830–1930*. Cambridge, Mass: Harvard University Press.
Tilly, Louise. 1992. *Politics and Class in Milan, 1881–1901*. Oxford University Press.
Tintner, G. 1940. *The Variate Difference Method*. Bloomington, Ind.: Principia Press.
Tomlins, Christopher. 1985. *The State and the Unions. Labor Relations, Law, and the Organized Labor Movement in America, 1880–1960*. Cambridge University Press.

Tonnies, Ferdinand. 1963. *Community & Society (Gemeinschaft und Gesellschaft)*. New York: Harper & Row.
Touraine, Alain. 1955. *L'évolution du travail ouvrier aux usines Renault*. Paris: Mouton.
⎯⎯⎯ 1966. *La Conscience Ouvrière*. Paris: Editions du Seuil.
Treu, Tiziano. 1971. *Sindacato e rappresentanze aziendali. Modelli ed esperienze di un sindacato industriale (FIM-CISL, 1954–1970)*. Bologna: Il Mulino.
⎯⎯⎯ 1972. "L'attacco all'occupazione operaia. Cassa integrazione guadagni, riduzioni d'orario, sospensioni dal lavoro e licenziamenti collettivi nel 1971." *Quale giustizia*, No. 13–14, pp. 6–16.
⎯⎯⎯ (ed.). 1975. *Sindacato e magistratura nei conflitti di lavoro. Vol. 1. L'uso politico dello Statuto dei Lavoratori*. Bologna: Il Mulino.
⎯⎯⎯ 1976a. "I governi centristi e la regolamentazione dell'attività sindacale." Pp. 553–88, in Aris Accornero (ed.), *Problemi del movimento sindacale in Italia 1943–1973*. Milan: Feltrinelli.
⎯⎯⎯ (ed.). 1976b. *Sindacato e magistratura nei conflitti di lavoro. Vol. 2. Lo statuto dei lavoratori: prassi sindacali e motivazioni dei giudici*. Bologna: Il Mulino.
⎯⎯⎯ 1979. "Forme, caratteri e obbiettivi dell'intervento sindacale sulle istituzioni." Pp. 5–18, in Tiziano Treu, Massimo Roccella, and Giuseppe Ferrari. *Sindacalisti nelle istituzioni*. Rome: Edizioni Lavoro.
⎯⎯⎯ 1984. "Una ricerca empirica sullo Statuto dei Lavoratori negli anni '80," *Giornale di diritto del lavoro e di relazioni industriali*, Vol. 6, No. 23, pp. 497–521.
Treu, Tiziano, Massimo Roccella, and Giuseppe Ferrari. 1979. *Sindacalisti nelle istituzioni*. Rome: Edizioni Lavoro.
Trigilia, Carlo. 1986. *Grandi partiti e piccole imprese. Comunisti e democristiani nelle regioni a economia diffusa*. Bologna: Il Mulino.
⎯⎯⎯ 1989. "Il distretto industriale di Prato." Pp. 283–334, in Marino Regini and Charles Sabel (eds.), *Strategie di riaggiustamento industriale*. Bologna: Il Mulino.
Troiani, Saverio. 1978. *Gli scioperi in Italia. Analisi statistica*. Bari: Cacucci Editore.
Trulli, Giuseppe, and Glauco Felici. 1968. "Movimenti di lotta e partiti," *Problemi del socialismo*, Vol. 10, No. 28–9, pp. 290–301.
Tukey, John W. 1957. "On the Comparative Anatomy of Transformations." *Annals of Mathematical Statistics*, Vol. 28, No. 3, pp. 602–32.
⎯⎯⎯ 1977. *Exploratory Data Analysis*. Reading, Mass.: Addison-Wesley.
Turner, H. A. 1969. *Is Britain Really Strike-Prone?* Cambridge University Press.
Turner, H. A., G. Clack, and G. Roberts. 1967. *Labour Relations in the Motor Industry*. London: Allen & Unwin.
Turone, Sergio. 1984. *Storia del sindacato in Italia*. Bari: Laterza.
Urbani, Giuliano. 1977a. "I piccoli e medi imprenditori lombardi di fronte alla politica: aspetti culturali e modelli di partecipazione." Pp. 377–414, in Federazione Regionale fra le Associazioni Industriali della Lombardia (ed.), *La piccola e media industria in Lombardia, Vol. 2, Relazioni del comitato scientifico*. Milan: Edizioni Industriali.
⎯⎯⎯ 1977b. "Atteggiamenti politici degli imprenditori: il caso della Lombardia," *Rivista italiana di scienza politica*, Vol. 7, No. 1, pp. 27–60.
Useem, Michael. 1979–80. "Which Business Leaders Help Govern?" *Insurgent Sociologist*, Vol. 9, No. 2–3, pp. 107–20.
⎯⎯⎯ 1982. "Classwide Rationality in the Politics of Managers and Directors of Large Corporations in the United States and Great Britain," *Administrative Science Quarterly*, Vol. 27, pp. 199–226.
Valcamonici, Roberto. 1977. "Struttura di mercato, accumulazione e produttività del lavoro nell'industria manifatturiera italiana, 1951–1971." Pp. 157–224, in Guido Carli (ed.), *Sviluppo economico e strutture finanziarie in Italia*. Bologna: Il Mulino.
Valcavi, Domenico. 1987. *Linee di sviluppo della contrattazione collettiva*. Turin: ISPER.

Valli, Vittorio. 1970. *Programmazione e sindacati in Italia*. Milan: Franco Angeli.
  1976. *L'economia e la politica economica italiana (1945–1975), Tendenze e problemi*. Milan: Etas Libri.
Vanderkamp, John. 1970. "Economic Activity and Strike Activity." *Industrial Relations* (University of California, Berkeley), Vol. 9, No. 2, pp. 215–30.
van Dijk, Teun. 1972. *Some Aspects of Text Grammars*. Paris: Mouton.
  1980. "Story Comprehension: An Introduction," *Poetics*, Vol. 8, No. 1–3, pp. 1–21.
  1986. "News Schemata." Pp. 155–86, in C. Cooper and S. Greenbaum (eds.), *Studying Writing: Linguistic Approaches*. Beverly Hills: Sage.
Velleman, F. Paul. 1980. "Definition and Comparison of Robust Nonlinear Data Smoothing Algorithms," *Journal of the American Statistical Association*, Vol. 75, No. 371, pp. 609–15.
Veneziani, Bruno (ed.). 1978. *La contrattazione collettiva in Italia (1945–1977)*. Bari: Cacucci.
Vento, Fulvio. 1980. "Delegati e consigli in una ricerca dei chimici," *Quaderni di rassegna sindacale*, Vol. 18, No. 86–87, pp. 44–55.
Viale, Guido. 1978. *Il sessantotto. Tra rivoluzione e restaurazione*. Milan: Mazzotta editore.
Vicarelli, Fausto. 1970. "L'esportazione di banconote nell'esperienza italiana dell'ultimo decennio: una analisi quantitativa." *Studi economici*, Vol. 25, No. 3–4, pp. 322–47.
Villa, Paola. 1986. *The Structuring of Labour Markets. A Comparative Analysis of the Steel and Construction Industries in Italy*. Oxford: Clarendon Press.
Visser, Jelle. 1989. *European Trade Unions in Figures*. Deventer: Kluwer Law and Taxation Publishers.
Wallace, Michael, Larry Griffin, and Beth Rubin. 1989. "The Positional Power of American Labor, 1963–1977," *American Sociological Review*, Vol. 54, No. 2, pp. 197–214.
Wallis, Kenneth F. 1972. "Testing for Fourth Order Auto-Correlation in Quarterly Regression Equations." *Econometrica*, Vol. 40, No. 4, pp. 617–36.
  1974. "Seasonal Adjustment and Relations Between Variables." *Journal of the American Statistical Association*, Vol. 69, No. 345, pp. 18–31.
Walsh, D. William. 1975. "Economic Conditions and Strike Activity in Canada." *Industrial Relations*, Vol. 14, No. 1, pp. 45–54.
Ward, R., and G. Zis. 1974. "Trade Union Militancy as an Explanation of Inflation, International Comparison." *The Manchester School of Economic and Social Studies*, Vol. 62, pp. 46–65.
Waxman, Chaim (ed.). 1969. *The End of Ideology Debate*. New York: Simon & Schuster.
Weintraub, Andrew. 1966. "Prosperity vs. Strikes: An Empirical Approach." *Industrial Labor Relations Review*, Vol. 19, No. 2, pp. 231–8.
Weiss, Linda. 1984. "The Italian State and Small Business." *European Journal of Sociology*, Vol. 5, No. 2, pp. 214–41.
Weitz, Peter R. 1975. "Labor and Politics in a Divided Movement: The Italian Case." *Industrial and Labor Relations Review*, Vol. 28, No. 2, pp. 226–42.
Westergaard, John. 1970. "The Rediscovery of the Cash Nexus," *Socialist Register*, pp. 111–38.
Whitt, J. Allen. 1979–80. "Can Capitalists Organize Themselves?" *Insurgent Sociologist*, Vol. 9, No. 2–3, pp. 51–9.
Wolleb, Enrico. 1988. "Belated Industrialization: The Case of Italy." Pp. 140–70, in Robert Boyer (ed.), *The Search for Labour Market Flexibility. The European Economies in Transition*. Oxford: Clarendon Press.
Woodward, Joan. 1965. *Industrial Organization: Theory and Practice*. Oxford University Press.
Wright, Erik Olin. 1979. *Class, Crisis and the State*. London: Verso.

Wright, Erik Olin, and Kwang-Yeong Shin. 1988. "Temporality and Class Analysis: A Comparative Analysis of Class Structure, Class Trajectory and Class Consciousness in Sweden and the United States," *Sociological Theory*, Vol. 6, No. 1, pp. 58–84.

Yoder, Dale. 1938. "Seasonality in Strikes." *Journal of the American Statistical Association*, Vol. 33, pp. 687–93.

Zaccone Derossi, Flavia. 1962. "L'inserimento nel lavoro degli immigrati meridionali a Torino," *Immigrazione e industria*. Milan: Comunità.

Zeuthen, F. 1930. *Problems of Monopoly and Economic Warfare*. London: Routledge & Sons.

Zolberg, Aristide. 1986. "How Many Exceptionalisms?" Pp. 397–456, in Ira Katznelson and Aristide Zolberg (eds.). *Working-Class Formation*. Princeton University Press.

Index

Abbatecola, Giuseppe, 145, 216, 267, 269, 280
Absenteeism, 87, 140–1, 181–2, 362, 419n, 422n, 428n
Accidents, work, 275–6, 386–7, 434n
Accornero, Aris, 16–17, 22, 145, 149, 151, 187, 204, 218, 220, 224, 236, 289, 319, 347, 393, 417n
ACLI. *See* Christian Association of Italian Workers
Aggregation
    sectoral, 401n
    temporal, 401n
Aglietta, Michel, 91, 336, 357
Agnelli, Giovanni, 123, 124, 206, 211, 219, 232, 237, 289, 331, 361, 364, 417n, 425n, 427n
    on *autunno caldo*, 307
    compromise policy of, 151–2, 314–15, 316–17
    on *scala mobile* agreement, 419n
    on small firm, 333
Agnelli, Umberto, 219, 359
Agreements, collective
    duration of, 418n
    industry-wide, 157–8, 185, 257, 352
    plant-level, 148, 157, 229, 352
    separate, 116–17
    See also Collective bargaining
Agriculture, 49, 50, 75, 211, 213, 399n
Aguet, Jean Pierre, 105, 224
Alasia, Franco, 50
Alberoni, Francesco, 50
Alfa-Romeo, 149, 265, 360, 389, 445n
Alfasud, 381–2
Alienation, 80, 403n
Alinari, Luigi, 169, 420n
Allende, Salvador, 205
Allum, P. A., 247

Almon polynomial distributed-lag procedure, 33, 35, 41, 67, 187, 396n, 402n
American Federation of Labor (AFL), 115, 198, 199, 273
Aminzade, Ronald, 39–40, 54, 103
Amoretti, Aldo, 140
Andreani, Edgard, 95
Apprentices, 332, 441n
Arbitration committees, 214–15
Aristocracy, labor, 231–2
Arrests. *See* Police
Articulated bargaining, 147
Artisans. *See* Craft production
Asap, 147, 201
Ascoli, Ugo, 49, 50, 52, 214, 399n
Ashenfelter, Orley, 32, 374, 430n
Ashenfelter and Johnson model, 10, 14, 17, 24, 32–8, 40, 41, 42–3, 57, 67, 95, 139, 143, 161–8, 187, 399n, 434n
Assemblee (mass meetings), 117, 291, 411–12n, 434n
Assembly line, 52, 80, 93, 274–5, 330–1, 336, 402n
Associazione Industriale Lombarda. *See* Assolombarda
Assolombarda, 50, 82, 120, 131, 132, 140, 176, 177, 179, 182, 262, 268, 309, 313, 323, 332, 334, 360, 362, 389, 399–400n, 421n, 428n, 433n
Authoritarianism, 272, 281, 282–3, 307, 310, 311
    See also Paternalism
Authority, 281–3, 291, 444n
Autobianchi, 269, 271, 272, 274–5, 281
Autocorrelation, 34–5, 40–1, 43, 45, 107, 239, 244, 398n, 401n, 402n, 431n
    See also Regression
Autocovariance function, 401n

Automation. *See* Technological innovation
Automobile industry, 77, 271, 402n
   See also Alfa-Romeo; Fiat
Autoregressive integrated moving-average (ARIMA) models, 6
Autunno caldo ("hot autumn"), 16, 17, 25, 26, 27, 40, 45, 52, 89, 98, 117, 118, 123, 149, 298, 301, 428n, 438n, 440n
   Communist Party and, 297
   defiance of authority in, 291, 293
   historical relevance of, 369–72
   hours lost in, 258, 259
   impact of, 53, 303–4, 306–8, 338–9, 344
   plant size in, 262
   radical intellectuals in, 288–9, 291, 293
   spontaneous actions in, 289–91
   as statistical outlier, 257–8
   structural/cultural factors in, 292–3
   student movement in, 283–8
   tactics in, 267–72
   workers' demands, 272–83
   workers' participation, 264–7, 294–7
   See also Strike waves
Avanguardia Operaia, 118, 269, 284, 286, 287

Baccetti, Carlo, 208
Baglioni, Guido, 50, 154, 155
Bagnara, Sebastiano, 152, 285, 392
Bagnasco, Arnaldo, 53, 124, 129, 133, 134, 176, 207, 211, 332, 333, 389–90, 438n, 441n, 446n
Balance-of-power theory, 238
Bank of Italy, 51, 305, 306, 345, 385
Barbagli, Marzio, 137, 295
Barca, Fabrizio, 85–6, 90, 237, 307, 329, 330, 338, 361, 362, 364
Bargaining. *See* Collective bargaining
Bassano del Grappa, 208, 211, 426n, 427n, 441n
Batstone, Eric, 18, 290
Battegazzorre, Francesco, 245
Bazzan, Nazareno, 271
Bean, R., 154, 419n
Beccalli, Bianca, 132, 271, 410n, 442n
Becchi Collida, Ada, 120, 153, 181, 197, 203, 264, 319, 330, 331, 360, 393
Bechelloni, Giovanni, 138
Becker, Howard, 377
Bellardi, Lauralba, 155
Belsley, A. David, 107

Bendix, Reinhard, 102, 240, 316, 438n
Benford, Robert D., 347
Bergamaschi, Tullia Myriam, 79, 335
Bergamo FLM survey, 175–6, 178, 391, 442n
Berger, Suzanne, 215
Berlinguer, Enrico, 205, 206, 359
Bertaux, Daniel, 23
Bezza, Bruno, 268, 393
Biagi, Marco, 219, 220
Biagioni, Eligio, 138
Bianchi, Giuseppe, 81, 275, 281, 393
Bias
   aggregation, 162, 177, 247, 419n
   simultaneous-equation, 67, 70, 74, 106, 410n
Bilateral bargaining, 228
Bishop, Robert, 32
Biz, Giovanni, 181, 275
Blackburn, Robin, 81–2, 404n
Black Death, 54
Blauner, Robert, 79–80, 86, 403n
Bloch, Marc, 343, 379
Block, Fred, 14, 235, 305
Blockades, 272, 422n
Bo, Giorgio, 201
Bobbio, Luigi, 284, 288, 297
Bonazzi, Giuseppe, 310, 390
Bonuses, 145, 274, 332, 362, 434n
Boraston, Ian, 18
Bordogna, Lorenzo, 34, 95, 103, 151, 183, 228, 229, 257, 261, 300, 422n
Borghese, Junio Valerio, 302
Borgomeo, L., 303
Bourgeoisie. *See* Class, capitalist
Bowles, Samuel, 92, 234, 306
Bratina, Darko, 392
Braudel, Fernand, 27, 371
Braverman, Harry, 82
Brecht, Bertold, 376
Brentano, Dominique, 49, 224
British strikes, 17, 135, 290, 292, 424n
Brusco, Sebastiano, 144, 178, 179, 332, 333, 334, 335, 337
Brutality. *See* Police
Bulgarelli, Aviana, 320, 321, 325, 327
Buratto, Fabio, 179, 265, 270
Burawoy, Michael, 431n
Burns, Arthur, 57, 385
Business-cycles, 10, 30, 31, 59, 60, 62
   Marxist view of, 90–2, 95
   strike frequency and, 24–5, 54–5, 72–5, 93, 95, 97, 98–9, 141
   strike waves and, 299–300

Butera, Federico, 331

Cabinet crises, 245–53, 299, 388–9
Cacciari, Massimo, 285, 286, 393
Cagnato, Alberto, 179, 337, 421n
Caleffi, Giuseppe, 213
Calhoun, Craig, 103, 293
Calosso, Giulio, 381
Camonico, Marina, 176, 177, 179
Campiglio, Luigi, 275
Candy, 269, 271, 272, 276, 280, 360, 446n
Canteri, Celestino, 50
Capacity utilization, 58, 59–60, 62–5, 67, 69, 385, 400n, 401n, 440n
Capecchi, Vittorio, 129, 209
Capital
   concentration of, 84
   flight, 437–8n
   investment, 329–30, 347, 426n, 443n
   -to-labor ratio, 329
Capitalism, 232, 233, 235, 237, 240, 278, 349–50, 353, 405n, 416n
   contradictions of, 84, 134
   development of, 340
   state, 147, 197, 305, 425n, 426n; *See also* ENI; IRI
   See also Employers; Capitalists
Capitalist class, 416n
Capitalists
   class consciousness, 416n
   internal divisions, 133, 145, 255
   See also Employers; Capitalism
Carabelli, Giuliana, 149, 269, 287
Carabinieri. See Police
Caracciolo, Alberto, 78, 84, 85
Cardulli, Alessandro, 151
Career, 405n
Car industry. *See* Automobile industry
Carli, Guido, 124, 308, 316
Carmignani, Fabrizio, 319
Carocci, Giovanni, 224
Carpo, Giampiero, 187, 273
Carrieri, Mimmo, 297
Cassa integrazione guadagni (CIG), 327, 363, 387, 441n
Castegnaro, Alessandro, 176, 332, 337, 338, 391
Castellano, Lucio, 287, 288
Catholic faction/Catholic church, 115, 196–7, 202, 206, 208, 295
Cattin, Carlo Donat, 305
Causality, 19, 20, 124, 140, 342, 373, 396n
Cavalli, Luciano, 50
Cavallo Perin, Maria Cristina, 126, 128, 131, 219, 415n

Celadin, Anna, 411n, 412n
Cella, Gian Primo, 81, 82, 83, 138, 146, 151, 152, 154, 241, 265, 266, 274, 277, 278
Center Left (*centro sinistra*), 122, 197, 202–4, 225, 243, 302, 344, 438n, 444n
Central Intelligence Agency (CIA), 205
Centro Studi Federlibro, 140, 332, 334, 415n
Cespe, 442n
CGIL. *See* Italian General Confederation of Labor
Charivari, 102, 434n
Chemical industry, 77–9, 83, 115, 119, 127, 128, 133, 144, 146, 148, 161, 218, 261, 297, 402n, 406n, 413n, 415n, 419n, 438n
Chomsky, Noam, 20
Chow test (stability of structural parameters), 399n
Christian Association of Italian Workers (ACLI), 178–9, 216, 217, 220, 222, 224, 302, 310, 323, 389
Christian Democrat Party (DC), 48, 115, 116, 117, 119, 120, 122, 139, 196, 197, 199–203, 206, 207, 208, 215, 225, 243, 252, 255, 418n, 425n, 426n, 427n
Ciarciaglino, Nico, 270, 285
CIG. See *Cassa integrazione guadagni*
CISL. *See* Italian Confederation of Workers Union
CISM. *See* Commissione indagini e Studi sull'Industria Meccanica
Clack, G., 381
Clark, Colin, 75
Clarke, Tom, 135, 235
Class
   capitalist, 416n, 425n
   compromise, 12, 233–7, 435n
   conflict, struggle, 11–12, 15, 233, 235–7, 294, 343–5, 352, 396n, 417n, 444–5n
   consciousness, 28, 293–5, 402n, 436n
   cooperation, 423n
   divisions within, 12, 153, 255, 296, 297
   formation, 293–4, 348, 349, 353
   middle class, 215, 423n
   new working class, 86, 266, 404n, 436n
   petty bourgeoisie, 84, 124, 409n
   structure, change in, 16–17, 83–4, 93–4, 267, 295, 347, 352, 353, 363, 402n, 422–3n
   unionism, 134–9

488 Index

working class, 215, 231–2, 233, 234, 423n
Classe Operaia, 284
Clawson, Dan, 240
Clegg, Hugh A., 11, 154, 155, 160, 419n
Clements, Laurie, 135, 235
Clientela, 200–1, 226
Cloward, Richard A., 17, 26, 105, 291, 297, 298, 303, 304, 443n
Cochrane, D., 34–5, 398n
Cochrane-Orcutt procedure, 34–5, 40, 41, 42, 45, 67, 165, 396n, 398n
Cohen, Joshua, 235
COLA (cost of living adustment). See *Scala mobile* agreement
Colasanti, Giuseppe, 105, 113
Cold War, 115, 198
Coldiretti, 120
Collective action, 10, 97–142, 212, 289
  proactive, 101
  reactive, 101, 102–3, 408–9n
  repertoires, 101–2, 103, 409n
  types of, 88, 102
Collective bargaining, 11, 12, 25, 28, 42, 419n, 424n, 431–2n, 446n
  bilateral, 228
  centralized, 145, 146, 154, 230, 243, 440n
  changes in, 344
  class compromise in, 233–5
  contract issues in, 151–3, 155, 175, 176–7, 178
  economic-bargaining theory and, 31–8, 55, 90, 212, 238
  economy-wide, 145, 154
  employer associations in, 120, 121–2
  industry-wide, 154, 230
  institutionalization of, 240–2, 430n
  interconfederal, 418n
  level of, 146, 152, 228
  perfect knowledge and, 36–7, 89–90
  plant-level, 12, 25, 115–16, 144–5, 147–9, 150–1, 152, 153, 154, 155, 157, 175–9, 180–1, 234, 322, 332, 420n
  profit-wages exchange in, 232–3, 237
  strike frequency and, 153–75, 187–9
  strikes during, 158–60, 177–8, 186, 352
  trilateral, 228–9
  two-tier (articulated), 147
  union power in, 226–7
  See also Agreements, collective; Demands (workers')
Collegi arbitrari, 215

Collingwood, R. G., 379
Comitati unitari di base (CUB), 118, 126, 269, 288, 412n
Commissione indagini e Studi sull'Industria Meccanica (CISIM), 78, 217, 310, 390
Commissione Parlamentare d'Inchiesta sulle Condizioni dei Lavoratori in Italia, 127, 179, 217, 219, 390, 399n,
Commissioni interne, 115–16, 118, 119, 126, 127, 128, 146, 147–8, 215, 219, 220, 221, 411n, 413n, 414n, 415n, 433n
Communist Party of Italy (Marxist-Leninist), 204
Communist Party (PCI), 115, 116, 119, 120, 138, 139, 196, 199, 203, 212, 230, 265, 283, 388, 417n, 418n, 427n, 428n, 430n, 444n
  autunno caldo and, 297
  in coalition government, 206–7, 213, 243–4, 339, 344
  compromesso storico strategy of, 205–6, 207, 236–7, 243, 244, 368
  electoral base of, 207, 208, 295–6
  political strength of, 137, 204, 206, 225–6, 338–9, 426n
  public attitude toward, 427n
  rejection of violence, 287
Competition (intraclass conflict), 317, 330, 337, 353, 354, 439n
Complete-system simultaneous methods, 70
Compromesso storico, 205–6, 207, 236–7, 243, 244, 317, 368
Confagricoltura, 120
Confapi, 120
Confcoltivatori, 120
Confcommercio, 120
Confesercenti, 120
Confindustria, 115, 177, 189, 201, 215, 361
  Agnelli/Carli leadership of, 151, 314–17
  in CIG agreement, 441n
  and electric industry nationalization, 122, 202–3
  member firms of, 120–2
  opposition to plant-level bargaining, 121, 144, 147
  organizational structure of, 120, 123, 314–15, 413–14n
  political affiliation of, 122–3, 199–200, 425

Index

in *scala mobile* agreement, 151, 227–8
Confindustria surveys, 87, 127–8, 140–1, 181, 182, 261–2, 295, 383, 390, 419–20n, 428n, 436n
Confintesa, 425n
Consigli di fabbrica (Cdf), 118–19, 126, 128, 130, 148, 412n, 415n, 428n, 435n, 438n
Consigli di gestione, 412n, 427n, 435n
Consigli di zona, 435n
Constituent Assembly, 196, 197
Constitution, 197–8
Consumer price index, 386
Contini, Bruno, 334–5
Corbetta, Piergiorgio, 137, 196, 295
Corporatism, 241, 429n
Correlation analysis, 6, 402n
Corriere della sera, 250, 252, 270, 312, 315, 393
Cosi, Cesare, 269, 285
Cosi, Dante, 225, 226
Cost-benefit analysis, 10, 14, 212
Cost of living, 386, 419n
Costa, Angelo, 121, 147, 233, 282–3
Coup d'état, 205
Courts, 132–3, 214, 226, 302–3, 305, 337
Cousineau, Jean-Michel, 31, 35, 37, 38
Cowden, Dudley J., 396n
Craft production, 50, 80, 82, 433
Crisis theory, 367–8
Cronin, James E., 99, 339, 357
Cross-sectional analysis, 257
Crouch, Colin, 191
Crouzel, Adrien, 101
CUB. See *Comitati unitari di base*
Cultural Revolution, 283
Culture, 289–93, 436n
Cycles
    long-term, 11–12, 91–2, 339, 340–1, 346
    medium-term, 41, 55, 93, 143, 144, 158, 161, 185, 187, 188, 355, 356, 397n, 420n, 424n
    nonperiodic, 6, 55, 143, 168, 346, 355, 356, 402n
    periodic, 6, 93, 143–4, 161–2, 346, 356–7
    short-term, 6, 93, 339, 346
    trend and, 347–8, 444n
    See also Business cycles
Cycles of struggle. *See* Strike waves

Da Empoli, Domenico, 384, 385
Dahrendorf, Ralf, 105, 355, 416n, 444n
D'Ambrosio, Mario, 81, 181, 275

Daneo, Camillo, 78
Dante, 377
Davies, James C., 97, 99
DC. *See* Christian Democrat Party
De Carlini, Lucio, 122
Decentralization of production. See *Decentramento produttivo*; Flexible specialization
Decentramento produttivo, 334–5, 445n
    See also Flexible specialization
Decomposition analysis, 6
De Gaspari, Alcide, 199, 214
Delegati (workers' delegates), 118, 148, 149–50, 285, 412n, 413n, 435n
Della Porta, Donatella, 204, 207
Dell'Aringa, Carlo, 178, 274, 278, 307, 319, 324, 325, 326, 362
Della Rocca, Giuseppe, 118, 126, 153, 213, 215, 216, 230
Del Lungo, Silvano, 218
Demands (workers'), 52–3, 272–83, 336
    authority structure, 281–3, 291
    bonuses, 145, 274, 332, 362
    corporatist, 280, 360
    egalitarian, 273–4, 288, 340
    environmental, 155, 178, 273
    health, 155, 178, 273, 277, 330, 434n
    investment decisions, 173, 230
    job classification, 273, 277–8, 360
    production structure, 274–7, 281
De Masi, Domenico, 87, 98, 117, 138, 265, 272, 295
De Micheli, Alighiero, 232
Demier, Francis, 54
Democratic Popular Front, 199
Demonstrations, 214, 215, 227, 247, 252, 267
Dente, Bruno, 225
Derossi, Flavia, 307, 309, 392
De Santis, Gustavo, 105
De Ste. Croix, D.E.M., 101
De Stefani, Pasquale, 49–50, 187, 272, 281, 285, 287, 291, 446n
Destruction of property, 268, 270, 271, 275, 282, 285, 288, 290, 292, 294, 298
    See also Violence
De Wasseige, Yves, 40
Diani, Marco, 152, 285, 392
Differentials, wage, 178, 215, 274, 278, 360, 361
Dimanico, Michele, 51, 268, 276
Distributed lag structure, 396n
Divide et impera strategy, 82
Division of labor, 405n

Doeringer, Peter, 179, 404n, 443n
Donolo, Carlo, 297
Donovan Commission, 290
Dozzo, Giovanni, 187, 216, 218, 220
Draper, N. R., 398n
Dubin, Robert, 143, 154
Duration of strikes. *See* Strikes, Italian, duration of
Durbin-Watson test, 34, 35, 40, 43, 45, 107, 431n
Durkheim, Emile, 136–7, 141–2

Econometric. *See* Regression
Economic-bargaining theory, 31–8, 55, 90, 96, 212, 238, 254, 349–50, 408n
Economic determinants of strikes, 12, 13, 17, 56–95, 254, 339–42
  See also Ashenfelter and Johnson model
Economic development, 47–8, 53, 133–4, 210, 365, 399n
Economic hardship theory, 10, 97, 98–9, 136–7, 142, 297, 408n
Economic miracle, 47, 49, 54, 81, 90, 95, 189, 202, 329, 345, 399n, 400n, 404n, 405n, 434n; *See also* Third Italy
Economic planning, 202, 203, 425n
Economic prosperity, 422n, 423n
Economism, 234, 255
Edwards, Richard, 240, 381
EFIM (Ente Partecipazioni e Finanziamenti Industria Manifatturiera), 425n
Egalitarianism, 273–4, 288, 340, 434n, 442n
EGAM (Ente Autonomo di Gestioni per le Aziende Minerarie), 425n
Elections
  administrative, 206
  commissioni interne, 111, 118, 130, 216, 218, 262, 433n
  delegati, 118
  divorce referendum, 206
  national, 199, 206, 295
  strikes and, 192, 424n
Electric industry, 122, 202–3
Elster, Jon, 353
Embourgeoisement thesis, 191, 231, 423n
Emilia-Romagna, 207, 208, 209, 254–5, 295, 417n
Employers
  associations of, 119–20, 123–4, 204, 314, 437n; *See also* Confindustria
  attitudes toward labor, 310–13, 364–5

  attitudes toward labor unions, 315–17, 438–9n
  authoritarianism, 272, 281, 282–3, 307, 310, 311
  autunno caldo impact on, 306–10, 313–14
  classification of, 312, 438n
  education levels of, 438n, 439n
  labor regulation and, 240–2
  large firm, 441-3n
  layoffs, 220–3, 226, 323–5, 326, 328, 359, 362, 383–4, 440n
  management of labor relations, 313
  padroni, 400n
  paternalism of, 145–6, 282, 307, 310–11, 435n
  profit strategy of, 237
  in Red *vs.* White regions, 209, 427n
  repressive methods of, 213–14, 215–24, 234, 311, 362, 435n, 438n
  small firm, 312–13, 441-3n
  violence against, 281–3
  Workers' Charter and, 313–14
  See also Collective bargaining; Industrial production; Plant size
Employment. *See* Jobs; Workers
Employement office (Ufficio di collocamento), 46, 48, 398n
Engels, Friedrich, 1, 134, 135
ENI. *See* Ente Nazionale Idrocarburi
Ente Nazionale Idrocarburi (ENI), 82, 200–1, 203, 425n, 426n
Error term. *See* Regression, residuals
Ethnographic research, 22–3, 185–7
Etzioni, Amitai, 100, 101, 301
EUR line, 230
Exploratory data analysis (EDA), 1, 6, 7, 19, 29, 34, 55, 109, 114, 245, 247, 252, 253, 398n
Extraparliamentary groups, 119, 204, 207, 285–288, 290, 292, 293, 303, 315, 443n

Factory councils. *See* Consigli di fabbrica (Cdf)
Factory regimes, 431n
Factory systems (factories)
  as industrial discipline, 50, 53
Factory town, 264, 267
Falck works, 271, 287
Falcone, Giovanni, 270, 285, 286
Family
  extended, 210–11
  financial responsibility to, 218

political culture of, 208
Fanfani, Amintore, 200, 202, 203
Farneti, Paolo, 86, 137, 196, 205, 255, 295–6, 297, 311, 312, 364, 391, 415n, 430n
Fascist Party (MSI), 196, 197, 201–2, 205, 424n
Federlombarda, 86–7, 129, 262, 278, 313, 335, 364, 391, 404, 438n
Federmeccanica, 87–8, 123–4, 314, 328, 364, 365, 391, 399n, 421n, 428n, 439n, 442–3n
Feltrin, Paolo, 139
Ferrante, Gianni, 139
Ferrara, 213
Ferrari, Giuseppe, 225, 226, 344, 444n
Ferraris, Pino, 79
Ferrerio, Pietro, 122
Fevola, Giuseppe, 98, 117, 138, 265, 272, 295
Fiat, 50, 122, 264, 267, 285, 288, 290, 419n, 425n, 436n, 439n
  absenteeism at, 419n
  antistrike march at, 359
  in *autunno caldo*, 269, 271, 272, 273, 276, 277
  CGIL defeat at, 146
  job rotation at, 439n
  layoffs at, 359, 362, 427n, 429n
  new technologies of, 330–1
  repressive methods of, 218, 219, 429n, 435n
  unionization of, 131, 433n
  wage differentials at, 360
Filippelli, Ronald, 115
FIM (Fondo per il Finanziamento dell'Industria Meccanica), 425n
Fines, 217, 220, 428n
FIOM, 138, 415n
Firm size. *See* Plant size
Fisher, R. A., 373
Flexible specialization, 336–7
FLM surveys, 175–6, 178, 391
Fluctuation, 190, 232, 241, 306
  See also Devaluation
Foa, Vittorio, 145, 146
Fogel, Robert William, 370
Fondazione Giovanni Agnelli, 48, 52, 77, 84, 330
Food riots, 101, 102, 409n
Forbice, Aldo, 303
Ford, Henry, 402n
Fordism, 79, 80, 83, 84, 89, 93, 151, 264, 336, 340, 341, 403n, 404n, 443n
Forecasting models, 355–6

Foremen, 282
  See also Supervisors; Workers
Franzosi, Roberto, 6, 34, 35, 40, 57, 143, 155, 185, 186, 257, 365, 382
Frau company, 145
Freedman, David, 19
French strikes, 14, 17, 54, 97, 241, 246–7, 290, 306, 307, 410n, 430–1n, 436n, 437n
Frenkel, Stephen, 18
Frequency of strikes. *See* Strike frequency
Fuguitt, Glenn V., 383
Full employment, 10, 31, 51, 90, 91, 328
Full information maximum likelihood (FIML), 70

Gallessi, Roberto, 268, 393
Galli, Giorgio, 208, 236
Gallie, Duncan, 404n
Gamson, William, 100
Garavini, Sergio, 146, 218, 393
Genoa, 47, 50, 201–2, 252
GEPI (Societa di Gestioni e Partecipazioni Industriali), 425n
Gianotti, Renzo, 265, 393
Giddens, Anthony, 231
Gilriches, Z., 396n
Ginzburg, Carlo, 375
Giolitti, 301
Giovani Imprenditori, 177
Giubilato, M., 176–7, 178, 179, 332, 391
Giugni, Gino, 64, 229, 271, 274, 289, 305, 393
Gobbi, Romolo, 284
Goetz-Girey, Robert, 100, 241, 299
Gomberg, Eugene L., 59
Gompers, Samuel, 273
Gordon, David M., 82, 92
Gorrieri, Ennio, 48
Gramm, Cynthia L., 31, 36, 38, 90, 397n
Gramsci, Antonio, 96, 135–6, 293, 348, 412n, 430n
Gramsci Institute, 442n
Granger, C. W., 40, 41, 66, 70, 143, 144, 397n, 398n, 402n
Grassini, Franco, 78, 79
Graziani, Augusto, 76
Graziosi, Andrea, 319, 320
Grievance committees. See *Commissioni interne*
Grievances. *See* Demands (workers')
Griffin, John I., 100, 398n
Griffin, Larry, 38
Gross national product (GNP), 47, 57, 58, 72, 384–5, 431n

Gruppi di studio, 48
Guala, Chito, 124
Guenther, A. L., 373
Guerci, Carlo Maria, 392
Guidetti Serra, Bianca, 219
Gullino, Giuseppe, 218
Gurr, Ted Robert, 97, 98

Halevi, Joseph, 257
Harbison, Frederick H., 143, 154, 181, 431n
Harsanyi, John C., 32
Hartman, Paul T., 2, 11, 99, 105, 181, 352
Hartman, Raymond, 331, 339
Heimler, Alberto, 329
Hibbs, Douglas, Jr., 11, 189, 192, 225
Hicks, J. R., 31, 32, 38
Hilton, Rodney, 54
Hiring freeze, 325
Historical change, 84, 153, 247, 253, 355, 370, 405n
Historical perspective, 47, 101–2, 104, 196, 231, 265, 274, 366, 368–72, 402n, 409n
History,
  histoire evenementielle, 371
  histoire structurelle, 371
  vs. Statistics, 23, 24, 242–5, 355, 359
Hobsbawm, Eric, 59, 75, 99, 257, 259, 261, 263, 275
Hoerl, Arthur E., 398n
Horowitz, Daniel, 146
Hyman, Richard, 90, 135, 232, 267, 353

Ideology, end of, 224, 423n
Ignis company, 145, 275, 328, 435n
Immigrants, 49, 50, 94, 214, 265, 266, 285, 292, 413n
Immiseration, 11, 12, 91, 136–7, 232–3, 354, 423n
  See also Economic hardship theory
Imperfect information, 37–8
Imperialism: The Last Phase of Capitalism (Lenin), 232
Income distribution, 211
Industrial conflict. *See* Strikes
Industrial production
  assembly line, 52, 80, 93, 274–5, 336, 402n, 443n
  backyard operations, 442n
  capital investment and, 329–30, 347
  continuous flow, 443n
  cost of strikes to, 179–82
  craft, 443n
  decentralized, 334–5, 336–7, 353, 443n
  Fordism-Taylorism, 78, 79, 80, 83, 84, 89, 93, 151, 264, 336, 340, 341, 402n, 404n
  index of, 384
  organization of, 16, 75, 78–80, 93, 269, 274, 275, 277, 278, 282, 290, 319, 329, 332, 335, 339–341, 345, 347, 352, 353, 358, 359, 367, 409n
  pace of, 275–7
  plant size and, 84–9, 94, 179, 337
  restructuring of, 274–7, 281
  small-scale, 53, 54, 84, 88, 134, 179, 209–11, 254–5, 332–3, 337, 345, 442–3n
  state-owned companies, 82, 200, 201
  strike frequency and, 58–62, 66–7, 69, 70, 72, 406n, 431n
  supervisory roles in, 359–60
  technological innovation in, 78–80, 93, 328, 330–1, 339, 347, 361–2
  types of technology, 403n, 442–3n
  working conditions in, 277
Industrial triangle, 47, 49, 127, 133, 295
Industrialization, 103–4, 409n, 417n, 423n
Inflation, 45, 51, 53, 361, 424n
Influence and influential observations, 171, 186, 253, 258–60
Ingham, Geoffrey, 154, 241
Injuries, work-related, 275–6, 386–7, 434n
Inquadramento unico (IU), 317–23, 439–40n
Institutional theories, 11, 430-1n
Integration tests, 440n
Intellectuals, 283–4, 288–9, 291, 293
Interests
  pursuit of, 14–17, 21, 22, 29, 92, 116, 255
Interindustry propensity to strike, 78, 402n
International Monetary Fund (IMF), 53
Intersind, 121–2, 147, 201
Investment, 52, 173, 230, 426n
IRI. *See* Istituto per la Ricostruzione Industriale
ISCO. *See* Istituto Italiano per lo Studio della Congiuntura
ISTAT. *See* Istituto Centrale di Statistica
Istituto Centrale di Statistica (ISTAT), 2, 16, 46, 158, 186, 250, 357, 380, 381, 383, 384–6, 396n, 428n
Istituto di Studi per la Programmazione Economica (ISPE), 305
Istituto Italiano per lo Studio della Congiuntura (ISCO), 58, 60, 61, 75, 385

Istituto Nazionale per l'Assicurazione contro gli Infortuni sul Lavoro (INAIL), 386–7
Istituto per la Ricostruzione Industriale (IRI), 82, 200, 201, 203, 425n
Isvet surveys, 87, 117, 138, 140, 265, 270, 272, 295, 392, 405n, 406n, 410n, 428n, 433n, 445n
Italian Confederation of Workers Union (CISL), 100–17, 106, 126, 134, 138, 139, 215, 216, 228, 235, 311, 360, 387–8, 390, 410–11n, 414n, 417n, 418n, 422n, 440n, 442n
Italian General Confederation of Labor (CGIL), 12, 106, 110–17, 125, 134, 137, 138, 139, 145, 146, 204, 209, 215, 216, 224, 228, 234–5, 236, 243, 311, 387–8, 390, 415n, 417n, 418n, 426n, 428n
Italian Workers Union (UIL), 111, 115, 116, 134, 215, 216, 228, 265, 311, 433n
Italy
  constitution of, 197–8
  economic growth in, 47–8, 53, 133–4, 365, 399n
  economic structure of, 72–89
  industrial capacity in, 78–80
  labor-market regulation in, 48–9
  labor-market structure in, 81–4
  labor migration in, 49–50
  occupational shifts in, 75–8
  organizational resources in. *See* Collective bargaining; Employers, associations; Labor unions; *specific names*
  political repression in, 213–15, 231
  political subcultures in, 207–12
  politics of postwar period, 196–207, 245–7, 302
  unemployment levels in, 50–1, 53, 74
  See also Strike frequency; Strikes, Italian; Strike waves

Jackson, Dudley, 98
Jobs
  change in class structure and, 16–17, 83–4, 93–4, 267, 347, 352, 353, 363
  classification of, 80–3, 93, 273, 277–8, 317–23, 332–3
  enlargement/enrichment, 277
  full employment, 10, 31, 51, 90, 91, 328
  hierarchies, 80–3, 93
  hiring, 399n
  for migrant workers, 49–50
  redesign, 277–8, 292, 307, 330–1
  rotation, 319, 320, 322, 439n
  screening, 48–9, 219
  sectoral shifts in, 75–8, 93–4
  security, 50, 82, 327
  turnover, 399–400n
  See also Workers
John XXIII, Pope, 202
Johnson, George E., 32, 374, 430n
  See also Ashenfelter and Johnson model
Johnston, J., 40, 69–70, 396n
Justice Ministry, 198

Kalecki, Michael, 90, 91, 235
Kaufman, Bruce, 37–8, 90, 397n
Kautsky, Karl, 135, 136, 232
Kelly, William R., 105
Kennedy, John F., 202
Kerr, Clark, 267, 423n
Keynesian economic policy, 91
Killed. *See* Police
Klein, Lawrence R., 58, 385
Knowles, Kenneth G.J.C., 56, 59, 100, 181, 275
Kocka, Jurgen, 215
Koenker, Diane P., 297
Kogan, Norman, 198, 202, 205
Kondratieff, N. D., 91, 339, 357, 407n
Kondratieff cycle, 339, 341, 443n
Koopmans, Ruud, 347
Kornhauser, Arthur, 98, 154, 181, 273, 422n
Korpi, Walter, 11, 14, 192, 213, 225, 238, 290, 344, 368, 380, 381, 445n
Kotz, David M., 91
Kuh, Edwin, 107
Kuhn, James, 380, 381

Labor aristocracy, 231–2
Labor market
  conditions in, 10, 24, 30–55, 74–8, 254, 405n
  dual, 179, 404n
  internal, 82, 404n
  noncompetitive, 404n
  primary, 445n
  rigidity of, 325–6, 327, 405n
  secondary, 443n, 445n
  sectors of, 404n
  structure of, 80–4, 93–4
Labor Ministry, 48, 214, 217, 305, 399n
Labor regulation, 240–2
Labor unions, 25, 83, 97, 397n
  aftermath of *autunno caldo*, 307–8

class, 134–9
dilemmas, 197, 231, 233, 235, 237
employer attitudes toward, 315–17, 438–9n
historical development of, 104
labor court appeals of, 304–5
membership in, 109–12, 114, 125–6, 140, 146, 209, 344, 387–8, 415n, 414n, 428n, 429n, 442n
moderation strategy of, 229–30, 237, 423–4n
as organizational measure, 106–7
organizational structure of, 114–19, 126, 133, 344
personnel of, 126, 139
plant size and, 127–33, 140, 209–10, 254, 312, 415–16n, 420n
political affiliations of, 113, 115, 116, 137–9, 141, 417–18n
political power of, 224–9
political subcultures and, 208–9
in public institutions, 444n
repression of, 215–24, 231
in small firms, 337–8, 345, 410n
technological change and, 361–2
territorial, 337
in triangular conferences, 204, 229
vs. mass movement, 149–50
See also Collective bargaining; Strike frequency; Strikes, Italian; *specific names*
Lacroix, Robert, 31, 35–6, 37, 38
Laissez-faire, 102
La Malfa, Ugo, 202
Lama, Luciano, 145, 225, 230, 234–5
Landrum-Griffith Act, 430n
Lange, Peter, 242, 368
Lanzalaco, Luca, 120, 123, 314
Lanzardo, Dario, 215, 216, 265, 267, 268, 276, 393
Lanzardo, Liliana, 361–2
La Palombara, Joseph, 115, 117, 122, 198, 200, 202, 203
Lapides, Kenneth, 38, 96, 134, 135, 232
La Valle, Davide, 126, 360
Laws, 214, 215, 217, 229, 313–14, 332
See also Workers' Charter
Lay, Adriana, 16, 100, 105
Layoffs, 220–3, 226, 323–5, 326, 328, 359, 362, 383–4, 429n, 440n
Leagues of resistance, 409n, 410n, 427n
Ledda, Gavino, 311
Lefebvre, Georges, 301
Left, radical, 264, 283–9
Legal framework, 215, 429n

Leisure, 271
Lenin, V. I., 1, 135, 136, 232, 283, 407n, 430n
Le Roy Ladurie, Emmanuel, 27, 358, 369, 370, 371, 372, 375
Lester, Richard A., 105, 233–4, 423n
Levi, Arrigo, 232, 237, 289, 315, 361, 364, 393, 419n
Levitt, Theodore, 423–4n
Liberal Party (PLI), 197, 203, 205, 425n
Lieberson, Stanley, 341, 357, 383
Limited information single equation (LISE), 70
Locke, Richard, 242, 331, 393
Lombardy, 81, 207, 208, 271, 415n, 417n
Long, Susan, 383
Long waves, 339
Lotta Continua, 284, 286, 435n
Lotta Continua, 284, 286, 287, 288
Lotte operaie e sindacato in Italia: 1968–1972 (Pizzorno), 1
Lovell, Michael C., 396n
Low-Beer, John, 266, 271, 436n
Luce, Clare Booth, 198–9, 425n
Lucifora, Claudio, 362
Ludtke, Alf, 224
Lukacs, Georg, 135, 136, 351, 416n
Lumley, Robert, 258, 283
Luppi, Laura, 269, 271, 272, 275, 280, 281
Luxemburg, Rosa, 124–5, 135, 136, 232, 235, 283, 290, 294, 343, 417n

McCabe, George P., 373
McCloskey, N. Donald, 373, 375, 377, 379
MacKinnon, James G., 396n
Magnani, Marco, 86, 90, 237, 307, 329, 330, 338, 361, 362, 364
Maier, Charles, 199
Makridakis, Spyros, 355
Malfatti, Eugenia, 383
Mallet, Serge, 80, 86
Mammarella, Giuseppe, 207
Management. *See* Confindustria; Employers
Mandel, Ernest, 331, 339, 357, 443n
Mandelli, Walter, 124
Manghi, Bruno, 237, 361
Mangiarotti, Gabriella, 266
Manifesto Party, 204
Mann, Michael, 81–2, 146, 236, 404n, 436n
Manufacturing industry, 81, 85, 157, 180, 441n
March, Lucien, 57, 95
Marcuse, Herbert, 283

Index

Marginal workers, 50–1
Marglin, Stephen A., 82, 276
Marino, Giuseppe Carlo, 115
Marshall Plan, 198, 199, 220, 254, 424n, 438n
Martinelli, Alberto, 120, 121, 122, 123, 124, 199, 200, 203, 255, 309, 310, 312, 313, 314, 316, 317, 392
Marucco, Dora, 16
Marx, Karl, 38, 84, 86, 96, 134–5, 231, 293, 416n, 430n
Marxist theory
  of class formation, 293–4, 423n, 445n
  of economic cycles, 90–2, 95, 141–2
  of organization, 12, 231–3, 289
  social relations and, 351
  of strikes, 11–12, 14–15, 352–5
  of working-class organization, 134–9, 416n
Marzotto mills, 282
Masiero, Attilio, 145
Mass Strike, The (Luxemburg), 124–5, 417n
Mattina, Enzo, 120, 121, 144, 199, 200, 215, 393
Mauro, Martin J., 31, 35, 37, 38, 49, 90, 154
Mayhew, K., 39, 397n
Mechanical industry, 77, 78–9
Media, radical press, 283–4, 435n
Mediobanca survey, 181–2
Meldolesi, Luca, 48, 51
Melucci, Alberto, 209, 304
Memoirs of Wool (Smith), 276
Merli, Stefano, 104, 105, 290
Mershon, Carol A., 42, 180, 420n
Metalworking industry, 48, 78, 79, 83, 87–8, 115, 117, 119, 123–4, 126, 127–30, 133, 138, 146–8, 154, 155, 163, 167, 168, 184, 189, 209, 216–17, 231, 261, 263, 265, 271, 273, 278, 280, 294, 296, 298, 310, 314, 320, 328, 334, 344, 360, 402n, 406n, 413n, 415n, 420n, 422n, 425n, 439n, 440n
  See also Automobile industry; Mechanical industry; Steel industry
Memoria storica, 212, 301
Michelin, 216, 267, 268
Michels, Robert, 435n
Mietto, Marco, 213
Migliaccio, Paolo, 22–3
Migration, labor, 49–50

Milan, 81, 118, 205, 220, 264, 267, 268, 269, 276, 285, 412n
Milana, Carlo, 329
Milanaccio, Alfredo, 393
Mill, John Stuart, 102
Mills, C. Wright, 1
Ministry of Labor. *See* Labor Ministry
Miracolo economico, 49, 329, 399–400n, 404n, 405n
  See also Economic miracle
Mitchell, Wensley C., 57, 385
Mobilità esterne, see Layoffs
Modena, 213
Monetary policy, 51, 305, 306, 345, 385
Moni, Adolfo, 140, 210
Montaldi, Danilo, 50
Montgomery, David, 54
Moore, Barrington, 103
Moore, David S., 373
Moral economy, 103
Morini plant, 334
Morisi, Massimo, 138
Moro, Aldo, 203, 206, 207, 368
Mortillaro, Felice, 88, 131, 314, 328, 364, 365
Mottura, Giovanni, 268
Mousnier, Roland, 102, 371
Movimento Sociale Italiano (MSI). *See* Fascist Party
MSI. *See* Fascist Party
Multinationals, 84
Multicollinearity, 107, 239, 245, 406n, 431n
Multivariate analysis, 67–72
Mutti, Antonio, 122, 200, 201
Mutual aid societies, 409n

Nash, John F., Jr., 32
Nass, G., 373
Natella, Alfonso, 264
National Bureau of Economic Research (NBER), 58
National Committee for Economic Programming (CNPE), 202
National income, 385
Nationalization of industry. *See* Confindustria
Necchi, 402n
Needs, 80, 98, 99, 280, 289, 290
Negrelli, Serafino, 152, 153, 181, 230, 264, 319, 330, 331, 360, 393
Nerlove, Marc, 397n
Neumann, George R., 36, 90, 154
Newbold, Paul, 41, 66, 70, 143, 144, 398n

Newby, Howard, 86, 409n
Nordhaus, William, 196
North, 49–50, 52, 94, 127, 202, 215, 261, 399n, 412n, 413n, 425n
Northeast, 53, 196, 207, 261, 295
Northwest, 127, 133, 261, 295, 436n
Novella, Agostino, 204
Number of hours lost. *See* Strikes, Italian, number of hours lost
Number of strikers. *See* Strikes, Italian, size of
Number of strikes. *See* Strike frequency

Obershall, Anthony, 100
Occupation
  factory, 359
  land, 76
Occupational structure, 75–8, 83, 93
Offe, Claus, 14, 15, 136, 235, 242, 305, 348, 416n
Oil shock, 53
Oligopolies, 84, 123, 404n
Olivetti, 131, 313, 403n, 435n, 440n
Ollman, Bertell, 436n
Onofri, Fabrizio, 221
Opportunism, 232, 244, 255, 416n, 435n
  See also Workers
Opportunities, 347, 367
Orcutt, G., 34–5
Ordinary least squares (OLS), 33, 69
Organizations
  employers, 119–20, 123–4, 204, 314, 437n
  See also Confindustria workers, 114–19, 411–13n
  See also *Commissioni interne*; Labor unions
Osservatorio Cesos, 176, 177
Ottone, Piero, 203, 232, 393
Outlier, statistical, 257–8
Overtime, 177, 333, 422n

Paci, Massimo, 49, 51, 52, 82
Pact of Rome, 114
Pagani, Massimo, 415n
Palanca, Vaifra, 179, 211
Paldman, Martin, 95
Palmieri, Stefania, 138
Paradoxes
  of the *genie d'un peuple*, 27, 98, 142, 191, 224, 254
  of large firms, 28, 89, 141, 188, 191, 254
  of the 1962 and 1966 strike shapes, 27, 94, 142, 189
  of the 1970s, 27, 88–9, 94, 98, 142, 189, 191, 254, 326–7, 351
  of small-scale production regions, 28, 179, 191, 209–10, 254
  of strike size, 27, 89, 94, 133, 141, 142, 161, 188
Parentela, 200–1, 226
Parisi, Arturo, 196
Parlanti, Luciano, 187
Parliament, 198–200, 203, 204, 224, 229, 252
Pasquino, Gianfranco, 204, 205, 206, 207
Pastore, Giulio, 117
Pastorino, Silvana, 177, 179, 332, 333, 391
Paternalism, 86, 145–6, 226, 272, 282, 307, 310–11, 409n, 435n
PCI. *See* Communist Party
Peasant family, 210–11
Peasant revolts, 371–2, 409n
Peasant workers, 211, 445n
Pedersen, Peder, 95
Pencavel, John H., 32, 100, 374, 424n
Pennacchi, Laura, 335
Perfect knowledge, 36–7, 89–90
Perrone, Luca, 38
Perrot, Michelle, 15, 39, 40, 104, 190, 217, 240, 289, 290, 327
Peruli, Paolo, 338
Pesante, Maria Luisa, 16
Phillips curve, 41
Pickets, 267–8, 273, 294
Pieces of the puzzle, 4, 7, 15, 24–6, 28, 43, 54, 94, 134, 142, 188, 189–91, 212, 253–4, 257, 258, 338, 342, 346, 372, 376
Piedmont, 208, 417n
Piore, Michael, 179, 404n, 443n
Pipan, Tatiana, 138, 319, 322, 323, 440n
Pirelli (firm), 269, 271, 286, 314, 419n, 436n
Pirelli, Leopoldo, 123, 124, 152, 153, 186
Pirzio Ammassari, Gloria, 122, 123, 124, 147, 152, 201, 206, 283, 314, 315
Piven, Frances Fox, 17, 26, 105, 291, 297, 298, 303, 304, 443n
Pizzorno, Alessandro, 1, 113, 116, 139, 149, 186–7, 191, 215, 240, 241–2, 263, 393
Planning. *See* Economic planning
Plant closings, 74
Plant-level bargaining, 12, 144–5, 147–9, 150–1, 152, 153, 157, 175–9, 234, 322, 332, 420n, 421n, 442n,
Plant size, 415n, 421n, 441n, 442n
  classification of, 442n

collective bargaining and, 176–7, 188, 421n
distribution of plants by, 405n
job classification and, 332–3
labor relations and, 177, 178–9, 219–20, 312–13
strike frequency and, 27–8, 84–9, 93, 132, 140–1, 254, 332, 406n
strike tactics and, 270
technological level and, 442–3n
unionization and, 127–33, 140, 254, 312, 415–16n, 421n
PLI. *See* Liberal Party
Plosser, Charles I., 41, 70, 398n
Police, 213–14, 215, 264, 265, 273, 303, 437n
Political approach, 12, 13–14
Political-crisis theory, 194
Political-exchange theory, 1, 11, 12, 13–14, 191–6, 212–13, 224–5, 241, 243, 244, 351
Political opportunity sctructure, 436n
Political parties
  class conflict and, 235–7
  electoral bases for, 207–12, 295–6, 426–7n
  employer associations and, 120, 122, 425n
  labor unions and, 115, 116, 117, 119, 137–9, 141, 417–18n
  in postwar period, 196–207, 225
  See also Elections; *specific names*
Political position of labor, 11, 12, 14, 192, 231, 238, 242, 245, 254, 299, 342, 346, 353, 368
Political strikes, 137–8, 243, 250, 253, 432n
Political subcultures, 207–12, 255, 295, 426–7n
Polo, Gabriele, 50, 270, 271, 272, 281, 285, 287, 290, 293, 307, 393
Potere Operaio, 284, 285–6
Power structure, labor in, 224–9
Prais, S. J., 406n
Preston, R. S., 58, 385
Prices, 56, 400n
  See also Inflation
Priest, 49, 215, 219
Principal component analysis, 6
Procacci, Giuliano, 104, 105
Process technology, 86, 403n, 406n
Production. *See* Industrial production
Productivity, 145, 146
Profits, 90, 146, 232–3

Provasi, Giancarlo, 34, 95, 103, 151, 183, 257, 261, 300, 422n
Przeworski, Adam, 206, 233, 237, 348
PSI. *See* Socialist Party
Pugliese, Francesco, 225, 226
Pugno, Emilio, 146, 218, 393

Quaderni Piacentini, 284
Quaderni Rossi, 283–4
Quantitative research, 15–16, 17, 19–20, 21, 23–4, 106, 186, 187, 237–8, 242–3, 373–5

Radicalism, 86, 283–9, 291
Radical press, 283–4, 435n
Ragazzoni, Alessandro, 177, 179, 332, 333, 391
Rallies, 272, 276, 294
Rao, P., 396n
Rapporto Pirelli, 123, 314
Rappresentanze sindacali aziendali (Rsa), 117, 118, 119, 126, 411n, 413n
Recession, 51–2, 99, 109–10, 305–6, 341, 353, 408n
Reconstruction, postwar, 78–9
Red Brigades, 207, 289
Reder, Melvin W., 36, 90, 154
Rees, Albert, 30–1, 32
Referendum, 206
Regalia, Ida, 52, 118, 119, 130, 145, 149, 150, 177, 268, 269, 312, 313, 392, 415n
Regini, Marino, 83, 243, 268, 269, 271, 272, 276, 280, 281, 282, 285, 293, 360, 398n
Regions (regional government)
  arbitration role of, 198, 202, 214
  Red, 207–212, 255, 296, 407n, 426n, 427n
  White, 207–212, 255, 296, 304, 407n, 426n, 427n
Regonini, Gloria, 225
Regression, 19–20, 186, 398n, 399n
  bivariate, 67, 164, 401n
  correlated errors, 34–5, 40–1, 43
  models, 19–20
  multivariate, 67
  problems with, 35–41
  residuals, 32, 34, 35, 40–3, 45, 55 107, 143, 162–8, 171, 244, 257, 398n, 399n, 420n
  univariate, 67, 355, 356
Regulation theory, 92, 340, 403n
Relative deprivation theory, 10, 97, 98, 298

498 · Index

Repertoires of collective actions, 101–3, 409n
Repression, 213–14, 215–24, 234, 311, 362, 446–7n
Republican Party (PRI), 196, 197, 202, 252
Residuals *see* Regression
Resource mobilization theory, 1, 10–11, 12, 13–14, 97, 99–101, 106–9, 127, 136, 140, 141, 212, 254, 289, 298, 350–1, 446n
Resta, Nicola, 124
Restivo, Franco, 302
Revolution, 370, 372, 407n, 416n
Revolving strikes, 267–9
Reyneri, Emilio, 48, 81, 82, 83, 117, 199, 225, 265, 266, 269, 271, 280, 325, 326, 327, 363
Rhetoric, 362, 373, 375–7
Ricolfi, Luca, 393
Rieser, Vittorio, 17, 22, 218, 224, 347, 393
Riforma Pirelli, 123, 414n
Right, 196–8, 203–5, 207, 237, 423n, 425n
Rinascita, 205
Rist, Charles, 30, 57, 59, 95
Riva, Massimo, 225, 235, 393
Roberts, G., 381
Robotgate system, 331, 441n, 443n
Roccella, Massimo, 204, 225, 226
Rogers, Joel, 235
Romagnoli, Guido, 116, 118, 119, 127, 220, 285, 387, 392, 412n
Rome, 174
Romeo, Rosario, 78
Romiti, Cesare, 237
Ronchi, Rossella, 392
Ronge, Volker, 14, 235, 305
Rosenberg, William G., 297
Rositi, Franco, 209, 304
Ross, Arthur H., 2, 11, 99, 105, 154, 181, 352
Rossi, Giovanna, 266
Rossi, Maurizio, 127, 204, 207, 387
Rubery, Jill, 82, 83
Rubin, Beth, 38
Rubinacci law, 214
Ruffolo, Giorgio, 233
Russian Revolution, 430n

Sabel, Charles, 335, 336, 360
Sabotage, 269
Salerni, Dario, 149, 319, 322, 323, 381–2, 393, 440n, 447n
Salvati, Michele, 47, 52, 53, 203, 214, 306, 310, 438n
Sample size, 446n

Sani, Ettore, 207
Santagata, Walter, 196, 424n
Santi, Ettore, 145, 269, 272, 275, 280, 287, 328, 387
Sapelli, Giulio, 78, 79
Sapsford, D., 40
Saraceno, Pasquale, 202
Scabs, 218, 219, 268, 270, 271
Scala mobile agreement, 151, 173, 227–8, 229, 230, 243–4, 327, 360, 419n, 441n
Scalfari, Eugenio, 151–2, 316, 393
Schadee, Hans, 196
Schmidt, Helmut, 429n
Schmidt, Peter, 35
Schuessler, Karl, 383
Schumpeter, Joseph, 407n
Schwert, G. William, 41, 70, 398n
Sclavi, Gastone, 146
Screpanti, Ernesto, 339, 357
Scuola di Formazione Superiore di Genova, 421n
Seasonality, 39–40, 169, 396–8n, 422n, 446n
Sebastiani, Chiara, 204, 206
Sectors
 primary (agriculture), 48–50, 76, 404n
 secondary (industry), 44, 47, 50, 67, 365, 396n, 397n, 404n
 tertiarty (services), 48, 50, 75, 76, 352, 358, 365
Segatori, Roberto, 319, 323, 359
Segatti, Paolo, 122, 200, 201
Sellier, Francois, 11, 154, 155
Service sector, 75, 76, 358, 363
Sezione sindacale aziendale (Ssa), 116, 118, 119
Shalev, Michael, 11, 192, 225, 368, 397n
Shorey, John, 406n
Shorter, Edward, 1, 2, 10, 14, 26, 96, 97, 100, 103, 104, 137, 146, 189, 190, 191–2, 194, 225, 246, 257, 259, 261, 298, 300, 301, 344
Sibona, Roberto, 187, 271, 272, 281, 290, 307
Siemens, 268
Single-equation simultaneous methods, 70
Size of strikes. *See* Strikes, Italian, size of
Skeels, Jack W., 95, 96, 220, 429n
Skipper, J. K., 373
Skocpol, Theda, 235–6
Slowdowns, 267, 269
Smith, H., 398n
Smith, John, 276
Smoothers, resistant, 414n

Index

Snow, David A., 347
Snyder, David, 14, 45, 47, 56, 95, 97, 105, 194, 196, 238–40, 241, 245, 430–1n
Social Democratic Party, 115, 116, 119, 120, 136, 202, 252, 296
Socialism
  Italian way to, 205–6
  political subculture of, 207–9
  See also Marxist theory; Marx, Karl
Socialist Party (PSI), 138, 197, 199, 201, 202, 225, 243, 252, 296, 344, 417n, 426n
Social-structure-of-accumulation theory, 92, 340, 367, 407n
Sociological approach, 1–2, 12, 13
Solidarity, 86, 158
Somaini, Eugenio, 151
Soskice, David, 98
South, 52, 196, 173, 196, 200, 202, 205, 215, 230, 261, 270, 271, 281, 286, 288–9, 293, 297, 400n, 402n, 426n, 430n, 436n, 438n
  migration from, 49–50, 94, 264, 265, 399n
Soviet Union, 201, 202, 205, 206, 236
Spectral analysis, 6, 62, 66, 70, 155, 400–1n
Speranza, Lorenzo, 319
Spies, 218–19, 222
Spoils system, 225
Spriano, Paolo, 105
Squarzon, Corrada, 337, 362, 414n
Standard of living, 444n
Stanford Research Institute, 78, 216–17, 310, 311
State
  capitalism, 200–1, 425n, 426n
  policies in labor conflict, 302–6
  role in labor relations, 214–15
Statuto dei lavoratori. See Workers' Charter
Stearns, Peter, 105, 437n
Steel industry, 81, 437n
  See also Metalworking industry
Stephenson, James A., 396n
Sterling, T. D., 373
Stern, Robert N., 382, 383, 397n
Stone, Katherine, 82
Stop-and-go strikes, 267, 268
Strategic interaction, 17, 18, 21, 22, 29, 346, 347, 374
Streeck, Wolfgang, 242, 418n, 432n
Strike demands. *See* Demands (workers')
Strike explosions. *See* Strike waves

Strike frequency, 51, 56, 398n, 414n, 420n, 421n
  balance-of-power model, 238
  business cycle and, 424n
  capacity utilization and, 58, 59–60, 62–5, 69
  collective bargaining and, 153–75, 187–9
  cyclical behavior in, 6, 13, 24–5, 54–5, 66, 72–5, 93, 95, 97, 98–9, 141–2, 143–4, 158, 161–2, 187–8, 339, 346–7, 348, 367, 446n
  decline in, 152, 153, 189, 243, 348, 423n
  economic hardship and, 97–9
  elections and, 192, 424n
  forecasting, 355–9
  government crises and, 245–53, 299
  industrialization and, 417n
  industrial production and, 58–62, 66–7, 69, 70, 72, 431n
  occupational sector and, 75–8
  plant size and, 27–8, 86–9, 93, 132, 140–1, 254, 332, 410n
  scala mobile agreement and, 243–4
  seasonal pattern in, 39–40, 169, 396–8n
  no strike clause, 147
  in strike waves, 261
  unemployment and, 30–1, 32–3, 42–3, 45–7, 48, 57, 67, 70, 88, 94, 106, 107, 139, 241, 349–50, 408n
  unionization and, 110, 112–14, 125–6, 140
  wages and, 31, 34, 41, 42–3, 48, 51, 53, 57, 67, 69, 106, 107, 182–5, 190, 399n, 410n
  work intensity and, 275–7
  See also Strike waves
Strike indicators, 382–3, 395n
Strike research
  automatic-pilot approach to, 19–21
  economic *vs.* organizational/political models, 237–40, 241
  ethnographic, 22–3, 185–7
  general theory in, 349
  historical change and, 21–2
  inductive approach to, 26–7
  Italian experience and, 2
  labor-market theories, 10, 24, 30–55
  lack of integration in, 16–18
  levels of analysis, 28–9
  paradoxes and, 27–8
  quantitative, 15–16, 17, 19–20, 21, 23–4, 106, 186, 187, 237–8, 242–3, 373–5

schemata for, 18–19
theoretical approaches to, 1–2, 7, 10–15, 345–6, 349–55
time-series data, 380–9
See also specific theories
Strikers, 31, 52, 54, 56–60, 62, 64–7, 70, 71, 73–5, 77, 93, 140, 106–10, 112–14, 125, 140–4, 150, 154–62, 164–6, 168–70, 172, 173, 183, 185, 187–9, 191, 193, 195, 196, 221–3, 230, 239, 243, 244, 247–51, 253, 258, 259, 268, 271, 275, 294, 300, 323, 354, 357, 366, 408n, 432n
Strikes
committees, 409–10n
historical perspective on, 101–6
length of, 94–5, 104–5
as multiple-action phenomena, 16, 346
success of, 105
See also Strike frequency; Strike waves
Strikes, Italian, 12, 25
characteristics of, 2–7, 432n
class structure change and, 16–17
contract renewal, 158–60, 177–8, 186, 352
cost of, 56, 179–82, 212–24
defensive, 408n
duration of, 94–5, 146, 149, 208
economic, 432n
economic determinants of, 56–95
general, 146, 173–5, 204, 252
labor-market conditions and, 40, 41–7, 51–3, 74–8
number of hours lost, 4–6, 25, 56–9, 62, 66, 72, 87, 93, 106–7, 110, 112, 152, 165, 170, 180, 222, 243, 258–9, 275, 356, 398n, 400n, 408n, 417n, 419n, 421n, 424n
political, 137–8, 243, 250, 253, 417n, 432n
political models of, 191–6
in Red *vs.* White regions, 208, 417n
shapes, 6, 25, 27, 52, 94, 103–4, 161, 189, 190, 192, 243, 254, 424n,
size of, 86, 89, 94, 133, 141, 149, 158, 161, 188, 420n
tactics in, 267–8
withering away of, 191, 224, 225, 231, 347–8
See also Strike frequency; Strike waves
Strikes in France: 1830–1968 (Shorter and Tilly), 1
Strike tactics, 267–72
blockades, 272, 422n

pickets, 267–8, 273
rallies, 267, 272
revolving strikes, 268–9, 422n
sabotage/violence, 269–72, 282, 287
slowdowns, 267, 269
stop-and-go, 267, 268, 270
symbolic/expressive, 432n, 434n
Strike waves, 17, 52–3, 74, 149, 227, 258–64, 434n, 446n
causes of, 297–300, 339–42
characteristics of, 25–6, 261
defined, 259, 261
diffusion process in, 261–3
effects of, 16, 338–9, 344, 353, 369
formal organizations in, 443n
qualitative aspects of, 263–4
state response to, 301–6
as war of movement, 348
See also *Autunno caldo*
Structure, 289–93, 436n
Student movement, 283–9, 297, 435n
Students, 119, 264, 273, 303
high school, 282
university, 282, 283–9, 297
Sullo, Fiorentino, 147
Summers, Robert, 58, 385
Superior Council of the Magistracy, 198
Supervisors, 281, 359–60, 365
Swidinsky, Robert, 397n

Talamo, Magda, 282, 311, 315, 316, 392
Tambroni, Fernando, 201, 202, 252
Tarantelli, Ezio, 226, 227
Tarrow, Sidney, 270, 283, 284–5, 298, 303–4, 347, 393, 436n
Taylor, Frederick, 402n
Taylorism, 78, 79, 93, 264, 336, 341, 404n
Tax rebellions, 101, 102, 409
Technicians, 79, 86, 266, 294, 295, 436
Technological innovation, 78–80, 93, 328, 330–1, 339, 347, 361–2, 442–3n
Tempia, Anna, 81, 82, 83, 266
Temporalities, 371, 373
Terrorism
leftist, 206–7, 289, 290
rightist, 204–5, 302
Terza Italia. See Third Italy
Textile industry, 54, 76, 77, 79, 81, 115, 119, 126, 127, 144, 146, 148, 173, 209, 210, 217, 218, 261, 278, 280, 282, 344, 402n, 426n, 433n
Third Italy, 53, 54, 88, 94, 134, 404n, 405n; *See also* Economic miracle
Thompson, E. P., 16, 101, 102, 103, 240, 276, 294, 436n

Three-stage least squares (3SLS), 70
Tilly, Charles, 1, 2, 10, 14, 16, 26, 96, 97, 98, 100, 101, 102, 103, 104, 137, 146, 189, 190, 191–2, 194, 213, 224, 225, 246, 255, 257, 259, 261, 298, 300, 301, 344, 350, 351, 371
Tilly, Louise, 104, 410n
Time-series data, 6, 380–9, 400–1n
Togliatti, Palmiro, 115, 205–6, 430n
Tonnies, Ferdinand, 100
Torresini, Daniela, 319, 323, 359
Trade unions. *See* Labor unions
Transfer rates, 321, 322, 328
Trend, 347–8, 402n, 440n, 444n
　elimination (differencing) 398n, 400–2n, 422n, 440,
Treu, Tiziano, 116, 120, 132, 151, 152, 154, 213, 214, 215, 216, 219, 225, 226, 304, 305, 437n
Triangolo industriale, 47
Triangular conferences, 204, 229
Trigilia, Carlo, 124, 129, 133, 176, 208, 209, 211, 313, 332, 333, 337–8, 389–90, 438n, 441n, 446n
Trilateral agreements, 228–9
Tripartite institutions. *See* Corporatism; Triangular conferences
Troiani, Saverio, 76, 398n, 417n
Troilo, Ettore, 430n
Trotsky, 135, 136, 233, 235, 283, 416n
Tukey, John W., 1, 398n
Turin, 47, 50, 81, 215, 262, 264–5, 267, 268, 272–3, 359, 412n, 415n, 434n
Turner, H. A., 98, 181, 381
Turone, Sergio, 115, 117, 199, 229, 265, 302
Tuscany, 207, 208, 210, 295, 417n
Two-stage least squares (2SLS), 70

UIL. *See* Italian Workers Union
Umbria, 207, 208, 295
Underemployment, 50, 74
Underground economy, 445n
Unemployment, 429n, 440n
　benefits, 74
　data on, 383, 396n
　indicator, 326
　levels of, 50–1, 52, 74, 326, 363, 446n
　in Marxist theory, 91
　strike frequency and, 10, 30–1, 32–3, 42–3, 45–7, 48, 57, 67, 70, 88, 94, 106, 107, 139, 242, 349–50, 408n
Unione Industriale di Torino, 120

Unionization, 110, 125–31, 132, 209, 262, 410n, 415n, 430n, 442n
Unions. *See* Labor unions
United Auto Workers, 306
United Federation (Federazione Unitaria), 117
United States
　in Italian politics, 198–9, 424–5n
　Italian unions and, 115
　strikes in, 54, 105, 194, 233–4, 234, 306, 424n, 430–1n
Urbani, Giuliano, 124, 313, 317, 364
Urbanization, 104, 409n
Ure, Andrew, 240

Vacante, Cetti, 138
Valcamonici, Roberto, 79, 84, 85
Valdagno, 282
Valdelsa, 208, 426–7n
Valletta, Vittorio, 122
Valli, Vittorio, 215, 306
Vanderkamp, John, 95, 397n
Vanoni Plan, 425n
Veneto, 178–9, 208, 295, 421n
Vento, Fulvio, 320, 322, 391
Vetere, Massimo, 361–2
Viale, Guido, 271, 273, 283, 286, 287, 288, 297
Vicarelli, Fausto, 309
Villa, Paola, 278, 308, 319, 320, 359, 437n
Violence, strike, 105, 270–1, 281–3, 284, 287, 302–3, 409n, 410n
Visser, Jelle, 154
Voting behavior, 207–8, 426–7n
　See also Elections

Wages
　CIG agreement, 441n
　in collective bargaining, 25, 151–3, 188, 192–3, 233, 237, 273–4
　differentials, 178, 215, 274, 278, 360, 361, 405n
　incentives, 362
　minimum, 385–6
　post–*autunno caldo* increase, 53, 306, 307
　scala mobile agreement, 151, 173, 227–8, 229, 230, 243–4, 357, 360
　in large firms, 327, 332
　in small firms, 178, 442n
　of skilled workers, 274, 318
　strike frequency and, 31, 34, 40, 41, 42–3, 48, 51, 53, 57, 67, 69, 106, 107, 182–5, 190, 410n

of unskilled workers, 274
vs. profits, 232–3, 237
Wallace, Michael, 38
Wallerstein, Michael, 206, 233
Wallis, Kenneth F., 35
Wallis test, 35, 40
Walsh, D. William, 95
Waud, Roger N., 35
Weiss, Linda, 215
Weitz, Peter R., 116
Welfare capitalism, 437n
Welfare spending, 192–3, 212
Welfare state, 213
Welsch, Roy E., 107
Westergaard, John, 86
What Is to Be Done? (Marx and Engels), 135, 232
Wheeler, David, 331, 339
Wheelwright, Steven, 355
Wiesenthal, Helmut, 15, 136, 235, 242, 348, 416n
Wilkinson, Frank, 98
Withering-away-of-strikes theories, 191, 224, 225, 231, 347–8
Woodward, Joan, 80, 86, 403n
Women, 83, 127, 182, 220, 277, 287, 295, 326, 332
Workers
  agricultural, 49, 50, 75, 213
  apprentices, 332, 441n
  blue collar/manual, 81, 82, 83, 88, 93, 106, 153, 179, 182, 207, 215, 217, 265, 266, 271, 278, 279, 285, 294, 295–6, 318, 320, 323, 335, 358, 360, 387, 423n, 428n, 436n, 439n
  communist, 412n
  craft, 433n
  male, 433n
  marginal, 50–1
  migrant, 49–50, 399n
  older, 217
  operaio massa, 266, 267, 284, 290,294, 296, 340, 347, 352, 357, 361, 362, 433n
  peasant, 211, 445n
  semi-skilled, 50, 80, 81, 323
  service sector, 358, 363
  skilled, 50, 78, 80, 81, 83, 94, 119, 126, 151, 153, 264–7, 266, 274, 278,
  shift, 265–6, 288
    280, 281, 287, 292, 295, 318, 319, 323, 328, 332, 333, 336, 337, 347, 354, 360, 361, 433n, 441n, 445n
  supervisors, 281, 359–60, 365
  technicians, 79, 86, 266, 294, 295, 436n
  unskilled, 16, 49, 50, 80, 81, 83, 93, 94, 119, 151–3, 209, 264–7, 270, 274, 278, 280, 283, 289, 292, 318, 319, 332, 333, 336, 354, 360, 404n, 440n, 442n
  white collar/clerical, 81, 151, 153, 182, 207, 215, 217, 261, 266, 271, 280, 281, 294–5, 318, 323, 352, 358, 360, 423n, 428n, 436n, 440n
  women, 48, 50, 52, 80, 217, 278, 358, 405n, 428n, 433n, 441n, 442n, 445n
  youth, 50, 229, 405n, 441n
  See also Jobs
Workers' Charter, 117, 119, 132, 148, 189, 208–9, 219, 226, 254, 255, 303–4, 306, 313–14, 332, 337, 411n, 437n, 440n, 442n
Work groups, 118, 277
  autonomous, 319
  homogeneous, 277, 320, 328, 334
Working conditions, 53, 178–9, 277
Wounded. *See* Police
Wright, Erik Olin, 343, 351

Yalta agreement, 236
Yoder, Dale, 398n
Youth, 50, 229, 405n

Zaccone Derossi, Flavia, 50
Zeuthen, F., 32
Zolberg, Aristide, 348